NEW YORK CITY SHSAT PREP 2024–2025

Lead Editor
Katy Haynicz-Smith, MA

Contributing Editors
Laura Aitcheson, MLIS; Melissa McLaughlin; J. Scott Mullison; Heather Waite

Special thanks to the following for their contributions to this text: Kelly Black, Connell Boyle, Michael Collins, Patrick Cox, Amy Craddock, Thomas Darragh, Megan Dusenbery, Mark Feery, Jonathan Habermacher, Peter Haynicz-Smith, Jesika Islam, Rebecca Knauer, Jo L'Abbate, Christine Lilley, Karen McCulloch, Camellia Mukherjee, Kristin Murner, Monica Ostolaza, Anne Marie Salloum, Gordon Spector, Caroline Sykes, Oscar Velazquez, Bonnie Wang, Shayna Webb-Dray, Ethan Weber, Michael Wolff, and Amy Zarkos.

© 2024 by Kaplan North America, LLC
Published by Kaplan North America, LLC dba Kaplan Publishing
1515 West Cypress Creek Road
Fort Lauderdale, Florida 33309

10 9 8 7 6 5 4 3 2 1

ISBN-13: 978-1-5062-9022-5

Kaplan North America, LLC print books are available at special quantity discounts to use for sales promotions, employee premiums, or educational purposes. For more information or to purchase books, call the Simon & Schuster special sales department at 866-506-1949

TABLE OF CONTENTS

PART ONE

GETTING STARTED

[CHAPTER 1]

THE SHSAT AND YOU

CHAPTER OBJECTIVES

By the end of this chapter, you will be able to:

- Answer common questions about the Specialized High Schools Admissions Test
- Take advantage of the test's structure
- Approach the questions strategically
- Describe the structure of the test, how it is scored, and the timing of each section
- Pace yourself effectively during the test

1. SHSAT Basics

Common Questions About the SHSAT

You're using this book because you're serious about attending high school at Brooklyn Latin, Stuyvesant, Bronx Science, Brooklyn Tech, City College, Lehman College, Staten Island Tech, or York College. You probably already know that if you want to go to one of these specialized high schools, you have to take the Specialized High Schools Admissions Test (SHSAT). Fortunately, you can take some steps to maximize your score. Essentially, you need to:

- Understand the structure of the test
- Hone your Math and English Language Arts skills
- Develop strategies and test-taking techniques
- Practice what you've learned

The Specialized High Schools Admissions Test (SHSAT) is a standardized test. It's certainly not easy, but it is a fairly predictable test. This means that you can prepare for the content and question types that you'll see on test day.

Before delving into the specific content and strategies you will need to perform well on the SHSAT, you should know some basic information about the test. Please note that Kaplan strives to provide the most up-to-date information based on the latest publicly released data provided by the New York City Department of Education.

Why Should I Take the SHSAT?

If you want to attend high school at Brooklyn Latin, Stuyvesant, Bronx Science, Brooklyn Tech, City College, Lehman College, Staten Island Tech, or York College, you must take the SHSAT. It is the sole criterion for admission. This means that your grades, extracurricular activities, and so on play no role in the admissions process. **Do not take the test if you are not serious about attending one of the schools!** If you score high enough to be accepted at a school, you will be expected to attend.

Who Administers the Test?

The New York City Department of Education administers the test. The Department of Education is composed of teachers and administrators who decide what students at New York City high schools need to learn.

SHSAT EXPERT NOTE

What does SHSAT stand for?

The full name of the test is the Specialized High Schools Admissions Test. SHSAT is just a bit easier to say.

How Is the Test Scored?

Composite Score

According to the test maker, the maximum Composite Score varies from year to year, but it is usually around 700 points. The number of correct answers from the Math and English Language Arts (ELA) sections determines the Composite Score. In calculating the Composite Score, the Math and ELA sections are weighted equally.

Raw Score

The Raw Score is the sum of the correct answers from each section. There are 57 questions per section; however, 10 questions per section are experimental. The experimental questions are not scored. Therefore, the maximum number of scored answers per section is 47. Overall, the highest Raw Score for the total test is 94. The Raw Score is converted to a scale of approximately 700 points to determine the Composite Score.

Experimental Questions

The 10 experimental questions per section are mixed in with the scored questions. You will not know if a question is experimental or scored. Therefore, you should answer all questions as if they will be scored.

What Is a "Good Score"?

That's a good question, but there is no magic number that will guarantee admission. Admission to each specialized high school works like this: The Department of Education identifies the number of places available at each school. If there are 500 spaces available at Stuyvesant, the Board of Education accepts the top 500 scorers who identified Stuyvesant as their first choice. Therefore, you should just work to get the best score you can.

What Should I Bring to the Test?

You need your admissions ticket, two or more No. 2 pencils, an eraser, and a watch that does not contain a calculator. You may not bring a calculator to the test.

Taking Advantage of the SHSAT's Structure

You can be confident that the test will look very similar to the test-like practice in this book. Therefore, you can take advantage of the test's predictability and use what you know about the structure to raise your score.

You Do Not Need to Answer the Questions in Order

Usually, when taking a test, you automatically answer the questions in the order that they're written. However, there are a lot of questions on the SHSAT, and you may be able to make it easier on yourself by doing the questions you find easier first. For example, if you're good at Reading Comprehension questions, build your confidence and grab some quick points by doing them first. Or if you have a tough time with percents questions, skip the percents questions and go back to them when you have time.

You Can Move Between Sections

Most standardized tests don't let you move between sections or go back and check your work on a section you've already completed. On the SHSAT, however, you can go back to the English Language Arts section after you've finished the Math section.

There Is No Penalty for Wrong Answers

A correct answer is a correct answer. It makes no difference to your score if you get the question correct by solving the question or by guessing. Of course, you should solve the questions you know, but there's no harm in guessing when you don't know how to answer a question or are running out of time. Remember, you have a 0 percent chance of getting a question correct if you leave it blank. Your chances of getting a multiple-choice question correct if you guess are at least 25 percent. Go with the odds.

Answer Grid Tips

Don't lose valuable points on the test by misgridding! The answer choices are labeled A–D and E–H to help you keep track of answers.

Always circle questions you skip in your test book.

Whenever you choose not to answer a question, circle the entire question in your test book. This can help you in two ways. The first is that it will be easier to find the questions you skipped if they're circled. The second is that you are less likely to misgrid when you skip questions if you clearly mark the ones you skip. Anything that will help you approach the test efficiently is worth doing. Circling questions that you skip is relatively effortless and can save you time. Just make sure to go back and erase any extra marks on your answer grid before you're done.

Always circle the answer you choose in your test book.

A great way to avoid careless gridding errors is to circle your answers in the test book. If you circle your answers, you can quickly check your circled answers against your gridded answers to make sure that you did not misgrid. Additionally, if you have time to recheck your answers, it's easier to do this if the answers are circled.

Grid your answers in blocks of five.

Don't grid in each answer after you answer each question. Instead, grid in your answers after every five questions. As you're entering the answers into the grid, think to yourself, "1, A," "2, G," and so on. This will help you to avoid any omissions. Since questions alternate between A–D choices and E–H choices, you should be able to catch a mistake if you skipped a question or entered answers onto the wrong line.

Approaching SHSAT Questions Strategically

As important as it is to know the setup of the SHSAT, it is equally important to have a system for attacking the questions. You wouldn't venture onto the subway for the first time without looking at a map, and you shouldn't approach the SHSAT without a plan. Remember, the more knowledge you have about the test and the questions, the better you'll be able to take control of the test. The following is the best way to approach SHSAT questions systematically.

Think About the Questions Before You Look at the Answers

It's hard to emphasize strenuously enough precisely how important this strategy is. Basically, it's **really, really** important! One of the most damaging mistakes that students make when taking the SHSAT is that they jump immediately from the question to the answer choices without stopping first to think. This is particularly true with the Reading Comprehension questions, but it is a problem with most question types. Here's what will happen if you read the questions and then go directly to the answer choices: you will be confronted with very tempting, but very incorrect, answer choices. If you take the time to think before looking at the choices, you will be much less likely to fall for the traps.

SHSAT EXPERT NOTE

Predict before you peek

Try to predict the answer—or at least think about it—before you look at the answer choices. If nothing else, you may realize what the answer won't be. This will help you to avoid the tempting "traps" set by the test maker.

Use Strategies and Guess Strategically

You'll learn more about Kaplan's strategies later, but the gist of them is that sometimes there are shortcuts to solving problems and guessing strategically. No one sees your work, so you do not have to solve problems the way you would in school. Any method that gets you the correct answer is the "right" way on the SHSAT. Additionally, because there is no penalty for wrong answers, don't leave any questions blank!

Pace Yourself

The SHSAT gives you a lot of questions in a relatively short period of time. To get through the test, you need to be in control of your pace. Remember, although you should enter an answer for every question, you don't have to answer every question correctly to score well. You can employ a few strategies to take control of your pace.

- Don't spend too much time on any one question. You can always circle a question and come back to it later.
- Give yourself a rough time limit for each question—move on if you run out of time.
- Be flexible—you can answer questions out of order.
- Don't spend more than 5 minutes on any one Reading passage—keep reading and move on. Remember, your points come from answering the questions.
- Practice under timed conditions.

> **SHSAT EXPERT NOTE**
>
> **Take control**
>
> Taking control of your pace and practicing test-like timing will help improve your testing experience.

Locate Quick Points If You're Running Out of Time

Some questions can be answered more quickly than others. Some are simply well-suited to shortcuts. For example, a Reading question that contains a line number or asks for the meaning of a specific phrase may be easier to answer quickly than one that does not give you such a clue. Other questions will be easier because of your particular strengths. For example, if you're comfortable with geometry and are running out of time, look for the geometry questions.

> **SHSAT EXPERT NOTE**
>
> **Play to your strengths and know your weaknesses**
>
> You know your strengths and weaknesses better than anyone else. Use this knowledge to work through the test efficiently.

2. Inside the SHSAT

Structure of the Test

The SHSAT is a standardized test, which means that it is predictable. Therefore, you can take control and build your confidence by knowing what to expect. When you sit down to take the test, you should know what the test will look like, how it will be scored, and how long you'll have to complete it.

On the SHSAT, you'll see 57 English Language Arts and 57 Math questions on the test. The English Language Arts and Math sections are equally weighted.

English Language Arts Section

The English Language Arts section is the first section on the test. It contains 57 questions and accounts for one-half of your total points on the SHSAT. The suggested time for the section is 90 minutes, or 1 hour and 30 minutes. All 57 questions are multiple-choice questions.

Based on the latest information available from the New York City Department of Education, the breakdown of the English Language Arts section is as follows:

ENGLISH LANGUAGE ARTS SUBSECTION	TOTAL NUMBER OF QUESTIONS
Revising/Editing Stand-Alone Questions	9–19 questions
Revising/Editing Passage(s)	
Reading Comprehension	38–48 questions

Math

The Math section is the second section on the test. It contains 57 questions and accounts for one-half of your total points on the SHSAT. The suggested time for the section is 90 minutes, or 1 hour and 30 minutes.

Based on the latest information available from the New York City Department of Education, the breakdown of the Math section is as follows:

MATH SUBSECTION	TOTAL NUMBER OF QUESTIONS
Grid-In Questions	5 questions
Multiple-Choice Questions	52 questions

Scoring

Scoring for the SHSAT is a little different. It's not that the scoring is difficult to understand; it's just that individual scores matter only to the extent that they are above or below a cutoff line, and that cutoff line changes each year depending on how that group of students performs on the test.

Here's how the scoring works. First, you get a Raw Score based on the number of questions you answer correctly. The test contains 114 questions. 94 of the questions are worth 1 "raw" point, and 20 are experimental questions that aren't scored. The maximum Raw Score is, therefore, 94.

Next, your Raw Score is multiplied by a formula known only to the Department of Education to arrive at a Scaled Score. You receive a Scaled Score for each section and a Composite Score for the entire test. According to the test makers, the highest possible Composite Score varies from year to year, but it is usually around 700.

Admission to all specialized high schools (except LaGuardia) is based solely on your Composite Score. The way this works is that all of the students are ranked from high score to low score and then assigned to the school of their first preference until all the available seats are filled. For example, if Stuyvesant had exactly 500 spaces available and the top 500 scorers all picked Stuyvesant as their first choice, all 500 scorers would be admitted. If the 501st scorer listed Stuyvesant as her first choice and Bronx Science as her second choice, she would be assigned to Bronx Science. Therefore, scores are relative; it matters only whether they are above the cutoff, but there is no way of accurately knowing what the cutoff score will be. All you know is that you should do your best to get the highest score possible and increase your chances.

Timing

Here's the way timing works on the SHSAT, which is different from a lot of other standardized tests. You'll have 180 minutes to complete the entire test. It is recommended that you spend approximately half the time (90 minutes, or 1 hour and 30 minutes) on each section. However, if you finish the English Language Arts section early, you can move on to the Math section without waiting for the 90 minutes to end. Similarly, if you finish the Math section with time to spare, you can go back over both the Math and English Language Arts sections of the test.

What this means is that you have both the freedom to structure your time and the responsibility to use your time wisely. Although you can spend more than 90 minutes working on the first section, it may not be wise to do so. However, the flexibility you have in skipping around and going back to one section after finishing the other gives you ample opportunity to play to your strengths.

The Schools

In addition to preparing for the test, you should be doing some research about the schools. Remember, if you get accepted into a school, you will be expected to attend. Therefore, you want to make an informed decision here. The best way to get information about the schools is to contact them or check out their websites. Here's the contact information for each school:

The Bronx High School of Science	75 West 205th Street Bronx, NY 10468 (718) 817-7700 *www.bxscience.edu*
The Brooklyn Latin School	223 Graham Avenue Brooklyn, NY 11206 (718) 366-0154 *www.brooklynlatin.org*
Brooklyn Technical High School	29 Fort Greene Place Brooklyn, NY 11217 (718) 804-6400 *www.bths.edu*
Fiorello H. LaGuardia High School of Music & Art and Performing Arts	100 Amsterdam Avenue New York, NY 10023 (212) 496-0700 *www.laguardiahs.org*

High School for Math, Science, and Engineering at the City College of New York	240 Convent Avenue New York, NY 10031 (212) 281-6490 *www.hsmse.org*
High School of American Studies at Lehman College	2925 Goulden Avenue Bronx, NY 10468 (718) 329-2144 *www.hsas-lehman.org*
Queens High School for the Sciences at York College	94-50 159th Street Jamaica, NY 11451 (718) 657-3181 *www.qhss.org*
Staten Island Technical High School	485 Clawson Street Staten Island, NY 10306 (718) 667-3222 *www.siths.org*
Stuyvesant High School	345 Chambers Street New York, NY 10282 (212) 312-4800 *stuy.enschool.org*

Do some research. Talk to your parents, teachers, and guidance counselor. Some factors that you may want to consider are these:

- Location
- Condition of facilities
- Class size
- School size
- Areas of concentration
- Advanced Placement courses
- Research programs
- Availability of hands-on tech courses
- College courses offered
- Extracurricular activities

PART TWO

SHSAT ENGLISH LANGUAGE ARTS

[CHAPTER 2]

INTRODUCING SHSAT ENGLISH LANGUAGE ARTS

CHAPTER OBJECTIVES

By the end of this chapter, you will be able to:

- Identify the format and timing of the SHSAT English Language Arts section
- Apply tips and strategies to the SHSAT English Language Arts section

1. Introducing SHSAT English Language Arts

English Language Arts Overview

The English Language Arts section is the first section on the test. It contains 57 questions and accounts for one-half of your total points on the SHSAT. The suggested time for the section is 90 minutes, or 1 hour and 30 minutes.

Based on the latest information available from the New York City Department of Education, the breakdown of the English Language Arts section is as follows:

ENGLISH LANGUAGE ARTS SUBSECTION	TOTAL NUMBER OF QUESTIONS	PACING
Revising/Editing Stand-Alone Questions	9–19 questions	1 minute per stand-alone question, $1\frac{1}{2}$ minutes per passage-based question
Revising/Editing Passage(s)		
Reading Comprehension	38–48 questions	Up to 5 minutes reading each passage, 1 minute per question

The Question Types

Revising/Editing Stand-Alone Questions

The beginning of the Revising/Editing section will look similar to the following:

Part 1—English Language Arts

57 QUESTIONS—SUGGESTED TIMING: 90 MINUTES

REVISING/EDITING

QUESTIONS 1–16 (Part A and Part B)

REVISING/EDITING Part A

DIRECTIONS: Answer the following questions, recognizing and correcting errors so that the sentences or paragraphs are grammatically correct. Reread relevant parts of the text before choosing the best answer for each question, but be mindful of time. You may write in your test booklet to take notes.

The SHSAT English Language Arts section stand-alone questions will require you to apply your knowledge of sentence structure, punctuation, usage, knowledge of language, organization, and topic development.

Revising/Editing Passages

The beginning of the Revising/Editing Part B section will look like this:

REVISING/EDITING Part B

DIRECTIONS: Read the passage and answer the questions following it, improving the writing quality and correcting grammatical errors. Reread relevant parts of the text before choosing the best answer for each question, but be mindful of time. You may write in your test booklet to take notes.

You will be asked to improve the organization and topic development of the passage(s).

Reading

The beginning of the Reading section will look like this:

READING COMPREHENSION

QUESTIONS 12–57

DIRECTIONS: Read the six passages and answer the corresponding questions. Reread relevant parts of the text before choosing the best answer for each question, but be mindful of time. Base your answers only on the content within each passage. You may write in your test booklet to take notes.

The Reading Comprehension questions test your ability to understand what you've read. The passages will appear on a variety of topics such as science, social studies, humanities, poetry, and literary fiction. The Reading Comprehension questions will test your understanding of what you've read in the passages as well as information provided in accompanying tables, charts, or graphs.

How to Approach SHSAT English Language Arts

To do well on the SHSAT English Language Arts (ELA) section, you need to be systematic in your approach. In other words, you need to know how you are going to deal with each question type and the section as a whole before you open the test booklet. Knowing your strengths ahead of time is an important part of using a strategic approach. For example, if you find the Revising/Editing questions more difficult than Reading Comprehension, you can leave the Revising/Editing questions for last. It's up to you.

In addition, pacing is crucial. Reading six passages is a lot. You have to be aware of your time and plan it well. In general, you want to spend no more than 15 minutes answering Revising/Editing questions and use at least 75 minutes for Reading passages and questions.

[CHAPTER 3]

THE KAPLAN METHOD FOR REVISING/EDITING TEXT

CHAPTER OBJECTIVES

By the end of this chapter, you will be able to:

- Efficiently apply the Kaplan Method for Revising/Editing Text

English

1. The Kaplan Method for Revising/Editing Text

Using the Method

You will use the Kaplan Method for Revising/Editing Text to optimize your score on the SHSAT English Language Arts section. Be sure to use this method for **every** Revising/Editing question you encounter, whether practicing, completing your homework, working on a Practice Test, or taking the official test. The more you use the Kaplan Method, the more it will be second nature on test day.

> **THE KAPLAN METHOD FOR REVISING/EDITING TEXT**
>
> **STEP 1:** Examine the question stem and answer choices
>
> **STEP 2:** Select the most correct, concise, and relevant choice

Let's take a closer look at each step.

Step 1: Examine the Question Stem and Answer Choices

Revising/Editing questions test sentence structure, usage, knowledge of language, organization, and topic development issues. Identifying what the question is asking before you carefully consider each answer choice will help you pinpoint your focus and save valuable time on test day.

1. Read this sentence.

> My science fair <u>project</u>, which took weeks for me to <u>complete</u> included information about how volcanoes are <u>formed</u>, how scientists predict eruptions, and how <u>lava</u> and magma differ.

Which edit should be made to correct the sentence?

    A. Delete the comma after **project**.

    B. Insert a comma after **complete**.

    C. Delete the comma after **formed**.

    D. Insert a comma after **lava**.

A. **What type of issue do the question stem and answer choices indicate?**

Step 2: Select the Most Correct, Concise, and Relevant Choice

Your goal is to select the text that creates the most correct, concise, and relevant response. This means that the text:

- Has no grammatical errors
- Is brief while retaining the writer's intended meaning
- Is appropriate for the surrounding text

All three of these elements are vital for a choice to be correct. You will notice that many choices will correct an error but will also incorrectly change the meaning of the text. In other instances, choices may keep the meaning the same and fix an error, but they might also incorrectly introduce an informal tone to an otherwise formal passage. Keep in mind, too, that although conciseness is a goal, the shortest answer choice will not always be the correct one, unless it accomplishes all three of the goals (correct, concise, and relevant).

B. The following table shows how the suggested edits in the answer choices, if implemented, would change the relevant text. Consider each of the options, decide to keep or eliminate the text, and indicate why.

EDITED TEXT	KEEP OR ELIMINATE?	WHY?
A. My science fair project which took weeks for me to complete included information about how volcanoes are formed, how scientists predict eruptions, and how lava and magma differ.		
B. My science fair project, which took weeks for me to complete, included information about how volcanoes are formed, how scientists predict eruptions, and how lava and magma differ.		
C. My science fair project, which took weeks for me to complete included information about how volcanoes are formed how scientists predict eruptions, and how lava and magma differ.		
D. My science fair project, which took weeks for me to complete included information about how volcanoes are formed, how scientists predict eruptions, and how lava, and magma differ.		

Practice: Revising/Editing Text Method

Revising/Editing Part A

2. Read this paragraph.

> (1) Given that they often spend a lot of time engaged in solitary <u>pursuits</u>, house cats <u>have</u> gained a reputation for being aloof. (2) Although they are capable of being sociable and affectionate with other felines and <u>humans</u>, adult cats <u>are</u> not known for voluntarily living in groups. (3) In fact, they are notorious for specific <u>behaviors</u>: they form dominance hierarchies and <u>refuse</u> to accept new cats. (4) Also, adult <u>cats</u>, protect their territory by chasing away any being perceived as a threat and <u>is</u> therefore considered nonsocial.

Which pair of revisions need to be made in the paragraph?

- **E.** Sentence 1: Delete the comma after *pursuits*, AND change *have* to **has**.
- **F.** Sentence 2: Delete the comma after *humans*, AND change *are* to **is**.
- **G.** Sentence 3: Delete the colon after *behaviors*, AND change *refuse* to **refuses**.
- **H.** Sentence 4: Delete the comma after *cats*, AND change *is* to **are**.

C. What type of issue do the question stem and answer choices indicate?

SHSAT EXPERT NOTE

If a sentence or paragraph includes two grammatical errors, the correct answer will fix **both** issues. Eliminate choices that do not fix both problems.

D. The following table shows how the suggested edits in the answer choices, if implemented, would change the relevant text. Consider each of the options, decide to keep or eliminate the text, and indicate why.

	EDITED TEXT	KEEP OR ELIMINATE?	WHY?
E.	(1) Given that they often spend a lot of time engaged in solitary pursuits house cats has gained a reputation for being aloof.		
F.	(2) Although they are capable of being sociable and affectionate with other felines and humans adult cats is not known for voluntarily living in groups.		
G.	(3) In fact, they are notorious for specific behaviors they form dominance hierarchies and refuses to accept new cats.		
H.	(4) Also, adult cats protect their territory by chasing away any being perceived as a threat and are therefore considered nonsocial.		

3. Read this sentence.

> After graduating from high school, the plan Kaylee has is to attend college in Vermont and to study American literature.

How should the sentence be revised?

A. After graduating from high school, attending college in Vermont and studying American literature is Kaylee's plan.

B. After graduating from high school, the plan Kaylee will follow is to attend college in Vermont and to study American literature.

C. After graduating from high school, Kaylee plans to attend college in Vermont and to study American literature.

D. After graduating from high school, the plan Kaylee has includes attending college in Vermont and studying American literature.

E. What type of issue do the question stem and answer choices indicate?

SHSAT EXPERT NOTE

To create a logical statement, an introductory phrase at the beginning of a sentence must both describe and be placed near the subject of the sentence. For this reason, the following sentence is illogical: "Standing tall at 305 feet, people can see the Statue of Liberty as far as 60 miles away on a clear day." As written, the sentence suggests that the people are 305 feet tall. The phrase "Standing tall at 305 feet" should instead be placed near what it describes, "the Statue of Liberty": "Standing tall at 305 feet, the Statue of Liberty can be seen as far as 60 miles away on a clear day."

F. The following table shows how the suggested edits in the answer choices, if implemented, would change the relevant text. Consider each of the options, decide to keep or eliminate the text, and indicate why.

EDITED TEXT	KEEP OR ELIMINATE?	WHY?
A. After graduating from high school, attending college in Vermont and studying American literature is Kaylee's plan.		
B. After graduating from high school, the plan Kaylee will follow is to attend college in Vermont and to study American literature.		
C. After graduating from high school, Kaylee plans to attend college in Vermont and to study American literature.		
D. After graduating from high school, the plan Kaylee has includes attending college in Vermont and studying American literature.		

4. Read this paragraph.

> Llamas, the South American relative of the camel, make excellent <u>pets, they</u> are very friendly and are well-liked by both people and other animals. In various parts of the world, people have herded llamas in <u>flocks, for they</u> are social animals that prefer to live in large packs. In South <u>America, llamas</u> helped the Andean civilization thrive in the high mountains; their high thirst tolerance, physical stamina, and ability to survive on a wide variety of plants make llamas important transport animals. Besides providing <u>transportation</u>, <u>llamas</u> offer wool, meat, and tallow for candles.

Which revision corrects the error in sentence structure in the paragraph?

E. pets. They

F. flocks. They

G. America. Llamas

H. transportation. Llamas

G. What type of issue do the question stem and answer choices indicate?

H. The following table shows how the suggested edits in the answer choices, if implemented, would change the relevant text. Consider each of the options, decide to keep or eliminate the text, and indicate why.

EDITED TEXT	KEEP OR ELIMINATE?	WHY?
E. Llamas, the South American relative of the camel, make excellent pets. They are very friendly and are well-liked by both people and other animals.		
F. In various parts of the world, people have herded llamas in flocks. They are social animals that prefer to live in large packs.		
G. In South America. Llamas helped the Andean civilization thrive in the high mountains; their high thirst tolerance, physical stamina, and ability to survive on a wide variety of plants make llamas important transport animals.		
H. Besides providing transportation. Llamas offer wool, meat, and tallow for candles.		

Revising/Editing Part B

The Industrial Revolution

(1) The first Industrial Revolution, which occurred in Great Britain in the latter half of the eighteenth century, represented a sudden acceleration of technological and economic development that would permeate all levels of British society. (2) New inventions supplanted the existing economy and led to a new one.

5. Which revision of sentence 2 uses the **most** precise language?

   A. Especially important was a change in the economy that had to do with manufacturing and machinery.

   B. In particular, manufacturing and machinery changed a traditional economy into a different kind of economy.

   C. Specifically, the traditional agrarian economy was supplanted by one based on manufacturing and machinery.

   D. They supplanted the traditional agrarian economy with an economy that was entirely different and included new technology.

I. What type of issue do the question stem and answer choices indicate?

J. The following table shows how the suggested edits in the answer choices, if implemented, would change the relevant text. Consider each of the options, decide to keep or eliminate the text, and indicate why.

EDITED TEXT	KEEP OR ELIMINATE?	WHY?
A. Especially important was a change in the economy that had to do with manufacturing and machinery.		
B. In particular, manufacturing and machinery changed a traditional economy into a different kind of economy.		
C. Specifically, the traditional agrarian economy was supplanted by one based on manufacturing and machinery.		
D. They supplanted the traditional agrarian economy with an economy that was entirely different and included new technology.		

(3) Very much an urban movement, the revolution gave rise to a new system of social class. (4) This was based primarily upon the relationship of the industrial capitalist to the factory worker. (5) These changes can be attributed to a number of favorable societal circumstances, including an increasing population that would provide both a larger workforce and expanding markets, a strong middle class, and stability in both the political environment and the monetary system.

6. What is the **best** way to combine sentences 3 and 4 to clarify the relationship between ideas?

E. Very much an urban movement, the revolution gave rise to a new system of society based primarily upon the relationship of the industrial capitalist to the factory worker.

F. Very much an urban movement, the revolution gave rise to a new system of social class, and that class was based primarily upon the relationship of the industrial capitalist to the factory worker.

G. Very much an urban movement, a new system of social class was given rise to primarily based on the relationship of the industrial capitalist to the factory worker.

H. Very much an urban movement, the revolution gave rise to a new system of social class based primarily upon the relationship of the industrial capitalist to the factory worker.

K. What type of issue do the question stem and answer choices indicate?

L. The following table shows how the suggested edits in the answer choices, if implemented, would change the relevant text. Consider each of the options, decide to keep or eliminate the text, and indicate why.

EDITED TEXT	KEEP OR ELIMINATE?	WHY?
E. Very much an urban movement, the revolution gave rise to a new system of society based primarily upon the relationship of the industrial capitalist to the factory worker.		
F. Very much an urban movement, the revolution gave rise to a new system of social class, and that class was based primarily upon the relationship of the industrial capitalist to the factory worker.		
G. Very much an urban movement, a new system of social class was given rise to primarily based on the relationship of the industrial capitalist to the factory worker.		
H. Very much an urban movement, the revolution gave rise to a new system of social class based primarily upon the relationship of the industrial capitalist to the factory worker.		

(6) In the United States, the Industrial Revolution had a similar effect, exemplified by the female factory workers in Lowell, Massachusetts. (7) Lowell had long been a textile manufacturing hub. (8) After the industrialization of textile production in 1815, the hand-spun textiles with which many families had supplemented their incomes could not compete with cheaper, factory-spun cloth. (9) While the factories diminished at-home work opportunities, they did create a new role for the farm daughter as a factory worker. (10) The family she left behind would profit from a share of her wages, while she kept a portion of the money—whether to save or to spend on the consumer goods created by the new industrial society.

7. Which sentence would **best** follow and support sentence 8?

   A. The factory-made cloth was less expensive to purchase, which made it popular, especially among the lower class.

   B. Men could still work the farm, but women found their traditional cloth-making work devalued.

   C. Factory-spun cloth could also be made faster, which was particularly advantageous for increasing profit margins.

   D. The textiles were just as well spun as was homemade cloth, both of which had to be well-constructed to stand up to wear and tear over time.

M. What type of issue do the question stem and answer choices indicate?

SHSAT EXPERT NOTE

Any new sentence should support the overall topic of the passage and fit in well with the previous and following sentences.

N. The following table shows how the suggested edits in the answer choices, if implemented, would change the relevant text. Consider each of the options, decide to keep or eliminate the text, and indicate why.

	EDITED TEXT	KEEP OR ELIMINATE?	WHY?
A.	After the industrialization of textile production in 1815, the hand-spun textiles with which many families had supplemented their incomes could not compete with cheaper, factory-spun cloth. The factory-made cloth was less expensive to purchase, which made it popular, especially among the lower class.		
B.	After the industrialization of textile production in 1815, the hand-spun textiles with which many families had supplemented their incomes could not compete with cheaper, factory-spun cloth. Men could still work the farm, but women found their traditional cloth-making work devalued.		
C.	After the industrialization of textile production in 1815, the hand-spun textiles with which many families had supplemented their incomes could not compete with cheaper, factory-spun cloth. Factory-spun cloth could also be made faster, which was particularly advantageous for increasing profit margins.		
D.	After the industrialization of textile production in 1815, the hand-spun textiles with which many families had supplemented their incomes could not compete with cheaper, factory-spun cloth. The textiles were just as well spun as was homemade cloth, both of which had to be well-constructed to stand up to wear and tear over time.		

(11) Millwork was often a deliberate step toward personal advancement for women from a limited, but not destitute, farm background. (12) The women, whose general ages ranged from 14 to 35 years, lived in company-owned, strictly controlled boarding houses. (13) These all-female establishments fostered strong friendships as well as a cohesive community of women of similar ages and socioeconomic backgrounds living and working together 24 hours a day.

8. Which transition should be added to the beginning of sentence 11?

    E. On the other hand,

    F. Nevertheless,

    G. Unfortunately,

    H. Furthermore,

O. What type of issue do the question stem and answer choices indicate?

P. The following table shows how the suggested edits in the answer choices, if implemented, would change the relevant text. Consider each of the options, decide to keep or eliminate the text, and indicate why.

EDITED TEXT	KEEP OR ELIMINATE?	WHY?
E. The family she left behind would profit from a share of her wages, while she kept a portion of the money—whether to save or to spend on the consumer goods created by the new industrial society. On the other hand, millwork was often a deliberate step toward personal advancement for women from a limited, but not destitute, farm background.		
F. The family she left behind would profit from a share of her wages, while she kept a portion of the money—whether to save or to spend on the consumer goods created by the new industrial society. Nevertheless, millwork was often a deliberate step toward personal advancement for women from a limited, but not destitute, farm background.		
G. The family she left behind would profit from a share of her wages, while she kept a portion of the money—whether to save or to spend on the consumer goods created by the new industrial society. Unfortunately, millwork was often a deliberate step toward personal advancement for women from a limited, but not destitute, farm background.		
H. The family she left behind would profit from a share of her wages, while she kept a portion of the money—whether to save or to spend on the consumer goods created by the new industrial society. Furthermore, millwork was often a deliberate step toward personal advancement for women from a limited, but not destitute, farm background.		

(14) In America, as in England, many previously rural workers moved to the cities. (15) Many people new to America were Irish immigrants fleeing from the potato famine. (16) In some cases, this led to improvements in their lives, with urban transportation and increased opportunities. (17) However, the rush to the cities also led to overcrowding, poor living conditions, health issues, and child labor. (18) Thus, the Industrial Revolution, which changed the basis of America's economy, brought both improvements and problems.

9. Which sentence is irrelevant to the argument made in the passage and should be deleted?

   A. sentence 14

   B. sentence 15

   C. sentence 16

   D. sentence 17

Q. **What type of issue do the question stem and answer choices indicate?**

SHSAT EXPERT NOTE

When determining which sentence to delete, find the one that is out of place with the topic, is unnecessary to the argument, or interrupts the flow of ideas.

R. **The following table shows how the suggested edits in the answer choices, if implemented, would change the relevant text. Consider each of the options, decide to keep or eliminate the text, and indicate why.**

	EDITED TEXT	KEEP OR ELIMINATE?	WHY?
A.	(15) Many people new to America were Irish immigrants fleeing from the potato famine. (16) In some cases, this led to improvements in their lives, with urban transportation and increased opportunities. (17) However, the rush to the cities also led to overcrowding, poor living conditions, health issues, and child labor. (18) Thus, the Industrial Revolution, which changed the basis of America's economy, brought both improvements and problems.		
B.	(14) In America, as in England, many previously rural workers moved to the cities. (16) In some cases, this led to improvements in their lives, with urban transportation and increased opportunities. (17) However, the rush to the cities also led to overcrowding, poor living conditions, health issues, and child labor. (18) Thus, the Industrial Revolution, which changed the basis of America's economy, brought both improvements and problems.		

EDITED TEXT	KEEP OR ELIMINATE?	WHY?
C. (14) In America, as in England, many previously rural workers moved to the cities. (15) Many people new to America were Irish immigrants fleeing from the potato famine. (17) However, the rush to the cities also led to overcrowding, poor living conditions, health issues, and child labor. (18) Thus, the Industrial Revolution, which changed the basis of America's economy, brought both improvements and problems.		
D. (14) In America, as in England, many previously rural workers moved to the cities. (15) Many people new to America were Irish immigrants fleeing from the potato famine. (16) In some cases, this led to improvements in their lives, with urban transportation and increased opportunities. (18) Thus, the Industrial Revolution, which changed the basis of America's economy, brought both improvements and problems.		

Answers and Explanations

1. The Kaplan Method for Revising/Editing Text

1.   **A.** There is a punctuation issue because the answer choices all contain suggestions about commas.

B.

	EDITED TEXT	KEEP OR ELIMINATE?	WHY?
A.	My science fair project which took weeks for me to complete included information about how volcanoes are formed, how scientists predict eruptions, and how lava and magma differ.	Eliminate	The phrase "which took weeks for me to complete" is not essential to the sentence and must be set apart with a comma before and after it.
B.	My science fair project, which took weeks for me to complete, included information about how volcanoes are formed, how scientists predict eruptions, and how lava and magma differ.	Keep	The phrase "which took weeks for me to complete" is not essential to the sentence and must be set apart with a comma before and after it.
C.	My science fair project, which took weeks for me to complete included information about how volcanoes are formed how scientists predict eruptions, and how lava and magma differ.	Eliminate	Three or more items in a list must be separated by commas.
D.	My science fair project, which took weeks for me to complete included information about how volcanoes are formed, how scientists predict eruptions, and how lava, and magma differ.	Eliminate	If a list—such as "lava and magma"—contains only two items (rather than three or more), a comma is not needed for that list.

Practice: Revising/Editing Text Method

2. **C** There are two issues: a punctuation error and a verb error. There is a punctuation error because the answer choices contain suggestions about commas and a colon. There is a verb error because all four choices include changing verb forms, either from plural to singular or from singular to plural.

D.

EDITED TEXT	KEEP OR ELIMINATE?	WHY?
E. (1) Given that they often spend a lot of time engaged in solitary pursuits house cats has gained a reputation for being aloof.	Eliminate	The comma after "pursuits" is necessary to separate the dependent clause "Given that they often spend a lot of time engaged in solitary pursuits" from the independent clause "cats have gained a reputation for being aloof." The plural verb "have" agrees with the plural noun "cats."
F. (2) Although they are capable of being sociable and affectionate with other felines and humans adult cats is not known for voluntarily living in groups.	Eliminate	The comma after "humans" is necessary to separate the dependent clause "Although they are capable of being sociable and affectionate with other felines and humans" from the independent clause "adult cats are not known for voluntarily living in groups." The plural verb "are" agrees with the plural noun "cats."
G. (3) In fact, they are notorious for specific behaviors they form dominance hierarchies and refuses to accept new cats.	Eliminate	The colon after "behaviors" is necessary to introduce the two examples of the notorious behaviors. The plural verb "refuse" agrees with the plural pronoun "they."
H. (4) Also, adult cats protect their territory by chasing away any being perceived as a threat and are therefore considered nonsocial.	Keep	The comma after "cats" is unnecessary because the noun "cats" should not be separated from the verb "protect." The verb "is" is singular, but "cats" is plural, so the verb must be changed to the plural "are."

3. **E.** The answer choices indicate that there is a modifier issue because they provide three different options that the phrase "After graduating from high school" could be modifying: "attending college in Vermont," "the plan," or "Kaylee."

F.

	EDITED TEXT	KEEP OR ELIMINATE?	WHY?
A.	After graduating from high school, attending college in Vermont and studying American literature is Kaylee's plan.	Eliminate	The phrase "after graduating from high school" is referring to "Kaylee," not "attending college in Vermont and studying American literature."
B.	After graduating from high school, the plan Kaylee will follow is to attend college in Vermont and to study American literature.	Eliminate	The phrase "after graduating from high school" is referring to "Kaylee," not "the plan Kaylee will follow."
C.	After graduating from high school, Kaylee plans to attend college in Vermont and to study American literature.	Keep	The phrase "after graduating from high school" is referring to the subject of the sentence ("Kaylee"); this version is correct because "Kaylee" appears directly after the modifying phrase.
D.	After graduating from high school, the plan Kaylee has includes attending college in Vermont and studying American literature.	Eliminate	The phrase "after graduating from high school" is referring to "Kaylee," not "the plan Kaylee has."

English

4. **G.** The question stem states that the paragraph has a sentence structure error. All of the answer choices change commas to periods, which is one way to correct a run-on sentence.

H.

	EDITED TEXT	KEEP OR ELIMINATE?	WHY?
E.	Llamas, the South American relative of the camel, make excellent pets. They are very friendly and are well-liked by both people and other animals.	Keep	"Llamas, the South American relative of the camel, make excellent pets" and "they are very friendly and are well-liked by both people and other animals" are two independent clauses that must be properly combined. Using only a comma is grammatically incorrect; separating the clauses into two sentences fixes the error.
F.	In various parts of the world, people have herded llamas in flocks. They are social animals that prefer to live in large packs.	Eliminate	Both of these sentences are independent clauses and can stand alone as complete sentences; however, they were originally connected with a comma and FANBOYS conjunction ("for"), which is also correct sentence structure. Therefore, this change is not needed, since it was not correcting an error.
G.	In South America. Llamas helped the Andean civilization thrive in the high mountains; their high thirst tolerance, physical stamina, and ability to survive on a wide variety of plants make llamas important transport animals.	Eliminate	"In South America" is not an independent clause because it does not have a verb or a complete thought, so it cannot stand alone as a sentence.
H.	Besides providing transporta-tion. Llamas offer wool, meat, and tallow for candles.	Eliminate	"Besides providing transportation" is not an independent clause because it does not have a subject or a complete thought, so it cannot be its own sentence.

5. I. The question stem states that precise language is needed. Sentence 2 does not provide specific information about the "New inventions," "the existing economy," or the "new" economy.

J.

EDITED TEXT	KEEP OR ELIMINATE?	WHY?
A. Especially important was a change in the economy that had to do with manufacturing and machinery.	Eliminate	The sentence does not specify the "change in the economy."
B. In particular, manufacturing and machinery changed a traditional economy into a different kind of economy.	Eliminate	The sentence does not provide details about the "traditional economy," and the phrase "different kind of economy" is vague.
C. Specifically, the traditional agrarian economy was supplanted by one based on manufacturing and machinery.	Keep	The sentence clearly states that the traditional economy was "agrarian" and that the new economy was "based on manufacturing and machinery."
D. They supplanted the traditional agrarian economy with an economy that was entirely different and included new technology.	Eliminate	While the sentence does clearly state that the traditional economy was "agrarian," it is unclear who "They" is referring to, and the phrases "entirely different" and "included new technology" are not specific.

6. **K.** The question stem asks you to combine two sentences in a clear, logical way.

L.

EDITED TEXT	KEEP OR ELIMINATE?	WHY?
E. Very much an urban movement, the revolution gave rise to a new system of society based primarily upon the relationship of the industrial capitalist to the factory worker.	Eliminate	This option changes the meaning from "new social class" to "society," which are not necessarily the same ideas.
F. Very much an urban movement, the revolution gave rise to a new system of social class, and that class was based primarily upon the relationship of the industrial capitalist to the factory worker.	Eliminate	This sentence adds the redundant words "and that class."
G. Very much an urban movement, a new system of social class was given rise to primarily based on the relationship of the industrial capitalist to the factory worker.	Eliminate	This choice deletes the original subject, which changes the meaning of the sentence and creates a modifier error. It also changes the active "gave rise to" to the passive voice "was given rise to," which is wordier and less clear.
H. Very much an urban movement, the revolution gave rise to a new system of social class based primarily upon the relationship of the industrial capitalist to the factory worker.	Keep	This option deletes the subject and verb from sentence 4 and adds the remainder of sentence 4 to the previous sentence. The result is a sentence that flows clearly and is logical.

7. **M.** An additional sentence is needed to support sentence 8 and connect its ideas to the rest of the paragraph.

N.

	EDITED TEXT	KEEP OR ELIMINATE?	WHY?
A.	After the industrialization of textile production in 1815, the hand-spun textiles with which many families had supplemented their incomes could not compete with cheaper, factory-spun cloth. The factory-made cloth was less expensive to purchase, which made it popular, especially among the lower class.	Eliminate	This sentence essentially repeats what the previous sentence said and adds no new information.
B.	After the industrialization of textile production in 1815, the hand-spun textiles with which many families had supplemented their incomes could not compete with cheaper, factory-spun cloth. Men could still work the farm, but women found their traditional cloth-making work devalued.	Keep	This sentence expands on the previous sentence, explaining an additional result of industrialization. It also provides a good introduction for the next sentence, which discusses the new roles for women as factory workers.
C.	After the industrialization of textile production in 1815, the hand-spun textiles with which many families had supplemented their incomes could not compete with cheaper, factory-spun cloth. Factory-spun cloth could also be made faster, which was particularly advantageous for increasing profit margins.	Eliminate	The topic is the female factory worker, so the profitability of factory-spun cloth does not fit well.
D.	After the industrialization of textile production in 1815, the hand-spun textiles with which many families had supplemented their incomes could not compete with cheaper, factory-spun cloth. The textiles were just as well spun as was homemade cloth, both of which had to be well-constructed to stand up to wear and tear over time.	Eliminate	The quality of the factory-spun cloth is off topic; the passage is about female factory workers and how industrialization affected their lives.

8. **O.** A transition is needed at the beginning of sentence 11 in order to connect the ideas of the previous paragraph to this new paragraph.

P.

	EDITED TEXT	KEEP OR ELIMINATE?	WHY?
E.	The family she left behind would profit from a share of her wages, while she kept a portion of the money—whether to save or to spend on the consumer goods created by the new industrial society. On the other hand, millwork was often a deliberate step toward personal advancement for women from a limited, but not destitute, farm background.	Eliminate	A transition that indicates an additional result is needed, so the contrast transition "on the other hand" will not work.
F.	The family she left behind would profit from a share of her wages, while she kept a portion of the money—whether to save or to spend on the consumer goods created by the new industrial society. Nevertheless, millwork was often a deliberate step toward personal advancement for women from a limited, but not destitute, farm background.	Eliminate	"Nevertheless" is a contrast transition, which is the opposite of the author's intended meaning.
G.	The family she left behind would profit from a share of her wages, while she kept a portion of the money—whether to save or to spend on the consumer goods created by the new industrial society. Unfortunately, millwork was often a deliberate step toward personal advancement for women from a limited, but not destitute, farm background.	Eliminate	"Unfortunately" does not reflect the generally positive tone of the third paragraph.
H.	The family she left behind would profit from a share of her wages, while she kept a portion of the money—whether to save or to spend on the consumer goods created by the new industrial society. Furthermore, millwork was often a deliberate step toward personal advancement for women from a limited, but not destitute, farm background.	Keep	Sentence 11 discusses another positive result of the Industrial Revolution, so the transition should indicate a continuation of the previous idea.

9. **Q.** The question stem indicates that the passage includes an irrelevant sentence. The answer choices are all from the last paragraph of the passage, which is about rural workers moving to the city.

R.

EDITED TEXT	KEEP OR ELIMINATE?	WHY?
A. (15) Many people new to America were Irish immigrants fleeing from the potato famine. (16) In some cases, this led to improvements in their lives, with urban transportation and increased opportunities. (17) However, the rush to the cities also led to overcrowding, poor living conditions, health issues, and child labor. (18) Thus, the Industrial Revolution, which changed the basis of America's economy, brought both improvements and problems.	Eliminate	Sentence 14 is the paragraph's topic sentence, so it should not be deleted.
B. (14) In America, as In England, many previously rural workers moved to the cities. (16) In some cases, this led to improvements in their lives, with urban transportation and increased opportunities. (17) However, the rush to the cities also led to overcrowding, poor living conditions, health issues, and child labor. (18) Thus, the Industrial Revolution, which changed the basis of America's economy, brought both improvements and problems.	Keep	The paragraph is about rural workers moving to cities; information about the Irish potato famine is off topic, and, therefore, this sentence should be deleted.
C. (14) In America, as in England, many previously rural workers moved to the cities. (15) Many people new to America were Irish immigrants fleeing from the potato famine. (17) However, the rush to the cities also led to overcrowding, poor living conditions, health issues, and child labor. (18) Thus, the Industrial Revolution, which changed the basis of America's economy, brought both improvements and problems.	Eliminate	Sentence 16 explains a result of moving to the cities, which fits with the paragraph's main focus; sentence 16 should be kept.
D. (14) In America, as in England, many previously rural workers moved to the cities. (15) Many people new to America were Irish immigrants fleeing from the potato famine. (16) In some cases, this led to improvements in their lives, with urban transportation and increased opportunities. (18) Thus, the Industrial Revolution, which changed the basis of America's economy, brought both improvements and problems.	Eliminate	Sentence 17 should not be deleted because it provides information about the effects of urban overpopulation.

[CHAPTER 4]

REVISING/EDITING TEXT SKILLS REVIEW

CHAPTER OBJECTIVES

By the end of this chapter, you will be able to:

- Determine the correct punctuation and/or conjunctions to form a complete sentence
- Identify and correct inappropriate modifier placement
- Identify and correct inappropriate uses of commas, dashes, semicolons, colons, and apostrophes
- Use punctuation to set off simple parenthetical elements
- Identify and correct verb agreement issues
- Identify and correct pronoun agreement issues
- Identify and correct modifier agreement issues
- Revise redundant or wordy writing
- Identify the wording that accomplishes the appropriate purpose
- Determine the need for transition words or phrases to establish logical relationships within and between paragraphs
- Determine the most logical place for a sentence in a paragraph or passage
- Determine the relevance of a sentence within a passage
- Provide an introduction or conclusion to a paragraph or passage
- Provide supporting text for a paragraph or passage

1. Sentence Structure and Modifier Placement

Sentence Structure

Fragments

A complete sentence must have both a subject and a verb and must express a complete thought. If any one of these elements is missing, the sentence is a **fragment**. You can recognize a fragment because the sentence will not make sense as written. Some examples are shown in the table below.

MISSING ELEMENT	EXAMPLE	CORRECTED SENTENCE
Subject	*Ran a marathon.*	*Lola ran a marathon.*
Verb	*Lola a marathon.*	
Complete thought	*While Lola ran a marathon.*	*While Lola ran a marathon, her friends cheered for her.*

The fragment "While Lola ran a marathon" is an example of a dependent clause: it has a subject (Lola) and a verb (ran), but it does not express a complete thought because it starts with a subordinating conjunction (while). Notice what the word "while" does to the meaning. While Lola ran a marathon, what happened? To fix this type of fragment, eliminate the subordinating conjunction or join the dependent clause to an independent clause using a comma. Subordinating conjunctions are words and phrases such as *since*, *because*, *therefore*, *unless*, *although*, and *due to*.

Run-Ons

Unlike a dependent clause, an independent clause can stand on its own as a complete sentence. If a sentence has more than one independent clause, however, those clauses must be properly joined. If they are not, the sentence is a **run-on**: *Lucas enjoys hiking, he climbs a new mountain every summer.* There are several ways to correct a run-on, as shown in the table below.

TO CORRECT A RUN-ON	EXAMPLE
Use a period	*Lucas enjoys hiking. He climbs a new mountain every summer.*
Use a semicolon	*Lucas enjoys hiking; he climbs a new mountain every summer.*
Use a colon	*Lucas enjoys hiking: he climbs a new mountain every summer.*
Make one clause dependent	*Since Lucas enjoys hiking, he climbs a new mountain every summer.*
Add a FANBOYS conjunction: for, and, nor, but, or, yet, so	*Lucas enjoys hiking, so he climbs a new mountain every summer.*
Use a dash	*Lucas enjoys hiking—he climbs a new mountain every summer.*

English

Semicolons

Semicolons can be confusing for some students. They are used in two specific ways.

USE SEMICOLONS TO . . .	EXAMPLE
Join two independent clauses that are not connected by a comma and FANBOYS conjunction, just as you would use a period	*Gaby knew that her term paper would take at least four hours to write; she got started in study hall and then finished it at home.*
Separate sublists within a longer list when those sublists contain commas	*The team needed to bring uniforms, helmets, and gloves; oranges, almonds, and water; and hockey sticks, pucks, and skates.*

How to Answer Fragment and Run-On Questions

To answer questions with fragment and run-on errors, familiarize yourself with the ways in which they are tested:

- Fragments
  - If a sentence is missing a subject, a verb, or a complete thought, it is a fragment.
  - Correct the fragment by adding the missing element.
- Run-ons
  - If a sentence includes two independent clauses, they must be properly joined.
  - Employ one of the following options to punctuate independent clauses properly:
    - Use a period.
    - Insert a semicolon or colon.
    - Make one clause dependent by using a subordinating conjunction (since, because, therefore, unless, although, due to, etc.).
    - Use a comma and a FANBOYS conjunction (for, and, nor, but, or, yet, so).
    - Use a dash.

Practice: Fragments and Run-Ons

Part 1

DIRECTIONS: Follow the instructions for each sentence to correct the grammatical error.

- **A.** **Correct the fragment by adding a subject:** Brought snacks to the weekend study session.
- **B.** **Correct the fragment by completing the thought:** After getting to the stadium.
- **C.** **Correct the run-on sentence with the proper punctuation:** The new arts center just opened it has a crafts room for children under thirteen.
- **D.** **Correct the run-on sentence with the proper punctuation:** Herodotus is known as one of the first historians he is even called "The Father of History."
- **E.** **Make one clause dependent to correct the run-on sentence:** Herodotus is sometimes accused of making up stories for his histories, he claimed he simply recorded what he had been told.

Part 2

1. Read this paragraph.

> (1) Colleges could give greater support to men's sports teams than to women's teams prior to 1972; today, women's and men's teams must receive equal funding. (2) Title IX of the Education Amendments prohibits gender discrimination at colleges and other federally funded institutions. (3) Resulted in more money in athletic departments allocated for women's sports. (4) Title IX has led to more interest in women's sports, greater competition among teams, and improvements in the quality of athletics for women.

Which sentence contains an error in its construction and should be revised?

A. sentence 1

B. sentence 2

C. sentence 3

D. sentence 4

F. **What type of issue do the question stem and answer choices indicate?**

G. **Consider each of the options, decide to keep or eliminate the choice, and indicate why.**

ANSWER CHOICE	KEEP OR ELIMINATE?	WHY?
A. (1) Colleges could give greater support to men's sports teams than to women's teams prior to 1972; today, women's and men's teams must receive equal funding.		
B. (2) Title IX of the Education Amendments prohibits gender discrimination at colleges and other federally funded institutions.		
C. (3) Resulted in more money in athletic departments allocated for women's sports.		
D. (4) Title IX has led to more interest in women's sports, greater competition among teams, and improvements in the quality of athletics for women.		

2. Read this sentence.

> White roses represent <u>unity</u>, yellow roses show friendship, and red roses signify <u>love however</u>, many people <u>believe</u> red roses are the most cherished within the genus *Rosa*.

Which edit should be made to correct this sentence?

E. Delete the comma after *unity*.

F. Insert a semicolon after *love*.

G. Delete the comma after *however*.

H. Insert a semicolon after *believe*.

H. What type of issue do the question stem and answer choices indicate?

I. The following table shows how the suggested edits in the answer choices, if implemented, would change the relevant text. Consider each of the options, decide to keep or eliminate the text, and indicate why.

	EDITED TEXT	KEEP OR ELIMINATE?	WHY?
E.	White roses represent unity yellow roses show friendship, and red roses signify love however, many people believe red roses are the most cherished within the genus *Rosa*.		
F.	White roses represent unity, yellow roses show friendship, and red roses signify love; however, many people believe red roses are the most cherished within the genus *Rosa*.		
G.	White roses represent unity, yellow roses show friendship, and red roses signify love however many people believe red roses are the most cherished within the genus *Rosa*.		
H.	White roses represent unity, yellow roses show friendship, and red roses signify love however, many people believe; red roses are the most cherished within the genus *Rosa*.		

Modifier Placement

A **modifier** is a word or phrase that describes, clarifies, or provides additional information about another part of the sentence. Modifier questions require you to identify the part of a sentence being described and use the appropriate modifier in the proper place.

In order to be grammatically correct, the modifier must be placed as close to the word it describes as possible. Use context clues in the passage to identify the correct placement of a modifier; a misplaced modifier can cause confusion and is always incorrect on test day.

Note that a common way the SHSAT tests modifiers is with modifying phrases at the beginning of a sentence. Just like any other modifier, the phrase grammatically modifies whatever is right next to it in the sentence. For example, consider the sentence, "While walking to the bus stop, the rain drenched Gina." The initial phrase, "While walking to the bus stop," grammatically modifies "the rain," but this creates a sentence that doesn't make sense; the rain can't walk to the bus stop. The writer meant that Gina was walking to the bus stop, so the sentence should read, "While walking to the bus stop, Gina was drenched by the rain." Here are some additional examples.

MODIFIER/MODIFYING PHRASE	INCORRECT	CORRECT
nearly	Andre **nearly** watched the play for four hours.	Andre watched the play for **nearly** four hours.
in individual containers	The art teacher handed out paints to the students **in individual containers**.	The art teacher handed out paints **in individual containers** to the students.
A scholar athlete	**A scholar athlete**, maintaining high grades in addition to playing soccer was expected of Maya.	**A scholar athlete**, Maya was expected to maintain high grades in addition to playing soccer.

How to Answer Modifier Placement Questions

If a question includes a modifier, determine whether the modifier is placed correctly:

- Is it as near as possible to the word it logically modifies?
- If it is not in the correct place, where should it be moved?

Practice: Modifier Placement

Part 1

DIRECTIONS: Edit each sentence to correct the modifier placement issue.

J. Wearing a brown collar, Cecilia walked the dog.

K. The dealer sold the Ford to the buyer with the hatchback.

L. The server placed rolls onto the warm table.

M. While looking toward the west, a breeze stirred the leaves on the trees as I watched.

N. I borrowed a blender from a neighbor that turned out to be broken.

Part 2

3. Read this sentence.

> To raise money for uniforms, a car wash will be held by members of the volleyball team on Saturday.

How should the sentence be revised?

A. Members of the volleyball team, on Saturday to raise money for uniforms, will hold a car wash.

B. To raise money for uniforms, on Saturday a car wash will be held by members of the volleyball team.

C. On Saturday to raise money for uniforms, members of the volleyball team will hold a car wash.

D. To raise money for uniforms, members of the volleyball team will hold a car wash on Saturday.

O. **What type of issue do the question stem and answer choices indicate?**

P. **Consider each of the options, decide to keep or eliminate the choice, and indicate why.**

ANSWER CHOICE	KEEP OR ELIMINATE?	WHY?
A. Members of the volleyball team, on Saturday to raise money for uniforms, will hold a car wash.		
B. To raise money for uniforms, on Saturday a car wash will be held by members of the volleyball team.		
C. On Saturday to raise money for uniforms, members of the volleyball team will hold a car wash.		
D. To raise money for uniforms, members of the volleyball team will hold a car wash on Saturday.		

4. Read this paragraph.

> (1) Most gems are crystallized minerals, but amber, coral, and pearls come from organic material. (2) Amber's buoyancy suggests organic origins; unlike most gemstones, this ancient fossilized resin floats in water. (3) Coral is a discarded limestone skeleton found in the sea. (4) Taking several years to form, oysters create white, black, or pink pearls.

Which sentence contains an error in its construction and should be revised?

E. sentence 1

F. sentence 2

G. sentence 3

H. sentence 4

Q. What type of issue do the question stem and answer choices indicate?

R. Consider each of the options, decide to keep or eliminate the choice, and indicate why.

ANSWER CHOICE	KEEP OR ELIMINATE?	WHY?
E. (1) Most gems are crystallized minerals, but amber, coral, and pearls come from organic material.		
F. (2) Amber's buoyancy suggests organic origins; unlike most gemstones, this ancient fossilized resin floats in water.		
G. (3) Coral is a discarded limestone skeleton found in the sea.		
H. (4) Taking several years to form, oysters create white, black, or pink pearls.		

2. Punctuation

Punctuation on the SHSAT

The SHSAT requires you to identify inappropriate commas, semicolons, colons, dashes, and apostrophes when they are used to indicate breaks in thought within a sentence. When you identify a Punctuation question, check to make sure the punctuation is used correctly in context.

Types of Punctuation

Commas

USE COMMAS TO . . .	EXAMPLE
Separate independent clauses connected by a FANBOYS conjunction (*for, and, nor, but, or, yet, so*)	*Jess finished her homework earlier than expected, so she started a project that was due the following week.*
Separate an introductory or modifying phrase from the rest of the sentence	*Knowing that soccer practice would be especially strenuous, Tia spent extra time stretching beforehand.*
Set off three or more items in a series or list	*Jeremiah packed a sleeping bag, a raincoat, and a lantern for his upcoming camping trip.*
Separate nonessential information from the rest of the sentence	*Professor Mann, who is the head of the English department, is known for the extensive assignments in his courses.*
Separate a dependent and an independent clause	*When it started to thunder, the lifeguards quickly ushered swimmers out of the pool.*
Separate coordinate adjectives	*Yogurt is a tasty, nutritious snack that is a good source of probiotics.*

SHSAT EXPERT NOTE

When deciding if you need a comma between two adjectives, make sure you can (1) replace the comma with the word "and" as well as (2) reverse the order of the adjectives without altering the meaning of the sentence. For example, "the large, heavy box" can be rewritten as "the large and heavy box" as well as "the heavy, large box," so it does require a comma.

Dashes

USE DASHES TO . . .	EXAMPLE
Indicate a hesitation or a break in thought	*Going to a history museum is a good way to begin researching prehistoric creatures—on second thought, researching on the computer would likely be much more efficient.*
Set off explanatory elements within a sentence	*Rockwell's Space Transportation Systems Division handled all facets—design, development, and testing—of the reusable orbiter.*

Parenthetical Elements

Parenthetical elements may appear at the beginning, in the middle, or at the end of a sentence. A phrase such as "the capital of France" is considered parenthetical if the rest of the sentence is grammatically correct when it is removed. A parenthetical phrase must be properly punctuated with parentheses, commas, or dashes for the sentence to be grammatically correct. Do not mix and match; a parenthetical element must begin and end with the same type of punctuation.

PARENTHETICAL ELEMENT PLACEMENT	PARENTHESES	COMMA(S)	DASH(ES)
Beginning	*N/A*	*The capital of France, Paris is a popular tourist destination.*	*N/A*
Middle	*Paris (the capital of France) is a popular tourist destination.*	*Paris, the capital of France, is a popular tourist destination.*	*Paris—the capital of France—is a popular tourist destination.*
End	*A popular tourist destination is Paris (the capital of France).*	*A popular tourist destination is Paris, the capital of France.*	*A popular tourist destination is Paris—the capital of France.*

Semicolons

As the lesson about Sentence Structure discussed, semicolons are used in two specific ways:

- A semicolon may join two independent clauses that are not connected by a FANBOYS conjunction, just as you would use a period.
- Semicolons may be used to separate items in a list if those items already include commas.

USE SEMICOLONS TO . . .	EXAMPLE
Join two independent clauses that are not connected by a FANBOYS conjunction	*Ramon looked at each option carefully; after a few minutes of deliberation, he selected the well-worn book on the bottom shelf.*
Separate items in a series or list if those items already include commas	*The recipe required pans, pots, and spoons; herbs, spices, and salt; and onions, carrots, and celery.*

Colons

USE COLONS TO . . .	EXAMPLE
Introduce a short phrase, quotation, explanation, example, or list	*Sanjay had two important projects to complete: a science experiment and an expository essay.*

Apostrophes

USE AN APOSTROPHE TO . . .	EXAMPLE
Indicate the possessive form of a single noun	*My oldest **sister's** soccer game is on Saturday.*
Indicate the possessive form of a plural noun	*My two older **sisters'** soccer games are on Saturday.*
Indicate a contraction (e.g., *don't, can't*)	***They've** won every soccer match this season.*

Note that plural nouns are formed without an apostrophe.

INCORRECT	CORRECT
Stingray's are cartilaginous fish related to shark's.	*Stingrays are cartilaginous fish related to sharks.*
There are many carnival's in this area every summer.	*There are many carnivals in this area every summer.*

To check whether *it's* is appropriate, replace it in the sentence with *it is* or *it has*. If the sentence no longer makes sense, *it's* is incorrect. The following sentence is correct:

The tree frog blends perfectly into its surroundings. When it holds still, it's nearly invisible.

Note that *its'* and *its's* are never correct.

Unnecessary Punctuation

Knowing when punctuation should not be used is equally important. If an underlined portion includes punctuation, take time to consider if it should be included at all.

DO NOT USE PUNCTUATION TO . . .	INCORRECT	CORRECT
Separate a subject from its verb	*The diligent student council, meets every week.*	*The diligent student council meets every week.*
Separate a verb from its object or a preposition from its object	*The diligent student council meets, every week.*	*The diligent student council meets every week.*
Set off elements that are essential to a sentence's meaning	*The, diligent student, council meets every week.*	*The diligent student council meets every week.*
Separate adjectives that work together to modify a noun	*The diligent, student council meets every week.*	*The diligent student council meets every week.*

How to Answer Punctuation Questions

If the question indicates that there is a punctuation error, evaluate the punctuation marks throughout the text, asking yourself:

- Is the punctuation used correctly?
  The punctuation needs to be the correct type (comma, dash, or colon) and in the correct location.
- Is the punctuation necessary?
  If you cannot identify a reason why the punctuation is included, the punctuation should be removed.

Practice: Punctuation

Part 1

> **DIRECTIONS:** Edit each sentence to correct the punctuation issue.

 A. For my birthday, I asked for my favorite dinner chicken and roasted vegetables.

 B. The story of Emperor Nero playing the fiddle while Rome burned has been debunked by historians but the saying based on it remains popular.

 C. Koalas' fingerprints are nearly indistinguishable from human fingerprints which has occasionally led to mistakes at crime scenes.

 D. Invented by Sir John Harrington in 1596 the flush toilet actually precedes modern indoor plumbing.

 E. Toni Morrison born Chloe Wofford was one of America's most celebrated writers.

Part 2

1. Read this sentence.

> Unable to decide between a career in <u>law</u> and one in <u>medicine</u> Jemma combined her two <u>interests</u> and studied <u>forensic</u> medicine.

Which edit should be made to correct this sentence?

 A. Insert a comma after *law*.

 B. Insert a comma after *medicine*.

 C. Insert a comma after *interests*.

 D. Insert a comma after *forensic*.

F. **What type of issue do the question stem and answer choices indicate?**

G. The following table shows how the suggested edits in the answer choices, if implemented, would change the relevant text. Consider each of the options, decide to keep or eliminate the text, and indicate why.

EDITED TEXT	KEEP OR ELIMINATE?	WHY?
A. Unable to decide between a career in law, and one in medicine Jemma combined her two interests and studied forensic medicine.		
B. Unable to decide between a career in law and one in medicine, Jemma combined her two interests and studied forensic medicine.		
C. Unable to decide between a career in law and one in medicine Jemma combined her two interests, and studied forensic medicine.		
D. Unable to decide between a career in law and one in medicine Jemma combined her two interests and studied forensic, medicine.		

2. Read this paragraph.

> (1) The winner of an election is often the candidate who best masters the art of the political advertisement. (2) Most voters have a stake in the issues of the day but cannot make sense of the rules and rhetoric of the real processes of government. (3) The 30-second commercial on prime-time television—making sense out of technical political jargon plays a crucial part in the political process. (4) Those who wish to speak for an electorate must make their case to that electorate, and the political advertisement is the most direct and effective way to achieve that goal.

Which sentence contains an error in its construction and should be revised?

E. sentence 1

F. sentence 2

G. sentence 3

H. sentence 4

H. What type of issue do the question stem and answer choices indicate?

I. **Consider each of the options, decide to keep or eliminate the choice, and indicate why.**

ANSWER CHOICE	KEEP OR ELIMINATE?	WHY?
E. (1) The winner of an election is often the candidate who best masters the art of the political advertisement.		
F. (2) Most voters have a stake in the issues of the day but cannot make sense of the rules and rhetoric of the real processes of government.		
G. (3) The 30-second commercial on prime-time television—making sense out of technical political jargon plays a crucial part in the political process.		
H. (4) Those who wish to speak for an electorate must make their case to that electorate, and the political advertisement is the most direct and effective way to achieve that goal.		

3. Read this paragraph.

> (1) Bicycling is a mainstream form of transportation in Japanese cities. (2) Nearly every type of person uses a bicycle, blue-collar workers, office workers in suits, parents toting babies, and students. (3) In the United States, however, bicycling is more often seen as a recreational activity or form of exercise than as a means of transportation. (4) An exception is that American children often rely on bikes because they have fewer transportation options.

Which sentence contains an error in its construction and should be revised?

A. sentence 1

B. sentence 2

C. sentence 3

D. sentence 4

J. **What type of issue do the question stem and answer choices indicate?**

K. Consider each of the options, decide to keep or eliminate the choice, and indicate why.

ANSWER CHOICE	KEEP OR ELIMINATE?	WHY?
A. (1) Bicycling is a mainstream form of transportation in Japanese cities.		
B. (2) Nearly every type of person uses a bicycle, blue-collar workers, office workers in suits, parents toting babies, and students.		
C. (3) In the United States, however, bicycling is more often seen as a recreational activity or form of exercise than as a means of transportation.		
D. (4) An exception is that American children often rely on bikes because they have fewer transportation options.		

4. Read this sentence.

> Although the statue was intended, in ancient times, to tower above the landscape, <u>it's presence</u> is now dominated by the enormous <u>skyscrapers</u> that came with the <u>city's</u> modernization.

Which edit should be made to correct the sentence?

E. Change *it's* to **its**.

F. Insert a comma after *presence*.

G. Insert a comma after *skyscrapers*.

H. Change *city's* to **cities**.

L. What type of issue do the question stem and answer choices indicate?

M. **Consider each of the options, decide to keep or eliminate the choice, and indicate why.**

ANSWER CHOICE	KEEP OR ELIMINATE?	WHY?
E. Although the statue was intended, in ancient times, to tower above the landscape, its presence is now dominated by the enormous skyscrapers that came with the city's modernization.		
F. Although the statue was intended, in ancient times, to tower above the landscape, it's presence, is now dominated by the enormous skyscrapers that came with the city's modernization.		
G. Although the statue was intended, in ancient times, to tower above the landscape, it's presence is now dominated by the enormous skyscrapers, that came with the city's modernization.		
H. Although the statue was intended, in ancient times, to tower above the landscape, it's presence is now dominated by the enormous skyscrapers that came with the cities modernization.		

3. Usage

Verbs

Verb Tense

Verb tense indicates when an action or state of being takes place: in the past, present, or future. The tense of the verb must fit the context of the passage. Each tense can express three different types of action.

TYPE OF ACTION	PAST	PRESENT	FUTURE
Single action occurring only once	Connor **planted** vegetables in the community garden.	Connor **plants** vegetables in the community garden.	Connor **will plant** vegetables in the community garden.
Action that is ongoing at some point in time	Connor **was planting** vegetables in the community garden this morning before noon.	Connor **is planting** vegetables in the community garden this morning before noon.	Connor **will be planting** vegetables in the community garden this morning before noon.
Action that is completed before a specific point in time	Connor **had planted** vegetables in the community garden every year until he gave his job to Jasmine.	Connor **has planted** vegetables in the community garden every season since the garden opened.	Connor **will have planted** vegetables in the community garden by the time the growing season starts.

Subject-Verb Agreement

A verb must agree with its subject in person and number:

- Person (first, second, or third)
  - First: *I* **ask** *a question.*
  - Second: *You* **ask** *a question.*
  - Third: *She* **asks** *a question.*
- Number (singular or plural)
  - Singular: *The apple* **tastes** *delicious.*
  - Plural: *Apples* **taste** *delicious.*

The noun closest to the verb is not always the subject. For example, in the sentence, "The chair with the lion feet is an antique," the singular verb, *is*, is closest to the plural noun *feet*. However, the verb's actual subject is the singular noun *chair*, so the sentence is correct as written.

When a sentence includes two nouns, only the conjunction *and* forms a compound subject requiring a plural verb form:

- Plural: *Saliyah and Taylor* **are** *in the running club.*
- Singular: *Either Saliyah or Taylor* **is** *in the running club.*
- Singular: *Neither Saliyah nor Taylor* **is** *in the running club.*

Collective nouns are nouns that name entities with more than one member, such as *group*, *team*, and *family*. Even though these nouns represent more than one person, they are grammatically singular and require singular verb forms:

- *The collection of paintings* **is** *one of the most popular art exhibits in recent years.*
- *The team* **looks** *promising this year.*

Parallelism

Verbs in a list, a compound, or a comparison must be parallel in form.

FEATURE	EXAMPLE	PARALLEL FORM
A list	*Chloe **formulated** a question, **conducted** background research, and **constructed** a hypothesis before starting the experiment.*	3 simple past-tense verb phrases
A compound	***Hunting** and **fishing** were essential to the survival of Midwestern Native American tribes such as the Omaha.*	2 *-ing* verb forms
A comparison	*Garrett enjoys **sculpting** as much as **painting**.*	2 *-ing* verb forms

Note that parallelism may be tested using other parts of speech besides verbs. In general, any items in a list, compound, or comparison must be in parallel form. For example, if a list starts with a noun, the other items in the list must also be nouns; if it starts with an adjective, the other items must also be adjectives.

INCORRECT	CORRECT
Naomi likes **oatmeal and drinking tea** on chilly weekend afternoons.	Naomi likes **oatmeal and tea** on chilly weekend afternoons. *or* Naomi likes **eating oatmeal and drinking tea** on chilly weekend afternoons.
Which of the dogs is the **most docile and better behaved?**	Which of the dogs is the **most docile and best behaved**? *or* Which of the dogs is the **more docile and better behaved**?

How to Answer Verb Questions

When answering questions that ask about verb errors, check that the verb:

- Reflects the correct tense (Does it fit the context?)
- Agrees with the subject in person and number
- Is parallel in form with other verbs in a series, list, or compound (if there is one in the sentence)

Practice: Verb Usage

Part 1

> **DIRECTIONS:** Edit each sentence to correct the verb issue.

A. Angel audition for the school play next week.

B. The song with the upbeat rhythm and catchy lyrics were wildly popular.

C. Either the governor or the lieutenant governor usually present the award.

D. By the time the last runner completed the marathon, the winner has crossed the finish line hours ago.

E. Few people know that Stephen Hawking both revolutionized physics and cowritten children's books with his daughter.

Part 2

1. Read this sentence.

> The most successful scientists, spanning <u>fields</u> from physics to geology, <u>sees</u> beyond the facts and <u>speculate</u> about the general principles that <u>provide</u> a foundation for new ideas.

   Which edit should be made to correct this sentence?

   A. Change *fields* to **field**.

   B. Change *sees* to **see**.

   C. Change *speculate* to **speculates**.

   D. Change *provide* to **provides**.

F. **What type of issue do the question stem and answer choices indicate?**

G. **The following table shows how the suggested edits in the answer choices, if implemented, would change the relevant text. Consider each of the options, decide to keep or eliminate the text, and indicate why.**

	EDITED TEXT	KEEP OR ELIMINATE?	WHY?
A.	The most successful scientists, spanning field from physics to geology, sees beyond the facts and speculate about the general principles that provide a foundation for new ideas.		
B.	The most successful scientists, spanning fields from physics to geology, see beyond the facts and speculate about the general principles that provide a foundation for new ideas.		
C.	The most successful scientists, spanning fields from physics to geology, sees beyond the facts and speculates about the general principles that provide a foundation for new ideas.		
D.	The most successful scientists, spanning fields from physics to geology, sees beyond the facts and speculate about the general principles that provides a foundation for new ideas.		

2. Read this sentence.

> During a time when women <u>are</u> generally not allowed to venture outside the domestic realm, Christine de Pisan <u>became</u> an acclaimed poet in the Middle Ages and <u>was</u> considered the first woman in France to have <u>earned</u> renown as a writer.

Which edit should be made to correct this sentence?

E. Change *are* to **were**.

F. Change *became* to **becomes**.

G. Change *was* to **is**.

H. Change *earned* to **earn**.

H. What type of issue do the question stem and answer choices indicate?

I. The following table shows how the suggested edits in the answer choices, if implemented, would change the relevant text. Consider each of the options, decide to keep or eliminate the text, and indicate why.

EDITED TEXT	KEEP OR ELIMINATE?	WHY?
E. During a time when women were generally not allowed to venture outside the domestic realm, Christine de Pisan became an acclaimed poet in the Middle Ages and was considered the first woman in France to have earned renown as a writer.		
F. During a time when women are generally not allowed to venture outside the domestic realm, Christine de Pisan becomes an acclaimed poet in the Middle Ages and was considered the first woman in France to have earned renown as a writer.		
G. During a time when women are generally not allowed to venture outside the domestic realm, Christine de Pisan became an acclaimed poet in the Middle Ages and is considered the first woman in France to have earned renown as a writer.		
H. During a time when women are generally not allowed to venture outside the domestic realm, Christine de Pisan became an acclaimed poet in the Middle Ages and was considered the first woman in France to have earn renown as a writer.		

Pronouns

Pronoun Forms

A pronoun is a word that takes the place of a noun. A pronoun can take three different forms, each of which is based on the grammatical role the pronoun plays in the sentence.

FORM	PRONOUNS	EXAMPLE
Subjective: The pronoun is used as the subject.	I, you, she, he, it, we, they, who	*Rivka is the student **who** will lead the presentation.*
Objective: The pronoun is used as the object of a verb or a preposition.	me, you, her, him, it, us, them, whom	*With **whom** will Rivka present the scientific findings?*
Possessive: The pronoun expresses ownership.	my, mine, your, yours, his, her, hers, its, our, ours, their, theirs, whose	*Rivka will likely choose a partner **whose** work is excellent.*

Pronoun-Antecedent Agreement

A pronoun's antecedent is the noun it logically represents in a sentence. If the noun is singular, the pronoun must be singular; if the noun is plural, the pronoun must be plural. Also, if the antecedent is a person or a group of people, use "who" instead of "that" because "that" can only refer to things.

ANTECEDENT	INCORRECT	CORRECT
selection	*The selection of books was placed in **their** designated location.*	*The selection of books was placed in **its** designated location.*
Addison	*Addison fed the giraffes all of the lettuce **they** had purchased.*	*Addison fed the giraffes all of the lettuce **she** had purchased.*
sapling	*The sapling, along with dozens of flowers, was relocated to where **they** would thrive.*	*The sapling, along with dozens of flowers, was relocated to where **it** would thrive.*
students	*If students are confused, **she** should ask for clarification.*	*If students are confused, **they** should ask for clarification.*
swimmers	*The swimmers **that** finish their laps first can head to the locker room.*	*The swimmers **who** finish their laps first can head to the locker room.*

SHSAT EXPERT NOTE

When there are two pronouns or a noun and a pronoun in a compound structure, drop the other noun or pronoun to confirm which case to use. Look at this example: "Leo and me walked into town." Would you say, "Me walked into town"? No, you would say, "I walked into town." Therefore, the original sentence should read: "Leo and I walked into town."

Possessive Nouns and Pronouns

Possessive nouns and pronouns indicate that something belongs to someone or something. In general, possessive nouns are written with an apostrophe, while possessive pronouns are not.

TO SPOT ERRORS IN POSSESSIVE NOUN OR PRONOUN CONSTRUCTION, LOOK FOR . . .	INCORRECT	CORRECT
Two nouns in a row	The **professors lectures** were both informative and entertaining.	The **professor's lectures** were both informative and entertaining.
Pronouns with apostrophes	The book is her's.	The book is **hers**.
Words that sound alike	The three friends decided to ride **there** bicycles to the park over **they're**, where **their** going to enjoy a picnic lunch.	The three friends decided to ride **their** bicycles to the park over **there**, where **they're** going to enjoy a picnic lunch.

How to Answer Pronoun Questions

If a question includes a pronoun, find the logical antecedent, which is the word(s) to which the pronoun is referring. Be sure to check that the pronoun:

- Agrees with its antecedent
  - A singular antecedent requires a singular pronoun; a plural antecedent requires a plural pronoun.
- Uses the correct form
  - If the pronoun is the subject of the sentence, use a subjective pronoun such as *I, you, she, he, it, we, they,* or *who.*
  - If the pronoun is an object within the sentence, use an objective pronoun such as *me, you, her, him, it, us, they,* or *whom.*
  - If the pronoun indicates possession, use a possessive pronoun such as *my, mine, your, yours, his, her, hers, its, our, ours, their, theirs,* or *whose.*

Practice: Pronoun Usage

Part 1

DIRECTIONS: Edit each sentence to correct the pronoun issue.

J. There planning to leave their bicycles over by the fence.

K. My uncle likes to go bowling with my sister and I.

L. The box of nails has been moved from their usual place in the shed.

M. My favorite singer, who I have wanted to see in person for years, will give a concert a week after my birthday.

N. The cathedral of Notre Dame, with vast vaulted ceilings and intricate carvings, never fails to amaze their visitors.

Part 2

3. Read this paragraph.

> (1) Sandstone, limestone, and shale are three common types of water-made rocks, and it all can play a role in fossil creation. (2) Shale is composed of mud, often containing distinct layers that have dried together, and it is usually formed by erosion from landmasses. (3) By contrast, sandstone and limestone typically come from the ocean bottom. (4) Sandstone is made up of grains of sand that, with the help of water, have adhered to one another over time, frequently trapping and fossilizing simple sea creatures and plants in the process.

Which sentence contains an error in its construction and should be revised?

A. sentence 1

B. sentence 2

C. sentence 3

D. sentence 4

O.   What type of issue do the question stem and answer choices indicate?

P.   Consider each of the options, decide to keep or eliminate the choice, and indicate why.

	ANSWER CHOICE	KEEP OR ELIMINATE?	WHY?
A.	(1) Sandstone, limestone, and shale are three common types of water-made rocks, and it all can play a role in fossil creation.		
B.	(2) Shale is composed of mud, often containing distinct layers that have dried together, and it is usually formed by erosion from landmasses.		
C.	(3) By contrast, sandstone and limestone typically come from the ocean bottom.		
D.	(4) Sandstone is made up of grains of sand that, with the help of water, have adhered to one another over time, frequently trapping and fossilizing simple sea creatures and plants in the process.		

4. Read this sentence.

> The wolf <u>spider</u>, with <u>its</u> large fuzzy body and hairy legs, is known for <u>their</u> agile hunting <u>skills</u> and excellent eyesight.

Which edit should be made to correct the sentence?

E. Change *spider* to **spiders**.

F. Change *its* to **their**.

G. Change *their* to **its**.

H. Change *skills* to **skill**.

Q. **What type of issue do the question stem and answer choices indicate?**

R. **The following table shows how the suggested edits in the answer choices, if implemented, would change the relevant text. Consider each of the options, decide to keep or eliminate the text, and indicate why.**

	EDITED TEXT	KEEP OR ELIMINATE?	WHY?
E.	The wolf spiders, with its large fuzzy body and hairy legs, is known for their agile hunting skills and excellent eyesight.		
F.	The wolf spider, with their large fuzzy body and hairy legs, is known for their agile hunting skills and excellent eyesight.		
G.	The wolf spider, with its large fuzzy body and hairy legs, is known for its agile hunting skills and excellent eyesight.		
H.	The wolf spider, with its large fuzzy body and hairy legs, is known for their agile hunting skill and excellent eyesight.		

Modifier Agreement

Adjectives and Adverbs

Use adjectives only to modify nouns and pronouns. Use adverbs to modify everything else.

- **Adjectives** are single-word modifiers that describe nouns and pronouns: *Ian conducted an **efficient** lab experiment.*

- **Adverbs** are single-word modifiers that describe verbs, adjectives, or other adverbs: *Ian **efficiently** conducted a lab experiment.*

Note that nouns can sometimes be used as adjectives. For example, in the phrase "the fashion company's autumn line," the word "fashion" functions as an adjective modifying "company," and the word "autumn" functions as an adjective modifying "line."

Comparative/Superlative

When comparing similar things, use adjectives that match the number of items being compared. When comparing two items or people, use the **comparative** form of the adjective. When comparing three or more items or people, use the **superlative** form.

COMPARATIVE (TWO ITEMS)	SUPERLATIVE (THREE OR MORE ITEMS)
better, more, newer, older, shorter, taller, worse, younger	best, most, newest, oldest, shortest, tallest, worst, youngest

How to Answer Modifier Agreement Questions

If the question includes a modifier, determine whether the modifier:

- Agrees with the word or words it is describing
    - Does the sentence require an adjective or an adverb?
    - If a comparative or superlative is used, does it match the number of items being compared?

Practice: Modifier Agreement

Part 1

> **DIRECTIONS:** Edit each sentence to correct the modifier agreement issue.

S. Computers have grown exponential more efficient since their invention.

T. Estella chose to take the route with the most attractively scenery.

U. The leaf-tailed gecko's amazing natural camouflage enables it to blend perfect into its surroundings.

V. Between basketball and baseball, basketball is the most popular sport in the United States.

W. Soccer is the more popular sport worldwide, with a fan base in the billions.

Part 2

5. Read this sentence.

> Between Hugo and Kai, Hugo is the <u>best sprinter</u>; however, Kai is <u>better</u> at the <u>long jump</u>.

Which edit should be made to correct this sentence?

A. Change *best* to **better**.

B. Change *sprinter* to **at sprinting**.

C. Change *better* to **best**.

D. Change *long jump* to **long jumping**.

X. **What type of issue do the question stem and answer choices indicate?**

Y. **The following table shows how the suggested edits in the answer choices, if implemented, would change the relevant text. Consider each of the options, decide to keep or eliminate the text, and indicate why.**

	EDITED TEXT	KEEP OR ELIMINATE?	WHY?
A.	Between Hugo and Kai, Hugo is the better sprinter; however, Kai is better at the long jump.		
B.	Between Hugo and Kai, Hugo is the best at sprinting; however, Kai is better at the long jump.		
C.	Between Hugo and Kai, Hugo is the best sprinter; however, Kai is best at the long jump.		
D.	Between Hugo and Kai, Hugo is the best sprinter; however, Kai is better at long jumping.		

6. Read this paragraph.

> (1) Translating any work is a much more complex process than simply exchanging one word for another, and the effect of a superbly translated play on an audience can be profound. (2) The script for a play is not a work to be appreciated on its own but rather a map used to create such a work. (3) Since the audience for a play will rarely view the script itself, all of the plot points, emotions, subtleties—all of the meaning—must be transmitted simply through spoken dialogue. (4) Granted, when translating between two close related languages, a near word-for-word process can sometimes be sufficient.

Which sentence contains an error and should be revised?

E. sentence 1

F. sentence 2

G. sentence 3

H. sentence 4

Z. **What type of issue do the question stem and answer choices indicate?**

AA. Consider each of the options, decide to keep or eliminate the choice, and indicate why.

	EDITED TEXT	KEEP OR ELIMINATE?	WHY?
E.	(1) Translating any work is a much more complex process than simply exchanging one word for another, and the effect of a superbly translated play on an audience can be profound.		
F.	(2) The script for a play is not a work to be appreciated on its own but rather a map used to create such a work.		
G.	(3) Since the audience for a play will rarely view the script itself, all of the plot points, emotions, subtleties—all of the meaning—must be transmitted simply through spoken dialogue.		
H.	(4) Granted, when translating between two close related languages, a near word-for-word process can sometimes be sufficient.		

4. Strategy Focus: One Error at a Time

One Error at a Time: Punctuation and Usage

Sometimes you will be asked to fix two issues within a single question. In those cases, knowing how to fix one of the two errors will help you narrow down the answer choices.

If the question asks you to fix two errors:

- Focus on one error at a time.
- Reread the text with the proposed changes, and select the option that creates the most correct, concise, and relevant text.

Note that many questions that ask you to correct two errors test both a punctuation issue and a usage issue; you reviewed both of these concepts in the previous lessons.

Practice: One Error at a Time

Part 1

> **DIRECTIONS:** Edit each sentence to correct both one punctuation error and one usage error.

A. Thorny dragons a type of Australian lizard, is covered entirely with spines shaped like upside-down cones.

B. The Pentagon building, located in Washington, D.C.; is known for it's unique five-sided shape, which was designed by American architect George Bergstrom.

C. The restaurant have three types of soups chicken noodle, minestrone, and split pea.

D. The math team newly formed this year—were astounded after winning first place.

E. The valuable, Victorian chairs with authentic upholstery was sold for an astronomical price.

Part 2

1. Read this paragraph.

> (1) Kira <u>spent</u> every day after school last week practicing for the <u>upcoming</u> speech and debate tournament. (2) She <u>rewrote</u> sections of her 10-minute original oratory speech on Monday and <u>Tuesday</u> to clarify her main points. (3) She <u>performs</u> her speech in front of her <u>friends</u>, and team members on Wednesday to simulate the way she planned to deliver her speech in front of people. (4) She <u>recited</u> it out loud over and over on Thursday and <u>Friday</u>, making sure she had every word memorized.

How should this paragraph be revised?

A. Sentence 1: Change *spent* to **had spent**, AND insert a comma after *upcoming*.

B. Sentence 2: Change *rewrote* to **rewrites**, AND insert a comma after *Tuesday*.

C. Sentence 3: Change *performs* to **performed**, AND delete the comma after *friends*.

D. Sentence 4: Change *recited* to **recites**, AND delete the comma after *Friday*.

F. What type of issue do the question stem and answer choices indicate?

G. The following table shows how the suggested edits in the answer choices, if implemented, would change the relevant text. Consider each of the options, decide to keep or eliminate the text, and indicate why.

	EDITED TEXT	KEEP OR ELIMINATE?	WHY?
A.	(1) Kira had spent every day after school last week practicing for the upcoming, speech and debate tournament.		
B.	(2) She rewrites sections of her 10-minute original oratory speech on Monday and Tuesday, to clarify her main points.		
C.	(3) She performed her speech in front of her friends and team members on Wednesday to simulate the way she planned to deliver her speech in front of people.		
D.	(4) She recites it out loud over and over on Thursday and Friday making sure she had every word memorized.		

2. Read this paragraph.

> (1) Okapis, which are also called forest <u>giraffes</u>, <u>are</u> native to central Africa. (2) The common ancestor of giraffes and <u>okapis</u>, the *Canthumeryx*, <u>lived</u> about 16 million years ago. (3) Animals that are now known as giraffes evolved to be quite tall and <u>lanky</u>, with necks that can reach leaves that <u>grow</u> high up on trees. (4) Okapis did not grow longer <u>necks</u>, but <u>develops</u> stripes similar to zebras to provide camouflage from predators.

How should this paragraph be revised?

E. Sentence 1: Delete the comma after *giraffes*, AND change *are* to **is**.

F. Sentence 2: Delete the comma after *okapis*, AND change *lived* to **lives**.

G. Sentence 3: Delete the comma after *lanky*, AND change *grow* to **grows**.

H. Sentence 4: Delete the comma after *necks*, AND change *develops* to **developed**.

H. What type of issue do the question stem and answer choices indicate?

I. **The following table shows how the suggested edits in the answer choices, if implemented, would change the relevant text. Consider each of the options, decide to keep or eliminate the text, and indicate why.**

	EDITED TEXT	KEEP OR ELIMINATE?	WHY?
E.	(1) Okapis, which are also called forest giraffes is native to central Africa.		
F.	(2) The common ancestor of giraffes and okapis the *Canthumeryx*, lives about 16 million years ago.		
G.	(3) Animals that are now known as giraffes evolved to be quite tall and lanky with necks that can reach leaves that grows high up on trees.		
H.	(4) Okapis did not grow longer necks but developed stripes similar to zebras to provide camouflage from predators.		

5. Knowledge of Language

Well-written text is concise, precise, and consistent in tone. The SHSAT rewards your ability to identify and correct these Knowledge of Language issues.

Conciseness

A concise sentence does not include any unnecessary words. Phrasing that is wordy is considered stylistically incorrect on the SHSAT and needs to be revised. All words must contribute to the meaning of the sentence; otherwise, they should be eliminated or replaced with more concise wording.

One common cause of wordiness is redundancy. A redundant sentence says something twice: "The new policy directly contributed to a crisis situation." A crisis is a type of situation, so there is no need to include both "crisis" and "situation." The sentence should be rephrased as "The new policy directly contributed to a crisis."

WORDY/REDUNDANT SENTENCE	CONCISE SENTENCE
The superb musical score **added enhancement to the experience of** the play's development.	The superb musical score **enhanced** the play's development.
*I **did not anticipate** the **surprising, unexpected** plot twist.*	*I **did not anticipate** the plot twist.*
The students **increased some of their knowledge of** Tuscan architecture.	The students **learned about** Tuscan architecture.

How to Answer Conciseness Questions

Choose the most concise, grammatically correct option that conveys the writer's intended meaning. When answering questions about conciseness:

- Identify the answer choice that creates the shortest sentence. (Note that this will not always be the correct answer, but it is an efficient place to start.)
- Identify words and phrases that have the same meaning (e.g., *thoughtful* and *mindful* or *end result* and *final outcome*). Find a choice that deletes one of the redundant expressions.

Practice: Conciseness

Part 1

> **DIRECTIONS:** Eliminate word(s) to make the sentences more concise without changing the writer's intended meaning.

- **A.** It is important to carefully consider and think about what kind of college you wish to attend.
- **B.** Often, a house cat will typically sleep for up to 16 hours per day.
- **C.** The whole team felt a sense of excited anticipation in the seconds before the whistle blew.
- **D.** My sister and I couldn't come to an agreement with each other about what movie we wanted to watch that afternoon.
- **E.** Noctilucent clouds appear approximately 82 kilometers above Earth's surface. This is an altitude which is seven times higher than commercial airlines fly.

Part 2

1.   Read this sentence.

> My sister and I spent <u>nearly</u> all of Saturday evening playing tennis at the park, but <u>we</u> had to stop when it became too difficult <u>and challenging to see the ball</u>.

Which edit should be made to correct this sentence?

A.   Delete *nearly*.

B.   Delete *we*.

C.   Delete *and challenging*.

D.   Delete *to see the ball*.

F.   What type of issue do the question stem and answer choices indicate?

G.   The following table shows how the suggested edits in the answer choices, if implemented, would change the relevant text. Consider each of the options, decide to keep or eliminate the text, and indicate why.

	EDITED TEXT	KEEP OR ELIMINATE?	WHY?
A.	My sister and I spent all of Saturday evening playing tennis at the park, but we had to stop when it became too difficult and challenging to see the ball.		
B.	My sister and I spent nearly all of Saturday evening playing tennis at the park, but had to stop when it became too difficult and challenging to see the ball.		
C.	My sister and I spent nearly all of Saturday evening playing tennis at the park, but we had to stop when it became too difficult to see the ball.		
D.	My sister and I spent nearly all of Saturday evening playing tennis at the park, but we had to stop when it became too difficult and challenging.		

2. Read this paragraph.

> (1) Although Jane Austen's novels are most often admired for their eloquence and imagery, they are also highly esteemed for their subtle yet shrewd observations of nineteenth-century English society and the people living in it. (2) Austen drew from her experiences with family and acquaintances in various situations to create the characters and settings in her novels. (3) In the novel *Sense and Sensibility*, she demonstrated her sophisticated literary technique even when portraying ordinary events. (4) Consequently, Austen is respected and often beloved by people worldwide.

How should the paragraph be revised?

E. Sentence 1: Change *society and the people living in it* to **society**.

F. Sentence 2: Change *family and acquaintances* to **family**.

G. Sentence 3: Change *even when* to **when**.

H. Sentence 4: Change *respected and often beloved* to **respected**.

H. **What type of issue do the question stem and answer choices indicate?**

I. **The following table shows how the suggested edits in the answer choices, if implemented, would change the relevant text. Consider each of the options, decide to keep or eliminate the text, and indicate why.**

	EDITED TEXT	KEEP OR ELIMINATE?	WHY?
E.	(1) Although Jane Austen's novels are most often admired for their eloquence and imagery, they are also highly esteemed for their subtle yet shrewd observations of nineteenth-century English society.		
F.	(2) Austen drew from her experiences with family in various situations to create the characters and settings in her novels.		
G.	(3) In the novel *Sense and Sensibility*, she demonstrated her sophisticated literary technique when portraying ordinary events.		
H.	(4) Consequently, Austen is respected by people worldwide.		

Precision

Detailed Wording

A common precision issue tested on the SHSAT is the lack of detailed wording in a sentence. The SHSAT prefers specific information such as "a four-hour train ride" to more general statements such as "a long trip."

GENERAL (INCORRECT)	SPECIFIC (CORRECT)
I ate **a big lunch**.	I ate **a turkey sandwich, crackers with peanut butter, and two apples for lunch**.
Jalen highly recommends **that book**.	Jalen highly recommends **The One and Only Ivan by Katherine Applegate, a Newbery Award–winning novel**.
The movie **had a surprising ending**.	The movie **ended with the shocking revelation that the magician had an identical twin sister who made the impressive illusions possible**.

Word Choice

Some questions test your knowledge of the correct word to use in context. You must identify which word(s) best convey the writer's intended meaning.

INCORRECT	CORRECT
The **initial** reason the students gather in the auditorium is that it is the only location large enough for all of them.	The **primary** reason the students gather in the auditorium is that it is the only location large enough for all of them.
It is common for children to **perform** the actions of their parents.	It is common for children to **mimic** the actions of their parents.

Ambiguous Pronouns

A pronoun is ambiguous if its antecedent (the noun to which it refers) is either missing or unclear.

AMBIGUOUS PRONOUN USE	CLEAR PRONOUN USE
Anthony walked with Cody to the store, and **he** bought a sandwich.	Anthony walked with Cody to the store, and **Cody** bought a sandwich.
When Kim dropped her phone on her foot, **it** broke.	When Kim dropped her phone on her foot, **the phone** broke.

How to Answer Precision Questions

Read the surrounding text to identify the writer's intended meaning. Then evaluate the answer choices. Eliminate the answer choices that:

- Do not convey the writer's intended meaning
- Do not make sense in context
- Create grammatical errors

If one or more of the words among the answer choices are unfamiliar, the process of elimination can help you get to the correct answer. If you recognize any of the options, decide whether to keep or eliminate them. For the words that remain, use roots, prefixes, and suffixes to make your decision. If all else fails, trust your instincts and guess; never leave a question blank.

Practice: Precision

Part 1

> **DIRECTIONS:** Rewrite each sentence to more precisely reflect the writer's intended meaning.

J. The audience laughed as the person performed on stage.

K. The teacher helped Graciela.

L. Zeke apologized for attending when he interrupted the private meeting.

M. The students walked toward the stage to receive their awards while a teacher arranged them alphabetically.

N. When Cia told her mom what happened at school, she was very surprised.

Part 2

3. Read this sentence.

> Cameron made his math grade better by doing extra work.

Which revision uses the **most** precise language?

A. Cameron made his math grade better by asking for, and completing, all available extra-credit projects.

B. Cameron worked on his math grade by his doing extra work, which made his grade not as low.

C. Cameron improved his math grade by completing all available extra-credit projects.

D. Cameron boosted his grade in math by working on and handing in all available extra-credit projects.

O. **What type of issue do the question stem and answer choices indicate?**

P. **Consider each of the options, decide to keep or eliminate the choice, and indicate why.**

	EDITED TEXT	KEEP OR ELIMINATE?	WHY?
A.	Cameron made his math grade better by asking for, and completing, all available extra-credit projects.		
B.	Cameron worked on his math grade by his doing extra work, which made his grade not as low.		
C.	Cameron improved his math grade by completing all available extra-credit projects.		
D.	Cameron boosted his grade in math by working on and handing in all available extra-credit projects.		

4. Read this sentence.

> The union agreed to concessions that included increasing wages and giving them more vacation time.

How should the sentence be revised?

E. Increasing wages and giving them more vacation time were concessions agreed upon by the union.

F. The union agreed to concessions that included increasing wages and giving full-time workers more vacation time.

G. The union agreed to two concessions: increasing wages and giving them more vacation time.

H. The two concessions the union agreed to were increasing wages and giving them more vacation time.

Q. What type of issue do the question stem and answer choices indicate?

R. Consider each of the options, decide to keep or eliminate the choice, and indicate why.

EDITED TEXT	KEEP OR ELIMINATE?	WHY?
E. Increasing wages and giving them more vacation time were concessions agreed upon by the union.		
F. The union agreed to concessions that included increasing wages and giving full-time workers more vacation time.		
G. The union agreed to two concessions: increasing wages and giving them more vacation time.		
H. The two concessions the union agreed to were increasing wages and giving them more vacation time.		

Style

A writer's style is the way in which the writer demonstrates a general attitude about a particular topic or idea. Writers select specific words to best convey their intended messages. The tone of SHSAT Revising/Editing text is usually more formal than casual, so you'll need to eliminate answer choices that use informal words and phrases. In particular, vague phrases such as "a lot of things" and "stay on top of" do not usually match the style of the surrounding text and would not be featured in a correct answer choice.

How to Answer Style Questions

Read the entire text to identify the writer's general style. Then evaluate the answer choices. Eliminate the answer choices that:

- Do not match the surrounding style
- Create grammatical errors
- Do not make sense in context
- Do not convey the writer's intended meaning

The process of elimination can help you identify the correct answer, so work through the options systematically. Cross out the choices that do not match the surrounding text, and then select the most clear, concise, and relevant option.

Practice: Style

Part 1

> **DIRECTIONS:** Select the word or phrase that best matches the general style of each sentence.

S. The dreary weather darkened the skies, dampened spirits, and spread <u>sad feelings/gloom</u> throughout the city.

T. The <u>jubilant/happy</u> contestant shrieked with delight when the host revealed what she had won.

U. The final episode of the sitcom was easily the funniest of the entire series; each character <u>gave a hilarious performance/told a lot of jokes</u> that made even casual fans laugh.

V. The baseball team rode home in silence after a devastating loss at the <u>merciless/mean</u> hands of their biggest rivals.

W. The runner breathed deeply, heart racing and palms sweating, <u>waiting with apprehension/feeling really scared while waiting</u> for the start of the race.

Part 2

5. Read this paragraph.

> (1) Before tourism became a mainstay of the economy, the value of land in Mexico was defined by how well its <u>soil could produce crops</u>. (2) To many Americans, <u>tropical tourist-oriented beach towns</u> such as Acapulco and Puerto Vallarta characterize Mexico. (3) These may be the common types of <u>destinations for foreign travelers</u>, but they are certainly not representative of the entire country. (4) For better or worse, these cities, and others like them, are set up to be <u>fun for lots of vacationers</u>.

How should the paragraph be revised?

A. Sentence 1: Change *soil could produce crops* to **dirt could make plants grow**.

B. Sentence 2: Change *tropical tourist-oriented beach towns* to **hot, sunny vacation spots**.

C. Sentence 3: Change *destinations for foreign travelers* to **spots for people who are on vacation**.

D. Sentence 4: Change *fun for lots of vacationers* to **attractive to tourists**.

X. **What type of issue do the question stem and answer choices indicate?**

Y. **The following table shows how the suggested edits in the answer choices, if implemented, would change the relevant text. Consider each of the options, decide to keep or eliminate the text, and indicate why.**

	EDITED TEXT	KEEP OR ELIMINATE?	WHY?
A.	(1) Before tourism became a mainstay of the economy, the value of land in Mexico was defined by how well its dirt could make plants grow.		
B.	(2) To many Americans, hot, sunny vacation spots such as Acapulco and Puerto Vallarta characterize Mexico.		
C.	(3) These may be the common types of spots for people who are on vacation, but they are certainly not representative of the entire country.		
D.	(4) For better or worse, these cities, and others like them, are set up to be attractive to tourists.		

6. Read this paragraph.

> (1) Before 1793, when Eli Whitney invented the cotton gin, the method used to separate seeds from cotton fiber was enormously labor-intensive. (2) The new gadget had a rotating drum with wire spikes that took the fibers people actually wanted and tossed out seeds, which were basically garbage. (3) Hodgen Holmes improved upon Whitney's cotton gin by removing the spikes and installing a circular saw that further streamlined the process. (4) Today's cotton gins make use of the same simple yet effective principles.

Which revision of sentence 2 **best** maintains the formal style established in the paragraph?

E. The cotton gin consisted of a rotating drum with wire spikes that efficiently caught the desired fibers and left behind the unwanted seeds.

F. The new machine had a rotating drum with wire spikes that took the fibers people actually wanted and tossed out seeds, which weren't useful anyway.

G. The cotton gin had a rotating drum with wire spikes that caught the cotton fibers and left the unwanted seeds out of things.

H. The new machine had a rotating drum with wire spikes that took the fibers that were worth some money and tossed out seeds, which couldn't be sold for any sort of profit.

Z. **What type of issue do the question stem and answer choices indicate?**

AA. **The following table shows how the suggested edits in the answer choices, if implemented, would change the relevant text. Consider each of the options, decide to keep or eliminate the text, and indicate why.**

	EDITED TEXT	KEEP OR ELIMINATE?	WHY?
E.	The cotton gin consisted of a rotating drum with wire spikes that efficiently caught the desired fibers and left behind the unwanted seeds.		
F.	The new machine had a rotating drum with wire spikes that took the fibers people actually wanted and tossed out seeds, which weren't useful anyway.		
G.	The cotton gin had a rotating drum with wire spikes that caught the cotton fibers and left the unwanted seeds out of things.		
H.	The new machine had a rotating drum with wire spikes that took the fibers that were worth some money and tossed out seeds, which couldn't be sold for any sort of profit.		

6. Organization and Topic Development

Organization

Organization questions require you to read specific text and decide how to most clearly convey the author's intended meaning. These questions differ in scope; you might be asked to organize writing at the level of a sentence, a paragraph, or even an entire passage.

Transitions

Writers use transitions to show relationships such as contrast, cause and effect, continuation, emphasis, and chronology (order of events). Knowing which words indicate which type of transition will help you choose the correct answer on test day.

CONTRAST TRANSITIONS	CAUSE-AND-EFFECT TRANSITIONS	CONTINUATION TRANSITIONS	EMPHASIS TRANSITIONS	CHRONOLOGY TRANSITIONS
although, but, despite, even though, however, in contrast, nonetheless, on the other hand, rather than, though, unlike, while, yet	as a result, because, consequently, since, so, therefore, thus	also, furthermore, in addition, moreover	certainly, in fact, indeed, that is	before, after, first (second, etc.), then, finally

Combining Sentences

Questions may ask you to combine sentences to clarify the relationship between ideas. These questions may be stand-alone or accompany a passage. Your goal is to ensure that information and ideas are logically conveyed using correct grammar.

Moving Sentences

Some Organization questions task you with moving a sentence to improve the organization of a paragraph within the passage (or a paragraph within a passage, though this is rare). To answer these questions effectively, evaluate each answer choice by looking for keywords that indicate where the sentence should be placed. If the sentence you are moving starts with "For example," you need to place the sentence after a statement that it would best support. If the sentence includes a chronological transition such as "next" or "after that," it must be placed in the most logical spot within a sequence of events the writer is discussing.

Other questions will ask you to check and potentially fix the placement of a sentence within a paragraph. Others will ask you for the best place to insert a new sentence. Your approach in both cases should be the same.

How to Answer Organization Questions

Transitions

If a question asks about a transition word, phrase, or sentence, determine the writer's intended meaning and select the transition that best conveys this information.

Combining Sentences

The process of elimination is an important strategy for combining sentences. Eliminate any option that creates a comparison or relationship the writer did not intend. For example, if a writer presents two related ideas that convey similar information, you can cross out choices that use contrast transitions such as "but," "however," or "although."

Moving Sentences

Look for specific clues that indicate the best organization. Common clues include:

- **Chronology:** If the information is presented in order by the time when it occurred, place the sentence within the correct time frame.

- **Explanation of a term or phrase:** If the passage features a term, the writer will explain what it is before using the term in other contexts.

- **Introduction of a person:** If the passage introduces someone, such as Grace Hopper, the writer will first refer to the person by first and last name before referring to the person by either first name (Grace) or last name (Hopper) only.

- **Examples:** A general statement is often followed by support in the form of examples.

- **Logic:** Transition words such as "however," "also," "furthermore," and "therefore" may signal the logic of the paragraph. For example, the word "therefore" indicates that a conclusion is being drawn from evidence that should logically come before it.

Practice: Organization

Part 1

> **DIRECTIONS:** Select the transition that most accurately reflects the writer's intended meaning.

- **A.** The train was delayed; (<u>therefore/in addition</u>), we arrived at our destination two hours late.

- **B.** (<u>Since/Although</u>) the critics agreed that the movie was terrible, I went to see it anyway.

- **C.** We need to finish our project (<u>consequently/before</u>) we leave this afternoon.

- **D.** The hiking trail was difficult to navigate; (<u>finally/indeed</u>), state park guidelines recommend that only experienced hikers attempt the climb.

- **E.** The morphology of the amoeba is more complex than you might expect; (<u>furthermore/in contrast</u>), the mechanism underlying amoeboid motion is still not fully understood.

Part 2

The Vinland Map

(1) One of the most notorious pieces in the Yale University Library is the Vinland map. (2) Valued at $1 million when it was donated in the 1950s, the map's authenticity has been hotly debated for years. (3) It is alleged to be a fifteenth-century artifact of the Vikings' first voyage to North America. (4) Chemical analyses of its ink indicate that it could be a modern forgery on previously blank fifteenth-century parchment. (5) Although many experts are convinced that the map is a reproduction, controversy remains.

1. What is the best way to combine sentences 3 and 4?

    A. It is alleged to be a fifteenth-century artifact of the Vikings' first voyage to North America, and chemical analyses of its ink indicate that it could be a modern forgery on previously blank fifteenth-century parchment.

    B. While it is alleged to be a fifteenth-century artifact of the Vikings' first voyage to North America, chemical analyses of its ink indicate that it could be a modern forgery on previously blank fifteenth-century parchment.

    C. Because it is alleged to be a fifteenth-century artifact of the Vikings' first voyage to North America, chemical analyses of its ink indicate that it could be a modern forgery on previously blank fifteenth-century parchment.

    D. Chemical analyses of the ink in the Vinland map, which is alleged to be a fifteenth-century artifact of the Vikings' first voyage to North America, indicate that it could be a modern forgery on previously blank fifteenth-century parchment.

F. **What type of issue do the question stem and answer choices indicate?**

G. **Consider each of the options, decide to keep or eliminate the choice, and indicate why.**

ANSWER CHOICE	KEEP OR ELIMINATE?	WHY?
A. It is alleged to be a fifteenth-century artifact of the Vikings' first voyage to North America, and chemical analyses of its ink indicate that it could be a modern forgery on previously blank fifteenth-century parchment.		
B. While it is alleged to be a fifteenth-century artifact of the Vikings' first voyage to North America, chemical analyses of its ink indicate that it could be a modern forgery on previously blank fifteenth-century parchment.		
C. Because it is alleged to be a fifteenth-century artifact of the Vikings' first voyage to North America, chemical analyses of its ink indicate that it could be a modern forgery on previously blank fifteenth-century parchment.		
D. Chemical analyses of the ink in the Vinland map, which is alleged to be a fifteenth-century artifact of the Vikings' first voyage to North America, indicate that it could be a modern forgery on previously blank fifteenth-century parchment.		

(6) Given that the Vinland map is not the only map for which authentication is difficult, experts have developed a variety of techniques to assess such documents. (7) First and foremost, there are several categories of evidence, including ink and paper, that experts use to determine authenticity. (8) A team of specialists identified titanium dioxide in the ink of the Vinland map in 1972. (9) That component in ink has been used in certain pigments only since the 1920s, providing support that the Vinland map is a forgery. (10) Early paper was handmade from the pulp of rags mixed with liquid, then spread out to dry. (11) The result was paper that was usually of uneven thickness. (12) Paper can also provide essential clues that help experts determine if a map is genuine.

2. Where should sentence 12 be moved to improve the organization of the second paragraph (sentences 6–12)?

   E. to the beginning of the paragraph (before sentence 6)

   F. between sentences 7 and 8

   G. between sentences 9 and 10

   H. between sentences 10 and 11

H. What type of issue do the question stem and answer choices indicate?

I. Consider each of the options, decide to keep or eliminate the choice, and indicate why.

ANSWER CHOICE	KEEP OR ELIMINATE?	WHY?
E. to the beginning of the paragraph (before sentence 6)		
F. between sentences 7 and 8		
G. between sentences 9 and 10		
H. between sentences 10 and 11		

(13) Even with more recently made maps, paper is often a helpful indicator of a map's provenance. (14) As machine-made paper became available, thickness was more regular, but paper quality continued to vary. (15) Authentic maps were most often produced on high-quality, low-acidity paper. (16) Experts have found that color, printing techniques, text, and stitching can provide useful clues about the date and authenticity of a map.

3. Which transition should be added to the beginning of sentence 16?

   A. Although

   B. In addition,

   C. However,

   D. Because

J. What type of issue do the question stem and answer choices indicate?

K. **The following table shows how the suggested edits in the answer choices, if implemented, would change the relevant text. Consider each of the options, decide to keep or eliminate the text, and indicate why.**

EDITED TEXT	KEEP OR ELIMINATE?	WHY?
A. Authentic maps were most often produced on high-quality, low-acidity paper. Although experts have found that color, printing techniques, text, and stitching can provide useful clues about the date and authenticity of a map.		
B. Authentic maps were most often produced on high-quality, low-acidity paper. In addition, experts have found that color, printing techniques, text, and stitching can provide useful clues about the date and authenticity of a map.		
C. Authentic maps were most often produced on high-quality, low-acidity paper. However, experts have found that color, printing techniques, text, and stitching can provide useful clues about the date and authenticity of a map.		
D. Authentic maps were most often produced on high-quality, low-acidity paper. Because experts have found that color, printing techniques, text, and stitching can provide useful clues about the date and authenticity of a map.		

(17) Forged maps have value since it takes time and effort to make them. (18) Some reproductions are products of highly skilled artistic talent achieved only after years of diligence and dedication. (19) For the Vinland map—and others shown to be superb but fake—a question remains: if these maps do not have the same value as true artifacts, will they retain historical worth as great forgeries of modern times?

4. Which revision of sentence 17 provides the **best** topic sentence for the fourth paragraph (sentences 17–19)?

E. Forged maps may have anywhere from a little to a lot of value.

F. The amount of skill required to make forged maps is directly proportional to their value.

G. It is worth considering how much value forged maps may have.

H. Experts often believe that forged maps do not have any value because it is illegal to create forgeries.

L. What type of issue do the question stem and answer choices indicate?

M. Consider each of the options, decide to keep or eliminate the choice, and indicate why.

ANSWER CHOICE	KEEP OR ELIMINATE?	WHY?
E. Forged maps may have anywhere from a little to a lot of value.		
F. The amount of skill required to make forged maps is directly proportional to their value.		
G. It is worth considering how much value forged maps may have.		
H. Experts often believe that forged maps do not have any value because it is illegal to create forgeries.		

Topic Development

Topic Development questions test your ability to determine why a passage is written and whether particular information helps accomplish that purpose. Some Topic Development questions task you with adding or replacing sentences to better support the information in the passage, while other questions ask you to delete information that is not relevant to the passage.

How to Answer Topic Development Questions

Take the time to determine the writer's intended purpose before selecting an answer. Correct answers will include information that the writer would agree is relevant and that fits well within the context of the passage.

To answer questions about **adding or replacing** sentences, first eliminate answer choices that do not reflect the writer's purpose. Then choose the most correct and relevant option.

To answer questions that require **deleting** information, determine which sentence does not specifically relate to the development of the passage. The passage should flow smoothly and logically once the irrelevant sentence is removed.

SHSAT EXPERT NOTE

Although conciseness is important, it should not be a primary goal when answering Topic Development questions. Instead, focus on selecting the choice that makes the most sense logically, given your understanding of the writer's tone and purpose.

Practice: Topic Development

Part 1

> **DIRECTIONS:** Underline a single phrase within each sentence that best conveys the main idea.

N. The plane ride was long because we had two long layovers, one in Dallas and one in Los Angeles.

O. After walking up and down each aisle at least three times, I chose a perfect present for my sister.

P. My dog, Bailey, is stubborn; no matter what I do, Bailey will not sit, shake, or roll over even though she knows how.

Q. Before the library opened for the day, I helped the librarian organize various books and toys as well as several games because we wanted story hour to go well.

R. I was very hungry, so I helped myself to soup, salad, chicken, rice, and green beans.

Part 2

Irrigation

(1) Irrigation is a process in which plants are watered by controlled release of river or lake water, especially in areas with insufficient rainfall or during particularly dry seasons. (2) The need for irrigation is a major reason why early settlements formed near rivers; rivers were their source of water not only for drinking and cooking but also for watering crops.

5. Which sentence should follow sentence 2 to **best** state the main claim in the passage?

A. Irrigation was certainly a problem ancient groups of people had to solve to ensure that their crops would flourish.

B. The first irrigation processes in Australia were centered around the Murray-Darling system, located in the southwest portion of the continent.

C. If ancient people could not access water, they would not be able to ensure that their cities would survive.

D. There is considerable evidence that irrigation may have played a pivotal role in shaping both the earliest civilizations and modern irrigation techniques.

> **SHSAT EXPERT NOTE**
>
> Since you will need to determine the author's purpose for the passage as a whole, you may want to come back to this question once you have finished the passage.

S.   **What type of issue do the question stem and answer choices indicate?**

T. **Consider each of the options, decide to keep or eliminate the choice, and indicate why.**

ANSWER CHOICE	KEEP OR ELIMINATE?	WHY?
A. Irrigation was certainly a problem ancient groups of people had to solve to ensure that their crops would flourish.		
B. The first irrigation processes in Australia were centered around the Murray-Darling system, located in the southwest portion of the continent.		
C. If ancient people could not access water, they would not be able to ensure that their cities would survive.		
D. There is considerable evidence that irrigation may have played a pivotal role in shaping both the earliest civilizations and modern irrigation techniques.		

(3) Ancient civilizations harnessed the power of water in different ways, depending on the climate and their needs. (4) The ancient Egyptians controlled water coming from the annual flooding of the Nile River to irrigate lands used for planting. (5) Ancient Persians used a system of sloping wells and tunnels to direct water to their barley fields. (6) The Dujiangyan Irrigation System, built in 256 B.C.E. in the Sichuan region of China, irrigated an enormous area of farmland. (7) Historians estimate that the Sichuan farmland amounted to at least 5,000 square kilometers, amounting to approximately the size of the U.S. state of Delaware.

6. Which sentence presents information that shifts away from the main topic of the second paragraph (sentences 3–7) and should be removed?

    E. sentence 4

    F. sentence 5

    G. sentence 6

    H. sentence 7

U. **What type of issue do the question stem and answer choices indicate?**

V. Consider each of the options, decide to keep or eliminate the choice, and indicate why.

ANSWER CHOICE	KEEP OR ELIMINATE?	WHY?
E. sentence 4 (The ancient Egyptians controlled water coming from the annual flooding of the Nile River to irrigate lands used for planting.)		
F. sentence 5 (Ancient Persians used a system of sloping wells and tunnels to direct water to their barley fields.)		
G. sentence 6 (The Dujiangyan Irrigation System, built in 256 B.C.E. in the Sichuan region of China, irrigated an enormous area of farmland.)		
H. sentence 7 (Historians estimate that the Sichuan farmland amounted to at least 5,000 square kilometers, amounting to approximately the size of the U.S. state of Delaware.)		

(8) Modern irrigation systems, using powerful diesel and electric engines, have enormously increased the amount of water that can be directed toward crops. (9) However, such irrigation methods can have the negative effect of depleting water faster than it can be replenished.

7. Which sentence would **best** follow sentence 9?

   A. Additional problems with modern irrigation, such as wasteful runoff, are not surprising, given irrigation's long history.

   B. Despite some negative results of irrigation, it has been and remains crucial to the development of communities.

   C. There are several reasons why irrigation is important, from providing much-needed hydration for crops to controlling unpredictable access to water.

   D. Ancient civilizations took the drawbacks and the benefits of irrigation in stride, knowing that it was essential to their survival.

W. What type of issue do the question stem and answer choices indicate?

X.   Consider each of the options, decide to keep or eliminate the choice, and indicate why.

ANSWER CHOICE	KEEP OR ELIMINATE?	WHY?
A. Additional problems with modern irrigation, such as wasteful runoff, are not surprising, given irrigation's long history.		
B. Despite some negative results of irrigation, it has been and remains crucial to the development of communities.		
C. There are several reasons why irrigation is important, from providing much-needed hydration for crops to controlling unpredictable access to water.		
D. Ancient civilizations took the drawbacks and the benefits of irrigation in stride, knowing that it was essential to their survival.		

(10) The reasons for the influence of irrigation are twofold. (11) The development of irrigation allowed for extremely efficient agricultural production, creating the surplus of food resources that must serve as the foundation for any civilization. (12) Furthermore, constructing the elaborate system of canals and drainage networks was a task of tremendous complexity. (13) The difficult work that made irrigation possible was worth the effort because it led to important developments.

8.   Which concluding sentence should replace sentence 13 to **best** follow and support sentence 12?

   E.   Some historians may argue that if ancient people had not endeavored to create irrigation systems, ancient civilization would not have developed in the way that it did.

   F.   The centers of commerce, administration, and science that accomplished the task eventually blossomed into the cities that served as the cornerstones of many ancient civilizations.

   G.   Irrigation was impressive in two particular ways: its construction and the resulting advancements.

   H.   There were noteworthy improvements in not only the irrigation-related features but also the extensive canal systems.

Y.   What type of issue do the question stem and answer choices indicate?

Z. **Consider each of the options, decide to keep or eliminate the choice, and indicate why.**

ANSWER CHOICE	KEEP OR ELIMINATE?	WHY?
E. Some historians may argue that if ancient people had not endeavored to create irrigation systems, ancient civilization would not have developed in the way that it did.		
F. The centers of commerce, administration, and science that accomplished the task eventually blossomed into the cities that served as the cornerstones of many ancient civilizations.		
G. Irrigation was impressive in two particular ways: its construction and the resulting advancements.		
H. There were noteworthy improvements in not only the irrigation-related features but also the extensive canal systems.		

Answers and Explanations

1. Sentence Structure and Modifier Placement

Practice: Fragments and Run-Ons

Note: These are not the only ways to correct the sentences; your answers may differ.

A. **My friend** brought snacks to the weekend study session.

B. After getting to the stadium, **we went looking for our seats.**

C. The new arts center just opened. **It** has a crafts room for children under thirteen.

D. Herodotus is known as one of the first historians; he is even called "The Father of History."

E. **Although** Herodotus is sometimes accused of making up stories for his histories, he claimed he simply recorded what he had been told.

1. **F.** The question stem states that there is a sentence construction error. Sentence construction errors include run-ons, fragments, and misplaced modifiers.

G.

ANSWER CHOICE	KEEP OR ELIMINATE?	WHY?
A. (1) Colleges could give greater support to men's sports teams than to women's teams prior to 1972; today, women's and men's teams must receive equal funding.	Eliminate	This is a grammatically correct sentence with two independent clauses. Both independent clauses have a subject, a verb, and a complete thought, and they are correctly separated by a semicolon.
B. (2) Title IX of the Education Amendments prohibits gender discrimination at colleges and other federally funded institutions.	Eliminate	This sentence does not contain any errors.
C. (3) Resulted in more money in athletic departments allocated for women's sports.	Keep	This is a fragment because it is missing a subject and does not express a complete thought.
D. (4) Title IX has led to more interest in women's sports, greater competition among teams, and improvements in the quality of athletics for women.	Eliminate	This is a grammatically correct sentence.

2. **H.** The answer choices give the options of either deleting a comma or inserting a semicolon. Likely, this is a run-on sentence that must be properly punctuated to fix the issue.

I.

EDITED TEXT	KEEP OR ELIMINATE?	WHY?
E. White roses represent unity yellow roses show friendship, and red roses signify love however, many people believe red roses are the most cherished within the genus *Rosa*.	Eliminate	The comma after "unity" is necessary because it separates items in a list.
F. White roses represent unity, yellow roses show friendship, and red roses signify love; however, many people believe red roses are the most cherished within the genus *Rosa*.	Keep	The first independent clause ends with the word "love," so placing a semicolon after "love" will correct the run-on.
G. White roses represent unity, yellow roses show friendship, and red roses signify love however many people believe red roses are the most cherished within the genus *Rosa*.	Eliminate	The comma that follows "however" correctly separates the transition word from the rest of the independent clause.
H. White roses represent unity, yellow roses show friendship, and red roses signify love however, many people believe; red roses are the most cherished within the genus *Rosa*.	Eliminate	The first independent clause ends with the word "love," not "believe," so placing a semicolon after "believe" would not correct the sentence.

Practice: Modifier Placement

Note: These are not the only ways to correct the sentences; your answers may differ.

J. Cecilia walked the dog wearing a brown collar.

K. The dealer sold the Ford with the hatchback to the buyer.

L. The server placed warm rolls onto the table.

M. While looking toward the west, I watched as a breeze stirred the leaves on the trees.

N. I borrowed a blender that turned out to be broken from a neighbor.

3. **O.** The question stem indicates that a revision is necessary. Each answer choice includes an introductory phrase, and introductory phrases must be followed by what the phrase modifies.

P.

ANSWER CHOICE	KEEP OR ELIMINATE?	WHY?
A. Members of the volleyball team, on Saturday to raise money for uniforms, will hold a car wash.	Eliminate	Although this choice fixes the modifier issue, the phrase "on Saturday to raise money for uniforms" does not make sense in the middle of the sentence.
B. To raise money for uniforms, on Saturday a car wash will be held by members of the volleyball team.	Eliminate	As written, the phrase "To raise money for uniforms" describes "on Saturday," which is not logical.
C. On Saturday to raise money for uniforms, members of the volleyball team will hold a car wash.	Eliminate	The phrase "on Saturday" does not make sense before "to raise money for uniforms."
D. To raise money for uniforms, members of the volleyball team will hold a car wash on Saturday.	Keep	This correctly places "members of the volleyball team" after the introductory phrase.

4. **Q.** The question states that there is a sentence construction error, which could be a fragment, run-on, or misplaced modifier.

R.

ANSWER CHOICE	KEEP OR ELIMINATE?	WHY?
E. (1) Most gems are crystallized minerals, but amber, coral, and pearls come from organic material.	Eliminate	This is grammatically correct; two independent clauses are properly joined with a comma and a FANBOYS conjunction.
F. (2) Amber's buoyancy suggests organic origins; unlike most gemstones, this ancient fossilized resin floats in water.	Eliminate	There is no grammar error because the two independent clauses are correctly joined with a semicolon.
G. (3) Coral is a discarded limestone skeleton found in the sea.	Eliminate	This sentence is correct as written with a subject, verb, and complete thought.
H. (4) Taking several years to form, oysters create white, black, or pink pearls.	Keep	"Taking several years to form" is followed by "oysters," which does not make sense; it is the pearls that form over time.

2. Punctuation

Practice: Punctuation

Note: These are not the only ways to correct the sentences; your answers may differ.

A.   For my birthday, I asked for my favorite dinner: chicken and roasted vegetables.

B.   The story of Emperor Nero playing the fiddle while Rome burned has been debunked by historians, but the saying based on it remains popular.

C.   Koalas' fingerprints are nearly indistinguishable from human fingerprints—which has occasionally led to mistakes at crime scenes.

D.   Invented by Sir John Harrington in 1596, the flush toilet actually precedes modern indoor plumbing.

E.   Toni Morrison—born Chloe Wofford—was one of America's most celebrated writers.

1.   **F.**   The question states that an edit is required to make the sentence grammatically correct, and the answer choices show that there is a missing comma.

G.

	EDITED TEXT	KEEP OR ELIMINATE?	WHY?
A.	Unable to decide between a career in law, and one in medicine Jemma combined her two interests and studied forensic medicine.	Eliminate	A comma is only needed in front of "and" when separating items in a list or separating two independent clauses, neither of which is the case here. The phrase "a career in law and one in medicine" is a compound that does not need a comma.
B.	Unable to decide between a career in law and one in medicine, Jemma combined her two interests and studied forensic medicine.	Keep	A comma is needed to properly connect the introductory phrase "Unable to decide between a career in law and one in medicine" with the independent clause "Jemma combined her two interests and studied forensic medicine."
C.	Unable to decide between a career in law and one in medicine Jemma combined her two interests, and studied forensic medicine.	Eliminate	Use a comma before "and" only when separating items in a list or separating two independent clauses. The phrase "studied forensic medicine" is not an independent clause, so adding a comma is not grammatically correct.
D.	Unable to decide between a career in law and one in medicine Jemma combined her two interests and studied forensic, medicine.	Eliminate	Do not put a comma between an adjective and the word it's modifying; "forensic" is modifying "medicine," so no comma is needed.

2. **H.** The question says that one of the sentences contains an error, so look for common errors such as agreement or punctuation issues.

I.

ANSWER CHOICE	KEEP OR ELIMINATE?	WHY?
E. (1) The winner of an election is often the candidate who best masters the art of the political advertisement.	Eliminate	This sentence is grammatically correct.
F. (2) Most voters have a stake in the issues of the day but cannot make sense of the rules and rhetoric of the real processes of government.	Eliminate	This sentence is correct; no comma is needed before "but" because the sentence does not include two independent clauses.
G. (3) The 30-second commercial on prime-time television—making sense out of technical political jargon plays a crucial part in the political process.	Keep	The phrase "making sense out of technical political jargon" is a nonessential clause that must be set off from the rest of the sentence with either a pair of commas or a pair of dashes. This sentence just has one dash before "making," so another dash is needed after "jargon" to fix the error.
H. (4) Those who wish to speak for an electorate must make their case to that electorate, and the political advertisement is the most direct and effective way to achieve that goal.	Eliminate	Two independent clauses are properly combined with a comma and a FANBOYS conjunction (in this case, "and").

3. **J.** The question states that there is an error, so read each sentence carefully, looking for common errors such as incorrect punctuation.

K.

ANSWER CHOICE	KEEP OR ELIMINATE?	WHY?
A. (1) Bicycling is a mainstream form of transportation in Japanese cities.	Eliminate	This sentence is correct.
B. (2) Nearly every type of person uses a bicycle, blue-collar workers, office workers in suits, parents toting babies, and students.	Keep	A colon is used to introduce a list, so sentence 2 should use a colon instead of a comma after "bicycle."
C. (3) In the United States, however, bicycling is more often seen as a recreational activity or form of exercise than as a means of transportation.	Eliminate	This sentence correctly uses a comma before and after "however."
D. (4) An exception is that American children often rely on bikes because they have fewer transportation options.	Eliminate	This sentence is correct.

4. **L.** The question states that the sentence contains an error, and the answer choices indicate that there is either a comma or an apostrophe error.

M.

	ANSWER CHOICE	KEEP OR ELIMINATE?	WHY?
E.	Although the statue was intended, in ancient times, to tower above the landscape, its presence is now dominated by the enormous skyscrapers that came with the city's modernization.	Keep	The word "it's" means "it is," but the sentence requires the possessive "its."
F.	Although the statue was intended, in ancient times, to tower above the landscape, it's presence, is now dominated by the enormous skyscrapers that came with the city's modernization.	Eliminate	This does not fix the error and adds an unnecessary comma.
G.	Although the statue was intended, in ancient times, to tower above the landscape, it's presence is now dominated by the enormous skyscrapers, that came with the city's modernization.	Eliminate	This adds an unnecessary comma and does not fix the original error.
H.	Although the statue was intended, in ancient times, to tower above the landscape, it's presence is now dominated by the enormous skyscrapers that came with the cities modernization.	Eliminate	This option does not fix the original error and incorrectly changes the singular possessive "city's" to the plural noun "cities."

3. Usage

Practice: Verb Usage

Note: These are not the only ways to correct the sentences; your answers may differ.

A. Angel **will** audition for the school play next week.

B. The song with the upbeat rhythm and catchy lyrics **was** wildly popular.

C. Either the governor or the lieutenant governor usually **presents** the award.

D. By the time the last runner completed the marathon, the winner **had** crossed the finish line hours ago.

E. Few people know that Stephen Hawking both revolutionized physics and **cowrote** children's books with his daughter.

1. **F.** The question states that the sentence contains an error, and the answer choices show that the error is related to one of the verbs. Look for common verb errors such as incorrect verb tense, subjects and verbs that do not agree, and faulty parallelism.

English

G.

	EDITED TEXT	KEEP OR ELIMINATE?	WHY?
A.	The most successful scientists, spanning field from physics to geology, sees beyond the facts and speculate about the general principles that provide a foundation for new ideas.	Eliminate	The plural noun "fields" should not be changed to the singular noun "field" because the sentence is describing more than one field; the word must remain plural.
B.	The most successful scientists, spanning fields from physics to geology, see beyond the facts and speculate about the general principles that provide a foundation for new ideas.	Keep	The singular verb "sees" must be changed to the plural verb "see" to match the plural subject "scientists."
C.	The most successful scientists, spanning fields from physics to geology, sees beyond the facts and speculates about the general principles that provide a foundation for new ideas.	Eliminate	The plural verb "speculate" should not be changed to the singular verb "speculates" because it needs to agree with the plural noun "scientists."
D.	The most successful scientists, spanning fields from physics to geology, sees beyond the facts and speculate about the general principles that provides a foundation for new ideas.	Eliminate	The plural verb "provide" should not be changed to the singular verb "provides" because the noun to which it refers—"principles"—is plural.

2. **H.** The question says that the sentence contains an error, and the answer choices indicate a verb issue, which could be an incorrect verb tense, a subject and a verb that do not agree, or faulty parallelism.

I.

EDITED TEXT	KEEP OR ELIMINATE?	WHY?
E. During a time when women were generally not allowed to venture outside the domestic realm, Christine de Pisan became an acclaimed poet in the Middle Ages and was considered the first woman in France to have earned renown as a writer.	Keep	The Middle Ages happened in the past, so the present tense "are" does not make sense in context; it must be changed to the past tense "were."
F. During a time when women are generally not allowed to venture outside the domestic realm, Christine de Pisan becomes an acclaimed poet in the Middle Ages and was considered the first woman in France to have earned renown as a writer.	Eliminate	This choice changes the correct past tense "became" to the incorrect present tense "becomes."
G. During a time when women are generally not allowed to venture outside the domestic realm, Christine de Pisan became an acclaimed poet in the Middle Ages and is considered the first woman in France to have earned renown as a writer.	Eliminate	This option creates a parallelism error; verb phrases connected with "and" must have the same tense. The word "is" is present tense, which does not match the past tense "became."
H. During a time when women are generally not allowed to venture outside the domestic realm, Christine de Pisan became an acclaimed poet in the Middle Ages and was considered the first woman in France to have earn renown as a writer.	Eliminate	This changes the correct past tense "earned" to the incorrect present tense "earn."

Practice: Pronoun Usage

J.   **They're** planning to leave their bicycles over by the fence.

K.   My uncle likes to go bowling with my sister and **me**.

L.   The box of nails has been moved from **its** usual place in the shed.

M.   My favorite singer, **whom** I have wanted to see in person for years, will give a concert a week after my birthday.

N.   The cathedral of Notre Dame, with vast vaulted ceilings and intricate carvings, never fails to amaze **its** visitors.

3.   **O.**   The question indicates that one of the sentences in the paragraph contains an error; look for common issues such as agreement issues with verbs or pronouns.

P.

	ANSWER CHOICE	KEEP OR ELIMINATE?	WHY?
A.	(1) Sandstone, limestone, and shale are three common types of water-made rocks, and it all can play a role in fossil creation.	Keep	The singular pronoun "it" does not match the plural antecedent "Sandstone, limestone, and shale."
B.	(2) Shale is composed of mud, often containing distinct layers that have dried together, and it is usually formed by erosion from landmasses.	Eliminate	This sentence is written correctly.
C.	(3) By contrast, sandstone and limestone typically come from the ocean bottom.	Eliminate	There are no grammar errors.
D.	(4) Sandstone is made up of grains of sand that, with the help of water, have adhered to one another over time, frequently trapping and fossilizing simple sea creatures and plants in the process.	Eliminate	This option is grammatically correct.

4. **Q.** The question indicates that there is an error, and the answer choices show that it is a singular/plural issue.

R.

	EDITED TEXT	KEEP OR ELIMINATE?	WHY?
E.	The wolf spiders, with its large fuzzy body and hairy legs, is known for their agile hunting skills and excellent eyesight.	Eliminate	This changes the correct singular noun "spider" to an incorrect plural noun that does not match the singular pronoun "its."
F.	The wolf spider, with their large fuzzy body and hairy legs, is known for their agile hunting skills and excellent eyesight.	Eliminate	This option changes the correct singular possessive pronoun "its" to an incorrect plural possessive pronoun "their," which does not match the singular antecedent "spider."
G.	The wolf spider, with its large fuzzy body and hairy legs, is known for its agile hunting skills and excellent eyesight.	Keep	The sentence discusses a single spider species, so the plural possessive pronoun "their" is incorrect. This choice fixes the issue by changing the pronoun to the singular possessive pronoun "its."
H.	The wolf spider, with its large fuzzy body and hairy legs, is known for their agile hunting skill and excellent eyesight.	Eliminate	Although this option does not introduce a new error, it does not fix the original issue.

Practice: Modifier Agreement

S. Computers have grown **exponentially** more efficient since their invention.

T. Estella chose to take the route with the most **attractive** scenery.

U. The leaf-tailed gecko's amazing natural camouflage enables it to blend **perfectly** into its surroundings.

V. Between basketball and baseball, basketball is the **more** popular sport in the United States.

W. Soccer is the **most** popular sport worldwide, with a fan base in the billions.

5. **X.** The sentence contains an error, and the answer choices indicate that the error is either a comparative/superlative issue or a verb tense error.

Y.

	EDITED TEXT	KEEP OR ELIMINATE?	WHY?
A.	Between Hugo and Kai, Hugo is the better sprinter; however, Kai is better at the long jump.	Keep	Two people are being compared, so the comparative "better" is needed since the superlative "best" is used for three or more items, not two.
B.	Between Hugo and Kai, Hugo is the best at sprinting; however, Kai is better at the long jump.	Eliminate	Although this does not introduce a new error, it doesn't fix the original issue.
C.	Between Hugo and Kai, Hugo is the best sprinter; however, Kai is best at the long jump.	Eliminate	Two people are being compared, so the comparative "better" is correct; the superlative "best" is used for more than two items.
D.	Between Hugo and Kai, Hugo is the best sprinter; however, Kai is better at long jumping.	Eliminate	This choice does not introduce a new error, but it does not fix the issue in the original sentence.

6. **Z.** The question indicates that one of the sentences in the paragraph contains an error; look for common issues such as adjective or adverb errors. Adjectives can be used to describe only nouns and pronouns, whereas adverbs are used to describe everything else, including adjectives.

AA.

	ANSWER CHOICE	KEEP OR ELIMINATE?	WHY?
E.	(1) Translating any work is a much more complex process than simply exchanging one word for another, and the effect of a superbly translated play on an audience can be profound.	Eliminate	This sentence does not contain an error.
F.	(2) The script for a play is not a work to be appreciated on its own but rather a map used to create such a work.	Eliminate	This is grammatically correct.
G.	(3) Since the audience for a play will rarely view the script itself, all of the plot points, emotions, subtleties—all of the meaning—must be transmitted simply through spoken dialogue.	Eliminate	There is no issue with this sentence.
H.	(4) Granted, when translating between two close related languages, a near word-for-word process can sometimes be sufficient.	Keep	The word "related" is an adjective, so it needs to be described by the adverb "closely" rather than the adjective "close."

4. Strategy Focus: One Error at a Time

Practice: One Error at a Time

A. Thorny dragons**,** a type of Australian lizard, **are** covered entirely with spines shaped like upside-down cones.

B. The Pentagon building, located in Washington, D.C.**,** is known for **its** unique five-sided shape, which was designed by American architect George Bergstrom.

C. The restaurant **has** three types of soups**:** chicken noodle, minestrone, and split pea.

D. The math team—newly formed this year—**was** astounded after winning first place.

E. The valuable Victorian chairs with authentic upholstery **were** sold for an astronomical price.

1. F. The question indicates that part of the paragraph needs to be revised. The answer choices show that the paragraph contains a verb tense error and a comma error, so concentrating on one error at a time will help narrow down the answer choices.

G.

	EDITED TEXT	KEEP OR ELIMINATE?	WHY?
A.	(1) Kira had spent every day after school last week practicing for the upcoming, speech and debate tournament.	Eliminate	This option unnecessarily changes "spent" to "had spent"; it also incorrectly adds a comma between an adjective, "upcoming," and the noun it's modifying, "speech."
B.	(2) She rewrites sections of her 10-minute original oratory speech on Monday and Tuesday, to clarify her main points.	Eliminate	This incorrectly changes the past tense "rewrote" to the present tense "rewrites" and adds an unnecessary comma in front of a phrase that does not need to be separated from the rest of the sentence.
C.	(3) She performed her speech in front of her friends and team members on Wednesday to simulate the way she planned to deliver her speech in front of people.	Keep	The comma after "friends" is unnecessary because "friends and team members" is a compound that should not be interrupted with any punctuation. This choice also changes the incorrect present tense "performs" to the past tense "performed" to reflect the fact that Kira completed the action last week.
D.	(4) She recites it out loud over and over on Thursday and Friday making sure she had every word memorized.	Eliminate	This incorrectly changes the past tense "recited" to the present tense "recites" and deletes a necessary comma that separates extra information from the rest of the sentence.

2. **H.** The question indicates that a revision is necessary, and the answer choices show that there are two errors: a comma error and a verb error. Focus on one at a time to make the question more manageable.

I.

	EDITED TEXT	KEEP OR ELIMINATE?	WHY?
E.	(1) Okapis, which are also called forest giraffes is native to central Africa.	Eliminate	This deletes a necessary comma that separates the nonessential clause "which are also called forest giraffes" from the rest of the sentence and incorrectly changes the plural "are" to the singular "is," which does not match the plural "Okapis."
F.	(2) The common ancestor of giraffes and okapis the *Canthumeryx*, lives about 16 million years ago.	Eliminate	This option deletes a necessary comma that separates the nonessential phrase "the *Canthumeryx*" from the rest of the sentence and incorrectly changes the past tense "lived" to the present tense "lives," which does not make sense in context.
G.	(3) Animals that are now known as giraffes evolved to be quite tall and lanky with necks that can reach leaves that grows high up on trees.	Eliminate	This choice deletes a necessary comma that separates the nonessential phrase "with necks that can reach leaves that grows high up on trees" from the rest of the sentence and incorrectly changes the plural "grow" to the singular "grows," which does not match the plural "leaves."
H.	(4) Okapis did not grow longer necks but developed stripes similar to zebras to provide camouflage from predators.	Keep	A comma should be used with the FANBOYS conjunction "but" only when separating two complete sentences; however, the portion of the sentence after "but" cannot stand alone. In addition, the present tense "develops" should be changed to the past tense "developed" to reflect that this action happened in the past.

5. Knowledge of Language

Practice: Conciseness

Note: These are not the only ways to correct the sentences; your answers may differ.

A. It is important to carefully consider ~~and think about~~ what kind of college you wish to attend.

B. ~~Often, a~~ **A** house cat will typically sleep for up to 16 hours per day.

C. The whole team felt ~~a sense of~~ **excited** ~~anticipation~~ in the seconds before the whistle blew.

D. My sister and I couldn't ~~come to an~~ **agree** ~~ment with each other~~ about what movie we wanted to watch that afternoon.

E. Noctilucent clouds appear approximately 82 kilometers above Earth's surface. ~~This is an altitude~~, which is seven times higher than commercial airlines fly.

1. **F.** The question stem indicates that there is an error that needs to be corrected, and the answer choices show that a word or phrase should be removed. Look for redundant or unclear wording that should be deleted.

G.

	EDITED TEXT	KEEP OR ELIMINATE?	WHY?
A.	My sister and I spent all of Saturday evening playing tennis at the park, but we had to stop when it became too difficult and challenging to see the ball.	Eliminate	This changes the meaning of the sentence by saying that "My sister and I" spent the entire evening rather than most of the evening playing tennis at the park.
B.	My sister and I spent nearly all of Saturday evening playing tennis at the park, but had to stop when it became too difficult and challenging to see the ball.	Eliminate	This option creates a grammar error by removing the subject of the independent clause after the comma and FANBOYS ("but").
C.	My sister and I spent nearly all of Saturday evening playing tennis at the park, but we had to stop when it became too difficult to see the ball.	Keep	The phrase "difficult and challenging" is redundant because "difficult" and "challenging" have the same meaning in this sentence, so deleting "and challenging" fixes the error.
D.	My sister and I spent nearly all of Saturday evening playing tennis at the park, but we had to stop when it became too difficult and challenging.	Eliminate	This choice changes the writer's intended meaning by implying that tennis, not seeing the ball, became too difficult.

2. **H.** The question stem implies that there is an error, and the answer choices indicate that a phrase should be edited for conciseness.

I.

EDITED TEXT	KEEP OR ELIMINATE?	WHY?
E. (1) Although Jane Austen's novels are most often admired for their eloquence and imagery, they are also highly esteemed for their subtle yet shrewd observations of nineteenth-century English society.	Keep	The phrase "and the people living in it" is unnecessary because the word "society" directly refers to a group of people living in a community.
F. (2) Austen drew from her experiences with family in various situations to create the characters and settings in her novels.	Eliminate	Deleting "and acquaintances" incorrectly changes the meaning of the sentence.
G. (3) In the novel *Sense and Sensibility*, she demonstrated her sophisticated literary technique when portraying ordinary events.	Eliminate	Removing "even" changes the writer's intended meaning by removing the original emphasis on the phrase "when portraying ordinary events."
H. (4) Consequently, Austen is respected by people worldwide.	Eliminate	This choice is incorrect because deleting "and often beloved" removes part of the writer's intended message.

Practice: Precision

Note: These are not the only ways to correct the sentences; your answers may differ.

J. The audience laughed as the ~~person performed~~ **comedian told jokes** on stage.

K. The teacher ~~helped~~ **wrote down a bulleted list of detailed instructions for** Graciela.

L. Zeke apologized for ~~attending~~ **intruding** when he interrupted the private meeting.

M. The students walked toward the stage to receive their awards while a teacher arranged ~~them~~ **the awards** alphabetically.

N. When Cia told her mom what happened at school, ~~she~~ **her mom** was very surprised.

3. **O.** The question is asking for the most precise language, so look for an answer choice that includes clear, logical wording.

P.

ANSWER CHOICE	KEEP OR ELIMINATE?	WHY?
A. Cameron made his math grade better by asking for, and completing, all available extra-credit projects.	Eliminate	Although this option makes some improvements, "asking for, and completing," is unnecessarily wordy.
B. Cameron worked on his math grade by his doing extra work, which made his grade not as low.	Eliminate	This choice uses the informal and unnecessarily wordy phrase "made his grade not as low."
C. Cameron improved his math grade by completing all available extra-credit projects.	Keep	This is correct because "improved his math grade" and "completing all available extra-credit projects" replace the less-detailed phrases "made his math grade better" and "doing extra work."
D. Cameron boosted his grade in math by working on and handing in all available extra-credit projects.	Eliminate	This option includes the unnecessarily wordy phrase "working on and handing in."

4. **Q.** The question indicates that there is a grammar issue that needs to be fixed, and the answer choices offer different ways of rephrasing the original sentence. Look for a precision issue such as lack of clarity or ambiguity.

R.

ANSWER CHOICE	KEEP OR ELIMINATE?	WHY?
E. Increasing wages and giving them more vacation time were concessions agreed upon by the union.	Eliminate	This does not fix the ambiguous pronoun "them" and changes the sentence from active to passive voice.
F. The union agreed to concessions that included increasing wages and giving full-time workers more vacation time.	Keep	This fixes the error by changing the ambiguous pronoun "them" to a specific noun, "full-time workers."
G. The union agreed to two concessions: increasing wages and giving them more vacation time.	Eliminate	This does not introduce a new error, but it does not fix the ambiguity issue.
H. The two concessions the union agreed to were increasing wages and giving them more vacation time.	Eliminate	This changes the sentence from active to passive voice and does not fix the original error.

Practice: Style

S. The dreary weather darkened the skies, dampened spirits, and spread **gloom** throughout the city.

T. The **jubilant** contestant shrieked with delight when the host revealed what she had won.

U. The final episode of the sitcom was easily the funniest of the entire series; each character **gave a hilarious performance** that made even casual fans laugh.

V. The baseball team rode home in silence after a devastating loss at the **merciless** hands of their biggest rivals.

W. The runner breathed deeply, heart racing and palms sweating, **waiting with apprehension** for the start of the race.

5. **X.** The answer choices involve changing the language used in parts of the paragraph; look for the answer choice that best matches the language in the rest of the paragraph or that fixes unclear or informal language.

Y.

EDITED TEXT	KEEP OR ELIMINATE?	WHY?
A. (1) Before tourism became a mainstay of the economy, the value of land in Mexico was defined by how well its dirt could make plants grow.	Eliminate	This incorrectly changes the more formal "soil could produce crops" to the informal "dirt could make plants grow."
B. (2) To many Americans, hot, sunny vacation spots such as Acapulco and Puerto Vallarta characterize Mexico.	Eliminate	This option uses less formal language, which does not fit well with language like "characterize" later in the sentence.
C. (3) These may be the common types of spots for people who are on vacation, but they are certainly not representative of the entire country.	Eliminate	This choice changes the clear phrase "destinations for foreign travelers" to a wordier and less formal "spots for people who are on vacation."
D. (4) For better or worse, these cities, and others like them, are set up to be attractive to tourists.	Keep	The phrase "fun for lots of vacationers" is too informal to match the style of the rest of the paragraph and should be changed.

6. **Z.** The question indicates there is a stylistic issue. The paragraph has a straightforward, scholarly style that is not reflected in sentence 2. Look for the choice that uses higher-level, formal vocabulary while explaining the cotton gin like a textbook would.

AA.

	EDITED TEXT	KEEP OR ELIMINATE?	WHY?
E.	The cotton gin consisted of a rotating drum with wire spikes that efficiently caught the desired fibers and left behind the unwanted seeds.	Keep	This is both formal and informative, so it is correct.
F.	The new machine had a rotating drum with wire spikes that took the fibers people actually wanted and tossed out seeds, which weren't useful anyway.	Eliminate	The phrase "tossed out" is too informal.
G.	The cotton gin had a rotating drum with wire spikes that caught the cotton fibers and left the unwanted seeds out of things.	Eliminate	The phrase "out of things" does not fit within the scholarly tone of the paragraph.
H.	The new machine had a rotating drum with wire spikes that took the fibers that were worth some money and tossed out seeds, which couldn't be sold for any sort of profit.	Eliminate	The phrase "any sort of" does not match the tone of the surrounding text.

6. Organization and Topic Development

Practice: Organization

A. The train was delayed; **therefore**, we arrived at our destination two hours late.

B. **Although** the critics agreed that the movie was terrible, I went to see it anyway.

C. We need to finish our project **before** we leave this afternoon.

D. The hiking trail was difficult to navigate; **indeed**, state park guidelines recommend that only experienced hikers attempt the climb.

E. The morphology of the amoeba is more complex than you might expect; **furthermore**, the mechanism underlying amoeboid motion is still not fully understood.

1. **F.** The question asks you to combine two sentences, and the answer choices provide various ways to do so. The first step is to determine the relationship between them. Sentence 3 states that the map is thought to be from the fifteenth century, and sentence 4 states that ink indicates that it may be a forgery, or a copy, rather than a document that was actually created hundreds of years ago. The two sentences offer contrasting, or opposite, ideas, so using a contrast transition to combine them will work well.

G.

	ANSWER CHOICE	KEEP OR ELIMINATE?	WHY?
A.	It is alleged to be a fifteenth-century artifact of the Vikings' first voyage to North America, and chemical analyses of its ink indicate that it could be a modern forgery on previously blank fifteenth-century parchment.	Eliminate	The word "and" implies a continuation, which is the opposite of what is needed.
B.	While it is alleged to be a fifteenth-century artifact of the Vikings' first voyage to North America, chemical analyses of its ink indicate that it could be a modern forgery on previously blank fifteenth-century parchment.	Keep	"While" is a contrast transition that logically conveys the writer's intended meaning.
C.	Because it is alleged to be a fifteenth-century artifact of the Vikings' first voyage to North America, chemical analyses of its ink indicate that it could be a modern forgery on previously blank fifteenth-century parchment.	Eliminate	"Because" is used to show cause-and-effect, which the writer did not intend.
D.	Chemical analyses of the ink in the Vinland map, which is alleged to be a fifteenth-century artifact of the Vikings' first voyage to North America, indicate that it could be a modern forgery on previously blank fifteenth-century parchment.	Eliminate	This option does not indicate a contrast, and it sets off sentence 3 in commas as if it is unnecessary information, when actually it is needed to understand the importance of the Vinland map.

2. **H.** The question says that sentence 12 needs to be moved, so look for specific clues that indicate the best place to relocate it. Sentence 12 introduces the idea that paper can help experts determine if a map is authentic, and sentences 10 and 11 provide details about paper that was created hundreds of years ago.

I.

ANSWER CHOICE	KEEP OR ELIMINATE?	WHY?
E. to the beginning of the paragraph (before sentence 6)	Eliminate	Sentences 6, 7, 8, and 9 do not discuss paper, so moving the sentence to the beginning of the paragraph does not make sense.
F. between sentences 7 and 8	Eliminate	Moving sentence 12 between sentences 7 and 8 interrupts the discussion of ink as an important clue for dating historical documents.
G. between sentences 9 and 10	Keep	Moving sentence 12 between sentences 9 and 10 creates a logical introductory statement for sentences 10 and 11, which discuss details about paper used hundreds of years ago.
H. between sentences 10 and 11	Eliminate	Sentence 12 must appear before sentence 10, not after it, in order to properly introduce the idea that paper can also be used to analyze authenticity.

3. **J.** The question asks which transition should be added, so read sentence 16 and the text before it to determine the type of transition that is needed. Sentence 16 includes a list of features that can be used to assess a map. These features were not discussed in any of the previous sentences, so a transition that highlights further information will make the most sense.

K.

EDITED TEXT	KEEP OR ELIMINATE?	WHY?
A. Authentic maps were most often produced on high-quality, low-acidity paper. Although experts have found that color, printing techniques, text, and stitching can provide useful clues about the date and authenticity of a map.	Eliminate	Not only does the contrast transition "Although" not make sense, it also creates a fragment.
B. Authentic maps were most often produced on high-quality, low-acidity paper. In addition, experts have found that color, printing techniques, text, and stitching can provide useful clues about the date and authenticity of a map.	Keep	"In addition" correctly introduces the four other ways maps can be assessed.
C. Authentic maps were most often produced on high-quality, low-acidity paper. However, experts have found that color, printing techniques, text, and stitching can provide useful clues about the date and authenticity of a map.	Eliminate	"However" is a contrast transition, which is the opposite of the writer's intended meaning.
D. Authentic maps were most often produced on high-quality, low-acidity paper. Because experts have found that color, printing techniques, text, and stitching can provide useful clues about the date and authenticity of a map.	Eliminate	"Because" incorrectly implies a cause-and-effect relationship, and it creates a fragment.

4. **L.** The question is asking for the best topic sentence for this paragraph. A topic sentence introduces the main idea of the paragraph and maintains the established tone. The previous paragraph is written in an informative tone; it discusses how forged maps take great skill to create and do have value, although perhaps not as much as authentic maps.

M.

ANSWER CHOICE	KEEP OR ELIMINATE?	WHY?
E. Forged maps may have anywhere from a little to a lot of value.	Eliminate	This sentence is too informal to match the writer's tone.
F. The amount of skill required to make forged maps is directly proportional to their value.	Eliminate	This reflects an idea that is not mentioned; the writer does not say that skill and value are proportional.
G. It is worth considering how much value forged maps may have.	Keep	This matches both the tone and the main idea.
H. Experts often believe that forged maps do not have any value because it is illegal to create forgeries.	Eliminate	The writer does not indicate that experts think that forged maps do not have value.

Practice: Topic Development

N.   **The plane ride was long** because we had two long layovers, one in Dallas and one in Los Angeles.

O.   After walking up and down each aisle at least three times, **I chose a perfect present for my sister**.

P.   **My dog, Bailey, is stubborn;** no matter what I do, Bailey will not sit, shake, or roll over even though she knows how.

Q.   Before the library opened for the day, I helped the librarian organize various books and toys as well as several games because **we wanted story hour to go well**.

R.   **I was very hungry,** so I helped myself to soup, salad, chicken, rice, and green beans.

5.   S.   The question indicates that the correct answer will state the main claim of the passage. Be sure to take the time to read through the entire passage before answering this type of question.

T.

ANSWER CHOICE	KEEP OR ELIMINATE?	WHY?
A. Irrigation was certainly a problem ancient groups of people had to solve to ensure that their crops would flourish.	Eliminate	Although this statement is true, it leaves out the discussion of modern irrigation in paragraph 3.
B. The first irrigation processes in Australia were centered around the Murray-Darling system, located in the southwest portion of the continent.	Eliminate	This provides a specific example of early irrigation processes, which would fit better in paragraph 2 than in paragraph 1.
C. If ancient people could not access water, they would not be able to ensure that their cities would survive.	Eliminate	This statement is true, but it doesn't mention modern irrigation, so it cannot reflect the passage as a whole.
D. There is considerable evidence that irrigation may have played a pivotal role in shaping both the earliest civilizations and modern irrigation techniques.	Keep	This option reflects the discussion of irrigation in ancient civilizations in paragraph 2 as well as modern irrigation in paragraph 3.

6. **U.** The question stem indicates that there is an off-topic sentence in this paragraph; the answer choices narrow the options to four possible sentences. The passage is about irrigation, so anything other than that topic is irrelevant.

V.

ANSWER CHOICE	KEEP OR ELIMINATE?	WHY?
E. sentence 4 (The ancient Egyptians controlled water coming from the annual flooding of the Nile River to irrigate lands used for planting.)	Eliminate	This provides an example of ancient civilizations employing irrigation techniques, so it fits within the paragraph.
F. sentence 5 (Ancient Persians used a system of sloping wells and tunnels to direct water to their barley fields.)	Eliminate	This sentences adds to the paragraph's discussion of irrigation systems used in ancient times.
G. sentence 6 (The Dujiangyan Irrigation System, built in 256 B.C.E. in the Sichuan region of China, irrigated an enormous area of farmland.)	Eliminate	This provides another example of an irrigation system in an ancient civilization.
H. sentence 7 (Historians estimate that the Sichuan farmland amounted to at least 5,000 square kilometers, amounting to approximately the size of the U.S. state of Delaware.)	Keep	This sentence shifts away from the paragraph's focus on irrigation in ancient civilizations to the size of the Sichuan farmland. It is the sentence that should be removed.

7. **W.** The question stem asks for a sentence that will be added to the paragraph. The correct answer will include information that is relevant and fits well within the context of the paragraph.

X.

ANSWER CHOICE	KEEP OR ELIMINATE?	WHY?
A. Additional problems with modern irrigation, such as wasteful runoff, are not surprising, given irrigation's long history.	Eliminate	This sentence makes the illogical claim that the drawbacks of modern irrigation are due to irrigation's long history.
B. Despite some negative results of irrigation, it has been and remains crucial to the development of communities.	Keep	This option fits well within the context of the passage by connecting to the last sentence of paragraph 3 and introducing the topic of the next paragraph.
C. There are several reasons why irrigation is important, from providing much-needed hydration for crops to controlling unpredictable access to water.	Eliminate	This option simply repeats information already discussed in the passage.
D. Ancient civilizations took the drawbacks and the benefits of irrigation in stride, knowing that it was essential to their survival.	Eliminate	This does not fit well within the context because the paragraph does not discuss ancient civilizations.

8. **Y.** The question is asking for a sentence to best follow and support sentence 12, which discuses the complexity of creating canals and drainage networks.

Z.

ANSWER CHOICE	KEEP OR ELIMINATE?	WHY?
E. Some historians may argue that if ancient people had not endeavored to create irrigation systems, ancient civilization would not have developed in the way that it did.	Eliminate	While this may be true, it does not add relevant information to the discussion of irrigation systems.
F. The centers of commerce, administration, and science that accomplished the task eventually blossomed into the cities that served as the cornerstones of many ancient civilizations.	Keep	This option directly references the creation of canals and drainage networks, which fits well within the context of the paragraph.
G. Irrigation was impressive in two particular ways: its construction and the resulting advancements.	Eliminate	This is not specific enough to provide the best support for the previous sentence.
H. There were noteworthy improvements in not only the irrigation-related features but also the extensive canal systems.	Eliminate	This option is appropriate in tone but not specific enough to provide relevant information.

[CHAPTER 5]

THE KAPLAN METHOD FOR READING COMPREHENSION

CHAPTER OBJECTIVES

By the end of this chapter, you will be able to:

- Read SHSAT Reading passages strategically
- Apply the Kaplan Method for Reading Comprehension efficiently and effectively to SHSAT Reading questions

1. The Kaplan Method for Reading Comprehension and Strategic Reading

The Kaplan Method for Reading Comprehension

The SHSAT includes reading comprehension passages and accompanying questions. On test day, you want to spend no more than 5 minutes actively reading each passage and 1 minute answering each question.

It is in your best interest to approach the SHSAT systematically; the Method for Reading Comprehension will help you improve your efficiency and accuracy on these questions. When you first start practicing with this method, you'll likely find yourself spending more than 5 minutes on each passage. As you continue practicing, pay attention to your timing. The best way to cut down your time is to get used to utilizing the Kaplan Method. If you approach every passage the same way, you will work your way through the Reading Comprehension passages and questions efficiently.

> **THE KAPLAN METHOD FOR READING COMPREHENSION**
>
> **STEP 1:** Read actively
>
> **STEP 2:** Examine the question stem and predict
>
> **STEP 3:** Match and answer

You may notice that the first two steps of the Kaplan Method for Reading Comprehension are flipped, compared with the Kaplan Method for Revising/Editing Text. While you should examine *the question* first in Revising/Editing questions, you need to actively read *the whole passage* first when it comes to Reading Comprehension. This is because the Reading Comprehension section tests your knowledge of the passage as a whole as well as specific elements of it, so you need to have a solid understanding of the entire passage in order to best answer all of the questions that accompany it.

Step 1: Read Actively

Active reading means that as you read the passage, you are asking questions and taking notes. You should ask questions such as:

- What do the **keywords** indicate?
- What is a good **summary** of each paragraph?
- What **specific information** is provided in the passage?
- What **inferences** can be made based on the information the author provides?
- What is the **main idea** of the passage?

Keywords

Keywords in a passage are purposefully included by the author to help you understand the ideas in the passage. Common keywords include **transition words**, such as those that indicate contrast, continuation, and cause-and-effect, and words that signal the author's **emphasis or opinion**. Use the keywords in the paragraph to answer the accompanying questions.

Some literary experts would say that writing in verse form cannot qualify as poetry unless it awakens the senses on a nonverbal level or elevates the emotions. However, the question of whether a verse fulfills these criteria may depend on the reader. Many haikus, for example, may awaken the senses on a nonverbal level in some readers but not in others. Thus, their classification as poems, according to experts, may depend on what the haiku means to readers rather than on what they say.

A. What does the word "However" indicate about the second sentence?

B. What do the words "for example" indicate about the third sentence?

C. What does the word "Thus" indicate about the fourth sentence?

SHSAT EXPERT NOTE

Mark up the passage as you read!

The first sentence or two of a paragraph will usually express the topic of the paragraph.

Summarizing

Summaries cut out the details and focus on the big ideas of an individual paragraph or the passage as a whole. Actively read the following paragraph. Then answer the accompanying questions that ask about summarizing the paragraph.

The four brightest moons of Jupiter were the first objects in the solar system discovered with the use of the telescope, and they played an important role in Galileo's famous argument supporting the Copernican model of the solar system. For several hundred years after the moons' discovery by Galileo in 1610, scientific understanding of these moons increased slowly but regularly. However, the spectacular close-up photographs sent back by the 1979 Voyager missions forever changed scientists' impressions of these bodies.

D. Why wouldn't "the early history of astronomy" be a good summary for this paragraph?

E. Why wouldn't "discoveries of the Voyager missions" be a good summary?

F. If you had to summarize this paragraph in just a few words, what would they be?

Specific Information

Don't try to memorize all of the **specific information**, or details, in the passage as you read. Instead, make a summary note for each paragraph, and use those notes to help you identify which paragraph to research if you need to find a specific detail. For the short passage below, write a summary note for each paragraph. Then use your notes to help you determine which paragraph contains the details needed to answer each question.

A human body can survive without water for several days and without food for as many as several weeks. If breathing stops for as little as 3–6 minutes, however, death is likely to occur. All animals require a constant supply of oxygen to the body tissues, especially to the heart and brain. In the human body, the respiratory system performs this function by delivering air, containing oxygen, to the blood.

Respiration in large animals possessing lungs involves more than just breathing. It is a complex process that delivers oxygen to internal tissues while eliminating carbon dioxide waste produced by cells. More specifically, respiration involves two processes known as bulk flow and diffusion. Oxygen and carbon dioxide are moved in bulk through the respiratory and circulatory systems; gaseous diffusion occurs at different points across thin tissue membranes.

G. What bodily function mentioned is the most critical to human survival? Least critical?

H. What need is shared by all animals?

I. What two processes are involved in respiration in large animals?

J. Where does gaseous diffusion occur?

Inference

Read the following paragraph. Then answer the accompanying questions that ask about making inferences.

Between the ages of 1 and 17, the average person learns the meaning of about 14 words per day. Dictionaries and traditional classroom vocabulary lessons account for only part of this spectacular growth. Far more influential is individuals' verbal interaction with people whose vocabularies are larger than their own. Conversation offers several benefits that make vocabulary learning interesting: it supplies visual information, offers frequent repetition of new words, and gives students the chance to ask questions.

K. The author would most likely recommend which method of increasing a student's vocabulary: classroom lessons or conversation?

L. How would the author most likely describe traditional classroom vocabulary lessons?

Roadmap

As you read, create your own **Roadmap** of the passage. Creating a Roadmap helps keep you focused on the big ideas rather than the small details of a passage. You can also use your Roadmap to help you locate the information you need to answer each question. A passage Roadmap should include:

- A short summary note about the topic of each paragraph
- A summary of the passage's main idea

SHSAT EXPERT NOTE

Be an active reader:

- Look for the main idea.
- Identify the paragraph topics.

Move efficiently, and take short, straightforward notes in your passage Roadmap. You don't want to take valuable time writing too much; you can always return to part of a passage if you need to refresh your memory about the smaller details.

Step 2: Examine the Question Stem and Predict

A set of 6 to 10 questions will follow the passage. The first thing you'll need to do with each question is to **examine the stem** to determine exactly what is being asked before you can answer the question. Basically, you need to make the question make sense to you.

Next, use your Roadmap to help you research the part of the passage that has the information you need to answer the question. **Predict** an answer before you look at the answer choices; in other words, "predict before you peek."

Predicting before you peek helps you:

- Know precisely what you are looking for in the answer choices
- Avoid weighing each answer choice equally, which saves time
- Eliminate the possibility of falling into incorrect answer traps

Step 3: Match and Answer

Finally, look for the one answer choice that **matches** your prediction. If you find a match, select it and move on to the next question.

If you can't find a match, **eliminate** answer choices to help you narrow down your options.

Practice Passage

Step 1: Read Actively

Actively reading the passage includes taking notes to create a **Roadmap** of a passage, which should include the main idea of the passage and the topic of each paragraph.

The Evolution of Ancient Greek Poetry

1   The poems of the earliest Greeks, like those found in other ancient societies, consisted of magical charms, mysterious predictions, prayers, and traditional songs of work and war. We can infer that these poems were intended to be sung or recited, rather than written down, if only because they were created before the Greeks began to use writing for literary purposes. Unfortunately, little is known about these ancient Greek poems because all that remain are fragments mentioned by later Greek writers. Homer, for example, quoted an ancient work song for harvesters, and Simonides adapted the ancient poetry of ritual lamentation—songs of mourning for the dead—in his writing.

> **M.** What words are mentioned repeatedly throughout paragraph 1?
>
> **N.** What do the words "for example" tell us about the last sentence of paragraph 1?
>
> **O.** What is the topic of paragraph 1?

2   Although little is preserved of these earliest forms of Greek poetic expression, scholars have been able to ascertain some information. The different forms of early Greek poetry all had something in common: they described the way of life of a culture. This poetry expressed ideas and feelings that were shared by everyone in a community—their folktales, their memories of historical events, and their religion. What remains of these poems suggests that the works were of collective significance, with little emphasis on the individual achievements of particular characters. Greek poets didn't spend time developing imagined narrative stories. This style of retelling the everyday events and beliefs of everyday people was referred to as "folk poetry," and it stands in stark contrast to the style of expression that came later.

> **P.** What is similar in paragraph 1 and paragraph 2?
>
> **Q.** How does paragraph 2 differ from paragraph 1?
>
> **R.** What is the topic of paragraph 2?

3   In the "age of heroes," the content and purpose of Greek poetry shifted dramatically. By this later period, Greek communities had become more stratified into separate classes, including those who ruled and those who were ruled. In contrast to the way people lived before, now those living in the same community had different, even opposing, interests. As such, they shared fewer daily experiences and probably shared fewer ideas and even emotions. The poetry of the Greek people reflected this shift. Whereas the earliest Greek literature conveyed larger themes related to the whole culture, now the particular outlook of the warlike upper classes predominated.

    S. What phrase at the beginning of paragraph 3 indicates a change in the passage's focus?

    T. How is the content of paragraph 3 different from that of paragraph 2?

    U. How is later Greek poetry different from earlier Greek poetry?

    V. What is the topic of paragraph 3?

4   One need only study Homer's *Iliad* and *Odyssey*, which are recorded examples of the epic poetry that was sung in the Heroic Age, to understand the influence that the upper class had on poetry. Poetic content in this time period told stories of the lives of great individuals, including warriors and kings, and it lost much of its religious character. Thus, the poetry of the Heroic Age could no longer be called folk poetry because poets were assigned a new task: to celebrate the accomplishments of outstanding characters, whether real or imaginary, rather than to catalog and preserve the activity and history of the community as a whole. This focus is indeed the reason why the Heroic Age is so named.

    W. How is the focus of paragraph 4 different from the focus of paragraph 3?

    X. What is the topic of paragraph 4?

    Y. What is the main idea of the passage?

Step 2: Examine the Question Stem and Predict

Answer the questions below. Understanding these question stems on their own, and predicting an answer now, will help you to quickly and easily answer the full questions later.

1.   Which statement best describes the central idea of the passage?

    AA. Where will you look for the answer to this question?

    AB. Predict the answer to the question stem.

2.   Read this sentence from paragraph 2.

> **The different forms of early Greek poetry all had something in common: they described the way of life of a culture.**

The sentence contributes to the development of ideas in the excerpt by

    AC. What specific text is helpful?

    AD. Predict the answer to the question stem.

3. Read this sentence from paragraph 4.

> **Thus, the poetry of the Heroic Age could no longer be called folk poetry because poets were assigned a new task: to celebrate the accomplishments of outstanding characters, whether real or imaginary, rather than to catalog and preserve the activity and history of the community as a whole.**

The phrase "folk poetry" most clearly conveys that poetry created before the Heroic Age primarily focused on the

AE. What aspect of folk poetry is the question asking about?

AF. Predict the answer to the question stem.

4. Which sentence best explains the subject matter that Heroic Age poetry primarily celebrated?

AG. What aspect of this poetry is the question asking about?

AH. What specific text from the passage is helpful in answering this question?

AI. Predict the answer to the question stem.

5. Compared with communities in an earlier period, Greek communities during the Heroic Age most likely

AJ. What important elements in the question stem tell you where to direct your research?

AK. What can you infer about how Greek communities changed between these periods?

AL. Predict the answer to the question stem.

Step 3: Match and Answer

Now that you've practiced examining the question stems and predicting the answers, answer the full version of these questions below. Select the choice that best matches your prediction.

1. Which statement **best** describes the central idea of the passage?

A. The role of early Greek poetry changed over time.

B. Greek communities became separated into classes.

C. Early Greek poetry is more admired than later Greek poetry.

D. The *Iliad* and the *Odyssey* were written by the upper class.

2. Read this sentence from paragraph 2.

> **The different forms of early Greek poetry all had something in common: they described the way of life of a culture.**

The sentence contributes to the development of ideas in the excerpt by

E. revealing how royalty such as kings and queens became known throughout Greece.

F. identifying the fame and prestige early Greek poets sought.

G. suggesting that early Greek poetry expressed commonly held beliefs.

H. demonstrating the importance of celebrating the lives of warriors.

3.   Read this sentence from paragraph 4.

> **Thus, the poetry of the Heroic Age could no longer be called folk poetry because poets were
> assigned a new task: to celebrate the accomplishments of outstanding characters, whether
> real or imaginary, rather than to catalog and preserve the activity and history of the
> community as a whole.**

The phrase "folk poetry" **most** clearly conveys that poetry created before the Heroic Age primarily
focused on the

A.   adventures of warriors.

B.   viewpoint of a ruling class.

C.   problems of a new lower class.

D.   concerns of a whole culture.

4.   Which sentence **best** explains the subject matter that Heroic Age poetry primarily celebrated?

E.   "Unfortunately, little is known about these ancient Greek poems because all that remains are
fragments mentioned by later Greek writers." (paragraph 1)

F.   "This poetry expressed ideas and feelings that were shared by everyone in a community—their
folktales, their memories of historical events, and their religion." (paragraph 2)

G.   "The poetry of the Greek people reflected this shift." (paragraph 3)

H.   "Poetic content in this time period told stories of the lives of great individuals, including warriors
and kings, and it lost much of its religious character." (paragraph 4)

5.   Compared with communities in an earlier period, Greek communities during the Heroic Age **most** likely

A.   were less prosperous.

B.   were less unified.

C.   were better organized.

D.   were more peaceful.

Answers and Explanations

1. The Kaplan Method for Reading Comprehension

Keywords

A. "However" indicates a contrast, or change in direction.

B. The words "for example" indicate that the author is providing an instance that will demonstrate something that was discussed in the preceding sentence.

C. "Thus" indicates a conclusion.

Summarizing

D. The paragraph focuses on four of Jupiter's moons, so "the early history of astronomy" isn't specific enough to be a good summary.

E. Only one sentence mentions the Voyager missions, so "discoveries of the Voyager missions" isn't broad enough to be a good summary.

F. Jupiter's four brightest moons

Specific Information

G. Breathing is the most critical. ("If breathing stops for as little as 3–6 minutes, however, death is likely.") Eating is the least critical. ("A human body can survive . . . without food for as many as several weeks.")

H. Oxygen is a need shared by all animals. ("All animals require a constant supply of oxygen to the body tissues.")

I. The two processes are bulk flow and diffusion.

J. Gaseous diffusion occurs across tissue membranes.

Inference

K. The author would recommend conversation with people with larger vocabularies to increase a student's vocabulary ("Far more influential" and "offers several benefits that make vocabulary learning interesting").

L. The author would describe traditional classroom vocabulary lessons as not as influential as conversations with people with larger vocabularies. In addition, traditional classroom vocabulary lessons do not offer benefits that make vocabulary learning interesting.

Step 1: Read Actively

The Evolution of Ancient Greek Poetry

M. Words repeated in paragraph 1 include "poems" and "Greek."

N. The phrase "for example" tells you that this sentence provides an example of something that has already been mentioned.

O. Early Greek poetry characteristics

P. Both paragraph 1 and paragraph 2 are about early Greek poetry.

Q. Paragraph 2 elaborates on the topic of paragraph 1, focusing on a single common element of all early Greek poetry.

R. Early Greek poetry focused on community.

S. The phrase "shifted dramatically" indicates a change of direction in the passage.

T. Paragraph 2 discusses a common theme in early Greek poetry, while paragraph 3 Introduces later Greek poetry.

U. Early Greek poetry focused on the community. Later poetry focused on individuals.

V. Poetry changed as society changed, and there was more focus on individuals.

W. Paragraph 3 describes the purpose of later Greek poetry. Paragraph 4 describes the changed role of the poets who composed it.

X. Heroic Age poetry was influenced by the upper class and individualism.

Y. While early Greek poetry focused on the community as a whole, later Greek poetry was crafted by and about individuals.

Passage Analysis: The purpose of the passage is to contrast the characteristics of two periods of Greek poetry. The main idea of the passage is that, although the earliest Greek poetry focused on the community as a whole, later Greek poetry of the Heroic Age celebrated individuals. Paragraph 1 describes general characteristics of the earliest Greek poetry. Paragraph 2 explains that the earliest Greek poetry focused on the community. Paragraph 3 explains that, after Greek society became separated into classes, poetry of the Heroic Age came to focus on accomplishments of individuals.

Paragraph 4 explains that Heroic Age poets wrote epic poems focused on the upper class.

Sample Passage Notes:

¶1: early Greek poetry

¶2: community focus

¶3: age of hero poetry had upper-class view

¶4: epic poems about ind.

Main Idea: describes 2 types of Greek poetry

Step 2: Examine the Question Stem and Predict

1. **AA.** Look for the answer in the Roadmap notes.

   AB. Early Greek poetry focused on community; later poetry focused on individuals.

2. **AC.** The next sentence in the paragraph elaborates on some examples of the ideals that Greek communities shared ("their folktales, their memories of historical events, and their religion").

   AD. The sentence is introducing the idea that early Greek poetry represented shared culture, and the next sentence provides some examples.

3. **AE.** The phrase "primarily focused on" means that the question is asking about the general subject of this type of poetry.

   AF. Folk poetry's general subject was the whole community.

4. **AG.** The phrase "primarily celebrated" means that the question is asking about the purpose of this type of poetry.

   AH. Paragraph 4 states that the focus of Greek poetry had shifted to influential individuals. ("Poetic content in this time period told stories of the lives of great individuals, including warriors and kings. . . .")

   AI. Later Greek poetry celebrated extraordinary individuals.

5. **AJ.** Paragraph 2 states that early Greek poetry expressed ideas and feelings that everyone shared, while paragraph 3 states that people living in the same community began to have different interests.

AK. Later Greek communities became divided into different classes, so they were less unified than earlier ones.

AL. Greek communities during the Heroic Age were more diverse than during earlier periods.

Step 3: Match and Answer

1. **A**
Category: Global

Getting to the Answer: Global questions such as this one ask you for the main idea. Remember, the scope of the correct answer will incorporate everything discussed in the passage but no more. In this case, the main idea involves the change in Greek poetry from the earliest poets focused on the community to the Heroic Age poets focused on individuals. In other words, the passage is about how the role of early Greek poets changed. **(A)** is correct. The author does not discuss how Greek communities became separated into classes or the superiority of early Greek poetry, making **(B)** and **(C)** Out of Scope. **(D)** is incorrect because it only mentions examples, which are not the focus of the entire passage; also, the poems focused on the upper class, but the upper class did not necessarily write them.

2. **G**
Category: Function

Getting to the Answer: You know from the paragraph topic in your Roadmap that the earliest poets focused on the community, so look for the choice that is consistent with that focus. **(G)** is correct. **(E)** and **(H)** are both Distortions; celebrating kings and warriors is characteristic of later Heroic Age poetry, not early poetry. **(F)** is Out of Scope since the author never suggests that poets sought fame for themselves.

3. **D**
Category: Inference

Getting to the Answer: Go back to the passage and study the context in which this phrase is used. Paragraph 4 says that poetry that celebrates individuals of the upper class can no longer be called "folk poetry." You can infer from "no longer" that earlier Greek poetry must have been folk poetry. Because the key difference discussed in the passage is that earlier poetry was concerned with the community as a whole, you can infer that this must be a characteristic of folk poetry. **(D)** reflects this best. Paragraph 4 says that folk poetry is not about warriors and the ruling class, making **(A)** and **(B)** incorrect. **(C)** is Out of Scope; the problems of the lower class are never discussed.

4.   G

Category: Detail

Getting to the Answer: Use your Roadmap to find the answer. Paragraph 4 explains that Heroic Age poetry focused on individuals. **(H)** is correct. **(E)**, **(F)**, and **(G)** are incorrect because they do not provide specific details about the focus of Heroic Age poetry. **(F)** is incorrect because community life was a subject of earlier poetry.

5.   B

Category: Inference

Getting to the Answer: What does the passage tell you about changes in Greek communities between the two periods? Paragraph 3, which provides the transition from the early period into the Heroic Age, tells you that "Greek communities had become more stratified into separate classes." If the communities were separated, the inference is that they were less unified; **(B)** reflects this. The passage does not compare the communities in terms of prosperity, organization, or peace, making **(A)**, **(C)**, and **(D)** Out of Scope.

[CHAPTER 6]

SHSAT READING QUESTIONS

CHAPTER OBJECTIVES

By the end of this chapter, you will be able to:

- Distinguish among five SHSAT Reading question types
- Apply strategies to answer Reading questions correctly
- Identify the five SHSAT Reading incorrect answer traps

1. SHSAT Reading Question Types

Answering SHSAT Reading Questions

As you already know, you get points from answering the questions, not simply reading the passages. In order to increase your chances of getting the most points, you should approach Reading questions strategically; part of this is understanding the various types of questions you'll encounter on test day. There are five basic question types in the Reading section: Global, Detail, Function, Inference, and Infographic. Knowing how to tackle each question type is a key component for test day success.

Global Questions

Global questions ask you either to choose a correct summary of the passage as a whole or to identify key information and ideas within the passage. You can recognize Global questions because they often use phrases like "the central idea" or "overall tone/theme/plot."

To answer Global questions successfully:

- Identify the central idea or theme of the passage
- Use your Roadmap as a brief summary (do not reread the entire passage)

Avoid incorrect answer choices that focus on only a part of the passage.

> **SHSAT EXPERT NOTE**
>
> A key strategy for Global questions is to look for a choice that summarizes the entire passage—not just a detail that's mentioned once or discussed in a single paragraph. The information should be present throughout the whole passage.

Detail Questions

Detail questions ask you to track down a piece of information directly stated in the passage. Remember that you will not (and should not!) remember every detail from your reading of the passage. Your Roadmap can help you find the *location* of the detail in question; then you should research the passage text to find the answer. You can recognize Detail questions because they often use wording like "According to the passage/author/paragraph" or "The author states."

To answer Detail questions successfully:

- Use paragraph references or specific phrasing in the question to find the relevant section of the passage
- Quickly skim through the relevant section to find specific evidence for your prediction; you should be able to put your finger on the exact information required to answer the question
- Rephrase the evidence in the passage in your own words to make a prediction and find a match among the answer choices

Avoid incorrect answer choices that mention details from the passage but that don't answer the specific question asked.

Function Questions

Function questions ask about the purpose of a particular part of the passage. They can ask about the purpose of any of the following: a word, a sentence, a paragraph, a detail, a quote, or punctuation.

To answer Function questions successfully:

- Focus on the author's reason for including the cited feature
- Read around the cited text, and take note of any transition words to get context and understand the author's reasoning

Avoid incorrect answer choices that distort the author's reason for including the portion of the passage.

Inference Questions

An Inference question, like a Detail question, asks you to find relevant information in the passage. These questions use phrases such as "most likely" or "suggests," and they may ask with what the author would most likely agree. Once you've located the relevant details, you need to go one step further: figure out the underlying point of a particular phrase or example. The correct answer to an Inference question will not be directly stated in the passage, but it will be *supported by* the information in the passage.

To answer Inference questions successfully:

- Look for clues that show how the author connects relevant details within the passage
- Consider how the author's point of view limits the range of what could be true

Avoid incorrect answer choices that make inferences that cannot be supported by the details found in the passage.

Infographic Questions

An SHSAT Reading passage may be accompanied by up to two infographics, which are graphs, tables, or images that represent information related to the passage. For example, if a passage discusses the development of trade between two continents, a map of the trade routes or a bar graph showing the number of goods transported each year may accompany the passage.

Infographic questions ask you how the information in the graph, table, or image supports ideas presented in the passage. To answer Infographic questions successfully:

- Evaluate the information in the question stem (e.g., "topic," "central idea," "paragraph 7")
- Identify units, labels, and titles in the infographic
- Circle the parts of the infographic that relate to the question

Avoid incorrect answer choices that misrepresent either the infographic or the passage.

Practice Passage

Step 1: Read Actively

Actively read the following passage, taking notes to create a Roadmap. Be sure to write down the topic of each paragraph and the main idea of the passage.

Industrial Progress

1 Is industrial progress a mixed blessing? A hundred years ago, this question was seldom asked. Science and industry were flooding the world with products that made life easier. Inventions such as dishwashers and electric washing machines automated many of the tasks that used to take hours to perform by hand. Industrialization was a major driving factor behind the increased educational opportunities, disposable income, and time for leisure activities that characterized the twentieth century. In the face of such technological convenience, few gave thought to how these miraculous machines and the companies that made them affected the natural world.

2 Today, however, we know that many industrial processes create pollution that can destroy our environment. Industries produce toxic waste, discharging harmful chemicals directly into lakes, rivers, and the air. One of the most noticeable results of this growing contamination is acid rain.

3 Acid rain is caused by industrial processes that release compounds of nitrogen and sulfur. When these pollutants combine with clean air, the results are nitric and sulfuric acids. Air, clouds, and rain containing acids can have terrible effects on human, animal, and plant life. Acid droplets in the air can be inhaled, causing illness. When these acid droplets fall from clouds as rain, they can accumulate and kill plant life if natural chemical processes in soils do not deactivate the acids. In some parts of the Northeast and Midwest, 10 percent of all lakes show dangerous acid levels. In eastern mountains, large forest tracts have been lost at elevations where trees are regularly bathed in acidic clouds. This loss of vegetation creates a trickle-down effect, impacting countless species of animals that depend on these forests for food or shelter.

4 The main components of acid rain are oxides of nitrogen and sulfur dioxide, exhausted from oil- and coal-burning power plants. To reduce acid rain, emissions from these plants, particularly sulfur dioxide, must be restrained. One way is to install machines that remove sulfur dioxide from a plant's exhausts. Another is to build new industrial plants, modeled on experimental designs that produce less sulfur dioxide. Since acid rain poses such an immense risk to human, animal, and plant health, finding ways to reduce its impact is an important and ongoing area of research for industrialists.

5 Happily, it seems that many companies today are becoming increasingly aware of their impact on the environment. Tech behemoths such as Google and Facebook rely more and more on renewable energy sources to power their data centers and actively look for ways to reduce their carbon footprint. Car companies are reevaluating their manufacturing processes and looking for ways to do more with less. Even the average citizen is probably more environmentally conscious than a citizen from a century ago. Practices such as composting and recycling are gaining ground in the public consciousness, and being concerned with the state of the environment is no longer considered a radical, countercultural view.

6 A century ago, industrial progress was viewed as a battle against nature; for humanity to make progress, nature must recede. Contemporary opinion holds that humanity and nature must cooperate, or both will be destroyed.

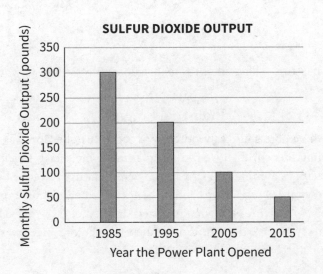

A. ¶1 Topic

B. ¶2 Topic

C. ¶3 Topic

D. ¶4 Topic

E. ¶5 Topic

F. ¶6 Topic

G. Passage Main Idea

Step 2: Examine the Question Stem and Predict & Step 3: Match and Answer

Now use your Roadmap and your researching skills to answer the following questions.

Global

1. Which statement **best** describes the central idea of the passage?

    A. The drawbacks of industrial progress far outweigh the economic and social benefits.

    B. People are now working to limit acid rain, as well as other types of pollution, to protect the environment.

    C. Industrial leaders have been irresponsible and should be held accountable for their poor environmental practices.

    D. To understand current environmental conditions, a comparison between industry in the nineteenth century and industry today is necessary.

Detail

2. Which sentence from the passage demonstrates a harmful effect of acid rain?

    E. "In the face of such technological convenience, few gave thought to how these miraculous machines and the companies that made them affected the natural world." (paragraph 1)

    F. "In eastern mountains, large forest tracts have been lost at elevations where trees are regularly bathed in acidic clouds." (paragraph 3)

    G. "To reduce acid rain, emissions from these plants, particularly sulfur dioxide, must be restrained." (paragraph 4)

    H. "A century ago, industrial progress was viewed as a battle against nature; for humanity to make progress, nature must recede." (paragraph 6)

Function

3. The question at the beginning of the passage contributes to the development of ideas by

    A. outlining why acid rain is so harmful to humans and plants.

    B. explaining the causes of acid rain as well as potential methods for its reduction.

    C. pointing out that the effect of industrial progress on the environment is a puzzling phenomenon.

    D. introducing a discussion about the benefits and detriments of industrial progress.

Inference

4. What is the **most** likely purpose of the "experimental designs" mentioned in paragraph 4?

    E. to increase sulfur dioxide output

    F. to reduce pollution-driven deforestation

    G. to deactivate sulfuric acid that falls in rain

    H. to neutralize the acidity of contaminated lakes

Infographic

5. How does the bar graph support the ideas in paragraph 4?

    A. It indicates how machines that remove sulfur dioxide are effective in plants built in the 1980s and 1990s.

    B. It reveals that dangerous acid levels in Northeast and Midwest lakes have decreased over time.

    C. It provides evidence that more recently built power plants emit less sulfur dioxide than older power plants.

    D. It shows how improvements in ecosystems have positively affected the amount of sulfur dioxide emitted each month.

2. Strategy Focus: Elimination Strategies

SHSAT Reading Elimination Strategies

One key strategy for determining the correct answer choice is to eliminate the incorrect choices. This can be especially helpful if you encounter a passage or question that you're not confident about. Most incorrect choices fall into specific categories. Once you know the categories, elimination is much easier!

INCORRECT ANSWER TRAP	DESCRIPTION
Distortion	The answer slightly alters details from a passage so they are no longer correct.
Extreme	The answer takes a stronger position (often more positive or more negative) than the passage takes.
Misused Detail	The answer is a true statement from the passage, but it doesn't answer the question.
Opposite	The answer contradicts information in the passage.
Out of Scope	The answer includes information that is not in the passage.

Global Questions

Global questions ask you to summarize the main idea of the passage. The correct answer choice should correspond to what you have written in your Roadmap. Out of Scope, Misused Detail, and Extreme are the most common incorrect answer traps for Global questions.

Detail Questions

Detail questions ask you to research information that is directly stated in the passage. There are two common types of incorrect answer choices for Detail questions: Misused Detail and Distortion.

Function Questions

Function questions ask about the purpose of a particular part of the passage. They can ask about the purpose of a word, sentence, paragraph, detail, or even punctuation. Distortion and Out of Scope incorrect answer traps are the most common incorrect answers that accompany Function questions.

Inference Questions

Inference questions ask you to figure out the underlying point of a particular phrase or example. The three common types of incorrect answer choices for Inference questions are Out of Scope, Extreme, and Misused Detail.

Infographic Questions

Infographic questions ask you how the information in the graph, table, or image supports ideas presented in the passage. Out of Scope and Distortion are the most common incorrect answer traps that accompany Infographic questions.

Practice Passage

Step 1: Read Actively

Actively read the following passage, taking notes to create a Roadmap. Be sure to write down the topic of each paragraph and the main idea of the passage.

Bird Courtship Behavior

1   Since there are thousands of species of birds in the natural world and many of these species tend to congregate in the same habitats, nearly every species has its own special courtship procedures and "identification checks." Identification checks allow birds to ensure that they are mating with members of their own species. Identification checks are important because if members of different species mate, the offspring are usually sterile or badly adapted to their surroundings. Once the species of a potential partner is confirmed, courtship rituals enable birds to assess the quality of their mates.

2   For many bird species, plumage plays a key role in both identification and courtship. During breeding season, male birds acquire distinctive plumage that they use to attract females, and the females respond only to males with the correct markings. The most striking example of such plumage is the magnificently colored head, chest, and tail feathers of the male bird of paradise. When attempting to attract a mate, the male perches on a branch and then gradually leans forward until he is hanging upside down, covered with his own brilliant feathers. A female bird of paradise will watch the display and then respond. Scientists refer to the bird displaying the plumage as the "actor," while the bird that observes is the "reactor." Although the male is the actor and the female is the reactor in the case of birds of paradise, the females of some species are more brightly colored than the males, and the courtship roles are reversed. Distinctive behavioral changes can also be important aspects of courtship and breeding activity.

3   Aggressiveness among males, and sometimes among females, is quite common. Some birds, such as whooping cranes and trumpeter swans, perform wonderfully elaborate courtship dances in which both sexes are enthusiastic participants. The purpose of the dance is to establish and maintain a "pair-bond" that will last between the male and female through the period of the reproductive season, or at least until the nesting has been completed. Each species has its own set of inherited courtship behaviors, which also helps prevent mating between birds of different species.

4   Birdcalls are another key part of identification between individuals in a given species. When a female migrates to her breeding region in the spring, she often encounters numerous birds of different species. The males of her species identify themselves by their singing and communicate to her that they are in breeding condition. This information allows the female to predict the response of a male to her approach. Later, after mating has taken place, the note patterns of a particular male's song enable the nesting female to continue to identify her partner.

5   Nature lovers do not need to travel to exotic lands to see these fascinating rituals take place. The northern cardinal, a common sight in the eastern and midwestern United States, is an excellent example of a territorial bird. Males perch on tall trees and sing high-pitched, piercing notes to announce that the surrounding area is their territory. They are so aggressive about defending it that they will sometimes mistake their reflection in a window or car as an invading male and attempt to fight it. During courtship, males will feed females, placing the food directly into her beak. Cardinals usually mate for life, and pairs will often sing to each other at dusk. Once the chicks have hatched, they are fed and cared for by the male cardinal, who listens carefully for their unique fledgling call.

6   The American goldfinch is another common bird with spectacular courtship behaviors. When a male is ready to mate, he will actually chase the prospective female. The female attempts to outmaneuver him by flying in zigzag patterns, and the male signals his fitness and worthiness as a mate by matching her move for move. Once the two birds are pair-bonded, the male will establish his territory by flying from tree to tree, singing a unique warbling song as he goes. He will circle the perimeter twice: once in a low, flat flight and again in "daredevil" display involving abrupt drops to the ground and loops. As with the cardinal, the male shoulders the responsibility of caring for the chicks once they have hatched. These displays and rituals illustrate how complex behavior can emerge from the most primitive of biological needs—reproduction.

Avian Identification Behaviors

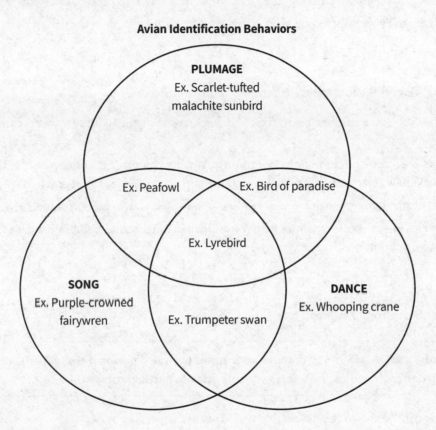

A. ¶1 Topic

B. ¶2 Topic

C. ¶3 Topic

D. ¶4 Topic

E. ¶5 Topic

F. ¶6 Topic

G. What is the Main Idea of the passage?

Step 2: Examine the Question Stem and Predict & Step 3: Match and Answer

Now use your Roadmap and your researching skills to answer the following questions.

Global

1. Which statement **best** describes the central idea of the passage?

   A. Birds create nests in a variety of ways, depending on their species and general habitat.

   B. The mating activities of birds involve several different types of behaviors and approaches.

   C. Birdcalls provide important migratory directions in addition to playing a key role in courtship.

   D. A "pair-bond" generally lasts at least as long as it takes the two birds to create a nest, if not longer.

Detail

2. Which sentence **best** demonstrates the function of male birdcalls?

   E. "Identification checks allow birds to ensure that they are mating with members of their own species." (paragraph 1)

   F. "During breeding season, male birds acquire distinctive plumage that they use to attract females, and the females respond only to males with the correct markings." (paragraph 2)

   G. "Aggressiveness among males, and sometimes among females, is quite common." (paragraph 3)

   H. "The males of her species identify themselves by their singing and communicate to her that they are in breeding condition." (paragraph 4)

Function

3. Read this sentence from paragraph 3.

   > **Some birds, such as whooping cranes and trumpeter swans, perform wonderfully elaborate courtship dances in which both sexes are enthusiastic participants.**

   The sentence contributes to the development of ideas in the passage by

   A. suggesting that some bird species seldom participate in courtship procedures.

   B. explaining how whooping cranes and trumpeter swans acquire distinctive breeding plumage.

   C. providing an example of species that behave in an unusual way during courtship.

   D. demonstrating a reversal of the typical male and female courtship roles.

Inference

4. In bird species for which sounds are a crucial form of identification check, the female bird **most** likely

   E. is unable to sing.

   F. is not aggressive.

   G. chooses the mate.

   H. must be in breeding condition.

Infographic

5. How does the Venn diagram contribute to the development of the topic of the passage?

    A. It emphasizes that the males of some avian species can use a variety of behaviors to attract a mate.

    B. It shows that birds are more likely to use a single courtship behavior rather than multiple techniques.

    C. It indicates that some species of birds may use more than one "identification check" behavior.

    D. It tells how male birds of paradise both develop distinctive plumage and perform a dance to attract females.

Answers and Explanations

1. SHSAT Reading Question Types

Step 1: Read Actively

Industrial Progress

A.   ¶1 Topic: Industrialization effects

B.   ¶2 Topic: Industrial pollution and acid rain

C.   ¶3 Topic: Why acid rain is so harmful

D.   ¶4 Topic: Methods for reducing acid rain

E.   ¶5 Topic: Companies and citizens working to reduce pollution

F.   ¶6 Topic: Industry and nature must find a healthy balance

G.   Passage Main Idea: Acid rain is harmful to the environment, but companies and citizens are reducing environmentally harmful effects.

Sample Passage Notes:

¶1: ind. effects

¶2: pollution & acid rain

¶3: why acid rain harmful

¶4: how reduce acid rain

¶5: companies & citizens reducing pollution

¶6: sum: need balance

Main Idea: acid rain harmful, but reducing effects

Steps 2 & 3

1.   B

Category: Global

Getting to the Answer: If you have already identified the main idea on your own, you will have a much easier time finding the correct answer choice. Remember that the correct choice will match both the tone and the scope of the passage. **(B)** does this best. **(A)** is a Misused Detail; the passage mentions economic and social benefits, but the author does not take a position about whether they are worth the environmental cost. Since the author is not openly critical of anyone, **(C)** doesn't match the tone of the passage either. **(D)** is Out of Scope since the nineteenth century (1800–1899) is never discussed.

2.   F

Category: Detail

Getting to the Answer: Use your Roadmap to find your way back to the paragraph that discusses the effects of acid rain. Paragraph 3 discusses why acid rain is so harmful, which matches **(F)**. **(E)**, **(G)**, and **(H)** are incorrect because they are from paragraphs 1, 4, and 6, which do not directly discuss the effects of acid rain.

3.   D

Category: Function

Getting to the Answer: The question at the beginning of the passage includes the phrase "mixed blessing," which indicates that industrial progress has created both good and bad results. **(D)** is correct. **(A)** describes the function of paragraph 3, and **(B)** describes the function of paragraph 4, so they are incorrect. **(C)** is a Distortion; the author is not puzzled or confused by the effects of industrial progress.

4.   F

Category: Inference

Getting to the Answer: The purpose of the experimental designs is to reduce pollution. One of the effects of pollution described in paragraph 3 is the loss of forests. You can infer, therefore, that by reducing pollution, the experimental designs would reduce pollution-driven deforestation; **(F)** is correct. **(E)** is Opposite because the experimental designs would reduce the sulfur dioxide that causes pollution, not increase it. **(G)** and **(H)** are both Distortions; the passage does not claim that the experimental designs would deactivate the acid that falls as rain or clean up the existing pollution.

5.   C

Category: Infographic

Getting to the Answer: Paragraph 4 discusses methods for reducing acid rain, which include building "new industrial plants, modeled on experimental designs that produce less sulfur dioxide." The graph shows how power plants that were opened more recently have lower monthly sulfur dioxide output. **(C)** correctly explains the relationship between the passage and the infographic. **(A)** is incorrect because, while paragraph 4 mentions machines that remove sulfur dioxide from a plant's exhausts, the plants built in 1985 and 1995 have higher emissions than the more recently built plants. **(B)** and **(D)** are incorrect because they are not mentioned in paragraph 4 and are not supported by the graph.

2. Strategy Focus: Elimination Strategies

Step 1: Read Actively

Bird Courtship Behavior

A. ¶1 Topic: Identification checks help ensure healthy offspring
B. ¶2 Topic: Bright plumage is used by some birds to identify and attract mates (ex. birds of paradise)
C. ¶3 Topic: Courtship dances help to establish and maintain "pair-bonds"
D. ¶4 Topic: Birdcalls help with determining identity and level of interest
E. ¶5 Topic: Northern cardinal mating behaviors
F. ¶6 Topic: American goldfinch mating behaviors
G. Passage Main Idea: Plumage, courtship dances, and birdcalls are important aspects of bird courtship and breeding behavior.

Sample Passage Notes:

¶1: need ID checks

¶2: use of bright plumage

¶3: use of dances

¶4: use of birdcalls

¶5: ex.: cardinal

¶6: ex.: goldfinch

Main Idea: plumage, dances, and calls important in bird courtship

Steps 2 & 3

1.   B

Category: Global

Getting to the Answer: **(B)** is correct because it states the basic theme that runs through all four paragraphs: key aspects of birds' mating activities. **(A)** and **(C)** are Out of Scope; how birds make nests and migration direction are not discussed. **(D)** is a Misused Detail because "pair-bonds" are mentioned only in paragraph 3.

2.   H

Category: Detail

Getting to the Answer: **(H)** is correct because it explains in paragraph 4 that male birds use their calls, or songs, to identify themselves as potential mates of the same species and to give females a way of determining the male's level of interest. **(E)**, **(F)**, and **(G)** are incorrect because they are from paragraphs 1, 2, and 3, all of which do not directly discuss birdcalls.

3.   C

Category: Function

Getting to the Answer: **(C)** is correct because whooping cranes and trumpeter swans are mentioned in paragraph 3 as examples of birds with unique courtship procedures. **(A)** is incorrect because it is Opposite: the whooping crane and the trumpeter swan **do** participate in courtship procedures. **(B)** is Out of Scope because the whooping crane's plumage is never discussed. **(D)** is a Distortion; the passage mentions that roles are reversed in different species, but it never establishes "typical" male and female courtship roles.

4.   G

Category: Inference

Getting to the Answer: **(G)** is correct because in the final paragraph, it is stated that males identify themselves by their singing and that the female interprets their singing in order to predict "the response of a male to her approach." Since the female makes the approach, it is implied that she chooses the male. **(E)** is Extreme; just because the female's singing ability is never mentioned does not mean that it doesn't exist. Aggression is not mentioned in regard to bird sounds, making **(F)** Out of Scope. The breeding condition of the females is never mentioned, making **(H)** also Out of Scope.

5. C

Category: Infographic

Getting to the Answer: The main idea of the passage is key aspects of identification checks within courtship behaviors of birds. The Venn diagram shows how birds can exhibit the three behaviors discussed in the passage in combination with one another or alone. The correct answer, **(C)**, features these behaviors and shows how they overlap for seven bird species. Eliminate **(A)** as a Distortion because paragraphs 3 and 4 state that both sexes participate in these behaviors, not just males. Eliminate **(B)** as Extreme because neither the passage nor the Venn diagram say that birds are limited to these behaviors. **(D)** is a Misused Detail; the question is asking how the graphic supports the whole passage, not just paragraph 2, where birds of paradise are discussed.

[CHAPTER 7]

SHSAT READING PASSAGES

CHAPTER OBJECTIVES

By the end of this chapter, you will be able to:

- Identify keywords that promote active reading and relate passage text to the questions
- Draw inferences about characters' motivations and relationships
- Apply strategies to answer fiction questions correctly
- Identify key information and ideas within a science passage

English

1. Fiction Passages

Literary Terms

SHSAT Reading Comprehension questions that accompany fiction and poetry passages may ask about **literary terms**. Knowing some common literary terms will help you as you tackle those passages. Two of the most prominent literary terms that you will be tested on are **tone** and **theme**.

Tone

Tone is an attitude, such as humorous, concerned, or sad, that a writer chooses to show to readers using specific words and phrases. Questions about tone will ask how a word, phrase, or sentence affects the tone of the passage.

When answering these questions, first identify the tone by locating keywords throughout the passage. If the author uses words such as "delightful," "joy," and "smiling," the tone is happy. If the author chooses words such as "terror," "distress," and "dread," the tone is fearful. Once you have pinpointed the tone, you can select the answer choice that best matches it.

Theme

The theme of a passage is the overall idea, moral, or lesson the author wants the reader to understand. For example, *The Outsiders* by S. E. Hinton is known for its theme of social class differences. The characters of two rival groups learn about both the contrasts and the similarities among social classes as the novel progresses.

An SHSAT Reading Comprehension question may ask, "How does the conversation in paragraphs 4–6 contribute to the development of the theme?" Before you look at the answer choices, ask yourself, "What does the author want me to know now that I've read the passage?" You can use your answer to find the best match.

More Literary Terms

Throughout a single passage, an author may use multiple literary devices along with tone and theme. Familiarizing yourself with these literary terms ahead of time will help you both to better understand the passage and to answer questions more efficiently and accurately. Below is a list of literary terms you may see on the SHSAT.

TERM	DEFINITION	EXAMPLE
Character	A person (or animal) who takes part in a story	Jo March is the main character in the novel *Little Women* by Louisa May Alcott.
Conflict	A problem between characters or a struggle within a character	The siblings argued nearly every day about who was the better athlete.
Dialogue	A conversation between characters	"Welcome to my home," Andres said, opening the front door. "Thank you," replied Jade as she stepped inside.
Imagery	Words and phrases that provide information about what someone may see, hear, feel, touch, or taste	The cool water tasted clean and crisp as I gulped it loudly, clutching the worn green canteen in my sweating palms.
Irony	A surprising contradiction or contrast	In the short story, "The Gift of the Magi" by O. Henry, a wife sells her hair to buy her husband a chain for his beloved watch, not knowing that her husband has just sold his watch to buy decorative combs for her beautiful long hair.
Metaphor	A comparison of two things that does not use the words "like" or "as"	The singer was a beautiful sparrow on stage.

TERM	DEFINITION	EXAMPLE
Moral	A lesson the author hopes readers will learn from the story	The moral of "The Tortoise and the Hare" is that you will be more successful if you work steadily than if you act quickly and carelessly.
Narrator	The speaker or character who tells the story	Jean Louise "Scout" Finch is the narrator of *To Kill a Mockingbird* by Harper Lee.
Personification	Words or phrases that give a nonhuman subject human characteristics	The flowers danced in the light breeze.
Plot	The sequence of events in a story	The plot of "Little Red Riding Hood" starts with Little Red meeting the wolf in the woods. The wolf goes to Granny's house before Little Red, Little Red sees the wolf impersonating her grandma, and the woodcutter arrives to rescue Little Red and Granny.
Point of view	A particular attitude about something	From an environmentalist's point of view, a factory that causes high levels of pollution should be closed; from the factory employees' point of view, it should remain open so they can keep their jobs.
Rhyme	The repetition of sounds at the end of words	The sun was done, but we felt like we won; we had run and spun having fun.
Setting	The time and place of a story	*Anne of Green Gables* by Lucy Maud Montgomery is set in Prince Edward Island, Canada, in the early 1900s.
Simile	A comparison of two things that uses "like" or "as"	She ran as swiftly as a deer.
Stanza	A group of lines in a poem	The first stanza of "Success" by Emily Dickinson is: Success is counted sweetest By those who ne'er succeed. To comprehend a nectar Requires sorest need.
Structure	The order and format of a passage or poem	The structure of the poem "I Have Found What You Are Like" by E. E. Cummings reinforces the poet's comparison of a person to falling raindrops: —in the woods which stutter and sing
Symbol	Something that is used to represent a particular idea	A red rose is a symbol of love.
Turning point	A specific moment in a story when something begins to change	The turning point in "The Three Little Pigs" is when the wolf cannot blow down the third house, which is made of bricks instead of sticks or straw.

Literary Terms Practice

> **DIRECTIONS:** Match the literary term on the left to the example on the right.

1.	Simile	A.	Hazel Lancaster shares her experiences in the novel *The Fault in Our Stars* by John Green.
2.	Conflict	B.	The parking lot was a lake after the rainstorm.
3.	Metaphor	C.	The story about the boy who cried wolf teaches the importance of telling the truth.
4.	Character	D.	*A Christmas Carol* by Charles Dickens takes place in the mid-1800s in London, England.
5.	Irony	E.	The wind howled outside my window.
6.	Moral	F.	A white dove represents peace.
7.	Personification	G.	The lake was as smooth as glass.
8.	Setting	H.	The rival teams played against each other each year in the regional semifinals.
9.	Symbol	I.	Lola raced to get to school on time only to find out when she arrived that it was Saturday.

> **DIRECTIONS:** Use the literary terms in the word bank to complete the sentences below. Use each word only once.

Plot	Rhyme	Point of view	Turning point
Narrator	Imagery	Structure	Stanza

10. Words that _____ have similar ending sounds, such as "tree," "key," and "plea."

11. Writers use _____ to provide vivid descriptions that help readers visualize what someone may see, hear, feel, touch, or taste.

12. The _____ is the sequence of events in a story.

13. A specific moment in a story when something begins to change is the _____.

14. The order and format of a passage or poem is called its _____.

15. The _____ is the speaker or character who tells the story.

16. A _____ is a group of lines in a poem.

17. A particular attitude about something is called _____.

Applying the Kaplan Method to Fiction Passages

You will use the same Kaplan Method for fiction passages that you use for other Reading Comprehension passages on the SHSAT.

> **Step 1:** Read actively
>
> **Step 2:** Examine the question stem and predict
>
> **Step 3:** Match and answer

However, there are some differences in what is involved with each of these steps that are particular to fiction passages.

Step 1: Read Actively

Active reading means that as you read the passage, you are asking questions and taking notes. As you read a fiction passage, you should:

Identify the characters, evaluate how the author describes them, and determine the relationships among the characters.

- Who are the characters?
- What are the characters doing?
- What adjectives describe each character?

Assess the characters' opinions of each other and themselves.

- Do they like or dislike each other?
- Why does each character make particular decisions or take particular courses of action?

Identify the tone and themes within the passage.

- What is the overall tone of the passage?
- What are the themes (morals, lessons, or messages) the author conveys?

Summarize the plot.

- What happens in the passage?
- What are the "turning points" in the passage?

Read the following passage and answer the questions to practice applying the Kaplan Method to fiction passages.

Identify the Characters

Excerpt from *The Story of Dr. Dolittle*
by Hugh Lofting

1 All the folks, young and old, knew him well by sight. And whenever he walked down the street in his high hat everyone would say, "There goes the Doctor!—He's a clever man." And the dogs and the children would all run up and follow behind him; and even the crows that lived in the church-tower would caw and nod their heads. The house he lived in, on the edge of the town, was quite small; but his garden was very large and had a wide lawn and stone seats and weeping willows hanging over. His sister, Sarah Dolittle, was housekeeper for him; but the Doctor looked after the garden himself.

    A. Who are the characters?

    B. What are the characters doing?

    C. What adjectives describe each character?

Assess the Characters' Opinions

2 He was very fond of animals and kept many kinds of pets. Besides the goldfish in the pond at the bottom of his garden, he had rabbits in the pantry, white mice in his piano, a squirrel in the linen closet and a hedgehog in the cellar. His sister used to grumble about all these animals and said they made the house untidy. And one day when an old lady with rheumatism came to see the Doctor, she sat on the hedgehog who was sleeping on the sofa and never came to see him anymore, but drove every Saturday all the way to Oxenthorpe, another town ten miles off, to see a different doctor. Then his sister, Sarah Dolittle, came to him and said, "John, how can you expect sick people to come and see you when you keep all these animals in the house? That's the fourth personage these animals have driven away. We are getting poorer every day. If you go on like this, none of the best people will have you for a doctor."

    D. Do they like or dislike each other?

    E. Why does each character make a particular decision or take a particular course of action?

Identify the Tone and Themes

3 But he kept on getting still more pets; and of course it cost a lot to feed them. And the money he had saved up grew littler and littler. And now, when he walked down the street in his high hat, people would say to one another, "There goes John Dolittle, M.D.! There was a time when he was the best known doctor in the West Country—Look at him now—He hasn't any money and his stockings are full of holes!" But the dogs and the cats and the children still ran up and followed him through the town—the same as they had done when he was rich.

    F. What is the overall tone of the passage?

    G. What are the themes (morals, lessons, or messages) the author conveys?

Summarize

    H. What happens in the passage?

    I. What are the "turning points" in the passage?

Step 2: Examine the Question Stem and Predict

Fiction passages, just like other SHSAT passages, will be accompanied by Global, Detail, Inference, and Function questions. The way a question stem is worded can tell you what type of question it is, and knowing this can help you get to the answer more quickly. The following are some reminders and tips about question types.

Global questions ask about the theme or central idea of the passage. Use your active reading notes to help you identify the main idea or theme of the passage. (Do not reread the entire passage.)

Detail questions ask about specific information from the passage. They may ask about a word, a phrase, or an idea. Use paragraph references or specific phrasing in the question to find the relevant section of the passage. Skim this section to find specific evidence; put your finger on the exact information required to answer the question.

Inference questions ask you about the underlying meaning of a particular phrase or example. These questions often use words like "imply" or "suggest." Look for clues that show the author's point of view or why the author chose to write in a certain way.

Function questions identify a feature of the passage—a line, a paragraph, an example, or an opinion—and ask you to consider either why or how the author uses the feature. Focus on the author's reason for including the cited feature. Take note of any transition words, and read around the cited text for context.

To answer fiction questions successfully, go back to the lines mentioned in the question or to the section of the passage where the idea in the question is discussed, and research the answer in the passage. Predict an answer using supporting information from the passage.

Step 3: Match and Answer

Finally, select the answer choice that matches your prediction. Don't rely on your memory or answer based on outside knowledge. It's an open-book test, so use the passage!

Practice Passage

Step 1: Read Actively

Actively reading a fiction passage includes taking notes to create a Roadmap. Complete the Roadmap questions below about the characters, their opinions, and the tone and themes of the passage as you read the excerpt that follows.

Excerpt from "The Shinansha"

compiled by Yei Theodora Ozaki

1 The compass, with its needle always pointing to the North, is quite a common thing, and no one thinks that it is remarkable now, though when it was first invented it must have been a wonder.

2 Now long ago in China, there was a still more wonderful invention called the shinansha. This was a kind of chariot with the figure of a man on it always pointing to the South. No matter how the chariot was placed the figure always wheeled about and pointed to the South.

3 This curious instrument was invented by Kotei, one of the three Chinese Emperors of the Mythological age. Kotei was the son of the Emperor Yuhi. Before he was born his mother had a vision which foretold that her son would be a great man.

4 One summer evening she went out to walk in the meadows to seek the cool breezes which blow at the end of the day and to gaze with pleasure at the star-lit heavens above her. As she looked at the North Star, strange to relate, it shot forth vivid flashes of lightning in every direction. Soon after this her son Kotei came into the world.

5 Kotei in time grew to manhood and succeeded his father the Emperor Yuhi. His early reign was greatly troubled by the rebel Shiyu. This rebel wanted to make himself King, and many were the battles which he fought to this end. Shiyu was a wicked magician, his head was made of iron, and there was no man that could conquer him.

6 At last Kotei declared war against the rebel and led his army to battle, and the two armies met on a plain called Takuroku. The Emperor boldly attacked the enemy, but the magician brought down a dense fog upon the battlefield, and while the royal army were wandering about in confusion, trying to find their way, Shiyu retreated with his troops, laughing at having fooled the royal army.

7 No matter however strong and brave the Emperor's soldiers were, the rebel with his magic could always escape in the end.

8 Kotei returned to his Palace, and thought and pondered deeply as to how he should conquer the magician, for he was determined not to give up yet. After a long time he invented the shinansha with the figure of a man always pointing South, for there were no compasses in those days. With this instrument to show him the way he need not fear the dense fogs raised up by the magician to confound his men.

1. Characters

   J. Who are the characters?

   K. What are the characters doing?

   L. What adjectives describe each character?

2. Characters' Opinions

   M. Do they like or dislike each other?

   N. Why does each character make particular decisions or take particular courses of action?

3. Tone and Themes

   O. What is the overall tone of the passage?

   P. What are the themes (morals, lessons, or messages) the author conveys?

4. Summarize

   Q. What happens in the passage?

   R. What are the "turning points" in the passage?

Step 2: Examine the Question Stem and Predict

The following section includes just the question stems of some test-like questions that you will see later, followed by guiding questions to help you make strong predictions. Answering these guiding questions will help you build your skills before you try your hand at the full questions and answer choices.

1. Read this sentence from paragraph 1.

> The compass, with its needle always pointing to the North, is quite a common thing, and no one thinks that it is remarkable now, though when it was first invented it must have been a wonder.

   How does the sentence contribute to the development of the plot?

   S. What are the "turning points" in the passage that contributed to the plot?

   T. Predict the answer to the question stem.

2. In paragraph 3, how does the phrase "of the Mythological age" affect the tone of the excerpt?

   U. What is the overall tone of the passage?

   V. Predict the answer to the question stem.

3. Which of the following best explains why Kotei's mother thought her son would be great?

   W. What is Kotei's mother's opinion of her son?

   X. Predict the answer to the question stem.

4. The phrase "strange to relate" in paragraph 4 shows that the author

   Y. What important element in the question stem tells you where to direct your research?

   Z. Predict the answer to the question stem.

Step 3: Match and Answer

Now that you've practiced examining the question stems and predicting the answers, try answering the full version of these questions below. Select the choice that best matches your prediction.

1. Read this sentence from paragraph 1.

> The compass, with its needle always pointing to the North, is quite a common thing, and no one thinks that it is remarkable now, though when it was first invented it must have been a wonder.

   How does the sentence contribute to the development of the plot?

   A. It defines what a compass is so that the reader better appreciates Kotei's invention of it.

   B. It explains the background of Kotei leading up to his birth.

   C. It suggests that the shinansha is a marvel on par with Shiyu's magical fog.

   D. It explains that "shinansha" is just a synonym for a north-pointing compass.

2. In paragraph 3, how does the phrase "of the Mythological age" affect the tone of the excerpt?

   E. It establishes the excerpt's factual tone, which matches the fact that events from recorded history are recounted.

   F. It highlights the excerpt's comedic tone, which highlights that magical events are presented as historical fact.

   G. It illustrates the excerpt's heroic tone about events that took place before China had any emperors.

   H. It establishes the excerpt's epic tone, which suggests to the reader that events are set in an era of heroes and magic.

3. Which of the following **best** explains why Kotei's mother thought her son would be great?

   A. "This curious instrument was invented by Kotei, one of the three Chinese Emperors of the Mythological age." (paragraph 3)

   B. "Kotei was the son of the Emperor Yuhi." (paragraph 3)

   C. "As she looked at the North Star . . . it shot forth vivid flashes of lightning in every direction." (paragraph 4)

   D. ". . . his head was made of iron, and there was no man that could conquer him." (paragraph 5)

4. The author **most** likely used the phrase "strange to relate" (paragraph 4) to show that

   E. the event he is about to describe is difficult to put into words.

   F. the event he is about to describe was hard for Kotei's mother to understand.

   G. the event he is about to describe is surprising and curious.

   H. the event Kotei's mother witnessed was unimportant.

2. Poetry Passages

Applying the Kaplan Method to Poetry Passages

Just like with fiction passages, you will use the same Kaplan Method you already know for poetry passages, but there are a few extra things to keep in mind that specifically apply to poetry.

Step 1: Read actively

Step 2: Examine the question stem and predict

Step 3: Match and answer

Step 1: Read Actively

As you read the poem, ask yourself questions and take notes. Be sure to:

Identify the topic and the narrator (when applicable).

- What is the poem about?
- Does the poem have a narrator? If yes, who (or what) is speaking?

Identify the mood.

- What feelings does the poem create in the reader?
- What words would you use to describe the mood?

Paraphrase the poet's words.

- What does the poem mean in your own words?
- What information is the poet trying to convey?

Read the following poem, and answer the accompanying questions to practice applying to Kaplan Method to poetry passages.

Identify the Topic

"The Road Not Taken"
by Robert Frost

Two roads diverged in a yellow wood,
And sorry I could not travel both
And be one traveler, long I stood
And looked down one as far as I could
(5)   To where it bent in the undergrowth;

Then took the other, as just as fair,
And having perhaps the better claim,
Because it was grassy and wanted wear;
Though as for that the passing there
(10)   Had worn them really about the same,

    A. What is the topic?
    B. Does the poem have a narrator? If yes, who (or what) is speaking?

Identify the Mood

And both that morning equally lay
In leaves no step had trodden black.
Oh, I kept the first for another day!
Yet knowing how way leads on to way,
(15)   I doubted if I should ever come back.

    C. What feelings does the poem create in the reader?
    D. What words would you use to describe the mood?

Paraphrase

I shall be telling this with a sigh
Somewhere ages and ages hence:
Two roads diverged in a wood, and I—
I took the one less traveled by,
(20)   And that has made all the difference.

    E. What does the poem mean in your own words?
    F. What information is the poet trying to convey?

Step 2: Examine the Question Stem and Predict

Poetry passages will be accompanied by Global, Detail, Inference, and Function questions. Here are some reminders and tips about the question types and how they may look when connected to a poem.

Global questions ask about the theme or central idea of the poem. This should be something you take note of while actively reading, so use your notes and avoid rereading the whole poem.

Detail questions ask about specific information in the poem. They may ask about a word, a phrase, or specific language the poet includes. Use line or stanza references, or specific phrasing in the question, to find the relevant section of the poem.

Inference questions ask you to support an idea that the poem conveys or to explain the meaning of imagery in the poem. Look for clues, and make sure you can always back up your answer with evidence in the poem.

Function questions identify a feature of the poem—a line, a stanza, or imagery—and ask you to consider either why or how the poet uses the feature. Think about why the author may have included this cited feature, and make sure to read a bit before and after the cited feature to get the proper context.

To answer poetry questions successfully, read each question carefully and thoroughly. Determine exactly what the question is asking. Go back to the lines or stanza mentioned in the question to look up the answer in the poem. Find support for your answer using information from the poem, and make a prediction before you peek at the answer choices.

Step 3: Match and Answer

Finally, select the answer choice that matches your prediction. If you have difficulty finding a match, narrow down the choices by analyzing each answer choice individually and eliminating any that you can determine are incorrect.

Practice Passage

Step 1: Read Actively

Actively reading a poetry passage includes taking notes to create a Roadmap. As you read the following poem, complete the Roadmap questions below about the topic, mood, and paraphrasing.

"Storm"
by Hilda Doolittle

You crash over the trees,
you crack the live branch—
the branch is white,
the green crushed,
(5)   each leaf is rent like split wood.

You burden the trees
with black drops,
you swirl and crash—
you have broken off a weighted leaf
(10)   in the wind,
it is hurled out,
whirls up and sinks,
a green stone.

1.   Topic

   G.   What is the topic?

   H.   Does the poem have a narrator? If yes, who (or what) is speaking?

2.   Mood

   I.   What feelings does the poem create in the reader?

   J.   What words would you use to describe the mood?

3.   Paraphrasing

   K.   What does the poem mean in your own words?

   L.   What information is the poet trying to convey?

Step 2: Examine the Question Stem and Predict

Answer the questions below. Understanding these question stems on their own, and predicting an answer now, will help you to quickly and easily answer the full questions later on.Step 2: Examine the Question Stem and Predict

1.   Lines 1–5 contribute to the development of ideas in the poem by

   M.   What is the topic?

   N.   What words would you use to describe the mood?

   O.   Predict the answer to the question stem.

2. What impact do the words "crash," "crack," and "crushed" in lines 1–4 have on the meaning of the poem?

    P. How do these words convey the author's message?

    Q. Predict the answer to the question stem.

3. Read lines 1–2 and 6–8 that begin the two stanzas.

> **You crash over the trees,**
> **you crack the live branch—**

> **You burden the trees**
> **with black drops,**
> **you swirl and crash—**

The purpose of the parallel structure of the two stanzas is to

R. How does the similar structure help convey the poet's meaning?

S. Predict the answer to the question stem.

4. Read lines 6–7.

> **You burden the trees**
> **with black drops,**

The lines help develop the theme of the poem by suggesting that the rain

T. What does this part of the poem mean in your own words?

U. Predict the answer to the question stem.

Step 3: Match and Answer

Now answer the full questions below by selecting the choice that best matches your prediction.

1. Lines 1–5 contribute to the development of ideas in the poem by

    A. depicting the dramatic way a leaf falls in a storm.

    B. mimicking the sound of a raging wind.

    C. using colors to evoke the devastation of the storm.

    D. describing the effect of a powerful storm on a tree.

2. What impact do the words "crash," "crack," and "crushed" in lines 1–4 have on the meaning of the poem?

    E. Their similar sounds unite the first and second stanzas.

    F. Their harsh sounds emphasize the fury of the storm.

    G. Their rhythmic, repeated beginnings imitate the sound of the rain.

    H. They provide a dramatic contrast to the quiet peace that follows the storm.

3. Read lines 1–2 and 6–8 that begin the two stanzas.

> **You crash over the trees,**
> **you crack the live branch—**

> **You burden the trees**
> **with black drops,**
> **you swirl and crash—**

The purpose of the parallel structure of the two stanzas is to

A. contrast the effects at the start of the storm with those at the end of the storm.

B. indicate that the wind mentioned in the first stanza is less important than the rain.

C. emphasize that the second stanza will be a continuation of the first.

D. show that the first stanza was more important than the second.

4. Read lines 6–7.

> **You burden the trees**
> **with black drops,**

The lines help develop the theme of the poem by suggesting that the rain

E. is so heavy it may damage the trees.

F. will harm the trees because it is black from pollution.

G. is necessary for the growth of the trees.

H. will cause widespread flooding.

3. Science Passages

Applying the Kaplan Method to Science Passages

You can expect to see at least one passage in the Reading section that deals with a scientific or technical topic. An important thing to remember is that you do not have to understand every word in the passage (such as specific terminology) in order to be able to answer the questions. For example, in the following passage, you don't need to stress about scientific phrases like "mathematical model" and "light densities." Additionally, keep in mind that you are **not** being tested on any outside science knowledge, so do not answer the questions based on anything other than the information contained in the passage.

A surefire way to keep your focus on the information in the passage is to follow the Kaplan Method. Practice the steps of the method as you read the following passage.

> **Step 1:** Read actively
>
> **Step 2:** Examine the question stem and predict
>
> **Step 3:** Match and answer

Practice Passage

Step 1: Read Actively

Actively reading the passage includes taking notes to create a Roadmap of a passage, which should include the Main Idea of the passage and the topic of each paragraph.

Green Sea Turtle Migration

1 Green sea turtles, shelled reptiles that plowed the oceans eons before mammals evolved, are known for their prodigious migrations. One group of green sea turtles makes a regular journey from feeding grounds near the Brazilian coast to breeding beaches on Ascension Island, a barren, relatively predator-free island in the central equatorial Atlantic. Notoriously slow on land, these turtles cover a distance of more than 2,000 kilometers in as little as two weeks. But how is this navigation of deep, featureless ocean accomplished? Scientists have several different hypotheses.

    A. What is the passage about?

    B. What is the topic of paragraph 1?

2 Green turtles appear to have an excellent sense of smell, so the turtles may orient themselves by detecting traces of substances released from Ascension Island itself. Because Ascension Island lies in the midst of a major westward-flowing ocean current, scientists believe that chemical substances picked up from the islands would tend to flow westward toward the feeding grounds of the turtle. As a result, these substances may provide a scented chemical trail that the turtles are able to follow. A mathematical model has been used to show that a concentration of substances delivered from Ascension to the turtles' feeding grounds, though diluted, may be sufficient to be sensed by the turtles. However, it is likely that other factors help the turtles orient themselves.

    C. What does the first sentence indicate?

    D. What is the topic of paragraph 2?

3 In addition to possessing a strong sense of smell, the turtles also have keen eyesight. This may help direct the turtles from their feeding grounds into the path of this chemical trail. It is an established fact that turtles are capable of distinguishing between different light densities. Turtles recognize at least four colors and are especially attuned to the color red because it often appears in their shell coloration.

Researchers believe that these turtles swim east toward the rising sun at the beginning of their migration, changing course toward Ascension's beaches as soon as their route intersects with the scented path.

> **E.** What new topic is discussed in detail here?
>
> **F.** What is the topic of paragraph 3?

4 Finally, turtles may also have the ability to orient themselves using Earth's magnetic field. Since this sense is deeper than either sight or smell, it may serve as an additional guide during cloudy days or times when the turtle has difficulty picking up the scent trail. Experimental results have shown that turtle hatchlings have the ability to use magnetic fields to determine the direction in which they are swimming. Furthermore, since turtles are known to return to the exact beach from which they hatched, they may "imprint" the magnetic field of this particular beach at a very young age.

> **G.** How is the focus of paragraph 4 different from the focus of paragraph 3?
>
> **H.** What is the topic of paragraph 4?

5 Green sea turtles are an endangered species, and their numbers are steadily decreasing throughout the world. Understanding how they accomplish their migrations will allow scientists to make intelligent recommendations to policy makers and help ensure the survival of this magnificent animal. For example, since the turtles use light to navigate, they are especially vulnerable to light pollution from coastal developments. Similarly, their acute sense of smell means that an excessive amount of foreign materials in the water may disorient them. Human decisions in the coming years will determine whether the seas will continue to be inhabited by the green sea turtle or if its celebrated migrations will be only a memory.

> **I.** What is the topic of paragraph 5?
>
> **J.** What is the Main Idea of the passage?

Step 2: Examine the Question Stem and Predict & Step 3: Match and Answer

Now use your Roadmap and your researching skills to answer the following questions.

1. Which statement **best** describes the central idea of the passage?

    A. Green sea turtles are an endangered species that cannot survive if their natural habitat continues to be polluted.

    B. The green turtle's outstanding eyesight and sense of smell have evolved over many eons.

    C. The tropical weather in the central equatorial Atlantic is an integral part of the 2,000-kilometer ocean migration.

    D. The migratory behavior of green sea turtles is made possible by a variety of factors.

2. What is the **most** likely reason green sea turtles breed on Ascension Island?

    E. There is an abundance of food there.

    F. It has a cooler climate than Brazil.

    G. The turtles have fewer natural enemies there.

    H. Its beaches are cleaner than Brazil's beaches.

3. The phrase "several different hypotheses" conveys the idea that

    A. scientists have not fully tracked the migration patterns of green sea turtles.

    B. green sea turtles use their sense of smell to compensate for their poor eyesight.

    C. knowledge about green sea turtles is limited by a lack of scientific evidence.

    D. there is more than one way to explain how green sea turtles navigate toward their breeding grounds.

4. What is one way turtles find the trail of chemical substances that are released from Ascension Island?

    E. the position of the rising sun

    F. an instinctive sense of direction

    G. the path of underwater ocean currents

    H. a mathematical model

5. Turtles are especially sensitive to the color red **most** likely because

    A. it helps them identify other turtles.

    B. it is the most intense of the primary colors.

    C. it matches the colors of the rising sun.

    D. it seems more attractive than other colors.

Answers and Explanations

1. Fiction Passages

Literary Terms

1. **G**

2. **H**

3. **B**

4. **A**

5. **I**

6. **C**

7. **E**

8. **D**

9. **F**

10. **rhyme**

11. **imagery**

12. **plot**

13. **turning point**

14. **structure**

15. **narrator**

16. **stanza**

17. **point of view**

Identify the Characters

A. Dr. Dolittle and his sister, Sarah Dolittle

B. Dr. Dolittle is a doctor who likes to garden. Sarah Dolittle is both his sister and his housekeeper.

C. Dr. Dolittle is clever and popular among the townspeople. His sister Sarah Dolittle is helpful.

Assess the Characters' Opinions

D. Dr. Dolittle is focused more on his fondness for animals than on his feelings toward his sister. Sarah Dolittle is frustrated with her brother because his obsession with animals is affecting their way of life.

E. Dr. Dolittle is more concerned about his animals than his human patients. Sarah Dolittle is afraid that Dr. Dolittle will lose all of his clients because there are so many animals in the house.

Identify the Tone and Themes

F. The tone is mixed; while it is a little sad that Dr. Dolittle used to be the best doctor in the West and now he is looked down upon by his community, the tone is also positive: Dr. Dolittle enjoys his work with animals, and the animals give him the same love and attention that they always did.

G. The author's messages include the importance of having compassion for animals and following one's passion even when others do not agree.

Summarize

H. Dr. Dolittle was a good doctor who was loved by many, but people thought he was foolish because he chose his love for animals over his medical practice.

I. Dr. Dolittle kept on getting more pets, but he couldn't afford to feed them all. He lost customers and spent his savings because of his love for animals.

Step 1: Read Actively

Excerpt from "The Shinansha"

J. Kotei, Kotei's mother, and Shiyu

K. Kotei grows up, becomes Emperor, and fights the rebel magician Shiyu.

L. Kotei is determined; Shiyu is wicked.

M. Kotei and Shiyu are enemies.

N. Shiyu creates a dense fog so Kotei's army cannot defeat him, but Kotei uses the shinansha to navigate through the fog and is triumphant.

O. The tone is admiring; the author says that Kotei's compass was a "wonderful invention."

P. The author's message is that it's important to keep working to achieve a goal; Kotei defeated Shiyu because he was determined not to give up.

Q. Emperor Kotei is faced with the rebel magician Shiyu, who wants to be King. Kotei and Shiyu go to war, but Kotei's forces are rendered helpless and confused by a magic fog that Shiyu spreads over the battlefield. It seems as if the Emperor's forces could never defeat Shiyu until Kotei develops the shinansha, which always points south and shows his soldiers the way, even in the densest magical fog.

R. In paragraph 8, Kotei invents the shinansha, which is the key to his victory.

Passage Analysis: This folktale from China describes the invention of the shinansha, a directional instrument that always points south. Paragraph 1 notes how common a compass is today, while paragraph 2 introduces an instrument invented even before the compass—the shinansha. Paragraph 3 describes Emperor Kotei, the inventor, while paragraph 4 tells of the strange event Kotei's mother witnessed while pregnant with Kotei, which seemed to be an omen of greatness. As the passage continues, Kotei grows up, becomes Emperor, and is faced with the rebel magician Shiyu, who wants to be King. In paragraph 6, Kotei and Shiyu go to war, but Kotei's forces are rendered helpless and confused by a magic fog that Shiyu spreads over the battlefield. It seems as if the Emperor's forces could never defeat Shiyu until, in paragraph 8, Kotei ponders how to overcome this fog and develops the shinansha, which always points south—thus, always showing his soldiers the way, even in the densest magical fog.

Sample Passage Notes:

¶1–2: compass & shinansha

¶3: invented by Kotei

¶4: K's mother's vision

¶5: threat of magician Shiyu

¶6–7: battle, S uses fog to escape

¶8: K uses shin. against fog

Main Idea: folktale about invention of shinansha

Step 2: Examine the Question Stem and Predict

S. Kotei invents the shinansha, which is the key to his victory.

T. The invention of the shinansha makes Emperor Kotei appear as impressive as the magical Shiyu.

U. The overall tone is admiring.

V. Knowing that this passage is considered part of the Mythological age helps convey the common folktale theme of good versus evil.

W. She thought he would achieve greatness when he grew up.

X. Before he was born, Kotei's mother saw the North Star flash with lightning.

Y. The quote shows exactly where to look in paragraph 4.

Z. The author is pointing out that the event is not an everyday occurrence; it is considered odd and surprising.

Step 3: Match and Answer

1. **C**

Category: Global

Getting to the Answer: Because a compass is a commonplace tool in the modern world, the author makes an effort to explain how wondrous it must have seemed when first invented. The author then uses the discussion of the compass as a springboard to talk about a similar invention, the mythic shinansha. This functions as a way to make Emperor Kotei appear as impressive as Shiyu's fog magic. Thus, **(C)** is correct. Kotei does not invent the compass, which points north, but the shinansha, which points south; **(A)** is incorrect. While the excerpt goes on to talk about omens that heralded Kotei's greatness ahead of his birth, this happens in paragraphs 3 and 4, not paragraph 1; **(B)** is incorrect. A shinansha, which points south, is not a compass, which points north; **(D)** is incorrect.

2. H

Category: Function

Getting to the Answer: As with so many folktales from around the world, this one pits good against evil. The magician rebel, with his iron head and magic fog, represents evil, while the Emperor, determined and intelligent, creates the shinansha, overcoming the evil magician. This is a mythological, or epic, style of story; **(H)** is correct. As mythological events are ones that did not actually occur, **(E)** is incorrect. Although events involving magic happen in the passage, the tone throughout is not comedic; **(F)** is incorrect. The excerpt defines Kotei as one of the three Chinese Emperors of the Mythological age; **(G)** is incorrect.

3. C

Category: Detail

Getting to the Answer: Kotei's mother was gazing at the night sky and saw "vivid flashes of lightning in every direction" (paragraph 4). This omen foreshadowed the greatness of her son; **(C)** is correct. Although **(A)** is tempting because Kotei did invent the shinansha, it is incorrect because Kotei's mother had no way of knowing that her son would create this specific invention many years later. While Kotei was the son of the Emperor, **(B)** is incorrect because that does not explain why his mother thought he would be especially great when he took the throne from his father. **(D)** is incorrect because it describes the rebel Shiyu rather than Kotei.

4. G

Category: Inference

Getting to the Answer: Inference questions will not be stated directly in the passage, but the answer will be evident by studying the passage. Look at paragraph 4: lightning shooting out from the North Star is not an everyday occurrence. The author uses the phrase "strange to relate" to acknowledge that it is considered odd and surprising. **(G)** is correct. Because the author managed to put the event into words, it could not have been too difficult to express; **(E)** is incorrect. The mother knew that the lightning signaled that her son would be a "great man" (paragraph 3). So, she did understand the strange omen, and there is no suggestion that the event was not significant; **(F)** and **(H)** are incorrect.

2. Poetry Passages

Identify the Topic

A. The narrator is considering which one of two different paths is better to take.

B. The poem does have a narrator, and the narrator is a person.

Identify the Mood

C. The poem creates a feeling of uncertainty.

D. The mood is thoughtful and cautious.

Paraphrase

E. A person comes to a place where one road branches into two, and the person must decide which path to choose.

F. There are times when people must choose between two options, and sometimes the better option is the hard one that most people prefer not to try.

Step 1: Read Actively

"Storm"

G. The topic is a raging storm and its effect on the trees.

H. The poem's narrator is a witness who is watching the storm.

I. The poem creates feelings of concern for the trees as well as awe of the storm.

J. The mood is stormy and powerful.

K. The wind roars, a branch breaks, and leaves are damaged. One leaf breaks off, is flung wildly around, and finally falls to the ground.

L. The poet is showing how nature is unstoppable.

Poem Analysis: This short poem by Hilda Doolittle, who wrote under the pen name H. D., displays her powerful imagery conveyed with an economy of words. There are two stanzas, together describing a raging storm and its effect on the trees. The first stanza tells of how the wind roars and, perhaps, of how lightning breaks a branch and rends leaves. The second stanza describes how a leaf breaks off, is flung wildly around, and finally falls to the ground.

Step 2: Examine the Question Stem and Predict

M. The topic is a raging storm and its effect on the trees.

N. The mood is stormy and powerful.

O. The first stanza shows that the storm crashes in, breaks off a branch, and tears the leaves of a tree.

P. The author uses these short, harsh words to emphasize how strong the storm is.

Q. The mood is stormy and powerful.

R. The two stanzas of the poem both describe the storm's fury.

S. The poet's repetition of the "You . . ." structure indicates that the second stanza will continue to discuss the topic introduced in the first stanza.

T. The storm weighs down the trees with big, heavy raindrops.

U. The raindrops are so heavy that the force of them may be bad for the trees.

Step 3: Match and Answer

1. D

Category: Global

Getting to the Answer: The poem describes how a storm wreaks havoc on a tree and its leaves. The first stanza shows that the storm crashes in, breaks off a branch, and tears the leaves on a tree; **(D)** is correct. **(A)** is incorrect because it describes the falling leaf of the second stanza. **(B)** is incorrect because the wind is merely an aspect of the poem, not a central idea. **(C)** is incorrect because the author uses colors to describe the tree branch, not the storm, and the branch is just one aspect of the storm's effects on the tree.

2. F

Category: Function

Getting to the Answer: The poem describes a violent storm, and the author's use of "crash," "crack," and "crushed" almost sounds like thunder. The author uses these short, harsh words to emphasize how strong the storm is; **(F)** is correct. While "crash" is repeated in the second stanza, the word doesn't appear until the end of the third line. The word is not being used to unite the stanzas; **(E)** is incorrect. **(G)** is incorrect because the author is not describing the sound of the rain but,

rather, the violent effects of the wind and the rain. **(H)** is incorrect because the poem does not close with a description of the calm that followed the storm.

3. C

Category: Function

Getting to the Answer: The two stanzas of the poem both describe the storm's fury, and the poet's repetition of the "You . . ." structure indicates that the second stanza will continue to discuss the topic introduced in the first stanza; **(C)** is correct. **(A)** is incorrect because there is no language in the poem to indicate that the storm is ending. **(B)** is incorrect because the second stanza discusses the violence of the wind, not the rain. Also, there is no comparison made between the wind and the rain. **(D)** is incorrect because the similar structure indicates the stanzas are basically similar. While parallel structure can be used to contrast two ideas, this poem does not contrast the two stanzas.

4. E

Category: Inference

Getting to the Answer: These lines are describing the heavy rain that accompanies the storm. Rain is usually helpful for trees, but in this storm, it is a "burden." The poet describes the drops as "black," a dark, heavy color that is usually a symbol for death or sadness. So **(E)** is correct. **(F)** is incorrect because "black" is a symbolic color, evoking a very heavy rain where the sun is darkened. There is no mention of pollution turning the rain black. **(G)** is incorrect because although water is certainly needed for the growth of trees, this rain is described as a "burden." **(H)** is incorrect because there is no mention in the poem of flooding.

3. Science Passages

Step 1: Read Actively

Green Sea Turtle Migration

A. Green sea turtles and their migrations—specifically, one group that goes from Brazil to Ascension Island to breed

B. ¶1 Topic: Green sea turtles make great migrations in short time spans.

C. The paragraph will discuss green sea turtles' sense of smell.

D. ¶2 Topic: Green turtles' strong sense of smell helps them detect a scented chemical trail.

E. The green sea turtles' eyesight

F. ¶3 Topic: The turtles' eyesight directs them toward the path of the chemical trail.

G. Paragraph 4 discusses how Earth's magnetic field, rather than the turtles' eyesight, helps them migrate.

H. ¶4 Topic: Earth's magnetic field is an additional guide that turtles use to find the scent trail.

I. ¶5 Topic: Green sea turtles are an endangered species.

J. Excellent sense of smell, good eyesight, and Earth's magnetic field help the green sea turtle migrate long distances.

Sample Passage Notes:

¶1: long migration

¶2: smell

¶3: sight

¶4: magnetic field

¶5: endangered, how understanding migration can help

Main Idea: how sea turtles migrate

Steps 2 & 3

1. D
Category: Global

Getting to the Answer: The point of the passage is to describe how green sea turtles make their "prodigious migrations." **(A)** is a Misused Detail because although the statement is true, it is mentioned only in the last paragraph and does not reflect the central idea of the entire passage. The passage doesn't discuss how turtles have evolved or weather conditions, making both **(B)** and **(C)** Out of Scope.

2. G
Category: Inference

Getting to the Answer: Ascension Island is described in paragraph 1 as "relatively predator-free," which supports **(G)**. The turtles leave their feeding grounds to go to Ascension Island, making **(E)** incorrect. The passage does not compare Brazil and Ascension Island

in terms of climate or cleanliness, making both **(F)** and **(H)** Out of Scope.

3. D
Category: Inference

Getting to the Answer: "Several different hypotheses" refers back to the question of how green sea turtles navigate the ocean. The passage states that the turtles use their eyesight to track the sun and their sense of smell to follow a chemical trail to Ascension Island. The phrase "several different hypotheses" suggests that green sea turtles use more than just their eyesight to navigate, which matches **(D)**. **(A)** is incorrect because the phrase "several different hypotheses" isn't referring to scientists' understanding. **(B)** is Opposite because the turtles have good eyesight. **(C)** is Out of Scope; the passage doesn't discuss the limitations of scientific evidence concerning green sea turtles.

4. E
Category: Detail

Getting to the Answer: According to paragraph 3, researchers think that the turtles swim toward the rising sun until they come across the chemical trail. Thus, the position of the sun leads turtles to the chemical trail, **(E)**. Paragraph 3 doesn't mention the turtles' sense of direction, making **(F)** incorrect. **(G)** and **(H)** are both Distortions of information provided in the passage.

5. A
Category: Inference

Getting to the Answer: Paragraph 3 states that the turtles are especially sensitive to red because it "appears in their shell coloration." This suggests that seeing red helps them to see other turtles' shells. This supports **(A)**. The passage doesn't compare the "intensity" of the primary colors or address the "attractiveness" of the color red, making **(B)** and **(D)** Out of Scope. **(C)** is incorrect because the passage doesn't make a connection between the color red and the sun.

SHSAT MATH

[CHAPTER 8]

INTRODUCING SHSAT MATH AND THE KAPLAN METHOD FOR MATH

CHAPTER OBJECTIVES

By the end of this chapter, you will be able to:

- Identify the format and timing of the SHSAT Math section
- Apply tips and strategies to the SHSAT Math questions
- Efficiently apply the Kaplan Method for SHSAT Math

1. Introducing SHSAT Math

Math Section Overview

The Math section is the second section on the test. It contains 57 questions and accounts for one-half of your total points on the SHSAT. The suggested total time for the section is 90 minutes, or 1 hour and 30 minutes.

Based on the latest information available from the New York City Department of Education, the math section will include:

MATH SUBSECTION	TOTAL NUMBER OF QUESTIONS	PACING
Grid-In	5 questions	$1\frac{1}{2}$ minutes per question
Multiple-Choice	52 questions	

The beginning of the Math section will look similar to the following:

Part 2—Mathematics

57 QUESTIONS—SUGGESTED TIMING: 90 MINUTES

IMPORTANT NOTES

(1) Definitions and formulas are **not** provided.
(2) Diagrams are **not** necessarily drawn to scale, with the exception of graphs.
(3) Diagrams are drawn in single planes unless the question specifically states they are not.
(4) Graphs are drawn to scale.
(5) Simplify all fractions to their lowest terms.

The directions include important information that helps you understand what you should expect on test day.

1. Definitions and formulas are not provided.

What this means: The Department of Education is not going to provide a reference sheet with common formulas, such as how to calculate the area of a parallelogram ($a = b \times h$), so memorize those math formulas.

2. Diagrams are not necessarily drawn to scale, with the exception of graphs.

What this means: You cannot take much for granted about diagrams unless you are specifically told that they are drawn to scale. For example, lines that look parallel may, in fact, not be parallel. Figures that look like squares may not be square. Lines that look like the diameter of a circle may not be the diameter.

3. Diagrams are drawn in single planes unless the question specifically states they are not.

What this means: One thing that you can assume is that diagrams are in one plane. In other words, assume that figures are flat unless you are told otherwise.

4. Graphs are drawn to scale.

What this means: You can use the way graphs look to your advantage. For example, if lines on graphs look parallel, you can assume that they are. You can also estimate and label coordinates of points on graphs.

5. Simplify all fractions to their lowest terms.

What this means: If you solve a problem that has a fraction for its answer and you do not simplify the fraction to its lowest terms, you will not find your answer among the choices.

The Question Types

Grid-In Questions

The beginning of the grid-in section will look like this:

GRID-IN QUESTIONS

QUESTIONS 58–62

DIRECTIONS: Answer each question. Write your answer in the boxes at the top of the grid on the answer sheet. Start on the left side of each grid, printing only one number or symbol in each box. **DO NOT LEAVE A BOX BLANK IN THE MIDDLE OF AN ANSWER.** Under each box, fill in the circle that matches the number or symbol you wrote above. **DO NOT FILL IN A CIRCLE UNDER AN UNUSED BOX.**

Multiple-Choice Questions

The multiple-choice section starts like this:

MULTIPLE-CHOICE QUESTIONS

QUESTIONS 63–114

DIRECTIONS: Answer each question, selecting the best answer available. On the answer sheet, mark the letter of each of your answers. You can do your figuring in the test booklet or on paper provided by the proctor.

SHSAT EXPERT NOTE

Save yourself time by knowing what to expect. The directions are not going to change, so learn them now so you can move more quickly through them on test day.

How to Approach SHSAT Math

You've most likely been exposed to the majority of the math concepts you'll see on the SHSAT, which include:

- Arithmetic
  - Number properties (odds, evens, positives, negatives)
  - Order of operations
  - Ratios and proportions
- Algebra
  - Expressions
  - Equations
  - Inequalities

- Geometry
  - Angles
  - Polygons
  - Circles
- Statistics and Probability
  - Mean, median, mode, and range
  - Probability of single and compound events

While you likely have seen most, if not all, of these concepts in school, you need to approach SHSAT math differently than you would approach any other math. You don't necessarily have to do the math *differently* than you would in class, it's just that you have to do it very methodically. You are being timed when you take the test, so you'll want to use your time well.

> **SHSAT EXPERT NOTE**
>
> Unlike the math tests you take at school, no one is going to check your work. Choose the *fastest* method to solve the question, even if it's not the way you would do your schoolwork.

Ultimately, the best way to take control of your testing experience is to approach every SHSAT math problem the same way. This doesn't mean that you will solve every *problem* the same way. Rather, it means that you'll use the same *process* to decide how to solve—or whether to solve—each problem.

Read Through the Question

You need to read the entire question carefully before you start solving the problem. When you do not read the question carefully, it's very easy to make careless errors. Consider the following problem:

1. For what negative value of x does $\left|\frac{1}{x}\right| = \frac{1}{4}$?

    A. -4

    B. $-\frac{1}{4}$

    C. $\frac{1}{4}$

    D. 4

It's crucial that you pay close attention to precisely what the question is asking. Question 1 contains a classic trap that's very easy to fall into if you don't read the question carefully. Did you notice how easy it would be to solve for the positive value of x and incorrectly choose **(D)**? When solved correctly, however, the answer is **(A)** because x is equal to -4. This is because the absolute value of $-\frac{1}{4}$ is $\frac{1}{4}$.

There are other reasons to read the whole question before you start solving the problem. One is that you may save yourself some work. If you start to answer too quickly, you may assume that a problem is more difficult than it actually is. Similarly, you might assume that the problem is less difficult than it actually is and skip a necessary step or two.

Decide Whether to Do the Question or Skip It for Now

Every time you approach a new math problem, you have the option of whether or not to answer the question. Therefore, you have to make a decision about how best to use your time. You have three options:

- If you can solve the problem relatively quickly and efficiently, go ahead and do it.
- If you think you can solve it but it will take you a long time, circle the number in your test booklet and go back to it later.
- If you have no idea what to do, skip the problem and mark it with an X. Save your time for the problems you can do.

SHSAT EXPERT NOTE

Remember that when you go back to the problems you skipped, you still want to fill in an answer even if you have to guess. You'll see more about this later, but you may very well be able to eliminate incorrect answers even when you do not know how to solve a problem. Every time you eliminate an incorrect answer, you increase your chances of guessing correctly.

2. Tamika, Becky, and Kym were investors in a new restaurant. Tamika and Becky each invested one-half as much as Kym invested. If the total investment made by these three was $5,200, how much did Kym invest?

   E. $900

   F. $1,300

   G. $1,800

   H. $2,600

Different test takers are going to have different reactions to question 2. Some test takers may quickly see the algebra and do the math. Others may see a word problem and want to run screaming from the room. If, despite practice, you know that you habitually have difficulty with algebra word problems, you may choose to save this problem for later or make an educated guess.

Here's the algebra, by the way. Kym, Tamika, and Becky contributed a total of $5,200. You can represent this algebraically as $K + T + B = \$5,200$. Since Tamika and Becky each contributed $\frac{1}{2}$ as much as Kym, you can represent these relationships as follows:

$$T = \frac{1}{2}K$$
$$B = \frac{1}{2}K$$

Now substitute variables so that you can solve the equation:

$$K + T + B = K + \frac{1}{2}K + \frac{1}{2}K$$
$$K + \frac{1}{2}K + \frac{1}{2}K = \$5,200$$
$$2K = \$5,200$$
$$K = \$2,600$$

Choice **(H)** is correct.

3.   Jenna is now x years old, and Amy is 3 years younger than Jenna. In terms of x, how old will Amy be in 4 years?

   A. $x - 1$

   B. x

   C. $x + 1$

   D. $x + 4$

Imagine a dialogue between Jenna and Amy:

Jenna:	This is an easy problem. If my age is x, then your age, Amy, is $x - 3$ because you're 3 years younger than me. Therefore, in 4 years, you'll be $(x - 3) + 4$ or $x + 1$.
Amy:	You may be right, but there's a much easier way to figure it out. Let's say you're 10 years old now. That makes me 7 because I'm 3 years younger. In 4 years, I'll be 11. Now let's just substitute your age, 10, for x in all the answer choices and see which answer gives us 11. Once you try all the answers, you see that only **(C)**, $x + 1$, works.
Jenna:	That's so much extra work. Why not just do the algebra?
Amy:	You can do the algebra, but my way feels like less work to me.

Here's the point: know your strengths, and make decisions about how to approach math problems accordingly!

Some people are very good at algebra. Some people have a harder time with it. The same is true for geometry, word problems, and so on. There is often more than one way to do a particular problem. The "best" method is the method that will get you the correct answer accurately and quickly. Know your strengths, and use them to your advantage.

Make an Educated Guess

Don't leave any answers blank on the SHSAT. Since there's no penalty for incorrect answers, there is no harm in guessing when you don't know the answer. Even if you answer a multiple-choice question randomly, you have a 1 in 4 chance of guessing correctly. Of course, you should still guess strategically whenever possible. Remember, every answer choice you eliminate increases your odds of guessing correctly.

4.   What is the greatest common factor of 95 and 114 ?

   E. 1

   F. 5

   G. 6

   H. 19

If you looked at this problem and either could not remember how to find the greatest common factor or were running out of time and wanted to save your time for other questions, you should be able to eliminate at least one answer choice pretty easily. Do you see which one?

Since all multiples of 5 end in either 5 or 0, 5 cannot be a factor of 114, so **(F)** can be eliminated.

Grid Strategically

The first five questions in the Math section are grid-in questions that you can either answer first or save for later. There is no incorrect answer penalty. So if you do not know the answer to the question, you can—and should—still guess. For every grid-in question, you'll enter your response into a grid that looks like this:

When gridding in your answer, begin on the left. Write only one number or decimal symbol in each box, using the "." symbol if your answer includes a decimal point. Fill in the circle under the box that matches the number or symbol that you wrote. The first column on the left of the grid is only for recording a negative sign. So if your answer is positive, leave the first column blank and begin recording your answer in the second column.

If you are gridding a value that doesn't take up the whole grid, do not leave a box blank in the middle of an answer. If there is a blank column in the middle of your answer, it will be scored as incorrect. If your answer is 50, you will leave the first column—the negative sign—blank, use the next two columns for 5 and 0, and then leave the last two columns blank.

If your answer is a fraction, such as $\frac{3}{4}$, you must first convert the fraction to a decimal because it is not possible to grid in a fraction on the SHSAT. To enter 0.75, the equivalent of $\frac{3}{4}$, fill in the circles under the 0, ".", 7, and 5. You would also receive credit if you entered .75 rather than 0.75 because they represent the same value.

SHSAT EXPERT NOTE

Memorize common decimals

The SHSAT does not allow you to grid in fractions, so memorizing common decimal equivalents such as $\frac{1}{4} = 0.25$, $\frac{1}{5} = 0.2$, and $\frac{1}{2} = 0.5$ can save you valuable time.

A repeating decimal can be either rounded or shortened, but it should be entered to as many decimal places as possible. This means it should fill four spaces. For example, you should grid $\frac{1}{6}$ as .166 or .167 rather than .16 or .17.

Note that you cannot grid any value greater than 9,999 or less than −9,999. If you get an answer that will not fit in the grid, you've made a mistake and should check your work.

Finally, make sure you fill in the circles that match all parts of your answer, and make sure that there is no more than one value bubbled in for each column. Always double-check the accuracy of your gridding so that you don't make errors that will cost you points.

2. The Kaplan Method for SHSAT Math

Using the Method

> **THE KAPLAN METHOD FOR SHSAT MATH**
>
> **STEP 1:** What is the question?
>
> **STEP 2:** What information is provided in the question?
> In what format do the answers appear?
>
> **STEP 3:** What can I do with the information?
> - Picking Numbers
> - Backsolving
> - Straightforward Math
>
> **STEP 4:** Am I finished?

The Kaplan Method for SHSAT Math helps you organize the information in a question and decide on the best approach to answer the question. This step-by-step approach applies to all multiple-choice questions. Let's apply the Kaplan Method to the question that follows:

1. If $3(x + y) = 12 + 3y$, what is the value of x?

    A. -4
    B. -1
    C. 1
    D. 4

Step 1: What is the question? The question asks for the value of x.

Step 2: What information is provided in the question? In what format do the answers appear? The question provides an equation to simplify. This is a multiple-choice question, which means you might be able to use the answer choices to help you answer the question.

Step 3: What can I do with the information? Using straightforward math will be the simplest way to solve. Begin by distributing the 3 over the terms inside the parentheses on the left side of the equation. This gives you $3x + 3y = 12 + 3y$.

Subtracting $3y$ from both sides results in $3x = 12$. Dividing both sides by 3 gives you $x = 4$.

Step 4: Am I finished? The question asks for the value of x, so you are finished. Select **(D)**.

The Method and Grid-In Questions

The Kaplan Method for Math will help you efficiently and accurately answer all multiple-choice as well as all grid-in questions. On grid-in questions, you aren't provided with answer choices, but you should still work through the steps.

2. If $3(x + y) = 12 + 3y$, what is the value of x?

Step 1: What is the question? The question asks for the value of x.

Step 2: What information is provided in the question? In what format do the answers appear? The question provides an equation to simplify. This is a grid-in question, so you'll have to calculate and grid-in your own answer to the question.

Step 3: What can I do with the information? Use straightforward math to solve for x. Begin by distributing the 3 over the terms inside the parentheses on the left side of the equation. This gives you $3x + 3y = 12 + 3y$. Subtracting $3y$ from both sides results in $3x = 12$. Dividing both sides by 3 gives you $x = 4$.

Step 4: Am I finished? The question asks for the value of x, so you are finished. Grid in **4**.

The SHSAT Math grid-in section requires you to stay organized as you answer the five grid-in questions you are guaranteed to see on test day. Some questions, like the one above, ask for straightforward calculations, while others are more complex. If the question is a word problem, work through the text systematically, breaking sentences into short phrases before calculating.

SHSAT EXPERT NOTE

Grid-in word problems with algebra

Approach these questions strategically:

- If variables are not defined, choose letters that make sense. Be careful not to use the same letter for different variables.
- Translate each phrase into a mathematical expression.
- Put the expressions together to form an equation.

[CHAPTER 9]

MATH FOUNDATIONS

CHAPTER OBJECTIVES

By the end of this chapter, you will be able to:

- Use properties of real numbers to perform basic operations
- Apply the strategies of Picking Numbers and Backsolving to solve SHSAT Math questions efficiently

1. Basic Terms and Translation

Basic Terms

The SHSAT tests your knowledge of fundamental math concepts and operations. Being comfortable with how numbers look and work can make your life easier on all sorts of math question types on the SHSAT.

Here are some essential rules and definitions to know:

- **Integers** include 0 and negative whole numbers. If a question says "x and y are integers," it's not ruling out numbers like 0 and -1.

- A **fraction** represents part of a whole. The bottom number (the denominator) indicates how many parts the whole is divided into, and the top number (the numerator) shows how many parts are present.

- The **reciprocal** of a fraction is the inverse of that fraction. For example, the reciprocal of $\frac{2}{3}$ is $\frac{3}{2}$. The reciprocal of a fraction has the same sign as the original fraction. For example, the reciprocal of $-\frac{2}{3}$ is $-\frac{3}{2}$.

- **Evens** and **odds** include 0 and negative whole numbers. 0 and -2 are even numbers; -1 is an odd number. Between 1 and 100, there are 50 even numbers and 50 odd numbers.

- **Consecutive numbers** follow each other in order from smallest to largest, with an equal gap between them. For example, 1, 2, 3, and 4 are consecutive numbers; 2, 4, 6, and 8 are consecutive even numbers; 1, 3, 5, and 7 are consecutive odd numbers; and 3, 6, 9, and 12 are consecutive multiples of 3. Consecutive numbers can be negative, such as -7, -6, -5, and -4.

- A **prime number** is a positive integer greater than 1 that is divisible by only 1 and itself. The smallest prime number is 2, and 2 is the only even prime number.

- A **set** is a collection of distinct elements. For example, {1, 4, 7, 8} and {2, 4, 6, 8, 10} are sets.

Translation

TRANSLATING FROM ENGLISH INTO MATH	
English	**Math**
equals, is, equivalent to, was, will be, has, costs, adds up to, the same as, as much as	$=$
times, of, multiplied by, product of, twice, double, by	$\times$
divided by, per, out of, each, ratio	$\div$
plus, added to, and, sum, combined, total, increased by	$+$
minus, subtracted from, smaller than, less than, fewer, decreased by, difference between	$-$
a number, how much, how many, what	x, n, etc.

DIRECTIONS: Translate the following expressions into mathematical operations or equations.

<u>STATEMENT:</u>   <u>TRANSLATION:</u>

A.   2 more than z is twice the value of z

B.   5 fewer than x equals y

C.   The product of 3 and x subtracted from 3

D.   What fraction of x is y ?

E.   One-fourth of the sum of 4 and x

DIRECTIONS: Translate the following equations or operations into words.

<u>**EQUATION OR OPERATION:**</u>   <u>**TRANSLATION:**</u>

F. $3z$

G. b^2

H. $\dfrac{a}{b-c}$

I. $8x = \dfrac{x^3}{2}$

J. $\dfrac{h}{g} = 4h$

DIRECTIONS: Translate the following more advanced statements into mathematical operations or equations.

<u>STATEMENT:</u>   <u>TRANSLATION:</u>

K.   An integer greater than 0, when divided by the
         square of itself, equals 2.

L.   The product of two distinct real numbers is
         2 greater than the sum of the numbers.

SHSAT EXPERT NOTE

Keys to translation success

1) Learn the common terms for all major operations.

2) Pay close attention to the order of operations when translating.

---

1. "Seven less than 4 times x is equal to twice x plus 9." Which of the following equations is a mathematical translation of the previous statement?

   A. $4x - 7 = 2 + 9x$

   B. $4x - 7 = 2x + 9$

   C. $7 - 4x = 2 + 9x$

   D. $7 - 4x = 2x + 9$

2. Moira started with D dollars in her wallet. If she placed B dollars that she withdrew from the bank into her wallet and then spent S dollars from her wallet at the store, how many dollars does Moira have in her wallet now?

   E. $D + B + S$

   F. $D + B - S$

   G. $D - B + S$

   H. $D - B - S$

3. Arwen has half as many pens as Adrienne. Adrienne gives Arwen 3 pens but still has 6 more than Arwen. How many pens did Arwen have originally?

   A. 12

   B. 15

   C. 21

   D. 24

4. The least of 4 consecutive integers is s, and the greatest is t. What is the value of $\dfrac{2t + s}{3}$ in terms of s?

   E. $s + 1$

   F. $s + 2$

   G. $s + 3$

   H. $s + 4$

2. Order of Operations, Number Properties, and Variables

Order of Operations

To find the correct answers to Math questions, you must perform your math calculations correctly. And to calculate correctly, you must follow the order of operations. For instance, multiplication must be performed before addition, from left to right. See the example below, and note how failing to follow the correct order of operations results in an incorrect answer:

Incorrect: $3 + 4 \times 2 = 7 \times 2 = 14$

Correct: $3 + 4 \times 2 = 3 + 8 = 11$

One common acronym for remembering the correct order of operations is **PEMDAS**. It stands for:

P: Parentheses (or other brackets)

E: Exponents

MD: Division and Multiplication (from left to right)

AS: Subtraction and Addition (from left to right)

Keep in mind that division/multiplication and subtraction/addition are each *pairs of operations* that must be performed from left to right. For example, $10 \div 2 \times 5 = 5 \times 5 = 25$, *not* $10 \div 2 \times 5 = 10 \div 10 = 1$. Remember: you must do all the division/multiplication operations from left to right.

When you do calculations involving parentheses or other types of brackets, be sure to distribute the term outside of the parentheses, paying close attention to its sign.

   A. $10 - 4 \div 2 \times 3 =$
   B. $(3 + 2)^2 - 6 \times 2^2 =$
   C. $3 + (2^2 - 6) \times 2^2 =$

1. $\left(\frac{1}{3} + \frac{2}{5}\right) \div \frac{3}{4} =$

   A. $\frac{9}{32}$

   B. $\frac{1}{2}$

   C. $\frac{11}{20}$

   D. $\frac{44}{45}$

SHSAT EXPERT NOTE

PEMDAS can be recalled using the expression "Please Excuse My Dear Aunt Sally." You may have heard other expressions for remembering the order of operations. However you remember it, the important thing is to perform the order of operations properly on test day. You will need to follow the order of operations for every calculation.

Number Properties

D. Odd $+/-$ Odd $=$

E. Odd $\times$ Odd $=$

F. Positive $-$ Negative $=$

G. Positive $\times/\div$ Positive $=$

H. Odd $+/-$ Even $=$

I. Odd $\times$ Even $=$

J. Negative $-$ Positive $=$

K. Positive $\times/\div$ Negative $=$

L. Even $+/-$ Even $=$

M. Even $\times$ Even $=$

N. Negative $+$ Negative $=$

O. Negative $\times/\div$ Negative $=$

SHSAT EXPERT NOTE

Don't attempt to memorize all the rules for odds/evens and positives/negatives. You can always Pick Numbers, such as 2 for an even and 3 for an odd, to help you figure out the rules.

Zero is an even number.

Adding and Subtracting Variables

A **variable** is a letter that represents an unknown value. For example, x is a variable in the expression $x + 3$.

To **add** or **subtract** variables, **combine like terms**:

$x + x = 2x$

$5x + x = 6x$

$7x - 3x = 4x$

$3 + 3 = 2(3)$

$5(3) + 3 = 6(3)$

$7(3) - 3(3) = 4(3)$

P. $4n + 5n =$

Q. $4x + x + 6x =$

R. $8g + 5g =$

S. $d + n + d + 2n =$

T. $8y + 7y =$

U. $5x - 3y + 2x - y =$

2. $5a - 3 + a =$

    E. $3a$

    F. $4a - 3$

    G. $5 + 2a$

    H. $6a - 3$

3. $2xy - y + 7 + xy =$

    A. $xy + 7$

    B. $2xy + x + 7$

    C. $3xy - y + 7$

    D. $2x^2y^3 + 7$

4. $(3d - 7) - (5 - 2d) =$

    E. $d - 12$

    F. $5d - 2$

    G. $5d + 12$

    H. $5d - 12$

5. $15x - 3y - 7x + 4y - 8x + x =$

    A. y

    B. $x + y$

    C. $31x + 7y$

    D. $8x + 7y$

SHSAT EXPERT NOTE

You should collect like terms whenever you are asked to add or subtract variables.

Multiplying and Dividing Variables

To **multiply** variables, multiply the numbers and the variables separately: $2a \times 3b = (2 \times 3)(a \times b) = 6ab$.

$x \times y = xy$

$2x \times 3y = 2 \times 3 \times x \times y = 6xy$

    V. $4g \times 6h = $ _____

    W. $2(5x \times 3y) = $ _____

    X. $\frac{1}{2}x(3y)(4z) = $ _____

Variables or numbers just outside of parentheses are multiplied by each term inside the parentheses:

$4(2x + y) = 8x + 4y$

Y. $3(5s - 3r) =$ _____

Z. $-b(4 - 3a) =$ _____

AA. $-2(3a - 2b) =$ _____

AB. $x(a + b - c) =$ _____

To **divide** variables with coefficients, simplify expressions and cancel like terms:

$x \div y = \dfrac{x}{y}$

$\dfrac{6x}{3y} = \dfrac{2x}{y}$

The same number or variable can be divided out from every term and placed outside parentheses:

$8x + 4y = 4(2x + y)$

AC. $\dfrac{12r}{4s} =$ _____

AD. $\dfrac{15j}{3k} =$ _____

AE. $\dfrac{21wx}{7} =$ _____

AF. $12x + 9y =$ _____

AG. $8ab - 6b + 2bc =$ _____

AH. $25g + 15h =$ _____

AI. $xy + 3x =$ _____

SHSAT EXPERT NOTE

Work carefully when you distribute negative signs! One of the choices will often entice test takers who neglect the signs.

Always look for common factors and variables to factor out of expressions.

---

6. $5r(3s) + 6r - 2rs =$

   E. $9rs$

   F. $11r + s - 2rs$

   G. $13rs + 6r$

   H. $19rs$

7. $2x(3y) + y =$

    A. $5xy$
    B. $5xy + y$
    C. $6xy$
    D. $6xy + y$

8. $3(x + y) - 3(-x - y) =$

    E. 0
    F. $3x + y$
    G. $6x + 6y$
    H. $3xy$

9. $-5n(3m - 2) =$

    A. $-15mn + 10n$
    B. $15mn - 10n$
    C. $-8mn + 7n$
    D. $8mn + 7n$

10. $\frac{25xyz}{5z} =$

    E. xy
    F. $5x$
    G. $5xy$
    H. Cannot be determined from the information given.

11. $a(3b) + b(-3a) =$

    A. 0
    B. $-ab$
    C. $6ab$
    D. $a + b - 3$

12. $12cd + 6c =$

    E. $3d(4c + 2)$
    F. $3c(4d + 2c)$
    G. $6c(2d + 1)$
    H. $6d(2c + 1)$

13. $3(x + 2) - (x - 4) =$

    A. $2x - 2$

    B. $2x + 2$

    C. $2(x + 5)$

    D. $3x + 10$

3. Strategy Focus: Picking Numbers

Picking Numbers

This strategy relates to questions that include unknown values. This type of question may contain variables or unknown quantities. You can Pick Numbers to make abstract problems—such as those that involve variables rather than numbers—more concrete. You may not even need to solve for the variables in an SHSAT question but, rather, determine how the variables would behave if they were real numbers. You simply pick a real number and see for yourself. Follow these guidelines:

Step 1: Pick a simple number to stand in for a variable or unknown quantity. Pick Numbers that are:

- *Permissible*: Make sure the numbers you pick follow any criteria stated in the question stem. Does the number have to be even or odd? Positive or negative?

- *Easy-to-use*: Pick Numbers that make your calculations easy. For instance, use small numbers such as 2 and 3 for a question about evens and odds, or choose 100 for a question about a percentage. Be careful when using 0 and 1, as they behave differently than most other numbers.

Step 2: Solve the *question* using the number(s) you picked.

Step 3: Test each of the *choices* using the number(s) you picked, eliminating those that give you a result that is different from the one you're looking for.

Step 4: If more than one choice remains, pick a different set of numbers and repeat steps 1–3 with the choices that remain.

> **SHSAT EXPERT NOTE**
>
> For questions with percents of an unknown number, 100 will almost always be the most manageable number to pick for the unknown number. Use 100 to make your calculations easier.

Picking Numbers is the perfect strategy to apply to story problems that ask for an expression that represents a given scenario. Let's use this strategy to answer the question that follows.

Maggie has at least 10 more toy cars than Ramón has. Which of the following inequalities gives the relationship between Maggie's toy cars (m) and Ramón's toy cars (r) ?

    A. $m - 10 \leq r$

    B. $m - r \leq 10$

    C. $r - m \geq 10$

    D. $m - r \geq 10$

Getting to the Answer: If the mere thought of this question gives you a headache, Picking Numbers can provide you with a safe way to quickly get to the answer. The efficient way to answer this question is to choose numbers that make the math easy for you. Because you know Maggie has at least 10 more toy cars than Ramón has, you can pick 13 for m and then subtract 11 to get 2 as a possible value for r. Now plug $m = 13$ and $r = 2$ into the answer choices. Often only one, maybe two, will yield a true statement. If needed, simply pick a second set of numbers.

Choice **(A)**: $13 - 10$ is not ≤ 2. Eliminate.

Choice **(B)**: $13 - 2$ is not ≤ 10. Eliminate.

Choice **(C)**: $2 - 13$ is not ≥ 10. Eliminate.

Choice **(D)**: $13 - 2 \geq 10$. Keep.

Only **(D)** works, so it must be correct. A second set of numbers isn't needed.

SHSAT EXPERT NOTE

When Picking Numbers, be sure to write down what numbers you picked and for which variables. This makes it less likely that you will make a mistake when checking the choices.

Be sure to check every choice. If the number you picked works for more than one choice, you'll need to pick another number.

Questions that involve properties of numbers (even/odd, prime/composite, rational/irrational, etc.) are another example of questions in which Picking Numbers can make your life easier. Let's give the next question a try.

If a is an odd integer and b is an even integer, which of the following must be odd?

    E. $2a + b$

    F. $a + 2b$

    G. ab

    H. a^2b

Getting to the Answer: Rather than trying to think this one through abstractly, it may be easier to Pick Numbers for a and b. There are rules for whether sums, differences, and products of integers are even or odd, but there's no need to memorize those rules.

The question states that a is odd and b is even, so let $a = 3$ (remember, 1 can be used but is not typically helpful) and $b = 2$. Plug those values into the answer choices, and identify any that produce an odd result:

Choice **(E)**: $2a + b = 2(3) + 2 = 8$. Eliminate.

Choice **(F)**: $a + 2b = 3 + 2(2) = 7$. Keep.

Choice **(G)**: $ab = (3)(2) = 6$. Eliminate.

Choice **(H)**: $a^2b = (3)^2(2) = 18$. Eliminate.

Choice **(F)** is the only odd result when $a = 3$ and $b = 2$, so it *must* be the one that's odd no matter what odd number a and even number b actually stand for. Even if you're not positive **(F)** will always be right, you know for a fact that all the others are definitely incorrect, which is just as good!

> **SHSAT EXPERT NOTE**
>
> If more than one of the answer choices returned an odd value, then you would simply try another pair of numbers with different properties, such as $a = -5$ and $b = -8$, in the remaining choices. Very rarely would you need to pick more than two sets of numbers before you find the correct answer.

1. While working together, x people earn y dollars per hour. Which of the following represents the number of dollars that z people earn if they work at this rate for 4 hours?

    A. $4xyz$

    B. $xy + 4z$

    C. $\dfrac{4yz}{x}$

    D. $\dfrac{4xy}{z}$

2. Each of the n members of an organization may invite up to 3 guests to a conference. What is the maximum number of members and guests who might attend the conference?

    E. $n + 3$

    F. $3n$

    G. $3n + 4$

    H. $4n$

3. Paolo sold x tickets, and Gina sold y tickets. The number of tickets that Gina sold is 10 less than 3 times as many tickets as Paolo sold. What is the value of y in terms of x?

    A. $10x - 3$

    B. $10 - 3x$

    C. $3x - 10$

    D. $3(x - 10)$

> **SHSAT EXPERT NOTE**
>
> When Picking Numbers, avoid picking fractions, 0, or 1.

4. Strategy Focus: Backsolving

Backsolving

For the multiple-choice questions on the SHSAT, you know for certain that one of the four answer choices is correct. Therefore, with some SHSAT Math multiple-choice questions, such as the one below, it may actually be easier to try out each answer choice until you find the one that works than to try to solve the problem using straightforward math and then look among the choices for the answer. This approach is called Backsolving.

When Backsolving, it can be helpful to start with a middle answer choice (B/F or C/G). The numerical answer choices on the SHSAT are always in either ascending or descending order. If you solve for the one in the middle and it comes out too big, you can eliminate it *and the larger number(s)*, and the same if it's too small. So trying *one* answer choice can eliminate up to three options.

> Suppose 200 tickets were sold for a particular concert. Some tickets cost $10 each, and the others cost $5 each. If total ticket sales were $1,750, how many of the more expensive tickets were sold?
>
> A. 20
>
> B. 75
>
> C. 100
>
> D. 150

You can solve this question by setting up two equations. However, if you're not comfortable using the algebraic approach for this one (or even if you are!), you should consider Backsolving. You know one of the answer choices will work, and, as a bonus, once you find one that works, you can stop. You're done!

Getting to the Answer: Start with **(C)**. If 100 tickets were sold for $10 each, then the other 100 have to have been sold for $5 each: 100 at $10 is $1,000, and 100 at $5 is $500, for a total of $1,500—too small. There *must* have been more than 100 tickets sold at the higher price point ($10).

This is great news! If you know it's not **(C)** and you know **(C)** is too small, you can eliminate **(A)** and **(B)**. By solving for one value, you have eliminated three answer choices.

If 150 tickets sold for $10, then the other 50 sold for $5. Do the math: 150 tickets at $10 is $1,500, and 50 tickets at $5 is $250, for a total of $1,750—that's it! The answer is **(D)**, so there is no need to go any further.

1. Bahar begins with three times as many tokens as Julia. Bahar gives Julia 5 tokens, but he still has 20 more than Julia. How many tokens did Bahar have to start with?

   A. 25

   B. 30

   C. 40

   D. 45

2. The perimeter of a rectangle is 728 inches. The ratio of the length to the width is 3:4. What are the dimensions of this rectangle?

   E. 120 in. by 135 in.

   F. 150 in. by 200 in.

   G. 156 in. by 208 in.

   H. 180 in. by 240 in.

3.   Today, Eraldo's age is $\frac{1}{3}$ of Paula's age. In 3 years, Eraldo's age will be $\frac{1}{2}$ of Paula's age. How old is Paula today?

    A.   1 year old

    B.   3 years old

    C.   9 years old

    D.   15 years old

4.   An unmarked straight rod will be laid end over end to measure a distance of exactly 72 inches. The same rod will be used in the same way to measure a distance of exactly 104 inches. What is the length of the longest possible rod that can be used for both measurements?

    E.   3 in.

    F.   6 in.

    G.   8 in.

    H.   9 in.

5.   Points A, B, and C are on a straight line, and B is between A and C. Length $\overline{BC} = \frac{5}{8}\,\overline{AB}$, and length $\overline{AB} = 16$ millimeters. What is the length of $\overline{AC}$?

    A.   10 mm

    B.   18 mm

    C.   24 mm

    D.   26 mm

6.   Agnes ate at least 5 more carrots than Miguel. Which of the following inequalities gives the relationship between the number of carrots Agnes ate (a) and the number of carrots Miguel ate (m) ?

    E. $5 - a \leq m$

    F. $5 - m \leq a$

    G. $a - m \geq 5$

    H. $a - m \leq 5$

Answers and Explanations

1. Basic Terms and Translation

A. $z + 2 = 2z$

B. $x - 5 = y$

C. $3 - 3x$

D. $\frac{y}{x}$

E. $\frac{1}{4}(4 + x)$

F. The product of 3 and z

G. The square of b

H. a divided by the quantity of b minus c

I. 8 times x is half as large as x cubed

J. The quotient of h and g is equivalent to 4 times the value of h

K. $\frac{x}{x^2} = 2$

L. $xy = x + y + 2$

1. B

Subject: Algebra

Getting to the Answer: Translate from English into math one phrase at a time:

Seven less than 4 times x	$4x - 7$
Is equal to	$4x - 7 =$
Twice x plus 9	$4x - 7 = 2x + 9$

2. F

Subject: Algebra

Getting to the Answer:

D dollars	In Moira's wallet originally
$+ B$ dollars	Withdrawn from bank (added to Moira's wallet)
$- S$ dollars	Spent (subtracted from Moira's wallet)
$D + B - S$	

3. A

Subject: Algebra

Getting to the Answer: First, set up equations. Arwen (R) has half as many pens as Adrienne (D):

$$R = \frac{1}{2}D$$

Adrienne gives Arwen 3 pens:

$$D - 3 \text{ and } R + 3$$

Adrienne still has 6 more pens than Arwen:

$$D - 3 = (R + 3) + 6$$

To find how many pens Arwen had originally, solve $R = \frac{1}{2}D$ for D, $D = 2R$, and substitute it into $D - 3 = (R + 3) + 6$:

$$2R - 3 = (R + 3) + 6$$
$$2R - 3 = R + 9$$
$$R = 12$$

4. F

Subject: Algebra

Getting to the Answer: Since the first integer is s, the second and third integers are $s + 1$ and $s + 2$. Thus, t is the fourth integer, or $s + 3$. Substitute $t = s + 3$ into $\frac{2t + s}{3}$ and simplify:

$$\frac{2t + s}{3} = \frac{2(s + 3) + s}{3} = \frac{2s + 6 + s}{3} = \frac{3s + 6}{3} = s + 2$$

2. Order of Operations, Number Properties, and Variables

A. $10 - 4 \div 2 \times 3 = 10 - 2 \times 3 = 10 - 6 = 4$

B. $(3 + 2)^2 - 6 \times 2^2 = (5)^2 - 6 \times 4 = 25 - 24 = 1$

C. $3 + (2^2 - 6) \times 2^2 = 3 + (4 - 6) \times 4 = 3 + (-2) \times 4 = 3 - 8 = -5$

1. D

Subject: Arithmetic

Getting to the Answer: Follow PEMDAS one step at a time:

$\left(\frac{1}{3} + \frac{2}{5}\right) \div \frac{3}{4} =$	
$\left(\frac{5}{15} + \frac{6}{15}\right) \div \frac{3}{4} =$	Add the fractions in parentheses.
$\frac{11}{15} \times \frac{4}{3} = \frac{44}{45}$	To divide fractions, multiply by the reciprocal of the divisor.

D. Even

E. Odd

F. Positive

G. Positive

H. Odd

I. Even

J. Negative

K. Negative

L. Even

M. Even

N. Negative

O. Positive

P. $9n$

Q. $11x$

R. $13g$

S. $2d + 3n$

T. $15y$

U. $7x - 4y$

2. H

Subject: Algebra

Getting to the Answer: Add the a-terms you have in the operation: $5a + a = 6a$. Then subtract 3.

3. C

Subject: Algebra

Getting to the Answer: Add like terms; in this case, add the xy-terms:

$2xy - y + 7 + xy =$	Combine like terms.
$3xy - y + 7$	

4. H

Subject: Algebra

Getting to the Answer:

$(3d - 7) - (5 - 2d) =$	Distribute to get rid of the parentheses.
$3d - 7 - 5 + 2d =$	Combine like terms.
$5d - 12$	

5. B

Subject: Algebra

Getting to the Answer: Simplify the equation.

$15x - 3y - 7x + 4y - 8x + x =$	Combine like terms.
$x + y$	

V. $24gh$

W. $30xy$

X. $6xyz$

Y. $15s - 9r$

Z. $-4b + 3ab$

AA. $-6a + 4b$

AB. $xa + xb - xc$

AC. $\frac{3r}{s}$

AD. $\frac{5j}{k}$

AE. $3wx$

AF. $3(4x + 3y)$

AG. $2b(4a - 3 + c)$

AH. $5(5g + 3h)$

AI. $x(y + 3)$

6. G

Subject: Algebra

Getting to the Answer:

$5r(3s) + 6r - 2rs =$	Do the multiplication first.
$15rs + 6r - 2rs =$	Now combine like terms.
$13rs + 6r$	

7. D

Subject: Algebra

Getting to the Answer: Following PEMDAS, multiply first and then add:

$$2x(3y) + y = 6xy + y$$

8. G

Subject: Algebra

Getting to the Answer:

$3(x + y) - 3(-x - y) =$	Multiply; distribute across parentheses.
$3x + 3y + 3x + 3y =$	Combine like terms.
$6x + 6y$	

9. A

Subject: Algebra

Getting to the Answer:

$-5n(3m - 2) =$	Distribute the $5n$ across the parentheses.
$-15mn + 10n$	

10. G

Subject: Algebra

Getting to the Answer:

$\dfrac{25xyz}{5z} =$	Cancel common factors in the numerator and the denominator.
$5xy$	

11. A

Subject: Algebra

Getting to the Answer:

$a(3b) + b(-3a) =$	Do the multiplication first.
$3ab - 3ab =$	Combine like terms.
0	

12. G

Subject: Algebra

Getting to the Answer: Pull out the common factors among the two terms in the expression:

$$12cd + 6c =$$
$$6c(2d + 1)$$

13. C

Subject: Algebra

Getting to the Answer:

$3(x + 2) - (x - 4) =$	Distribute to get rid of the parentheses.
$3x + 6 - x + 4 =$	Combine like terms.
$2x + 10 =$	Pull out the common factor.
$2(x + 5)$	

3. Strategy Focus: Picking Numbers

1.   C

Subject: Algebra

Getting to the Answer: With variables in the answer choices, pick easy numbers to work with: $x = 2$, $y = 6$, and $z = 3$.

If 2 people work 1 hour, they make 6 dollars, so each person makes $3 an hour. This means that 3 people working 4 hours at that rate will make $3 \times 4 \times \$3 = \$36$.

Now check each answer choice to see which one works out to $36.

A. $4xyz = 144$

B. $xy + 4z = 12 + 12 = 24$

C. $\dfrac{4yz}{x} = \dfrac{72}{2} = 36$

D. $\dfrac{4xy}{z} = \dfrac{48}{3} = 16$

Choice **(C)** is your answer.

2.   H

Subject: Algebra

Getting to the Answer: With variables in the question and the answer choices, you can Pick Numbers. Choose $n = 5$; this means that if 5 members each brought 3 guests, there are 15 guest attendees plus the original 5 members = 20. Check the choices:

E. $n + 3 = 8$, which is incorrect.

F. $3n = 15$, which is also incorrect.

G. $3n + 4 = 19$, which is also incorrect.

H. $4n = 20$, which matches your answer above.

3.   C

Subject: Algebra

Getting to the Answer: This question may be easier to solve with real numbers instead of variables. You could pick $x = 4$ for Paolo. To find out how many tickets Gina sold, follow the math in the question stem: $4 \times 3 = 12$ and $12 - 10 = 2$, so $y = 2$.

Now plug in 4 for x in the answer choices, looking for a value of 2:

A. $10x - 3 = 37$, which does not work.

B. $10 - 3x = -2$, which is incorrect.

C. $3x - 10 = 2$, which matches your choice of $y = 2$.

D. $3(x - 10) = -18$, which is incorrect.

Choice **(C)** is correct.

4. Strategy Focus: Backsolving

1.   D

Subject: Algebra

Getting to the Answer: Since solving this question using straightforward math would require setting up multiple equations, Backsolving may be an efficient approach. It might be helpful to set up a simple T-chart to test answer choices. To test **(B)**, Bahar would start with 30 and Julia would start with $30 \div 3 = 10$ tokens. If Bahar gave Julia 5 tokens, Bahar would have $30 - 5 = 25$ tokens and Julia would have $10 + 5 = 15$ tokens. This difference is 10, which is less than 20, so Bahar must begin with more than 30 tokens; eliminate **(A)** and **(B)**.

Bahar	Julia
30	10
25	15

Choice **(C)** can quickly be eliminated, as $\frac{1}{3}$ of 40 tokens would yield partial tokens. On test day, you can confidently choose **(D)**. To confirm that **(D)** is correct:

Bahar	Julia
45	15
40	20

The difference is 20; **(D)** is correct.

To solve using traditional math, you would need to set up and solve the equations $b = 3j$ and $(b - 5) = (j + 5) + 20$.

2. G
Subject: Geometry

Getting to the Answer: You could set up the equation $2(3x) + 2(4x) = 728$ to solve. Alternatively, you can solve by Backsolving. Starting with **(F)**, 150 and 200 satisfy the ratio of 3:4, but the perimeter would be $2(150) + 2(200) = 300 + 400 = 700$, which is too small; eliminate **(E)** and **(F)**. Choice **(G)** also satisfies the ratio of 3:4, since $3 \times 52 = 156$ and $4 \times 52 = 208$. The perimeter would be $2(156) + 2(208) = 312 + 416 = 728$; **(G)** is correct.

3. C
Subject: Algebra

Getting to the Answer: You could solve by setting up equations, but Backsolving is another effective strategy. Start by testing **(B)**. If Paula is 3 years old today, Eraldo would be $\frac{1}{3}(3) = 1$ year old today. In 3 years, Paula would be $3 + 3 = 6$ and Eraldo would be $1 + 3 = 4$. This would make Eraldo's age more than $\frac{1}{2}$ of Paula's age, so Paula's age today must be a larger number. Eliminate **(A)** and **(B)**; try **(C)**. If Paula is 9 years old today, Eraldo would be $\frac{1}{3}(9) = 3$ years old today. In 3 years, Paula would be $9 + 3 = 12$ and Eraldo could be $3 + 3 = 6$, which is $\frac{1}{2}$ of 12. Choice **(C)** is correct.

Alternately, you could set up the equations $e = \frac{1}{3}p$ and $e + 3 = \frac{1}{2}(p + 3)$, substitute $\frac{1}{3}p$ for e in the second equation, and solve for p.

4. G
Subject: Arithmetic

Getting to the Answer: The correct answer will be the greatest common factor (GCF) of 72 and 104, but rather than calculating the GCF, you can use Backsolving. Since the question asks for the "longest possible rod," start by testing the largest answer choice. For **(H)**, 9 is a factor of 72 ($8 \times 9 = 72$), but 9 is **not** a factor of 104 ($9 \times 11 = 99$, $9 \times 12 = 108$). You may also know that a number is a multiple of 9 only if its digits add to a multiple of 9 ($1 + 0 + 4 = 5$, which is not a multiple of 9). Eliminate **(H)**. For **(G)**, 8 is a factor of 72 ($8 \times 9 = 72$), and 8 is a factor of 104 ($104 \div 8 = 13$). Choice **(G)** is correct.

Alternatively, to solve by finding the GCF, make a factor tree for each number. The factors of 72 are $2 \times 2 \times 2 \times 3 \times 3$, and the factors of 104 are $2 \times 2 \times 2 \times 13$. The numbers have $2 \times 2 \times 2 = 8$ in common, so 8 is the greatest common factor.

5. D
Subject: Arithmetic

Getting to the Answer: Begin by making a sketch of the information provided in the question. Based on the sketch, note that the question is asking for the length of the entire line segment $\overline{AC}$. Since $\overline{AB}$ is 16 mm and is part of $\overline{AC}$, **(A)** can be eliminated. You can now use straightforward math to solve, or you can continue to use logic to eliminate answer choices. The other portion of $\overline{AC}$, $\overline{BC}$, is $\frac{5}{8}\overline{AB}$. So $\overline{BC}$ must be a little more than half of $\overline{AB}$ since 5 is a little more than half of 8. Half of $\overline{AB}$ is $16 \div 2 = 8$, so $\overline{BC}$ is a little more than 8. Since $\overline{AB} + \overline{BC} = 16 +$ a little more than 8, $\overline{AC}$ is a little more than 24. **(B)** and **(C)** can be eliminated, and **(D)** can be confirmed as correct without testing any of the answer choices. To verify the math, $\overline{BC} = \frac{5}{8}\overline{AB} = \frac{5}{8}(16) = 10$ and $\overline{AB} + \overline{BC} = 16 + 10 = 26$.

6. C
Subject: Algebra

Getting to the Answer: You can Backsolve by testing each of the answer choices. It does not make sense to subtract the number of carrots eaten from 5, so eliminate **(E)** and **(F)**. Test the remaining choices by Picking Numbers that are permissible and easy to use, such as 10 for a and 4 for m. These numbers are permissible because they reflect that Agnes "ate at least 5 more carrots" than Miguel since $10 - 4 = 6$, which is more than 5. Substituting these values into **(G)** shows that **(G)** is correct. $10 - 4 = 6$, and $6 \geq 5$.

CHAPTER 10

ARITHMETIC

CHAPTER OBJECTIVES

By the end of this chapter, you will be able to:

- Calculate fractions, decimals, and percents
- Round numbers to specific place values
- Calculate distance on a number line
- Calculate absolute value
- Identify factors and multiples
- Calculate percent change
- Calculate mean, median, mode, and range
- Use the three-part formula to solve for components of rates
- Set up and solve a proportion for a missing value
- Use ratios to perform unit conversions
- Interpret a point on the coordinate plane
- Calculate the constant of proportionality for a proportional relationship
- Calculate probabilities based on data sets
- Distinguish between and solve combinations and permutations

Math

Math

1. Fractions and Decimals

Fraction Operations

Any number that can be expressed as a fraction or a repeating decimal is a **rational number**. This includes numbers like 3, $\frac{2}{5}$, -0.1666, and $0.\overline{3}$.

- The process used to write a fraction in **lowest terms** is called **simplifying**. This simply means dividing out any common multiples from both the numerator and denominator so that the numerator and the denominator are not divisible by any common integer greater than 1. This process is also commonly called **canceling**. For example, the fraction $\frac{3}{6}$ is not in lowest terms because 3 and 6 are both divisible by 3. Simplifying $\frac{3}{6}$ gives $\frac{1}{2}$.

- To add or subtract fractions, first find a **common denominator**, and then add or subtract the numerators. Finding a common denominator often involves multiplying one or more of the fractions by a number so that the denominators will be the same. Note that multiplying both the numerator and denominator of a fraction by the same number is essentially just multiplying by 1, so it does not change the value of the original fraction. For example, $\frac{2}{15} \times \frac{2}{2} + \frac{3}{10} \times \frac{3}{3} = \frac{4}{30} + \frac{9}{30} = \frac{4+9}{30} = \frac{13}{30}$.

- To **multiply fractions**, multiply straight across—numerator times numerator and denominator times denominator. For example, $\frac{5}{7} \times \frac{3}{4} = \frac{5 \times 3}{7 \times 4} = \frac{15}{28}$.

- To **divide fractions**, invert the second fraction (or fraction in the denominator) and multiply. For example, $\frac{1}{2} \div \frac{3}{5} = \frac{1}{2} \times \frac{5}{3} = \frac{1 \times 5}{2 \times 3} = \frac{5}{6}$.

- To **convert a mixed number**, which is a whole number with a fraction, to an improper fraction, which is a fraction where the numerator is greater than the denominator, multiply the whole number part by the denominator and then add the numerator. The result is the new numerator over the same denominator. For example, to convert $7\frac{1}{3}$, first multiply 7 by 3 and then add 1 to get the new numerator of 22. Put that over the same denominator, 3, to get $\frac{22}{3}$.

- To **convert an improper fraction** to a mixed number, divide the denominator into the numerator, and the remainder will be the numerator of the fraction part with the same denominator. For example, to convert $\frac{108}{5}$, first divide 5 into 108, which yields 21 with a remainder of 3. Therefore, $\frac{108}{5} = 21\frac{3}{5}$.

- The **reciprocal** of a fraction is the inverse of that fraction. To find the reciprocal of a fraction, switch the numerator and the denominator. The reciprocal of $\frac{3}{7}$ is $\frac{7}{3}$, and the reciprocal of $-\frac{4}{9}$ is $-\frac{9}{4}$. The reciprocal of 5 (or $\frac{5}{1}$ because all whole numbers can be written over 1) is $\frac{1}{5}$. The product of two reciprocals is always 1.

- One way to **compare fractions** is to manipulate them so they have a common denominator. For instance, compare $\frac{3}{4}$ and $\frac{7}{10}$. Convert the denominator of each to 40: $\frac{3}{4} = \frac{30}{40}$ and $\frac{7}{10} = \frac{28}{40}$. Since $\frac{30}{40}$ is greater than $\frac{28}{40}$, that means $\frac{3}{4}$ is greater than $\frac{7}{10}$.

  Another way to compare fractions is to convert them both to decimals: $\frac{3}{4}$ converts to 0.75, $\frac{7}{10}$ converts to 0.7, and 0.75 is greater than 0.7.

DIRECTIONS: Use the information in the list above to complete the following fraction operations.

A. Simplify by canceling out common factors on top and bottom.

$$\frac{39}{72} = \underline{\hspace{1.5cm}} = \underline{\hspace{1.5cm}}$$

B. Find a common denominator, and then add the numerators and simplify.

$$\frac{5}{9} + \frac{2}{6} = \underline{\hspace{1.5cm}} + \underline{\hspace{1.5cm}} = \underline{\hspace{1.5cm}} = \underline{\hspace{1.5cm}}$$

C. Find a common denominator, and then subtract the numerators.

$$\frac{1}{2} - \frac{3}{7} = \underline{\hspace{1.5cm}} - \underline{\hspace{1.5cm}} = \underline{\hspace{1.5cm}}$$

D. Multiply the numerators to get the new numerator, and multiply the denominators to get the new denominator.

$$\frac{1}{3} \times \frac{2}{5} = \underline{\hspace{1.5cm}}$$

E. To divide by a fraction, multiply by the reciprocal.

$$\frac{1}{4} \div \frac{1}{3} = \frac{1}{4} \times \underline{\hspace{1.5cm}} = \underline{\hspace{1.5cm}}$$

F. To convert to an improper fraction, multiply the whole number by the denominator and then add the numerator. The resulting value becomes the new numerator over the same denominator.

$$4\frac{3}{7} = \underline{\hspace{1.5cm}}$$

G. To convert to a mixed number, divide the denominator into the numerator, and the remainder will be the numerator of the fraction part, with the same denominator.

$$\frac{43}{8} = \underline{\hspace{1.5cm}}$$

H. Find the reciprocal by switching the numerator and the denominator.

$$\frac{5}{9} = \underline{\hspace{1.5cm}}$$

I. Manipulate the fractions so they have a common denominator, and determine which value is greater.

$$\frac{2}{5} \text{ compared to } \frac{4}{11}$$

$$\underline{\hspace{1.5cm}} \text{ compared to } \underline{\hspace{1.5cm}}$$

$$\underline{\hspace{1.5cm}} \text{ is greater}$$

J. Convert the fractions to decimals, and then determine which value is greater

$$\frac{6}{8} \text{ compared to } \frac{8}{10}$$

$$\frac{6}{8} = \underline{\hspace{1cm}}.\underline{\hspace{1cm}}\ \underline{\hspace{1cm}}$$

$$\frac{8}{10} = \underline{\hspace{1cm}}.\underline{\hspace{1cm}}$$

$$\underline{\hspace{1.5cm}} \text{ is greater}$$

1. What is the value of $2\frac{2}{3} + 3\frac{3}{4} - 1\frac{1}{3} + 3\frac{1}{12}$?

   A. $7\frac{3}{4}$

   B. $7\frac{7}{16}$

   C. $8\frac{1}{12}$

   D. $8\frac{1}{6}$

SHSAT EXPERT NOTE

To add or subtract fractions, the denominators need to be the same.

Converting Fractions, Decimals, and Percents

To convert a fraction to a decimal, divide the numerator by the denominator. For example, to convert $\frac{3}{8}$, divide 3 by 8, which yields 0.375:

$$\frac{3}{8} = 8\overline{)3.000}$$

$$
\begin{array}{r}
0.375 \\
\hline
8\,)\,3.000 \\
-2.4 \\
\hline
60 \\
-56 \\
\hline
40 \\
-40 \\
\hline
0
\end{array}
$$

Often, numbers in the quotient will start repeating, such as with $\frac{1}{6}$. When 1 is divided by 6, the decimal starts repeating almost right away, 0.16666666 . . . , so it can be written as $0.1\overline{66}$ (the line over the 66 means "repeating"). To find a particular digit in a repeating decimal, note the number of digits in the cluster that repeats. If there are two digits in that cluster, then every second digit to the right of the decimal point is the same. For example, for $\frac{23}{99} = 0.\overline{23}$, the second digit, fourth digit, sixth digit, and so on is 3. If there are three digits in that cluster, then every third digit to the right of the decimal point is the same. For example, for $\frac{152}{333} = 0.\overline{456}$, the third digit, sixth digit, ninth digit, and so on is 6. To find the nth digit to the right of the decimal point, divide the number of the digit you are looking for by the number of digits that are repeated. The remainder (R) will correspond to the position that digit will hold. For the previous example, since there are 3 digits in the repeating decimal, to find the 13th digit divide 13 by 3: $\frac{13}{3} = 4$ R1. The remainder of 1 means the 13th digit is the same as the 1st digit, which is 4.

To convert a decimal to a fraction, put each number to the right of the decimal point over the power of 10 that corresponds to that number's digit. Note that the number to the left of the decimal is an integer and thus does not need to be converted into a fraction.

For example, to convert 3.246 to a fraction, place 2 over 10, 4 over 100, and 6 over 1,000 and then add them using a common denominator.

$$3 \;.\; \underset{\text{tenths}}{2} \quad \underset{\text{hundredths}}{4} \quad \underset{\text{thousandths}}{6}$$

$$3 + \frac{2}{10} + \frac{4}{100} + \frac{6}{1000} = 3\frac{246}{1000}$$

Then simplify: $3\frac{246}{1,000} = 3\frac{123}{500}$.

To convert a decimal to a percent, multiply by 100%: Percent = Decimal × 100%. For example, 0.45 as a percent is $0.45 \times 100\% = 45\%$.

To convert a percent to a decimal, divide by 100%: Decimal $= \frac{\text{Percent}}{100\%}$. For example, 15% as a decimal is $\frac{15\%}{100\%} = 0.15$.

To convert a fraction to a percent, first convert the fraction to a decimal. For example, $\frac{3}{5}$ as a percent is $0.6 \times 100\% = 60\%$.

	Fraction	Decimal	Percent
K.	$\frac{1}{4}$		
L.	$\frac{1}{6}$		
M.			99%
N.		0.35	

2. The decimal 0.16 can be expressed as the fraction $\frac{x}{25}$. What is the value of x?

   E. 2
   F. 4
   G. 8
   H. 16

$$\frac{2}{7} = 0.\overline{285714}$$

3. In the decimal above, 2 is the first digit in the repeating pattern. What is the 415th digit?

   A. 1
   B. 2
   C. 5
   D. 8

Multiplying and Dividing with Decimals

Multiplying decimals is also a lot like multiplying whole numbers. Multiply each digit in the first number by each digit in the second number. The number of decimal places in the product will equal the total number of decimal places in the original numbers.

For example, to multiply 9.76 by 0.4:

First, multiply the digits as whole numbers.

$$\begin{array}{r} 976 \\ \times\ \underline{04} \\ 3904 \end{array}$$

Then find the total number of decimal places.

- There are 2 decimal places in 9.76.
- There is 1 decimal place in 0.4.
- The product must have $2 + 1 = 3$ decimal places. Write 3.904.

Dividing decimals is similar to dividing whole numbers.

First, make the divisor (the number doing the dividing) a whole number by multiplying it by a power of 10. Then, multiply the dividend (the number being divided by the divisor) by the same power of 10.

For example, to divide 18.93 by 1.5:

- Change the divisor to a whole number by multiplying by a power of 10. So, $1.5 \times 10 = 15$.
- Multiply the dividend by the same power of 10. So, $18.93 \times 10 = 189.3$.
- Divide. Line up the decimal point in the quotient.
- Continue dividing until there is no amount left over or you see a repeating pattern. You can add zeros to the end of the dividend.

$$\begin{array}{r} 12.62\ \ \\ 15\overline{)189.30} \\ \underline{-15}\ \ \ \ \ \ \ \\ 39\ \ \ \ \ \\ \underline{-30}\ \ \ \ \\ 93\ \ \\ \underline{-90}\ \\ 30\\ \underline{-30}\\ 0 \end{array}$$

2. Rounding, Number Lines, Absolute Value, Factors, and Multiples

Rounding

To **round** a number, look at the value to the right of the digit in question. If the number is 4 or less, round down. If the number is 5 or greater, round up. For example, to round 28.935 to the nearest tenth, look at the 3, which is to the right of the tenths place. Since 3 is less than 4, round 28.935 down to 28.9.

Scenarios that involve countable items may also require you to round your answer up or down. For instance, a store does not sell $1\frac{2}{7}$ bags of flour, so a person would need to purchase 2 bags of flour to meet his or her needs. A pitcher containing 100 fluid ounces of lemonade can completely fill 12 8-ounce bottles, since $\frac{100}{8} = 12.5$.

1. Wes is buying plates for a graduation party. The plates are sold 12 in a pack, and there will be 80 guests. How many packs of plates does Wes need to buy in order for each of the guests to have a plate?

    A. 5

    B. 6

    C. 7

    D. 8

Number Lines

Number lines show values placed at intervals. Values may be whole numbers, negative numbers, fractions, or decimals. As you move to the left, values decrease, and as you move to the right, values increase. For the number line shown, A < B < C < D.

The midpoint is the point halfway between two points. If B is halfway between A and C, then B is the midpoint of AC. You can find the midpoint of a line segment on a number line by calculating the average of the two endpoints. If A = 2 and C = 6, then the midpoint is $\frac{2+6}{2} = \frac{8}{2} = 4$.

2. The intervals between the tick marks on the number line above are equal. What is the value of point B ?

    E. $\frac{1}{18}$

    F. $\frac{1}{6}$

    G. $\frac{2}{9}$

    H. $\frac{1}{3}$

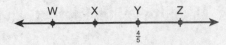

3. On the number line above, $YZ = 2\frac{1}{4}$, $WZ = 5\frac{1}{10}$, and $WX = 1\frac{3}{5}$. What is the value of point X ?

    A. $-2\frac{1}{20}$

    B. $-\frac{9}{20}$

    C. $\frac{11}{20}$

    D. $3\frac{1}{20}$

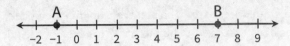

4. On the number line above, Point M (not shown) is the midpoint of line segment AB. What is the location of point M ?

    E. 2

    F. 3

    G. 4

    H. 5

5. On a number line, points A, B, C, and D represent -7, -5, -1, and 3, respectively. How many units is the midpoint of $\overline{AB}$ from the midpoint of $\overline{CD}$?

    A. 4

    B. 7

    C. 14

    D. 21

> **SHSAT EXPERT NOTE**
>
> A number line shows the distance between real numbers in a positive or negative direction from a point.
>
> A midpoint is a point that is the same distance from both ends of a line segment.

Absolute Value

The **absolute value** of a number (integers, fractions, and decimals alike) is its distance from zero on the number line, which is why absolute value is greater than or equal to 0. Treat absolute value signs a lot like parentheses: do what's inside them first and then take the absolute value of the result. Don't take the absolute value of each piece between the bars before calculating. For example, in order to calculate $|(-12) + 5 - (-4)| - |5 + (-10)|$, first do what's inside the bars to arrive at $|-3| - |-5|$, which is $3 - 5$, or -2.

    A. What is $|3|$?
    B. What is $|-3|$?

> **SHSAT EXPERT NOTE**
>
> When following the order of operations, absolute value signs should be treated as parentheses.

6. $|9 + (-3.4)| - |(-4) + 1.6| =$

    E. -7

    F.   2

    G.   3.2

    H.   8

Factors and Multiples

A **factor** of an integer is any number that divides precisely into that integer (with no remainder).

A **multiple** of an integer is that integer times any number. In other words, factor × factor = multiple.

> **DIRECTIONS:** For each statement, determine whether the first number is a factor, a multiple, or both a factor and a multiple of the second number.

    C.   4 is a factor/multiple of 24.

    D.   49 is a factor/multiple of 7.

    E.   8 is a factor/multiple of 8.

> **SHSAT EXPERT NOTE**
>
> 2 is the only even prime, and 1 is not a prime number.
>
> There are only a few factors of a number but an infinite number of multiples.
>
> When a question seems to involve a lot of complex multiplication or division, consider looking at the prime factors to break it down.

Consecutive Multiples

To calculate **multiples** of a given number, multiply the number by positive integers. To calculate consecutive multiples, multiply that number by positive integers that increase by 1 each time.

    F.   List the three smallest multiples of both 6 and 8.

    _____

    G.   Four consecutive multiples of 6 yield a sum of 156. What are these multiples?

    _____

    H.   Five consecutive multiples of 3 yield a sum that is equal to the product of 7 and 15. What are these multiples?

    _____

7.   How many positive odd factors of 30 are greater than 3 and less than 30 ?

    A. 2

    B. 3

    C. 4

    D. 5

8.   In the set of consecutive integers from 8 to 25 inclusive, two integers are multiples of both 3 and 4. How many integers in this set are multiples of neither 3 nor 4 ?

    E. 2

    F. 4

    G. 6

    H. 9

Divisibility Rules

DIVISIBLE BY:	RULE:	EXAMPLE:
2	The last digit must be even.	2,002
3	The sum of the digits is a multiple of 3.	813
4	The last two digits are a multiple of 4.	456
5	The last digit must be 5 or 0.	705
6	The rules for both 2 and 3 must apply.	924
9	The sum of the digits is a multiple of 9.	891

    I.   Is 115, 370, 465, or 890 a multiple of 3 ?

    J. Is 12,420 or 20,242 a multiple of 6 ?

SHSAT EXPERT NOTE

Knowing these divisibility rules by memory will save you time on test day. The SHSAT will never explicitly ask you for these definitions, but knowing them will save you a lot of time and calculations on test day.

Greatest Common Factor

A **prime number** is a positive integer that is divisible without a remainder by only 1 and itself. The number 2 is the smallest prime number and the only even prime number; 1 is not considered prime.

To find the **prime factorization** of an integer, use a factor tree to keep breaking the integer into factors until all the factors are prime numbers. To find the prime factorization of 36, for example, you could begin by breaking it into 4×9. Then break 4 into 2×2 and break 9 into 3×3. The prime factorization of 36 is $2 \times 2 \times 3 \times 3$.

The **greatest common factor (GCF)** of two numbers is the highest number that divides into each of them without a remainder. To find the greatest common factor, break down both numbers into their prime factorizations and take all the prime factors they have in common. For example, try 36 and 48: $36 = 2 \times 2 \times 3 \times 3$ and $48 = 2 \times 2 \times 2 \times 2 \times 3$. What they have in common is two 2s and one 3, so the GCF is $2 \times 2 \times 3 = 12$.

For a GCF problem, you can Backsolve by simply checking the largest answer choice to see if it divides evenly into both numbers. If not, proceed to the second-largest answer choice. Keep going until you've found the greatest factor of both numbers.

DIRECTIONS: To find the greatest common factor of 240 and 980, identify all of the prime factors the two have in common.

K. They share a _____, another _____, and a _____.

L. The greatest common factor is _____.

9. What is the greatest common factor of 48 and 180 ?

   A. 4

   B. 12

   C. 16

   D. 18

Least Common Multiple

The **least common multiple (LCM)** of two numbers is the smallest multiple that both of those numbers divide into. To find the LCM of two or more numbers, check out the multiples of the larger number until you find one that's also a multiple of the smaller number. For example, to find the LCM of 12 and 15, identify which multiple of 15 is also a multiple of 12: $1 \times 15 = 15$ is not divisible by 12; $2 \times 15 = 30$ is not divisible by 12; nor is 45, which is 3×15. However, the next multiple of 15, $4 \times 15 = 60$, is divisible by 12, so it's the LCM.

To find the LCM, begin with the smallest answer choice. Check to see if it is a multiple of both numbers. If not, proceed to the second-smallest answer choice. Keep going until you've found the smallest multiple of both numbers.

To find the LCM using **prime factorization**, first write the prime factorization of each value. Then take out each factor (not just factors common to both numbers), and raise each factor to the highest power at which it appears.

DIRECTIONS: Use the steps below to find the LCM of 24 and 28.

M. What is the prime factorization of 24 ?

N. What is the prime factorization of 28 ?

O. What are all the distinct factors?

P. Now raise them to the highest power at which they appear:

10. What is the least common multiple of 12, 4, and 32 ?

   E. 64

   F. 72

   G. 96

   H. 384

Math

For a GCF or LCM problem with prime factorization, all of the choices are presented in prime factorization. This means there is no need to multiply out any of the numbers!

3. Percents

Calculating Percents

Percents are one of the most commonly used mathematical relationships and are quite popular on the SHSAT:

$$\text{Percent} = \frac{\text{Part}}{\text{Whole}} \times 100\%$$

Percent is just another word for *hundredth*. For example, 27% (27 percent) means:

$$27\% = \frac{27}{100} \times 100\%$$

Other ways to express 27% include:

27 hundredths

$\frac{27}{100}$

0.27

27 out of every 100 things

27 parts out of a whole of 100 parts

In percent questions, you can use the same **three-part percent formula** whether you need to find the part, the whole, or the percent: part = percent × whole.

When you work with a percent in a formula, be sure to convert the percent into decimal form:

Example:	What is 12% of 25 ?
Setup:	Part $= 0.12 \times 25$
Example:	15 is 3% of what number?
Setup:	$15 = 0.03 \times$ whole
Example:	45 is what percent of 9 ?
Setup:	$45 =$ percent $\times 9$

Here are some other types of questions that may involve percents:

- To **increase a number by a percent**, add the percent to 100%, convert to a decimal, and multiply. For example, to increase 40 by 25%, add 25% to 100%, convert 125% to 1.25, and multiply by 40. The result is $1.25 \times 40 = 50$. To decrease, subtract the percent from 100%, convert to a decimal, and multiply. For example, to decrease 40 by 25%, subtract 25% from 100%, convert 75% to 0.75, and multiply by 40 to get $0.75 \times 40 = 30$.

- To calculate a **percent increase** (or decrease), use the formula:

$$\text{Percent Change} = \frac{\text{Amount of Change}}{\text{Original Amount}} \times 100\%$$

- When there are **multiple percent increases** and/or decreases, and when the question asks for the combined percent increase or decrease, the easiest and most effective strategy is to Pick Numbers. Pick 100 for the original value and see what happens in each step.

    Example: A price went up 10% one year, and the new price went up 20% the next year. What was the combined percent increase over the two-year period?

    Setup: First year: $100 + (10\%$ of $100) = 110$. Second year: $110 + (20\%$ of $110) = 132$. That's a combined 32% increase (which does not equal $10\% + 20\% = 30\%$).

SHSAT EXPERT NOTE

You cannot just add or subtract the percents to get the total percent increase or decrease.

- To find the **original whole before a percent increase or decrease**, set up an equation with a variable in place of the original number. Suppose you have a 15% increase over an unknown original amount, such as x. You would follow the same steps as always: 100% plus 15% is 115%, which is 1.15 when converted to a decimal. Then multiply by the number, which in this case is x, and you get $1.15x$. Finally, set that equal to the new amount.

    Example: After a 5% increase, the population was 59,346. What was the population *before* the increase?

    Setup: $1.05x = 59{,}346 \rightarrow x = 56{,}520$

SHSAT EXPERT NOTE

Questions may ask for a part, the whole, or a percent. No matter which of them the question asks for, the question will give you the other two pieces of information you need to find the missing one.

A.   Regina wants to donate 15% of her paycheck to charity. If she receives a paycheck of $300, how much money will she donate?

_____

B.   Andrew has a coupon for 20% off of the price of any CD. If he purchases a CD originally priced at $16, what will the discounted price be?

Solve the above problem by using decimals.

_____

1. In a certain class, 15 students are seniors. This is 30% of the total number of students in the class. How many students are in the class?

   A. 45
   B. 50
   C. 200
   D. 450

2. A light bulb filament is one-hundredth of an inch thick, with an allowable error of 2 percent. What is the **least** allowable thickness of the filament?

   E. 0.00098 in.
   F. 0.0002 in.
   G. 0.0098 in.
   H. 0.0102 in.

3. A sweater is on sale for 20% less than the original price. Julie has a coupon for an additional 10% off. What discount off the original amount does Julie receive?

   A. 15%
   B. 28%
   C. 30%
   D. 34%

4. Mandy buys a toaster that is on sale for 20% less than the original price, and then she uses a coupon worth an additional 15% off of the sale price. What percentage of the original price has she saved?

   E. 32%
   F. 34%
   G. 35%
   H. 38%

SURVEY OF TABLETS PER HOUSEHOLD

Number of Tablets	Number of Households
0	11
1	60
2	75
3	23

5. The table above gives the number of tablets per household in Sumir's neighborhood. By what percent is the number of households with 2 tablets greater than the number of households with 1 tablet?

    A.   15

    B.   25

    C.   60

    D.   80

SHSAT EXPERT NOTE

For any percent problem, you can use the formula, set up two proportions, or use decimals. On test day, use the approach with which you are most comfortable.

4. Statistics Terms

Mean, Median, Mode, and Range

Suppose Jake took five quizzes in an algebra class and earned scores of 85, 92, 85, 80, and 96. Descriptions of three fundamental statistical measures you can find for this data set follow:

- **Mean (also called average):** The sum of the values divided by the number of values. The mean of Jake's quiz scores is $\frac{85 + 92 + 85 + 80 + 96}{5} = \frac{438}{5} = 87.6$.
- **Median:** The value that is in the middle of the set *when the values are arranged in order (ascending or descending)*. The test scores in ascending order are 80, 85, 85, 92, and 96, making the median 85. Be careful: the SHSAT could give you a set of numbers that is not in order. Make sure you properly arrange them before determining the median.

SHSAT EXPERT NOTE

To find the median of a data set that contains an even number of terms, first arrange the terms in ascending order and then find the average of the two middle terms.

- **Mode:** The value that occurs most frequently. The score that appears more than any other is 85 (twice vs. once), so it is the mode. If more than one value appears the most often, that's okay: a set of data can have multiple modes. If no value appears the most often because they all appear the same number of times, that's okay, too: a set of data can have no mode.
- **Range:** The difference between the highest and lowest values. In this data set, the lowest and highest values are 80 and 96, respectively, so the range is $96 - 80 = 16$.

> **SHSAT EXPERT NOTE**
>
> The SHSAT won't ask you for these definitions, but you will be expected to know them.

DIRECTIONS: As with the percent formula, if you have two components of the average formula, you can find the missing piece. Use the average formula to answer the following questions.

A. Juan went to the bookstore 3 times. The first time, he bought 3 books. On both of the other trips, he bought 6 books. What is the average number of books he bought per trip?

_____

B. Alyssa has an average of 90 in English class after taking 4 tests. What is the sum of her scores?

_____

C. Muriel makes an average of $30 a day babysitting. If she made $270 in one month, how many days did she work?

_____

1. Zuri bought 4 apples at the farmer's market for a mean price of $1.35 per apple. She bought 5 pears at the local grocery store. If the total price of the apples is equal to the total price of the pears, what was the mean price of the pears?

    A. $1.01
    B. $1.08
    C. $1.21
    D. $1.68

2. A museum records 16 visitors to an exhibit on Monday, 21 on Tuesday, 20 on Wednesday, 17 on Thursday, 19 on Friday, 21 on Saturday, and 17 on Sunday. What is the median number of visitors for the week?

    E. 18.5
    F. 18.75
    G. 19
    H. 19.5

3. The scores of Garrett's last 5 quizzes are 80, 90, 80, 70, and 100. What is Garrett's mode quiz score?

    A. 30
    B. 80
    C. 84
    D. 85

LIFTS IN WEIGHTLIFTING COMPETITION

Class	Lowest Lift	Range
I	55	54
II	58	52
III	61	50

4. At a weightlifting competition, competitors were divided into three weight classes. The table above shows the lowest lift and the range of lifts for each class. What is the overall range of all the lifts in all three weight classes?

    E. 50
    F. 52
    G. 54
    H. 56

SHSAT EXPERT NOTE

Don't be intimidated by complex problems. Break them down into manageable pieces.

Box Plots

A **box plot**, or box and whisker plot, can be used to show a summary of a set of data.

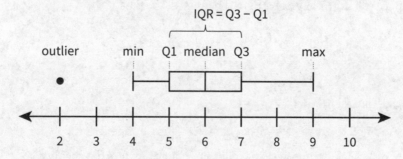

The box plot above shows the following about the data set it represents:

- **Median:** 6
- **Minimum value:** 4
- **Maximum value:** 9

- **First quartile:** 5
  - The first quartile value is calculated by finding the median of the data points to the *left* of the median.
- **Third quartile:** 7
  - The third quartile value is calculated by finding the median of the data points to the *right* of the median.
- **Interquartile range:** $7 - 5 = 2$
  - The interquartile range is the distance between the first and third quartiles.
- **Outlier:** 2
  - Outliers are data points that fall outside the box and whisker plot.

A box plot also provides information about the distribution of the data points:

- About 25% of the data points are below the first quartile value.
- About 25% of the data points are between the first quartile value and the median.
- About 25% of the data points are between the median and the third quartile value.
- About 25% of the data points are above the third quartile value.

5. A teacher used the box plot below to display the distribution of scores on a 10-point math quiz.

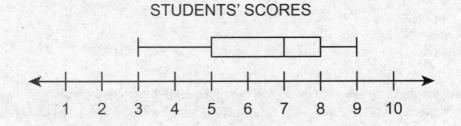

STUDENTS' SCORES

Which statement about the distribution of scores is true?

A. Approximately half of the scores are exactly 7.

B. The data contain an outlier.

C. Approximately one-fourth of the scores are at least 8.

D. The interquartile range is 3 greater than the range of the data.

5. Rates

Calculating Rates

Rate formula: $\text{Rate} = \dfrac{\text{Distance}}{\text{Time}}$

This formula can be modified to $\text{Rate} = \dfrac{\text{Dollars}}{\text{Hour}}$ or $\text{Rate} = \dfrac{\text{Pages}}{\text{Minute}}$, as needed.

Speed is a measure of distance per time, such as miles per hour or meters per second.

When two objects are moving, their average speed is the *total* distance traveled divided by the *total* time.

SHSAT EXPERT NOTE

As you saw with percent and average, if you have two components of the formula, then you can find the third.

A. Regina drove 325 miles in 5 hours. What was her average speed?

_____

B. Bob produces 70 widgets every hour. If he worked 3.5 hours, how many widgets did he make?

_____

C. A grocery store has salmon on sale for $5.50 per pound. If Andres spent $13.75 on salmon, how many pounds did he buy?

_____

D. A car travels at 20 mph for 1 hour and then at 40 mph for 2 hours. What is the average speed for the entire trip?

_____

Math

1. If Jordan took 3 hours to bike 48 miles and 1 mile $= 5,280$ feet, which of the following calculations would give his average speed in feet per minute?

   A. $\dfrac{16 \times 60}{5,280}$

   B. $\dfrac{16 \times 3,600}{5,280}$

   C. $\dfrac{16 \times 5,280}{3,600}$

   D. $\dfrac{16 \times 5,280}{60}$

2. Henry traveled 225 miles in 5 hours, and Demi traveled 350 miles in 7 hours. How much greater was Demi's mean speed, in miles per hour (mph), than Henry's?

   E. 3

   F. $4\dfrac{1}{2}$

   G. 4

   H. 5

3. Last week, Jennifer babysat on 4 different days for the Fosters. She babysat for $3\dfrac{1}{2}$ hours each day. If her total pay for the week was $77.00, how much was she paid per hour?

   A. $4.75

   B. $5.50

   C. $6.20

   D. $22.00

4. Annaliese can clean 3 fish tanks in 45 minutes. Angelina can clean 3 fish tanks in 54 minutes. What is the total number of fish tanks they can clean together in 1.5 hours?

   E. 5

   F. 6

   G. 11

   H. 30

SHSAT EXPERT NOTE

The SHSAT rewards you for being able to manipulate a formula as opposed to just using it in its most basic form. Be flexible on test day!

6. Ratios and Proportions

Calculating Ratios and Proportions

A **ratio** expresses the **relationship** between numbers.

A ratio is a comparison. In a ratio of two numbers, the numerator is often associated with the word *of* and the denominator with the word *to*. For example, the ratio *of* 1 *to* 2 is $\frac{of\ 1}{to\ 2} = \frac{1}{2}$.

A **part-to-part ratio** can be turned into two **part-to-whole ratios** by putting each number in the original ratio over the sum of the parts. If a flower arrangement has two types of flowers and if the ratio of lilies to daisies is 1 to 2, the lilies-to-flowers ratio is $\frac{1}{1+2} = \frac{1}{3}$, and the daisies-to-flowers ratio is $\frac{2}{1+2} = \frac{2}{3}$. This is the same as saying $\frac{1}{3}$ of all the flowers are lilies and $\frac{2}{3}$ are daisies.

A **proportion** is two ratios set equal to each other. Proportions are an efficient way to solve certain problems, but you must exercise caution when setting them up. Watching the units of each piece of the proportion will help you with this. To solve a proportion, cross multiply:

$$\frac{x}{8} = \frac{3}{4}$$
$$4x = 8(3)$$
$$x = \frac{24}{4} \text{ or } 6$$

In a proportional relationship, the **constant of proportionality (k)** is calculated by $k = \frac{y}{x}$. The y-value is always dependent upon the x-value. For instance, in a flower shop, if the number of bouquets made is proportional to the number of roses in stock, the y-value would be the number of bouquets and the x-value would be the number of roses in stock, since the number of bouquets is dependent upon the number of roses. If the store has 24 roses and makes 4 bouquets, the constant of proportionality would be $k = \frac{y}{x} = \frac{4}{24} = \frac{1}{6}$.

SHSAT EXPERT NOTE

Ratios get reduced to their simplest form the same way that fractions do. In fact, fractions are really just a way to express part-to-whole ratios.

1. If $\frac{36}{8} = \frac{9}{y}$, what is the value of y ?

   A. 2

   B. 4

   C. 8

   D. 32

2. There are 60 people in a movie theater. The ratio of people who have seen the movie before to those who haven't seen the movie before is 3:2. How many people have not seen the movie before?

   E. 24

   F. 30

   G. 90

   H. 120

3. Kate began a novel on Monday and read $\frac{1}{4}$ of it. If she reads an additional $\frac{1}{6}$ of the novel on Tuesday, what is the ratio of the amount of the novel she has read to the amount of the novel she has not read?

   A. 1:6

   B. 1:4

   C. 5:12

   D. 5:7

4. The number of hot dogs sold by a food truck is proportional to the amount of time that the food truck is open. The food truck sells 120 hot dogs in 6 hours. What is the constant of proportionality for this relationship?

   E. 2

   F. 6

   G. 20

   H. 120

5. The sum of the numbers a, b, and c is 110. The ratio of a to c is 1:7, and the ratio of b to c is 3:7. What is the value of c ?

   A. 20

   B. 40

   C. 70

   D. 110

SHSAT EXPERT NOTE

On test day, a question may ask for a part-to-part, part-to-whole, or whole-to-part ratio. Pay careful attention to exactly what the question is asking for, and remember that order matters when it comes to ratios.

If you are given a proportion with one missing value, you can cross multiply to solve it.

Conversions

You can set up a proportion to perform unit conversions. This is especially useful when there are multiple conversions or when the units are unfamiliar. For example, there are 8 furlongs in a mile and 3 miles in a league. (These units of measurement are no longer commonly used and may therefore be unfamiliar to you.) Say you're asked to convert 4 leagues into furlongs. A convenient way to do this is to set up a proportion so that equivalent units cancel:

$$4 \text{ leagues} \times \frac{3 \text{ miles}}{1 \text{ league}} \times \frac{8 \text{ furlongs}}{1 \text{ mile}} = 4 \times 3 \times 8 \text{ furlongs} = 96 \text{ furlongs}$$

Notice that all the units cancel out except the furlongs, which is the one you want. You need to do this: set up a proportion to make equivalent units cancel. (Keep track of the units by writing them next to the numbers in the proportion.) You should be left with the units you're converting into.

Learn to look past unfamiliar units to determine what a question is really asking and then solve accordingly.

DIRECTIONS: Use the conversion provided to solve the following questions.

A. 1 calorie = 4.184 joules. How many joules are in 3 calories?

_____

B. 3 slugs = 43.77 kilograms. How many kilograms are in 9 slugs?

_____

1 bushel = 60 pounds of potatoes
1 bushel = 48 pounds of barley

6. Adien has 1,800 pounds of potatoes and 960 pounds of barley. According to the rates above, if he fills bins that hold 1 bushel each, how many bins will he need?

    E. 20

    F. 30

    G. 50

    H. 108

7. On a map legend, 0.675 inches represents 67.5 miles. How many inches represent 1 mile?

    A. 0.001

    B. 0.01

    C. 10

    D. 100

8. The maximum capacity of a water tower is 4,500,000 liters. The tower is $\frac{3}{5}$ full of water. How many kiloliters need to be added to completely fill the tower?

    E. 900

    F. 1,800

    G. 2,700

    H. 3,600

SHSAT EXPERT NOTE

When converting units, set up proportions so that the units you don't want cancel out and leave you with the units you want.

7. The Coordinate Plane

Coordinate Plane Basics

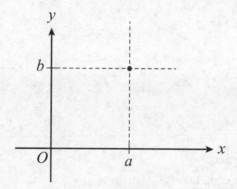

The horizontal line is the **x-axis**.

The vertical line is the **y-axis**.

The two dotted lines meet at the point (a, b).

A location is given by two numbers in parentheses:

- The first is the *x*-coordinate.
- The second is the *y*-coordinate.

If you start at the origin and move:

- To the right, *x* is positive.
- Up, *y* is positive.

SHSAT EXPERT NOTE

Understanding the basics of the coordinate plane will help you unlock more difficult problems and get more points on test day!

Interpreting Graphs

Some questions may ask you to explain what the components of a graph represent. When interpreting a graph:

- Determine what variable is represented on each axis.
- Remember that a point represents (x, y).

The graph below shows cookies baked for a bake sale.

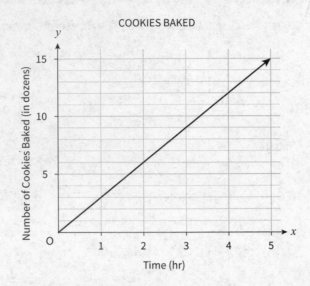

On this graph:

- The *x*-axis shows the time in hours.
- The *y*-axis shows the number of cookies baked in dozens.
- A point (x, y) indicates the number of cookies (y) baked in x hours.

The point $(2, 6)$, for example, indicates that in 2 hours, 6 dozen cookies were baked.

Proportional Relationships

Some graphs depict a **proportional relationship**. The graph of a proportional relationship:

- Passes through the origin $(0, 0)$.
- Reflects a proportional relationship between the *x*- and *y*-values. Every increase (or decrease) in one variable has a proportional increase (or decrease) in the other variable.

The graph of cookies baked shows a proportional relationship for two reasons:

- It passes through the point $(0, 0)$.
- For every increase of 1 hour on the *x*-axis, the number of cookies baked increases by 3 dozen on the *y*-axis.

Recall that the **constant of proportionality** is calculated using $k = \frac{y}{x}$ and that the *y*-value is dependent upon the *x*-value. Plug in any point on the graph, such as $(1, 3)$, to find the constant of proportionality for the cookie graph: $k = \frac{y}{x} = \frac{3}{1} = 3$.

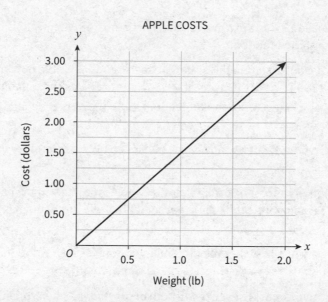

APPLE COSTS

1. A family is buying apples for snacks. The graph shows the cost of apples, in dollars, in relation to the weight, in pounds. What is the meaning of the point (1.5, 2.25) on the graph?

   A. Every 1.0 lb of apples costs $2.25.

   B. Every 2.25 lb of apples costs $1.50.

   C. Every 1.0 lb of apples costs $2.25.

   D. Every 1.5 lb of apples costs $2.25.

2. The number of calories a swimmer burns is proportional to the number of laps she swims. The swimmer completes 20 laps and burns 500 calories. What is the constant of proportionality for this relationship?

   E. 20

   F. 25

   G. 500

   H. 10,000

8. Probability, Combinations, and Permutations

Probability

Probability measures the likelihood of an event taking place. It can be expressed as a fraction ("The probability of snow tomorrow is $\frac{1}{2}$"), a decimal ("There is a 0.5 chance of snow tomorrow"), or a percent ("The probability of snow tomorrow is 50%").

To compute a probability, divide the number of desired outcomes by the number of possible outcomes.

$$\text{Probability} = \frac{\text{Number of Desired Outcomes}}{\text{Number of Possible Outcomes}}$$

Example: If you have 12 shirts in a drawer and 9 of them are white, what is the probability of picking a white shirt at random?

Setup: When picking a shirt in this situation, there are 12 possible outcomes, 1 for each shirt. Of these 12 shirts, 9 of them are white, so there are 9 desired outcomes. Therefore, the probability of picking a white shirt at random is $\frac{9}{12} = \frac{3}{4}$. This probability can also be expressed as 0.75 or 75%.

A **probability of 0** means that the event has no chance of happening. A **probability of 1** means that the event will always happen.

Thus, probability is just another ratio, specifically a part-to-whole ratio. How many parts are desired? How many total parts are there? Finding the probability that something will **not** happen is simply a matter of taking the other piece of the pie.

If the probability of picking a white shirt is $\frac{3}{4}$, the probability of not picking a white shirt is $\frac{1}{4}$, or 1 minus the probability that it will happen. These two events are called **complementary events**.

To find the probability that **two separate events** will both occur, *multiply* the probabilities.

A. There are 24 marbles in a bag: 6 green, 8 red, and 10 white. If one marble is chosen at random, what is the probability that it will be green?

_____

What is the probability that it will **not** be red?

_____

B. Express the probabilities in the above questions as decimals.

Will be green: _____

Will **not** be red: _____

C. The probability that a single cookie taken from a jar will be chocolate chip is $\frac{1}{5}$. If there are 6 chocolate chip cookies in the jar, how many are **not** chocolate chip?

_____

SHSAT EXPERT NOTE

Probability can also be expressed as a fraction or a decimal. Convert probability fractions and decimals as you would any other fractions and decimals.

1. In a drawer, there are 6 white socks, 5 blue socks, and 4 black socks. If one sock is pulled out at random, what is the probability that it will **not** be white?

A. $\frac{4}{15}$

B. $\frac{1}{3}$

C. $\frac{2}{5}$

D. $\frac{3}{5}$

2. There are 10 blue marbles, 4 black marbles, 5 white marbles, and 6 red marbles in a box. If two marbles are drawn at random without replacement, what is the probability that both marbles removed are **not** blue?

E. $\frac{42}{125}$

F. $\frac{7}{20}$

G. $\frac{7}{12}$

H. $\frac{13}{20}$

Number of Pairs of Shoes	Number of Students
1	6
2	29
3	95
4	68
5 or more	32

3. Lacie surveyed students at her school to determine the number of pairs of shoes they owned. Using the table above, what is the probability that a student surveyed owns at least 4 pairs of shoes?

A. $\frac{34}{115}$

B. $\frac{10}{23}$

C. $\frac{13}{23}$

D. $\frac{99}{115}$

SHSAT EXPERT NOTE

Probability falls between 0 and 1, inclusive (meaning that you can have a probability of 0 or 1). Something with a probability of 0 will *never* happen, and something with a probability of 1 will *always* happen.

Permutations and Combinations

Permutations are sequences in which order matters. Permutation questions ask "how many distinct ways" an element can be arranged. A computer password would be an example of a permutation—even if you have the right numbers, letters, and/or special characters, the password won't work if they're out of order.

D. How many different ways can Sydney, Jed, Corinne, and Devin stand in a line?

_____

Combinations are groups in which order does not matter. Combination questions ask "how many ways" might elements of a set be arranged or "how many arrangements" are possible. Choosing from a selection of ice cream flavors would be an example of a combination—the order in which you choose doesn't change the end result.

E. Amy packed 3 shirts and 4 pairs of pants for her vacation. Assuming that an outfit consists of one shirt and one pair of pants, how many different outfits are possible?

_____

F. Miguel has 4 cans of soda and 6 pieces of fruit. He plans to make himself a snack consisting of one can of soda and one piece of fruit. How many snack possibilities does he have?

_____

The previous two problems deal with the possible arrangements of multiple objects. However, the SHSAT is also known to test the possible arrangements of a single type of object.

G. Anita owns 4 different books and will place 2 of them onto her desk. How many combinations of books are possible?

_____

> **SHSAT EXPERT NOTE**
>
> If the same object cannot be used twice, there are fewer possibilities for the second option than there are for the first.

4. An interior designer plans to place 2 potted plants in 1 of 3 possible locations in the house. There are 6 varieties of plant to choose from. If the designer chooses 2 different varieties, how many different combinations of plants are possible?

    E. 12
    F. 15
    G. 36
    H. 45

5. Jennifer has 9 cookie cutters but only enough dough left for 2 cookies, which she will position side by side on the baking sheet. How many different arrangements of cookies on the baking sheet are possible, assuming she uses each cookie cutter no more than once?

    A. 2
    B. 9
    C. 72
    D. 81

6. How many 4-digit numbers can be created using 1, 2, 4, 7, and 9 if each number is used only once?

    E. 20
    F. 30
    G. 60
    H. 120

Answers and Explanations

1. Fractions and Decimals

A. $\frac{39}{72} = \frac{3 \times 13}{3 \times 24} = \frac{13}{24}$

B. $\frac{5}{9} + \frac{2}{6} = \frac{10}{18} + \frac{6}{18} = \frac{16}{18} = \frac{8}{9}$

C. $\frac{1}{2} - \frac{3}{7} = \frac{7}{14} - \frac{6}{14} = \frac{1}{14}$

D. $\frac{1}{3} \times \frac{2}{5} = \frac{2}{15}$

E. $\frac{1}{4} \div \frac{1}{3} = \frac{1}{4} \times \frac{3}{1} = \frac{3}{4}$

F. $4\frac{3}{7} = \frac{(4 \times 7) + 3}{7} = \frac{31}{7}$

G. $\frac{43}{8} = \frac{(5 \times 8) + 3}{8} = \frac{5 \times 8}{8} + \frac{3}{8} = 5\frac{3}{8}$

H. $\frac{9}{5}$

I. $\frac{2}{5}$ compared to $\frac{4}{11}$

LCD of 5 and 11 is 55

$\frac{2 \times 11}{5 \times 11}$ compared to $\frac{4 \times 5}{11 \times 5}$

$\frac{22}{55}$ compared to $\frac{20}{55}$

$\frac{22}{55} = \frac{2}{5}$ is greater

J. $\frac{6}{8}$ compared to $\frac{8}{10}$

$\frac{6}{8} = \frac{3}{4} = 0.75$

$\frac{8}{10} = 0.80$

$0.80 = \frac{8}{10}$ is greater

1. D

Subject: Arithmetic

Getting to the Answer: To add fractions, you need a common denominator. The lowest common denominator of 3, 4, and 12 is 12. Convert all the fractions so they have a denominator of 12, and then calculate their sum.

$$2\frac{2}{3} + 3\frac{3}{4} - 1\frac{1}{3} + 3\frac{1}{12}$$
$$2\frac{8}{12} + 3\frac{9}{12} - 1\frac{4}{12} + 3\frac{1}{12}$$
$$(2 + 3 - 1 + 3) + \left(\frac{8 + 9 - 4 + 1}{12}\right)$$
$$7 + \frac{14}{12}$$
$$7 + 1\frac{2}{12}$$
$$7 + 1\frac{1}{6}$$
$$8\frac{1}{6}$$

Note that you could have also converted the mixed numbers to improper fractions:

$$2\frac{2}{3} + 3\frac{3}{4} - 1\frac{1}{3} + 3\frac{1}{12}$$
$$2\frac{8}{12} + 3\frac{9}{12} - 1\frac{4}{12} + 3\frac{1}{12}$$
$$\frac{32}{12} + \frac{45}{12} - \frac{16}{12} + \frac{37}{12}$$
$$\frac{98}{12}$$
$$8\frac{1}{6}$$

	Fraction	Decimal	Percent
K.	$\frac{1}{4}$	0.25	25%
L.	$\frac{1}{6}$	$0.1\overline{6}$	$16.\overline{6}\%$
M.	$\frac{99}{100}$	0.99	99%
N.	$\frac{7}{20}$	0.35	35%

2. F

Subject: Arithmetic

Getting to the Answer: Write the decimal as a fraction and then simplify: $0.16 = \frac{16}{100} = \frac{4}{25}$. Thus, the value of x is 4.

3. B

Subject: Arithmetic

Getting to the Answer: In the repeating decimal (285714), there are 6 digits. Since 2 is the first digit, it will also be the 1st + 6 = the 7th digit, the 1st + 6 + 6 = the 13th digit, and so on. To find the 415th digit, divide 415 by 6:

$$6\overline{)415} \quad 69\,R1$$

The remainder of 1 means the 415th digit is the same as the 1st digit, which is 2.

2. Rounding, Number Lines, Absolute Value, Factors, and Multiples

1. C

Subject: Arithmetic

Getting to the Answer: Divide the number of guests by the number of plates per pack: $\frac{80}{12} = 6.67$. Since Wes cannot buy 0.67 of a package, round up to 7 so there will be enough plates for all the guests.

2. H

Subject: Arithmetic

Getting to the Answer: To find the value of point B, you need to determine the interval between the tick marks. First determine the distance between A and C, and then divide by the number of sections between A and C. The distance between A and C is $\frac{7}{18} - \frac{2}{9} = \frac{7}{18} - \frac{4}{18} = \frac{3}{18} = \frac{1}{6}$.

There are 6 sections between A and C, so the interval between the tick marks is $\frac{1}{6} \div 6 = \frac{1}{6} \times \frac{1}{6} = \frac{1}{36}$.

B is 4 sections away from A. So the value of point B is $\frac{2}{9} + 4\left(\frac{1}{36}\right) = \frac{2}{9} + \frac{1}{9} = \frac{3}{9} = \frac{1}{3}$.

3. B

Subject: Arithmetic

Getting to the Answer: To find the value of point X, first use $YZ = 2\frac{1}{4}$ to find the value of Z:

$$Z = \frac{4}{5} + 2\frac{1}{4} = \frac{16}{20} + \frac{45}{20} = \frac{61}{20}$$

Next, use $WZ = 5\frac{1}{10}$ to find the value of W:

$$W = \frac{61}{20} - \frac{51}{10} = \frac{61}{20} - \frac{102}{20} = -\frac{41}{20}$$

Then use $WX = 1\frac{3}{5}$ to find the value of X:

$$X = -\frac{41}{20} + \frac{8}{5} = -\frac{41}{20} + \frac{32}{20} = -\frac{9}{20}$$

Note that you also could have converted the fractions to decimals if you find decimals easier to work with.

4. F

Subject: Arithmetic

Getting to the Answer: The difference in value between the two endpoints is 8. Since the midpoint is halfway between the endpoints, it must be 4 units from each end. Four units to the right of -1 and to the left of 7 puts the midpoint at 3.

5. B

Subject: Arithmetic

Getting to the Answer: First find the midpoint of $\overline{AB}$ and the midpoint of $\overline{CD}$:

The midpoint of $\overline{AB}$ is $\frac{-7 + -5}{2} = \frac{-12}{2} = -6$.

The midpoint of $\overline{CD}$ is $\frac{-1 + 3}{2} = \frac{2}{2} = 1$.

Thus, the distance between the two midpoints is $1 - (-6) = 7$ units.

A. 3

B. 3

6. G

Subject: Arithmetic

Getting to the Answer: Keep in mind what the absolute value symbol affects:

$$|9 + (-3.4)| - |(-4) + 1.6| = |5.6| - |-2.4|$$
$$= 5.6 - 2.4 = 3.2$$

C.   Factor

D.   Multiple

E.   Both a factor and multiple

F.   The first three multiples of both 6 and 8 are 24, 48, 72.

G.   Four multiples of 6 can be expressed as $6x$, $6(x + 1)$, $6(x + 2)$, and $6(x + 3)$. Add the multiples and set them equal to 156:

$$6x + 6(x + 1) + 6(x + 2) + 6(x + 3) = 156$$
$$6x + 6x + 6 + 6x + 12 + 6x + 18 = 156$$
$$24x + 36 = 156$$
$$24x = 120$$
$$x = 5$$

Therefore, the multiples are $6(5)$, $6(5 + 1)$, $6(5 + 2)$, $6(5 + 3)$, or 30, 36, 42, 48.

H. Five multiples of 3 can be expressed as $3x$, $3(x + 1)$, $3(x + 2)$, $3(x + 3)$, and $3(x + 4)$. Add the multiples and set them equal to 105:

$$3x + 3(x + 1) + 3(x + 2) + 3(x + 3) + 3(x + 4) = 105$$
$$3x + 3x + 3 + 3x + 6 + 3x + 9 + 3x + 12 = 105$$
$$15x + 30 = 105$$
$$15x = 75$$
$$x = 5$$

The multiples are $3(5)$, $3(5 + 1)$, $3(5 + 2)$, $3(5 + 3)$, $3(5 + 4)$, or 15, 18, 21, 24, and 27.

7. A

Subject: Arithmetic

Getting to the Answer: First list the factors of 30, and then identify how many factors greater than 3 and less than 30 are odd. The positive factors of 30 are 1 and 30, 2 and 15, 3 and 10, and 5 and 6. The factors greater than 3 and less than 30 are 5, 6, 10, and 15. Thus, there are 2 positive odd factors of 30 greater than 3 and less than 30.

8. H

Subject: Arithmetic

Getting to the Answer: To determine which integers are **not** multiples of 3 or 4, list all the numbers in the set and then eliminate those that are multiples of 3 and 4. The set of consecutive integers from 8 to 25 inclusive is [8, 9, 10, 11, 12, 13, 14, 15, 16, 17, 18, 19, 20, 21, 22, 23, 24, 25]. Eliminate the multiples of 3: 9, 12, 15, 18, 21, 24. From the remaining integers in the set, eliminate the multiples of 4: 8, 16, 20.

That leaves [10, 11, 13, 14, 17, 19, 22, 23, 25]. Thus, there are 9 numbers in the set that are not multiples of 3 or 4.

I. 465

J. 12,420

K. 2, 2, 5 (Note: $240 = 2 \times 2 \times 2 \times 2 \times 3 \times 5$, and $980 = 2 \times 2 \times 5 \times 7 \times 7$)

L. 20

9. B

Subject: Arithmetic

Getting to the Answer: To determine the greatest common factor, Backsolve by starting with the largest answer choice and working your way down.

(D) This is a factor of 180 but not of 48.

(C) This is a factor of 48 but not of 180.

(B) This is a factor of both and therefore is the correct answer.

Note that 4, although a factor of both 48 and 180, is not the **greatest** common factor.

Alternatively, you can use prime factorization. The prime factorization of 48 and 180 is $48 = 2 \times 2 \times 2 \times 2 \times 3$ and $180 = 2 \times 2 \times 3 \times 3 \times 5$. Thus, the GCF is $2^2 \times 3 = 12$, **(B)**.

M. $2 \times 2 \times 2 \times 3$

N. $2 \times 2 \times 7$

O. 2, 3, 7

P. $2^3 \times 3 \times 7 = 168$

10. G

Subject: Arithmetic

Getting to the Answer: Since 12 and 32 are both multiples of 4, you only need to check whether the answer choice is a common multiple of 12 and 32. To find the least common multiple, Backsolve by starting with the smallest number and working your way up.

(E) This is a multiple of 32 but not of 12.

(F) This is a multiple of 12 but not of 32.

(G) This is a multiple of both numbers and, therefore, is the correct answer.

Note that although 384 is also a multiple of both 12 and 32, it is not the **least** common multiple.

Alternatively, you could use prime factorization to determine the LCM of 12 and 32. The prime factorization of 12 and 32 is $12 = 2 \times 2 \times 3$ and $32 = 2 \times 2 \times 2 \times 2 \times 2$. So the LCM is $2^5 \times 3 = 96$, **(G)**.

3. Percents

A. $\$300 \times 15\% = \$300 \times 0.15 = \$45$

B. $\$16 - \$16(0.20) = \$16 - \$3.20 = \$12.80$ or $\$16(0.8) = \$12.80$

1. B

Subject: Arithmetic

Getting to the Answer: Plug the known values for part and percent into the Percent $= \dfrac{\text{Part}}{\text{Whole}} \times 100\%$ formula to solve for the whole:

$$30\% = \frac{15}{\text{Whole}} \times 100\%$$

Divide both sides by 100% and isolate the whole:

$$\frac{30\%}{100\%} = \frac{15}{\text{Whole}}$$

$$0.3 \times \text{Whole} = 15$$

$$\text{Whole} = \frac{15}{0.3}$$

$$\text{Whole} = 50$$

2. G

Subject: Arithmetic

Getting to the Answer: First find 2% of one-hundredth of an inch, and then determine the least allowable thickness. One-hundredth of an inch is 0.01, so 2% of 0.01 equals $\dfrac{2}{100} \times 0.01 = 0.0002$. Thus, the least allowable thickness of the filament would be $0.01 - 0.0002 = 0.0098$ inch.

3. B

Subject: Arithmetic

Getting to the Answer: Pick a Number like $100 for the original value. Evaluate each percent discount one at a time. Then calculate the total percent change. Let S represent the sale price.

First, determine the sale price of the sweater: $S = \$100 - 0.2 \times \$100$. So, $S = \$80$.

Next, determine the price Julie paid for the sweater. Let P represent the paid price: $P = \$80 - 0.1 \times \$80$. The price Julie paid is $72.

The question is asking what discount Julie received off of the original price: $\$100 - \$72 = \$28$ and $28 out of $100 is 28%.

4. E

Subject: Arithmetic

Getting to the Answer: Picking Numbers is a good approach for questions that ask about a percentage of an unknown number, and the easiest number to pick is 100. If the original price was 100, then:

$\$100 \times 20\% = \$20$

$\$100 - \$20 = \$80$

$\$80 \times 15\% = \$12$ and $\$12 + \$20 = \$32$ less than the original price

$\dfrac{32}{100} = 32\%$

5. B

Subject: Arithmetic

Getting to the Answer: Calculate the difference between the number of households with 2 tablets and the number of households with 1 tablet, and then divide by the number of households with 1 tablet and multiply by 100%.

The difference between the number of households with 2 tablets and the number of households with 1 tablet is $75 - 60 = 15$. Thus, the percent by which the number of households with 2 tablets is greater than the number of households with 1 tablet is:

$$\frac{15}{60} \times 100\% = 25\%$$

4. Statistics Terms

A. $\text{Average} = \dfrac{\text{Sum of Terms}}{\text{Number of Terms}}$

$$= \frac{3 + 6 + 6}{3}$$

$$= \frac{15}{3}$$

$$= 5$$

B. $\text{Average} = \dfrac{\text{Sum of Terms}}{\text{Number of Terms}}$

$\text{Average} \times \text{\# of Tests} = \text{Sum of Scores}$

$$90 \times 4 = 360$$

C. $\text{Average} = \dfrac{\text{Sum of Terms}}{\text{Number of Terms}}$

$\text{Average Earnings} = \dfrac{\text{Total Earnings}}{\text{\# of Days}}$

$\text{\# of Days} = \dfrac{\text{Total Earnings}}{\text{Average Earnings}}$

$\text{\# of Days} = \dfrac{\$270}{\$30}$

$$= 9$$

1.   B

Subject: Arithmetic

Getting to the Answer: First determine the total cost of the 4 apples, and then use the average formula. Average $= \dfrac{\text{Sum}}{\text{Number of Items}}$ to calculate the mean price for 5 pears.

The total cost of the 4 apples is $4 \times \$1.35 = \$5.40$. Therefore, the mean price of 5 pears is $\dfrac{\$5.40}{5} = \$1.08$.

2.   G

Subject: Statistics and Probability

Getting to the Answer: You need to put the numbers in sequential order and determine which is the middle number: 16, 17, 17, 19, 20, 21, 21. The middle number is 19.

3.   B

Subject: Statistics and Probability

Getting to the Answer: The mode is the number that appears most often. Garrett scored 80 twice, while he scored 70, 90, and 100 only once. Thus, Garrett's mode quiz score is 80.

4.   H

Subject: Statistics and Probability

Getting to the Answer: First calculate the highest lift for each weight class by adding the range to the lowest lift:

Class I: $55 + 54 = 109$

Class II: $58 + 52 = 110$

Class III: $61 + 50 = 111$

The overall lowest lift is 55, and the overall highest lift is 111. Therefore, the overall range of all the lifts is $111 - 55 = 56$.

5.   C

Subject: Statistics and Probability

Getting to the Answer: Test the answer choices against the box plot to determine which is correct. For **(A)**, the *median* of the scores is 7, but this does not mean that half of the scores are *exactly* 7. Rather, half of the scores fall between the minimum (3) and the median (7). Eliminate **(A)**. For **(B)**, the box plot does not show any outliers, or data points outside the box plot. Eliminate **(B)**. For **(C)**, the value of the third quartile is 8, meaning that about one-fourth of the scores are between 8 and the maximum; **(C)** is correct. For the record, **(D)** is incorrect because it mixes up the ranges. The interquartile range is the difference between the value of the third quartile and the value of the first quartile ($8 - 5 = 3$). The range is the difference between the maximum and the minimum ($9 - 3 = 6$). The *range* is 3 greater than the *interquartile range*, not the other way around.

5. Rates

A. $R = \dfrac{d}{t} = \dfrac{325}{5} = 65$ mph

B.   # of widgets $=$ (rate)(time) $= 70 \times 3.5 =$ 245 widgets

C.   # of pounds $= \dfrac{\text{total price}}{\text{price per pound}} = \dfrac{\$13.75}{\$5.50} = 2.5$ pounds

D. $\dfrac{\text{total number of miles}}{\text{total number of hours}} = \dfrac{20 + 40 + 40}{3} = \dfrac{100}{3} = 33.\overline{3}$ mph

1.   D

Subject: Arithmetic

Getting to the Answer: First determine Jordan's rate in miles per hour, and then convert his speed to feet per minute.

To find Jordan's rate in miles per hour, use the information you have about distance (miles) and time (hours): $\dfrac{48 \text{ miles}}{3 \text{ hours}} = 16$ miles per hour. Then use 1 mile $=$ 5,280 feet and 1 hour equals 60 minutes to convert miles per hour to feet per minute:

$$\frac{16 \text{ miles}}{\text{hour}} \times \frac{5{,}280 \text{ feet}}{1 \text{ mile}} \times \frac{1 \text{ hour}}{60 \text{ minutes}} = \frac{16 \times 5{,}280}{60} \text{ feet per minute}$$

2.   H

Subject: Arithmetic

Getting to the Answer: First calculate the mean speeds for Henry and Demi, and then find the difference between their mean speeds.

Henry's mean speed is $\dfrac{225}{5} = 45$ mph.

Demi's mean speed is $\dfrac{350}{7} = 50$ mph.

The difference between their mean speeds is $50 - 45 = 5$ mph, so Demi's speed is 5 mph greater than Henry's.

Math

3. B

Subject: Arithmetic

Getting to the Answer: Use Rate $= \frac{\text{Total Pay}}{\text{Total Hours}}$ to calculate the rate:

$$\text{Rate} = \frac{\$77}{4 \times 3\frac{1}{2} \text{ hours}} = \frac{\$77}{14 \text{ hours}}$$

$$\text{Rate} = \$5.50/\text{hour}$$

4. G

Subject: Arithmetic

Getting to the Answer: First determine how many tanks Annaliese and Angelina can each clean in 1.5 hours. Then calculate how many they can clean together. First calculate for Annaliese:

$$\frac{3}{45} = \frac{x}{90}$$
$$\frac{1}{15} = \frac{x}{90}$$
$$90 = 15x$$
$$6 = x$$

Annaliese can clean 6 tanks in 1.5 hours. Note that reducing the fraction to its lowest terms simplifies the calculations. Now calculate for Angelina:

$$\frac{3}{54} = \frac{y}{90}$$
$$\frac{1}{18} = \frac{y}{90}$$
$$90 = 18y$$
$$5 = y$$

Angelina can clean 5 tanks in 1.5 hours.

Thus, Annaliese and Angelina can clean together $6 + 5 = 11$ tanks in 1.5 hours.

6. Ratios and Proportions

1. A

Subject: Arithmetic

Getting to the Answer: Cross multiply to solve for y.

$$\frac{36}{8} = \frac{9}{y}$$
$$36y = 72$$
$$y = 2$$

2. E

Subject: Arithmetic

Getting to the Answer: First determine the part-to-whole ratio from the given information, and then set up a proportion to solve for the number of people who have not seen the movie before, x.

The ratio given is a part-to-part ratio. Since the question gives the total number of people in the movie theater, you need to use the part-to-whole ratio. The number of people who have not seen the movie before to the total number of movie attendees is $\frac{2}{2+3} = \frac{2}{5}$.

Setting up the proportion to solve for x gives:

$$\frac{x}{60} = \frac{2}{5}$$
$$5x = 120$$
$$x = 24$$

3. D

Subject: Arithmetic

Getting to the Answer: First calculate how much of the book Kate has read: $\frac{1}{4} + \frac{1}{6} = \frac{3}{12} + \frac{2}{12} = \frac{5}{12}$. She read 5 parts. Then calculate the amount of the book she has not read: $1 - \frac{5}{12} = \frac{7}{12}$. Kate did not read 7 parts. Compare the parts read to the parts unread in a ratio; in this case, parts read to parts unread equals 5:7.

4. G

Subject: Arithmetic

Getting to the Answer: The constant of proportionality (k) is calculated by dividing the y-value by the x-value: $k = \frac{y}{x}$. The y-value is always dependent upon the x-value. Here, since the number of hot dogs sold is dependent upon how long the food truck is open, the number of hot dogs sold (120) is the y-value and the number of hours open (6) is the x-value. Plug in these values to calculate the constant of proportionality:

$$k = \frac{y}{x} = \frac{120}{6} = 20$$

5. C

Subject: Arithmetic

Getting to the Answer: Since both ratios have a c in common, solve each ratio in terms of c:

$$\frac{a}{c} = \frac{1}{7}$$
$$7a = c$$
$$a = \frac{c}{7}$$

$$\frac{b}{c} = \frac{3}{7}$$
$$7b = 3c$$
$$b = \frac{3c}{7}$$

Since $a + b + c = 110$, substitute a and b and solve for c:

$$\frac{c}{7} + \frac{3c}{7} + c = 110$$
$$\frac{11c}{7} = 110$$
$$c = 70$$

A. $3 \text{ calories} \times \frac{4.184 \text{ joules}}{1 \text{ calorie}} = 3 \times 4.184 \text{ joules}$, so there are 12.552 joules in 3 calories.

B. $9 \text{ slugs} \times \frac{43.77 \text{ kilograms}}{3 \text{ slugs}} = \frac{(9 \times 43.77)}{3} \text{ kilograms}$, and since $9 \div 3 = 3$ and $3 \times 43.77 = 131.31$, there are 131.31 kilograms in 9 slugs.

6. G

Subject: Arithmetic

Getting to the Answer: Use proportions to make the conversion from pounds to bushels.

Potatoes:

$$\frac{1,800}{x} = \frac{60}{1}$$
$$1,800 = 60x$$
$$30 = x$$

Barley:

$$\frac{960}{y} = \frac{48}{1}$$
$$960 = 48y$$
$$20 = y$$

Total bushels $= 30 + 20 = 50$.

7. B

Subject: Arithmetic

Getting to the Answer: Set up a proportion to solve for the number of inches representing 1 mile. Let x be the number of inches:

$$\frac{x}{1} = \frac{0.675}{67.5}$$
$$67.5x = 0.675$$
$$x = 0.01$$

8. F

Subject: Arithmetic

Getting to the Answer: First find the number of liters that need to be added to fill the tower. The tower is $\frac{3}{5}$ full, so it is $\frac{2}{5}$ empty. $\frac{2}{5} \times 4,500,000 = 1,800,000$. Use the conversion 1 kiloliter $= 1,000$ liters to calculate the number of kiloliters: $\frac{1,800,000}{1,000} = 1,800$ kiloliters.

7. The Coordinate Plane

1. D

Subject: Arithmetic

Getting to the Answer: A point on a graph represents (x, y). On this graph, the x-axis is the weight in pounds, and the y-axis is the cost in dollars. Thus, for the point $(1.5, 2.25)$, 1.5 corresponds to the weight of the apples in pounds, and 2.25 corresponds to the cost in dollars. Choice **(D)** is correct.

2. F

Subject: Arithmetic

Getting to the Answer: If the number of calories burned is proportional to the number of laps completed, the number of calories burned is dependent upon the number of laps completed. Thus, the number of calories is the y-variable, and the number of laps is the x-variable. A proportional relationship can be modeled by the equation $k = \frac{y}{x}$, in which k is the constant of proportionality. Plug in the given information and solve for k:

$$k = \frac{y}{x}$$
$$k = \frac{500}{20}$$
$$k = 25$$

8. Probability, Combinations, and Permutations

A. The probability of picking a green marble is $\frac{6}{24} = \frac{1}{4}$. There are 8 red out of 24 total marbles, so 16 are not red. The probability of picking a marble that is not red is $\frac{16}{24} = \frac{2}{3}$.

B. Probability that it is green $= 0.25$
Probability that it is not red $= 0.67$

C. $\frac{1}{5}$ of the cookies are chocolate chip; 6 is $\frac{1}{5}$ of 30, so there must be 30 total cookies. Therefore, 24 are not chocolate chip.

1. D

Subject: Statistics and Probability

Getting to the Answer: Use the probability formula, Probability $= \dfrac{\text{Number of Desired Outcomes}}{\text{Number of Possible Outcomes}}$. The non-white socks are all of the blue and black socks, so there are 9 socks that are not white out of a total of 15 socks:

$$\text{Probability} = \frac{9}{15} = \frac{3}{5}$$

2. F

Subject: Statistics and Probability

Getting to the Answer: The total number of marbles is $10 + 4 + 5 + 6 = 25$. The number of marbles that are not blue are $4 + 5 + 6 = 15$.

The probability of the first marble not being blue is $\frac{15}{25}$. Now, there are 14 marbles left that are not blue. The probability of the second marble not being blue is $\frac{14}{24}$. Multiply these two probabilities to get

$$\frac{15}{25} \times \frac{14}{24} = \frac{3}{5} \times \frac{7}{12} = \frac{3 \times 7}{5 \times 12} = \frac{7}{5 \times 4} = \frac{7}{20}.$$

3. B

Subject: Statistics and Probability

Getting to the Answer: First determine the total number of students surveyed: $6 + 29 + 95 + 68 + 32 = 230$. Then determine the number of students who own at least 4 pairs of shoes. Students who own 4 pairs of shoes (68) + students who own 5 or more (32) $= 68 + 32 = 100$.

The probability of a student who was surveyed owning at least 4 pairs of shoes is $\frac{100}{230} = \frac{10}{23}$.

D. The total number of ways 4 people can stand in a line is $4 \times 3 \times 2 \times 1 = 24$.

E. For each of the 3 shirts, 4 pairs of pants are possible. That makes 12 total combinations (the product of 3 and 4).

F. For each of the 4 cans of soda, 6 pieces of fruit are possible. That makes 24 total combinations (the product of 4 and 6).

G. Figure out how many different combinations of pairs of books are possible by using A, B, C, and D for each book and listing the combinations: AB, AC, AD, BC, BD, CD.

4. H

Subject: Statistics and Probability

Getting to the Answer: First figure out how many different combinations of pairs of plants are possible. Use 1, 2, 3, 4, 5, and 6 to represent the varieties, and list the possible pairs:

1, 2; 1, 3; 1, 4; 1, 5; 1, 6

2, 3; 2, 4; 2, 5; 2, 6

3, 4; 3, 5; 3, 6

4, 5; 4, 6

5, 6

There are 15 different possible pairs for one location. Since there 3 possible locations, multiply the total number of combinations by 3 to get the total number of arrangements the designer can create: $3 \times 15 = 45$.

5. C

Subject: Statistics and Probability

Getting to the Answer: For each of the 9 cookie cutters Jennifer could make the first cookie with, she has 8 others left to make the second cookie. So the total number of cookie arrangements possible on the baking sheet is $9 \times 8 = 72$.

6. H

Subject: Statistics and Probability

Getting to the Answer: Determine the number of choices for each digit, and then multiply to get the total number of possibilities. For the first digit, there are 5 choices; for the second digit, there are 4 choices; for the third digit, there are 3 choices; and for the fourth digit, there are 2 choices. The total number of possibilities is thus $5 \times 4 \times 3 \times 2 = 120$.

[CHAPTER 11]

ALGEBRA

CHAPTER OBJECTIVES

By the end of this chapter, you will be able to:

- Evaluate an algebraic expression
- Isolate a variable
- Solve an inequality for a range of values
- Identify the graph of an inequality or a system of inequalities

1. Algebraic Expressions and Equations with One Variable

Evaluate an Algebraic Expression

Evaluating an expression typically involves substituting a given value (or values) for the variables into the expression and then simplifying. For example, the value of $3x + 4y$ when $x = 5$ and $y = -2$ is $3(5) + 4(-2) = 15 - 8 = 7$.

- **A.** If $a = 3$, then $a(5 - a) =$
- **B.** If $a = 3$, then $a(5) - a =$
- **C.** If $b = -7$, then $4 - b =$
- **D.** If $b = 7$, then $4 - b =$
- **E.** When $c = 3$ and $d = 2$, what is the value of $c^d - d^c$?
- **F.** If $n = 4$, then $2\left(\dfrac{n}{n+1}\right) =$
- **G.** If $x = 2$, then $x(3^x) =$

1. What is the value of $x(y - 2) + xz$ if $x = 2$, $y = 5$, and $z = 7$?

   A. 12

   B. 20

   C. 22

   D. 28

2. If $x = 3$, $y = 2$, and $z = 0.5$, then $x^2 - 5yz + y^2 =$

   E. 1

   F. 4

   G. 8

   H. 12

3. If $a + b = 17$ and $c = 2$, then $ac + bc =$

   A. 17

   B. 18

   C. 34

   D. Cannot be determined from the information given.

SHSAT EXPERT NOTE

You must always follow the order of operations when solving algebraic equations. PEMDAS = Parentheses; Exponents; Multiplication/Division from left to right; Addition/Subtraction from left to right.

Solve Equations with One Variable

To **solve an equation**, isolate the variable. To solve $5x - 12 = -2x + 9$, first get all the x-terms on one side by adding $2x$ to both sides: $7x - 12 = 9$. Then add 12 to both sides: $7x = 21$. Finally, divide both sides by 7 to get $x = 3$. As long as you do the same thing to both sides of the equation, the equation is still balanced.

DIRECTIONS: Solve each of the following equations for the variable.

H. $2x + 4 = 8$

I. $\frac{x}{3} + 1 = 5$

J. $x - 5 = 3x - 10$

K. If $\left(\frac{1}{3}\right)x = 8$, then $\left(\frac{1}{4}\right)x =$

4. If $0.5n + 2 = 3$, what is the value of n?

    E. 0.5

    F. 1

    G. 2

    H. 2.5

5. For what value of x is $2x - 13 = 25$ true?

    A. 6

    B. 6.5

    C. 19

    D. 38

6. The sum of five consecutive multiples of 2 is 130. What are the five numbers?

    E. 12, 14, 16, 18, 20

    F. 18, 20, 22, 24, 26

    G. 22, 24, 26, 28, 30

    H. 26, 28, 30, 32, 34

SHSAT EXPERT NOTE

When manipulating an equation, always perform the same operation on both sides of the equal sign.

2. Equations with Two Variables

Solve Equations with Two Variables

Equations often contain more than one variable. When two variables are present, solve the equation piece by piece. If you are given a value for one or more variables, substitute the value for its variable. Then isolate the remaining variable and solve.

A. What is the value of a in the equation $3a - 6 = b$ if $b = 18$?

B. If $k = \frac{1}{3}$ in the equation $2m + \frac{1}{3}k = \frac{1}{3}k^2$, then $m =$

C. If $\frac{4a + b}{b} = 7$ and $b = 2$, $a =$

D. If x is a positive odd number less than 10, list all of the potential solutions for y in the following equation:

$$x^2 + 2x + 1 = y$$

x	y

SHSAT EXPERT NOTE

Always set up an equation and write it down rather than trying to work it out in your head.

---

1. What is the value of x in the equation $5x - 7 = y$ if $y = 8$?

    A. -1

    B. 1

    C. 3

    D. 33

2. If $q \neq 0$, for what value of p is $p(12q) = 6q$?

    E. 0.5

    F. 2

    G. 4

    H. 8

3.   If $m = 2$ and $2m(2m - 3n) = 34$, what is the value of n ?

   A. -6

   B. $-\frac{3}{2}$

   C. -1

   D. $\frac{3}{2}$

4.   If $\frac{x}{y} = \frac{2}{5}$ and $x = 10$, $y =$

   E.   4

   F.   10

   G.   15

   H.   25

5.   The set of possible values of a is $\{1, 4, 7\}$. If $3b = 10 - a$, what is the set of possible values of b ?

   A. $\{1, 2, 3\}$

   B. $\{3, 6, 9\}$

   C. $\{6, 12, 18\}$

   D. $\{9, 18, 27\}$

SHSAT EXPERT NOTE

Perform only one step at a time. First substitute, then simplify the resulting equation, and then isolate the remaining variable.

Solve for One Variable in Terms of the Other

Even if you aren't given numerical values to substitute, you can still solve for one variable in an equation in terms of the other variable(s).

   E.   If $2r + 8s = 24$, then $r =$

   F.   Solve for c in the equation $b(a - 1) = \frac{bc}{2}$.

   G. $3x + 2y + 4z = 12$

   Solve for each of the variables.

   $x =$

   $y =$

   $z =$

SHSAT EXPERT NOTE

When you perform the same operation to both sides of an equation, you are not altering the equation but merely rearranging it.

6. If $\dfrac{(a+b)}{2} = 8$, then $a =$

   E. $b + 4$

   F. $4 - b$

   G. $16 - b$

   H. $\dfrac{16}{b}$

7. If $3(a - 2) = 5m - 6 + 2a$, what is the value of a in terms of m ?

   A. $\dfrac{3m}{2}$

   B. 3

   C. $5m$

   D. $3m - 3$

8. If $3(2t + 6) = 12s$, then $t =$

   E. $2s + 3$

   F. $2s - 3$

   G. $4s$

   H. $3s - 8$

Expressions and Equations

   H. Solve $2(3 + 1)^2 + 5 - 6 \div 3 =$

   I. When $x = 2$, what is the value of $2x + 3$?

   J. When $x = \frac{1}{4}$, $y = \frac{1}{5}$, and $z = \frac{1}{6}$, what is the value of $\frac{x}{15} + \frac{y}{6} + \frac{z}{5}$?

   K. What is x when $4x + 3 = 19$?

   L. Solve for x in terms of y: $7xy = 3$

SHSAT EXPERT NOTE

Always perform the same mathematical operation on both sides of an equation.

---

9. If $3x + 7 = 14$, then $x =$

   A. -14

   B. 0

   C. $\dfrac{7}{3}$

   D. 7

10. If $4z - 3 = -19$, then $z =$

    E. -16

    F. -5

    G. -4

    H.   4

11. For what value of y is $4(y - 1) = 2(y + 2)$?

    A.   0

    B.   2

    C.   4

    D.   6

12. If $5p + 12 = 17 - 4\left(\dfrac{p}{2} + 1\right)$, what is the value of p ?

    E. $\dfrac{1}{7}$

    F. $\dfrac{1}{3}$

    G. $\dfrac{6}{7}$

    H. $1\dfrac{2}{7}$

13. If $-2x + xy = 30$ and $y = 8$, then what is the value of x ?

    A. $-\dfrac{15}{4}$

    B. $-\dfrac{15}{16}$

    C.   3

    D.   5

14. $15 + xy \div 3 = 35$ and $x = 5$. What is the value of y ?

    E. $-\dfrac{2}{3}$

    F. $5\dfrac{1}{4}$

    G.   12

    H.   18

15. If $\dfrac{2x}{5y} = 6$, what is the value of y in terms of x ?

    A. $\dfrac{x}{15}$

    B. $\dfrac{x}{2}$

    C. $\dfrac{15}{x}$

    D. $15x$

16. If $3ab = 6$, what is the value of a in terms of b ?

    E. 2

    F. $\dfrac{2}{b}$

    G. $2b^2$

    H. $2b$

17. If $2(a + m) = 5m - 3 + a$, what is the value of a in terms of m ?

    A. $\dfrac{3m}{2}$

    B. 3

    C. $m - 1$

    E. $3m - 3$

SHSAT EXPERT NOTE

Questions that ask for one variable "in terms of" another can also be answered effectively by Picking Numbers for the variables. Always pick numbers that fit the rules, and be sure to check every answer choice.

---

3. Inequalities

Standard Inequalities

Solving an inequality means finding the set of all values that satisfy the given statement. They work just like equations: your task is to isolate the variable on one side of the inequality symbol. The only significant difference is that **if you multiply or divide by a negative number, you must reverse the direction** of the inequality symbol.

    A. Solve for a: $4a + 5 > 9a + 15$

    B. Solve for y: $2y - 3 < 9 + y$

    C. Solve for y: $3y - 10 > 11$

    D. Solve for x: $7 - 2x > 3y$

1. Which of the following is equivalent to the inequality $9 > 5x - 6$?

    A. $x > -3$

    B. $x > 3$

    C. $x < 3$

    D. $x > 5$

2. Which of the following is equivalent to $13 - 2y < 7$?

    E. $y < -\dfrac{7}{13}$

    F. $y < 3$

    G. $y > 3$

    H. $y < 10$

3. What is the range of possible values of y when $2y - 3 < 6$?

    A. $y > \dfrac{2}{9}$

    B. $y > \dfrac{3}{2}$

    C. $y < \dfrac{9}{2}$

    D. $y < 6$

SHSAT EXPERT NOTE

Always perform the same operation on both sides of the inequality.

Always reverse the inequality sign when multiplying or dividing by a negative number.

Ranges

Ranges are inequalities with three parts. When you perform a mathematical operation on one part, you have to do the same thing to all three parts.

DIRECTIONS: Find the range of values for each of these variables.

E. y when $(y - 2)$ is greater than 3 and less than 10

F. z when $(2z)$ is less than 6 and greater than -2

G. x^2 when x lies between 8 and 9

H. a when $-a$ lies between -4 and 7

4. Which of the following is equivalent to the inequality $7 > -3x > -12$?

    E. $-7 < x < 12$

    F. $\dfrac{7}{3} < x < 4$

    G. $-\dfrac{7}{3} < x < 4$

    H. $-4 < x < -\dfrac{7}{3}$

5. Which of the following is equivalent to the inequality $-8 < -2x < 12$?

   A. $-3 < x < 2$

   B. $-4 < x < 6$

   C. $-6 < x < 4$

   D. $-12 < x < 8$

6. The number a is a number less than -3. What is the range of possible values of $\frac{1}{a^2}$?

   E. $\frac{1}{a^2} < -9$

   F. $\frac{1}{a^2} < -3$

   G. $-\frac{1}{9} < \frac{1}{a^2} < \frac{1}{9}$

   H. $0 < \frac{1}{a^2} < \frac{1}{9}$

> ### SHSAT EXPERT NOTE
>
> When you divide or multiply the parts of a range by a negative number, you must change the direction of the inequality signs.

Number Lines

The solution to an inequality can be represented on a number line. For example, $x > 4$ could be graphed like this:

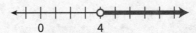

Notice the open dot at 4, indicating that 4 is not a solution to the inequality. This is called a **strict** inequality. By contrast, the graph of $x \le 4$ looks like this:

Notice the closed (solid) dot, indicating that 4 should be included in the solution set for the inequality.

DIRECTIONS: Draw the following ranges on the number lines provided.

I. $-6 < x < 4$

J. $4 > -2y > -2$

K. $3 \leq z \leq 5$

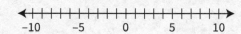

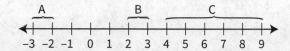

7. The value x^2 is greater than 4 and less than 9. Which region or regions on the number line above represent the range of values for x ?

A. A

B. B

C. C

D. A and B

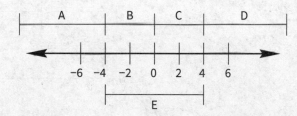

8. Which region(s) on the number line above is the set of all possible values of $-4x$, where $x > 1$?

E. A

F. B

G. C

H. D and E

Answers and Explanations

1. Algebraic Expressions and Equations with One Variable

A. $a(5 - a) = 3(5 - 3) = 3(2) = 6$

B. $a(5) - a = 3(5) - 3 = 15 - 3 = 12$

C. $4 - b = 4 - (-7) = 4 + 7 = 11$

D. $4 - b = 4 - 7 = -3$

E. $c^d - d^c = 3^2 - 2^3 = 9 - 8 = 1$

F. $2\left(\dfrac{n}{n+1}\right) = 2\left(\dfrac{4}{4+1}\right) = 2\left(\dfrac{4}{5}\right) = \dfrac{8}{5}$

G. $x(3^x) = 2(3^2) = 2(9) = 18$

H. $2x + 4 = 8$
$2x = 4$
$x = 2$

I. $\dfrac{x}{3} + 1 = 5$
$\dfrac{x}{3} = 4$
$x = 12$

J. $x - 5 = 3x - 10$
$-5 = 2x - 10$
$5 = 2x$
$\dfrac{5}{2} = x$

K. $\left(\dfrac{1}{3}\right)x = 8$
$x = 24$
$\left(\dfrac{1}{4}\right)x = \left(\dfrac{1}{4}\right)(24) = 6$

1. B
Subject: Algebra

Getting to the Answer: The equation is ready for substitution as it stands. Just substitute:

$$x(y - 2) + xz = (2)[(5) - 2] + (2)(7) = 6 + 14 = 20$$

2. G
Subject: Algebra

Getting to the Answer: Substitute carefully:

$$x^2 - 5yz + y^2 =$$
$$(3)^2 - 5(2)(0.5) + (2)^2 =$$
$$9 - 5 + 4 = 8$$

3. C
Subject: Algebra

Getting to the Answer: Given that you are looking for $ac + bc$, you can simplify by factoring:

$$ac + bc = c(a + b)$$

You know that $c = 2$ and $a + b = 17$; therefore $c(a + b) = 2(17) = 34$.

4. G
Subject: Algebra

Getting to the Answer: You need to isolate the variable:

$0.5n + 2 = 3$	
$0.5n = 1$ or $\frac{1}{2}n = 1$	Multiply by 2.
$n = 2$	

5. C
Subject: Algebra

Getting to the Answer: Isolate the x:

$2x = 13 + 25$	
$2x = 38$	Divide by 2.
$x = 19$	

6. G

Subject: Arithmetic

Getting to the Answer: Each multiple of 2 is 2 more than the previous. Let x represent the smallest number:

$$x + (x + 2) + (x + 4) + (x + 6) + (x + 8) = 130$$
$$5x + 20 = 130$$
$$5x = 110$$
$$x = 22$$

Thus, 22 is the smallest of the five numbers.

2. Equations with Two Variables

A. $3a - 6 = b$; plug in $b = 18$
$3a - 6 = (18)$
$3a = 24$
$a = 8$

B. $2m + \frac{1}{3}k = \frac{1}{3}k^2$; plug in $k = \frac{1}{3}$
$2m + \frac{1}{3}\left(\frac{1}{3}\right) = \frac{1}{3}\left(\frac{1}{3}\right)^2$
$2m + \frac{1}{9} = \frac{1}{27}$
$2m = -\frac{2}{27}$
$m = -\frac{1}{27}$

C. $\frac{4a + b}{b} = 7$; plug in $b = 2$
$\frac{4a + (2)}{(2)} = 7$
$4a + 2 = 14$
$4a = 12$
$a = 3$

D.

x	y
1	4
3	16
5	36
7	64
9	100

1. C

Subject: Algebra

Getting to the Answer: Plug in 8 for y and isolate x:

$5x - 7 = y$	
$5x - 7 = (8)$	Substitute $y = 8$.
$5x = 15$	Isolate.
$x = 3$	Simplify.

2. E

Subject: Algebra

Getting to the Answer: Solve for p:

$p(12q) = 6q$	
$p = \frac{6q}{12q}$	Divide by $12q$.
$p = \frac{1}{2}$ or 0.5	Simplify.

3. B

Subject: Algebra

Getting to the Answer: Substitute:

$$2m(2m - 3n) = 34$$
$$2(2)[2(2) - 3n] = 34$$
$$4(4 - 3n) = 34$$
$$16 - 12n = 34$$
$$-12n = 18$$
$$n = -\frac{18}{12} = -\frac{3}{2}$$

4. H

Subject: Algebra

Getting to the Answer: Cross multiply and then substitute the value given for x:

$$\frac{x}{y} = \frac{2}{5}$$
$$5x = 2y$$
$$5(10) = 2y$$
$$50 = 2y$$
$$25 = y$$

Math

5. A

Subject: Algebra

Getting to the Answer: $3b = 10 - a$, so $b = \dfrac{10 - a}{3}$. Substitute each value of a into the equation to find the set of values of b:

$$b = \frac{10 - (1)}{3} = 3$$
$$b = \frac{10 - (4)}{3} = 2$$
$$b = \frac{10 - (7)}{3} = 1$$

The set of possible values of b is $\{1, 2, 3\}$.

E. $2r + 8s = 24$

$2r = 24 - 8s$

$r = 12 - 4s$

F. $b(a - 1) = \dfrac{bc}{2}$

$2b(a - 1) = bc$

$2(a - 1) = c$

$2a - 2 = c$

G. $3x + 2y + 4z = 12$

Solve for x:

$3x = 12 - 2y - 4z$

$x = 4 - \dfrac{2}{3}y - \dfrac{4}{3}z$

Solve for y:

$2y = 12 - 3x - 4z$

$y = 6 - \dfrac{3}{2}x - 2z$

Solve for z:

$4z = 12 - 3x - 2y$

$z = 3 - \dfrac{3}{4}x - \dfrac{1}{2}y$

6. G

Subject: Algebra

Getting to the Answer: Keep in mind what question you are answering:

$\dfrac{(a + b)}{2} = 8$ $(a + b) = 16$ $a = 16 - b$	After you have eliminated the fraction, isolate a.

7. C

Subject: Algebra

Getting to the Answer: Simplify and then isolate a:

$3(a - 2) = 5m - 6 + 2a$	
$3a - 6 = 5m - 6 + 2a$	Subtract $2a$.
$a - 6 = 5m - 6$	Add 6.
$a = 5m$	

8. F

Subject: Algebra

Getting to the Answer: In this case, you have to distribute through and then isolate:

$3(2t + 6) = 12s$	
$6t + 18 = 12s$	Divide each side by 6 to simplify.
$t + 3 = 2s$	
$t = 2s - 3$	

H. $2(3 + 1)^2 + 5 - 6 \div 3 =$

$2(4)^2 + 5 - 6 \div 3 =$

$2(16) + 5 - 6 \div 3 =$

$32 + 5 - 6 \div 3 =$

$32 + 5 - 2 =$

$37 - 2 =$

35

I. When $x = 2$, $2x + 3 = 2(2) + 3 = 4 + 3 = 7$.

J. When $x = \dfrac{1}{4}$, $y = \dfrac{1}{5}$, and $z = \dfrac{1}{6}$,

$$\frac{x}{15} + \frac{y}{6} + \frac{z}{5} =$$

$$\frac{\left(\frac{1}{4}\right)}{15} + \frac{\left(\frac{1}{5}\right)}{6} + \frac{\left(\frac{1}{6}\right)}{5} =$$

$$\frac{1}{60} + \frac{1}{30} + \frac{1}{30} =$$

$$\frac{1}{60} + \frac{2}{60} + \frac{2}{60} =$$

$$\frac{5}{60} = \frac{1}{12}$$

K. $4x + 3 = 19$

$4x = 16$

$x = 4$

L. $7xy = 3$

$x = \dfrac{3}{7y}$

9. C

Subject: Algebra

Getting to the Answer: Isolate the terms with x in them and then solve:

$$3x + 7 = 14$$
$$3x = 7$$
$$x = \frac{7}{3}$$

10. G

Subject: Algebra

Getting to the Answer: Solve for z. Once you have the z-terms on one side, simplify:

$$4z - 3 = -19$$
$$4z = -16$$
$$\frac{4z}{4} = \frac{-16}{4}$$
$$z = -4$$

11. C

Subject: Algebra

Getting to the Answer: The problem is straightforward. Distribute and solve:

$$4(y - 1) = 2(y + 2)$$
$$4y - 4 = 2y + 4$$
$$2y = 8$$
$$\frac{2y}{2} = \frac{8}{2}$$
$$y = 4$$

12. E

Subject: Algebra

Getting to the Answer: Distribute, combine like terms, and solve for p:

$$5p + 12 = 17 - 4\left(\frac{p}{2} + 1\right)$$
$$5p + 12 = 17 - 2p - 4$$
$$5p + 12 = 13 - 2p$$
$$7p = 1$$
$$p = \frac{1}{7}$$

13. D

Subject: Algebra

Getting to the Answer: Substitute 8 for y:

$$-2x + xy = 30$$
$$-2x + x(8) = 30$$
$$6x = 30$$
$$x = 5$$

14. G

Subject: Algebra

Getting to the Answer: Substitute 5 for x:

$15 + xy \div 3 = 35$	
$15 + (5)y \div 3 = 35$	
$5y \div 3 = 20$	Subtract 15 from both sides.
$5y = 60$	Multiply both sides by 3 to isolate the y-term.
$y = 12$	Divide by 5 to solve for y.

15. A

Subject: Algebra

Getting to the Answer:

$$\frac{2x}{5y} = 6$$
$$2x = 30y$$
$$\frac{2x}{30} = \frac{30y}{30}$$
$$\frac{x}{15} = y$$

16. F

Subject: Algebra

Getting to the Answer: Isolate a:

$3ab = 6$	
$a = \dfrac{6}{3b}$	Divide by $3b$.
$a = \dfrac{2}{b}$	Simplify.

17. D

Subject: Algebra

Getting to the Answer: You'll need to get the *a*-terms on one side of the equation:

$2(a + m) = 5m - 3 + a$	Distribute the 2.
$2a + 2m = 5m - 3 + a$	Combine like terms.
$a = 3m - 3$	Isolate *a*.

3. Inequalities

A. $4a + 5 > 9a + 15$
$-10 > 5a$
$-2 > a$

B. $2y - 3 < 9 + y$
$y < 12$

C. $3y - 10 > 11$
$3y > 21$
$y > 7$

D. $7 - 2x > 3y$
$-2x > 3y - 7$
$x < -\dfrac{3y + 7}{2}$

1. C

Subject: Algebra

Getting to the Answer: Solve it like an equation:

$$9 > 5x - 6$$
$$9 + 6 > 5x$$
$$15 > 5x$$
$$3 > x$$
$$x < 3$$

2. G

Subject: Algebra

Getting to the Answer: Solve for *y*:

$$13 - 2y < 7$$
$$-2y < -6$$
$$y < 3 \quad \text{Divide by } -2, \text{ and reverse}$$
the inequality sign.
$$y > 3$$

3. C

Subject: Algebra

Getting to the Answer: Solve for *y*:

$$2y - 3 < 6$$
$$2y < 9$$
$$y < \frac{9}{2}$$

E. $3 < y - 2 < 10$
$5 < y < 12$

F. $-2 < 2z < 6$
$-1 < z < 3$

G. $8 < x < 9$
$64 < x^2 < 81$

H. $-4 < -a < 7$
$4 > a > -7$
$-7 < a < 4$

4. G

Subject: Algebra

Getting to the Answer: Solve for the range of *x*:

$7 > -3x > -12$	Divide through by -3, and reverse the signs.
$-\dfrac{7}{3} < x < 4$	

5. C

Subject: Algebra

Getting to the Answer: Solve for the range of *x*:

$$-8 < -2x < 12$$
$$-4 < -x < 6$$
$$4 > x > -6 \text{ or } -6 < x < 4$$

Math

6. H

Subject: Algebra

Getting to the Answer: Pick Numbers to help solve this abstract range. If a is a number less than -3, to find the range of values for $\frac{1}{a^2}$, you have to plug in values for a starting with -3 and working downward (-4, -5, etc.).

If $a = -3$, then $\frac{1}{a^2} = \frac{1}{9}$. This sets the upper boundary.

If $a = -4$, then $\frac{1}{a^2} = \frac{1}{16}$. If $a = -5$, then $\frac{1}{a^2} = \frac{1}{25}$.

As a gets smaller, the value gets closer to zero but never reaches zero, so 0 is the lower boundary:

$$0 < \frac{1}{a^2} < \frac{1}{9}$$

I. Put open dots at -6 and 4, and then shade between.

J. Simplify the range first by dividing all sides by -2, so that $-2 < y < 1$. Put open dots at -2 and 1, and then shade between -2 and 1.

K. Put closed dots at 3 and 5, and then shade between.

7. G

Subject: Algebra

Getting to the Answer: First, set up the inequality described in the question stem: x is the square root of x^2, so the parameters of x will be the square roots of the given parameters of x^2:

$$4 < x^2 < 9$$
$$\sqrt{4} < \sqrt{x^2} < \sqrt{9}$$
$$2 < x < 3 \text{ or } -2 > x > -3$$

8. E

Subject: Algebra

Getting to the Answer: Consider the original inequality.

$x > 1$	
$-4x$	Consider what you must do to x to produce the new expression.
$(-4)x < 1(-4)$	Multiply both sides of the inequality by -4. Remember to change the sign.
$-4x < -4$	Look for the values that are less than -4.

Math

CHAPTER 12

GEOMETRY

CHAPTER OBJECTIVES

By the end of this chapter, you will be able to:

- Solve questions involving lines, angles, quadrilaterals, triangles, and circles
- Solve questions involving complex figures and three-dimensional shapes

1. Lines and Angles

Calculating Angle Measures

Angles are formed by two line segments that begin at the same point. Adjacent angles can be added to find the measure of a larger angle. The following diagram demonstrates this.

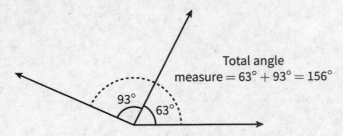

Total angle
measure $= 63° + 93° = 156°$

There are 180 degrees in a straight line, and 90 degrees in a right angle. Two angles that sum to 180° are called **supplementary angles**. Two angles that sum to 90° are called **complementary angles**.

DIRECTIONS: Use the information provided to solve for the angle measures.

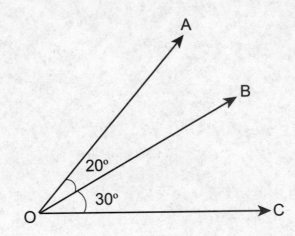

A. ∠AOC =

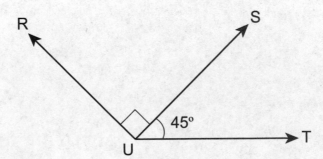

B. ∠RUT =

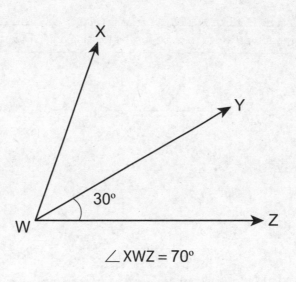

∠ XWZ = 70°

C.   ∠XWY =

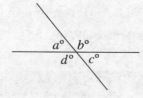

D.   ∠XOZ =

SHSAT EXPERT NOTE

Figures on the SHSAT may not necessarily be drawn to scale. Don't guess solely based on how a figure looks.

When two lines intersect, **adjacent angles** are supplementary because they add up to 180 degrees, and **vertical angles** (two angles opposite a vertex) are equal, or **congruent**. The symbol ≅ is used to show that angles are congruent.

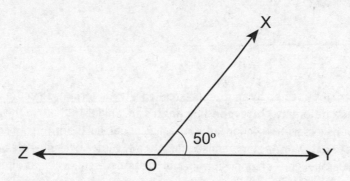

The angles marked $a°$ and $b°$ are supplementary; therefore, $a° + b° = 180°$. The angle marked $a°$ is vertical (and thus equal) to the one marked $c°$, so $a° = c°$.

Math

Math

DIRECTIONS: Use the information provided to solve for the missing angle measures.

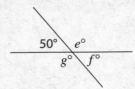

E. $e =$

F. $f =$

G. $g =$

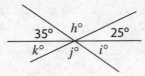

H. $h =$

I. $i =$

J. $j =$

K. $k =$

When two parallel lines are intersected by another line (called a **transversal**), all acute angles are equal and all obtuse angles are equal. Additionally, **corresponding angles** are angles that are in the same position but on different parallel lines/transversal intersections; they are also equal. Furthermore, **alternate interior angles** are all equal and **alternate exterior angles** are all equal. Alternate interior angles are angles that are positioned between the two parallel lines on opposite sides of the transversal, whereas alternate exterior angles are positioned on the outside of the parallel lines on opposite sides of the transversal. Consider the following figure:

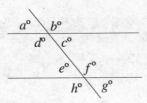

- Angles a, c, e, and g are acute and equal.
- Angles b, d, f, and h are obtuse and equal.
- Angle pairs (b and f), (c and g), (a and e), and (d and h) are corresponding angles.
- Angle pairs (a and g) and (b and h) are alternate exterior angles.
- Angle pairs (d and f) and (c and e) are alternate interior angles.

SHSAT EXPERT NOTE

Having the rules for parallel lines memorized for test day will translate into easy points!

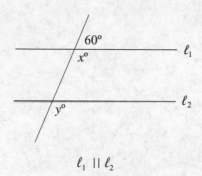

$\ell_1 \parallel \ell_2$

L. $\angle x =$

M. $\angle y =$

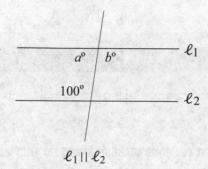

$\ell_1 \parallel \ell_2$

N. $\angle a =$

O. $\angle b =$

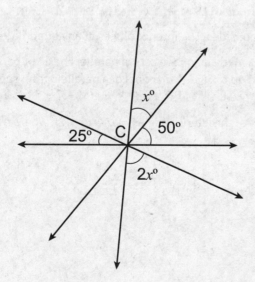

1. In the figure above, four straight lines intersect at point C. What is the value of x ?

   A. 25

   B. 35

   C. 75

   D. 105

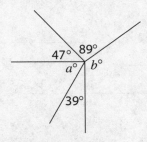

2. In the figure above, what is the value of $a + b$?

    E.   145

    F.   175

    G.   185

    H.   275

SHSAT EXPERT NOTE

Two intersecting lines create two sets of congruent angles called vertical angles.

If two lines intersect at a 90° angle, they are perpendicular. If one intersection is 90°, then all four angles are 90°.

If a question asks for the value of $a + b$, see if you can find the answer without solving for a and b separately.

Degrees of Triangles and Quadrilaterals

The interior angles of any triangle sum to 180°.

Quadrilaterals are shapes with four sides. The interior angles of any quadrilateral sum to 360°.

Parallelograms are quadrilaterals made up of two sets of parallel lines. For parallelograms, opposite angles are equal and adjacent angles add up to 180°. A diagonal of a parallelogram separates it into two congruent triangles.

For any polygon, the total degrees of the interior angles $= 180°(n - 2)$, where n is the number of sides.

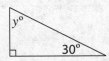

P. $y = $ _____

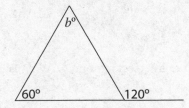

Q. $b = $ _____

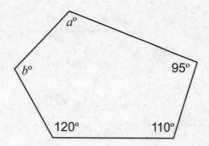

R. $a + b =$ _____

S. A quadrilateral has angles measuring 56°, 78°, and 90°. How large is the missing angle?

_____

T. The measure of one angle in a parallelogram is 46°. What is the measure of the adjacent angle?

_____

SHSAT EXPERT NOTE

For test day, you must know that the interior angles of a triangle sum to 180° and the interior angles of a quadrilateral sum to 360°.

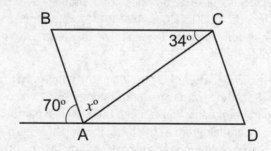

3. In the given figure, ABCD is a parallelogram. What is the value of x ?

A. 36

B. 56

C. 66

D. 76

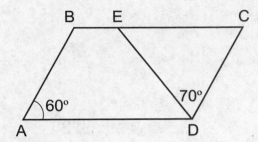

4.   In the given figure, ABCD is a parallelogram. The measure of ∠BAD is 60°, and the measure of ∠EDC is 70°. What is the measure of ∠CED ?

   E.   50°

   F.   60°

   G.   70°

   H.   80°

2. Perimeter and Area

Perimeter and Area of Quadrilaterals

Perimeter and area are basic properties that all two-dimensional shapes have. The **perimeter** of a quadrilateral can be calculated by adding the lengths of all its sides. **Area** is the amount of two-dimensional space a shape occupies. The most common shapes for which you'll need these two properties on test day are squares, rectangles, parallelograms, and trapezoids.

The area (A) of a **square** is given by $A = s^2$, where s is the side of the square. To find the area of a **rectangle**, multiply the length by the width. **Parallelograms** are quadrilaterals with two pairs of parallel sides. Rectangles and squares are subsets of parallelograms. You can find the area of a parallelogram using $A = bh$. As with triangles, you can use any side of a parallelogram as the base; the height is perpendicular to the base. Use the side perpendicular to the base as the height for a rectangle or square; for any other parallelogram, the height (or enough information to find it) will be given. A **trapezoid** is a quadrilateral with only one set of parallel sides. Those parallel sides form the two bases. To find the area, average those bases and multiply by the height.

Scaling involves changing the size of one or more sides of a shape and then evaluating the difference in the new shape's area or perimeter.

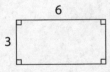

   A.   Perimeter =

   B.   Area =

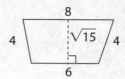

C. Perimeter =

D. Area =

E. Perimeter =

F. Area =

G. Draw a rectangle with an area of 40, labeling the sides. What is the perimeter?

H. A fence surrounds a rectangular field whose length is 3 times its width. If the entire length of the fence is 240 meters, what is the width of the field?

I. How much will the area change when the side lengths of a square with an area of 16 are doubled?

1. A rectangular doormat that is 1 foot by 2 feet is placed on a square porch that has a perimeter of 16 feet. What is the area, in square feet, of the porch **not** covered by the doormat?

    A. 4

    B. 8

    C. 14

    D. 16

SHSAT EXPERT NOTE

The SHSAT will test your ability to handle geometry problems that do not have a diagram. Be sure to draw your own diagram if none is provided on test day.

---

2. The length of a rectangle is 56 centimeters. The ratio of the length to the width is 7:4. What is the perimeter of the rectangle?

    E. 32 cm

    F. 88 cm

    G. 176 cm

    H. 1,792 cm

SHSAT EXPERT NOTE

Be careful to answer exactly what the question asks. If a question asks for the area, the perimeter is often among the incorrect answers and vice versa.

Perimeter and Area of Triangles

Perimeter of a triangle: The perimeter of a triangle is the distance around the triangle. In other words, the perimeter is equal to the sum of the lengths of the sides.

An **isosceles triangle** is a triangle that has at least two sides of equal length. The two equal sides are called the legs, and the third side is called the base. Because the two legs have the same length, the two angles opposite the legs must have the same measure.

An **equilateral triangle** is a triangle that has three equal sides. Because all the sides are equal, all the angles are also equal. All three angles in an equilateral triangle measure 60°, regardless of the lengths of the sides. All equilateral triangles are also isosceles, but not all isosceles triangles are equilateral.

A **right triangle** has one interior angle of 90°. The longest side, which lies opposite the right angle, is called the **hypotenuse**. The other two sides are called the **legs**.

Area of a triangle: The area of a triangle refers to the space it takes up. The area of a triangle is $\frac{1}{2} \times$ base $\times$ height.

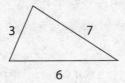

J. Perimeter = _____

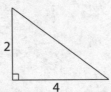

K. Area = _____

L. Area = _____

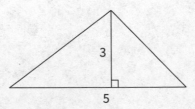

M. Area = _____

SHSAT EXPERT NOTE

The height of a triangle is the perpendicular distance from any side chosen as the base to the opposite vertex.

---

3. A square sandwich that is 4 inches wide is diagonally cut in half, and half of the sandwich is placed on a square napkin that is 5 inches wide. What is the area of the napkin **not** covered by half of the sandwich?

    A. 9 sq in.

    B. 16 sq in.

    C. 17 sq in.

    D. 25 sq in.

4. The perimeter of an isosceles triangle is 50 centimeters. The ratio of the two equal sides to the third side is 3:4. What are the dimensions of the triangle?

    E. 3 cm × 3 cm × 4 cm

    F. 6 cm × 6 cm × 8 cm

    G. 15 cm × 15 cm × 20 cm

    H. 18 cm × 18 cm × 30 cm

Circumference and Area of Circles

A circle's **perimeter** is known as its **circumference** (C) and is found using $C = 2\pi r$, where r is the radius (distance from the center of the circle to its edge). The lowercase Greek letter π (pronounced "pie") is approximately $\frac{22}{7}$ or 3.14. One revolution of a wheel equals the circumference of the wheel. The **area** of a circle is given by $A = \pi r^2$.

DIRECTIONS: Find the missing measurement for each circle.

N. Radius = 8
   Circumference =

O. Radius = 5
   Area =

P. Area = 16π
   Radius =

Q. Circumference = 6π
   Area =

5. Six circular lights, each with a circumference of 10π feet, are installed in a ceiling that is 11 feet by 20 feet. What is the area of the ceiling **not** covered by the lights?

    A. $62 - 25\pi$ sq ft

    B. $62 - 150\pi$ sq ft

    C. $220 - 25\pi$ sq ft

    D. $220 - 150\pi$ sq ft

6. A bicycle travels 22 feet per minute. If the radius of each wheel is 12 inches, how many revolutions does one wheel make in 1 hour? $\left(\pi \approx \frac{22}{7} \right)$

    E. $\frac{7}{2}$

    F. $\frac{44}{7}$

    G. 17.5

    H. 210

SHSAT EXPERT NOTE

Identify whether the question asks you to calculate the actual area or circumference or whether the answer is expressed in terms of π.

3. Geometric Figures

Figures in the Coordinate Plane

For some questions, you'll have to combine what you know about different geometric figures with what you know about the coordinate plane.

> **DIRECTIONS:** Find the areas of the shapes graphed below.

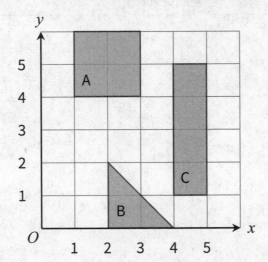

A. A = _____

B. B = _____

C. C = _____

SHSAT EXPERT NOTE

Often, coordinate plane questions ask you to use your knowledge of basic shapes as well as your understanding of the coordinate plane.

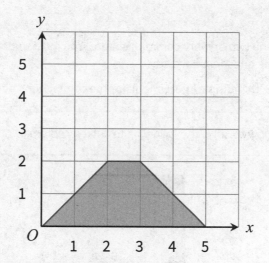

1.   In the graph above, what is the area of the shaded region?

   A.   4 sq units

   B.   6 sq units

   C.   8 sq units

   D.   12 sq units

SHSAT EXPERT NOTE

To find the length of a line segment that is parallel to either axis, take the absolute value of the difference between the coordinates that are at either end of the line segment.

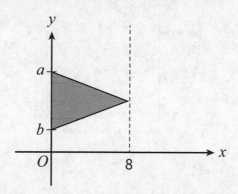

2.   In the figure above, what is the area of the shaded triangle?

   E. $\frac{1}{2}(a - b)$

   F. $2(a - b)$

   G. $4(a - b)$

   H. $8(a - b)$

Math

Complex Figures

Many geometry questions combine two or more common shapes. You must understand the relationships between the shapes to answer the questions correctly.

When you encounter questions with multiple figures, look for the connections between the shapes.

DIRECTIONS: Use the steps below to solve the following test-like problem.

In the figure above, a circle is inscribed within a square. If the area of the circle is 25π, what is the total perimeter of the shaded region?

    D. First, determine the connection between the shapes:

    E. Next, decide what information you need to find and solve for unknown variables:

    F. Finally, solve the question:

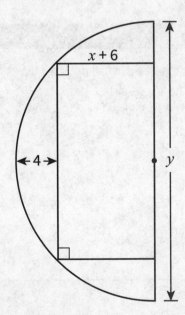

3.   In the figure above, what is y in terms of x ?

    A. $x + 10$

    B. $2x + 10$

    C. $2x + 20$

    D. $4x + 24$

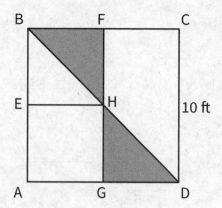

4. In the figure above, E, F, and G are midpoints of the sides of square ABCD, and H is the center of square ABCD. What is the total area, in square feet, of the shaded portions?

E. 12.5

F. 25

G. 50

H. 100

Math

SHSAT EXPERT NOTE

There are no new rules to memorize for multiple-figure problems. Just take them step by step, using a bit of information from one figure and plugging it into the equation for another figure.

Each step of the math is standard geometry. It is the combination of steps that makes these problems challenging.

Label the diagram in the test booklet whenever possible. You can and should write in the test booklet.

4. Three-Dimensional Shapes

Geometric Solids

Three-dimensional (3D) shapes are also called solids. The following diagram shows the basic anatomy of a 3D shape:

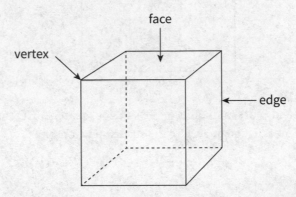

A **face** (or **surface**) is a two-dimensional (2D) shape that acts as one of the sides of the solid. Two faces meet at a line segment called an **edge**, and three faces meet at a single point called a **vertex**.

Commonly tested three-dimensional shapes on the SHSAT are prisms, which have two parallel faces, and pyramids, which have a base and three or more triangular faces that meet at a point. Note that a cube is a rectangular prism with all sides equal.

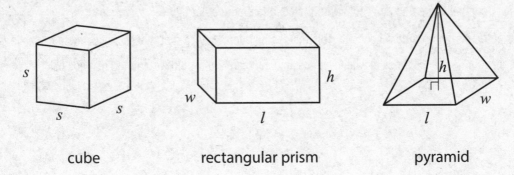

cube   rectangular prism   pyramid

Volume

Volume is the amount of 3D space occupied by a solid. Volume is analogous to the area of a 2D shape. You can find the volume of prisms by finding the area of the base and multiplying it by the height: $V = A_{base} \times h$.

When you are not explicitly given the area of the base of a 3D shape, you'll need to rely on your knowledge of two-dimensional geometry to find it before calculating the volume of the prism.

Surface Area

Surface area is the sum of the areas of all faces of a solid. To calculate the surface area of a solid, simply find the area of each face using your 2D geometry skills and then add them all together.

You might think that finding the surface area of a solid with many sides, such as a square pyramid, is a tall order. However, you can save time by noticing a vital trait: a square pyramid has four identical triangular faces and one square base. Don't waste time finding the area of each of the surfaces. Find the area of only one triangular face and the square base. Then multiply the area of the triangular face by 4 and add it to the area of the square base, and you're done. The same is true for other 3D shapes.

Because formulas are not given on the SHSAT, you will need to memorize the ones that will help you most. Be smart when you memorize—sometimes you can break up a solid into polygons with area formulas you already know.

SHAPE	SURFACE AREA	VOLUME
Cube	$6s^2$	s^3
Rectangular prism	$2lw + 2hw + 2lh$ Think: find the area of each rectangle and then add	$l \times w \times h$ Think: area of the base times the height
Cylinder	$2\pi rh + 2\pi r^2$ Think: find the area of each circle and then the area of the curved surface, which is a rectangle	$\pi r^2 h$ Think: area of the base times the height
Pyramid	base area $+ \frac{1}{2} \times$ base perimeter $\times$ slant length	$\frac{1}{3} \times$ base area $\times$ height
Cone	*Not tested*	$\frac{1}{3}\pi r^2 h$ Note how this relates to the volume of a cylinder

A. A rectangular prism is 5 inches long, 3 inches wide, and 2 inches high. What is the volume of the prism, in cubic inches?

B. A cube has a surface area of 294 square centimeters. What is the length of each edge of the cube, in centimeters?

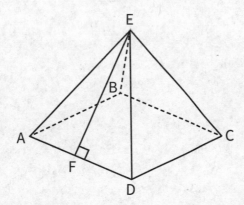

1. In the figure above, the areas of each triangular face are equal, and the sides of the square base ABCD are each 4 inches. If EF = 6 inches, what is the surface area of the pyramid **including** the base?

   A. 48 sq in.

   B. 52 sq in.

   C. 60 sq in.

   D. 64 sq in.

SHSAT EXPERT NOTE

To calculate the surface area of a three-dimensional shape, find the sum of the areas of each face. Save time by identifying identical faces and multiplying the area of that face by the number of identical faces.

2. A storage bench has a rectangular base. The length of the base is three times the width of the base. The height is equal to the width of the bench. If the length of the bench is 120 centimeters, what is the volume of the bench?

    E.   43,200 cu cm

    F.   192,000 cu cm

    G.   576,000 cu cm

    H.   728,000 cu cm

SHSAT EXPERT NOTE

You can calculate the volume of prisms by finding the area of the base and multiplying it by the height: $V = A_{base} \times h$.

Answers and Explanations

1. Lines and Angles

A. $\angle AOC = 50°$

B. $\angle RUT = 90° + 45° = 135°$

C. $\angle XWY = 70° - 30° = 40°$

D. $\angle XOZ = 180° - 50° = 130°$

E. $e = 180° - 50° = 130°$

F. $f = 50°$

G. $g = 130°$

H. $h = 180° - 60° = 120°$

I. $i = 35°$

J. $j = 120°$

K. $k = 25°$

L. $x = 120°$

M. $y = 120°$

N. $a = 80°$

O. $b = 100°$

1.   B

Subject: Geometry

Getting to the Answer: Let y represent the missing angle in the top half of the figure. The sum of the top four angles is equal to $180°$: $x° + y° + 25° + 50° = 180°$.

Since y is vertical to $2x$, $y = 2x$. Use that to solve for x:

$$x° + 2x° + 25° + 50° = 180°$$
$$3x° + 75° = 180°$$
$$3x° = 105°$$
$$x° = 35°$$

2.   G

Subject: Geometry

Getting to the Answer: Angles around a single point total $360°$, so set up an equation with what you know. Then solve for $a + b$:

$$a° + 47° + 89° + b° + 39° = 360°$$
$$a° + b° + 175° = 360°$$
$$a° + b° = 185°$$

P. $y = 60$

Q. $b = 60$

R. Total degrees in polygon: $(n - 2)(180°)$

For 5 sides: $(5 - 2)(180°) = 540°$

$95 + 110 + 120 + a + b = 540$

$a + b = 215$

S. Quadrilaterals have $360°$ inside:

$56° + 78° + 90° = 224°$

Missing angle: $360° - 224° = 136°$

T. Adjacent angles in a parallelogram add up to $180°$: $180° - 46° = 134°$

3.   D

Subject: Geometry

Getting to the Answer: Remember, the diagonal of a parallelogram divides it into two congruent triangles. Thus, $\angle BCA = \angle CAD = 34°$. The sum of the angles that form a line is $180°$, so $70° + x° + 34° = 180°$. Solve for x: $x° = 180° - 70° - 34° = 76°$.

4.   E

Subject: Geometry

Getting to the Answer: In a parallelogram, opposite angles are equal, so $\angle ECD = \angle BAD = 60°$. Since the sum of the interior angles of a triangle is $180°$, $\angle CED + 60° + 70° = 180°$. Thus, $\angle CED = 50°$.

2. Perimeter and Area

A. $2(6 + 3) = 2(9) = 18$

B. $6 \times 3 = 18$

C. 22

D. $\frac{1}{2}\sqrt{15}(8 + 6) = 7\sqrt{15}$

E. 20

F. 25

G. The perimeter depends on knowing the side lengths of the rectangle. Since we only know the area is 40, we do not know the exact dimensions. To see that we get different perimeters, let's pick values based on a rectangle having an area of 40. If we pick sides of 4 and 10, the perimeter is $2(4 + 10) = 28$. If we pick sides of 20 and 2, the perimeter is $2(20 + 2) = 44$.

H. Label the width x and the length $3x$. The problem provides the total length of the fence, so use the perimeter equation: $x + 3x + x + 3x = 240$. Simplify: $8x = 240$, $x = 30$.

I. Since $A = 16$, the length of each side $= 4$. Double the original side length to get the new side length $= 8$. Then find the new area:

$$A = 8^2 = 64$$

$$\frac{64}{16} = 4$$

Therefore, the new area is 4 times larger.

1. C

Subject: Geometry

Getting to the Answer: Drawing your own diagram may seem like it will take up valuable time, but it will actually prevent you from making careless errors on test day.

Calculate the area of the doormat using the dimensions of the doormat: $A = l \times w = 1 \text{ ft} \times 2 \text{ ft} = 2$ sq ft.

Use the perimeter of the porch to find the side length of the porch. Then use the side length to calculate the area the porch. Since $P = 4s$ and $P = 16$ ft, then $16 \text{ ft} = 4s$ and $4 \text{ ft} = s$.

Thus, the area of the porch is $A = s^2 = 4^2 = 16$ sq ft.

Subtract the area of the doormat from the area of the porch: $16 - 2 = 14$ sq ft.

2. G

Subject: Geometry

Getting to the Answer: Set up a proportion to find the width of the rectangle. Let w represent the width:

$$\frac{56}{w} = \frac{7}{4}$$
$$224 = 7w$$
$$32 = w$$

Thus, the perimeter is $2 \times 56 + 2 \times 32 = 176$ centimeters.

J. Perimeter $= 16$

K. Area $= 4$

L. Area $= 6$

M. Area $= 7.5$

3. C

Subject: Geometry

Getting to the Answer: First calculate the area of the napkin: $A = s^2 = 5^2 = 25$ sq in. Then calculate the area of half of the sandwich. Diagonally cutting the square sandwich in half creates two triangular halves that each have a base of 4 inches and a height of 4 inches. Thus, the area of half of the sandwich is $\frac{1}{2}bh = \frac{1}{2}(4)(4) = 8$ sq in. Subtract the area of the half sandwich from the area of the napkin: $25 - 8 = 17$ sq in.

4. G

Subject: Geometry

Getting to the Answer: Let $3x$, $3x$, and $4x$ represent the sides of the triangle. The perimeter is $3x + 3x + 4x = 50$, $10x = 50$, $x = 5$. So the sides of the triangle are $3 \times 5 = 15$, 15, and $4 \times 5 = 20$ centimeters.

N. Circumference $= 16\pi$

O. Area $= 25\pi$

P. Radius $= 4$

Q. Area $= 9\pi$

5. D

Subject: Geometry

Getting to the Answer: First, use the circumference of one light to find the radius of one light:

$$C = 2\pi r$$
$$10\pi = 2\pi r$$
$$5 = r$$

Then use the radius to calculate the area of one light:

$$A = \pi r^2$$
$$= \pi(5)^2$$
$$= 25\pi$$

Multiply by 6 to get the area of the 6 lights: $6 \times 25\pi = 150\pi$ sq in.

Next, use the dimensions of the ceiling to find its area:

$$A = l \times w$$
$$= 11 \times 20$$
$$= 220$$

Subtract the area of the ceiling from the area of the 6 lights: $220 - 150\pi$ sq ft.

6. H

Subject: Geometry

Getting to the Answer: One revolution equals the circumference of the wheel. Note the radius in feet is 1 foot:

$$C = 2\pi r = 2\left(\frac{22}{7}\right)(1) = \frac{44}{7} \text{ feet}$$

Since the bicycle travels 22 feet per minute, the number of revolutions one wheel makes is $22 \div \frac{44}{7} = 22 \times \frac{7}{44} = \frac{7}{2}$ revolutions per minute. Multiply by 60 minutes to get $\frac{7}{2} \times 60 = 210$ revolutions per hour.

3. Geometric Figures

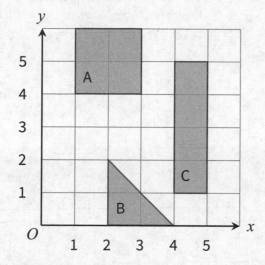

A. $A = 4$ square units

B. $B = 2$ square units

C. $C = 4$ square units

1. B
Subject: Geometry

Getting to the Answer: The shaded region is a trapezoid. The length of the top side is 1 unit, the length of the base is 5 units, and the height is 2 units. Thus, the area is $\frac{1}{2}(1 + 5) \times 2 = 6$ square units. Alternatively, you can divide the trapezoid into two right triangles and one rectangle, which gives an area of $2 \times \frac{1}{2}(2 \times 2) + 1 \times 2 = 4 + 2 = 6$ square units.

2. G
Subject: Geometry

Getting to the Answer: Recall the area of a triangle is $\frac{1}{2}bh$. The length of the base of the triangle is $a - b$, and the height of the triangle is 8 units. Thus, the area is $\frac{1}{2}(a - b)8 = 4(a - b)$.

D. Since the circle is inscribed in a square, the circle's diameter is equal to the length of a side of the square.

E. Here, the perimeter of the square provides the outside perimeter of the shaded area, and the circumference of the circle provides the inside perimeter. Add them together to find the total perimeter. Since the area of the circle is 25π, the radius is 5. The diameter of the circle and the length of a side of the square are both 10.

F. The circumference of the circle is 10π. The perimeter of the square is $4(10) = 40$. Add these together to get the total perimeter of the shaded area: $40 + 10\pi$.

3. C
Subject: Geometry

Getting to the Answer: In the figure, the diameter is y and the radius is $(x + 6) + 4$. Since the diameter is twice the radius, set $y = 2[(x + 6) + 4]$ and solve for y:

$$y = 2(x + 10)$$
$$= 2x + 20$$

4. F
Subject: Geometry

Getting to the Answer: The length of the side of the square is 10 ft. Since E, F, and G are midpoints and H is the center, then BF, FH, GH, and GD all equal 5 ft. The two shaded triangles, BFH and HGD, are right triangles, so the area of one of the triangles is $\frac{1}{2}(5)(5) = \frac{25}{2}$. The sum of the areas is $\frac{25}{2} + \frac{25}{2} = \frac{50}{2} = 25$ sq ft.

4. Three-Dimensional Shapes

A. Volume $= l \times w \times h = 5 \times 3 \times 2 = 30$

B. Surface area of a cube $= 6s^2 = 294$
$s^2 = 49$
$s = 7$

1. D

Subject: Geometry

Getting to the Answer: The height of triangle AED is
$EF = 6$. The length of AD is 4. Thus, the area of each
triangular face is $\frac{1}{2}bh = \frac{1}{2}(4)(6) = 12$ sq in. The base of
the pyramid is $A = s^2 = 4^2 = 16$. Since there are 4 congruent triangular faces, the total surface area of the pyramid
is $4 \times 12 + 16 = 64$ sq in.

2. F

Subject: Geometry

Getting to the Answer: First use the length of the bench
to find the width and height of the bench. Then use the
dimensions to calculate the volume.

The length is three times the width of the bench:
$l = 3w$. Since the length is 120 centimeters, the width of
the base is $\frac{120}{3} = 40$ cm. The height equals the width, so
the height is also 40 cm. Thus, the volume of the bench
is $l \times w \times h = 120 \times 40 \times 40 = 192{,}000$ cu cm.

[CHAPTER 13]

WORD PROBLEMS

CHAPTER OBJECTIVES

By the end of this chapter, you will be able to:

- Translate word problems into mathematical terms
- Solve SHSAT word problems

1. Word Problems: Arithmetic

Ratios

The ratio of *a* to *b* can be written as *a:b* or as $\frac{a}{b}$.

    A. A grocery store stocks 3 apples for every 4 oranges. What is the ratio of apples to oranges?

    B. If the store has 28 pieces of fruit and they are all either apples or oranges, how many apples are there?

Percents

$$\text{Percent} = \frac{\text{Part}}{\text{Whole}} \times 100\%$$

$$\text{Percent Change} = \frac{\text{Change}}{\text{Original}} \times 100\%$$

$$\text{Simple Interest Earned} = \text{Initial Deposit } (p) \times \text{Annual Interest Rate } (r) \times \text{Years } (t)$$

    C. What percentage of 50 is 35 ?

    D. 12 is 20% of what number?

    E. How much interest will a $3,600 deposit that earns 2% simple interest annually earn in 4 years?

Rates

Common rate equations:

$$\text{Rate} = \frac{\text{Distance}}{\text{Time}}$$

$$\text{Distance} = \text{Time} \times \text{Rate}$$

$$\text{Time} = \frac{\text{Distance}}{\text{Rate}}$$

    F. John travels 80 miles in 2 hours. What is his average speed?

    G. Mary makes $72 on Friday. If she works for 8 hours, how much does she make per hour?

SHSAT EXPERT NOTE

As with all word problems questions, first translate the English into equations. Only when you are sure you have the translation correct should you begin the actual math.

---

1.   If the price of a stock decreases by 20%, and then by an additional 25%, by what percentage has the price decreased from its original value?

    A. 40

    B. 45

    C. 50

    D. 55

2. At Mattress Shop, 75% of the mattresses are memory foam and 20% of the mattresses are extra firm. Of the total mattresses at Mattress Shop, 12% are extra-firm memory foam mattresses. What percentage of the total mattresses are not memory foam and not extra firm?

   E. 8
   F. 17
   G. 63
   H. 80

3. In a piggy bank, there are 12 bills. Of the four types of coins, 42 coins are pennies. The bill-to-coin ratio for the piggy bank is 1 to 25. What is the total number of nickels, dimes, and quarters in the piggy bank?

   A. 258
   B. 300
   C. 342
   D. 479

4. Three students are each giving a slide show presentation with 12 slides each. Astrid presents 1 slide every 3 minutes. Steven presents 1 slide every 8 minutes, and Anna presents 1 slide every 4 minutes. How many minutes did the three students spend giving their presentations?

   E. 48
   F. 96
   G. 180
   H. 210

5. At Eddie's convenience store, 2 of every 21 items purchased are returned. If 441 items are purchased, how many items will be returned?

   A. 24
   B. 28
   C. 36
   D. 42

6. A sheet of one-ply paper towel has a thickness of 0.2 millimeters, with an error of 5%. What is the least possible thickness of a sheet of one-ply paper towel?

   E. 0.01
   F. 0.1
   G. 0.19
   H. 0.9

7. Ken turned on his oven at noon to bake a casserole. The starting temperature of the oven was 195°F. The temperature increased 10 degrees every minute. How many minutes did it take the oven to reach 375°F ?

   A. 12

   B. 14

   C. 18

   D. 20

8. A rope with a specific length is used to measure a horizontal distance of 39 yards. The same rope is also used to measure a distance of 45 yards. What is the greatest possible length, in yards, of the rope?

   E. 3

   F. 6

   G. 9

   H. 18

9. Paulo opened a savings account with a deposit of $1,800. The account earns 3% simple interest annually. How many years will it take to earn $486 on the deposit?

   A. 6

   B. 7

   C. 8

   D. 9

SHSAT EXPERT NOTE

Picking Numbers often works well when a question includes variables in the answer choices, percentages, number properties, or unknown values.

---

2. Word Problems: Statistics and Probability

Mean, Median, Mode, Range

- **Mean (or average):**

$$\text{Average} = \frac{\text{Sum of Items}}{\text{Number of Items}}$$

- **Median:** Middle value in a data set when values are in ascending or descending order.
- **Mode:** Most frequent value in a data set (can have multiple modes).
- **Range:** The highest value in a data set minus the lowest value.

Xiaomei ran 5 laps. The times of each lap are 4.0, 4.8, 4.2, 4.5, and 4.0 minutes.

   A. What is the average time it took Xiaomei to complete one lap?

   B. What is Xiaomei's median lap time?

   C. What is the mode of Xiaomei's lap time?

   D. What is the range of Xiaomei's lap time?

Probability

$$\text{Probability} = \frac{\text{Number of Desired Outcomes}}{\text{Number of Possible Outcomes}}$$

Jean spins a prize wheel that is divided into 6 even slices that are colored red, orange, yellow, green, blue, and purple.

E. What is the probability of landing on the green slice?

F. What is the probability of landing on the green or blue slice?

G. What is the probability of not landing on the green or blue slice?

1. Rishi received a mean score of 88 per quiz for his first four quizzes in physics. On his 5th quiz, he scored 93. What is his mean quiz score for the first 5 quizzes?

   A. 89

   B. 90

   C. 91

   D. 92

2. Kelsey bought 5 pairs of pants at the department store for a mean price of $24 per pair of pants. She bought 2 pairs of shoes at the footwear store. If the total price of the pants equals the total price of the shoes, what was the mean price of the shoes?

   E. $56

   F. $60

   G. $64

   H. $72

3. A zoo records 127 visitors to an exhibit on Monday, 178 on Tuesday, 112 on Wednesday, 103 on Thursday, 196 on Friday, 271 on Saturday, and 217 on Sunday. What is the median number of visitors for the week?

   A. 103

   B. 172

   C. 178

   D. 271

4. The average weight of Jake, Ken, and Larry is 60 kilograms. If Jake and Ken each weigh 50 kilograms, how much does Larry weigh, in kilograms?

   E. 40

   F. 50

   G. 60

   H. 80

5. The high temperature on Monday, measured in degrees Fahrenheit, was 34°. If the low temperature was 3° below zero, what was the range of temperatures on Monday?

   A. −3°

   B. 31°

   C. 34°

   D. 37°

6. On a shelf, there are 7 comic books, 3 joke books, and 5 space books. If one book is pulled out at random, what is the probability that it will **not** be a comic book?

   E. $\frac{1}{5}$

   F. $\frac{7}{15}$

   G. $\frac{8}{15}$

   H. $\frac{4}{5}$

7. There are 2 red scarves, 7 purple scarves, 6 yellow scarves, and 3 green scarves in a hat. If two scarves are drawn at random without replacement, what is the probability that both scarves removed are **not** purple?

   A. $\frac{55}{153}$

   B. $\frac{70}{153}$

   C. $\frac{98}{153}$

   D. $\frac{121}{153}$

3. Word Problems: Algebra

Translation

Label your own variables to translate problems in which the variables you're trying to solve for aren't explicitly labeled.

> **DIRECTIONS:** Identify the variable(s) in each of the phrases below, and translate the statements into appropriate equations:

STATEMENT:	TRANSLATION:
A. Martha is 3 times as old as Ann.	
B. There are 5 more orange marbles than blue marbles in a bag.	
C. There are 3 empty boxes for every full box.	

SHSAT EXPERT NOTE

When translating, try to avoid using *o*, *l*, *s*, and *z* if you can. These letters can be easily confused with numbers. If those variables are already included in a question, take care to keep your numbers and letters straight.

Linear Models

A linear model is generally defined by two parameters: the rate of change, or slope, and the initial value, or *y*-intercept. Real-world scenarios that involve a constant rate of change—such as the position of a car moving at a constant speed—can be represented by linear models.

> **DIRECTIONS:** Write a linear equation for each of the following scenarios.

<u>SCENARIO:</u>	<u>EQUATION:</u>

D. A fitness club has 45 members and plans to increase membership by 4 members every month.

E. The cost of a pizza starts at $5, and each additional topping costs $1.

F. The value of a car initially is $22,500 and declines by $2,000 a year.

1. Anna is now *y* years old, and Marco is 3 years younger. In terms of *y*, how old was Marco 5 years ago?

   A. $y - 2$

   B. $y - 3$

   C. $y - 5$

   D. $y - 8$

2. Cade's age now is two times Taylor's age. If Taylor will be 15 in three years, how old was Cade two years ago?

   E. 10

   F. 18

   G. 22

   H. 23

3. Christopher is at least 7 years younger than Lillian. Which of the following inequalities represents the relationship between Christopher's age (C) and Lillian's age (L) ?

A. $C + L \leq 7$

B. $C + L \geq 7$

C. $7 + C \geq L$

D. $7 + C \leq L$

4. A tank when full can hold 16 gallons. There are g gallons in the tank. If 2 gallons are drained from the tank, the tank would be a quarter full. What is the value of g ?

E. 4

F. 6

G. 10

H. 12

5. Levi has a phone plan that charges $20 per month plus $6 per 1 gigabyte of data. Jayden has a phone plan that charges $44 per month for unlimited data. At the end of the month, Levi's charges are equal to Jayden's charges. How many gigabytes of data did Levi use?

A. 4

B. 7

C. 10

D. 12

6. Dylan rented a studio for four years. He paid a one-time security deposit of $250 and an additional $875 per month for the full four years. What is the total amount Dylan paid to rent the studio for four years?

E. $3,750

F. $12,875

G. $41,750

H. $42,250

7. The monthly expenses for Addison's music shop are $360. It costs Addison $290 to build a guitar, and she sells each guitar for $510. What is Addison's profit if she builds and sells 6 guitars in 1 month?

A. $220

B. $960

C. $1,320

D. $2,770

8. Mason bought 3 apples for $1.29 each and 2 pounds of salmon. His total purchase for these items, not including tax, was $24.95. What was the price per pound of the salmon?

    E. $7.46

    F. $10.54

    G. $11.83

    H. $21.08

9. To make lemonade, Skylar could buy a bag of lemons for $5.40, or she could buy x individual lemons for $0.60 each. What is the largest value of x that would make buying individual lemons less expensive than buying the bag?

    A. 7

    B. 8

    C. 9

    D. 10

> **SHSAT EXPERT NOTE**
>
> Problems with numbers in the answer choices are often solved quickly with Kaplan's Backsolving strategy.

4. Word Problems: Geometry

Geometry

Translation of geometry problems typically involves putting information from the question directly into the given diagram or, occasionally, drawing a brand-new figure.

    A. If the width of a rectangle is 4 and the length is twice the width, what is the area?

    B. ABC is an isosceles triangle. Sides $\overline{AB}$ and $\overline{AC}$ are 7 units each, and side $\overline{BC}$ is 3 units. The measure of angle ABC is 78°. What is the measure of angle CAB ?

    C. Six bridges are connected at points A, B, C, D, E, and F in a hexagon. The points appear clockwise when viewed from above, from A to F. If Jenny starts at point A and walks 725 bridges in a clockwise direction, at what point will she be when she has stopped?

1. A cup with a circumference of 2π inches is placed in the center of a circular coaster that has a radius of 2 inches. What is the area, in square inches, of the coaster **not** covered by the bottom of the cup?

    A. π

    B. 3π

    C. 4π

    D. 5π

2. A toy chest has a rectangular base. The length of the base is four times the width of the base. The height of the chest is one-half the length of the base. If the height of the chest is 10 inches, what is the volume of the chest in cubic inches?

   E. 400
   F. 500
   G. 1,000
   H. 8,000

3. A right triangle in a diagram has a base of 3 centimeters and a height of 4 centimeters. A copy machine enlarges the diagram. The base of the enlarged triangle is 9 centimeters. What is the area, in square centimeters, of the triangle in the enlarged diagram?

   A. 12
   B. 21
   C. 54
   D. 108

4. A nine-sided polygon has two sides that each have a length of x, three sides that each have a length of $x + 1$, one side with a length of $x + 3$, and three sides that each have a length of $x + 4$. What is the value of x if the perimeter is 108 ?

   E. 9
   F. 10
   G. 11
   H. 12

5. The perimeter of a rectangle is 32 inches. The ratio of the length to the width is 5:3. What is the area of the rectangle?

   A. 52
   B. 56
   C. 60
   D. 64

Answers and Explanations

1. Word Problems: Arithmetic

A. 3 apples to 4 oranges

B. 12 apples because 3 apples $+$ 4 oranges $=$ 7 pieces of fruit, which means the ratio of apples to fruit is 3:7. Set up a proportion and solve:

$$\frac{3}{7} = \frac{x}{28}$$
$$7x = 84$$
$$x = 12$$

C. $\frac{\text{part}}{\text{whole}} \times 100\% = \frac{35}{50} \times 100\% =$
$\frac{70}{100} \times 100\% = 70\%$

D. $12 = 20\%$ of x

$12 = 0.2x$

$\frac{12}{0.2} = \frac{0.2x}{0.2}$

$60 = x$

E. simple interest earned $= p \times r \times t =$
$3,600 \times 0.02 \times 4 = 288$

F. Rate (speed) $= \frac{\text{Distance}}{\text{Time}} = \frac{80 \text{ miles}}{2 \text{ hours}}$
$= 40$ miles per hour

G. Rate $= \frac{\text{Total \$ Earned}}{\text{Time}} = \frac{\$72}{8 \text{ hours}}$
$= \$9$ per hour

1. A

Subject: Arithmetic

Getting to the Answer: Since the original price of the stock is not given, use the Picking Numbers strategy. Picking 100 for percent problems simplifies the calculations:

Price of the stock = $100

$100 - ($100 \times 0.20) = $100 - $20 = $80

$80 - ($80 \times 0.25) = $80 - $20 = $60

$100 - $60 = $40

$\frac{40}{100} = 40\%$	Always divide the difference by the original number to find the percent change.

2. F

Subject: Arithmetic

Getting to the Answer: Solve this problem step by step. Put all the given information into a table and determine the unknown information.

	Memory Foam	Not Memory Foam	Total
Extra firm	12%	20% − 12% = 8%	20%
Not extra firm	75% − 12% = 63%	80% − 63% = 17%	100% − 20% = 80%
Total	75%	25%	100%

17% of the mattresses at Mattress Shop are not memory foam and not extra firm.

3. A

Subject: Arithmetic

Getting to the Answer: Let x represent the number of nickels, dimes, and quarters. Set up a proportion and solve for x:

$$\frac{1}{25} = \frac{12}{42 + x}$$
$$42 + x = 300$$
$$x = 258$$

4. G

Subject: Arithmetic

Getting to the Answer: Calculate the number of minutes each student spent presenting. Astrid spent $12 \times 3 = 36$ minutes, Steven spent $12 \times 8 = 96$ minutes, and Anna spent $12 \times 4 = 48$ minutes. The total time is $36 + 96 + 48 = 180$ minutes.

5. D

Subject: Arithmetic

Getting to the Answer: Let r represent the number of items returned. Set up a proportion and solve for r:

$$\frac{r}{441} = \frac{2}{21}$$
$$21r = 882$$
$$r = 42$$

Math

6. G

Subject: Arithmetic

Getting to the Answer: First find 5% of 0.2 millimeters, and then determine the least possible thickness. 5% of 0.2 millimeters equals 0.01 millimeters. Thus, the least possible thickness of the paper towel would be $0.2 - 0.01 = 0.19$ millimeters.

7. C

Subject: Arithmetic

Getting to the Answer: Find the difference between the starting temperature and the final temperature: $375°F - 195°F = 180°F$. Use the rate of 10° per minute to calculate the number of minutes:

$$180° \times \frac{1 \text{ min}}{10°} = 18 \text{ min}$$

8. E

Subject: Arithmetic

Getting to the Answer: The length of the rope is the greatest common factor (GCF) of 39 and 45. The factors of 39 are 1, 3, 13, and 39. The factors of 45 are 1, 3, 5, 9, 15, and 45. The GCF is 3. The rope is 3 yards long.

Note that you could also determine the GCF from the prime factors. The prime factorization of 39 is 3×13, and the prime factorization of 45 is $3 \times 3 \times 5$. The only prime factor that 39 and 45 have in common is 3, so the GCF is 3.

9. D

Subject: Arithmetic

Getting to the Answer: The formula for simple interest earned is $p \times r \times t$. Plug in the initial deposit for p, the annual interest rate for r, and the amount of interest earned. Then solve for t to find the number of years.

$$\text{simple interest earned} = p \times r \times t$$
$$486 = (1,800)(0.03)t$$
$$486 = 54t$$
$$9 = t$$

2. Word Problems: Statistics and Probability

A. $\frac{21.5}{5} = 4.3$ minutes

B. 4.2 minutes

C. 4.0 minutes

D. 0.8 minutes

E. $\frac{1}{6}$

F. $\frac{2}{6} = \frac{1}{3}$

G. $1 - \frac{1}{3} = \frac{2}{3}$

1. A

Subject: Statistics and Probability

Getting to the Answer: Use the average formula to calculate the mean score of the first 5 quizzes. Rishi scored a mean of 88 points per quiz on the first 4 quizzes, so he earned a total of $4 \times 88 = 352$ points. Thus, the sum of the 5 quizzes is $352 + 93 = 445$, and the mean score of the 5 quizzes is Average $= \frac{445}{5} = 89$.

2. F

Subject: Statistics and Probability

Getting to the Answer: First determine the total cost of the 6 pairs of pants. Then use the average formula, $\text{Average} = \frac{\text{Sum}}{\text{Number of Items}}$, to calculate the mean price for 2 pairs of shoes.

The total cost of the 5 pairs of pants is $5 \times \$24 = \$120$. Therefore, the mean price of 2 pairs of shoes is $\frac{\$120}{2} = \$60$.

3. C

Subject: Statistics and Probability

Getting to the Answer: You need to put the numbers in sequential order and determine which is the middle number: 103, 112, 127, 178, 196, 217, 271.

The middle number is 178.

4. H

Subject: Statistics and Probability

Getting to the Answer: You can always use Backsolving if you cannot find the answer algebraically. Use the average formula to find the sum: $\frac{(\text{Jake} + \text{Ken} + \text{Larry})}{3} = 60$. So, Jake + Ken + Larry = 180.

If Jake and Ken each weigh 50 kilograms, then:

$$50 + 50 + \text{Larry} = 180$$
$$100 + \text{Larry} = 180$$
$$\text{Larry} = 80$$

Alternatively, you might note that Larry's weight must be greater than the average weight of 60 kilograms, since Jake and Ken each weigh less than the average.

5.   D

Subject: Statistics and Probability

Getting to the Answer: To find the range, subtract the lowest temperature from the highest temperature. Since $3°$ below zero is $-3°$, the range is $34° - (-3°) = 37°$.

6.   G

Subject: Statistics and Probability

Getting to the Answer: Use the probability formula: $\text{Probability} = \dfrac{\text{Number of Desired Outcomes}}{\text{Number of Possible Outcomes}}$. The non–comic books are all of the joke and space books, so there are 8 books that are not comic books out of a total of 15 books:

$\text{Probability} = \dfrac{8}{15}$

7.   A

Subject: Statistics and Probability

Getting to the Answer: The total number of scarves is $2 + 7 + 6 + 3 = 18$. The number of scarves that are not purple are $2 + 6 + 3 = 11$.

The probability of the first scarf not being purple is $\dfrac{11}{18}$. Now there are 10 scarves left that are not purple. The probability of the second scarf not being purple is $\dfrac{10}{17}$. Multiply these two probabilities to get $\dfrac{11}{18} \times \dfrac{10}{17}$ $= \dfrac{11 \times 10}{18 \times 17} = \dfrac{11 \times 5}{9 \times 17} = \dfrac{55}{153}$.

3. Word Problems: Algebra

A. $M = 3A$

B. $O = B + 5$

C. $E = 3F$

D. $N = 4M + 45$

E. $C = 1T + 5$

F. $V = 22{,}500 - 2{,}000Y$

1.   D

Subject: Algebra

Getting to the Answer: Assign a variable for Anna's age, and write Marco's age as an expression with that variable. Then Pick a Number for Anna's age and solve for Marco's age 5 years ago:

Anna's age now $= y$

Marco's age now $= y - 3$

Let $y = 20$

Marco's age now $= 20 - 3 = 17$

Marco's age 5 years ago $= 17 - 5 = 12$

Find the answer choice that matches.

A. $y - 2 = 20 - 2 = 18$. Eliminate it.

B. $y - 3 = 20 - 3 = 17$. Eliminate it.

C. $y - 5 = 20 - 5 = 15$. Eliminate it.

D. $y - 8 = 20 - 8 = 12$. This is the answer.

2.   G

Subject: Algebra

Getting to the Answer: Let $C =$ Cade's age now and let $T =$ Taylor's age now:

$T + 3 = 15$ so $T = 12$ (Taylor's age now)

$C = 2T$

$C = 2(12) = 24$ (Cade's age now)

$C - 2 = 24 - 2 = 22$ (Cade's age two years ago)

3.   D

Subject: Algebra

Getting to the Answer: Translate "Christopher is at least 7 years younger than Lillian": $C \leq L - 7$.

Rewrite the inequality to find the match among the answer choices: $7 + C \leq L$.

4.   F

Subject: Algebra

Getting to the Answer: First, determine how many gallons are in the tank when a quarter full. Since a full tank is 16 gallons, one-quarter of 16 is 4. Then determine the number of gallons initially in the tank: $g - 2 = 4$, so $g = 6$.

5.   A

Subject: Algebra

Getting to the Answer: Let *d* represent the number of gigabytes of data Levi used. Levi's monthly charges were $20 + $6*d*. Set Levi's charges equal to Jayden's charges and solve for *d*:

$$\$20 + \$6d = \$44$$
$$\$6d = \$24$$
$$d = 4$$

Levi used 4 gigabytes of data.

6.   H

Subject: Algebra

Getting to the Answer: First, determine the number of months in four years. Since there are 12 months in a year, there are $12 \times 4 = 48$ months in four years. Write an expression to calculate the total amount Dylan paid: $250 + $875(48) = $42,250.

7.   B

Subject: Algebra

Getting to the Answer: First, calculate the profit Addison makes from one guitar. Each guitar costs Addison $290 to build, and she sells the guitar for $510. Thus, her profit equals the selling price minus the cost: $510 − $290 = $220. If Addison builds and sells 6 guitars in a month, her initial profit is 6 × $220 = $1,320. However, she has monthly expenses of $360, so her final profit is $1,320 − $360 = $960.

8.   F

Subject: Algebra

Getting to the Answer: First, assign a variable for the price per pound of salmon, *S*. Then set up an equation for the total cost:

$$3(\$1.29) + 2S = \$24.95$$
$$\$3.87 + 2S = \$24.95$$
$$2S = \$21.08$$
$$S = \$10.54$$

9.   B

Subject: Algebra

Getting to the Answer: Set up an inequality:

$$\$0.60x < \$5.40$$
$$x < 9$$

Thus, 9 lemons would cost $5.40. So 8 is the greatest number of individual lemons Skylar could buy that would be less expensive than the bag.

4. Word Problems: Geometry

A. $w = 4$, $l = 8$, Area $= 4 \times 8 = 32$

B.   Draw an isosceles triangle with A at the apex. Side $\overline{AB}$ = side $\overline{AC}$ = 7, and base $\overline{BC}$ = 3.

∠ACB must be equal to ∠CBA (78°) since they are opposite equal sides.

∠CAB $= 180° − 78° − 78° = 24°$

C.   Draw a regular hexagon. Label the points A through F. Since Jenny she walks over 725 bridges, divide 725 by 6 to find how many times she goes all the way around the hexagon:

$$\frac{725}{6} = 120 \text{ R5}$$

Her final trip around will take her over 5 bridges. Since she starts at point A, Jenny stops at point F.

1.   B

Subject: Geometry

Getting to the Answer: Use the circumference of the cup to find the radius of the cup first:

$$C = 2\pi r$$
$$2\pi r = 2\pi r$$
$$1 = r$$

Then use the radius to calculate the area of the bottom of the cup: $A = \pi r^2 = \pi (1)^2 = \pi$ sq in.

Next use the radius of the coaster to calculate the area of the coaster: $A = \pi (2)^2 = 4\pi$ sq in.

Subtract the area of the bottom of the cup from the area of the coaster: $4\pi − \pi = 3\pi$ sq in.

2.   G

Subject: Geometry

Getting to the Answer: First use the height of the chest to find the length and width of the base. Then use the dimensions to calculate the volume.

The height is one-half the length of the base. Since the height is 10 inches, the length of the base is $2 \times 10 = 20$ inches. The length is four times the width of the base, so the width is $20 \div 4 = 5$ inches.

Thus, the volume of the chest is $l \times w \times h = 20 \times 5 \times 10 = 1,000$ in^3.

3.   C

Subject: Geometry

Getting to the Answer: First calculate the height of the larger triangle. If the enlarged base is 9, the triangle tripled in size. Multiply 4×3 to find the new height: 12. Then calculate the area of the enlarged triangle:

$$A = \tfrac{1}{2}bh = \tfrac{1}{2}(9)(12) = 54 \text{ cm}^2$$

4.   F

Subject: Geometry

Getting to the Answer: Calculate x using the perimeter given. The perimeter is 108, so $2x + 3(x+1) + (x+3) + 3(x+4) = 108$. Simplify and solve for x:

$$\begin{aligned}
2x + 3(x+1) + (x+3) + 3(x+4) &= 108 \\
2x + 3x + 3 + x + 3 + 3x + 12 &= 108 \\
9x + 18 &= 108 \\
9x &= 90 \\
x &= 10
\end{aligned}$$

5.   C

Subject: Geometry

Getting to the Answer: Let $5x$ represent the length and $3x$ represent the width. The perimeter is $2(5x) + 2(3x) = 32$. Calculate the value of x:

$$\begin{aligned}
10x + 6x &= 32 \\
16x &= 32 \\
x &= 2
\end{aligned}$$

So, the sides of the rectangle are $5 \times 2 = 10$ and $3 \times 2 = 6$.

The area of the rectangle is $10 \times 6 = 60$ sq in.

Math

CHAPTER 14

ADVANCED MATH

CHAPTER OBJECTIVES

By the end of this chapter, you will be able to:

- Draw inferences about data presented in a variety of graphical formats
- Draw inferences about surveys and data samples

Math

1. Charts and Data Interpretation

Interpreting Charts

To excel at data interpretation, you must recognize the many ways that charts communicate information. The most common types of charts and graphs include pie charts, line graphs, bar graphs, and pictographs.

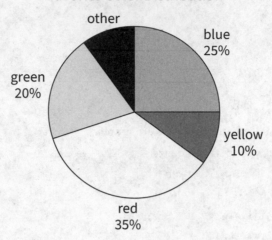

Favorite Color Distribution

A. What conclusions can you draw from the circle graph above?

_____

B. What's missing from the circle graph?

_____

C. If 200 people were surveyed, how many more people picked red than picked yellow as their favorite color?

_____

SHSAT EXPERT NOTE

Before working on data interpretation questions, briefly study the graph, table, or chart; determine what it represents and what patterns are apparent in the data.

NUMBER OF NATIONAL PARKS
IN FOUR STATES

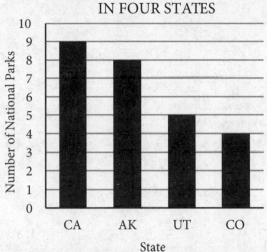

1. The graph above shows the number of national parks in each of four states. CA has 10 million visitors per park per year, and AK has 5 million visitors per park per year. UT and CO each have 4.5 million visitors per park per year. Which of the states has the **least** number of national park visitors per year?

A. CA

B. AK

C. UT

D. CO

SHSAT EXPERT NOTE

When tackling charts and graphs, first identify the title and what the chart represents. Next, determine what the *x*-axis represents and what the *y*-axis represents. Your success will be determined by your ability to keep track of different pieces of information.

2. Data Tables

Interpreting Data Tables

Questions with data tables usually ask about percent, average, range, and probability.

A **frequency distribution** shows the number of times each value appears in the data set.

- To find the mean, multiply each value by the number of times it occurs, add all of these products, and then divide by the total number of values.
- To find the median, add the frequencies to find the number of values, and then determine into which group the middle value falls.

VALUE	FREQUENCY
4	5
5	2
6	4
7	4
8	6

A. What is the mean of the data in the table above?

_____

B. What is the median of the data in the table above?

_____

SHSAT EXPERT NOTE

The mean is the average of the values in a data set. The median is the value in the middle when the terms are arranged in order. The mode is the value that occurs most frequently in the data set. The range of a data set is the difference between the largest and smallest values in the set.

Number of Framed Artworks	Percent of Rooms
1	12%
2	60%
3	25%
4 or more	3%

1. A study reported the number of framed artworks in a hotel room. The table above shows the percent distribution for 500 rooms. How many of the 500 rooms had at least 2 framed artworks?

A. 60
B. 140
C. 300
D. 440

Number of Notebooks	Number of Backpacks
0	8
1	10
2	25
3	11
4	3
5	3

2. The table above shows the number of notebooks that students on campus carried in their backpacks. What is the mean number of notebooks per backpack?

E. 1
F. 2
G. 3
H. 4

Team	Lowest Score	Range
Portal	1,850	98
J & J	1,733	101
Danger	1,910	68
Bots	1,512	215

3. Four teams participated at a cybersecurity competition. The table above shows the lowest score and the range of scores for each team. What is the overall range of all the scores for all four teams?

A. 147

B. 215

C. 398

D. 466

Number of Pieces	Color on Piece
6	blue
9	green
4	white
2	yellow
3	purple

4. A box contains jigsaw pieces. Using the table above, which color has exactly a 1 in 6 chance of being selected at random from the box?

E. blue

F. green

G. white

H. purple

3. Surveys with Two Responses

Interpreting Surveys

For questions that involve a survey with two responses (A and B), the total number surveyed is the number of responses for A plus the number of responses for B minus the number of responses for both A and B plus the number of responses for neither A nor B:

$$total = (A + B) - both + neither$$

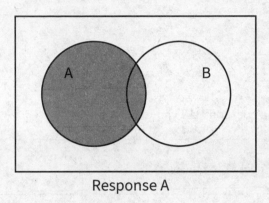

Response A

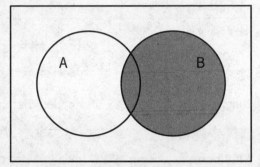

Response B

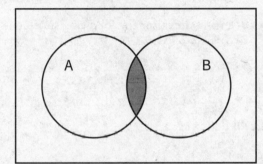

Both Response A and B

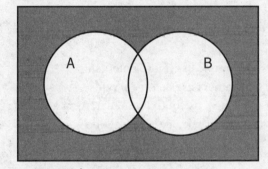

Neither Response A nor B

A survey polled students to determine whether they liked the summer and winter seasons. Below are the results of the survey:

- 50 students answered that they like summer.
- 40 students answered that they like winter.
- 15 students said that they like both summer and winter.
- 20 students said that they like neither summer nor winter.

A. How many students answered summer only?

_____

B. How many students answered winter only?

_____

C. How many students were surveyed?

_____

Another approach to solving survey questions is to organize the given information into a table and logically fill in the boxes until you find the answer to what the question asked.

Out of a class of 200 high school students, 60 play soccer, 25 play football, and 130 play neither sport. How many students play soccer but not football?

D. What given information can you fill in?

	Soccer	Not Soccer	Total
Football			
Not Football			
Total			

E. Which box represents the information that the question asks you to solve for?

_____

F. What boxes can you logically fill in to help you get to the answer?

_____

1. A survey polled customers to determine what type of detergent they use. The following statements are the results of the survey:

   - 15 customers use liquid detergent.
   - 25 customers use detergent pods.
   - 4 customers use both liquid detergent and detergent pods.
   - 2 customers use neither liquid detergent nor detergent pods.

   How many customers were surveyed?

   A. 38

   B. 40

   C. 42

   E. 46

2. At a restaurant, a survey asked two "yes/no" questions. Of the 290 diners who responded to the survey, 220 answered "yes" to the first question, and 150 answered "yes" to the second question. What is the **least** possible number of diners who answered "yes" to both questions?

   E. 50

   F. 60

   G. 70

   H. 80

Answers and Explanations

1. Charts and Data Interpretation

A. The greatest number of people chose red, then blue, then green.

B. No percentage is given for "other."

C. First find how many people picked red and yellow if 200 people were surveyed: $200 \times 0.35 = 70$ picked red; $200 \times 0.10 = 20$ picked yellow. Then subtract $70 - 20 = 50$ more picked red.

1. D
Subject: Statistics and Probability

Getting to the Answer: The question asks for the state with the least number of national park visitors per year. See if you can logically eliminate any of the states. Eliminate CA, as it has both the largest number of parks and the highest number of visitors per park. Also eliminate AK, as it has both more parks and more visitors per park than UT and CO. Finally, eliminate UT, as it has the same number of visitors per park as CO but more total parks than CO. CO has the least number of national park visitors per year.

2. Data Tables

A. The sum of the products is $4(5) + 5(2) + 6(4) + 7(4) + 8(6) = 20 + 10 + 24 + 28 + 48 = 130$. The number of data points is $5 + 2 + 4 + 4 + 6 = 21$. Now divide: the mean is $\frac{130}{21} \approx 6.2$.

B. Since there are 21 values, the 11th value is the median. The 8th through 11th values are all 6, so the median is 6.

1. D
Subject: Arithmetic

Getting to the Answer: Add the percentage of rooms that have 2, 3, and 4 or more framed artworks: $60\% + 25\% + 3\% = 88\%$.

Multiply that percentage by the total number of rooms to calculate the number of rooms that had at least 2 framed artworks: $500 \times 0.88 = 440$ rooms.

Alternatively, you could find the number of rooms with 1 framed artwork and then subtract it from the total: $500 - 0.12(500) = 440$.

2. F
Subject: Arithmetic

Getting to the Answer: First determine the total number of notebooks by multiplying the number of notebooks by the number of students.

Number of Notebooks	Number of Backpacks	Total Number of Notebooks
0	8	0
1	10	10
2	25	50
3	11	33
4	3	12
5	3	15
		120

Then add to get the total number of notebooks. To calculate the mean, divide the total number of notebooks by the number of backpacks: $\text{average} = \frac{120}{60} = 2$. The mean number of notebooks per backpack is 2.

3. D
Subject: Statistics and Probability

Getting to the Answer: First calculate the highest score for each team by adding the range to the lowest score:

Portal: $1,850 + 98 = 1,948$

J & J: $1,733 + 101 = 1,834$

Danger: $1,910 + 68 = 1,978$

Bots: $1,512 + 215 = 1,727$

The overall lowest score is 1,512, and the overall highest score is 1,978. Therefore, the overall range of all the scores is $1,978 - 1,512 = 466$.

4.   G

Subject: Statistics and Probability

Getting to the Answer: First determine the total number of jigsaw pieces in the box: $6 + 9 + 4 + 2 + 3 = 24$.

Then set up a proportion to find which color has exactly a 1 in 6 chance of being picked:

$$\frac{x}{24} = \frac{1}{6}$$
$$6x = 24$$
$$x = 4$$

There are 4 white pieces in the box, so a white piece has a 1 in 6 chance of being randomly selected.

3. Surveys with Two Responses

A. $50 - 15 = 35$

B. $40 - 15 = 25$

C.   total $= (A + B) -$ both $+$ neither $= (50 + 40) - 15 + 20 = 95$

D.

	Soccer	Not Soccer	Total
Football			25
Not Football		130	
Total	60		200

E.   The intersection of "Soccer" and "Not Football"

F.   One way to fill in the table is to realize that there are $200 - 25 = 175$ students who do not play football. Therefore, there are $175 - 130 = 45$ students who play soccer but not football.

	Soccer	Not Soccer	Total
Football			25
Not Football	**45**	130	**175**
Total	60		200

1.   A

Subject: Statistics and Probability

Getting to the Answer: The total number of customers surveyed can be found using the formula total $= (A + B) -$ both $+$ neither, in which A represents the number of customers who use liquid detergent and B represents the

number of customers who use pods: $(A + B) -$ both $+$ neither $= (15 + 25) - 4 + 2 = 40 - 4 + 2 = 36 + 2 = 38$.

Alternatively, fill in a table to solve:

	Liquid	Not Liquid	Total
Pods	4		25
Not Pods		2	
Total	15		

Now fill in information until you can determine the total. You can determine that $15 - 4 = 11$ customers use liquid but not pods. Thus, $11 + 2 = 13$ customers do not use pods. Therefore, $25 + 13 = 38$ total customers were surveyed.

	Liquid	Not Liquid	Total
Pods	4		25
Not Pods	**11**	2	**13**
Total	15		**38**

2.   H

Subject: Statistics and Probability

Getting to the Answer: The number of diners who answered "yes" to either question is $220 + 150 = 370$. Given that there were only 290 diners surveyed, some of the diners must have answered "yes" to both questions. The least possible number of diners who answered "yes" to both questions is $370 - 290 = 80$.

Alternatively, you can solve for the least possible value of "both" in the formula total $= (A + B) -$ both $+$ neither. The variable A is the number of diners who answered "yes" to the first question, and the variable B is the number of diners who answered "yes" to the second question. Set the "neither" value to 0, since the least possible value of "both" (answering "yes" to both questions) would occur when no one answered "no" to both questions. (The more overlap—or "yes" answers to both questions—the higher the "neither" value would need to be to add up to 290 total diners surveyed.) Solve for "both" in the equation $290 = (220 + 150) -$ both $+ 0$. This equation yields "both" $= 80$.

PART FOUR

READY, SET, GO!

CHAPTER 15

PREPARING FOR TEST DAY

CHAPTER OBJECTIVES

By the end of this chapter, you will be able to:

- Identify what to do the week before, the night before, and the morning of the test
- Describe specific strategies for managing your stress during the weeks before test day

1. Countdown to the Test

It's normal to have some pre-test nervousness. This chapter provides a helpful plan for the week before test day so that you can feel prepared and confident.

The Week Before the Test

Focus on pacing and strategy.

Decide how you are going to approach each section and question type.

Sit down and do practice problems in the Practice Sets, or complete extra drills you skipped the first time through.

Practice waking up early and eating breakfast on the weekend so that you will be alert on test day.

Two Days Before the Test

Do your last studying—a few more practice problems—and then relax. Don't start making hundreds of flash cards or take practice test after practice test.

The Night Before the Test

Do NOT study. Instead, get together the following items:

- Your admission/registration ticket
- Your ID
- A watch (choose one that is easy to read)
- Slightly dull No. 2 pencils (so they fill in the ovals faster)
- A pencil sharpener
- Erasers
- The clothes you will wear (layers)
- Snacks (easy to open and eat quickly)
- Money
- A packet of tissues

Know exactly where you're going and exactly how you're getting there.

Relax the night before the test, and get a good night's sleep. Go to bed at a reasonable hour, and leave yourself extra time in the morning.

The Morning of the Test

Eat breakfast. Make it something substantial and nutritious, but don't deviate too much from your everyday pattern.

Dress in layers so that you can adjust to the temperature of the test room. The climate at the test location may vary, as may your body temperature. Make sure you can warm up or cool down easily.

Be sure to get there early. Leave enough time to allow for traffic, mass transit delays, getting lost on the way, or any other snag that could slow you down.

Don't stress! Check out the next lesson for more information on how to manage your stress before and during the test.

2. Stress Management

Make the Most of Your Prep Time

The countdown to the SHSAT has begun. Your test date is looming on the horizon, and your anxiety is probably on the rise. Your stomach may feel twisted, or your thinking may be getting cloudy. You might be worried that you won't be ready in time. Worst of all, you may not be sure of what to do about these feelings.

First, don't panic! It is possible to conquer that anxiety and stress—both before and during the test. Lack of control is a common cause of stress. Research shows that if you don't have a sense of control over what's happening in your life, you can easily end up feeling helpless and hopeless. This means that just having specific things to do and to think about may help reduce your stress. This chapter discusses how to take control, including stress management strategies for both your remaining time leading up to the test and for the SHSAT itself.

> **SHSAT EXPERT NOTE**
>
> **Avoid Must-y Thinking**
>
> Let go of "must-y" thoughts: those notions that you must do something in a certain way. For example, thoughts like "I must get a great score, or else!" or "I must meet everyone's expectations!" can have a negative influence on your actions.

Identify the Sources of Stress

In the space provided below, jot down anything you identify as a source of your test-related stress. The idea is to pin down as much free-floating anxiety as possible so that you can take control of it. Here are some common examples to get you started:

- I always freeze up on tests.
- I'm nervous about the English Language Arts section.
- I'm never any good at math.
- I need a good/great score to go to Brooklyn Tech.
- My older brother/sister/best friend got in. I need to get in, too.
- People will be really disappointed if I don't get in.
- I'm afraid of losing my focus and concentration.
- I'm afraid that I'm not spending enough time preparing.
- I study like crazy, but nothing seems to stick.
- I always run out of time and get nervous or anxious during a test.

Sources of Stress

_____

_____

_____

_____

Take a few minutes to think about the sources of stress you've just written down. Then, rewrite them, listing the statements that contribute most to your stress first and putting the least stressful items last. Chances are that the top of the list is a fairly accurate description of your test anxiety, both physically and mentally. The items at the bottom of the list usually describe your more general fears. As you write the list, you're creating a prioritized list of sources of stress so that you can start by dealing with the sources that affect you most. Often, taking care of the most stressful sources at the top of the list goes a long way toward relieving overall testing anxiety, and you may not even need to bother with the worries you placed last.

> **SHSAT EXPERT NOTE**
>
> Create a study space. Don't study in a messy, cramped, or loud area if at all possible. Before you sit down to work, clear yourself an uncluttered space. Make sure you have whatever tools you will need—such as books, pencils, or highlighters—within easy reach before you sit down to study. Put your phone on silent, and turn it over so that you're not tempted by notifications. Set up a study space that allows you to focus on your work with minimal distractions.

Know Your Strengths

Research shows that reframing your thoughts in a positive way can actually influence how you act; reflecting on positive experiences can influence positive behaviors. The following exercise is most effective when completed multiple times, so you should plan to complete it at least once before you take the SHSAT. First, spend one minute listing the areas of the test that you are good at. These areas can be general ("reading") or specific ("math grid-in questions"). Write down as many as you can think of and, if possible, write for the entire minute. If you have trouble brainstorming, think about more than just the SHSAT. In which areas have you succeeded recently in school?

Strong Subjects

_____

_____

_____

Next, spend one minute listing the areas of the test you're not so good at yet. These are your areas of opportunity. Again, keep it to one minute, but do your best to continue writing until you reach the cutoff. Don't be afraid to identify and write down your weak spots; everyone has them! In all probability, as you write both lists, you'll find that you are strong in some areas and not so strong in others. Taking note of both your strengths and your areas of opportunity boosts your confidence and focuses your studying.

Areas of Opportunity

_____

_____

_____

_____

Identifying your areas of opportunity gives you some distinct advantages over those who choose to focus only on their strengths. First, doing this helps you to determine where you need to spend extra effort, especially if you have a lot of time to study. Increased exposure to tough material makes it feel more familiar and less intimidating. So reviewing a topic, even if you don't feel that you have time to master it, can reduce your stress level when you encounter a question about that topic on test day. Also, you'll feel better about your own progress because you'll be dealing directly with areas of the test that bring on your anxiety. It's easier to feel confident when you know you're actively strengthening your chances of earning a higher overall test score.

Now that you have identified both your strengths and your areas of opportunity, go back to your list of strengths and expand on it for two minutes. Start with the general items on that first list and make them more specific. If anything new comes to mind, jot it down. For now, focus all of your attention and effort on your strengths. Don't underestimate yourself or your abilities; at the same time, don't list strengths you don't really have.

Expanding from general to specific might go like this: If you listed "reading" as a broad topic you feel strong in, you would then narrow your focus to include the parts of reading about which you are particularly knowledgeable. Your areas of strength related to "reading" might include identifying the main idea of a passage, locating key details, being able to answer complicated questions about a passage, etc.

Strong Subjects: An Expanded List

_____

_____

_____

_____

After you've stopped, check your time. Did you find yourself going beyond the allotted two minutes? Did you write down more things than you thought you knew? Is it possible you know more than you've given yourself credit for?

Here's another way to think about this type of exercise: Every area of strength and confidence you can identify is like having a reserve of solid gold in a safe, protected place. You can then use these reserves to solve difficult questions, maintain confidence, and keep test stress and anxiety at a distance. The most encouraging part is that every time you recognize another area of strength, succeed at coming up with a solution, or get a good score on a test, you increase your reserves, and there is absolutely no limit to how much self-confidence you can have or how good you can feel about yourself.

SHSAT EXPERT NOTE

Just by completing these brief exercises, you have taken an active step toward helping yourself. Do you notice any increased feelings of confidence? Enjoy them: you've earned it!

Imagine Yourself Succeeding

These two exercises are both physical and mental. For both exercises, you will want to find a comfortable chair and get yourself into a comfortable sitting position in a quiet setting. Wear loose clothes. If you wear glasses, take them off.

Start by closing your eyes and breathing in a deep, satisfying breath of air. Really fill your lungs until your rib cage is fully expanded and you feel like you can't take in any more. Hold your breath for a moment, and then slowly exhale the air completely. Imagine you're blowing out a candle with your last little puff of air. Do this two or three more times, filling your lungs to their maximum and emptying them totally. Keep your eyes closed comfortably but not tightly. Let your body sink deeper into the chair as you become even more comfortable.

With your eyes shut, you may notice something very interesting. When you sit comfortably, close your eyes, and focus on your breathing, you're no longer focusing on the world outside of you. Now, you can concentrate on what happens *inside* you. The more you recognize your own physical reactions to stress and anxiety, the more you can do about them. You might not realize it, but as this happens, you're beginning to regain a sense of being in control.

Once you've settled into a relaxed, comfortable breathing pattern, imagine yourself in a relaxing situation. Your situation might take place in a special place you've visited before, or it can be one you've only heard about. It can even be a fictional location that you create in your imagination, but using a real-life memory of a place or situation usually requires less effort. Imagine the scene with as much detail as possible, and notice as much as you can about it. Once you feel that you have noticed everything there is to notice about the situation, allow the first relaxing situation to fade away and another to take its place. Do what you can to allow the images to come easily and naturally; don't force them.

Stay focused on these images as you sink farther back into your chair. Breathe easily and naturally. You might have the sensation of stress or tension draining from your muscles and flowing downward, out your feet, and away from you. If you're having trouble seeing anything, that's okay. Focus on your relaxed breathing, noticing how you feel as you breathe in and out. If an image comes to mind, examine it. If not, just keep breathing.

After two or three images (or approximately 20–30 breaths), take a moment to check how you're feeling. Notice how comfortable you've become, and imagine how much easier it would feel if you could take the test feeling this comfortable. If you were successful, you've coupled the images of your special place with sensations of comfort and relaxation. You've also found a way to become relaxed simply by visualizing your own safe, special place. If you weren't successful today, that's okay . . . try again tomorrow!

Once you've completed this relaxation exercise, close your eyes and start remembering a real-life situation in which you did well on a test. If you can't come up with one, remember a situation in which you did something (academic or otherwise) that you were really proud of—just make sure that it's a genuine accomplishment.

Now, make this memory as detailed as possible. Think about the sights, the sounds, the smells, and even the tastes associated with this memory. Remember how confident and motivated you felt as you accomplished your goal. Now, start thinking about the upcoming SHSAT. Keep your thoughts and feelings in line with that successful experience. Don't try to make comparisons between them. Instead, focus on imagining yourself taking the upcoming test with the same feelings of confidence and relaxed control.

These exercises are a great way to manage your stress, especially stress related to the SHSAT. You should practice them often, especially whenever the prospect of taking the exam starts to stress you out. The more you practice, the more effective these exercises will be for you.

SHSAT EXPERT NOTE

Your school likely has counseling available. If you've tried multiple strategies for conquering test stress on your own and don't feel like you're making progress, make an appointment with your counselor for one-on-one support.

Get Active

Whether your choice is walking, jogging, biking, dance, push-ups, or even a pickup basketball or baseball game, physical exercise is a very effective way to stimulate both your mind and body and to improve your ability to think and concentrate. Also, it's a medical fact that sedentary people get less oxygen to the blood and, therefore, to the head than active people do. You can live fine with a little less oxygen, but you definitely can't think as well. Ironically, a surprising number of students get out of the habit of regular exercise because they're spending so much time prepping for exams. In the long term, however, making time for exercise will pay off as part of your stress management efforts.

> **SHSAT EXPERT NOTE**
>
> When you're in the middle of studying and start feeling tired, take a short, brisk walk. Breathe deeply and swing your arms as you walk to clear your mind.

There's something else that happens when students don't make exercise an integral part of their test preparation. Like all natural things, you operate best if all your "energy systems" are in balance. Studying uses a lot of energy, but that energy is (usually) only mental energy. When you take a study break, try to do something active (instead of scrolling through social media or trying to take a very short nap). Set a timer, and take a 5- to 10-minute movement break for every hour that you study.

Need some inspiration? A quick Internet search should pull up some easy activities for short movement breaks. The physical exertion helps use up your physical energy, which helps to keep your mind and body in sync. Then, when you finish studying for the night and go to bed, it's less likely that you will lie there tense and unable to sleep because your head is overtired and your body wants to get out and do something.

One warning about physical activity: it's not a good idea to exercise vigorously during the hour or two before you go to bed. It takes some time for your body to relax after physical activity, so doing physical activity close to bedtime could easily cause sleep problems. For the same reason, it's also not a good idea to study right up to bedtime. Make time for a "buffer period" for 30 to 60 minutes before you go to bed that's designed to help you transition from being awake to being asleep.

Here's another natural route to relaxation and invigoration. It's an exercise that you can do whenever you get stressed out—including right before the test begins or even *during* the test. It's very simple and takes just a few minutes.

First, close your eyes. Start with your eyes, and—without holding your breath—gradually tighten every muscle in your body (noticeably but not to the point of pain) in the following sequence:

1. Close your eyes tightly.
2. Squeeze your nose and mouth together so that your whole face is scrunched up. (If it makes you self-conscious to do this in the test room, skip the face-scrunching part.)
3. Pull your chin into your chest and pull your shoulders together.
4. Tighten your arms to your body and then clench your hands into tight fists.
5. Pull in your stomach.
6. Squeeze your thighs together and tighten your calves.
7. Stretch your feet and then curl your toes (watch out for cramping in this part).

At this point, every muscle should be tightened. Now, relax your body, one part at a time, *in reverse order*, starting with your toes. Let the tension drop out of each muscle. The entire process might take five minutes from start to finish when you are not in a timed situation (but probably only a minute or two during the test). This clenching and unclenching exercise should help you to feel very relaxed.

Keep Breathing

Dedicated attention to breathing is an excellent way of managing stress. Often, those who are struggling (either with physical or mental stress) end up taking shallow breaths. They breathe using only their upper chest and shoulder muscles, and they may even hold their breath for long periods of time. Conversely, those who continue to breathe normally and rhythmically while experiencing stress are more likely to be relaxed and in control during the entire experience. This means that now is the time to get used to the practice of relaxed breathing. Practice the next exercise to learn to breathe in a natural, easy rhythm.

With your eyes still closed, breathe in slowly and *deeply* through your nose. Hold the breath for a bit, and then release it through your mouth. The key is to breathe slowly and deeply by using your diaphragm (the big band of muscle that spans your body just above your waist) to draw air in and out naturally and effortlessly. Breathing deeply with your diaphragm (as opposed to your shoulders and chest) encourages relaxation and helps minimize tension. Try it, and notice how relaxed and comfortable you feel, especially compared with breathing more shallowly.

This is yet another stress management technique you can use during the test to collect your thoughts and ward off excess stress. The entire exercise should take no more than three to five minutes. Again, though, this is suggested timing while you are in an untimed situation; during the test, you should plan to spend a minute or less on this activity at any one time.

Handling Stress During the Test

The biggest stress generator is often the test itself. Fear not; there are methods designed to reduce your stress during the test.

- Remind yourself to keep moving forward instead of getting bogged down in a difficult question. Remember, you don't have to get everything right to achieve a good score. The best test takers skip difficult material temporarily (sometimes permanently!) in search of the easier questions. They mark the questions that require extra time and thought, and they strategically skip questions if doing so increases the number of questions they can answer correctly. This strategy buys time and builds confidence so they can handle the tough questions later, and you can use this strategy regardless of how much content you have mastered.

- Keep breathing! Test takers often tend to forget to breathe properly as the test proceeds. They may start holding their breath without realizing it, or they may breathe erratically. Improper breathing interferes with clear thinking, so use the breathing exercises from this chapter to help you overcome stress during the test.

- Some quick, small physical activity during the test—especially if your concentration is wandering or your energy is waning—can help. Try this: Put your palms together and press intensely for a few seconds. Concentrate on the tension you feel through your palms, wrists, forearms, and up into your biceps and shoulders. Then, quickly release the pressure. Feel the difference as you let go. Focus on the warm relaxation that floods through the muscles. Now you're ready to return to the task.

- Here's another quick activity that will relieve tension in both your neck and eye muscles. Slowly rotate your head from side to side, turning your head and eyes to look as far back over each shoulder as you can. Feel the muscles stretch on one side of your neck as they contract on the other. Repeat five times in each direction.

- If it feels like something is going really wrong, don't panic. If the test booklet is defective—two pages are stuck together or the ink has run—stay calm. Raise your hand to tell the proctor you need a new book. If you accidentally skip a page and realize you have more questions left than you originally thought, just work through each question strategically; be sure to fill in an answer for every question even if it's a complete guess.

- Don't be thrown if other test takers seem to be working faster or with more exertion than you are. Continue to spend your time working systematically through your answers; this process leads to better results. Don't mistake the other test takers' activity as a sign of progress and higher scores.

- If you find yourself starting to worry, remind yourself of how well you've prepared. Try to change your mindset: Think of any nerves as excitement for being able to prove what you know. You know the structure of the test, you know the instructions, and you've studied for every question type. You've got this!

CHAPTER 16

STRATEGIC REVIEW

CHAPTER OBJECTIVES

By the end of this chapter, you will be able to:

- Reinforce the Kaplan Method for Revising/Editing Text and the Kaplan Method for Reading Comprehension
- Review active reading, question types, and common incorrect answers
- Reinforce the Kaplan Method for SHSAT Math and other good habits for the math section of the test
- Review important math concepts and skills

1. Strategic Review: SHSAT English Language Arts

Reading

> **THE KAPLAN METHOD FOR READING COMPREHENSION**
>
> **STEP 1:** Read actively
>
> **STEP 2:** Examine the question stem and predict
>
> **STEP 3:** Match and answer

Read Actively

Actively read the following passage, taking notes to create a Roadmap. Be sure to write down the topic of each paragraph and the main idea of the passage.

Daniel Webster

1 Though he later became known as one of the greatest orators of his time, the prominent attorney and statesman Daniel Webster suffered from a debilitating fear of public speaking in his youth. Webster was the son of a farmer, born in New Hampshire in 1782 and brought up in a large family. As a boy, he was encouraged to read and had a strong natural intellect and a passion for learning that convinced his parents to prioritize a formal education for him. Unfortunately, when he was 14 years old, Webster's introduction to schooling at the prestigious Phillips Exeter Academy was nothing short of traumatic for him. A significant curricular requirement for students of the Academy was "declamation," the act of public speaking. Historical records indicate that Webster became so petrified when asked to speak in front of an audience that he simply refused to stand up in front of his classmates, retreating to his room in fear.

2 Although Webster's time at Exeter Academy was short-lived, it is not known whether he left school due to the trauma of the educational model employed there or for other reasons, perhaps financial. In any case, just a year later, Webster enrolled at Dartmouth College where he was able to finally overcome this powerful phobia. Webster dealt with his fear of public speaking, technically termed glossophobia, by plunging himself into activities that demanded he speak before an audience. He became an active member of the United Fraternity where he was required to deliver many speeches. He relied on his other great skills, such as his remarkable memory and writing talent, to enhance his performance in public debates. When he graduated from Dartmouth in 1801, Webster was already so polished a speaker that he was invited to deliver the Independence Day oration on campus.

3 After graduating from college, Webster began his career as a teacher before ultimately finding his calling in the practice of law. Webster, known for his relentless determinationand lofty aspirations, was not satisfied with merelygiving speeches for colleagues at annual holiday parties. He soon opened his own law practice in Portsmouth in 1807. His reputation as a lawyer grew rapidly, and he quickly rose to prominence. Webster took an active interest in the political landscape of the time, expressing criticism of the Jefferson administration's actions leading up to the War of 1812. In fact, it was in 1812 that Webster officially entered politics with his election to the U.S. House of Representatives. Historians credit Webster's fervently articulated opposition to the War of 1812 as the reason for his successful entrée into political office.

4 Webster's political career is marked by an interesting shift from being an advocate of states' rights to that of a staunch nationalist championing the importance of a unified nation without international influences and entanglements. He served as a U.S. congressman and senator from Massachusetts, did a stint as U.S. secretary of state under President William Harrison, and even made a bid for president. Perhaps his most influential role continued to be that of debater, as Webster argued many important cases in front of the Supreme Court that influenced judicial decision-making. Under Chief Justice John Marshall, Webster's arguments helped shape policy that fostered a strong federal government and powerful judicial branch.

5 As an orator, Daniel Webster had no equal. He spoke with eloquence and dramatic expression. His talent for persuasion is legendary. It is remarkable indeed that such great triumphs can be traced back to that young student who found himself literally sick with fear, attempting to address his classmates. Webster's accomplishments powerfully demonstrate that talent can evolve, that tapping into one's other strengths can help overcome adversity, and that even the most intense of fears can be overcome through concerted effort.

FAMOUS PEOPLE WITH GLOSSOPHOBIA[1]		
NAME	**PROFESSION**	**BORN**
Demosthenes	Greek Politician	384 B.C.E.
Thomas Jefferson	U.S. Politician	1743
Daniel Webster	U.S. Politician	1782
Mahatma Gandhi	Activist	1869
Maya Angelou	Poet	1928
Warren Buffet	Investor	1930
Harrison Ford	Actor	1942
Ricky Williams	Football Player	1977
Adele	Singer	1988

[1] The fear of public speaking

Global

A. What is the subject of the passage?

B. What does the author say about that subject?

1. Which statement **best** describes the central idea of the passage?

   A. Webster was scared of speaking before a large audience for much of his life.

   B. Webster laid his phobias to rest and became the most effective politician of his time.

   C. Webster's lofty aspirations for the presidency were never fulfilled.

   D. Webster overcame his aversion to public speaking to become a successful politician.

Detail

    C. Where in the passage are Webster's skills as a public speaker addressed?

    D. Based on the information in the passage, what is a good prediction for the answer to the question below?

2. Which sentence **best** explains why Webster was able to become such an effective public speaker?

    E. "Webster was the son of a farmer, born in New Hampshire in 1782 and brought up in a large family." (paragraph 1)

    F. "He relied on his other great skills, such as his remarkable memory and writing talent, to enhance his performance in public debates." (paragraph 2)

    G. "After graduating from college, Webster began his career as a teacher before ultimately finding his calling in the practice of law." (paragraph 3)

    H. "Under Chief Justice John Marshall, Webster's arguments helped shape policy that fostered a strong federal government and powerful judicial branch." (paragraph 4)

Function

    E. Why does the author begin the passage with a discussion of Webster's fear of public speaking?

    F. Why does the author characterize Webster's phobia as "powerful" in paragraph 2?

3. Read the sentence from paragraph 2.

> **In any case, just a year later, Webster enrolled at Dartmouth College where he was able to finally overcome this powerful phobia.**

The author **most** likely uses the word "powerful" in order to

    A. highlight that Webster's ability to overcome such an all-consuming fear was impressive.

    B. foreshadow Webster's eventual failure within the political sphere.

    C. assert that Webster was regarded as a particularly effective lawyer.

    D. introduce the idea that Webster's efforts to overcome his considerable fear were ineffective.

Inference

    G. What does the passage say about "giving [holiday] speeches" specifically?

    H. Based on the information in the passage, what is a good prediction for the answer to the question below?

4. What does the author suggest by mentioning that Webster "was not satisfied with merely giving speeches for colleagues at annual holiday parties"? (paragraph 3)

    E. Webster was famous for his determination.

    F. Webster refused future invitations to speak in front of colleagues.

    G. Webster was driven by passionate nationalism.

    H. Webster's ambition led to his rise as a prominent statesman.

Infographic

    I.   What does the table below the passage show?

    J.   How does this information relate to the passage as a whole?

5. The table below the passage contributes to the development of the topic of the passage by

    A. suggesting that Webster was inspired to overcome glossophobia by other famous people who overcame their fear of public speaking.

    B. implying that Webster was only one person among many famous people, past and present, affected by glossophobia.

    C. comparing Webster's accomplishments with those of other famous people who suffered from glossophobia.

    D. proving that overcoming a fear of public speaking through facing the fear has been common from ancient times to the present.

Revising/Editing

THE KAPLAN METHOD FOR REVISING/EDITING TEXT

STEP 1: Examine the question stem and answer choices

STEP 2: Select the most correct, concise, and relevant choice

REVISING/EDITING PART A

DIRECTIONS: Answer the following questions, recognizing and correcting errors so that the sentences or paragraphs are grammatically correct. Reread relevant parts of the text before choosing the best answer for each question, but be mindful of time. You may write in your test booklet to take notes.

6. Read this paragraph.

A new music class, eagerly anticipated by new <u>students, includes</u> exercises for developing vocal range and for making musical notation understandable to beginner <u>musicians. The</u> course provides instruction in a variety of topics, such as tonality and <u>harmony, formal</u> and contemporary styles of music are also part of the curriculum. Students will explore the interaction of theory and technique as well as how these features apply to rhythm, scales, improvisation, and creative <u>expression. The</u> class culminates in a highly anticipated concert at the end of the semester.

Which revision corrects the error in sentence structure in the paragraph?

    E. students. Includes

    F. musicians; the

    G. harmony. Formal

    H. expression, the

7. Read this paragraph.

> (1) Built in 1889 for the World's Fair, the Eiffel Tower was almost destroyed due to Parisians' dislike of this architectural wonder. (2) Fortunately, the tower became home to a radio antenna in 1909 and has since had over 200 million visitors who have taken the elevator to the top level. (3) Visitors might notice that every seven years the tower receives a new coat of paint, which takes 15 months to apply to its network of beams. (4) While taking a sightseeing tour of Paris, the Eiffel Tower is often a tourist's first stop.

Which sentence contains an error in its construction and should be revised?

A. sentence 1

B. sentence 2

C. sentence 3

D. sentence 4

8. Read this paragraph.

> (1) Canada's ten <u>provinces</u> and two territories <u>cover</u> an extremely large portion of North America. (2) The country includes forests, mountains, rivers, and <u>grasslands,</u> which <u>can be</u> influenced by extreme seasonal temperatures. (3) Canadians speak English and <u>French,</u> and tend to live in the southern part of the country, where they generally <u>inhabiting</u> urban locations. (4) Since it shares a long border with America, <u>Canada</u> has <u>developed</u> trading arrangements and various shared interests with the United States.

Which revisions correct the errors in the paragraph?

E. Sentence 1: Insert a comma after *provinces*, AND change *cover* to **covers**.

F. Sentence 2: Delete the comma after *grasslands*, AND change *can be* to **are**.

G. Sentence 3: Delete the comma after *French*, AND change *inhabiting* to **inhabit**.

H. Sentence 4: Insert a comma after *Canada*, AND change *developed* to **develop**.

9. Read these sentences.

> (1) The first magnetic resonance imaging (MRI) scan was completed on July 3, 1977. (2) An MRI scan creates detailed images of the organs and tissues within the body that help physicians diagnose a variety of medical conditions.

What is the **best** way to combine the sentences to clarify the relationship between the ideas?

A. Even though the first magnetic resonance imaging (MRI) scan was completed on July 3, 1977, MRI scans create detailed images of the organs and tissues within the body that help physicians diagnose a variety of medical conditions.

B. An MRI scan, the first of which was completed on July 3, 1977, creates detailed images of the organs and tissues within the body that help physicians diagnose a variety of medical conditions.

C. Today, an MRI scan creates detailed images of the organs and tissues within the body that help physicians diagnose a variety of medical conditions, but the first magnetic one was completed on July 3, 1977.

D. While the first magnetic resonance imaging (MRI) scan was completed on July 3, 1977, MRI scans create detailed images of the organs and tissues within the body that help physicians diagnose a variety of medical conditions.

10. Read this sentence.

> During the pivotal moment in the murder mystery novel, the main character—a highly respected detective—talked to people who seemed to be lying about some things.

Which revision of the sentence uses the **most** precise language?

E. questioned the two main suspects

F. spoke to a few untrustworthy people

G. discussed the case with suspects

H. yelled loudly at the criminals

REVISING/EDITING PART B

DIRECTIONS: Read the passage and answer the questions following it, improving the writing quality and correcting grammatical errors. Reread relevant parts of the text before choosing the best answer for each question, but be mindful of time. You may write in your test booklet to take notes.

Milton Hershey

(1) Who has not enjoyed a Hershey Bar or a Hershey Kiss? (2) Both were created by master confectioner Milton Hershey, born into a Pennsylvania farm family in 1857. (3) His education was limited—he went only as far as the fourth grade—and after a disastrous first apprenticeship to a printer, his mother arranged for his training with a local caramel candy maker. (4) Hershey not only learned his craft but also began a lifelong dedication to quality ingredients. (5) In 1883, Hershey opened the highly successful Lancaster Caramel Company, which packaged caramels in bulk. (6) This was a new and profitable innovation.

(7) Hershey's interest in chocolate was sparked by his 1893 visit to the World's Columbian Exposition. (8) He sold the caramel company and used the money to open the Hershey Chocolate company. (9) Because of its location near the farmland of Lancaster, Pennsylvania, Hershey was able to buy fresh milk. (10) At the time, it was considered a luxury product, but the mass production of the Hershey products made chocolate more popular. (11) This purchase was strategic since he was able to incorporate it into his own milk chocolate recipe.

(12) In 1905, Hershey's huge new factory opened and became the center of a town that grew up around it. (13) With his workers in mind, Hershey oversaw the construction of houses, schools, churches, public transportation, and even a zoo. (14) Today the town is a tourist attraction, popularly called Chocolatetown, USA; Hershey called it "the sweetest place on Earth." (15) It is one of several locations named after their founders, such as Disneyland.

(16) Hershey and his wife Catherine had no children, so they focused a great deal of their attention to philanthropic endeavors. (17) Their best known project was an orphanage, called the Hershey Industrial School (later renamed the Milton Hershey School). (18) In 1918, Hershey put all his shares of the Hershey's Chocolate Company into a trust for the school, which today provides an excellent education for children from troubled backgrounds. (19) Milton Hershey died peacefully in 1945 at the age of 88, having happily given away most of his money in his lifetime.

11. Which is the **best** way to combine sentences 5 and 6 to clarify the relationship between ideas?

   A. In 1883, Hershey opened the highly successful Lancaster Caramel Company, packaging caramels in bulk, this was a new and profitable innovation.

   B. In 1883, Hershey opened the highly successful Lancaster Caramel Company, packaging caramels in bulk, however this was a new and profitable innovation.

   C. In 1883, Hershey opened the highly successful Lancaster Caramel Company, packaging caramels in bulk, a new and profitable innovation.

   D. In 1883, Hershey opened the highly successful Lancaster Caramel Company, packaging caramels in bulk, starting a new and profitable innovation.

12. Which transition should be added to the beginning of sentence 8?

    E. Nonetheless,

    F. Even so,

    G. Unfortunately,

    H. Afterward,

13. Which revision of sentence 10 uses the **most** precise language?

    A. At the time, chocolate was considered a luxury product, but the mass production of the Hershey Bar, introduced in 1903, and Hershey's Kisses, first sold in 1907, made chocolate widely available and affordable.

    B. During that period in the United States, milk was considered a luxury product, but the mass production of the Hershey products, made chocolate widely available and affordable.

    C. At the time, chocolate was considered a product, but the mass production of the Hershey Bar, introduced in 1903, and Hershey's Kisses, first sold in 1907, made chocolate widely available and affordable.

    D. Milk, being a luxury product, was first introduced in 1903, and Hershey's Kisses, first sold in 1907, made chocolate widely available and affordable.

14. Where should sentence 11 be moved to improve the organization of the second paragraph (sentences 7–11)?

    E. to the beginning of the paragraph (before sentence 7)

    F. between sentences 7 and 8

    G. between sentences 8 and 9

    H. between sentences 9 and 10

15. Which sentence presents information that shifts away from the main topic of the third paragraph (sentences 12–15) and should be removed?

    A. sentence 12

    B. sentence 13

    C. sentence 14

    D. sentence 15

16. Which sentence would **best** follow and support sentence 16?

    E. Indeed, Milton Hershey is in the Philanthropy Hall of Fame.

    F. The two were equal partners in philanthropic contributions.

    G. Not every married couple without children gives to charity, though.

    H. Their contributions went to all manner of charitable organizations.

2. Strategic Review: SHSAT Math

THE KAPLAN METHOD FOR SHSAT MATH

STEP 1: What is the question?

STEP 2: What information is provided in the question? In what format do the answers appear?

STEP 3: What can I do with the information?
- Picking Numbers
- Backsolving
- Straightforward Math

STEP 4: Am I finished?

Arithmetic

1. Points A, B, and C are on a number line. A is between B and C. $\overline{AC} = \frac{2}{3}\overline{BA}$, and $\overline{BA} = 15$ units. What is the distance between points B and C ?

   A. 20 units

   B. 22.5 units

   C. 25 units

   D. 30 units

2. How many positive odd factors of 60 are greater than 2 and less than 20 ?

   E. 1

   F. 3

   G. 5

   H. 7

Minimum Wage	Number of States
$7.25	16
$8.25	3
$13.25	1

3. What is the mean minimum wage of the 20 states in the table above?

   A. $7.19

   B. $7.70

   C. $8.75

   D. $9.58

4. A package of cups contains exactly 6 blue cups. The probability of choosing a blue cup from the package is $\frac{3}{5}$. How many of the cups in the package are **not** blue?

   E. 4

   F. 10

   G. 12

   H. 16

Algebra

5. An air mattress is partially filled with a liters of air. Gwen adds 80 liters of air to the air mattress such that it is 80% inflated. If Gwen adds 30 more liters of air, the air mattress will be 90% full. What is the value of a?

   A. 100

   B. 121

   C. 160

   D. 209

6. Which of the following number lines shows the solution set for $4x + 1 \leq y$ or $y < 2x - 5$ when $y = 2$?

   E.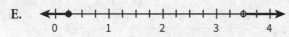

   F.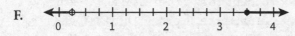

   G.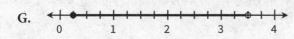

   H.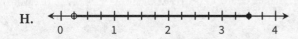

7. Today, Weiwei is half as old as Caleb. In 3 years, Weiwei will be $\frac{2}{3}$ as old as Caleb. How old is Caleb today?

   A. 3

   B. 6

   C. 9

   D. 12

8. Ester and Noel each rented a 20-cubic foot dumpster for 2 weeks. The total cost of Ester's dumpster rental was $365 plus $1.25 per pound over 3,000 pounds. Noel paid a flat fee of $430 for his dumpster rental. If Ester's and Noel's total costs were identical, how many pounds over 3,000 pounds did Ester go?

   E. 52

   F. 65

   G. 82

   H. 292

Geometry

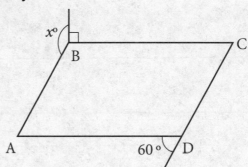

9. In the figure above, ABCD is a parallelogram. What is the value of x?

   A. 110

   B. 120

   C. 140

   D. 150

10. A truck travels 88 inches per second. If the diameter of each tire is 20 inches, how many revolutions does one tire make in 1 minute? $\left(\pi \approx \frac{22}{7} \right)$

   E. $\frac{7}{5}$

   F. 43

   G. $\frac{440}{7}$

   H. 84

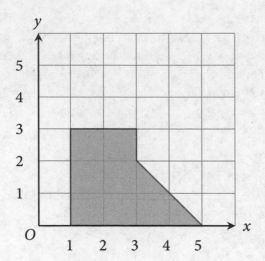

11. In the graph above, what is the area of the shaded region?

    A. 8

    B. 10

    C. 11

    D. 13

Advanced Math

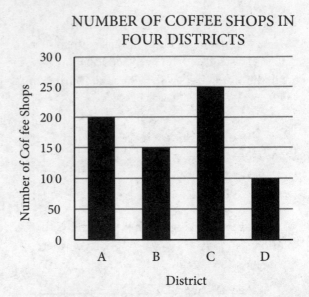

NUMBER OF COFFEE SHOPS IN FOUR DISTRICTS

12. The graph above shows the number of coffee shops in four districts. Districts A and B each have 150 patrons per coffee shop. Districts C and D each have 100 patrons per coffee shop. Which of the districts has the **greatest** number of coffee shop patrons?

    E. District A

    F. District B

    G. District C

    H. District D

Math Grid-In Questions

When answering SHSAT grid-in questions, the goal is to stay organized. Work quickly but carefully through the questions that require straightforward calculations. If the question is a word problem, break the sentences into short phrases before calculating.

DIRECTIONS: Answer each question. Write your answer in the boxes at the top of the grid. Start on the left side of each grid, printing only one number or symbol in each box. **DO NOT LEAVE A BOX BLANK IN THE MIDDLE OF AN ANSWER.** Under each box, fill in the circle that matches the number or symbol you wrote above. **DO NOT FILL IN A CIRCLE UNDER AN UNUSED BOX.**

$$6 + 4 \div |-2| + (-4)^3 \times \frac{1}{2}$$

13. What is the value of the expression shown above?

14. Solve for x:

$$8x + 2 - 4(x + 4) = 6$$

15. In the equation $\frac{h}{12} - 10 = -6$, what is the value of h?

16. What is the value of the expression $2(a - 5)^2 + 3a \div 4$ if $a = 8$?

17. If Maria ran 2.1 miles on Monday, 6 miles on Tuesday, and 4.2 miles on Wednesday, what is the mean number of miles she ran over the course of three days?

18. In a cupboard with only red and blue cups, the ratio of red cups to blue cups is 3:4. If there are 48 red cups, how many total cups are in the cupboard?

19. Mark paints houses as part of his job. In a given week, he has 28 houses to paint. If he paints $\frac{1}{4}$ of these houses on Monday and $\frac{1}{7}$ of the remaining houses on Tuesday, how many houses does Mark still have to paint after Tuesday?

20. A magazine pays authors by the word for essays that are submitted. Authors are paid $0.10 per word for the first 250 words and $0.05 per word for every word after 250 words. Sam submitted three essays: a 300-word essay, a 400-word essay, and a 500-word essay. How much did the magazine pay Sam for his three essays?

21. What number is halfway between −5 and 23 on a number line?

22. An art instructor is buying tubes of paint and paintbrushes for an upcoming class. If a tube of paint costs $5 and a paintbrush costs $1.50, how much does the instructor spend if the class has 8 students and each student needs 5 tubes of paint and a paintbrush?

23. Maria recently took a nonstop flight from Miami, Florida, to Quito, Ecuador. If the airplane flew at a constant speed of 436 miles per hour and the flight took 4.5 hours, what is the distance from Miami to Quito?

25. Danielle and Emma participated in a book-reading contest over the summer. Danielle read 13 books, and Emma read 15 fewer than 3 times the number of books that Danielle read. How many books did Danielle and Emma read over the summer?

24. William is enrolled in a book-of-the-month club. This club sends members leather-bound editions of classic books the same day each month. As a reward for loyalty, William receives a free book at the end of each year. If William pays $468 per year for the club, what is the average price he pays for each book?

26. Patricia ate lunch at a restaurant yesterday. She ordered three items: a salad, a bowl of soup, and a glass of iced tea. The salad cost $3, the soup cost $4, and the iced tea cost $1. If there is a 6% tax on food but not on drinks, how much did Patricia pay for lunch?

27. A recipe calls for $1\frac{2}{3}$ cups of water, $\frac{1}{2}$ cup of oil, and $\frac{5}{6}$ cup of milk. If these are the only three liquids used in the recipe, how many total cups of liquid are used?

28. Krista and Dana are both avid tea drinkers and have many different tea mugs. Dana has 4 more than half the number of mugs that Krista has, and together they have 19 tea mugs. How many tea mugs does Krista have?

29. Plow trucks are used to clear snow off highways after snowstorms as well as to spread anti-skid material on the road to help snow melt and give drivers more traction. A certain anti-skid material is 3 parts gravel to 2 parts salt. If 300 tons of salt were used in this material last year, how many total tons of anti-skid material were used?

LAST YEAR'S TOTAL SALES

Bicycle Type	Number
Road	600
Mountain	900
Hybrid	1,200
Total	2,700

30. The table above shows the number of each type of bicycle sold at a local shop last year. If 300 bikes will be sold next month, what is the best estimate (based on last year's sales) of the number of mountain bicycles that will be sold?

31. Elli opens an account with a deposit of $1,200. This account earns 4% simple interest annually. How many years will it take for her $1,200 deposit to earn $432 interest?

32. A camp counselor has 54 paintbrushes, 72 tubes of paint, and 90 sheets of paper to distribute to the children in the camp. If each child receives an equal number of each item and there are no items remaining, what is the greatest possible number of children in the camp?

Answers and Explanations

1. Strategic Review: SHSAT English Language Arts

A. Daniel Webster was one of the most outspoken politicians of his time.

B. Webster overcame a huge fear of public speaking in order to achieve his goals.

1.   D
Category: Global

Getting to the Answer: If you have already identified the main idea on your own, you will have a much easier time finding the correct answer choice. Remember that the correct choice will match both the tone and the scope of the passage. **(D)** does this best. **(A)** is a Misused Detail; the passage discusses Webster's fear, but it is how he overcomes his fear that is the focus. **(B)** is Extreme; the passage does not say that Webster was the "most effective" politician of his time. **(C)** is a Misused Detail; the author mentions that Webster did not become president, but it is not the primary idea of the passage.

C. Paragraph 2

D. Webster used his great memory and writing skills to do well in public debates.

2.   F
Category: Detail

Getting to the Answer: Paragraph 2 tells you that Webster used his memory and skills as a writer to excel at public debate, which matches **(F)**. **(E)**, **(G)**, and **(H)** are Misused Details; they are mentioned in the passage, but they do not specifically answer the question.

E. To provide information about a fear that Webster was eventually able to overcome

F. To show that Webster's fear was considerable, which makes it all the more admirable that he was able to move past his phobia

3.   A
Category: Function

Getting to the Answer: The author describes Webster's fear of public speaking as greatly affecting his life before he courageously overcame it, which matches **(A)**. **(B)** is a Distortion. Although Webster did not become president,

the author does not characterize his political career as a failure. **(C)** is incorrect because Webster's success as a lawyer is mentioned in paragraph 3, not paragraph 2. **(D)** is Opposite; Webster did, in fact, overcome his fear.

G. Webster wanted to do more than speak in front of colleagues at holiday parties.

H. Webster did more than give holiday speeches; he became a lawyer and politician.

4.   H
Category: Inference

Getting to the Answer: Paragraph 3 discusses Webster's pursuit of political esteem. The phrase "merely giving speeches for colleagues" introduces the idea that Webster wished to fulfill greater goals—in this case, a political career, which matches **(H)**. Although **(E)** and **(G)** may be true, the primary purpose of the phrase is to point out that Webster had goals that extended beyond practicing law. The passage does not include information to support the idea that Webster refused to give speeches in front of coworkers, so **(F)** is incorrect.

I. The table shows additional famous people over time and in different professions who had or have a fear of public speaking.

J. The main idea of the passage is that Daniel Webster overcame his fear of public speaking and became a great orator and, according to the table, many other famous people also suffered from a fear of public speaking.

5.   B
Category: Infographic

Getting to the Answer: Daniel Webster was greatly affected by his fear of public speaking, and other famous people such as Mahatma Gandhi and Maya Angelou have had to overcome glossophobia too; **(B)** is correct. **(A)** and **(D)** are Out of Scope because the passage does not say that Webster was inspired by others, and it does not provide information to support the idea that glossophobia is common. **(C)** is incorrect because the table does not provide specific information about the accomplishments of the famous people listed; it provides only names, professions, and years of birth.

6.   G

Category: Sentence Structure

Getting to the Answer: The question indicates that there is an error that needs to be fixed. Check each underlined segment systematically to locate the issue. The second sentence of the paragraph is a run-on because both clauses—"The course provides instruction in a variety of topics, such as tonality and harmony" and "formal and contemporary styles of music are also part of the curriculum"—are independent clauses. **(G)** fixes this error with a period. The other answer choices are incorrect because they do not address the original error, and they each create a new issue.

7.   D

Category: Sentence Structure

Getting to the Answer: Modifying words and phrases must be properly placed to accurately reflect the author's intended meaning. As written in sentence 4, it is "the Eiffel Tower" that is "taking a . . . tour of Paris," which is not logical; **(D)** is correct. Eliminate the other answer choices because they are grammatically correct sentences.

8.   G

Category: Punctuation & Usage

Getting to the Answer: The question indicates that the paragraph includes two errors. In sentence 3, the comma after "French" is unnecessary and must be deleted, and "inhabiting" should be "inhabit" to keep it consistent with the verbs "speak" and "tend"; **(G)** is correct. Eliminate the other answer choices because they are grammatically correct.

9.   B

Category: Organization

Getting to the Answer: When combining two sentences, determine the relationship between the two. The first sentence states when the first MRI scan was conducted, and the second sentence provides details about what an MRI scan does and how it is used. **(B)** correctly reflects the relationship between the two by putting the information from the first sentence between two commas, which indicates that the two ideas are closely related. The other answer choices are incorrect because they use the contrast transitions "Even though," "but," and "While," which do not accurately reflect the writer's

intention to express two pieces of related information about a single topic.

10.   E

Category: Knowledge of Language

Getting to the Answer: The question asks you to use precise, or specific, language to express the phrase "talked to people who seemed to be lying about some things." **(E)** precisely states the detective's action ("questioned") as well as with whom the detective spoke ("the two main suspects"). **(F)** and **(G)** do not provide specific information about exactly what the detective was doing, and **(H)** adds information that the writer may not have intended to include. Be sure to eliminate any choices that change the original meaning of the text.

11.   C

Category: Organization

Getting to the Answer: Since both sentences are about packaging in bulk, the two can be logically joined by making the second sentence dependent and adding it to the first with a comma. **(C)** is correct. **(A)** Incorrectly joins two independent clauses with a comma. **(B)** contrasts the two, whereas one is a continuation of the other. **(D)** is redundant; both "new" and "innovation" imply "starting."

12.   H

Category: Organization

Getting to the Answer: In context, it can be inferred that after visiting the exposition and becoming interested in chocolate, Hershey sold the caramel company to make chocolate candies instead. The best word to describe this change of events is **(H)**, "Afterward." **(E)** and **(F)** are contrast words, which do not convey the intended meaning, and **(G)** adds a point of view that the author doesn't state.

13.   A

Category: Knowledge of Language

Getting to the Answer: "It" does not provide specific details, but **(A)** makes the sentence clear: it was chocolate that was considered a luxury product until Hershey began to mass produce it. **(B)** and **(D)** refer to the wrong product—milk instead of chocolate—and **(C)** omits the important word "luxury."

14. H

Category: Organization

Getting to the Answer: When relocating a sentence, look for context clues that indicate where it must be placed to make the paragraph as logical as possible. Sentence 11 uses the phrase "This purchase" to refer to how Hershey was able to buy fresh milk, which is first mentioned in sentence 9; sentence 11 should be placed directly after this reference, so **(H)** is correct. The other answer choices place the sentence in locations that do not make logical sense given the information provided in sentence 11.

15. D

Category: Topic Development

Getting to the Answer: The entire passage is about Milton Hershey, including the fact that the town he built is named after him. It's true that this is just one example of towns or other locations named after their founders, but that is irrelevant in a passage about a specific person. **(D)** is correct. All other sentences make sense in the passage.

16. H

Category: Topic Development

Getting to the Answer: The previous sentence introduces the Hersheys' charity work, and **(H)** provides a logical transition from the introduction of this philanthropy to the example provided in sentence 16. None of the other answers provides a supporting example of sentence 16.

2. Strategic Review: SHSAT Math

1. C

Subject: Arithmetic

Getting to the Answer: First use $\overline{BA} = 15$ units and $\overline{AC} = \frac{2}{3}\overline{BA}$ to find the distance between A and C:

$$\overline{AC} = \frac{2}{3}\overline{BA} = \frac{2}{3}(15) = 10 \text{ units}$$

Since points A, B, and C are on a number line and A is between B and C, then $\overline{BC} = \overline{BA} + \overline{AC}$. Thus, $\overline{BC} = 15 + 10 = 25$ units.

2. F

Subject: Arithmetic

Getting to the Answer: First list the factors of 60, and then identify how many factors greater than 2 and less than 20 are odd. The positive factors of 60 are 1 and 60, 2 and 30, 3 and 20, 4 and 15, 5 and 12, and 6 and 10. The factors greater than 2 and less than 20 are 3, 4, 5, 6, 10, 12, and 15. Thus, there are 3 positive odd factors of 60 greater than 2 and less than 20.

3. B

Subject: Arithmetic

Getting to the Answer: Use Average $= \dfrac{\text{Sum}}{\text{Number of Items}}$ to find the mean. To calculate the sum, first multiply the number of states by the minimum wage for each row and then add them together:

$$\text{Average} = \frac{6(\$7.25) + 3(\$8.25) + 1(\$13.25)}{20}$$
$$= \frac{\$154}{20}$$
$$= \$7.70$$

4. E

Subject: Statistics and Probability

Getting to the Answer: Let c be the total number of cups in the package. Set up a proportion to find c:

$$\frac{3}{5} = \frac{6}{c}$$
$$30 = 3c$$
$$10 = c$$

If there are 10 total cups and 6 are blue, 4 cups are not blue.

5. C

Subject: Algebra

Getting to the Answer: Let t be the total number of liters the air mattress can hold, and use Percent $= \dfrac{\text{Part}}{\text{Whole}}$ to write two equations: $\dfrac{a + 80}{t} = 80\%$ and $\dfrac{a + 80 + 30}{t} = 90\%$.

Solve each equation for t.

Equation 1:

$$\frac{a + 80}{t} = \frac{80}{100}$$

$$\frac{a + 80}{t} = \frac{4}{5}$$

$$5(a + 80) = 4t$$

$$\frac{5a + 400}{4} = t$$

Equation 2:

$$\frac{a + 80 + 30}{t} = \frac{90}{100}$$

$$\frac{a + 110}{t} = \frac{9}{10}$$

$$10(a + 110) = 9t$$

$$\frac{10a + 1,100}{9} = t$$

Set the two equations equal to each other and solve for a:

$$\frac{5a + 400}{4} = \frac{10a + 1,100}{9}$$

$$9(5a + 400) = 4(10a + 1,100)$$

$$45a + 3,600 = 40a + 4,400$$

$$5a = 800$$

$$a = 160$$

6. E

Subject: Algebra

Getting to the Answer: Solve each side of the inequality separately. Then substitute $y = 2$ and solve for x.

Left side of the inequality:

$$4x + 1 \leq y$$

$$4x + 1 \leq 2$$

$$4x \leq 1$$

$$x \leq \frac{1}{4}$$

Right side of the inequality:

$$y < 2x - 5$$

$$2 < 2x - 5$$

$$7 < 2x$$

$$\frac{7}{2} < x$$

The solution set is $x \leq \frac{1}{4}$ or $3\frac{1}{2} < x$, which matches **(E)**.

7. B

Subject: Algebra

Getting to the Answer: Let W represent Weiwei's age and C represent Caleb's age today. Set up equations expressing the relationship between Weiwei's age and Caleb's age today and in 3 years: $W = \frac{1}{2}C$ and $W + 3 = \frac{2}{3}(C + 3)$.

Substitute W, and solve for C:

$$\frac{1}{2}C + 3 = \frac{2}{3}(C + 3)$$

$$\frac{1}{2}C + 3 = \frac{2}{3}C + 2$$

$$1 = \frac{2}{3}C - \frac{1}{2}C$$

$$1 = \frac{4}{6}C - \frac{3}{6}C$$

$$1 = \frac{1}{6}C$$

$$6 = C$$

Alternatively, you can Backsolve and test the answer choices.

8. E

Subject: Algebra

Getting to the Answer: Let p be the number of pounds Ester went over 3,000 pounds. Ester's total cost is $\$365 + \$1.25p$. Noel's total cost is identical to Ester's, so $\$365 + \$1.25p = \$430$. Solving for p gives:

$$\$365 + \$1.25p = \$430$$

$$\$1.25p = \$65$$

$$p = 52$$

Ester went 52 pounds over 3,000 pounds.

9. D

Subject: Geometry

Getting to the Answer: Angle ADC and 60° add up to 180° because they form a straight line. Therefore, $\angle ADC = 180° - 60° = 120°$. Remember that in parallelograms, opposite angles are equal. Thus, $\angle ABC = \angle ADC = 120°$. The sum of the angles around B is 360°, so $x° + 120° + 90° = 360°$. Solving for x gives $x = 150$.

10. H

Subject: Geometry

Getting to the Answer: One revolution equals the circumference of the tire. The radius is half the diameter, or 10 inches:

$$C = 2\pi r = 2\left(\frac{22}{7}\right)(10) = \frac{440}{7} \text{ inches}$$

Since the truck travels 88 inches per second, the number of revolutions one tire makes is $88 \div \frac{440}{7} = 88 \times \frac{7}{440} = \frac{7}{5}$ revolutions per second. Multiply by 60 seconds to get $\frac{7}{5} \times 60 = 84$ revolutions in 1 minute.

11. A

Subject: Geometry

Getting to the Answer: The shaded region is composed of one rectangle and one right triangle. The rectangle has a width of 2 units and a height of 3 units. The right triangle has a base of 2 units and a height of 2 units.

Thus, the total area of the shaded region is $(2 \times 3) + \frac{1}{2}(2 \times 2) = 6 + 2 = 8$ square units.

12. E

Subject: Statistics and Probability

Getting to the Answer: Multiply each district's number of coffee shops by the number of patrons. Note that since Districts A and B have the same number of patrons, you only need to calculate the number of patrons for District A, which has a greater number of coffee shops. Similarly, since Districts C and D have the same number of patrons, you only need to calculate the number of patrons for District C, which has a greater number of coffee shops.

District A: $200 \times 150 = 30,000$

District C: $250 \times 100 = 25,000$

District A has the greatest number of patrons.

13. −24

Subject: Arithmetic

Getting to the Answer: Apply the order of operations, or PEMDAS, and calculate carefully:

$$6 + 4 \div |{-2}| + (-4)^3 \times \frac{1}{2}$$
$$6 + 4 \div 2 + (-4)^3 \times \frac{1}{2}$$
$$6 + 4 \div 2 + -64 \times \frac{1}{2}$$
$$6 + 2 + (-32) = -24$$

Grid in **−24**.

14. 5

Subject: Algebra

Getting to the Answer: Solve this question as you would any other equation. Isolate the variable by subtracting 16 from both sides and then dividing by −4:

$$8x + 2 - 4(x + 4) = 6$$
$$8x + 2 - 4x - 16 = 6$$
$$4x - 14 = 6$$
$$4x = 20$$
$$x = 5$$

Grid in **5**.

15. 48

Subject: Algebra

Getting to the Answer: To solve this equation, begin by adding 10 to both sides. The final step is to multiply both sides by 12 to undo the fraction:

$$\frac{h}{12} - 10 = -6$$
$$\frac{h}{12} = 4$$
$$h = 48$$

Grid in **48**.

16. 24

Subject: Algebra

Getting to the answer: Substitute 8 in for *a* everywhere it appears in the given expression. Compute and simplify, keeping in mind the correct rules for the order of operations, or PEMDAS:

$$2(a-5)^2 + 3a \div 4$$
$$2[(8)-5]^2 + 3(8) \div 4$$
$$2(3)^2 + 24 \div 4$$
$$18 + 6 = 24$$

Grid in **24**.

17. 4.1

Subject: Arithmetic

Getting to the Answer: To find the mean, or average, distance that Maria ran over the three days, add the three distances and divide by the number of days:

$2.1 + 6 + 4.2 = 12.3$ miles

12.3 miles $\div$ 3 days $= 4.1$ miles per day

Grid in **4.1**.

18. 112

Subject: Algebra

Getting to the Answer: First, create a proportion that expresses the given information. You know that the ratio of red cups to blue cups is 3:4 and there are 48 red cups:

$$\frac{3}{4} = \frac{48}{x}$$
$$3x = 192$$
$$x = 64$$

Don't grid in 64, though! That's the number of blue cups. You are asked how many total cups there are, so add 48 and 64 together to get 112. Grid in **112**.

19. 18

Subject: Arithmetic

Getting to the Answer: On Monday, Mark paints $\frac{1}{4}$ of the 28 houses, or 7 houses. On Tuesday, he paints $\frac{1}{7}$ of the remaining 21 (not 28!) houses, which is 3 houses. This means that he paints $7 + 3 = 10$ houses on Monday and Tuesday, leaving 18 houses for the rest of the week. Grid in **18**.

20. 97.5

Subject: Arithmetic

Getting to the Answer: Start by calculating how much Sam was paid for each essay. Essay 1 was 300 words, so he received $250(\$0.10) + 50(\$0.05) = \$25 + \$2.50 = \$27.50$. Essay 2 was 400 words, so he received $250(\$0.10) + 150(\$0.05) = \$25 + \$7.50 = \$32.50$. Essay 3 was 500 words, so he received $250(\$0.10) + 250(\$0.05) = \$25 + \$12.50 = \$37.50$. Together, Sam was paid $\$27.50 + \$32.50 + \$37.50 = \$97.50$. Grid in **97.5**.

21. 9

Subject: Arithmetic

Getting to the Answer: Finding the halfway point between two numbers is the same as finding the midpoint of two numbers. To find the midpoint, add the two numbers together and divide by 2. This yields $\frac{-5+23}{2} = \frac{18}{2} = 9$. Grid in **9**.

22. 212

Subject: Arithmetic

Getting to the Answer: Each of the 8 students needs a paintbrush, so the cost of 8 paintbrushes is $8 \times \$1.50 = \$12$. Each student needs 5 tubes of paint, meaning that $8 \times 5 = 40$ tubes of paint are needed. 40 tubes of paint cost $40 \times \$5 = \$200$. Thus, the instructor spends $\$12 + \$200 = \$212$ on supplies. Grid in **212**.

23. 1962

Subject: Arithmetic

Getting to the Answer: If an airplane flies 436 miles per hour and the flight takes 4.5 hours, then the distance the airplane flies is simply 436×4.5 using $d = rt$. This product is 1,962, meaning the distance between Miami and Quito is 1,962 miles. Grid in **1962**.

24. 36

Subject: Statistics and Probability

Getting to the Answer: The question tells you that the book club sends William a book each month, which would be 12 books over the course of a year. However, don't forget about the free book! If William receives a free book at the end of the year, then he receives 13 books total for the year. If you are computing the average price per book, you need to consider all 13 books. The answer is simply $468 divided by 13, which is $36. Grid in **36**.

25. 37

Subject: Arithmetic

Getting to the Answer: You know that Danielle read 13 books and that Emma read 15 fewer than 3 times this amount. That means Emma read 15 fewer than 3(13) books, or $3(13) - 15 = 24$ books. The question asks for the number of books that Danielle and Emma read combined, which is $13 + 24 = 37$ books. Grid in **37**.

26. 8.42

Subject: Arithmetic

Getting to the Answer: First, consider which items are taxed and which aren't. The question tells you that food is taxed, so the salad and the soup are taxed at 6%. Thus, these two items cost $3 + $4 = $7, but you also need to consider the tax, which is $7(0.06) = $0.42. Including tax, these two items cost $7.42. You also need to include the cost of the iced tea, which is $1, giving you a total of $8.42. Grid in **8.42**.

27. 3

Subject: Arithmetic

Getting to the Answer: To determine how much liquid is used, simply add the three numbers together. Remember to use a common denominator when adding or subtracting fractions. Also, converting the mixed number to an improper fraction first is a good idea:

$$\frac{5}{3} + \frac{1}{2} + \frac{5}{6} \Rightarrow \frac{10}{6} + \frac{3}{6} + \frac{5}{6} = \frac{18}{6} = 3$$

Grid in **3**.

28. 10

Subject: Algebra

Getting to the Answer: Let t be the number of tea mugs that Krista has. If Dana has four more than half of this number of mugs and they have a total of 19 mugs, the following equation can be constructed:

$$t + \frac{1}{2}t + 4 = 19$$

$$\frac{3}{2}t + 4 = 19$$

$$\frac{3}{2}t = 15$$

$$t = 10$$

The question asks for the number of mugs that Krista has, so grid in **10**.

29. 750

Subject: Algebra

Getting to the Answer: Start by calculating how much gravel was used in the anti-skid material last year. You know that the ratio of gravel to salt was 3:2 and 300 tons of salt were used, so the following proportion can be set up: $\frac{3}{2} = \frac{x}{300}$. Multiplying by 2 and dividing by 3 will give you 450, so 450 tons of gravel were used. This isn't the correct answer, though! The question asks how much total material was used, so add up both numbers to get $300 + 450 = 750$ tons of material. Grid in **750**.

30. 100

Subject: Arithmetic

Getting to the Answer: Let m represent the number of mountain bicycles that will be sold next month. Use the information in the table to set up a proportion:

$$\frac{m}{300} = \frac{900}{2,700}$$

$$2,700m = 900(300)$$

$$m = \frac{900(300)}{2,700}$$

$$m = 100$$

Grid in **100**.

31. 9

Subject: Arithmetic

Getting to the Answer: Calculate simple interest by multiplying the initial deposit (p), the interest rate (r), and the number of years (t) together and set that equal to the interest earned:

$$(p)(r)(t) = \text{Interest Earned}$$

$$(1,200)(0.04)t = 432$$

$$48t = 432$$

$$t = 9$$

Grid in **9**.

32. 18

Subject: Arithmetic

Getting to the Answer: The greatest possible number of children in the camp is equal to the greatest common factor (GCF) of 72, 60, and 84. Write the prime factorization of each number to find the factors that all three have in common:

$$54 = 2 \times 3^3$$
$$72 = 2^3 \times 3^2$$
$$90 = 2 \times 3^2 \times 5$$

The factors they have in common are 2, 3, and 3. Multiply those together to find the GCF: $2 \times 3 \times 3 = \textbf{18}$. Grid in **18**.

PART FIVE

SHSAT PRACTICE TESTS AND EXPLANATIONS

PRACTICE TEST 1

SHSAT Practice Test 1

ANSWER SHEET

Part 1—English Language Arts

1. Ⓐ Ⓑ Ⓒ Ⓓ
2. Ⓔ Ⓕ Ⓖ Ⓗ
3. Ⓐ Ⓑ Ⓒ Ⓓ
4. Ⓔ Ⓕ Ⓖ Ⓗ
5. Ⓐ Ⓑ Ⓒ Ⓓ
6. Ⓔ Ⓕ Ⓖ Ⓗ
7. Ⓐ Ⓑ Ⓒ Ⓓ
8. Ⓔ Ⓕ Ⓖ Ⓗ
9. Ⓐ Ⓑ Ⓒ Ⓓ
10. Ⓔ Ⓕ Ⓖ Ⓗ

11. Ⓐ Ⓑ Ⓒ Ⓓ
12. Ⓔ Ⓕ Ⓖ Ⓗ
13. Ⓐ Ⓑ Ⓒ Ⓓ
14. Ⓔ Ⓕ Ⓖ Ⓗ
15. Ⓐ Ⓑ Ⓒ Ⓓ
16. Ⓔ Ⓕ Ⓖ Ⓗ
17. Ⓐ Ⓑ Ⓒ Ⓓ
18. Ⓔ Ⓕ Ⓖ Ⓗ
19. Ⓐ Ⓑ Ⓒ Ⓓ
20. Ⓔ Ⓕ Ⓖ Ⓗ

21. Ⓐ Ⓑ Ⓒ Ⓓ
22. Ⓔ Ⓕ Ⓖ Ⓗ
23. Ⓐ Ⓑ Ⓒ Ⓓ
24. Ⓔ Ⓕ Ⓖ Ⓗ
25. Ⓐ Ⓑ Ⓒ Ⓓ
26. Ⓔ Ⓕ Ⓖ Ⓗ
27. Ⓐ Ⓑ Ⓒ Ⓓ
28. Ⓔ Ⓕ Ⓖ Ⓗ
29. Ⓐ Ⓑ Ⓒ Ⓓ
30. Ⓔ Ⓕ Ⓖ Ⓗ

31. Ⓐ Ⓑ Ⓒ Ⓓ
32. Ⓔ Ⓕ Ⓖ Ⓗ
33. Ⓐ Ⓑ Ⓒ Ⓓ
34. Ⓔ Ⓕ Ⓖ Ⓗ
35. Ⓐ Ⓑ Ⓒ Ⓓ
36. Ⓔ Ⓕ Ⓖ Ⓗ
37. Ⓐ Ⓑ Ⓒ Ⓓ
38. Ⓔ Ⓕ Ⓖ Ⓗ
39. Ⓐ Ⓑ Ⓒ Ⓓ
40. Ⓔ Ⓕ Ⓖ Ⓗ

41. Ⓐ Ⓑ Ⓒ Ⓓ
42. Ⓔ Ⓕ Ⓖ Ⓗ
43. Ⓐ Ⓑ Ⓒ Ⓓ
44. Ⓔ Ⓕ Ⓖ Ⓗ
45. Ⓐ Ⓑ Ⓒ Ⓓ
46. Ⓔ Ⓕ Ⓖ Ⓗ
47. Ⓐ Ⓑ Ⓒ Ⓓ
48. Ⓔ Ⓕ Ⓖ Ⓗ
49. Ⓐ Ⓑ Ⓒ Ⓓ
50. Ⓔ Ⓕ Ⓖ Ⓗ

51. Ⓐ Ⓑ Ⓒ Ⓓ
52. Ⓔ Ⓕ Ⓖ Ⓗ
53. Ⓐ Ⓑ Ⓒ Ⓓ
54. Ⓔ Ⓕ Ⓖ Ⓗ
55. Ⓐ Ⓑ Ⓒ Ⓓ
56. Ⓔ Ⓕ Ⓖ Ⓗ
57. Ⓐ Ⓑ Ⓒ Ⓓ

Part 2—Mathematics

58.
59.
60.
61.
62.

63. Ⓐ Ⓑ Ⓒ Ⓓ
64. Ⓔ Ⓕ Ⓖ Ⓗ
65. Ⓐ Ⓑ Ⓒ Ⓓ
66. Ⓔ Ⓕ Ⓖ Ⓗ
67. Ⓐ Ⓑ Ⓒ Ⓓ
68. Ⓔ Ⓕ Ⓖ Ⓗ
69. Ⓐ Ⓑ Ⓒ Ⓓ
70. Ⓔ Ⓕ Ⓖ Ⓗ
71. Ⓐ Ⓑ Ⓒ Ⓓ

72. Ⓔ Ⓕ Ⓖ Ⓗ
73. Ⓐ Ⓑ Ⓒ Ⓓ
74. Ⓔ Ⓕ Ⓖ Ⓗ
75. Ⓐ Ⓑ Ⓒ Ⓓ
76. Ⓔ Ⓕ Ⓖ Ⓗ
77. Ⓐ Ⓑ Ⓒ Ⓓ
78. Ⓔ Ⓕ Ⓖ Ⓗ
79. Ⓐ Ⓑ Ⓒ Ⓓ
80. Ⓔ Ⓕ Ⓖ Ⓗ

81. Ⓐ Ⓑ Ⓒ Ⓓ
82. Ⓔ Ⓕ Ⓖ Ⓗ
83. Ⓐ Ⓑ Ⓒ Ⓓ
84. Ⓔ Ⓕ Ⓖ Ⓗ
85. Ⓐ Ⓑ Ⓒ Ⓓ
86. Ⓔ Ⓕ Ⓖ Ⓗ
87. Ⓐ Ⓑ Ⓒ Ⓓ
88. Ⓔ Ⓕ Ⓖ Ⓗ
89. Ⓐ Ⓑ Ⓒ Ⓓ

90. Ⓔ Ⓕ Ⓖ Ⓗ
91. Ⓐ Ⓑ Ⓒ Ⓓ
92. Ⓔ Ⓕ Ⓖ Ⓗ
93. Ⓐ Ⓑ Ⓒ Ⓓ
94. Ⓔ Ⓕ Ⓖ Ⓗ
95. Ⓐ Ⓑ Ⓒ Ⓓ
96. Ⓔ Ⓕ Ⓖ Ⓗ
97. Ⓐ Ⓑ Ⓒ Ⓓ
98. Ⓔ Ⓕ Ⓖ Ⓗ

99. Ⓐ Ⓑ Ⓒ Ⓓ
100. Ⓔ Ⓕ Ⓖ Ⓗ
101. Ⓐ Ⓑ Ⓒ Ⓓ
102. Ⓔ Ⓕ Ⓖ Ⓗ
103. Ⓐ Ⓑ Ⓒ Ⓓ
104. Ⓔ Ⓕ Ⓖ Ⓗ
105. Ⓐ Ⓑ Ⓒ Ⓓ
106. Ⓔ Ⓕ Ⓖ Ⓗ
107. Ⓐ Ⓑ Ⓒ Ⓓ

108. Ⓔ Ⓕ Ⓖ Ⓗ
109. Ⓐ Ⓑ Ⓒ Ⓓ
110. Ⓔ Ⓕ Ⓖ Ⓗ
111. Ⓐ Ⓑ Ⓒ Ⓓ
112. Ⓔ Ⓕ Ⓖ Ⓗ
113. Ⓐ Ⓑ Ⓒ Ⓓ
114. Ⓔ Ⓕ Ⓖ Ⓗ

Practice Test 1

Directions: Mark your answers on the separate sheet provided. You will receive credit only for answers marked on the answer grid. **DO NOT MAKE ANY STRAY MARKS ON THE ANSWER GRID.** You can write in the test booklet, or use the paper provided for scratchwork.

Each question has only one correct answer. Select the **best** answer for each question. Your score is determined by the number of questions you answered correctly. **It is to your advantage to answer every question, even though you may not be certain which choice is correct.**

You have 180 minutes to complete the entire test. How you split the time between the English Language Arts and Mathematics sections is up to you. **If you begin with the English Language Arts section, you may go on to the Mathematics section as soon as you are ready. If you begin with the Mathematics section, you may go on to the English Language Arts section as soon as you are ready.** It is recommended that you do not spend more than 90 minutes on either section. If you complete the test before the allotted time (180 minutes) is over, you may go back to review questions in either section.

Work as rapidly as you can without making mistakes. Don't spend too much time on a difficult question. Return to it later if you have time. If time remains, you should check your answers.

Part 1—English Language Arts

REVISING/EDITING

QUESTIONS 1–14 (Part A and Part B)

REVISING/EDITING Part A

DIRECTIONS: Answer the following questions, recognizing and correcting errors so that the sentences or paragraphs are grammatically correct. Reread relevant parts of the text before choosing the best answer for each question, but be mindful of time. You may write in your test booklet to take notes.

---

1. Read this sentence.

> One of the most predictable <u>problems</u> that New England gardeners <u>encounter</u> is rocky <u>soil</u>, another issue that plagues these gardeners is the destruction of cultivated plants by local wildlife.

Which edit should be made to correct this sentence?

A. Insert a comma after *problems*.

B. Insert a comma after *encounter*.

C. Delete the comma after *soil*.

D. Replace the comma after *soil* with a semicolon.

2. Read this sentence.

> Many theater critics agree that Patti <u>LuPone</u>, a famous Broadway <u>performer</u> is nearly as <u>dramatic</u> an <u>actor</u> as she is a singer.

Which edit should be made to correct this sentence?

E. Delete the comma after *LuPone*.

F. Insert a comma after *performer*.

G. Insert a comma after *dramatic*.

H. Insert a comma after *actor*.

GO ON TO THE NEXT PAGE ➡

3. Read these sentences.

> (1) Young figure skaters need to make a tremendous commitment in order to earn a place on the Olympic team. (2) This commitment is impossible without the help and support of their families.

What is the best way to combine the sentences to clarify the relationship between the ideas?

A. Young figure skaters have a tremendous commitment they need to make in order to earn a place on the Olympic team; however, they also need the support of their families.

B. While young figure skaters have a tremendous commitment they need to make in order to earn a place on the Olympic team, they also need the support of their families.

C. The tremendous commitment that young figure skaters have to make in order to earn a place on the Olympic team is impossible without the help and support of their families.

D. The tremendous commitment that young figure skaters have, along with the support of their families, is needed to make the Olympic team.

4. Read these sentences.

> (1) The River Seine cuts through <u>Paris,</u> <u>forming</u> the Left Bank and Right Bank.
> (2) Although the riverbanks no longer <u>have</u> any <u>factories,</u> they include many famous attractions. (3) On a river <u>cruise,</u> tourists <u>can view</u> the Eiffel Tower, artistic bridges, and lush gardens. (4) They can also see the famous Musée d'Orsay, a renovated train station that <u>becomes</u> a <u>museum,</u> after it was filled with paintings and sculptures.

Which revisions correct the errors in the paragraph?

E. Sentence 1: Change *forming* to **forms**, AND delete the comma after *Paris*.

F. Sentence 2: Change *have* to **has**, AND delete the comma after *factories*.

G. Sentence 3: Change *can view* to **view**, AND delete the comma after *cruise*.

H. Sentence 4: Change *becomes* to **became**, AND delete the comma after *museum*.

5. Read this paragraph.

> (1) With <u>its</u> dramatic canyons and gushing geysers in sections of Wyoming, Idaho, and Montana, Yellowstone National Park <u>offers</u> unique hydrothermal and geologic wonders. (2) While many tourists <u>visited</u> the park each year, <u>they are</u> a permanent home for thousands of animals, including bears, elk, and wolves. (3) During the spring, Yellowstone <u>becomes</u> a dynamic landscape, prompting nature lovers to flock to <u>it</u> to see the rushing rivers and flourishing plant and animal life. (4) Hundreds of animal species, including nearly 300 species of birds, 16 species of fish, and 67 species of mammals, <u>have been</u> observed making the park <u>their</u> home.

How should the paragraph be revised?

A. Sentence 1: Change *its* to **their**, AND change *offers* to **offered**.

B. Sentence 2: Change *visited* to **visit**, AND change *they are* to **it is**.

C. Sentence 3: Change *becomes* to **became**, AND change *it* to **them**.

D. Sentence 4: Change *have been* to **had been**, AND change *their* to **its**.

6. Read this paragraph.

> (1) There is considerable evidence that the earliest civilizations were greatly influenced by how well the land could be adapted to provide a stable water supply, such as Sumer and Babylonia in the Tigris-Euphrates valley. (2) The development of irrigation allowed for extremely efficient agricultural production, which created a surplus of food resources. (3) In addition to irrigating crops, early civilizations often developed an elaborate system of canals and drainage networks. (4) Greater resources and improved infrastructure allowed civilizations in these locations to grow faster than was possible in areas where such development was more difficult.

Which sentence should be revised to correct an error in sentence structure?

E. sentence 1

F. sentence 2

G. sentence 3

H. sentence 4

GO ON TO THE NEXT PAGE

7. Read this paragraph.

> Consumers have shown a preference for organic fruits and vegetables since the early <u>1990s, the</u> boom in the organic produce market has encouraged the spread of Community Supported Agriculture farms, or CSAs. In addition to selling produce at traditional outlets such as farmers' markets, small farmers grow a wide variety of crops and sell membership subscriptions for the <u>season. Members</u> pay a set rate for a <u>subscription and then</u> come to the farm or to a centrally located pick-up site each week to receive a selection of the week's harvest. Small-scale CSA farming is a sustainable alternative to traditional <u>agriculture</u>, <u>with</u> many advantages for both producers and consumers.

Which revision corrects the error in sentence structure in the paragraph?

A. 1990s, and the

B. season, and members

C. subscription, and then they

D. agriculture, which includes

REVISING/EDITING Part B

DIRECTIONS: Read the passage and answer the questions following it, improving the writing quality and correcting grammatical errors. Reread relevant parts of the text before choosing the best answer for each question, but be mindful of time. You may write in your test booklet to take notes.

Nikola Tesla

(1) Movies and television shows often portray the scientist as an adherent to the rules—a square, upstanding member of society. (2) Consider the brainy Lisa Simpson in *The Simpsons*, the geeks in *The Big Bang Theory*, and even Mr. Spock in the *Star Trek* series. (3) However, the stupidity of this stereotype is revealed by the life and work of Nikola Tesla, the scientist, inventor, and thinker. (4) Born in 1856 in what is today Croatia, Tesla became interested in electricity while in high school. (5) As a college student, his performance prompted one professor to write to a member of Tesla's family that "Your son is a star of the first rank."

(6) Having immigrated to the United States in 1884, Tesla was hired by Thomas Edison to work first on simple electrical programs, then on more complicated problems. (7) After resigning over a pay dispute, Tesla and two partners founded the Tesla Electric Light and Manufacturing Company. (8) A disagreement with these partners resulted in them pushing out Tesla. (9) In 1887, he and two new investors set up another company in which Tesla was free to develop his innovative ideas. (10) He became a naturalized American citizen in 1891.

(11) His most well-known invention, at least to the general public, was probably the Tesla coil, a power supply with lightning bolt-like fingers of electricity shooting from the base. (12) Indeed, it was this coil that brought the monster to life in the movie version of *Frankenstein*. (13) He also developed wireless lighting systems and the AC generator. (14) Tesla developed a number of devices, including an induction motor using the then-controversial alternating current.

(15) Tesla was far from the mild-mannered and unobtrusive caricature of a scientist. (16) He once nearly toppled New York's landmark Brooklyn Bridge in testing his theory of sympathetic vibration. (17) By placing a small oscillator on a supporting pillar and tuning the device to a special frequency, Tesla demonstrated the possibility of exponentially increasing vibration energy, sending giant, wavelike ripples through the bridge. (18) While he did not see fit to topple the structure, he did completely destroy the fallacy of the scientist as a conformist. (19) He was the picture-perfect example of the America Dream.

GO ON TO THE NEXT PAGE ➡

8. Which transition should be added to the beginning of sentence 2?

   E. For example,

   F. In essence,

   G. Therefore,

   H. Conversely,

9. Which revision of sentence 3 best maintains the formal style established in the passage?

   A. The stupidity of this stereotype is revealed by the life and work of Nikola Tesla.

   B. Nonetheless, this stereotype falls way too short, as revealed by the life and work of Nikola Tesla, the scientist, inventor, and thinker.

   C. However, the inadequacy of this stereotype is revealed by the life and work of Nikola Tesla, the scientist, inventor, and thinker.

   D. As you may know, the weakness of this stereotype is unveiled by the work of Nikola Tesla, the scientist, inventor, and thinker.

10. In sentence 5, which revision uses the most precise language for the words *his performance prompted one professor to write to a member of Tesla's family*?

   E. his incredible performance prompted one professor to write to his father

   F. he prompted one professor to write to Tesla's father

   G. his incredible performance prompted one professor to write to Tesla's family members

   H. his incredible performance prompted one professor to write to Tesla's father

11. Which sentence presents information that shifts away from the main topic of the second paragraph (sentences 6–10) and should be removed?

   A. sentence 7

   B. sentence 8

   C. sentence 9

   D. sentence 10

12. Where should sentence 14 be moved to improve the organization of the third paragraph?

   E. to the beginning of the paragraph (before sentence 11)

   F. between sentences 11 and 12

   G. between sentences 12 and 13

   H. at the end of the paragraph (where it is now)

13. Which sentence should follow sentence 15 to best support the main claim in the paragraph?

   A. In fact, he did some odd and dangerous things.

   B. People often found him hard to work with.

   C. Nevertheless, he was a great scientist and inventor.

   D. Tesla disproves the character of the unobtrusive scientist.

14. Which concluding sentence should replace sentence 19 to best support the topic presented in the passage?

   E.   Thanks to his restraint, the Brooklyn Bridge is still standing.

   F.   An intellectual pioneer, Tesla was anything but "square."

   G.   In fact, some modern scientists have invented important devices that help everyone.

   H.   Nevertheless, the stereotype of the rules-bound scientist persists.

READING COMPREHENSION

QUESTIONS 15–57

DIRECTIONS: Read the six passages and answer the corresponding questions. Reread relevant parts of the text before choosing the best answer for each question, but be mindful of time. Base your answers only on the content within each passage. You may write in your test booklet to take notes.

The Ball that Defied Logic

1 In the 1870s, a baseball pitcher named William "Candy" Cummings threw a ball that astounded crowds across the eastern United States. Instead of flying through the air in a straight line, as one might expect it to do, Cummings's ball seemed to change its path midway to the batter. To the naked eye, this pitch appeared to curve, not only impressing spectators but also completely fooling batters of the day who attempted to make contact. This "curveball" changed the way baseball was played and continues to be an essential tool for the professional game.

2 Interest in this phenomenon excited the world of sports and compelled scientists to investigate the mechanism by which a thrown baseball could change its path mid-flight. Some posited that the rotation of Earth played a factor. Others theorized that the effect was simply the work of a foreign object upon the ball. In reality, the curve of a curveball involves a complex scientific process called the Magnus effect, named after German physicist H. G. Magnus. While this effect was eventually identified in the late nineteenth century as the reason for the curveball, the origins of the explanation actually date back as far as the time of Isaac Newton. The physics of an object moving inside a fluid substance such as a liquid or a gas—in this case, a baseball flying through the air—can be complex and unexpected. When a ball leaves the pitcher's hand with a bit of a spin, its turning motion drags some of the surrounding air with it. While the ball spins in the air, the speed of the air changes, and the air moves slower on one side of the ball than it does on the other side. This difference in speed causes the ball to depart from its straight path, making the ball curve. A skilled pitcher can learn to create this effect by imparting a spin upon the ball as it is released.

3 This unexpected movement of the ball can have devastating results for the batter. Because of the Magnus effect, a curveball will begin its directional change, or "break," in the opposite direction of the pitcher's throwing hand (e.g., toward the right side if the pitcher is left-handed). A ball that spins in this manner is now referred to as a "regulation curve." In the early 1900s, pitchers began throwing curveballs in the opposite direction as well; these have come to be known as "fadeaways" or "screwballs." In both types of curves, the effect is generally the same. The ball reaches the batter at a slower rate of speed than a more direct pitch would have and fools the batter into thinking the ball will continue to move in a straight line. Contrary to how it appears, the ball has already changed its direction, and the batter has swung at a ball that was never really there. Today, the curveball is still alive and well, living in the nightmares of batters who have attempted—and failed—to hit it.

RESULTS OF ALL PITCHES IN MAJOR LEAGUE BASEBALL GAMES, 2007 SEASON

Pitch Type	Ball	Strike	Foul	Hit
Fastball	36%	26%	19%	19%
Curveball	40%	30%	14%	16%
Slider	36%	27%	17%	20%
Changeup	40%	25%	14%	21%
Average for all types	38%	27%	16%	19%

HOW "CURVE" BALLS CURVE

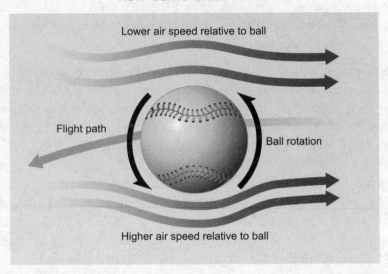

15. Which sentence best supports the idea that baseball pitches prior to the 1870s moved differently than the curveball?

   A. "In the 1870s, a baseball pitcher named William 'Candy' Cummings threw a ball that astounded crowds across the eastern United States." (paragraph 1)

   B. "This 'curveball' changed the way baseball was played and continues to be an essential tool for the professional game." (paragraph 1)

   C. "When a ball leaves the pitcher's hand with a bit of a spin, its turning motion drags some of the surrounding air with it." (paragraph 2)

   D. "While the ball spins in the air, the speed of the air changes, and the air moves slower on one side of the ball than it does on the other side." (paragraph 2)

GO ON TO THE NEXT PAGE

16. Which of the following best explains one early theory about the curveball?

    E. "To the naked eye, this pitch appeared to curve, not only impressing spectators but also completely fooling batters of the day who attempted to make contact." (paragraph 1)

    F. "Some posited that the rotation of Earth played a factor." (paragraph 2)

    G. "While the ball spins in the air, the speed of the air changes, and the air moves slower on one side of the ball than it does on the other side." (paragraph 2)

    H. "In the early 1900s, pitchers began throwing curveballs in the opposite direction as well; these have come to be known as 'fadeaways' or 'screwballs.'" (paragraph 3)

17. The table contributes to the development of the topic of the passage mainly by

    A. detailing how pitchers choose to pitch curveballs, fastballs, sliders, and changeups during a baseball game.

    B. suggesting that pitchers should throw curveballs all the time because they are impossible to hit.

    C. revealing that curveballs always have results greater than the averages for all pitches.

    D. emphasizing that curveballs are harder to hit than other types of pitches.

18. The image supports the central ideas of paragraph 2 mainly by

    E. providing a graphic that illustrates how the Magnus effect impacts the speed of a pitched ball.

    F. illustrating that the difference in air speeds on opposite sides of the ball causes the curveball to arc.

    G. proving that the theory that the rotation of Earth causes a curveball to curve is incorrect.

    H. showing that the Magnus effect causes curveballs to turn into screwballs due to air speed relative to the ball.

19. Read this sentence from paragraph 2.

> **Interest in this phenomenon excited the world of sports and compelled scientists to investigate the mechanism by which a thrown baseball could change its path mid-flight.**

How does the sentence contribute to the structure and development of ideas in the passage?

    A. It signals a shift from a neutral perspective in paragraph 1 to positive opinions in paragraphs 2 and 3.

    B. It presents a claim about why athletes and scientists often have contrasting ideas regarding sports data.

    C. It highlights the reason why baseball fans were impressed by the new type of pitch described in paragraph 1.

    D. It introduces the discussion of a scientific explanation for the physics of a curveball.

20. What is the most likely reason that the curveball is "in the nightmares of batters" (paragraph 3)?

    E. The Magnus effect still occurs today.

    F. The curveball leads batters to swing at balls that aren't there.

    G. "Candy" Cummings is still a professional baseball pitcher.

    H. There are two kinds of "curves" today.

21. The phrase "spins in this manner" in paragraph 3 conveys the idea that

    A. the pitch deliberately fools both the batter and the spectators.

    B. the ball shifts to the direction opposite the pitcher's throwing arm.

    C. the pitch follows the same direction as the pitcher's throwing arm.

    D. the pitch continues on one path as it approaches the batter.

Excerpt from "Rain"

by W. Somerset Maugham

1 It was nearly bed-time and when they[1] awoke next morning land would be in sight. Dr. Macphail lit his pipe and, leaning over the rail, searched the heavens for the Southern Cross. After two years at the front and a wound that had taken longer to heal than it should, he was glad to settle down quietly at Apia for twelve months at least, and he felt already better for the journey. Since some of the passengers were leaving the ship next day at Pago-Pago they had had a little dance that evening and in his ears hammered still the harsh notes of the mechanical piano. But the deck was quiet at last. A little way off he saw his wife in a long chair talking with the Davidsons, and he strolled over to her. When he sat down under the light and took off his hat you saw that he had very red hair, with a bald patch on the crown, and the red, freckled skin which accompanies red hair; he was a man of forty, thin, with a pinched face, precise and rather pedantic; and he spoke with a Scots accent in a very low, quiet voice.

2 Between the Macphails and the Davidsons, who were missionaries, there had arisen the intimacy of shipboard, which is due to propinquity rather than to any community of taste. Their chief tie was the disapproval they shared of the men who spent their days and nights in the smoking-room playing poker or bridge and drinking. Mrs. Macphail was not a little flattered to think that she and her husband were the only people on board with whom the Davidsons were willing to associate, and even the doctor, shy but no fool, half unconsciously acknowledged the compliment. It was only because he was of an argumentative mind that in their cabin at night he permitted himself to carp.

3 "Mrs. Davidson was saying she didn't know how they'd have got through the journey if it hadn't been for us," said Mrs. Macphail, as she neatly brushed out her transformation. "She said we were really the only people on the ship they cared to know."

4 "I shouldn't have thought a missionary was such a big bug that he could afford to put on frills."

5 "It's not frills. I quite understand what she means. It wouldn't have been very nice for the Davidsons to have to mix with all that rough lot in the smoking-room."

6 "The founder of their religion wasn't so exclusive," said Dr. Macphail with a chuckle.

7 "I've asked you over and over again not to joke about religion," answered his wife. "I shouldn't like to have a nature like yours, Alec. You never look for the best in people."

8 He gave her a sidelong glance with his pale, blue eyes, but did not reply. After many years of married life he had learned that it was more conducive to peace to leave his wife with the last word. He was undressed before she was, and climbing into the upper bunk he settled down to read himself to sleep.

9 When he came on deck next morning they were close to land. He looked at it with greedy eyes. There was a thin strip of silver beach rising quickly to hills covered to the top with luxuriant vegetation. The coconut trees, thick and green, came nearly to the water's edge, and among them you saw the grass houses of the Samoaris; and here and there, gleaming white, a little church.

---

[1]In this excerpt, two couples are aboard a ship bound for a South Seas island.

10   Mrs. Davidson came and stood beside him. She was dressed in black, and wore round her neck a gold chain, from which dangled a small cross. She was a little woman, with brown, dull hair very elaborately arranged, and she had prominent blue eyes behind invisible pince-nez. Her face was long, like a sheep's, but she gave no impression of foolishness, rather of extreme alertness; she had the quick movements of a bird. The most remarkable thing about her was her voice, high, metallic, and without inflection; it fell on the ear with a hard monotony, irritating to the nerves like the pitiless clamour of the pneumatic drill.

11   "This must seem like home to you," said Dr. Macphail, with his thin, difficult smile.

12   "Ours are low islands, you know, not like these. Coral. These are volcanic. We've got another ten days' journey to reach them."

13   "In these parts that's almost like being in the next street at home," said Dr. Macphail facetiously.

14   "Well, that's rather an exaggerated way of putting it, but one does look at distances differently in the South Seas. So far you're right." Dr. Macphail sighed faintly.

15   "I'm glad we're not stationed here," she went on. "They say this is a terribly difficult place to work in. The steamers' touching makes the people unsettled; and then there's the naval station; that's bad for the natives. In our district we don't have difficulties like that to contend with. There are one or two traders, of course, but we take care to make them behave, and if they don't we make the place so hot for them they're glad to go."

16   Fixing the glasses on her nose she looked at the green island with a ruthless stare.

17   "It's almost a hopeless task for the missionaries here. I can never be sufficiently thankful to God that we are at least spared that."

22.   In paragraph 2, how does the phrase "intimacy of shipboard" affect the tone of the excerpt?

   E.   It creates a tone of calm serenity by evoking the peaceful life at sea.

   F.   It contributes to a tone based on the close relationship that will emerge between the characters.

   G.   It suggests a skeptical tone based on a relationship that is forced by circumstances.

   H.   It introduces a humorous tone because the characters met aboard the ship.

23.   How does paragraph 2 contribute to the plot of the excerpt?

   A.   It reveals the character of the Davidsons.

   B.   It describes the motivations of Mrs. Macphail.

   C.   It introduces a topic of controversy between the Macphails.

   D.   It illustrates the Davidsons' concerns for the Macphails.

GO ON TO THE NEXT PAGE ▶

24. Read this sentence from paragraph 2.

> **It was only because he was of an argumentative mind that in their cabin at night he permitted himself to carp.**

How does the sentence contribute to the development of the plot?

E. It introduces Dr. Macphail's tendency to be very disagreeable and combative.

F. It reveals Dr. Macphail's concerns about his wife's relationship with the Davidsons.

G. It shows the discord in the Macphails' relationship caused by the Davidsons.

H. It highlights Dr. Macphail's true feelings about the Davidsons despite his dialogue.

25. Which sentence from the excerpt best supports the idea that Dr. Macphail suspects the Davidsons of hypocrisy?

A. "I shouldn't have thought a missionary was such a big bug that he could afford to put on frills." (paragraph 4)

B. "It wouldn't have been very nice for the Davidsons to have to mix with all that rough lot in the smoking-room." (paragraph 5)

C. "The founder of their religion wasn't so exclusive." (paragraph 6)

D. "You never look for the best in people." (paragraph 7)

26. Read this sentence from paragraph 8.

> **He was undressed before she was, and climbing into the upper bunk he settled down to read himself to sleep.**

Which statement best describes how the sentence fits into the overall structure of the excerpt?

E. It illustrates the relationship among the characters.

F. It emphasizes the intensity and difficulty of the journey.

G. It serves as a summary of the descriptions and the conversations in the first part of the passage.

H. It marks the transition from the characters' descriptions and conversations to the arrival at the island.

27. How does the descriptive language in paragraphs 9 and 10 help support the theme of the excerpt?

A. They create a sense of welcome after the difficult voyage.

B. They establish background details that explain Mrs. Davidson's attraction to the island.

C. They extend the close relationship established on the ship to that relationship on land.

D. They contrast the rich, natural beauty of the island with the austerity of Mrs. Davidson.

Practice Tests

28. Which sentence from the excerpt best supports the idea that Dr. Macphail was tired of traveling by ship?

    E. "After two years at the front and a wound that had taken longer to heal than it should, he was glad to settle down quietly at Apia for twelve months at least, and he felt already better for the journey." (paragraph 1)

    F. "He was undressed before she was, and climbing into the upper bunk he settled down to read himself to sleep." (paragraph 8)

    G. "He looked at it with greedy eyes." (paragraph 9)

    H. "Dr. Macphail sighed faintly." (paragraph 14)

29. In paragraph 16, how does the phrase "she looked at the green island with a ruthless stare" affect the tone in the latter part of the excerpt?

    A. It creates a welcoming tone by emphasizing the beauty of the island and Mrs. Davidson's desire to return.

    B. It introduces a hopeful tone as Mrs. Davidson compares the island before them with the island where she serves.

    C. It develops the humorous tone introduced earlier by Dr. Macphail's comment to Mrs. Davidson.

    D. It reinforces the severe tone introduced earlier in the passage by suggesting Mrs. Davidson's feelings about her return.

Cheetahs: Fascinating Creatures

1 The cheetah—whose name comes from the Sanskrit word *chitkara*, meaning "spotted one"—can be found hunting in the African savanna, the vast, uninhabited grassy plains of sub-Saharan Africa. Although the cheetah is certainly famous for its incredible speed, which has been recorded in excess of 70 miles per hour by biologists, the significant vulnerabilities of this wild cat are less well-known. Ironically, it is largely because of its ability to run so blindingly fast that the cheetah has evolved to be quite defenseless when it stands still. This combination of great strengths and significant weaknesses makes the cheetah a fascinating creature.

2 The phrase "built for speed" is a perfect descriptor for this magnificent animal. It is almost as if every aspect of the cheetah's biological makeup were designed with the intention of prioritizing fast movement over every other consideration. For instance, to reach its full sprinting stride the cheetah utilizes a remarkably flexible spine that works as a spring for its powerful back legs. This mechanism is incredibly effective for fast acceleration, yet the springlike movement of the spine comes at a significant cost; it quickly drains the cheetah's energy. In fact, the cheetah is limited to 300-yard bursts of sprinting before it is exhausted. This limitation, in turn, affects the cheetah's predatory behavior. The cheetah's tendency is to creep close to its intended prey, using its exceptional eyesight to scan its surroundings; not until it is within 50 yards will the cheetah typically open chase, allowing it to reach its target before its body tires. It may be surprising to realize that, for such an incredibly powerful runner, the cheetah's chase usually lasts only about 20 seconds. It never stays in pursuit for longer than a minute, and when successful, the chase ends quickly, culminating in a suffocating clamp of the cheetah's jaw on the windpipe of its victim.

3 Other adaptations seem similarly designed for swift movement above all else. For instance, the cheetah possesses rather blunt, nonretractable claws that provide great traction while running; it has further adapted a light bone structure for a lithe, streamlined body that is ideal for speed. But both of these characteristics can also be vulnerabilities, especially when the cheetah is in close contact with other predators. Blunt claws and a light body (not to mention small teeth) make it difficult for the cheetah to defend itself against other more aggressive and powerful predators. Thus, if ever challenged for a meal, the cheetah is far more likely to flee than fight. Pragmatists in their habits, cheetahs are also known to hunt during the day in order to avoid competition from more powerful predators such as lions and leopards at night. Thus, despite its impressive hunting skills, the cheetah must be classified as a particularly nonaggressive predator. As a result, these cats usually seek out similarly docile prey, like small antelopes, birds, and rabbits. Nevertheless, no other land animal on Earth can come close to matching the speed of these remarkable cats. A study in contrasts, cheetahs are fascinating creatures worth taking the time to get to know but, sadly, are now considered threatened due to loss of habitat and prey as well as conflict with humans.

30. Which of the following best describes what this passage is about?

    E. Cheetahs reach sprinting speeds that outpace most predators.

    F. Cheetahs dominate the grassy plains of sub-Saharan Africa.

    G. The cheetah is a surprisingly ill-protected species.

    H. The cheetah's biological makeup makes it fast but vulnerable.

31. The phrase "significant vulnerabilities" in paragraph 1 conveys the idea that cheetahs

    A. more than compensate for them by their speed.

    B. conduct frequent, but often futile, hunting.

    C. are generally unable to hunt during the day.

    D. are susceptible to attack when stationary.

32. Read this sentence from paragraph 2.

> This mechanism is incredibly effective for fast acceleration, yet the springlike movement of the spine comes at a significant cost; it quickly drains the cheetah's energy.

The sentence contributes to the development of ideas in the passage by

    E. suggesting that cheetahs can easily catch prey that moves more slowly than they do.

    F. revealing how cheetahs require far more rest than other animals such as small antelopes, birds, and rabbits.

    G. supporting the idea that cheetahs face limitations that affect their hunting tendencies.

    H. demonstrating the challenge cheetahs face when the energy they spend is greater than their daily caloric intake.

33. The author refers to the cheetah as a "fascinating creature" (paragraph 1) most likely to

    A. emphasize the juxtaposition of great speed with a tendency to flee.

    B. confirm the classification of this particular predator as nonaggressive.

    C. explain the cheetah's remarkable ability to run at speeds exceeding 70 miles per hour.

    D. highlight the idea that such a fast animal could also be so vulnerable.

34. With which statement would the author of the passage most likely agree?

    E. The cheetah's spots help it to blend into the savanna.

    F. The cheetah's speed creates too many weaknesses.

    G. The cheetah has a tendency to frantically eat its prey.

    H. The cheetah can run better than it can fight.

35. According to the passage, the grassy plains of sub-Saharan Africa are

    A. made up of completely flat, grassy plains.

    B. the hunting grounds of the cheetah.

    C. strictly savannas.

    D. populated mostly by antelopes, birds, and rabbits.

GO ON TO THE NEXT PAGE →

Practice Tests

36. The cheetah's tendency to creep close to its prey before giving chase is behavior caused by the cheetah's

   E. incredible sprinting speed.

   F. need to catch its prey before fatigue sets in.

   G. relatively small teeth.

   H. prey being nonaggressive antelopes, birds, and rabbits.

37. Which sentence from the passage indicates that cheetahs must be selective hunters?

   A. "This combination of great strengths and significant weaknesses makes the cheetah a fascinating creature." (paragraph 1)

   B. "The phrase 'built for speed' is a perfect descriptor for this magnificent animal." (paragraph 2)

   C. "It is almost as if every aspect of the cheetah's biological makeup were designed with the intention of prioritizing fast movement over every other consideration." (paragraph 2)

   D. "As a result, these cats usually seek out similarly docile prey, like small antelopes, birds, and rabbits." (paragraph 3)

Restoring the Respite: Urban Parks

1   Plots of urban land set aside for recreation have a long history in Europe. In the United States, such city parks date back to the late nineteenth century. These urban oases were initially created to provide the local populace with a convenient refuge from the crowding and chaos of its surroundings. As modern cities continued to grow in complexity and population, the ability to achieve some respite in nature served an essential function. Whether city dwellers wanted to sit under a shady tree to think or take a vigorous stroll to get some exercise, they looked forward to visiting these nearby places of serenity. Filled with trees, shrubs, flowers, meadows, and ponds, city parks were a tranquil spot in which to unwind from the daily pressures of urban life. They were places where people met their friends for picnics or sporting events. They were also places to get some sun and fresh air in the midst of an often dark and dreary environment, with its seemingly endless rows of buildings.

2   For most of their history, these parks have served their purpose admirably, and their ability to add to the quality of life in cities has been well-recognized by urban planners. Yet city parks around the world have been allowed to deteriorate to an alarming extent in recent decades. The degradation has occurred on many fronts. They have become centers of crime, some now so dangerous that local residents are even afraid to enter them. And the great natural beauty that was once their hallmark has been severely diminished, not only through lack of proper care and maintenance of walkways, benches, and structures, but also from active attack by the forces of humanity. For instance, trees, shrubs, flowers, and meadows have withered under the impact of intense air pollution and littering, while ponds have been fouled by untreated sewage. The diminution of beauty further adds to the lack of interest in visiting city parks, and a vicious cycle of neglect is perpetuated.

3   This sad process of decline, though it seems to be the order of the day, is hardly inevitable. A few key changes could turn this situation around. First, special police units, whose only responsibility would be to patrol city parks, should be created to ensure that the urban parks remain safe for those who wish to enjoy them. Ensuring the safety of visitors must be primary, but additional measures could reestablish a beautiful and serene space that could be inviting to urban residents once again. For instance, more caretakers should be hired to care for the grounds and, in particular, to collect trash. Beyond the increased staffing requirements, it will also be necessary to insulate city parks from their surroundings. Total isolation is, of course, impossible, but many beneficial measures in that direction could be implemented without too much trouble. Vehicles, for instance, should be banned from city parks to cut down on air pollution. Sewage pipes should be rerouted away from park areas to prevent the contamination of land and water. Such measures are self-reinforcing. More care will make parks attractive to more residents; the more law-abiding residents use parks, the less crime infested they will be, and the more citizens will wish to see their tax dollars go toward preserving and maintaining such spaces. If urban planners are willing to make these changes, city parks can be restored to their proud tradition and place of former glory for the benefit of all.

38. What is the most likely reason the natural beauty of city parks has deteriorated in recent decades?

   E.   Fewer people have been visiting the parks.

   F.   Air pollution has spoiled the trees and flowers.

   G.   Criminals have made the parks centers of crime.

   H.   Urban planners have cut funding for the parks.

GO ON TO THE NEXT PAGE

39. According to the passage, by the end of the nineteenth century, urban planners were beginning to

    A. neglect the urban dweller's need for outdoor leisure space.

    B. consider the harmful effects of the urban environment.

    C. worry about the safety of citizens when designing public areas.

    D. address the issue of sewage disposal regulations.

40. With which statement would the author of the passage most likely agree?

    E. Few urban planners recognize the value of city parks.

    F. The extent of urban crime makes city parks impossible to police.

    G. City parks are unlikely to ever recover their former glory.

    H. City parks are beneficial to the well-being of city residents.

41. What is the most likely reason the author recommends the establishment of a police force dedicated to public parks?

    A. In the past, cities have had too few police officers to be able to patrol parks.

    B. People will visit parks only if they feel they will be safe there.

    C. Patrol cars should not be able to enter because all vehicles will be banned from parks.

    D. Most police officers do not appreciate nature.

42. The phrase "such measures are self-reinforcing" in paragraph 3 conveys the idea that

    E. repairing the damaged benches, walkways, and structures will improve the experience of park visitors.

    F. if the problems in the parks had been addressed more quickly, their condition may not have become so serious.

    G. if positive changes are begun, the responses to those changes will enable more improvements to continue.

    H. further improvements to the parks are not necessary.

43. Read this sentence from paragraph 3.

> **Vehicles, for instance, should be banned from city parks to cut down on air pollution.**

The sentence contributes to the development of ideas in the paragraph by

    A. emphasizing how parks have deteriorated.

    B. introducing the importance of urban parks.

    C. suggesting a way to improve parks.

    D. highlighting the failure of urban planning.

The Evolution of Airships

1 Today, airships are seen mostly as advertisements hovering in the sky over sporting events. Such companies as Goodyear®, Metropolitan Life®, and Fuji Film® have all made use of "blimps" in this way to the delight of spectators. But there was a time, before World War II, that blimps—as well as other lighter-than-air vehicles—were not just a charming diversion but actually used as a mode of transportation. One in particular, the German ship *Hindenburg*, was an incredible example of a commercial passenger aircraft capable of crossing the Atlantic Ocean. Tragically, on one fateful day, the path of airships was changed forever when, in spectacular fashion, the *Hindenburg* revealed the downside of the use of airships as transportation.

2 Airships enjoyed many advantages in the early twentieth century, and the *Hindenburg* was considered a one-of-a-kind example. When the 804-foot *Hindenburg* was launched in 1936, it was the largest airship in the world. Like most airships of the period, the *Hindenburg* was built with a solid frame that encased a simple balloon filled with a light gas—in this case, hydrogen. The *Hindenburg* was a product of some of the newest technology of its time with a frame constructed of an early aluminum alloy called duralumin, while its gas cells were reinforced with a new material known as latex. In an age when airplanes could not carry more than 10 passengers at a time, the *Hindenburg* could hold an astounding 1,002 passengers, twice as many as a modern jetliner. Thus, in many ways, it was an incredible specimen of modern advancements.

3 Despite these advantages, however, the *Hindenburg* was hampered by many of the same drawbacks that plagued other airships. Tickets to fly in the *Hindenburg* were not affordable for most people, so the customer base was extremely limited. This was due in part to the massive amount of fuel needed not only to fill the balloon but also to power its propellers, making this airship very expensive to operate. Even with all of that fuel, the *Hindenburg* flew at a mere 78 miles per hour—a snail's pace considering that it was used for transatlantic passenger service. Because any airship is essentially a balloon with an engine, it is extremely vulnerable to air currents and stormy weather, and the *Hindenburg*, despite its massive size, was no different.

4 The *Hindenburg*'s fate, however, rested on its most dangerous characteristic and one it shared with other airships: the use of highly flammable hydrogen gas. Any spark or flame that came near the gas could cause a horrific explosion, which is exactly what happened. On May 6, 1937, as the *Hindenburg* was landing in Lakehurst, New Jersey, it suddenly burst into flames, killing 36 of the 97 passengers on board. This explosion destroyed the ship quickly; in a matter of just 34 seconds, the entire ship was engulfed in flames. Although the exact cause is still unknown, it is believed to have been caused by a discharge of static electricity in the air that reacted to gas that had escaped from a small leak in the balloon. Though there had been other airship mishaps before this date, something about this particular disaster captured the public imagination—maybe the fact that it was famously witnessed and reported live by radio reporter Herbert Morrison, who gave a dramatic account of the event as it unfolded, or maybe it was just a final symbolic end to a mode of travel that had become passé.

5 At the time of the *Hindenburg* disaster, the airship was already obsolete as a mode of transportation. By the 1940s, commercial airplanes had advanced in development far beyond the airship's capacity. Now, modern airplanes cost much less to operate and fly at more than seven times the speed of the *Hindenburg*. Meanwhile, airline tickets are also far more affordable than airship travel ever was. The airship thus sank into permanently outdated status as a passenger service and acquired its modern-day role as a quirky advertising platform.

GO ON TO THE NEXT PAGE ➡

44. Which statement best describes the central idea of the passage?

   E. Commercial airships often have flaws.

   F. The *Hindenburg* played an important role in the history of airships.

   G. Commercial airlines of today are vastly different from the *Hindenburg*.

   H. Airships are an integral part of modern transportation.

45. Read this sentence from the passage.

> But there was a time, before World War II, that blimps—as well as other lighter-than-air vehicles—were not just a charming diversion but actually used as a mode of transportation.

How does this sentence contribute to the development of a central idea in the passage?

   A. It confirms that blimps were developed in Germany.

   B. It introduces the idea that in the past, airships had different uses than today.

   C. It shows why airships, including blimps, are dangerous.

   D. It indicates why airships continue to be used for transportation.

46. The author contrasts the airship's modern use with the airship's previous role mainly by

   E. providing examples of companies that use airships to advertise at sporting events.

   F. detailing the versatile nature of airships, including vast passenger capacities.

   G. showing that the *Hindenburg* had limitations similar to those of other airships.

   H. discussing the cost of airline tickets versus airship tickets.

47. Read this sentence from paragraph 2.

> Thus, in many ways, it was an incredible specimen of modern advancements.

The sentence contributes to the development of ideas in the passage by

   A. revealing that the *Hindenburg* had great speed.

   B. suggesting that the *Hindenburg* had many advantages.

   C. emphasizing the *Hindenburg's* enormous size.

   D. demonstrating that the *Hindenburg* had a solid frame.

48. The details about hydrogen in paragraph 4 convey which of the following?

   E. They suggest that it was not surprising the *Hindenburg* burst into flames.

   F. They explain why the customer base for airship tickets was so limited.

   G. They indicate that by the end of the 1930s, airships had become passé.

   H. They confirm that the exact cause of the *Hindenburg* disaster is still unknown.

49. Which sentence from the excerpt best supports the idea that the *Hindenburg* had a dangerous flaw?

   A. "Like most airships of the period, the *Hindenburg* was built with a solid frame that encased a simple balloon filled with a light gas—in this case, hydrogen." (paragraph 2)

   B. "Despite these advantages, however, the *Hindenburg* was hampered by many of the same drawbacks that plagued other airships." (paragraph 3)

   C. "Any spark or flame that came near the gas could cause a horrific explosion, which is exactly what happened." (paragraph 4)

   D. "At the time of the *Hindenburg* disaster, the airship was already obsolete as a mode of transportation." (paragraph 5)

50. According to the passage, why are airships used primarily as advertisements today?

   E. Their huge capacity makes airships ideal for large advertisements.

   F. They are susceptible to wind currents.

   G. They are not as effective as airplanes in modern transportation.

   H. They are too expensive for use as advertisements.

GO ON TO THE NEXT PAGE

"I like to see it lap the Miles"

by Emily Dickinson

I like to see it[1] lap the Miles,
And lick the Valleys up,
And stop to feed itself at Tanks;
And then, prodigious, step

5 Around a Pile of Mountains,
And, supercilious, peer
In shanties by the sides of Roads;
And then a Quarry pare

To fit its sides, and crawl between,
10 Complaining all the while
In horrid, hooting stanza;
Then chase itself down Hill

And neigh like Boanerges;
Then, punctual as a Star,
15 Stop—docile and omnipotent—
At its own stable door.

[1] the train

51. How does the line "I like to see it lap the Miles" (line 1) contribute to the development of ideas in the stanza?

    A. It illustrates a preference of the speaker.

    B. It explains how quickly a horse is drinking water.

    C. It describes a fast-moving subject.

    D. It foreshadows the speaker's own thirst.

52. The description in the first stanza (lines 1–4) helps establish a central idea of the poem by

    E. following the progression of a horse on a long trip.

    F. describing the sights in the country and a town.

    G. evoking feelings of the progress of a train.

    H. illustrating the author's trip through the countryside.

53. Read lines 6–7.

> **And, supercilious, peer**
> **In shanties by the sides of Roads;**

What impact do these lines have on the meaning of the poem?

- **A.** The lines emphasize that the train is something to be disdained.
- **B.** The lines act as a simile, which is continued throughout the other stanzas.
- **C.** The lines introduce personification for the first time in the poem.
- **D.** The lines continue personification that was introduced in the first stanza.

54. Which detail of the poem reflects the speaker's view that the subject is very large?

- **E.** "And then, prodigious, step" (line 4)
- **F.** "To fit its sides, and crawl between," (line 9)
- **G.** "Then chase itself down Hill" (line 12)
- **H.** "Stop—docile and omnipotent—" (line 15)

55. What impact does the phrase "In horrid, hooting stanza" (line 11) have on the meaning of the poem?

- **A.** It illustrates that the sounds of the subject are rhythmic.
- **B.** It suggests that the subject voices its unhappiness.
- **C.** It implies that the subject uses poetry to state its opinions.
- **D.** It indicates that the sounds of the subject often can be heard from miles away.

56. How does the phrase "punctual as a Star" (line 14) contribute to the development of ideas in the stanza?

- **E.** It describes how the subject appears at night.
- **F.** It alludes to the fact that the subject always appears in the same place.
- **G.** It defines how the subject twinkles from far away.
- **H.** It emphasizes how steady and predictable the subject is.

57. Which line from the poem best supports the idea that the subject is quite powerful?

- **A.** "Around a Pile of Mountains," (line 5)
- **B.** "And then a Quarry pare" (line 8)
- **C.** "To fit its sides, and crawl between," (line 9)
- **D.** "And neigh like Boanerges;" (line 13)

Part 2—Mathematics

57 QUESTIONS—SUGGESTED TIMING: 90 MINUTES

IMPORTANT NOTES

1. Definitions and formulas are **not** provided.

2. Diagrams are **not** necessarily drawn to scale, with the exception of graphs.

3. Diagrams are drawn in single planes unless the question specifically states they are not.

4. Graphs are drawn to scale.

5. Simplify all fractions to lowest terms.

GRID-IN QUESTIONS

QUESTIONS 58–62

DIRECTIONS: Answer each question. Write your answer in the boxes at the top of the grid on the answer sheet. Start on the left side of each grid, printing only one number or symbol in each box. **DO NOT LEAVE A BOX BLANK IN THE MIDDLE OF AN ANSWER.** Under each box, fill in the circle that matches the number or symbol you wrote above. **DO NOT FILL IN A CIRCLE UNDER AN UNUSED BOX.**

$$4 - 6 \div |-2| + (-3)^3 \times 2\frac{1}{3}$$

58. What is the value of the expression shown above?

59. If $3x + 8 = 44$, what is the value of x ?

60. Carin opened a money market account with a deposit of $3,000. This account earns 2% simple interest annually. How many years will it take for her $3,000 deposit to earn $420 in interest, assuming she does not withdraw any of the money?

61. In a scale drawing of a rectangular patio, the length is 14 inches and the width is 10 inches. In the drawing, 4 inches represents 5 yards. What is the length of the actual patio, in yards?

62. A certain test consists of multiple-choice questions and essay questions in the ratio of 5:2. If the test contains 6 essay questions, what is the total number of questions on the test?

MULTIPLE-CHOICE QUESTIONS

QUESTIONS 63–114

DIRECTIONS: Answer each question, selecting the best answer available. On the answer sheet, mark the letter of each of your answers. You can do your figuring in the test booklet or on paper provided by the proctor.

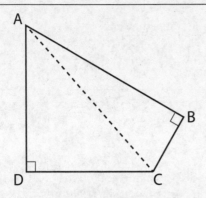

63. If AD = 20 centimeters, DC = 15 centimeters, BC = 7 centimeters, and AB = 24 centimeters, what is the area of quadrilateral ABCD?

    A. 66 sq cm

    B. 117 sq cm

    C. 234 sq cm

    D. 468 sq cm

64. In a pond of 1,600 fish, 25% of the fish are trout. The remaining fish are bass. How many fewer trout are there than bass?

    E. 200

    F. 400

    G. 800

    H. 1,200

65. Which of the following numbers does **not** have factors that include the smallest factor (other than 1) of 119 ?

    A. 28

    B. 35

    C. 40

    D. 63

66. Lucia speed walks 3 kilometers in $\frac{2}{3}$ of an hour. At that rate, how many **meters** does she speed walk per minute?

    E. 0.75

    F. 75

    G. 750

    H. 7,500

$$\frac{72}{7} = \frac{12}{x}$$

67. What value of x makes the equation above true?

    A. 1

    B. $1\frac{1}{6}$

    C. 6

    D. $7\frac{1}{6}$

GO ON TO THE NEXT PAGE ➔

$$-2 < \frac{x}{3} < 1$$

68. Which number line shows the solution to the inequality above?

E.
F.
G.
H.

69. Between which two consecutive integers is the fraction $\frac{43}{8}$?

A. 3 and 4
B. 4 and 5
C. 5 and 6
D. 6 and 7

70. Isabel has 10 boards that are x meters long. She has 5 boards that are $2x$ meters long. She also has 4 boards that measure 3 meters, 6 meters, 9 meters, and 13 meters, respectively. If she were to lay all her boards in a straight line with no gaps between them, the boards would measure 271 meters. What is the value of x?

E. 5 meters
F. 6 meters
G. 10 meters
H. 12 meters

BASEBALL TICKET PRICES

Price Paid	# of Customers
$25	50
$40	30
$100	20

71. What is the mean price paid by the 100 customers in the table above?

A. $25
B. $33.33
C. $44.50
D. $55

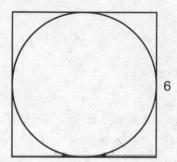

6

72. What is the circumference of the circle inscribed in the square above?

E. 2π
F. 3π
G. 6π
H. 9π

73. If $x + y = 12$ and $x = 15$, then what is $-\frac{x}{y}$?

A. -5
B. -3
C. 3
D. 5

MEAT SOLD AT DELI COUNTER

Meat	Pounds Sold
Ham	9
Turkey	6
Salami	?
Chicken	3
Roast Beef	4
Total	25

74. According to the table above, salami made up what percentage of the total number of pounds of meat sold at the deli counter?

    E. 3
    F. 8
    G. 10
    H. 12

75. There are 250 giggles in one laugh and 3 laughs in a burst. How many giggles are in 2 bursts?

    A. 250
    B. 500
    C. 750
    D. 1,500

76. Daniel is packing crates of tires for storage in a warehouse. Each crate can hold 9 tires. If Daniel has 469 tires to store and fills all but the last crate, how many full crates of tires will Daniel have to put in the warehouse?

    E. 5
    F. 50
    G. 52
    H. 53

77. A bus travels 1,070 miles from Jacksonville, FL, to Syracuse, NY. The bus covers the first 310 miles in 5 hours. If the bus continues to travel at this rate, how many **more** hours will it take to reach Syracuse? Round your answer to the nearest whole hour.

    A. 12
    B. 14
    C. 16
    D. 17

$$\frac{n}{100} = \frac{x}{y}$$

78. In the equation above, if $n = 30$ and $y = 300$, what is the value of x ?

    E. 3
    F. 9
    G. 90
    H. 900

79. What is the average of all the even numbers in the set $\{2, 3, 4, \ldots, 12, 13, 14\}$?

    A. 7
    B. 8
    C. 8.5
    D. 9

80. Jennifer has $200 in her checking account. She makes $6.48 per hour babysitting her cousins. If she wants to buy a guitar that costs $310.04 (including tax), how many hours must she work?

    E. 10
    F. 15
    G. 16
    H. 17

GO ON TO THE NEXT PAGE →

81. Suppose point Z is halfway between points W and X on a standard number line, and point X is halfway between points Z and Y. Where is W if Z is located at $\frac{1}{3}$ and Y is located at $\frac{11}{3}$?

    A. −2
    B. $-\frac{4}{3}$
    C. $-\frac{1}{3}$
    D. 2

82. If *n* is an even integer that is greater than −3.75, what is the least possible value of *n*?

    E. −5
    F. −4
    G. −3
    H. −2

83. What is the least common multiple of 8, 32, and 48?

    A. 64
    B. 96
    C. 128
    D. 144

84. David is now 4 years more than twice the age of Henry. If Henry will be 18 in 3 years, how old was David 2 years ago?

    E. 13
    F. 15
    G. 32
    H. 34

85. Joe answered 37 out of 50 questions correctly on his history exam. What percentage of the questions did he get wrong?

    A. 13%
    B. 26%
    C. 37%
    D. 74%

86. Angle A and angle B are supplementary. If the measure of angle B is one-third the measure of angle A, what is the measure of angle B?

    E. 22.5°
    F. 45°
    G. 67.5°
    H. 135°

87. Jin completed 8 pages in his math workbook and 12 pages in his science workbook. This is 25% of the total number of pages in both workbooks together. If there are 32 pages in his math workbook, how many pages are there in his science workbook?

    A. 20
    B. 48
    C. 80
    D. 128

88. In March, the electricity used in New York was 5,000,000 watts. In April, the number of watts used was 4,000,000. By what percentage did the electricity usage decrease from March to April?

    E. 20%
    F. 25%
    G. 50%
    H. 75%

89. The population of a particular bacteria doubles in size every 19 hours. If the population is 100 at 2:15 p.m. on a given day, at what time of day will the bacteria have doubled twice?

    A. 2:15 a.m.

    B. 4:15 a.m.

    C. 6:15 a.m.

    D. 4:15 p.m.

90. The sum of 6 consecutive odd numbers is 36. What is the difference between the highest and the lowest of these numbers?

    E. 1

    F. 6

    G. 7

    H. 10

WEEKNIGHT BEDTIMES, AGE 11

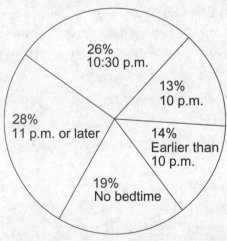

91. If 5,000 children were surveyed, how many have bedtimes that are 10:30 p.m. or earlier, according to the circle graph above?

    A. 53

    B. 1,350

    C. 2,650

    D. 3,600

92. $(11 + 4x) - (2 - x) =$

    E. $9 - 5x$

    F. $9 + 3x$

    G. $9 + 5x$

    H. $13 + 3x$

93. A can contains 40 chips: 10 each of red and blue, 12 white, and the remaining black. If Susan were to remove 3 black and 2 red chips, what is the probability that the next one she removes is black?

    A. $\frac{3}{35}$

    B. $\frac{1}{8}$

    C. $\frac{1}{7}$

    D. $\frac{1}{5}$

94. For what value of x does $6(8 - x) = 3(x - 2)$?

    A. -9

    B. -6

    C. 3

    D. 6

95. Bob, Ted, and Carol are all splitting a reward they received for returning someone's wallet. If Bob and Ted each take one-quarter of the reward, and Carol gets $40, how much was the reward in total?

    A. $50

    B. $60

    C. $80

    D. $120

Practice Tests

96. $\left(\frac{3}{4} - \frac{2}{7}\right) \div \frac{1}{4} =$

   E. $-\frac{3}{2}$

   F. $-\frac{1}{2}$

   G. $\frac{7}{112}$

   H. $\frac{13}{7}$

97. A survey asked students what types of exercise they regularly do. Based on the results, the following statements are all true.

   - 40 students jog.
   - 36 students lift weights.
   - 12 students both jog and lift weights.
   - 16 students neither jog nor lift weights.

   How many students were surveyed?

   A. 72

   B. 76

   C. 80

   D. 104

98. Larissa spends 3 times as many hours reading as Tom does, and Nela spends half as many hours as Tom does. If all 3 people read for a total of 18 hours, for how many hours did Tom read?

   E. 3

   F. 4

   G. 6

   H. 8

99. On Monday, 100 people played golf at a certain golf course. The pro shop sold 14 dozen golf balls that day. At this rate, approximately how many dozens of golf balls can the pro shop expect to sell on Tuesday if 150 people are scheduled to play?

   A. 18 dozen

   B. 20 dozen

   C. 21 dozen

   D. 24 dozen

100. The side length of square A is shorter than the side length of square B by 5 inches. The perimeter of square A is 100 inches. What is the difference, in square inches, between the area of square A and the area of square B?

   E. 10

   F. 25

   G. 125

   H. 275

101. N belongs to the set of rational numbers $\{0.4, 0.5, 1.1, 2.0, 3.5\}$. If $\frac{4.9N}{1.4}$ is an integer, what is N?

   A. 0.4

   B. 0.5

   C. 1.1

   D. 2.0

102. A painter uses a certain shade of green paint made from $\frac{1}{3}$ ounces of blue paint and $1\frac{2}{3}$ ounces of yellow paint. What is the ratio of blue paint to yellow paint in this shade of green?

   E. 1:6

   F. 1:5

   G. 1:3

   H. 1:2

103. If $x = 2$ and $2x(2y - x) = 16$, what is the value of y?

   A.   1

   B.   3

   C.   6

   D.   12

104. A mixed box of frozen yogurt bars contains exactly 8 strawberry bars. The probability of choosing a strawberry bar from the box is $\frac{2}{5}$. How many of the yogurt bars in the box are **not** strawberry?

   E.   12

   F.   16

   G.   20

   H.   32

105. Margo bowled a mean of 110 points per game in her first 4 games. In her 5th game, she bowled 160 points. What is her mean score for the first 5 games?

   A.   120

   B.   132

   C.   135

   D.   142

106. Nick and Alex worked on a paper together. If Nick wrote $\frac{2}{7}$ of the paper and Alex wrote 20 pages, then what was the total length of the paper?

   E.   7 pages

   F.   21 pages

   G.   28 pages

   H.   35 pages

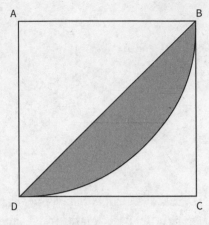

107. In the figure above, point A is both a vertex of square ABCD and the center of a circle that contains arc BD. If the area of square ABCD is 100 square meters, what is the area of the shaded region?

   A. 100π sq m

   B. $(100\pi - 50)$ sq m

   C. 25π sq m

   D. $(25\pi - 50)$ sq m

108. At summer camp, campers are randomly assigned to one of 25 cabins and one of 4 cafeterias. Josef likes 8 of the cabins and 2 of the cafeterias. What is the probability that he is assigned to both a cabin and a cafeteria that he likes?

   E.   16%

   F.   20%

   G.   34%

   H.   82%

109. How many numbers in the set of consecutive integers from 1 to 99, inclusive, have 3 as a factor but do not have 6 as a factor?

   A.   1

   B.   3

   C.   9

   D.   17

GO ON TO THE NEXT PAGE ▶

110. The probability of picking a red marble from a bag of 30 red and blue marbles is $\frac{1}{5}$. How many blue marbles must be removed from the bag to increase the probability to $\frac{1}{4}$?

    E. 4
    F. 5
    G. 6
    H. 24

111. Burt has b action figures, and Cho has c action figures. If Burt gives 4 action figures to Cho, Burt will have twice as many action figures as Cho. Which equation shows the relationship between b and c?

    A. $b - 4 = 2(c + 4)$
    B. $b - 4 = 2c + 4$
    C. $2(b - 4) = c$
    D. $2(b - 4) = c + 4$

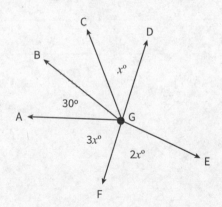

112. In the figure above, the measure of $\angle BGC$ is 10° less than the measure of $\angle CGD$, and the measure of $\angle DGE$ is 25° more than the measure of $\angle EGF$. What is the measure of $\angle DGE$?

    E. 25°
    F. 35°
    G. 70°
    H. 95°

113. The sum of the numbers m, n, and p is 24. The ratio of m to n is 2:5, and the ratio of n to p is 5:3. What is the value of n?

    A. 6
    B. 8
    C. 12
    D. 14

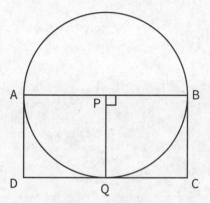

114. P is the center of the circle shown above. AB is a diameter. The perimeter of rectangle ABCD is 72 cm. PQ is a radius, and Q is on CD. What is the circumference of the circle?

    E. 12π
    F. 18π
    G. 24π
    H. 144π

Practice Tests

SHSAT Practice Test 1

Answer Key

PART 1—ENGLISH LANGUAGE ARTS

1. D	16. F	31. D	46. E
2. F	17. D	32. G	47. C
3. C	18. F	33. D	48. E
4. H	19. D	34. H	49. C
5. B	20. F	35. B	50. G
6. E	21. B	36. F	51. C
7. A	22. G	37. D	52. G
8. E	23. A	38. F	53. D
9. C	24. H	39. B	54. E
10. H	25. C	40. H	55. A
11. D	26. H	41. B	56. H
12. E	27. D	42. G	57. B
13. A	28. G	43. C	
14. F	29. D	44. F	
15. A	30. H	45. B	

PART 2—MATHEMATICS

58. —62	73. D	88. E	103. B
59. 12	74. H	89. B	104. E
60. 7	75. D	90. H	105. A
61. 17.5	76. G	91. C	106. G
62. 21	77. A	92. G	107. D
63. C	78. G	93. C	108. E
64. G	79. B	94. H	109. D
65. C	80. H	95. C	110. G
66. F	81. B	96. H	111. A
67. B	82. H	97. C	112. H
68. F	83. B	98. F	113. C
69. C	84. G	99. C	114. G
70. H	85. B	100. H	
71. C	86. F	101. D	
72. G	87. B	102. F	

Answers and Explanations

Part 1—English Language Arts

1. D

Category: Sentence Structure

Getting to the Answer: When the question includes a complex sentence, check that it is not a run-on. This sentence includes two parts that could each stand on their own as a complete sentence, but they are connected with only a comma, so the sentence is a run-on. **(D)** corrects the error by joining the two independent clauses with a semicolon. **(A)** and **(B)** do not fix the original issue and add unnecessary commas. **(C)** is incorrect because the sentence would still be a run-on.

2. F

Category: Punctuation

Getting to the Answer: Nonessential information should be set apart from the rest of the sentence with a pair of commas, parentheses, or dashes. As written, "a famous Broadway performer" is not set apart, so **(F)** correctly completes the pair of commas. **(E)** removes the first comma that sets off the nonessential information, which is incorrect. Both **(G)** and **(H)** place the second comma in an incorrect location.

3. C

Category: Organization

Getting to the Answer: Make sure to keep the main ideas of both sentences when combining the two. Sentence 1 states, "Young figure skaters need to make a tremendous commitment," and sentence 2 adds that this is possible only with the "help and support of their families." **(C)** accurately reflects the relationship between these ideas. **(A)**, **(B)**, and **(D)** all change the meaning by not showing that the commitment is "impossible" without "the help and support of their families."

4. H

Category: Usage

Getting to the Answer: Although the first part of sentence 4 is correct in the present tense, since the tourists can currently see the Musée d'Orsay, saying the former train station "becomes" a museum in the present is incorrect. It "was filled" with art in the past, so it

must have become a museum in the past. **(H)** fixes this by replacing "becomes" with "became." Additionally, the comma after museum is unnecessary and should be deleted. **(E)**, **(F)**, and **(G)** use correct verb tenses and contain necessary commas.

5. B

Category: Usage

Getting to the Answer: Notice that each answer choice contains a change to a verb and a change to a pronoun. Therefore, check each sentence for a verb and a pronoun error. Sentence 1 correctly uses "its" to refer to "Yellowstone National Park" and the present tense "offers" to describe what is happening currently; eliminate **(A)**. Sentence 2 incorrectly uses the past tense "visited" to describe a situation occurring in the present tense and the incorrect plural pronoun "they" to refer to singular Yellowstone, so **(B)** is correct. Sentences 3 and 4 are correct as written; eliminate **(C)** and **(D)**.

6. E

Category: Sentence Structure

Getting to the Answer: Read each sentence, looking for an error in sentence structure such as a run-on sentence or a misplaced modifier, which happens when part of the sentence is in an incorrect place. **(E)** is correct because sentence 1 should be revised to correct the misplaced modifier "such as Sumer and Babylonia in the Tigris-Euphrates valley." As written, the phrase incorrectly modifies "water supply." The correct placement of the phrase is after "civilizations" because Sumer and Babylonia are examples of ancient civilizations: "There is considerable evidence that the earliest civilizations, such as Sumer and Babylonia in the Tigris-Euphrates valley, were greatly influenced by how well the land could be adapted to provide a stable water supply." Sentences 2, 3, and 4 are correct as written, so **(F)**, **(G)**, and **(H)** are incorrect.

7. A

Category: Sentence Structure

Getting to the Answer: Systematically read each underlined portion, looking for an error. The first sentence is a run-on because "consumers have shown a preference for organic fruits and vegetables since the early 1990s" and "the boom in the organic produce market has encouraged the spread of Community Supported Agriculture farms, or CSAs" are each independent clauses that must be properly joined. **(A)** correctly fixes the run-on by adding the coordinating conjunction "and." **(B)**, **(C)**, and **(D)** are incorrect because even though they do not introduce new errors, they do not fix the error in sentence 1.

8. E

Category: Organization

Getting to the Answer: When a question asks you to add a transition to the beginning of a sentence, think about that sentence's relationship to the sentence before. In this case, sentence 2 provides examples of a trend described in sentence 1, so an example transition is needed. **(E)** is correct. **(F)** introduces a restatement of an idea, and **(G)** offers a conclusion. **(H)** suggests a contrast from the previous sentence.

9. C

Category: Knowledge of Language

Getting to the Answer: The author takes an academic tone in this passage, and the word "stupidity" does not fit with this tone. **(C)** matches the more formal tone needed for this passage and is correct. **(A)** does not change "stupidity." **(B)** and **(D)** both add phrases that retain the incorrect informal tone.

10. H

Category: Knowledge of Language

Getting to the Answer: Precise language means language that is specific or detailed. **(H)** is correct because it tells us the family member was Tesla's father and specifies that Tesla's performance was good. The remaining choices are incorrect because they alter the meaning of the sentence. **(E)** is not clear whose father it is, while **(F)** gets less precise because it removes the part about performance. **(G)** changes the number of people to whom the professor wrote.

11. D

Category: Topic Development

Getting to the Answer: Every sentence in a paragraph should be connected to the paragraph's main topic. This paragraph is about Tesla's work in the United States, so the sentence to remove will be about something else. **(D)**, sentence 10, which mentions the fact that Tesla

became a naturalized citizen, is irrelevant to the topic and should be removed. All other sentences are about his work and are therefore on topic.

12. E

Category: Organization

Getting to the Answer: Sentence 14 introduces the idea that "Tesla developed a number of devices" and provides an example. This makes it a good introduction sentence for the paragraph. **(E)** is correct. The other choices interrupt the flow of the paragraph.

13. A

Category: Topic Development

Getting to the Answer: Any new sentence must fit with the topic of the paragraph and with the sentences around it. Sentence 15, the topic sentence of the paragraph, reiterates that Tesla did not fit the popular image of a scientist, and sentence 16 gives an example of why this is so. **(A)** is correct because it fits well with both, supporting the idea of Tesla's nonconformity and leading into specifics about his unusual actions. **(B)** could be true, but it doesn't fit with the specific example provided. **(C)** uses a contrast phrase where no contrast is needed. **(D)** is redundant; this fact has already been stated.

14. F

Category: Topic Development

Getting to the Answer: A concluding sentence should wrap up the passage well and not introduce anything new. **(F)** summarizes the passage well and ties the ending back to the beginning. **(E)** is redundant, repeating information from the previous sentence, and **(G)** introduces new and irrelevant ideas. **(H)** is related to the topic of the passage but is too focused on the continuation of the stereotype rather than on how Tesla breaks it.

Passage Analysis: The passage is about the mechanics and uses of a curveball pitch in baseball. Paragraph 1 gives a historical anecdote about the beginnings of the curveball. Paragraph 2 mentions the differing theories of the curveball and then explains the Magnus effect. Paragraph 3 illustrates the different kinds of "curves" and their effects on batters.

15. A

Category: Detail

Getting to the Answer: Since the curveball "astounded crowds across the eastern United States" (paragraph 1), it must have been a new phenomenon—something that was not seen before that time—and it must have been something that was easy for the crowds to see: its motion. **(A)** is correct. The importance of the curveball to baseball is described in **(B)**, but nothing in that sentence describes the motion of a baseball. **(C)** and **(D)** are portions of the explanation of how a ball curves, but neither describes the ball's motion nor identifies this motion as a change that occurred in the 1870s.

16. F

Category: Detail

Getting to the Answer: The clue "one early theory" in the question sends you to paragraph 2, which provides two early theories about the curveball: the rotation of Earth and the use of a foreign object. See which choice fits either of these details. **(F)** is the correct answer. **(E)** is a Misused Detail; the curveball's effect on baseball is hinted at in the last sentence of paragraph 1. However, this detail is never used as a theory to explain the curveball itself. **(G)** and **(H)** are Opposite choices that describe the *current* theory, a phenomenon called the Magnus effect, not the *early* theories.

17. D

Category: Infographic

Getting to the Answer: The table compares curveballs to other kinds of pitches. If you don't know what those other kinds of pitches (fastball, slider, changeup) are, or what the results (ball, strike, foul, hit) are, don't panic. You will always be able to answer the question based only on the information in the text. The passage's focus is how curveballs function and why they are a hard pitch to hit. Predict that the correct answer will discuss how hard a curveball is to hit as evidenced by the data in the table; the correct answer is **(D)**. **(A)** is Out of Scope because the table does not describe how pitchers decide pitch types, just what they decided in 2007. The word "impossible" in **(B)** is a clue that this is an Extreme choice; the table indicates that curveballs are hit 16% of the time, so they are not "impossible" to hit. **(C)** is incorrect because the curveball's results for Foul are 14% compared with the average of 16% and

the curveball's results for Hit are 16% compared with the average of 19%, so the results are not always greater than the average.

18. F

Category: Infographic

Getting to the Answer: Both paragraph 2 and the image describe the mechanics of how a curveball curves, and **(F)** correctly reflects that connection. Be careful not to confuse details about how this happens, as in Distortion choices like **(E)**; according to the paragraph, the Magnus effect changes the path, not the speed, of the curveball. The central idea of the paragraph is not to disprove other theories but to explain how the Magnus effect works on a curveball, so **(G)** is incorrect. **(H)** is incorrect both because it is a Distortion (screwballs are just curveballs thrown in the opposite direction) and screwballs are discussed in paragraph 3, not paragraph 2.

19. D

Category: Function

Getting to the Answer: The sentence in the question is the opening sentence of paragraph 2. Within the entire passage, this paragraph discusses the mechanism by which a curveball can be made to travel in an arc rather than a straight line. **(D)** is correct. The entire passage has a neutral tone, and the author does not present an opinion, so **(A)** is incorrect. The text also never discusses sports data or the opinions of athletes and scientists, so **(B)** is incorrect. **(C)** is a Misused Detail. Fans were impressed by the new type of pitch but not by the exact mechanics that the pitcher was using to make the ball curve.

20. F

Category: Inference

Getting to the Answer: Always look for a clear detail to support the answer to the question, and never get attached to the exact wording of the text. Here, paragraph 3 states how the batter is fooled by the curveball and how it still terrifies batters. The last sentence tells you why: batters fail to hit it. **(F)** is a good match and is correct. The detailed explanation of how "the batter has swung at a ball that was never really there" is found in the next-to-the-last sentence in paragraph 3. **(E)** is an irrelevant detail; since the Magnus effect is the current theory for the motion of curveballs, it is likely occurring today, but the passage does not directly connect the Magnus effect to batters' "nightmares." **(G)** is another irrelevant detail; the current status of "Candy" Cummings is never discussed in the passage and is never related to batters' "nightmares." **(H)** is a Misused Detail; the types of "curves" are listed earlier in the paragraph, but their existence alone does not explain why they trouble batters so much.

21. B

Category: Inference

Getting to the Answer: The pronoun "this" in the question means that the "manner" will be described in the previous sentence. Return to paragraph 3, which states that the term "regulation curve" is used for a pitch that curves in the opposite direction of the pitcher's throwing arm. **(B)** is correct. **(A)** and **(D)** are Distortions of information in the passage. The passage states that both kinds of curves are used to fool the batter, and a "regulation curve" cannot continue on one path as it approaches the batter. The passage describes all curveballs as changing direction. **(C)** is an Opposite choice from what is stated in the passage; a "regulation curve" does not follow the *same* direction as the pitcher's arm but follows the *opposite* direction.

Passage Analysis: This W. Somerset Maugham excerpt describes an unlikely friendship begun on a ship taking passengers to a Pacific island. Paragraphs 1 and 2 introduce the two main couples: the self-righteous, stern missionary Davidson and his wife, and the more open, informal Dr. Macphail and his wife. The Macphails discuss how and why they became friendly with the Davidsons on board the ship. Paragraphs 3 through 6 continue this discussion: Mrs. Macphail believes that the Davidsons felt uncomfortable with the "rough" people on board, so they chose to spend time with the respectable doctor and his wife. Dr. Macphail tries to make jokes about the situation. In paragraph 7, Mrs. Macphail chastises her husband for making fun of religion and seeing only the worst in people. Paragraph 8 describes the doctor's calm and somewhat bemused reaction. Paragraph 9 depicts the lush and inviting island Dr. Macphail sees from the deck the next morning. Paragraph 10 describes Mrs. Davidson, the missionary's wife, who has joined the doctor on deck. Paragraphs 11 through 17 chronicle the conversation

between Dr. Macphail and Mrs. Davidson as they approach the island.

22. G

Category: Global

Getting to the Answer: The "intimacy of shipboard" is explained in the phrase that follows. If you don't know the word "propinquity" (the state of being in close proximity), remember that the two couples are aboard a ship, a place in which people are confined together in a limited space. **(G)** is correct because the passage goes on to describe "their chief tie" as a dislike of the other people on board, not as a friendship or an association due to a shared interest. **(E)** and **(F)** are incorrect because the mildly critical discussion that follows, as well as the stern description of Mrs. Davidson, does not create a tone of calm serenity or unity. **(H)** is incorrect because, while Dr. Macphail does make jokes occasionally, the overall tone of the excerpt is not humorous.

23. A

Category: Global

Getting to the Answer: The second paragraph describes how the Davidsons and Macphails became acquainted. The Davidsons are missionaries who chose their acquaintances so carefully that only the Macphails were deemed suitable. This behavior of the Davidsons becomes the focus of the Macphails' later conversation; **(A)** is correct. **(B)** is incorrect because, while Mrs. Macphail is "flattered" by the Davidsons' attention, that is not described as her "motivation." **(C)** is incorrect because no controversy arises in the text. Dr. Macphail also considers the Davidsons' attention a "compliment" and teases his wife only because he's in an "argumentative" mood. **(D)** is incorrect because the passage does not mention any "concerns" the Davidsons have about the Macphails.

24. H

Category: Global

Getting to the Answer: The author paints a picture of two couples who have become friendly aboard a ship, primarily because they both disapprove of "the men who spent their days and nights in the smoking-room playing poker or bridge and drinking" (paragraph 2). It is this shared opinion, along with the opinions expressed later by the Macphails, that characterizes the excerpt's general purpose. The line mentioned follows the statement that "even the doctor . . . acknowledged the compliment" (paragraph 2). So the doctor disagrees with his wife because he wants to banter, not because he disagrees with his wife's assessment. Thus, **(H)** is correct. **(E)** is incorrect because Dr. Macphail is not disagreeable and combative; his comments are gentle teasing. **(F)** is incorrect because Dr. Macphail is not concerned about his wife's relationship with the Davidsons; he considers their exclusive company a compliment. **(G)** is incorrect because there's no discord in the Macphails' relationship presented in the passage. After teasing his wife, Dr. Macphail chuckles, and Mrs. Macphail recognizes the joke, even if she doesn't find it funny. Dr. Macphail then drops the discussion in the interest of keeping peace with his wife.

25. C

Category: Detail

Getting to the Answer: In paragraph 6, Dr. Macphail negatively contrasts the behavior of the Davidsons with that of the founder of their religion, indicating that the Davidsons are not behaving as the founder would. Since, as missionaries, the Davidsons would likely be teaching the founder's behavior as an example, they seem to be living in a way that is inconsistent with what they are teaching. **(C)** is correct. **(A)** is incorrect because it indicates that Dr. Macphail thinks the Davidsons may be arrogant but not hypocritical. **(B)** and **(D)** are incorrect because they are Mrs. Macphail's words and thus indicate her opinions, not Dr. Macphail's.

26. H

Category: Function

Getting to the Answer: Dr. Macphail calmly goes to bed, ending the conversation with his wife and the discussion about the Davidsons. The next paragraph begins the description of the ship's arrival at the island and the conversation between Dr. Macphail and Mrs. Davidson; **(H)** is correct. **(E)** is incorrect because, although the sentence does illustrate an aspect of the relationship between the Macphails, that relationship is not at the center of this excerpt; the Davidsons are the focus. **(F)** is incorrect because Dr. Macphail is planning to "read himself to sleep" after a party on board the ship. There is no indication that the journey has been difficult. **(G)** is incorrect because, although the sentence does end those discussions, it does not summarize them.

27. D

Category: Function

Getting to the Answer: The author uses pleasant descriptions—"silver beach," "luxuriant vegetation," and "gleaming white"—to describe the island. However, Mrs. Davidson is described with "brown, dull hair," a long face "like a sheep," and a voice "irritating to the nerves." **(D)** is correct. **(A)** is incorrect because, while paragraph 9 does describe the island as welcoming, paragraph 10 does not. **(B)** is incorrect because Mrs. Davidson is not attracted to the island. She goes on to say that she's grateful she is **not** assigned to that island. **(C)** is incorrect because the paragraphs do not describe a relationship between the characters nor do they describe a relationship on land.

28. G

Category: Detail

Getting to the Answer: There are two mentions in the excerpt of Dr. Macphail's feelings about the trip. The second mention is in paragraph 9, where Dr. Macphail looks at the land with "greedy eyes." If Dr. Macphail is "greedy," he wants the island very much, so he must be ready to get off the ship, at least for a little while. Thus, **(G)** is correct. In the first mention in paragraph 1, he is described as feeling "better for the journey." That is, the trip is helping him heal from his wound, so that would not be a reason he would want the trip to end; **(E)** is incorrect. **(F)** is incorrect because although Dr. Macphail is tired, he's tired from the party and the evening, not the journey. **(H)** is incorrect because Dr. Macphail is sighing because of Mrs. Davidson's reaction to his little joke, not because he's tired of the trip.

29. D

Category: Global

Getting to the Answer: Paragraph 16 appears in the middle of the stark description of Mrs. Davidson's opinion of the island begun in paragraph 15 and continuing in paragraph 17, so **(D)** is correct. **(A)** is incorrect because Mrs. Davidson expresses only negative feelings toward the island. **(B)** is incorrect because Mrs. Davidson is critical of the island and she does not mention anything hopeful. The geography of the islands is not central to the theme of the excerpt. **(C)** is incorrect because Dr. Macphail tries to make a humorous comment to Mrs. Davidson, but she doesn't understand the joke, and the humor of the situation ends there.

Passage Analysis: The purpose of this passage is to describe the remarkable sprinting speed of the cheetah and the vulnerabilities created as a result of this ability. The purpose of paragraph 1 is to introduce this topic. The purpose of paragraph 2 is to explore how the cheetah's flexible spine is both a strength and a weakness. The purpose of paragraph 3 is to describe other strengths and weaknesses of the cheetah as well as to state that no other land animal is as fast.

30. H

Category: Global

Getting to the Answer: When identifying the central idea of a passage, make sure to take into account the focus of the passage as a whole. In this case, all three paragraphs of the passage center on the fact that the cheetah's body gives it great speed but also makes it vulnerable; look for an answer choice that takes into account both the strengths and weaknesses of this animal. **(H)** is correct. **(E)** is a Misused Detail; although the passage mentions several physical characteristics that describe how the cheetah is able to reach such great speeds, this information is not the focus of the entire passage. **(F)** is a Distortion; the passage characterizes the cheetah as vulnerable to other predators in its habitat, not as the dominant species. **(G)** is too narrow, capturing only part of the focus of the passage.

31. D

Category: Detail

Getting to the Answer: In the sentence following this reference, the author states that the "cheetah is quite defenseless when stationary." It makes sense, then, that the vulnerabilities make it hard for the cheetah to defend itself; match this with the correct answer, **(D)**. **(A)** is the opposite of the information given; the passage states that the cheetah's speed causes, not makes up for, these weaknesses. **(B)** is not mentioned in the passage and is incorrect. There is no suggestion that the cheetah's hunts are often futile. In fact, the author notes its "impressive hunting skills" (paragraph 3). **(C)** is incorrect because this sentence doesn't refer to the time when cheetahs hunt; that comes later, in paragraph 3, which says that they do tend to hunt during the day.

32. G

Category: Global

Getting to the Answer: This question asks about the "development of ideas" in the entire passage, so refresh your memory of the purpose: to describe the speed of the cheetah and the vulnerabilities this speed causes. The sentence in the question describes one reason the cheetah is so fast, followed by a problem this adaptation may cause, so **(G)** is correct. **(E)** may be true; cheetahs may be able to easily catch slower prey, but this is not the idea of the sentence in the question. Also, this choice does not include any of the costs of the cheetah's speed that are mentioned in the question. **(E)** is incorrect. **(F)** is incorrect because the text never compares the rest the cheetah needs with that of other animals. **(H)** is incorrect because the text never discusses the cheetah's caloric needs nor relates those needs to the cheetah's use of energy.

33. D

Category: Inference

Getting to the Answer: The author mentions earlier in the paragraph that the cheetah combines "great strengths and significant weaknesses"; look for an answer choice that focuses on this interesting combination. **(D)** is correct. **(A)** is a Misused Detail; the fact that the cheetah is fast and also flees is not juxtaposed in the text but is shown to be a logical combination. **(B)** is a Misused Detail; the passage never indicates that the cheetah being classified as a nonaggressive predator is particularly fascinating. **(C)** is also a Misused Detail; although this ability is mentioned and even described as "remarkable" by the author, it does not connect with the context of the aforementioned line referring to both strengths and weaknesses.

34. H

Category: Inference

Getting to the Answer: You will be able to "prove" the correct answer from the passage, even for an Inference question, so match each choice strictly to the information in the text. The last paragraph states that "no other land animal on Earth can come close to matching the speed" of the cheetah, and paragraph 2 says that the cheetah's adaptations for speed "make it difficult for the cheetah to defend itself." If the cheetah is the fastest animal on Earth yet struggles to defend itself, **(H)** must be correct. **(E)** is never mentioned in the passage and is incorrect. There is no discussion of the cheetah's spots helping cheetahs to blend into the savanna. **(F)** is Extreme; the author doesn't say the cheetah has "too many" weaknesses. **(G)** is not discussed in the passage and is incorrect. There is no mention of how quickly (or slowly) the cheetah eats.

35. B

Category: Detail

Getting to the Answer: The clue in the question, "grassy plains of sub-Saharan Africa," is mentioned only at the start of paragraph 1, and the plains are simply described as the home of the cheetah. **(B)** is correct; cheetahs are said to be found hunting in these grassy plains. **(A)** is Extreme; the passage mentions grassy plains but never suggests that they are "completely" flat. **(C)** is a Distortion; the passage says that sub-Saharan Africa contains savannas but does not suggest that it is made up **only** of savannas. **(D)** is Extreme; although these animals are found in the grassy plain, the passage does not suggest that they are "most" of the population.

36. F

Category: Detail

Getting to the Answer: The question asks what causes the cheetah's stalking behavior. In paragraph 2, the author notes that cheetahs, while hunting, creep up on their prey to ensure that "once the cheetah opens chase, it will reach its target before its body tires." Look for an answer choice that best captures this information: **(F)** is correct. **(E)** and **(G)** accurately describe the cheetah, but these characteristics are not connected to its stalking behavior. Although the passage describes the cheetah's prey as nonaggressive, this fact is not connected to the behavior described in the question, so **(H)** is also incorrect.

37. D

Category: Detail

Getting to the Answer: The clue in the question, "selective hunters," means that cheetahs do not attack every type of animal but, instead, choose their prey. This idea is discussed in the last part of paragraph 3, so check the choice from that section first. **(D)** is correct. Because of its poor fighting skills, the cheetah chooses "docile" prey, which it can hunt without putting itself in a defensive situation. The incorrect choices, **(A)**, **(B)**, and **(C)**, do not address the cheetah's selection of prey.

Passage Analysis: This social studies passage concerns city parks and what has gone wrong with them. Paragraph 1 outlines the original purpose that city planners had in mind for their parks. Paragraph 2 describes some of the ways in which parks have been allowed to deteriorate. Paragraph 3 describes a few measures the author would recommend to turn around the situation.

38. F

Category: Inference

Getting to the Answer: Use the clue in the question, "natural beauty of city parks," to find the location of the information in the passage. Paragraph 2 describes the decline in the natural beauty of city parks and lists three reasons—intense air pollution, littering, and sewage pollution, so **(F)** is correct. **(E)** is a result, not a cause, of the loss of natural beauty. **(G)** is incorrect because crime is not mentioned as affecting natural beauty. Funding of parks is never discussed, making **(H)** Out of Scope.

39. B

Category: Detail

Getting to the Answer: The only place in the passage that mentions the nineteenth century is the beginning of paragraph 1. Return there and carefully read the first three sentences to find out what urban planners were doing at that time. These sentences state that parks In the United States were started in the late nineteenth century, and they were intended to provide citizens with "a convenient refuge" from "crowding and chaos" and "sun and fresh air in the midst of an often dark and dreary environment." **(B)** is correct. If urban planners—those responsible for designing public spaces—were creating spaces to "provide a refuge," they were mindful of the harmful effects of the urban environment on city dwellers. **(A)** is Opposite since paragraph 1 is all about how urban planners attended to these needs of the residents. **(C)** is a Distortion; according to the second paragraph, crime in the parks did not become a problem until recent decades. **(D)** is also a Distortion; paragraph 2 says that sewage pipes have become an issue only in recent decades.

40. H

Category: Inference

Getting to the Answer: The main idea of the passage is that parks should be restored, so the author obviously thinks parks are important for city residents and would agree with **(H)**. **(E)** is Opposite; at the start of paragraph 2, the author says urban planners have long recognized the importance of parks. **(F)** contradicts the author's own policing recommendations in paragraph 3. **(G)** goes against the author's optimistic conclusion at the end of paragraph 3.

41. B

Category: Inference

Getting to the Answer: The author's recommendations are in paragraph 3. Research the section of the passage that discusses policing parks. In paragraph 3, the author suggests that cities should establish "special police units, whose only responsibility would be to patrol city parks . . . to ensure that the urban parks remain safe for those who wish to enjoy them." **(B)** is correct. **(A)** is incorrect because it may or may not be true. The text does not discuss the number of police officers. **(C)** is incorrect because although the author does suggest that vehicles should be banned, this recommendation has no connection to policing the parks. **(D)** is not mentioned in the passage.

42. G

Category: Function

Getting to the Answer: Paragraph 3 contains the author's recommendations for improving parks, so locate the phrase and reread that section carefully. The sentence following the phrase explains that more attention to the parks will draw more visitors to the parks, more visitors will lead to less crime, and more citizens will be willing to support funding further improvements to the parks. This describes **(G)**, the correct answer. For the incorrect choices, **(E)** and **(F)** may be true in real life but are not mentioned in the passage, so they are Out of Scope choices. **(H)** is Opposite; the author's argument is that park improvements **are** necessary.

43. C

Category: Function

Getting to the Answer: A quick scan of paragraph 3 shows that it details ways in which deteriorating parks can be brought back to beauty and safety; thus, the correct answer is **(C)**. **(A)** reflects paragraph 2, and **(B)** is discussed in paragraph 1. Although urban planners are mentioned in paragraph 3, the author doesn't say that urban planning has failed, so **(D)** is incorrect.

Passage Analysis: The purpose of this passage is to tell the story of the *Hindenburg* and the way that the airship became obsolete as a mode of transportation. Paragraph 1 describes the modern use of airships, contrasting their former uses and introduces the *Hindenburg*. Paragraph 2 details the advantages of airships in general and the *Hindenburg* in particular. Paragraph 3 focuses on the airship's flaws. Paragraph 4 describes the airship's most fatal flaw and its role in the *Hindenburg's* demise. Paragraph 5 tells how advances in airplanes have made airships like the *Hindenburg* obsolete.

44. F

Category: Global

Getting to the Answer: A Global question will ask for the main idea of the passage—the one idea that is mentioned throughout the piece. Your Roadmap should have as a main idea something about the *Hindenburg*—the *Hindenburg's* story and how it relates to the death of the airship as a mode of transportation. Look at the answer choices and see which of them fits this best. **(F)** is correct. **(E)** is a Misused Detail; paragraph 3 discusses the flaws of airships, but this is not a central idea of the passage. **(G)** gives a detail discussed only in paragraph 5, not the whole passage. **(H)** is Opposite; airships are not used for transportation anymore.

45. B

Category: Global

Getting to the Answer: Since the question asks about "a central idea," keep the main focus of the passage in mind—the *Hindenburg*, why it was distinctive, how it was destroyed, and the effects of its destruction. The sentence quoted in the question marks a transition from the current uses of airships to their historical uses, making **(B)** the correct answer. Though the *Hindenburg* was a German blimp, it cannot be inferred that lighter-than-air crafts were developed there; eliminate **(A)**. Similarly, hydrogen in the *Hindenburg* was enormously dangerous, but **(C)** is incorrect because the sentence the question is asking about does not show blimps to be dangerous. **(D)** is Opposite of the information in the passage. Blimps are no longer used for passenger transportation.

46. E

Category: Function

Getting to the Answer: Predict an answer to this question by identifying the modern use of airships (advertising novelties) with the previous role mentioned in the passage (passenger transportation). **(E)** is correct. **(F)** is a Distortion. The modern use of airships does not include the transportation of large numbers of passengers. **(G)** is also a Distortion. The limitations of the *Hindenburg* do not describe any modern use of airships. **(H)** is too narrow; the price comparison between airline and airship tickets serves to illustrate why airships became obsolete, but it says nothing about their modern use.

47. C

Category: Global

Getting to the Answer: For questions like this, use the clues in the rest of the paragraph to place the phrase in context. Paragraph 2 contains two details that describe the *Hindenburg* as unique or special: its use of new materials and the number of passengers it could carry. Look for an answer choice that includes at least one of these facts; **(C)** is correct. **(A)** is incorrect because the *Hindenburg* did not have great speed. **(B)** is incorrect because the unique materials used in the *Hindenburg* are not described as providing the airship with any advantages. **(D)** is incorrect because the passage indicates that airships in general have solid frames, which would, therefore, not be considered a unique feature of the *Hindenburg*.

48. E

Category: Function

Getting to the Answer: Reread paragraph 4, which relates the events of the loss of the *Hindenburg*. Hydrogen is described as "highly flammable" and capable of causing a "horrific explosion," which, the author states, is "exactly what happened" to the *Hindenburg*. **(E)** is correct. **(F)** is incorrect because none of the details about hydrogen relate to airship tickets. **(G)** is a

Distortion; airships did become obsolete, and the problems with hydrogen may have been part of the reason, but that is not why the author mentioned those problems. Similarly, **(H)** is a Distortion. The exact cause of the *Hindenburg* disaster is still unknown, but again, the author did not use the details about hydrogen to make that point.

49. C

Category: Detail

Getting to the Answer: Always be aware of the details in the passage and be on the lookout for different wordings of the same concept. In this case, paragraph 4 states that the most dangerous flaw of airships was the flammable hydrogen and gives the *Hindenburg* explosion as evidence. See which of the answer choices fits this. **(C)** is correct. **(A)** is incorrect because the problems with hydrogen are not mentioned in that excerpt. **(B)** simply states that the flaws of the *Hindenburg* were shared with other airships but doesn't identify the flaws; furthermore, this quote doesn't establish that these drawbacks were dangerous. **(D)** is incorrect because it is a historical fact, not a reason the *Hindenburg* was flawed.

50. G

Category: Detail

Getting to the Answer: The question asks why airships are used only for advertisements, or why they are **not** used for other things. Paragraph 5 states that advances in airplanes have made airships ineffective for transportation, leading to **(G)**, the correct answer. **(E)** is a Distortion; their huge capacity allowed airships to carry many passengers, not advertisements. **(F)** is incorrect because, while airships are susceptible to wind currents, this is not a reason why they are used in advertisements. **(H)** is incorrect because nothing in the passage indicates that airplanes are too expensive for advertisements.

Poem Analysis: This short poem has four stanzas of four lines each. All stanzas describe the trip of a train, which was a relatively new technology in 1891. The first stanza starts the trip out in valleys, the next moves to mountains, the third to hills, and the fourth to home—"its own stable door."

51. C

Category: Function

Getting to the Answer: The line "I like to see it lap the Miles" describes something that is moving so quickly that it seems to be drinking up the miles; **(C)** is correct. **(A)** and **(D)** are incorrect because the preferences of the speaker are not a main point of the stanza. **(B)** is incorrect because there is no indication that the stanza is describing a horse.

52. G

Category: Global

Getting to the Answer: The poem's extended metaphor, likening a train to a horse, is meant to evoke the power and endurance of a train, a relatively new technology in 1891, making **(G)** the correct answer. **(E)** is incorrect because, as noted, the horse is a metaphor; Dickinson is not writing about an actual horse. Though the author mentions some sights along the way, **(F)** is not the primary theme of the poem. There is no suggestion that the author herself is making this trip, so **(H)** is incorrect.

53. D

Category: Function

Getting to the Answer: In lines 6–7, the speaker grants the train a human-like trait in stating that it peers into shanties in a snobby manner. This offers a continuation of the personification seen in the first stanza, where the speaker describes the train as being so large that it steps over mountain ranges; **(D)** is correct. The word "supercilious" suggests that the shanties are to be disdained, not the train, eliminating **(A)**. The speaker uses the metaphor (not a simile) of a horse to describe the train throughout the poem; **(B)** is incorrect. **(C)** is incorrect because this is not the first time the speaker personifies the train.

54. E

Category: Detail

Getting to the Answer: "Prodigious" refers to something that is very large, and lines 4–5 illustrate that this subject is large enough to step around a mountain range, making **(E)** correct. "To fit its sides, and crawl between" indicates that the train is very small and flexible in relation to the mountains, so **(F)** is incorrect. **(G)** is incorrect since the subject does not necessarily need to be large to chase itself down a hill. Docile means

submissive, and omnipotent means all powerful—neither of which require something to be large, making **(H)** incorrect.

55. A

Category: Function

Getting to the Answer: The third stanza focuses on the sounds of the train, which are heard in a "horrid, hooting stanza." This line reflects the rhythmic qualities of the subject, the train; **(A)** is correct. **(B)** and **(C)** are incorrect because the train itself is not unhappy and does not voice any opinions. While trains can typically be heard from blocks away, there is no indication in this stanza that the train can be heard from miles away, making **(D)** incorrect.

56. H

Category: Function

Getting to the Answer: Although they move about the night sky depending on Earth's rotation, stars are always there, steady and predictable in their return, just as the train will always come to rest at its home, the station at which it is based; **(H)** is correct. **(E)** is incorrect because the poem does not indicate that the train appears at night, only that it is predictable like a star. Stars are not always in the same place, so eliminate **(F)**. Although stars are twinkling and bright, a train, at least as Dickinson describes it, is not, making **(G)** incorrect.

57. B

Category: Detail

Getting to the Answer: The power of the subject is noted in line 8: it can carve a quarry out of rock. **(B)** is correct. **(A)** and **(C)** are incorrect because "Around a pile of mountains" and "To fit its sides, and crawl between" point to only the subject's route, not its power. Line 13 refers to the sound of the object rather than its power, eliminating **(D)**.

Part 2—Mathematics

58. −62

Subject: Arithmetic

Getting to the Answer: Follow the order of operations: PEMDAS. Remember that absolute value bars act like parentheses, so evaluate that part first.

$$4 - 6 \div \boxed{|-2|} + (-3)^3 \times 2\tfrac{1}{3}$$

$$= 4 - 6 \div 2 + \boxed{(-3)^3} \times 2\tfrac{1}{3}$$

$$= 4 - \boxed{6 \div 2} + (-27) \times 2\tfrac{1}{3}$$

$$= 4 - 3 + \boxed{(-27) \times 2\tfrac{1}{3}}$$

$$= 4 - 3 + \boxed{\left(-27 \times \tfrac{7}{3}\right)}$$

$$= 4 - 3 + (-63)$$

$$= -62$$

59. 12

Subject: Algebra

Getting to the Answer: To solve the equation for x, first subtract 8 from both sides of the equation. Then, divide both sides by 3.

$$3x + 8 = 44$$
$$3x = 36$$
$$x = 12$$

60. 7

Subject: Algebra

Getting to the Answer: Use the simple interest formula $I = Prt$, where I is the interest earned, P is the principal (starting amount), r is the interest rate written as a decimal, and t is the time in years. Here, you are looking for the number of years, so you must solve for t.

$$I = \$420;\ P = \$3,000;\ r = 2\% = 0.02$$

$$I = Prt$$
$$420 = 3,000 \times 0.02 \times t$$
$$420 = 60t$$
$$7 = t$$

It will take 7 years for this account to earn $420 in interest.

61. 17.5

Subject: Geometry

Getting to the Answer: The dimensions of the scale drawing are given in inches, so start by simplifying the scale to determine how many yards 1 inch represents. If 4 inches represent 5 yards, then 1 inch represents $5 \div 4 = 1.25$ yards. The length of the patio in the drawing is 14 inches, so the actual length is $14 \times 1.25 = 17.5$ yards.

62. 21

Subject: Arithmetic

Getting to the Answer: To determine the total number of questions on the test, first figure out how many multiple-choice questions there are. The question states that the ratio of multiple-choice questions to essay questions is 5:2 and that there are 6 essay questions. Because 6 is 3×2, there must be $3 \times 5 = 15$ multiple-choice questions. Thus, the total number of questions on the test is $6 + 15 = 21$.

63. C

Subject: Geometry

Getting to the Answer: The diagonal divides the quadrilateral into two right triangles. To find the area of the quadrilateral, find the area of the two triangles and then add them together. One of the right triangles has legs of lengths 20 cm and 15 cm, so its area is $\frac{1}{2}(20)(15) = 150$ sq cm. The other right triangle has legs of lengths 7 cm and 24 cm, so its area is $\frac{1}{2}(7)(24) = 84$ sq cm. The total area of the quadrilateral is thus $150 + 84 = 234$ sq cm.

64. G

Subject: Arithmetic

Getting to the Answer: Pay close attention to what is being asked. You are looking for the *difference* between the number of trout and bass. First, figure out how many trout there are:

$1,600 \times 0.25 = 400$ trout

The remaining fish are bass, so there are:

$1,600 - 400 = 1,200$ bass

Subtract to determine how many fewer trout there are than bass:

$1,200 - 400 = 800$

65. C

Subject: Arithmetic

Getting to the Answer: Begin by listing the factors of 119: 1, 7, 17, and 119. The smallest factor (other than 1) is 7. Of the options listed (28, 35, 40, and 63), only 40 does not have a factor of 7.

66. F

Subject: Arithmetic

Getting to the Answer: Pay careful attention to the units. You are asked for the rate in meters per minute, so convert kilometers to meters and hours to minutes.

$$3 \text{ km} = 3 \times 1,000 = 3,000 \text{ m}$$
$$\frac{2}{3} \text{ hr} = \frac{2}{3} \times 60 = 40 \text{ minutes}$$

Thus, Lucia speed walks 3,000 meters in 40 minutes, or $3,000 \div 40 = 75$ meters per minute.

67. B

Subject: Algebra

Getting to the Answer: Since this is a proportion, you could cross multiply and solve for x. However, you can save time by considering the relationships between the numbers. Because $72 \div 6 = 12$, the value of x must be $7 \div 6$, which is $\frac{7}{6}$, or $1\frac{1}{6}$.

68. F

Subject: Algebra

Getting to the Answer: Multiply each term in the equation by 3 to clear the fraction. This will isolate the x.

$$-2(3) < \left(\frac{x}{3}\right)(3) < 1(3)$$
$$-6 < \quad x \quad < 3$$

Since x is between -6 and 3, choose the number line that is shaded between -6 and 3, **(F)**.

69. C

Subject: Arithmetic

Getting to the Answer: To place an improper fraction between two consecutive integers, rewrite the fraction as a mixed number.

$$\frac{43}{8} = 5\frac{3}{8}$$

The mixed number is bigger than 5 and smaller than 6, so **(C)** is the correct answer.

70. H

Subject: Algebra

Getting to the Answer: First, subtract the lengths of the 4 boards that are given from the total length of all of the boards:

$$271 - 13 - 9 - 6 - 3 = 240$$

Next, create an algebraic equation to solve for x.

$$10(x) + 5(2x) = 240$$
$$10x + 10x = 240$$
$$20x = 240$$
$$x = 12 \text{ meters}$$

71. C

Subject: Statistics and Probability

Getting to the Answer: For each column in the table, multiply the number of customers by the price paid. Add the results together and divide by the total number of customers to find the mean (average) of the 100 customers.

$$\frac{50(\$25) + 30(\$40) + 20(\$100)}{100}$$
$$= \frac{\$1,250 + \$1,200 + \$2,000}{100}$$
$$= \frac{\$4,450}{100} = \$44.50$$

72. G

Subject: Geometry

Getting to the Answer: Recall that the circumference of a circle is π times its diameter. If the circle is inscribed in a square with a side length of 6, it must have a diameter of 6. Therefore, the circle has a circumference of 6π.

73. D

Subject: Algebra

Getting to the Answer: You know the value of x, so plug it in to find the value of y.

$$x + y = 12$$
$$15 + y = 12$$
$$y = -3$$

Next, substitute the values of *x* and *y* in the equation and simplify. Be careful of the negative signs.

$$-\frac{x}{y} = -\frac{15}{-3}$$
$$= -(-5)$$
$$= 5$$

74. H

Subject: Arithmetic

Getting to the Answer: Read the question carefully before selecting your answer. The question asks for the *percentage* that salami represents, not its actual number of pounds. **(E)** is a trap.

Start by finding the number of pounds of salami that were sold at the deli counter. Subtract all the other amounts from the total pounds sold (25) to obtain $25 - 22 = 3$ pounds. Next, write 3 out of 25 pounds as a percent:

$$\frac{3}{25} = \frac{3 \times 4}{25 \times 4} = \frac{12}{100} = 12\%$$

75. D

Subject: Arithmetic

Getting to the Answer: Apply each conversion factor one step at a time, cancelling out units as you go.

$$2 \text{ bursts} \times \left(\frac{3 \text{ laughs}}{1 \text{ burst}}\right) \times \left(\frac{250 \text{ giggles}}{1 \text{ laugh}}\right)$$
$$= 1,500 \text{ giggles}$$

76. G

Subject: Arithmetic

Getting to the Answer: Divide the total number of tires by how many fit in each crate.

$$\frac{469}{9} = 52 \text{ remainder } 1$$

So, there will be 52 full crates and 1 additional crate holding 1 tire.

77. A

Subject: Arithmetic

Getting to the Answer: This question requires several steps, so proceed methodically. All calculations center around the basic formula $d = rt$.

First, find the rate at which the bus is traveling: $310 \div 5 = 62$ miles per hour.

Next, find how many miles remain in the trip: $1,070 - 310 = 760$.

Finally, divide the remaining miles by the rate: $760 \div 62 \approx 12.3$, which is about 12 hours, **(A)**.

78. G

Subject: Algebra

Getting to the Answer: Substitute the two given values into the equation. Then cross multiply to solve for *x*.

$$\frac{30}{100} = \frac{x}{300}$$
$$100x = 30(300)$$
$$100x = 9,000$$
$$x = 90$$

79. B

Subject: Statistics and Probability

Getting to the Answer: Because you are asked to take the average of a set of consecutive even numbers, you can simply take the average of the highest and lowest numbers: $\frac{2 + 14}{2} = \frac{16}{2} = 8$. If you didn't remember this property, you could also find the sum of all the even numbers in the set (which is 56) and divide by the number of even numbers in the set (which is 7). The result is still $56 \div 7 = 8$.

80. H

Subject: Arithmetic

Getting to the Answer: First, determine how much money Jennifer still needs: $310.04 - $200 = $110.04. Now Backsolve, starting with **(G)**. If Jennifer makes $6.48 per hour and works for 16 hours, she will make $103.68 ($6.48 \times 16 = $103.68). Because this isn't enough, move on to **(H)**: $6.48 \times 17 = $110.16. This is sufficient. Note that once you realize that **(G)** is too small, you know that the answer must be **(H)**, as this is the only larger answer choice.

81. B

Subject: Arithmetic

Getting to the Answer: If a question mentions a diagram or a number line, make a sketch so that you can visualize the situation. If point Z is at $\frac{1}{3}$ and point Y is at $\frac{11}{3}$, the distance between Z and Y is $\frac{10}{3}$. Since point X is halfway between them, X is half that distance, or $\frac{5}{3}$, from Z. Thus, X is at $\frac{1}{3} + \frac{5}{3} = \frac{6}{3}$, or 2. You are looking for point W, so keep going.

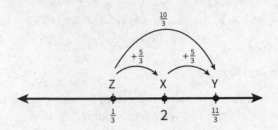

Since Z is halfway between W and X, W must be the same distance from Z that X is, but in the opposite direction. Subtract $\frac{5}{3}$ from $\frac{1}{3}$.

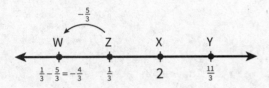

The answer is $-\frac{4}{3}$.

82. H

Subject: Arithmetic

Getting to the Answer: When comparing numbers, especially negative numbers, it is helpful to draw a number line. Here, mark a couple of numbers on each side of -3.75.

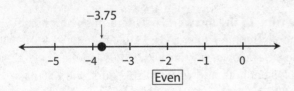

Numbers that are greater than -3.75 are to the right of -3.75 on the number line. The smallest of these numbers that is *even* is -2.

83. B

Subject: Arithmetic

Getting to the Answer: Since 48 and 32 are both multiples of 8, find the least common multiple of 48 and 32 only.

Multiples of 48: 48, **96**, 144, 192, …

Multiples of 32: 32, 64, **96**, …

Thus, the least common multiple of 8, 32, and 48 is 96.

84. G

Subject: Algebra

Getting to the Answer: The ages are given in three different time frames. Do not confuse them!

Let Henry's age now $= x$.

David's age now $= 2x + 4$.

Henry's age in 3 years $= x + 3 = 18$. Thus, Henry's age now $= 15$.

David's age now $= 2(15) + 4 = 34$.

David's age 2 years ago $= 34 - 2 = 32$.

85. B

Subject: Arithmetic

Getting to the Answer: If Joe answered 37 out of 50 questions correctly, then he got 13 out of 50 questions wrong. Write this as a fraction and set it equal to $\frac{x}{100}$ to determine what percentage of questions Joe got wrong.

$$\frac{13}{50} = \frac{x}{100} \rightarrow \frac{13 \times 2}{50 \times 2} = \frac{26}{100} = 26\%$$

86. F

Subject: Geometry

Getting to the Answer: The sum of the measures of supplementary angles is $180°$, so the measure of angle A plus the measure of angle B is $180°$. Since the measure of angle B is one-third the measure of angle A, you can write $B = \frac{1}{3}A$, or $A = 3B$. Set up an equation and solve for B.

$$A + B = 180°$$
$$3B + B = 180°$$
$$4B = 180°$$
$$B = 45°$$

87. B

Subject: Algebra

Getting to the Answer: Start by finding the total number of pages, P, in both workbooks together. Then figure out how many pages are in each workbook. Jin completed $8 + 12 = 20$ pages, which represents 25% of P. Set up an equation and solve for P.

$$20 = \frac{25}{100}P$$
$$2000 = 25P$$
$$80 = P$$

You're not done! The question asks for the number of pages in the science workbook, so subtract away the number of pages in the math workbook: $80 - 32 = 48$ pages. **(B)** is correct.

88. E

Subject: Arithmetic

Getting to the Answer: To find a percent change, find the amount of *change* and divide by the *original* amount.

$5,000,000 - 4,000,000 = 1,000,000$. This is the amount of change. Now divide by the original amount.

$$\frac{1,000,000}{5,000,000} = \frac{1}{5} = \frac{20}{100} = 20\%$$

89. B

Subject: Arithmetic

Getting to the Answer: When you encounter questions like this on Test Day, don't let the clutter get in your way. This question is simply asking what time of day it will be 38 hours after 2:15 p.m.

Determine how much time will pass between the moment the bacteria count is at 100 and the moment the count has doubled twice. The first doubling will happen after 19 hours, and the second doubling will happen 19 hours after that, or 38 hours after the start time. Break the 38 hours into manageable "time chunks" that are easy to calculate. 24 hours after 2:15 p.m. it will be 2:15 p.m. again. 12 hours after that it will be 2:15 a.m. Finally, the remaining 2 hours will take you to 4:15 a.m.

90. H

Subject: Algebra

Getting to the Answer: The typical way to set up questions that contain unknown consecutive numbers is to make the first number a variable, like x, and construct the relationship described. Remember that the difference between two consecutive odd numbers is always 2, no matter what those numbers are. For this question, you could write:

$$x + (x + 2) + (x + 4) + (x + 6) + (x + 8) + (x + 10) = 36$$

At this point, you could solve for x, which would give you 1. The largest number is $(x + 10)$, or $1 + 10 = 11$. The difference between 1 and 11 is 10, **(H)**.

You might also notice that the smallest number is x and the largest number is $(x + 10)$. The difference between x and $(x + 10)$ is 10. Here, the fact that the numbers add up to 36 is irrelevant, since you do not have to find the actual value of x to answer the question.

91. C

Subject: Arithmetic

Getting to the Answer: Read the question carefully—10:30 p.m. or earlier includes 10:30 p.m., 10 p.m., and earlier than 10 p.m. Refer to the circle graph to find the percentages: $26\% + 13\% + 14\% = 53\%$ of the children surveyed have bedtimes that are 10:30 p.m. or earlier. Finally, find 53% of 5,000.

$$\frac{53}{100} \times 5,000 = \frac{265,000}{100} = 2,650$$

92. G

Subject: Algebra

Getting to the Answer: Be careful when simplifying algebraic equations that involve parentheses. Here, you're subtracting a parenthetical expression, so distribute the negative through both terms in the parentheses.

$$(11 + 4x) - (2 - x)$$
$$= 11 + 4x - 2 + x$$
$$= 11 - 2 + 4x + x$$
$$= 9 + 5x$$

93. C

Subject: Statistics and Probability

Getting to the Answer: First, you need to figure out how many black chips there are to start:

40 total $-$ 10 red $-$ 10 blue $-$ 12 white $=$ 8 black chips

Next, figure out how many total chips there will be once Susan removes the 2 red and 3 black.

40 total $-$ 2 red $-$ 3 black $=$ 35 new total

Finally, figure out how many black chips there are before Susan chooses the final chip.

8 black $-$ 3 black removed $=$ 5 black

Plug this into the probability formula:

probability $= \dfrac{\text{desired}}{\text{total}}$, to obtain **(C)**: $\dfrac{5}{35} = \dfrac{1}{7}$.

94. H

Subject: Algebra

Getting to the Answer: Be careful with your work, especially when manipulating positive and negative terms. Sloppy calculations can cost you points on Test Day.

$$6(8 - x) = 3(x - 2)$$
$$48 - 6x = 3x - 6$$
$$48 = 9x - 6$$
$$54 = 9x$$
$$6 = x$$

95. C

Subject: Algebra

Getting to the Answer: If Bob and Ted each receive one-quarter of the reward, then together they received half of the reward. This means that Carol received the other half. Since Carol received $40, the total reward must have been double that, or $80.

96. H

Subject: Arithmetic

Getting to the Answer: When adding or subtracting fractions, you must have a common denominator.

$$\left(\frac{3}{4} - \frac{2}{7}\right) \div \frac{1}{4}$$
$$= \left(\frac{3 \times 7}{4 \times 7} - \frac{2 \times 4}{7 \times 4}\right) \div \frac{1}{4}$$
$$= \left(\frac{21}{28} - \frac{8}{28}\right) \div \frac{1}{4}$$
$$= \frac{13}{28} \div \frac{1}{4}$$

To divide by a fraction, multiply by its reciprocal.

$$\frac{13}{28} \times \frac{4}{1} = \frac{52}{28} = \frac{13}{7}$$

97. C

Subject: Statistics and Probability

Getting to the Answer: Although this is not an algebra problem, defining variables helps keep all the information organized.

Let j = number of students who only jog.

Let w = number of students who only lift weights.

Calculate j and w using the given information. There are 40 students who jog, and of those 40 students, 12 both

jog and lift weights. Thus, $j = 40 - 12 = 28$. There are 36 students who lift weights, and of those 36 students, 12 both jog and lift weights. Thus $w = 36 - 12 = 24$.

To find the total number of students surveyed, add the number of students who only jog (j), the number of students who only lift weights (w), the number of students who do both (12), and the number of students who do neither (16): $28 + 24 + 12 + 16 = 80$.

98. F

Subject: Algebra

Getting to the Answer: When you encounter a word problem that involves multiple steps, begin by translating the language into algebraic equations. Since Larissa spends 3 times as many hours reading as Tom does, then you know that $L = 3T$. If Nela spends half as many hours as Tom does, then $N = \frac{1}{2}T$. You also know that $L + N + T = 18$.

Plug in the expressions for L and N and solve for T.

$$L + N + T = 18$$
$$3T + \frac{1}{2}T + T = 18$$
$$\frac{6}{2}T + \frac{1}{2}T + \frac{2}{2}T = 18$$
$$\frac{9}{2}T = 18$$
$$9T = 36$$
$$T = 4$$

The question asks how many hours Tom read, so **(F)** is correct.

Note that if you can't determine an adequate starting point, a problem like this one could also be Backsolved.

99. C

Subject: Algebra

Getting to the Answer: There is no need to convert dozens into total number of balls because all the information and answer choices are given in dozens.

Let b be the number of dozens of golf balls for 150 people. Set up a proportion and solve:

$$\frac{b}{150} = \frac{14}{100}$$
$$100b = 14(150)$$
$$100b = 2,100$$
$$b = 21$$

100. H

Subject: Geometry

Getting to the Answer: The perimeter of a square is 4 times its side length. The area of a square is its side length multiplied by itself.

First, use the information given about the perimeter of square A to find its side length. If the perimeter is 100 inches, then its side length is $100 \div 4 = 25$ inches. Now, use that information to find the side length of square B. The side length of square A is shorter than the side length of square B by 5 inches, so the side length of square B is 30 inches. Thus, the area of square B is $(30 \times 30) = 900$ sq in. Similarly, the area of square A is $(25 \times 25) = 625$ sq in. Finally, take the difference between these areas to obtain $900 - 625 = 275$ sq in.

101. D

Subject: Arithmetic

Getting to the Answer: First, simplify the fraction:

$$\frac{4.9N}{1.4} = \frac{49N}{14} = \frac{7N}{2}$$

Look carefully at this fraction. Since there is a 2 in the denominator, N must be an integer that is divisible by 2 in order for the entire fraction to be equal to an integer. The only integer divisible by 2 in the given set of numbers is 2.0, so **(D)** must be the answer.

102. F

Subject: Arithmetic

Getting to the Answer: Write the desired ratio in words first. Then fill in the numbers. Convert the mixed number into an improper fraction to make it easier to simplify.

$$\text{blue paint: yellow paint}$$
$$\frac{1}{3} : 1\frac{2}{3} \quad \text{or} \quad \frac{1}{3} : \frac{5}{3}$$

Notice that the first number in each of the answer choices is 1. Because 1 is $3 \times \frac{1}{3}$, there must be $3 \times \frac{5}{3} = 5$ ounces of yellow paint. Thus, the ratio of blue paint to yellow paint is 1:5.

103. B

Subject: Algebra

Getting to the Answer: Plug in 2 for x and simplify carefully.

$$2x(2y - x) = 16$$
$$(2 \times 2)(2y - 2) = 16$$
$$4(2y - 2) = 16$$
$$8y - 8 = 16$$
$$8y = 24$$
$$y = 3$$

104. E

Subject: Statistics and Probability

Getting to the Answer: Use the given probability to set up a proportion. Let T be the total number of yogurt bars in the box. Solve for T:

$$\frac{2}{5} = \frac{\text{strawberry}}{\text{total}}$$
$$\frac{2}{5} = \frac{8}{T}$$
$$2T = 40$$
$$T = 20$$

You now know that there are 20 total bars in the box. If there are 8 strawberry bars, then the number of bars that are not strawberry is $20 - 8 = 12$. **(E)** is correct.

105. A

Subject: Statistics and Probability

Getting to the Answer: Margo bowled a mean of 110 points per game in each of the first 4 games, so she earned a total of $110 \times 4 = 440$ points for the first 4 games. Use this information to calculate the mean over the first 5 games:

$$\frac{440 + 160}{5} = \frac{600}{5} = 120$$

106. G

Subject: Algebra

Getting to the Answer: If Nick wrote $\frac{2}{7}$ of the paper, then Alex must have written the other $\frac{5}{7}$ of the paper. This means $\frac{5}{7}$ of the paper is equal to 20 pages.

$$\frac{5}{7}P = 20$$

To solve for P, multiply both sides of the equation by the reciprocal of $\frac{5}{7}$, which is $\frac{7}{5}$.

$$P = \frac{7}{5} \times 20$$
$$P = 28$$

The paper is 28 pages long.

107. D
Subject: Geometry

Getting to the Answer: The quarter circle is part of a complete circle whose radius is the same as the length of a side of the square. If the square has an area of 100 square meters, each side must have a length of 10 meters. Since the area of the full circle is $A = \pi r^2 = \pi(10)^2 = 100\pi$ square meters, the area of the quarter circle must be $\frac{100\pi}{4} = 25\pi$ square meters. The shaded region is not an entire quarter circle, but a quarter circle with a right triangle cut out of it. The right triangle has legs that are each 10 meters long, so its area must be $\frac{1}{2}(10)(10) = 50$ square meters. The area of the shaded region is the difference between these two areas, or $(25\pi - 50)$ square meters.

108. E
Subject: Statistics and Probability

Getting to the Answer: To find the probability that Josef likes *both* the cabin and the cafeteria he is assigned, find the probability of each and multiply the results. The probability that he will be assigned one of the 8 out of 25 cabins that he likes is $\frac{8}{25}$, and the probability that he will be assigned one of the 2 out of 4 cafeterias that he likes is $\frac{2}{4}$. The product is $\frac{8}{25} \times \frac{2}{4} = \frac{16}{100}$, or 16%.

109. D
Subject: Arithmetic

Getting to the Answer: Do not try to count every number. Instead, jot down the first several numbers and look for patterns.

$$1, 2, 3, 4, 5, 6, \ldots, 98, 99$$

First, determine how many numbers are divisible by 3. Every third number is divisible by 3, so there are $99 \div 3 = 33$.

Now, determine how many are divisible by 6. Every sixth number is divisible by 6, so there are $99 \div 6 = 16.5$. Only

whole numbers matter here, so you can ignore the decimal and use 16. Now take the difference: $33 - 16 = 17$.

110. G
Subject: Statistics and Probability

Getting to the Answer: Use the given probability to figure out how many red marbles are in the bag.

$$\frac{1}{5} = \frac{\text{red}}{30} \rightarrow \text{red} = 6$$

If only blue marbles are removed from the bag, then the new number of marbles will not affect the 6 red marbles already in the bag. Set up a proportion to figure out how many red marbles total would give you a $\frac{1}{4}$ probability.

$$\frac{1}{4} = \frac{6}{\text{total}} \rightarrow \text{total} = 24$$

If the new total needs to be 24 marbles and the original total was 30, then $30 - 24 = 6$ blue marbles need to be removed.

111. A
Subject: Algebra

Getting to the Answer: When you are given a lot of general information about variables, start by writing down what you know. Divide the information into before and after Burt gives 4 of his action figures to Cho.

Before: Burt $= b$ and Cho $= c$

After: Burt $= b - 4$ and Cho $= c + 4$

After: Burt $=$ twice Cho, so $b - 4 = 2(c + 4)$

(A) is correct.

112. H
Subject: Geometry

Getting to the Answer: The sum of the measures of the angles around a full circle is 360°. Set up an equation and solve for x. Then use this result to answer the question.

$$360° = AGB + BGC + CGD + DGE + EGF + AGF$$
$$360° = 30° + (x° - 10°) + x° + (2x° + 25°) + 2x° + 3x°$$
$$360° = 30° - 10° + 25° + x° + x° + 2x° + 2x° + 3x°$$
$$360° = 45° + 9x°$$
$$315° = 9x°$$
$$35° = x°$$

Thus, $m\angle DGE = 2x° + 25° = 2(35°) + 25° = 95°$.

113. C

Subject: Algebra

Getting to the Answer: Since the two ratios have n in common, you can write two equations using the ratios and solve each equation for n. Start by writing the given ratios as fractions:

$$\frac{m}{n} = \frac{2}{5} \rightarrow m = \frac{2}{5}n$$

$$\frac{n}{p} = \frac{5}{3} \rightarrow p = \frac{3}{5}n$$

The question states that $m + n + p = 24$. Substitute in the two equations above and solve for n.

$$m + n + p = 24$$
$$\frac{2}{5}n + n + \frac{3}{5}n = 24$$
$$\frac{2}{5}n + \frac{5}{5}n + \frac{3}{5}n = 24$$
$$\frac{10}{5}n = 24$$
$$2n = 24$$
$$n = 12$$

114. G

Subject: Geometry

Getting to the Answer: From the information given, you know that AB is one side of the rectangle and also the diameter of the circle. You also know that PQ is the radius of the circle and equal to AD, which is another side of the rectangle.

Since the diameter is twice the radius, you can designate the short and long sides of the rectangle as x and $2x$, respectively.

Find the perimeter of the rectangle by adding up all the sides.

$$72 \text{ cm} = x + x + 2x + 2x$$
$$72 \text{ cm} = 6x$$
$$12 \text{ cm} = x$$

The radius of the circle is thus 12 cm.

Therefore, the circumference $= 2\pi r = 2\pi(12) = 24\pi$.

PRACTICE TEST 2

SHSAT Practice Test 2

ANSWER SHEET

Part 1—English Language Arts

1. Ⓐ Ⓑ Ⓒ Ⓓ	11. Ⓐ Ⓑ Ⓒ Ⓓ	21. Ⓐ Ⓑ Ⓒ Ⓓ	31. Ⓐ Ⓑ Ⓒ Ⓓ	41. Ⓐ Ⓑ Ⓒ Ⓓ	51. Ⓐ Ⓑ Ⓒ Ⓓ
2. Ⓔ Ⓕ Ⓖ Ⓗ	12. Ⓔ Ⓕ Ⓖ Ⓗ	22. Ⓔ Ⓕ Ⓖ Ⓗ	32. Ⓔ Ⓕ Ⓖ Ⓗ	42. Ⓔ Ⓕ Ⓖ Ⓗ	52. Ⓔ Ⓕ Ⓖ Ⓗ
3. Ⓐ Ⓑ Ⓒ Ⓓ	13. Ⓐ Ⓑ Ⓒ Ⓓ	23. Ⓐ Ⓑ Ⓒ Ⓓ	33. Ⓐ Ⓑ Ⓒ Ⓓ	43. Ⓐ Ⓑ Ⓒ Ⓓ	53. Ⓐ Ⓑ Ⓒ Ⓓ
4. Ⓔ Ⓕ Ⓖ Ⓗ	14. Ⓔ Ⓕ Ⓖ Ⓗ	24. Ⓔ Ⓕ Ⓖ Ⓗ	34. Ⓔ Ⓕ Ⓖ Ⓗ	44. Ⓔ Ⓕ Ⓖ Ⓗ	54. Ⓔ Ⓕ Ⓖ Ⓗ
5. Ⓐ Ⓑ Ⓒ Ⓓ	15. Ⓐ Ⓑ Ⓒ Ⓓ	25. Ⓐ Ⓑ Ⓒ Ⓓ	35. Ⓐ Ⓑ Ⓒ Ⓓ	45. Ⓐ Ⓑ Ⓒ Ⓓ	55. Ⓐ Ⓑ Ⓒ Ⓓ
6. Ⓔ Ⓕ Ⓖ Ⓗ	16. Ⓔ Ⓕ Ⓖ Ⓗ	26. Ⓔ Ⓕ Ⓖ Ⓗ	36. Ⓔ Ⓕ Ⓖ Ⓗ	46. Ⓔ Ⓕ Ⓖ Ⓗ	56. Ⓔ Ⓕ Ⓖ Ⓗ
7. Ⓐ Ⓑ Ⓒ Ⓓ	17. Ⓐ Ⓑ Ⓒ Ⓓ	27. Ⓐ Ⓑ Ⓒ Ⓓ	37. Ⓐ Ⓑ Ⓒ Ⓓ	47. Ⓐ Ⓑ Ⓒ Ⓓ	57. Ⓐ Ⓑ Ⓒ Ⓓ
8. Ⓔ Ⓕ Ⓖ Ⓗ	18. Ⓔ Ⓕ Ⓖ Ⓗ	28. Ⓔ Ⓕ Ⓖ Ⓗ	38. Ⓔ Ⓕ Ⓖ Ⓗ	48. Ⓔ Ⓕ Ⓖ Ⓗ	
9. Ⓐ Ⓑ Ⓒ Ⓓ	19. Ⓐ Ⓑ Ⓒ Ⓓ	29. Ⓐ Ⓑ Ⓒ Ⓓ	39. Ⓐ Ⓑ Ⓒ Ⓓ	49. Ⓐ Ⓑ Ⓒ Ⓓ	
10. Ⓔ Ⓕ Ⓖ Ⓗ	20. Ⓔ Ⓕ Ⓖ Ⓗ	30. Ⓔ Ⓕ Ⓖ Ⓗ	40. Ⓔ Ⓕ Ⓖ Ⓗ	50. Ⓔ Ⓕ Ⓖ Ⓗ	

Part 2—Mathematics

58.   59.   60.   61.   62.

63. Ⓐ Ⓑ Ⓒ Ⓓ	72. Ⓔ Ⓕ Ⓖ Ⓗ	81. Ⓐ Ⓑ Ⓒ Ⓓ	90. Ⓔ Ⓕ Ⓖ Ⓗ	99. Ⓐ Ⓑ Ⓒ Ⓓ	108. Ⓔ Ⓕ Ⓖ Ⓗ
64. Ⓔ Ⓕ Ⓖ Ⓗ	73. Ⓐ Ⓑ Ⓒ Ⓓ	82. Ⓔ Ⓕ Ⓖ Ⓗ	91. Ⓐ Ⓑ Ⓒ Ⓓ	100. Ⓔ Ⓕ Ⓖ Ⓗ	109. Ⓐ Ⓑ Ⓒ Ⓓ
65. Ⓐ Ⓑ Ⓒ Ⓓ	74. Ⓔ Ⓕ Ⓖ Ⓗ	83. Ⓐ Ⓑ Ⓒ Ⓓ	92. Ⓔ Ⓕ Ⓖ Ⓗ	101. Ⓐ Ⓑ Ⓒ Ⓓ	110. Ⓔ Ⓕ Ⓖ Ⓗ
66. Ⓔ Ⓕ Ⓖ Ⓗ	75. Ⓐ Ⓑ Ⓒ Ⓓ	84. Ⓔ Ⓕ Ⓖ Ⓗ	93. Ⓐ Ⓑ Ⓒ Ⓓ	102. Ⓔ Ⓕ Ⓖ Ⓗ	111. Ⓐ Ⓑ Ⓒ Ⓓ
67. Ⓐ Ⓑ Ⓒ Ⓓ	76. Ⓔ Ⓕ Ⓖ Ⓗ	85. Ⓐ Ⓑ Ⓒ Ⓓ	94. Ⓔ Ⓕ Ⓖ Ⓗ	103. Ⓐ Ⓑ Ⓒ Ⓓ	112. Ⓔ Ⓕ Ⓖ Ⓗ
68. Ⓔ Ⓕ Ⓖ Ⓗ	77. Ⓐ Ⓑ Ⓒ Ⓓ	86. Ⓔ Ⓕ Ⓖ Ⓗ	95. Ⓐ Ⓑ Ⓒ Ⓓ	104. Ⓔ Ⓕ Ⓖ Ⓗ	113. Ⓐ Ⓑ Ⓒ Ⓓ
69. Ⓐ Ⓑ Ⓒ Ⓓ	78. Ⓔ Ⓕ Ⓖ Ⓗ	87. Ⓐ Ⓑ Ⓒ Ⓓ	96. Ⓔ Ⓕ Ⓖ Ⓗ	105. Ⓐ Ⓑ Ⓒ Ⓓ	114. Ⓔ Ⓕ Ⓖ Ⓗ
70. Ⓔ Ⓕ Ⓖ Ⓗ	79. Ⓐ Ⓑ Ⓒ Ⓓ	88. Ⓔ Ⓕ Ⓖ Ⓗ	97. Ⓐ Ⓑ Ⓒ Ⓓ	106. Ⓔ Ⓕ Ⓖ Ⓗ	
71. Ⓐ Ⓑ Ⓒ Ⓓ	80. Ⓔ Ⓕ Ⓖ Ⓗ	89. Ⓐ Ⓑ Ⓒ Ⓓ	98. Ⓔ Ⓕ Ⓖ Ⓗ	107. Ⓐ Ⓑ Ⓒ Ⓓ	

Practice Test 2

Directions: Mark your answers on the separate sheet provided. You will receive credit only for answers marked on the answer grid. **DO NOT MAKE ANY STRAY MARKS ON THE ANSWER GRID.** You can write in the test booklet, or use the paper provided for scratchwork.

Each question has only one correct answer. Select the **best** answer for each question. Your score is determined by the number of questions you answered correctly. **It is to your advantage to answer every question, even though you may not be certain which choice is correct.**

You have 180 minutes to complete the entire test. How you split the time between the English Language Arts and Mathematics sections is up to you. **If you begin with the English Language Arts section, you may go on to the Mathematics section as soon as you are ready. If you begin with the Mathematics section, you may go on to the English Language Arts section as soon as you are ready.** It is recommended that you do not spend more than 90 minutes on either section. If you complete the test before the allotted time (180 minutes) is over, you may go back to review questions in either section.

Work as rapidly as you can without making mistakes. Don't spend too much time on a difficult question. Return to it later if you have time. If time remains, you should check your answers.

Part 1—English Language Arts

57 QUESTIONS—SUGGESTED TIMING: 90 MINUTES

REVISING/EDITING

QUESTIONS 1–14 (Part A and Part B)

REVISING/EDITING Part A

DIRECTIONS: Answer the following questions, recognizing and correcting errors so that the sentences or paragraphs are grammatically correct. Reread relevant parts of the text before choosing the best answer for each question, but be mindful of time. You may write in your test booklet to take notes.

1. Read this paragraph.

> (1) A talented geographer, the professor, who teaches college students, is an expert at locating cities and countries on maps. (2) In his lectures, he explains cartography, or map-making, which involves surveying the Earth's surface to represent its physical structures. (3) Geographers use maps with different projections that can display the Earth's various features, including mountains, the magnetic poles, and oceans. (4) Studying the field of geography provides knowledge about its connections to biology, sociology, and history, among other subjects.

Which sentence should be revised to correct a wordiness issue?

A. sentence 1
B. sentence 2
C. sentence 3
D. sentence 4

GO ON TO THE NEXT PAGE

2. Read this paragraph.

> (1) After graduating from college, the next five years of a software engineer's life are spent working toward a graduate degree in computer science. (2) The coursework revolves around programming, which is the preparation of instructions that tell the computer which operations it needs to perform. (3) Students learn formulas as well as programs that translate complex computer languages. (4) With new advancements every day, the computer science field requires professionals to constantly learn about applying the latest technology.

Which sentence contains an error in its construction and should be revised?

E. sentence 1

F. sentence 2

G. sentence 3

H. sentence 4

3. Read this sentence.

> The federal government <u>provides</u> low-interest loans that <u>allow</u> students <u>of deferring</u> payment until they graduate and <u>begin to</u> work.

Which edit should be made to correct this sentence?

A. Change *provides* to **provide**.

B. Change *allow* to **allowed**.

C. Change *of deferring* to **to defer**.

D. Change *begin to* to **begin with**.

4. Read this sentence.

> The helicopter, <u>which offers</u> the advantages of flight without requiring <u>large amounts of space</u> for <u>takeoff and landing</u>, <u>allowing</u> relatively easy access to places as remote as islands, mountain villages, and snow-bound communities.

Which edit should be made to correct the sentence?

E. Change *which offers* to **offering**.

F. Change *large amounts of space* to **space in large amounts**.

G. Change *takeoff and landing* to **the takeoff as well as the landing**.

H. Change *allowing* to **allows**.

5. What is the best way to combine the sentences?

> (1) New York state has more than 70,000 miles of rivers and streams.
>
> (2) One of New York's rivers is the Hudson River.
>
> (3) The Hudson River is home to dozens of rare birds and more than a hundred rare plants.

A. The Hudson River, one of New York's rivers, is home to dozens of rare birds and more than a hundred rare plants, and New York state has more than 70,000 miles of rivers and streams.

B. New York state has more than 70,000 miles of rivers and streams, and one of them is the Hudson River, which is home to dozens of rare birds and more than a hundred rare plants.

C. The Hudson River, home to dozens of rare birds and more than a hundred rare plants, is one of New York State's rivers, and New York state has more than 70,000 miles of rivers and streams.

D. New York state has more than 70,000 miles of rivers and streams, including the Hudson River, which is home to dozens of rare birds and more than a hundred rare plants.

REVISING/EDITING Part B

DIRECTIONS: Read the passage and answer the questions following it, improving the writing quality and correcting grammatical errors. Reread relevant parts of the text before choosing the best answer for each question, but be mindful of time. You may write in your test booklet to take notes.

States of Consciousness

(1) Consciousness is a topic that has captivated psychologists since the beginning of experimental psychology in the late 1800s. (2) Wilhelm Wundt and William James, both notable founders of psychology, were fascinated with studying consciousness, both from the perspective of how it was organized and how it worked.

(3) Consciousness refers to the active processing of information in the brain. (4) It is your awareness of yourself and your environment, and the features of your consciousness at any given point in time are referred to as your state of consciousness. (5) While in a normal state of consciousness, you are awake and alert. (6) In an altered state of consciousness, however, you experience a disruption to your normal state—such as falling asleep or drifting off into a daydream. (7) You may not realize that you experience different states of consciousness throughout each day. (8) You are likely not actively aware of your breathing, heartbeat, and other biological functions, for instance. (9) These body processes, which are being controlled by your brain, are happening on a nonconscious level.

(10) According to psychoanalytic theory, all of the memories that you have stored and could actively start thinking about, if prompted, represent the preconscious level. (11) For example, what did you have for breakfast this morning?

(12) Psychologists have found that people are affected by information that they are not aware of consciously. (13) This information is acting on a subconscious level. (14) According to Austrian psychologist Sigmund Freud, people possess subconscious longings that are often socially unacceptable. (15) Two examples that illustrate subconscious processing are priming and the mere-exposure effect. (16) Priming refers to the processing of information from stimuli that are outside of conscious awareness. (17) In fact, studies show that people can correctly answer questions that they have seen previously—even when they do not remember seeing the questions. (18) The mere-exposure effect happens when people prefer stimuli they have seen previously over new stimuli—even when they do not remember the old stimuli.

(19) Psychologists design and conduct experiments that explore different states of consciousness to better understand how the brain processes information. (20) These experiments probe the inner workings of normal conscious, nonconscious, preconscious, and subconscious levels of being.

6. Which sentence should follow sentence 2 to introduce the main claim of the passage?

   E. Altered states of consciousness include falling asleep, daydreaming, and experiencing hallucinations.

   F. Today, researchers continue to explore what consciousness is, how we are able to understand it, and what it means to be in a "state of consciousness."

   G. Some psychology research investigates consciousness with the hope of discovering the key to curing, or at least better managing, neurological disorders such as epilepsy.

   H. Based on their studies of consciousness, these fathers of psychology founded the field's first two great "schools": voluntarism and functionalism.

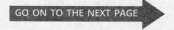

7. Which sentence could best follow sentence 11 to support the ideas in the third paragraph (sentences 10–11)?

   A. If someone asked you about what you ate, you would be able to transfer that memory from the preconscious level to the conscious level in just a few seconds.

   B. If you are not able to come up with an answer, it is likely because the memory is stored at the unconscious level.

   C. Many studies have linked eating breakfast to better memory and concentration, lower risks of heart disease, and a healthier body weight.

   D. If you were prompted to think about what you had for breakfast, you would think about exactly what you ate, such as cereal and milk or yogurt and fruit.

8. Which sentence presents ideas irrelevant to the topic of paragraph 4 and should be deleted?

   E. sentence 14

   F. sentence 15

   G. sentence 16

   H. sentence 17

9. Which concluding sentence should follow sentence 20 to best support the information presented in the passage?

   A. Scientists create and facilitate experiments that investigate different states of consciousness to better comprehend how people sift through and internalize information.

   B. Psychological experiments focus on the intricacies of multiple levels of consciousness, which range from active, normal consciousness to completely unconscious states.

   C. The goal of investigating consciousness is to learn more about the awareness of one's self and environment, the ways consciousness can be altered, and the various levels and states of consciousness.

   D. Hypnosis involves a change in the way a person senses, thinks, feels, perceives, or behaves while following the suggestions of a hypnotist; a state of altered consciousness appears to take over while normal conscious control is seemingly suspended.

GO ON TO THE NEXT PAGE

Weaving

(1) Handweaving, traditionally the province of home spinners and weavers, has been practiced throughout recorded history. (2) Silk weaving has been known in China since 3500 B.C.E and in Egypt since 3600 B.C.E. (3) By 700 C.E., looms were common in Africa, Asia, and Europe. (4) In particular, they were found throughout the Islamic world.

(5) In mythology, weaving is typically the province of women. (6) In Pre-Dynastic Egypt, Neith was the goddess of weaving; in Greece, it was the goddess Athena; in Scandinavia, it was the goddess Frigg, the wife of chief god Odin. (7) These goddesses and other protectors of weavers show the importance of the craft to ancient peoples: each was not only prominent in her pantheon but also associated with other crucial domains, such as childbirth, wisdom, the creation of the stars, and fate itself.

(8) Tales about weaving are numerous as well. (9) Theseus emerges from the maze of the Minotaur by following Ariadne's woven thread. (10) A crane weaves a gorgeous cloth of her own feathers as a gift for those who rescued her. (11) In the fable "The Old Man and Death," Aesop warns of being careful of what you wish for. (12) Sleeping Beauty pricks her finger on a spindle and is cursed. (13) Indeed, the English word *text* derives from the Latin word *textare*—weaving, as in "weaving a story."

(14) Weaving continues to be an important part of many modern cultures as well. (15) In Ukraine, the *rushnyk*, a ritual cloth, accompanies people throughout their lives; a newborn is placed immediately upon it and the dead are covered with it. (16) Without question, the importance of weaving goes far beyond the practical into cultural meanings that still resonate today. (17) Navajo weaving often features the symbol of Spider Woman, who gave the art of weaving to Navajo women. (18) Andean peoples, living in close connection with nature, incorporate symbols for the sun and rivers. (19) A pattern or motif may be specific to the weaver herself and can convey piety, cultural or family traditions, daily life, folklore characters, and even humor.

10. Which transition should be added to the beginning of sentence 2?

   E. However,

   F. Indeed,

   G. As a result,

   H. Even so,

11. Which is the best way to combine sentences 3 and 4 to clarify the relationship between ideas?

   A. By 700 C.E., looms were common in Africa, Asia, and Europe, and evidence has shown that they could also be found throughout the Islamic world.

   B. As long ago as the year 700 C.E., looms were common in Africa, Asia, Europe, as well as in parts of the Islamic world.

   C. By 700 C.E., looms were common in Africa, Asia, and Europe, though they were also found throughout the Islamic world.

   D. By 700 C.E., looms were common in Africa, Asia, and Europe, as well as throughout the Islamic world.

12. Which sentence should be added after sentence 4 to introduce the main topic of the passage?

    E. Given the widespread use and long history of weaving, it is unsurprising that the art is deeply intertwined with folklore and tradition.

    F. Cultures are reflections of people's beliefs and attitudes, and weaving has impacted the course of many societies.

    G. Weaving materials vary significantly between cultures and can include everything from tree bark to caterpillar cocoons, depending on local resources.

    H. Since the art of weaving is so widely practiced, many weavers find inspiration in the traditions of other cultures as well as in their own.

13. Which sentence presents information that shifts away from the main topic of the third paragraph (sentences 8–13) and should be removed?

    A. sentence 9

    B. sentence 10

    C. sentence 11

    D. sentence 12

14. Where should sentence 16 be moved to improve the organization of the fourth paragraph (sentences 14–19)?

    E. to the beginning of the paragraph (before sentence 14)

    F. between sentences 14 and 15

    G. between sentences 17 and 18

    H. to the end of the paragraph (after sentence 19)

Practice Tests

READING COMPREHENSION

QUESTIONS 15–57

DIRECTIONS: Read the six passages and answer the corresponding questions. Reread relevant parts of the text before choosing the best answer for each question, but be mindful of time. Base your answers only on the content within each passage. You may write in your test booklet to take notes.

Did an Asteroid Kill the Dinosaurs?

1 The question of why dinosaurs became extinct has puzzled paleontologists since the first dinosaur fossil was found almost two centuries ago. These great reptiles dominated the Earth for nearly 160 million years but mysteriously died out approximately 65 million years ago. Although various explanations for this disappearance have been offered, ranging from an epidemic to a sudden, catastrophic drop in temperature, no theory has yet been conclusively proven.

2 One of the most recent theories was posited in 1980 by Luis Alvarez, a Nobel Prize-winning physicist. According to Alvarez and his geologist son Walter, a huge meteor crashed into the Earth's surface 65 million years ago, sending up a massive cloud of dust and rock particles. The cloud blocked out sunlight for a period of months or even years, disrupting plant growth and the global food chain. The lack of plants as a food source, coupled with a significant drop in temperature, resulted in the extinction of the dinosaurs.

3 Alvarez based his theory on an unusual piece of evidence. Geologists discovered that a thin layer of the metal iridium had been deposited all over the world at approximately the time the dinosaurs died out. Since iridium is rarely found on the Earth's surface, Alvarez reasoned that it had either come up from the Earth's core by volcanic action or been deposited by meteorite strikes from space. Because the iridium was deposited evenly in sediments worldwide, Alvarez found the meteorite theory more likely.

4 But paleontologists—scientists who study dinosaurs—scoffed at the Alvarez extinction theory. Neither Luis nor Walter Alvarez was a paleontologist, yet they claimed to have solved a mystery that had defied the efforts of paleontologists for over a century. Some scientists pointed out that, in order to create worldwide fallout of iridium on the scale suggested by Alvarez, the "doomsday" meteorite would have had to be about 5 miles in diameter, and its impact would have formed a crater perhaps a hundred miles wide. If such a meteorite had hit the Earth, where was the crater? Because of the absence of evidence of such a catastrophic collision, these critics were skeptical of the Alvarez theory.

5 Finally, a decade after the cosmic extinction theory was first proposed, the crater was found. Lying partly underwater on the northern edge of Mexico's Yucatan Peninsula, the crater is 110 miles wide, with the center of impact close to the city of Chicxulub, which has given the crater its name. Long-buried under sediment, the Chicxulub crater had actually been discovered in 1981 by oil geologists, but dates of nearby rock samples taken at that time suggested that it was significantly older than 65 million years. New deepwater samples of melted rock from the crater itself were recently analyzed by an advanced dating process, however, and were found to be 64.98 million years old. Many scientists now feel that, thanks to the Alvarez theory, the mystery of dinosaur extinction has finally been solved.

GO ON TO THE NEXT PAGE

15. According to the passage, the Alvarez theory that the iridium layer was deposited by a meteorite rather than by volcanic action is supported by evidence that

    A. proves that the Yucatan crater was created by a meteor strike.

    B. describes the only way in which a large enough dust and rock cloud could be generated to disrupt the food chain.

    C. indicates that iridium is evenly distributed in sediments worldwide.

    D. shows that geologists agree that iridium is rare on the surface of the Earth.

16. Based on the passage, what is the main reason that opponents of the Alvarez theory criticized both Luis and Walter Alvarez?

    E. The Alvarezes published incomplete research.

    F. The Alvarezes were being personally abrasive.

    G. The Alvarezes were theorizing outside their own fields.

    H. The Alvarezes misinterpreted experimental data.

17. The author mentions the global food chain in paragraph 2 in order to

    A. refute the theory that an epidemic was responsible for dinosaur extinction.

    B. illustrate the importance of a clean atmosphere for life on Earth.

    C. support the contention that dinosaurs were primarily plant-eaters.

    D. explain how the cloud of dust caused the extinction of dinosaurs.

18. What is the most likely reason the discovery of a layer of iridium in geologic sediments was considered unusual?

    E. Iridium had never been detected there before.

    F. Iridium is normally quite scarce at the Earth's surface.

    G. Iridium only occurs in meteoric craters.

    H. Few volcanoes had been active during the era when those sediments accumulated.

19. Read this sentence from paragraph 2.

    > **The lack of plants as a food source, coupled with a significant drop in temperature, resulted in the extinction of the dinosaurs.**

    The phrase "coupled with" conveys the idea that the lack of plants

    A. resulted from the meteorite impact.

    B. combined with the weather to cause dinosaur extinction.

    C. led to the even worldwide distribution of iridium in snowfall.

    D. caused the dinosaurs to go extinct due to starvation.

GO ON TO THE NEXT PAGE ➡

20. Which sentence best supports the idea that paleontologists initially had reason to be critical of the Alvarez theory?

    E. "Although various explanations for this disappearance have been offered, ranging from an epidemic to a sudden, catastrophic drop in temperature, no theory has yet been conclusively proven." (paragraph 1)

    F. "Geologists discovered that a thin layer of the metal iridium had been deposited all over the world at approximately the time the dinosaurs died out." (paragraph 3)

    G. "[T]he 'doomsday' meteorite would have had to be about 5 miles in diameter, and its impact would have formed a crater perhaps a hundred miles wide." (paragraph 4)

    H. "New deepwater samples of melted rock from the crater itself were recently analyzed by an advanced dating process, however, and were found to be 64.98 million years old." (paragraph 5)

21. Paragraph 5 contributes to the development of the central idea of the passage by

    A. rejecting the majority opinion of paleontologists.

    B. revealing the impact crater was far older than 65 million years.

    C. showing how the Alvarez theory was accepted a decade later.

    D. highlighting the lack of iridium at the impact site.

New Research in Repairing Bone

1 Surgeons perform phenomenal feats such as replacing clogged coronary arteries with blood vessels from the leg, reconnecting capillaries and tendons to reattach severed fingers, and even refashioning parts of intestines to create new bladders. However, surgeons find it difficult to reconstruct complicated bones like the jawbone or those of the inner ear, and only rarely can they replace large bones lost to disease or injury.

2 This challenge stems from the nature of bones. Unlike other types of tissue, bones with one normal shape cannot be reworked into other shapes, nor can doctors move large bones from one part of the body to another without severely disabling a person. Many existing treatments for bone defects are short-term and limited. Surgeons can replace some diseased joints with plastic or metal implants, but artificial hips or knees steadily loosen and must be reconstructed several times during a patient's life.

3 Several new procedures have been developed that enable surgeons to treat a larger number of bone defects. Bone grafting involves replacing a damaged section of bone with bone removed from another part of the body such as the rib or hip, or from bone donated from a cadaver. The living cells within the bone graft grow and attach to those in the original bone, repairing the injury. Distraction osteogenesis is now also another option available to surgeons. In this process, a bone that needs to be lengthened is cut surgically, and the ends of the cut bone are held apart by a mechanical device. As the body's natural healing process begins to refill the gap in the bone, the gap is slowly widened, stretching the newly formed soft bone and lengthening it. Distraction osteogenesis is used to correct a number of problems in the jawbones and palate and may reduce the number of surgeries needed by patients with these issues.

4 The most radical approach to overcoming the obstacles presented by bones is to create bone substitutes from, of all things, muscle. Although this may sound peculiar, muscle, bone, fat, blood vessels, and bone marrow all develop in human embryos from the same loosely organized tissue, so the idea of making bones from muscle is not all that strange. In 1987, scientists isolated a bone-inducing protein called osteogenin from cows and discovered that osteogenin can make undifferentiated human tissue produce cartilage and bone. However, few surgeons have used osteogenin because it is hard to control. If sprinkled directly onto a defect, for instance, the entire area might stiffen to bone if even a tiny bit of osteogenin fell on the surrounding blood vessels and nerves.

5 More recently, plastic surgeons are working on circumventing that snag by prefabricating bones away from the immediate site of a defect. Flaps of animal thigh muscles are removed, placed in osteogenin-coated molds, and implanted in the same animal's abdomen. This implantation provides a suitable biologic environment for transforming muscle into bone. Within weeks, the molds yield tiny, perfectly detailed bone segments. So far, surgeons have made bones from muscles in small animals but have not yet tried the process in humans. One limitation on the process is that osteogenin is available only in small amounts. Second, the safety and effectiveness of the process must first be tested on larger animals before human trials can begin.

GO ON TO THE NEXT PAGE ▶

Practice Tests

22. Which statement best describes the central idea of the passage?

    E. The drawbacks and limitations of osteogenin make it an ineffective treatment for bone-related medical issues.

    F. There are various approaches that doctors and scientists can use to cultivate bone tissue.

    G. The approval process for new medical procedures to be used on humans is a complex one.

    H. The recent major advances in reconstructive surgery offer hope to those with previously incurable medical issues.

23. What do the details about animal testing described in paragraph 5 convey?

    A. They highlight that osteogenin bone replacement in humans can be tried only after extensive animal testing.

    B. They imply that success in large animals assures success in human bone transplants.

    C. They convey that all bones can be regenerated from undifferentiated muscle tissue.

    D. They show how cows are unique in producing osteogenin.

24. How does the word "challenge" in paragraph 2 contribute to the meaning of the paragraph?

    E. It conveys how hard it is to match bone to be grafted from a donor to that of the recipient.

    F. It highlights the problems of learning how to reconfigure the natural shapes of bones.

    G. It emphasizes the issues with designing better types of plastic or metal substitutes for bone.

    H. It references how difficult it is to find ways of reconstructing or replacing certain bones.

25. Which sentence from the passage best supports the author's claim that "the idea of making bones from muscle is not all that strange" (paragraph 4)?

    A. "Surgeons perform phenomenal feats such as replacing clogged coronary arteries with blood vessels from the leg[.]" (paragraph 1)

    B. "The living cells within the bone graft grow and attach to those in the original bone, repairing the injury." (paragraph 3)

    C. "[M]uscle, bone, fat, blood vessels, and bone marrow all develop in human embryos from the same loosely organized tissue[.]" (paragraph 4)

    D. "In 1987, scientists isolated a bone-inducing protein called osteogenin from cows and discovered that osteogenin can make undifferentiated human tissue produce cartilage and bone." (paragraph 4)

26. Which sentence from the passage best supports the idea that plastic surgeons will be able to circumvent the "snag" osteogenin presents?

    E. "If sprinkled directly onto a defect, for instance, the entire area might stiffen to bone if even a tiny bit of osteogenin fell on the surrounding blood vessels and nerves." (paragraph 4)

    F. "Flaps of animal thigh muscles are removed, placed in osteogenin-coated molds, and implanted in the same animal's abdomen." (paragraph 5)

    G. "So far, surgeons have made bones from muscles in small animals but have not yet tried the process in humans." (paragraph 5)

    H. "One limitation on the process is that osteogenin is available only in small amounts." (paragraph 5)

27. The passage suggests that osteogenin-coated molds are most likely placed inside the animal's abdomen during the bone growth procedure because

    A. osteogenin-coated molds need a living environment in order to work properly.

    B. the abdominal muscles are the easiest to transform into replacement bone.

    C. doctors cannot move large bones in the body without disabling the test subject.

    D. osteogenin is available only in small amounts.

28. The author most likely used the phrase "this may sound peculiar" in paragraph 4 to convey the idea that

    E. mending bones artificially rather than letting them heal on their own is surprisingly beneficial for patients.

    F. the process involving osteogenin has proven shockingly successful in animal trials.

    G. mending bones artificially is a complex time-consuming process that even researchers do not fully understand.

    H. the process involving the use of osteogenin may seem strange to the uninformed.

29. How does paragraph 4 fit into the overall structure of the passage?

    A. It explains how osteogenin can be used safely.

    B. It argues that replacing bone is more difficult than other procedures.

    C. It describes how a protein can turn other human tissue into bone.

    D. It indicates that artificial bones and joints do not last long.

GO ON TO THE NEXT PAGE →

Chain Mail

1   Flexible body armor made from interlocking iron or steel rings was known as far back as the ancient Roman era. Used primarily as protection for elite heavy cavalry troops, various forms of so-called "chain mail" armor were relatively rare and expensive at that time, and less practical in many ways than the Roman infantryman's segmented steel breastplate. For centuries after the fall of Imperial Rome, the craft of fashioning mail armor fell into disuse. In the medieval period, however, the techniques were revived and became more popular than ever. By the fourteenth century, entire armies were often outfitted with practical and effective linked-metal armor suits.

2   The type of armor historians sometimes call "chain mail," but which was called by the people of the time merely "mail," had many advantages for the individual fighting man in the age of steel weapons. It combined the flexibility and suppleness of cloth with the impact-absorbing mass and cut resistance of rigid metal plates. Edged weapons, no matter how sharp, are incapable of slashing or sawing through a well-fashioned mail suit. Moreover, when struck with a blunt object, the links transfer much of the force through the mass of the garment, absorbing a significant amount of impact instead of allowing it to pass to the soft tissues of the wearer beneath.

3   The process of manufacturing a mail shirt was very labor-intensive in preindustrial times. Each of the thousands of individual links that made up a full suit, or "harness," had to be individually cut from a coil of hand-drawn wire. The ends of each link were flattened and drilled with tiny holes, and then the link was added into the garment and riveted closed. Each of these steps was accomplished by a small group of specialists in that task to reduce the amount of time needed to produce a suit. The master mailer was then able to grow or shrink the metal garment to "knit" sleeves, mittens, hoods, and other garments by varying the pattern of interlocking links. Modern mail-makers, or "maillers," use these traditional techniques to create historically accurate chain mail and may work alone for a year to produce a full set of mail.

4   At first, the expense of chain mail meant that it was used exclusively by the wealthy nobility. As soon as a soldier fell in battle, however, his coveted chain mail would quickly be taken for use by another. Eventually, as improved stabbing and piercing weapons became more widespread, linked mail armor became obsolete and was relegated to the common foot soldier, the peasant recruit, or just discarded completely. For the nobility, the need for greater protection spurred the development of armors revolving around cleverly articulated rigid steel plates instead. Because of this, only a few examples of medieval mail armor survive into the present.

5   Today, in addition to traditional maillers, modern maillers produce chain mail with premade wire, electric motors, and pneumatic tools for costumes for Renaissance festivals, movies, theme parks, medieval restaurants, and fantasy hobbyists. Although these modern techniques make the process go faster, "mail making" remains a tedious, time-consuming pursuit.

30. Which statement best describes the central idea of the passage?

    E. The armor used in the medieval era was closely related to the types of weapons used in warfare.

    F. Medieval mail armor has a long history, including a complicated production process and some modern uses.

    G. The revival of Roman arms technology in the medieval era enabled the use of chain mail to spread.

    H. Body armor and its production process has continued to evolve since Roman times.

31. In paragraph 3, how does the word "master" contribute to the meaning of the paragraph?

    A. It emphasizes that the maillers owned the armor they made.

    B. It indicates that the makers of mail shirts were elders.

    C. It defines the maillers as teachers.

    D. It describes the makers of mail shirts as experts.

32. How does paragraph 3 fit into the overall structure of the excerpt?

    E. It contrasts the initial exclusivity of chain mail to wealthy medieval elites with its later spread to the lower classes.

    F. It elaborates on the advantages of chain mail against various types of weapons on the medieval battlefield.

    G. It highlights how the development of weaponry affects offensive and defensive military technology over time.

    H. It describes the manufacturing process for chain mail in order to establish why only the wealthy initially owned it.

33. What is the most likely reason chain mail was not commonly used in the ancient Roman era?

    A. Ancient Roman "linked mail armor" was less effective than the armor made in the fourteenth century.

    B. The improved stabbing and piercing weapons used by Rome's military opponents made flexible mail armor impractical.

    C. Armor made from segmented steel plates was unsuitable for wear by Roman cavalry troops.

    D. The segmented breastplate was a more practical form of protection for Roman infantry than flexible mail armor.

Practice Tests

34. Which sentence best supports the idea that chain mail became less effective as a form of defense on the battlefield?

    E. "It combined the flexibility and suppleness of cloth with the impact-absorbing mass and cut resistance of rigid metal plates." (paragraph 2)

    F. "Moreover, when struck with a blunt object, the links transfer much of the force through the mass of the garment, absorbing a significant amount of impact instead of allowing it to pass to the soft tissues of the wearer beneath." (paragraph 2)

    G. "For the nobility, the need for greater protection spurred the development of armors revolving around cleverly articulated rigid steel plates instead." (paragraph 4)

    H. "Today, in addition to traditional maillers, modern maillers produce chain mail with premade wire, electric motors, and pneumatic tools for costumes for renaissance festivals, movies, theme parks, medieval restaurants, and fantasy hobbyists." (paragraph 5)

35. In paragraph 4, the idea that chain mail was once considered very valuable is illustrated mainly through the

    A. tedious, labor-intensive process for creating mail armor.

    B. use of chain armor by the peasant class.

    C. superior durability of medieval mail armor.

    D. immediate theft of an armor suit after a soldier's death.

36. With which statement would the author of this excerpt most likely agree?

    E. Linked-metal armor represented a practical solution to a technological need in a particular historical era.

    F. Military technologies in the era of steel hand weapons succeeded primarily because of the existence of an adequate network of skilled craftsmen to support them.

    G. The availability of practical mail armor was limited mainly to the fourteenth century.

    H. Linked-metal armor was of such limited usefulness that it became obsolete as soon as the superior technology of articulated metal plates became widespread.

"The Flying Gang"

by Andrew Barton Paterson

I served my time, in the days gone by,
In the railway's clash and clang,
And I worked my way to the end, and I
Was the head of the 'Flying Gang.'
5 'Twas a chosen band that was kept at hand
In case of an urgent need,
Was it south or north we were started forth,
And away at our utmost speed.
If word reached town that a bridge was down,
10 The imperious summons rang—
'Come out with the pilot engine sharp,
And away with the flying gang.'

Then a piercing scream and a rush of steam
As the engine moved ahead,
15 With a measured beat by the slum and street
Of the busy town we fled,
By the uplands bright and the homesteads white,
With the rush of the western gale,
And the pilot swayed with the pace we made
20 As she rocked on the ringing rail.
And the country children clapped their hands
As the engine's echoes rang,
But their elders said: 'There is work ahead
When they send for the flying gang.'

25 Then across the miles of the saltbush plain
That gleamed with the morning dew,
Where the grasses waved like the ripening grain
The pilot engine flew,
A fiery rush in the open bush
30 Where the grade marks seemed to fly,
And the order sped on the wires ahead,
The pilot *MUST* go by.
The Governor's special must stand aside,
And the fast express go hang,
35 Let your orders be that the line is free
For the boys of the flying gang.

GO ON TO THE NEXT PAGE

37. The first stanza (lines 1–12) conveys a central idea of the poem by

    A. showing how the members of the flying gang were chosen.

    B. explaining the occupation of the narrator.

    C. comparing the work of the flying gang to the jobs performed by other railroad workers.

    D. implying that the narrator was required to travel long distances.

38. Read lines 5–6 from the first stanza.

    > 'Twas a chosen band that was kept at hand
    > In case of an urgent need,

    How do the lines contribute to the development of ideas in the stanza?

    E. The lines emphasize the immediacy and importance of the narrator's work.

    F. The lines indicate how musicians were an integral part of railroad work.

    G. The lines reveal the narrator's intention to persevere in a difficult situation.

    H. The lines show how the narrator began his employment at the railroad.

39. Which line from the poem best supports the idea that the flying gang was used for the largest, most important repairs the railroad needed?

    A. "I served my time, in the days gone by,

    In the railway's clash and clang," (lines 1–2)

    B. "And I worked my way to the end, and I

    Was the head of the 'Flying Gang.'" (lines 3–4)

    C. "If word reached town that a bridge was down,

    The imperious summons rang—" (lines 9–10)

    D. "'Come out with the pilot engine sharp,

    And away with the flying gang.'" (lines 11–12)

40. The poet develops the speaker's point of view in the second stanza (lines 13–24) by

    E. describing the beautiful, desolate countryside through which the flying gang travels.

    F. showing how the train thrills the city dwellers as it moves through the town.

    G. illustrating all the preparations necessary before the flying gang can leave.

    H. contrasting the children's cheerful excitement with the adults' recognition of the job ahead.

41. How do the phrases "piercing scream," "rush of steam," and "she rocked on the ringing rail" in the second stanza affect the tone of the poem?

    A. They suggest that the flying gang must urgently respond to its orders.

    B. They imply that the flying gang is very noisy when it works.

    C. They indicate the sounds that one might expect close to a railroad.

    D. They contrast the quiet of the countryside with the noise the train makes as it passes.

42. Which line from the poem best supports the idea that the children do not understand the work of the flying gang?

   E. "Then a piercing scream and a rush of steam
      As the engine moved ahead," (lines 13–14)

   F. "And the pilot swayed with the pace we made
      As she rocked on the ringing rail." (lines 19–20)

   G. "And the country children clapped their hands
      As the engine's echoes rang," (lines 21–22)

   H. "But their elders said: 'There is work ahead
      When they send for the flying gang.'" (lines 23–24)

43. Read lines 29–30.

   > **A fiery rush in the open bush**
   > **Where the grade marks seemed to fly,**

   Which of the following supports the most likely meaning of these lines?

   A. "By the uplands bright and the homesteads white,
      With the rush of the western gale," (lines 17–18)

   B. "But their elders said: 'There is work ahead
      When they send for the flying gang.'" (lines 23–24)

   C. "Then across the miles of the saltbush plain
      That gleamed with the morning dew," (lines 25–26)

   D. "Let your orders be that the line is free
      For the boys of the flying gang." (lines 35–36)

44. How does the form of the poem contribute to its meaning?

   E. The use of an equal number of lines in each stanza emphasizes that each stage of the journey is equally important.

   F. The regular rhyme scheme and meter reflect the repetitive sound and motion of the train.

   G. The different stanzas are used to illustrate different aspects of the flying gang and its work.

   H. The first-person narrator is used to emphasize the dangerous conditions faced by the flying gang.

GO ON TO THE NEXT PAGE ➤

The Panama Canal

1 In 1880, Ferdinand de Lesseps, the force behind the successful completion of the Suez Canal in Egypt, attempted to finance the construction of a canal in Panama. After he successfully shortened many long ocean voyages by connecting the Mediterranean Sea with the Red Sea and eliminated the need for the perilous passage around the entire continent of Africa, he turned his attention to Panama. As he had done in Suez, de Lesseps planned to trim the journey between the Atlantic and Pacific Oceans by cutting across the Isthmus of Panama, the shortest distance between the two oceans. However, by 1888, de Lesseps retreated, discouraged by the many logistical problems he faced in the construction of the canal. For example, the volume of excavation that the canal would require was beyond the capabilities of the era's technology. Likewise, all materials to be used on the canal had to be imported, and communities to house the canal's workers had to be constructed from scratch.

2 The Isthmus of Panama also presented many environmental obstacles that had to be overcome before progress could be made on the canal. The unique geology of the area resulted in frequent landslides, and tropical diseases plagued the workers. In fact, during the six years that de Lesseps' work on the canal continued, between 10,000 and 20,000 workers died from various diseases, most notably malaria and yellow fever. As a result of these hardships, de Lesseps was forced to abandon his project, though his company still retained the right to complete it.

3 Just after the turn of the century, the United States began taking an active interest in the Panama Canal. The United States had been mulling over the idea of investing in a canal in Nicaragua, but experts managed to convince American leaders that the Panama site was better suited for this type of project. However, de Lesseps's Compagnie Nouvelle refused to sell its contracts and equipment for less than $100 million. As the Nicaraguan site was far less expensive, Compagnie Nouvelle came to fear that the Americans would decide on the Nicaraguan canal, so it agreed to sell its Panama site for $40 million. Now, America had only to convince Panama and Colombia—since, at the time, Panama was under Colombian rule—to sell them the land. The Americans approached the Panamanians, who were eager to sell, but the Colombians refused.

4 With support from the United States, which sent warships to prevent Colombia from sending troops by sea, Panama declared its independence. Despite vocal protestations from some Panamanians, some United States lawmakers, and the press, a treaty, giving the United States the right to build and defend the canal as well as administer the territory immediately adjacent to that canal, was signed three days later.

5 America's next step was to control the rampant diseases of the area. Colonel William Crawford Gorgas helped to rid the Isthmus of yellow fever and limit the outbreaks of malaria. Though this was a praiseworthy accomplishment, many of the obstacles that had faced de Lesseps remained. Landslides were still common, so a system of dredges was designed to remove debris from the locks that would be used to move ships across the canal. Once these problems were solved, it still took a decade and the labor of more than 70,000 workers to construct the canal, all at a cost of nearly half a billion dollars and the lives of almost 40% of the workers. The first ship passed through the canal on August 15, 1914, and throughout the twentieth century, nearly a million vessels have crossed the Isthmus via the Panama Canal, not only saving 7,800 miles on the ocean journey from New York to San Francisco, but also sparing ships from the treacherous passage around Cape Horn.

6 After the Second World War, the devious inception of the United States' control of the Panama Canal began to show its effects: more Panamanians began to demand the United States return the territory to Panama. Riots erupted in the Canal Zone in 1964, and the United States reinforced the military assigned to defend the Canal. Pressure continued to build on the United States to return the Canal, and in 1974, the United States' president began negotiations to do so. Three years later, a new treaty was signed which returned the land, the Canal, and its operation to Panama, in return for Panama guaranteeing the permanent neutrality of the Canal. Today, the Canal provides the largest portion of Panama's annual revenue.

OCEAN TRADE ROUTES BETWEEN NEW YORK CITY AND SAN FRANCISCO

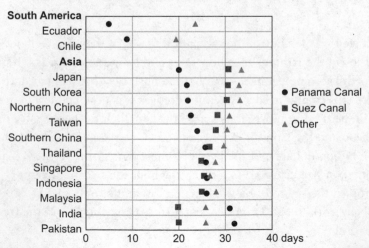

APPROXIMATE VOYAGE TIME FROM U.S. GULF COAST
THROUGH PANAMA CANAL OR OTHER ROUTES

45. Which statement best describes the central idea of the passage?

    A.   The Panama Canal is key to the history of the entire region of Central America in the late 1800s.

    B.   The Panama Canal represented the failure of the Panamanian revolution as the canal fell under United States control.

    C.   The Panama Canal had a massive impact on international trade.

    D.   The Panama Canal faced difficulties in its planning and construction.

46. The map contributes to the development of the topic of the passage mainly by

    E.   illustrating that Panama was a more advantageous location than Nicaragua for the building of a canal that would shorten the journey from the East and West coasts of the United States.

    F.   suggesting that the much shorter ocean voyage between the North American coasts through the Isthmus of Panama was a compelling reason for the building of the Panama Canal.

    G.   revealing that the route through the Panama Canal is not the only ocean trade route between New York City and San Francisco.

    H.   showing that the environmental, logistical, and political obstacles standing in the way of building the Panama Canal can eventually be overcome.

47. The hardships that de Lesseps experienced in building his canal are best illustrated through the

    A.   hurdles necessary to gain Panama's political independence from Columbia.

    B.   financial problems he faced in securing funding for its construction.

    C.   Colombian government's stance against allowing the United States to build and operate a canal in Panama.

    D.   logistical and environmental challenges he faced while operating in the isthmus of Panama.

48. Which evidence from the passage best supports the claim in paragraph 3 that "the Americans would decide on the Nicaraguan canal"?

    E.   the assertion that it would be cheaper to build a canal at the Nicaraguan site

    F.   the recommendation of the experts that a canal be built at the Nicaraguan site

    G.   the revelation that the Nicaraguans had nearly completed their canal already

    H.   the description of the Nicaraguan site as the shortest span of distance between the Atlantic and Pacific

49. How does the graph support the development of ideas in paragraph 1?

    A. It provides evidence that the voyage time from the U.S. Gulf coast to many other countries through the Panama Canal is shorter on average than via other routes.

    B. It proves that the time it takes to travel from the U.S. Gulf coast to other countries using the Suez canal rather than the Panama Canal is shorter in most cases.

    C. It illustrates the surprising fact that it takes approximately the same amount of time for a ship to reach Indonesia from the U.S. Gulf coast no matter which route is taken.

    D. It shows that leaders in the United States were inspired by Ferdinand de Lesseps to complete building the canal in Panama rather than in Nicaragua.

50. With which statement would the author of this excerpt most likely agree?

    E. The United States spent much more to build the canal than was expected.

    F. The diseases in the area were a major impediment to U.S. construction of the canal.

    G. Ferdinand de Lesseps did not want the United States to have control over the canal.

    H. The canal project damaged relations between the United States and Panama.

51. Read this sentence from paragraph 5.

> **Once these problems were solved, it still took a decade and the labor of more than 70,000 workers to construct the canal, all at a cost of nearly half a billion dollars and the lives of almost 40% of the workers.**

How does the sentence contribute to the structure and development of ideas in the passage?

    A. It contrasts the success achieved by the United States with the failure of de Lesseps to overcome the environmental and logistical issues of the site.

    B. It criticizes the huge expense and the human cost required to successfully complete the Panama Canal.

    C. It indicates that the cost of constructing the canal was worthwhile because of the time saved and the revenues generated by the canal.

    D. It emphasizes the continued challenges presented earlier in the passage while recognizing that they were eventually overcome.

Practice Tests

In this excerpt, renowned detective Sherlock Holmes and his companion and chronicler Dr. Watson have received an early morning visit from a distraught woman, afraid for her life. The stepdaughter of Dr. Grimesby Roylott, she has witnessed the mysterious death of her sister and been ill-treated by her stepfather, a violent and unpredictable man, who has unexpectedly burst in on Holmes and Watson.

Excerpt from "The Adventure of the Speckled Band"
by Sir Arthur Conan Doyle

1 [O]ur door had been suddenly dashed open, and . . . a huge man had framed himself in the aperture. His costume was a peculiar mixture of the professional and of the agricultural, having a black top-hat, a long frock-coat, and a pair of high gaiters, with a hunting crop swinging in his hand. So tall was he that his hat actually brushed the crossbar of the doorway, and his breadth seemed to span it across from side to side. A large face, seared with a thousand wrinkles, burned yellow with the sun, and marked with every evil passion, was turned from one to the other of us, while his deep-set, bile-shot eyes, and his high, thin, fleshless nose, gave him somewhat the resemblance to a fierce old bird of prey.

2 "Which of you is Holmes?" asked this apparition.

3 "My name, sir; but you have the advantage of me," said my companion quietly.

4 "I am Dr. Grimesby Roylott, of Stoke Moran."

5 "Indeed, Doctor," said Holmes blandly. "Pray take a seat."

6 "I will do nothing of the kind. My stepdaughter has been here. I have traced her. What has she been saying to you?"

7 "It is a little cold for the time of the year," said Holmes.

8 "What has she been saying to you?" screamed the old man furiously.

9 "But I have heard that the crocuses promise well," continued my companion imperturbably.

10 "Ha! You put me off, do you?" said our new visitor, taking a step forward and shaking his hunting crop. "I know you, you scoundrel! I have heard of you before. You are Holmes, the meddler."

11 My friend smiled.

12 "Holmes, the busybody!"

13 His smile broadened.

14 "Holmes, the Scotland Yard Jack-in-office!"

15 Holmes chuckled heartily. "Your conversation is most entertaining," said he. "When you go out close the door, for there is a decided draught."

16 "I will go when I have said my say. Don't you dare to meddle with my affairs. I know that Miss Stoner has been here. I traced her! I am a dangerous man to fall foul of! See here." He stepped swiftly forward, seized the poker, and bent it into a curve with his huge brown hands.

17 "See that you keep yourself out of my grip," he snarled, and hurling the twisted poker into the fireplace he strode out of the room.

18 "He seems a very amiable person," said Holmes, laughing. "I am not quite so bulky, but if he had remained I might have shown him that my grip was not much more feeble than his own." As he spoke he picked up the steel poker and, with a sudden effort, straightened it out again.

19 "Fancy his having the insolence to confound me with the official detective force! This incident gives zest to our investigation, however, and I only trust that our little friend will not suffer from her imprudence in allowing this brute to trace her. And now, Watson, we shall order breakfast, and afterwards I shall walk down to Doctors' Commons, where I hope to get some data which may help us in this matter."

20 It was nearly one o'clock when Sherlock Holmes returned from his excursion. He held in his hand a sheet of blue paper, scrawled over with notes and figures.

21 "I have seen the will of the deceased wife," said he. "To determine its exact meaning I have been obliged to work out the present prices of the investments with which it is concerned. The total income, which at the time of the wife's death was little short of 1100 pounds, is now, through the fall in agricultural prices, not more than 750 pounds. Each daughter can claim an income of 250 pounds, in case of marriage. It is evident, therefore, that if both girls had married, this beauty would have had a mere pittance, while even one of them would cripple him to a very serious extent. My morning's work has not been wasted, since it has proved that he has the very strongest motives for standing in the way of anything of the sort. And now, Watson, this is too serious for dawdling, especially as the old man is aware that we are interesting ourselves in his affairs; so if you are ready, we shall call a cab and drive to Waterloo. I should be very much obliged if you would slip your revolver into your pocket. An Eley's No. 2 is an excellent argument with gentlemen who can twist steel pokers into knots. That and a toothbrush are, I think, all that we need."

52. How does paragraph 9 fit into the overall structure of the excerpt?

E. It establishes that this is a meeting between two satiric adversaries.

F. It illustrates the calmness of Holmes in the face of possible danger.

G. It highlights the somewhat unseasonable weather.

H. It describes the degree of Dr. Roylott's anger.

GO ON TO THE NEXT PAGE ➡

53. With which statement would the author of this excerpt most likely agree?

    A. Dr. Roylott's stepdaughter speaking with Holmes influences Dr. Roylott to threaten Holmes in order to find out what his stepdaughter has said.

    B. Dr. Roylott's stepdaughter speaking with Holmes influences Dr. Roylott to burst into the room and physically assault both Holmes and Dr. Watson.

    C. Dr. Roylott's stepdaughter speaking with Holmes influences Dr. Roylott to furiously deny the accusations that his stepdaughter has made.

    D. Dr. Roylott's stepdaughter speaking with Holmes influences Dr. Roylott to threaten his stepdaughter's life if Holmes doesn't stop investigating.

54. The words "scoundrel" and "meddler" in paragraph 10 contribute to the meaning of the paragraph by

    E. conveying that Dr. Roylott is a violent, unhinged person who does not care whom he attacks.

    F. underlining that Dr. Roylott knows enough about Holmes to view him as a threat.

    G. emphasizing that Dr. Roylott is taking care not to come across as potentially guilty.

    H. revealing that Dr. Roylott knows exactly who Holmes is and what he does for a living.

55. How does the author's use of various insults in paragraphs 10–14 contribute to the development of ideas in the passage?

    A. They reveal that Dr. Roylott will insult every man that he meets.

    B. They illustrate that Holmes is calm until his profession is called into question.

    C. They demonstrate that Dr. Roylott is trying and failing to make Holmes afraid of him.

    D. They highlight the ever-increasing outrage that Holmes feels.

56. How does paragraph 17 fit into the overall structure of the excerpt?

    E. It introduces a shift from the perspective of Dr. Roylott to that of Dr. Watson.

    F. It emphasizes that neither Dr. Roylott nor his stepdaughter can intimidate Holmes.

    G. It offers a practical explanation for why Holmes is not afraid of Dr. Roylott.

    H. It indicates that the conversation between Holmes and Dr. Roylott is now over.

57. Which sentence best supports the idea that Dr. Roylott poses no actual threat to the safety of Holmes?

    A. "'Pray take a seat.'" (paragraph 5)

    B. "Holmes chuckled heartily. 'Your conversation is most entertaining,' said he." (paragraph 15)

    C. "'He seems a very amiable person,' said Holmes, laughing." (paragraph 18)

    D. "' . . . my grip was not much more feeble than his own.'" (paragraph 18)

Part 2—Mathematics

57 QUESTIONS—SUGGESTED TIMING: 90 MINUTES

IMPORTANT NOTES

1. Definitions and formulas are **not** provided.

2. Diagrams are **not** necessarily drawn to scale, with the exception of graphs.

3. Diagrams are drawn in single planes unless the question specifically states they are not.

4. Graphs are drawn to scale.

5. Simplify all fractions to lowest terms.

GRID-IN QUESTIONS

QUESTIONS 58–62

DIRECTIONS: Answer each question. Write your answer in the boxes at the top of the grid on the answer sheet. Start on the left side of each grid, printing only one number or symbol in each box. **DO NOT LEAVE A BOX BLANK IN THE MIDDLE OF AN ANSWER.** Under each box, fill in the circle that matches the number or symbol you wrote above. **DO NOT FILL IN A CIRCLE UNDER AN UNUSED BOX.**

---

58. Alicia can choose 2 of her 5 best friends to go with her to the amusement park. Her best friends are Connie, Dale, Eric, Finley, and Georgette. How many different pairs of 2 friends can she choose from the 5 ?

59. What value of m makes the proportion $\frac{3m}{5} = \frac{12}{4}$ true?

60. Sidney is eating lunch at a salad bar where you create your own salad. An 8-ounce salad costs $2.49. Each additional ounce of salad costs $0.25. How much does Sidney's salad cost if it weighs 1 pound, 8 ounces?

61. If $2x + 3y = 194$ and $x = 28$, what is the value of y ?

62. In a scale drawing of a triangular stained-glass window, the base measures 12 inches and the other two sides each measure 8 inches. On the actual window, the two congruent sides each measure 6 feet. What is the length in feet of the base of the actual window?

GO ON TO THE NEXT PAGE ➤

MULTIPLE-CHOICE QUESTIONS

QUESTIONS 63–114

DIRECTIONS: Answer each question, selecting the best answer available. On the answer sheet, mark the letter of each of your answers. You can do your figuring in the test booklet or on paper provided by the proctor.

$$\left\{ \frac{2}{11}, \frac{3}{11}, \frac{4}{11}, \frac{5}{11}, \frac{6}{11}, \frac{7}{11} \right\}$$

63. If Deena chooses a number at random from the set above, what is the probability that the number she chooses is less than $\frac{1}{2}$?

   A. $\frac{5}{11}$

   B. $\frac{1}{2}$

   C. $\frac{2}{3}$

   D. $\frac{5}{6}$

Education/Career Plans for Centerville High School Graduates

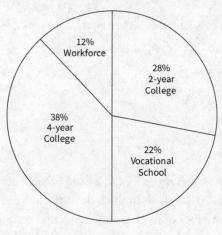

2019
Total Number of Graduates: 600

64. In 2019, how many graduates from Centerville High School chose either to enter the workforce or to continue their education at a vocational school?

   E. 72

   F. 132

   G. 168

   H. 204

65. If $2(x + y) = 8 + 2y$, then what is x?

   A. -1

   B. 2

   C. 3

   D. 4

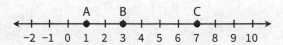

66. On the number line above, how many units is point B from the midpoint of AC?

   E. 1

   F. 2

   G. 3

   H. 4

67. A certain machine caps 5 bottles every 2 seconds. At this rate, how many bottles can the machine cap in 1 minute?

   A. 120

   B. 150

   C. 240

   D. 300

SECOND QUARTER SALES

68. According to the bar graph above, April sales accounted for approximately what percent of the total second-quarter sales?

E. $12\frac{1}{2}\%$

F. 25%

G. $37\frac{1}{2}\%$

H. 50%

69. If $a + b < 5$, and $a - b > 6$, which of the following pairs could be the values of a and b ?

A. $(4, -3)$
B. $(4, -2)$
C. $(3, -2)$
D. $(1, 3)$

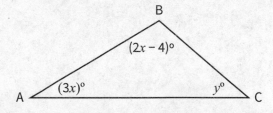

70. In the triangle above, if the measure of $\angle ABC$ is 60°, then what is the value of y ?

E. 24
F. 26
G. 28
H. 30

71. In a certain building, there are 10 floors and the number of rooms on each floor is R. If each room has exactly C chairs, which of the following expresses the total number of chairs in the building?

A. $\dfrac{10}{RC}$

B. $10RC$

C. $10R + C$

D. $10R + 10C$

72. The mean of a set of 10 numbers is 16. Two of the numbers (7 and 13) are removed. What is the mean of the 8 remaining numbers?

E. 6
F. 13.5
G. 17.5
H. 18

73. If 4% of r is 6.2, then what is 20% of r ?

A. 25
B. 26
C. 30
D. 31

74. At a certain school, the ratio of teachers to students is 1:10. Which of the following could be the total number of teachers and students?

E. 100
F. 121
G. 144
H. 222

GO ON TO THE NEXT PAGE ➤

75. Points A, B, C, D, E, F, G, and H are all on a straight line in that order. The distance between each pair of adjacent points is the same. If the distance between points A and H is 56, what is the distance between points B and E?

    A. 16
    B. 18
    C. 21
    D. 24

76. The perimeter of a decagon is 160 centimeters. The length of one side is 36 centimeters. The length of another side is 44 centimeters. All the remaining sides are equal in length to each other. What is the length of each of the remaining sides, in centimeters?

    E. 6
    F. 8
    G. 10
    H. 16

77. The sum of two consecutive integers is -9. If the smaller integer is doubled and 3 is added to the larger integer, what is the sum of the two resulting integers?

    A. -14
    B. -11
    C. -10
    D. -9

78. If the ratio of a to b is 4:5 and the ratio of a to c is 2:7, what is the ratio of c to b ?

    E. 8:35
    F. 5:7
    G. 14:5
    H. 35:8

79. If $k = 15$, what is $(4k + 30) - (2k + 15)$?

    A. 15
    B. 30
    C. 45
    D. 60

AVERAGE TICKET PRICE AT VARIOUS ONLINE TICKET RESELLERS

Average Price	Number of Online Resellers
$60	2
$68	5
$75	4
$82	4

80. The table above shows the average price of a ticket to a certain baseball game at 15 different online ticket reseller websites. What is the median of this set of average prices for a ticket to this particular game?

    E. $68
    F. $71.50
    G. $75
    H. 78.50

81. On a town map, 3 inches represents 5 miles. The points on this map that represent the library and the water tower are 7 inches apart. How many miles apart are the library and the water tower, to the nearest mile?

    A. 10
    B. 12
    C. 13
    D. 15

82. Clarissa bought a new freezer and plugged it in first thing in the morning. At 2:00 p.m., the temperature inside the freezer was 40 degrees above zero. Over the rest of the day, the temperature inside the freezer fell 7 degrees per hour. What was the temperature inside the freezer at 8:00 p.m. that day?

    E. $-42°$

    F. $-12°$

    G. $-2°$

    H. $2°$

83. Solve for x in terms of y if $3x - 5 = y$.

    A. $x = \dfrac{y - 5}{3}$

    B. $x = 3(y + 5)$

    C. $x = \dfrac{y + 5}{3}$

    D. $x = 3(5 - y)$

84. Jung's average (arithmetic mean) on 2 biology quizzes is 70. What must Jung's score on the next quiz be in order to have an average of 80 for the three quizzes?

    E. 80

    F. 85

    G. 90

    H. 100

85. Which percentage is closest in value to 0.0201 ?

    A. 0%

    B. 0.2%

    C. 2%

    D. 200%

86. What is the value of $\dfrac{4g - 150}{h}$ if $h = 100$ and $g = 300$?

    E. 1.5

    F. 10.5

    G. 105

    H. 1,000

87. If $x = 2$, $y = 3$, and $z = 4$, then what is $\left(\dfrac{4y}{2x}\right)\left(\dfrac{9z}{3x}\right)$?

    A. 6

    B. 12

    C. 18

    D. 36

88. How many positive **even** factors of 120 are greater than 20 and less than 120 ?

    E. 1

    F. 3

    G. 4

    H. 6

89. What is the surface area, in square centimeters, of a cube with volume 27 cubic centimeters?

    A. 24

    B. 27

    C. 36

    D. 54

GO ON TO THE NEXT PAGE

Practice Tests

Population of City X, 2014-2018
(in Hundred Thousands)

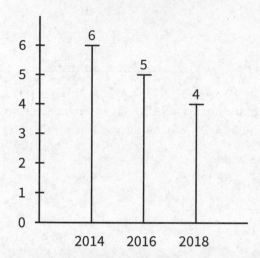

90. Based on the graph above, if the percent decrease from the 2018 population to the 2020 population of City X is the same as the percent decrease from the 2016 population to the 2018 population, what should the 2020 population in City X be?

   E. 280,000

   F. 300,000

   G. 320,000

   H. 350,000

91. If x is an even number, what is the sum of x and the previous two even numbers less than x ?

   A. $x - 4$

   B. $2x - 6$

   C. $3x - 3$

   D. $3x - 6$

92. Lisa completed a math competition problem in 33.24 seconds. Deidra completed the same problem in 33.09 seconds. What was the difference between their times, expressed as a fraction of a second?

   E. $\dfrac{1}{20}$

   F. $\dfrac{1}{15}$

   G. $\dfrac{3}{20}$

   H. $\dfrac{1}{5}$

93. How many negative **odd** numbers satisfy the inequality $4x + 100 \geq 20$?

   A. 9

   B. 10

   C. 19

   D. 20

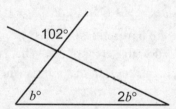

94. What is the value of b in the figure above?

   E. 26

   F. 28

   G. 30

   H. 31

$\{1, 2, 3, 4, \ldots, 297, 298, 299, 300\}$

95. How many members of the set shown above are multiples of 10 but not multiples of 15 ?

   A. 20

   B. 24

   C. 25

   D. 30

GO ON TO THE NEXT PAGE

VOWEL CARDS

Number of Cards	Letter on Card
7	A
6	E
5	I
8	O
4	U

96. The cards in the table above are shuffled and placed in a deck. Assuming there are no other cards in the deck, which vowel has exactly a 1 in 5 chance of being picked at random from the deck?

    E. A

    F. E

    G. I

    H. O

97. A brass washer used in a mechanical device is intended to have a thickness of 0.4 centimeter, with an allowable error of 2%. What is the greatest allowable thickness of the brass washer?

    A. 0.008 cm

    B. 0.048 cm

    C. 0.408 cm

    D. 0.48 cm

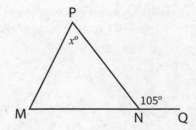

98. In the figure above, MQ is a straight line segment. If PM = PN, what is the value of x ?

    E. 30

    F. 45

    G. 60

    H. 75

99. In a certain 3,000-meter race, 2 people finished in under 10 minutes, 7 people finished between 10 and 11 minutes, 18 people finished between 11 and 12 minutes, and the other 473 people finished in more than 12 minutes. What percentage of the people in the competition finished in 12 minutes or less?

    A. 0.0054%

    B. 0.054%

    C. 0.54%

    D. 5.4%

100. Erin has a box of quarters from various states in the Northeast. The box contains 6 quarters from New York, 4 from Pennsylvania, 2 from Delaware, and 3 from New Jersey. If Erin selects 2 quarters at random from this box, without replacing them, what is the probability that both coins are **not** from New York?

    E. $\dfrac{12}{35}$

    F. $\dfrac{7}{13}$

    G. $\dfrac{4}{7}$

    H. $\dfrac{6}{7}$

$$(-1)^0 + 0^2 + (-1)^2 + \left(\frac{1}{2}\right)^2$$

101. What is the decimal form of the sum above?

A.   −1.75

B.   0.25

C.   2.25

D.   3

102. If a bucket contains 4 ounces of sand and 16 ounces of water, how many ounces of water would need to evaporate in order to make the ratio of the number of ounces of sand to the number of ounces of water 2 to 3 ?

E.   6

F.   7

G.   8

H.   10

103. If $x(b - c) = y + x$ and $2b = 3c = 7$, what is the value of $\frac{y}{x}$?

A. $\frac{1}{7}$

B. $\frac{1}{6}$

C. $\frac{1}{3}$

D. $\frac{5}{7}$

104. The perimeter of a rectangle is 12 inches. If the rectangle has a width that is 2 inches less than its length, what is its area in square inches?

E.   6

F.   8

G.   10

H.   20

105. The speed 5 feet per second is equivalent to how many meters per hour? (Use the approximation 1 foot = 0.3 meter.)

A.   1.5

B.   16.67

C.   5,400

D.   60,000

106. Suppose A is the sum of the first 50 consecutive multiples of 3, and B is the sum of the first 50 consecutive multiples of 6. What percent of A is B ?

E.   50%

F.   75%

G.   100%

H.   200%

107. In a recent survey, 80% of the people polled were registered voters and 75% of the registered voters voted in the last election. What fraction of all those surveyed were registered voters who did **not** vote in the last election?

A. $\frac{1}{10}$

B. $\frac{1}{5}$

C. $\frac{1}{4}$

D. $\frac{2}{5}$

108. What is $\frac{\ell m}{\ell p} + \ell$ given that $\ell = 24$, $m = 2\ell + 2$, and $p = \ell - 14$?

E.   5.1

F.   29

G.   240

H.   1,200

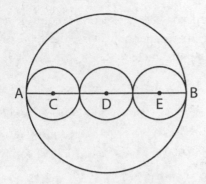

109. Three small circles of equal area have centers on line segment AB, as shown in the figure above. The centers of the small circles are C, D, and E. The area of the large circle with center D is 900π square units. What is the circumference of the circle with center C, assuming the circles just touch, but do not overlap?

    A. 5π

    B. 10π

    C. 20π

    D. 40π

110. If $x = \dfrac{1}{4}$ and $y = \dfrac{1}{2} - \dfrac{1}{3}$, what is the value of $x - y$?

    E. $-\dfrac{7}{12}$

    F. $-\dfrac{5}{12}$

    G. 0

    H. $\dfrac{1}{12}$

$$2.\overline{56} + 1.\overline{32}$$

111. Which improper fraction has the same value as the expression above?

    A. $\dfrac{41}{11}$

    B. $\dfrac{19}{5}$

    C. $\dfrac{97}{25}$

    D. $\dfrac{35}{9}$

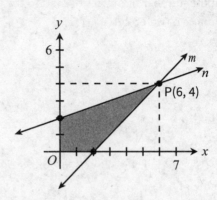

112. In the figure above, lines m and n intersect at point P (6, 4). What is the area, in square units, of the shaded region?

    E. 10

    F. 11

    G. 12

    H. 14

Practice Tests

113. Diego selects a marble from a bag and then returns it to the bag. When he does this 4 times, the probability of choosing a blue marble all 4 times is $\frac{1}{81}$. Based on this information, what is the probability of Diego choosing a blue marble the first time he selects a marble?

A. $\frac{4}{81}$

B. $\frac{1}{9}$

C. $\frac{2}{9}$

D. $\frac{1}{3}$

114. A particular brand of asphalt used to pave driveways is made by mixing the following ingredients: 1 part asphalt cement, 12 parts sand, 4 parts gravel, and 3 parts porous stone. Covering one driveway requires 200 cubic feet of this asphalt. How many total cubic feet of sand are required to cover 6 identical driveways?

E. 100

F. 120

G. 360

H. 720

THIS IS THE END OF THE TEST. IF TIME REMAINS, YOU MAY CHECK YOUR ANSWERS. BE SURE THAT THERE ARE NO STRAY MARKS, PARTIALLY FILLED ANSWER CIRCLES, OR INCOMPLETE ERASURES ON YOUR ANSWER SHEET.

STOP

Answer Key

PART 1—ENGLISH LANGUAGE ARTS

1.	A	16.	G	31.	D	46.	F
2.	E	17.	D	32.	H	47.	D
3.	C	18.	F	33.	D	48.	E
4.	H	19.	B	34.	G	49.	A
5.	D	20.	G	35.	D	50.	H
6.	F	21.	C	36.	E	51.	D
7.	A	22.	F	37.	B	52.	F
8.	E	23.	A	38.	E	53.	A
9.	C	24.	H	39.	C	54.	F
10.	F	25.	C	40.	H	55.	C
11.	D	26.	F	41.	A	56.	H
12.	E	27.	A	42.	H	57.	D
13.	C	28.	H	43.	D		
14.	H	29.	C	44.	F		
15.	C	30.	F	45.	D		

PART 2—MATHEMATICS

58. 10	73. D	88. G	103. B
59. 5	74. F	89. D	104. F
60. 6.49	75. D	90. G	105. C
61. 46	76. G	91. D	106. H
62. 9	77. B	92. G	107. B
63. C	78. G	93. B	108. F
64. H	79. C	94. E	109. C
65. D	80. G	95. A	110. H
66. E	81. B	96. F	111. D
67. B	82. G	97. C	112. E
68. H	83. C	98. E	113. D
69. A	84. H	99. D	114. H
70. E	85. C	100. E	
71. B	86. F	101. C	
72. G	87. C	102. H	

Answers and Explanations

Part 1—English Language Arts

1.   A

Category: Knowledge of Language

Getting to the Answer: In sentence 1, the clause "who teaches college students" is redundant because the sentence already uses the word "professor." **(A)** is correct. The sentences in **(B)**, **(C)**, and **(D)** do not contain errors.

2.   E

Category: Sentence Structure

Getting to the Answer: Modifying phrases must be placed directly next to the thing they are intended to modify. In sentence 1, the modifying phrase "after graduating from college" is placed next to "the next five years of a software engineer's life." This makes it sound like the "next five years" graduated from college, which is illogical. **(E)** is correct. The sentences in **(F)**, **(G)**, and **(H)** do not contain structural errors.

3.   C

Category: Usage

Getting to the Answer: Check each answer choice systematically. Since the subject of the singular verb "provides" is the singular noun "the federal government," no change is necessary, so **(A)** is incorrect. There are no context clues to indicate that the past tense is needed, so **(B)** is incorrect. The prepositional phrase "of deferring" is not idiomatically correct, so this change should be made. **(C)** is correct. For the record, the phrase "begin to work" is idiomatically correct as written; thus, **(D)** is incorrect as well.

4.   H

Category: Sentence Structure

Getting to the Answer: As written, this sentence lacks a predicate verb and is thus a fragment. Eliminate **(F)** and **(G)** immediately, since they do not address the issue. **(E)** may look tempting since it removes "which" and changes a verb. However, "offering" is not a predicate verb, so **(E)** is incorrect. **(H)** supplies a predicate verb without introducing other structural errors, so it is correct.

5.   D

Category: Sentence Structure

Getting to the Answer: Read through each answer, looking for a complex sentence that presents ideas clearly and precisely while logically connecting the ideas in the three sentences. **(D)** is correct because it starts broadly with the statement that New York state has extensive rivers and streams, then narrows the focus specifically to the Hudson River. The dependent clause "which is home to dozens of rare birds and more than a hundred rare plants" immediately follows the phrase "the Hudson River" to provide additional information about the river. **(A)** and **(C)** are incorrect because they place "New York state has more than 70,000 miles of rivers and streams" at the end of the sentence rather than at the beginning, disrupting the logical organization, which in this case is general-to-specific. **(B)** is incorrect because it unnecessarily uses the wordier phrase "and one of them is the Hudson River" instead of the clearer, shorter phrase "including the Hudson River."

6.   F

Category: Topic Development

Getting to the Answer: When identifying the main claim of the passage, use the main ideas of each paragraph as guidance. Paragraph 1 introduces the topic of consciousness, paragraphs 2, 3, and 4 talk about different states of consciousness, and paragraph 5 states that scientists conduct experiments that explore these different states, which is best reflected by **(F)**. **(E)** is too specific; an altered state of consciousness is mentioned only in paragraph 2, so it cannot reflect the main claim of the entire passage. **(G)** is incorrect because although the sentence mentions psychological research that investigates consciousness, the topic of the passage is related to the different states of consciousness rather than neurological disorders. Although sentence 2 mentions Wilhelm Wundt and William James, this sentence references two "schools" of psychology—voluntarism and functionalism—that the passage does not discuss; **(H)** is incorrect.

7. A

Category: Topic Development

Getting to the Answer: Use the information in the sentences indicated in the question to identify the correct answer. Sentence 10 discusses how people can access their memories if they are prompted to do so. Sentence 11 provides an example of a question that would prompt someone to access a memory, which would bring the information from preconscious level to the conscious level; **(A)** describes this transfer perfectly. **(B)** is incorrect because it contradicts the information in the paragraph; sentence 10 says that memories are stored on a preconscious level, not an unconscious level. **(C)** is incorrect because the sentence focuses on the importance of eating breakfast rather than the preconscious level of consciousness. **(D)** is incorrect because "you would think about what you ate" is too vague to sufficiently support the ideas in the third paragraph.

8. E

Category: Topic Development

Getting to the Answer: Every sentence in a paragraph should be connected to the paragraph's main topic. Paragraph 4 is about two types of subconscious processing: priming and the mere-exposure effect. Sentence 14 is not about either process, so it should be removed; **(E)** is correct. Sentence 15 introduces the two types of subconscious processing, so **(F)** is incorrect. Sentences 16 and 17 are about priming, so they are on topic; eliminate **(G)** and **(H)**.

9. C

Category: Topic Development

Getting to the Answer: A concluding sentence should reflect the passage's general topic and main ideas while not introducing new information. The passage is about consciousness and researchers' interest in studying the different states of consciousness. **(C)** fits well with the passage's topic and ties the concluding paragraph back to paragraph 1 where studying consciousness is first mentioned. **(A)** and **(B)** are incorrect because they do not provide any additional support for the passage; they are restatements of sentences 19 and 20, respectively. **(D)** is incorrect because hypnosis is not mentioned in the passage.

10. F

Category: Organization

Getting to the Answer: When you are asked to add a transition, think about the relationship between the sentences in the paragraph. Sentence 1 describes how weaving has a long history. Sentence 2 continues this train of thought by showing how it also features in two early civilizations. The continuation transition word "indeed" is appropriate here, so **(F)** is correct. **(E)** and **(H)** are incorrect because they express contrast, not a continuation. **(G)** is incorrect because weaving's ancient past did not cause it to be a part of Chinese or Egyptian culture.

11. D

Category: Organization

Getting to the Answer: Both sentences identify where looms were used, so it is not necessary to separate them. Since conciseness is important on the SHSAT, look for a revision that connects the sentences logically and concisely. **(D)** is correct. **(A)** is unnecessarily wordy. **(B)** changes the sentence's meaning by changing "By" to "As long ago as" and "throughout" to "parts of." **(C)** introduces the contrast word "though," which is incorrect since there is no contrast between the two parts of the sentence.

12. E

Category: Topic Development

Getting to the Answer: When you are asked which sentence best introduces the main topic, be sure to take the whole passage into account. Paragraphs 2 and 3 talk about weaving in mythology and folktales, and paragraph 4 describes modern weaving practices. Though all the answer choices mention culture in some way, **(E)** best expresses this cultural importance of weaving. **(F)** is vague and "the course of many societies" is off-topic. **(G)** is overly specific and off-topic. **(H)** twists what the passage says; although the passage discusses weavers and traditions across many cultures, it does not say anything about them inspiring each other.

13. C

Category: Topic Development

Getting to the Answer: To determine which sentence is out of place, identify the main idea of the paragraph from which the sentences are taken. This paragraph describes stories involving weaving and gives several examples. Aesop's fable, however, is not about weaving; thus, sentence 11 is irrelevant and should be deleted. **(C)** is correct. All other sentences support the main idea of the paragraph.

14. H

Category: Organization

Getting to the Answer: Before looking at each answer choice, consider the structure and function of the sentence in question. The transition phrase "without question" indicates emphasis, and the sentence itself reads like a conclusion. Therefore, this sentence must be placed near the end of the paragraph and after a sentence that discusses the cultural meanings of weaving. **(H)** is correct. **(E)**, **(F)**, and **(G)** are incorrect because sentence 16 functions as a conclusion, not as an introduction or as part of the paragraph's body.

Passage Analysis: This passage describes the Alvarez theory that dinosaurs became extinct due to a giant meteor strike. Paragraph 1 introduces the topic of dinosaur extinction and explains that paleontologists provided many theories of dinosaur extinction, but none had been proven. Paragraph 2 explains how a physicist named Luis Alvarez and his son, a geologist, proposed a new theory: that a meteor strike caused the temperature to drop and plants to die. Their evidence is discussed in paragraph 3, which describes a layer of iridium across the whole Earth from the time when the dinosaurs died. Paragraph 4 states that paleontologists refused to believe them because no crater had been found, but paragraph 5 describes how a crater was found a decade later in Mexico, solving the mystery.

15. C

Category: Detail

Getting to the Answer: The Alvarez theory is discussed in paragraph 3, which states that the iridium could have occurred either from a meteor strike or by volcanic action, but concludes that the meteorite theory Is more likely. Therefore, **(C)** is correct and **(B)** is incorrect. The Yucatan crater seems to support the Alvarez theory, but the theory is not proven, since the last sentence of the passage indicates that many (but not all) scientists are convinced; eliminate **(A)**. **(D)** is Out of Scope because this choice doesn't support the meteorite explanation; also, the passage focuses on paleontologists, not geologists.

16. G

Category: Detail

Getting to the Answer: Criticism of the Alverez theory is found in paragraph 4, so look up the answer to the question there. The second sentence states, "Neither Luis nor Walter Alvarez was a paleontologist." Match this phrase to **(G)**, the correct answer. Incomplete or improper research, **(E)**, being abrasive, **(F)**, and misinterpreting data, **(H)**, are all Out of Scope for this passage.

17. D

Category: Function

Getting to the Answer: Paragraph 2 explains the Alvarez theory of dinosaur extinction: a huge meteor crash created a cloud of dust, which disrupted vegetation and led to a break in the global food chain. When the dinosaurs could not find enough to eat, they died out. **(D)** is correct. All the incorrect choices are Out of Scope. Although the passage presents an alternative theory, the epidemic theory, **(A)**, is only mentioned, not refuted. A clean atmosphere, **(B)**, and the primary diet of the dinosaurs, **(C)**, are never mentioned in the excerpt.

18. F

Category: Inference

Getting to the Answer: The iridium evidence is discussed in paragraph 3, so look up the answer there. The correct answer comes from the start of the third sentence, "Since iridium is rarely found on the Earth's surface. . ." This information matches **(F)**. For the incorrect choices, **(E)** and **(H)** are not discussed in the passage and are Out of Scope. **(G)** is Extreme. The passage states that iridium can be deposited by meteors or volcanoes, not "only" meteors.

19. B

Category: Function

Getting to the Answer: In the context of the passage, the phrase "coupled with" means "combined with" or "together with." So the sentence is saying that two factors, lack of plants and a drop in temperature, caused the extinction of the dinosaurs. This prediction matches the correct answer, **(B)**. **(A)** and **(D)** are Misused Details from the passage; the lack of plants may have been a result of the meteor impact and caused the dinosaurs to starve, but these ideas are not conveyed by the phrase "coupled with." **(C)** is Out of Scope, since there is no mention in the passage of iridium being distributed in snowfall.

20. G

Category: Detail

Getting to the Answer: The criticisms of the paleontologists are found in paragraph 4. Return there to look up the answer to the question. The last sentence gives the reason for the paleontologists' skepticism: there was no evidence of a crater from the meteor's impact. The correct answer is **(G)**. None of the other choices identify the paleontologists' early criticisms.

21. C

Category: Global

Getting to the Answer: The main idea of the passage is the Alvarez theory for the extinction of the dinosaurs. Review your Roadmap and determine the information paragraph 5 provides: how the Yucatan crater provides

evidence for the Alvarez theory of dinosaur extinction. **(C)** is correct. **(A)** is Out of Scope, as the excerpt never identifies or rejects the "majority opinion of paleontologists." **(B)** is a Misused Detail. The crater is indeed older than 65 million years, but this fact does not support the main idea of the whole passage. **(D)** is Out of Scope; the passage does not discuss a lack of iridium at the impact site.

Passage Analysis: This passage describes how materials used to replace bone in living organisms have been made from muscles. Paragraph 1 explains that replacing bone is much more difficult for surgeons than many other procedures. Paragraph 2 explains that bones are difficult to work with because they cannot be moved or reshaped, and that artificial bones and joints do not last long. Paragraph 3 goes into detail about existing procedures for bone defects, including distraction osteogenesis. Paragraph 4 describes how a protein called osteogenin can cause other human tissues to turn into bone, but it is hard to control because it can turn unintended body parts into bone. Paragraph 5 describes how osteogenin can be more safely used by removing muscle tissue from animals, and that experiments are underway to resolve potential issues before this method can be used on humans.

22. F

Category: Global

Getting to the Answer: Science passages like this one tend to explain new discoveries or theories, so predict an answer such as the following: reasons a method to repair or replace bone is needed, some ways bones are repaired now, or a new method of growing bones from muscle with osteogenin. These match **(F)**, the correct answer. **(E)** may be tempting, but it is incorrect because the passage talks about benefits as well as limitations. **(G)** is too general and brings up a point that is only mentioned in one part of the passage. **(H)** is also too broad; the passage is about bone growth specifically, not all reconstructive surgery.

23. A

Category: Function

Getting to the Answer: Start by locating the information about animal testing in paragraph 5. There, the passage states that "surgeons have made bones from muscles in small animals but have not yet tried the process in humans," and "the safety and effectiveness of the process must first be tested on larger animals." So, scientists do not perform procedures on humans until they are first tried and evaluated in animals. This matches the correct answer, **(A)**. **(B)** and **(C)** are Extreme; the words "assures success" in **(B)** and "all" in **(C)** go beyond what is stated in the text. The passage states that osteogenin has been isolated in cows, but that doesn't mean that it exists *only* in cows. It is possible that the protein may also be found in other animals, so **(D)** is incorrect.

24. H

Category: Function

Getting to the Answer: The pronoun "this" in front of the word "challenge" in paragraph 2 tells you to look back to the previous sentence to find the description of the "challenge." At the end of paragraph 1, the author talks about the difficulty of restructuring and replacing bones, so **(H)** is correct. The author does not mention bone grafting until paragraph 3 and then does not discuss difficulties in matching the bone between donor and recipient; **(E)** is Out of Scope and incorrect. **(F)** is incorrect because the author indicates that it is impossible to reconfigure the shapes of bones. While the author mentions plastic and metal substitutes for bones, there is no discussion of designing better types; **(G)** is incorrect.

25. C

Category: Detail

Getting to the Answer: Return to paragraph 4 and find the phrase given in the question. The sentence starts with a contrast keyword phrase, "Although this may sound peculiar," and then gives a reason why the idea isn't peculiar: different types of tissues all develop from the same tissue in embryos. **(C)** is correct. **(A)** and **(B)** are not related to the reason why making bone from muscle is not a strange idea. **(D)** is a fact describing a way scientists can produce bone, but it is not the reason the author uses to explain why this is not a peculiar idea.

26. F

Category: Detail

Getting to the Answer: The "snag," or difficulty, with osteogenin is mentioned at the start of paragraph 5. The pronoun "this" indicates that the "snag" is defined in the previous sentence: osteogenin is hard to work with; a tiny mistake could turn nearby tissues to bone. The first sentence of paragraph 5 introduces the solution: building the new bones in a different location. **(F)** is correct. All of the incorrect choices, **(E)**, **(G)**, and **(H)**, describe limitations with osteogenin, but not a way to circumvent, or overcome these difficulties.

27. A

Category: Inference

Getting to the Answer: The answer to an Inference question will always be based on information in the passage. The process of growing bone with osteogenin is discussed in paragraph 5, so research the answer there. The second and third sentences say that placing the mold in the animal's abdomen provides a "suitable biologic environment" for growth—in other words, the mold needs to be inside something that is alive. The correct answer is **(A)**. **(B)** is Opposite; it contradicts the passage, which says that thigh muscles are transformed, not abdominal muscles. **(C)** and **(D)** are Misused Details from other parts of the passage; these choices are true but do not address the reason the molds are placed in the animal's abdomen.

28. H

Category: Inference

Getting to the Answer: Paragraph 4 discusses growing bones from muscle using osteogenin. The phrase "this may sound peculiar," is found in the second sentence, introduced by the contrast keyword "although." It is also set up by the first sentence, which uses language such as "most radical approach" and "to create bone substitutes from, of all things, muscle." The author is making it clear that it would be easy to think this approach is strange, when it is in fact very possible. **(H)** is correct. **(E)** and **(G)** are incorrect because the author has not provided any opinions on the benefits or complexities of mending bones artificially. **(F)** is incorrect because the word "shockingly" is Extreme. The passage only indicates that bones have been made for "small animals."

29. C
Category: Global

Getting to the Answer: Consult your Roadmap to identify the topic of paragraph 4: a protein, osteogenin, can turn other human tissue into bone. **(C)** is correct. **(A)** is incorrect because paragraph 5, not paragraph 4, explains how osteogenin can be used safely. Paragraph 1 explains that replacing bone is more difficult than other procedures; **(B)** is incorrect. Finally, **(D)** is incorrect because paragraph 2 indicates that artificial bones and joints do not last long.

Passage Analysis: This passage describes how chain mail was created, how it works, and why it is no longer used. Paragraph 1 explains that chain mail was used by cavalry (horse) troops in the Roman era and again in the fourteenth century. Paragraph 2 describes how it functioned to protect the wearer. Paragraph 3 discusses the difficult and labor-intensive process of making mail. Paragraph 4 explains why mail stopped being used in battle, and paragraph 5 describes the production and uses of mail in modern times.

30. F
Category: Global

Getting to the Answer: The passage begins with a history of chain mail armor, goes on to discuss how it works, how it's made, why people stopped using it, and how it's used today. This matches **(F)**. The incorrect choices, **(E)**, **(G)**, and **(H)**, are Misused Details; they are located in the text but are too narrow to capture the main idea of the entire passage.

31. D
Category: Function

Getting to the Answer: In paragraph 3, the author states that the "master mailler" or armor maker "was able to grow or shrink the metal garment to 'knit' sleeves, mittens, hoods, and other garments." Such an artisan must have been an expert at making chain mail; **(D)** is correct. **(A)** is incorrect because it is not mentioned in the paragraph. There is also no indication that the armor makers were elders or teachers; **(B)** and **(C)** are incorrect.

32. H
Category: Global

Getting to the Answer: Use your Roadmap to identify how paragraph 3 contributes to the main idea of the passage: it describes how difficult and time-consuming it was to make chain mail, so **(H)** is correct. The passage does not contrast the use of chain mail by the wealthy and the lower classes, but simply recounts how this change came about; **(E)** is incorrect. **(F)** describes the role of paragraph 2, not paragraph 3. **(G)** is too general; the text only discusses chain mail, not all "offensive and defensive military technology."

33. D
Category: Inference

Getting to the Answer: The only location in the passage where the "ancient Roman era" is mentioned is in paragraph 1. There, the second sentence tells us that chain mail was "relatively rare and expensive . . . and less practical . . . than the Roman infantryman's segmented steel breastplate." This information matches **(D)**. **(A)** makes an unsupported comparison between Roman and fourteenth-century armor. **(B)** is a Distortion; the passage implies that "improved stabbing and piercing weapons" capable of defeating flexible mail did not come along until after the medieval period, so this could not be the reason that such armor was impractical for Roman troops. **(C)** is also unsupported; some cavalry may have preferred mail armor, but nowhere in the passage do we have evidence that segmented-plate armor was "unsuitable" for cavalry.

34. G
Category: Detail

Getting to the Answer: The decline in the use of chain mail is described in paragraph 4, so reread that paragraph, looking for the reason chain mail stopped working. The third sentence states "as improved stabbing and piercing weapons became more widespread . . . the need for greater protection spurred the development of armors [with] steel plates instead." The correct answer is **(G)**. **(E)** and **(F)** describe the advantages of mail armor, not reasons it became less effective. **(H)** describes how modern maillers produce mail today, not why it became a less effective defense on the battlefield.

35. D

Category: Detail

Getting to the Answer: Paragraph 4 discusses the transition *away* from mail armor, so focus your research on the first part of the paragraph where the expense of chain mail is discussed. The first sentence says only the wealthy owned it, and the second describes how a fallen soldier's suit would be immediately taken. The correct answer is **(D)**. The tedious production process that made mail expensive, and thus valuable, is discussed in paragraph 3, not paragraph 4, so **(A)** is incorrect. **(B)** is evidence that armor was *not* valuable, and **(C)** is Out of Scope.

36. E

Category: Inference

Getting to the Answer: When there are no clues in the question that point to a location in the passage, work through the choices individually, eliminating any that are not supported by the information in the text. **(E)** is correct because it makes a statement that is well supported by the passage. Chain mail was, in fact, "a practical solution to a technological need" during the late medieval era, according to the last sentence in paragraph 1. **(F)** is Extreme; there is not sufficient evidence that a network of skilled craftsmen was always the primary reason for the success of older military technologies. **(G)** is Out of Scope; mail armor was widely available in the fourteenth century, but the passage does not discuss other centuries in comparison. **(H)** is Opposite because it incorrectly describes mail armor as being of "limited usefulness" and thus quickly becoming out-of-date; the passage actually says it was "practical and effective."

Poem Analysis: The poem describes a special railroad repair crew that was called out to do the most important, urgent repairs. The first stanza introduces the narrator and describes the type of repair the crew does. The second stanza describes the start of the flying gang's journey and the excitement generated by the gang's train as it rushes to the repair site. The third stanza continues this theme and emphasizes the importance of the flying gang: even the "fast express" and the "Governor's special" must wait to allow the train carrying the flying gang to pass.

37. B

Category: Global

Getting to the Answer: The first stanza introduces the narrator, who, after long employment with the railroad, is now head of "the flying gang," and goes on to explain what the flying gang is: a "chosen band . . . kept at hand in case of an urgent need." In other words, they are a select group of workers who were reserved so they would be available for important repairs; **(B)** is correct. **(A)** is Out of Scope because the poem doesn't explain how the members of the flying gang were chosen. **(C)** is also Out of Scope because no comparison is made with the work done by other railroad workers. **(D)** is incorrect because the stanza indicates the flying gang would travel in any direction "south or north" as quickly as it could with "utmost speed," but there is no indication that the gang is traveling long distances.

38. E

Category: Function

Getting to the Answer: The stanza describes the flying gang as a select group of workers who were reserved so they would be available for important repairs, and this is supported by wording such as "chosen" and "urgent need"; **(E)** is correct. **(F)** is incorrect because "band" refers to a group of railroad workers, not musicians. **(G)** is incorrect because the lines are a factual description, not a statement of the narrator's intentions. **(H)** is incorrect because the narrator is head of the flying gang after a long period of employment with the railroad, not at the beginning of his career.

39. C

Category: Detail

Getting to the Answer: The first stanza describes the flying gang as a special team of railroad repair experts. Lines 9–10 describe the type of job they would be called for—a broken bridge, a major repair that would prevent any trains from running—and how they would respond with utmost speed. This matches **(C)**. **(A)** and **(B)** are Misused Details because these lines describe the narrator's experience, not the type of work done by the flying gang. **(D)** is incorrect because it describes how the flying gang responds to the call, not the nature of the job they are called to do.

40. H

Category: Global

Getting to the Answer: Throughout the poem, the narrator is conveying the urgent, difficult work of the flying gang. The second stanza describes the flying gang responding to a call for an urgent repair. The vivid description in the first part of the stanza reflects the excitement the fast-moving train creates; the children are happily clapping their hands as they see the train go by, but their "elders," the adults, know the flying gang is on its way to serious, urgent work. This matches **(H)**. **(E)** is incorrect because the beauty of the countryside is not the theme of the poem. **(F)** is incorrect because, while the train is exciting, that excitement is not the focus of the poem. **(G)** is Out of Scope because the preparations of the flying gang are not mentioned in the poem.

41. A

Category: Global

Getting to the Answer: The central theme of the poem is the urgent, important work of the flying gang. The phrases in the question stem are sharp descriptions that emphasize how quickly the flying gang travels to where they are needed, so **(A)** is correct. **(B)** is a Misused Detail because the noise is made by the pilot engine on the trip to where the flying gang will work, not by the flying gang itself. **(C)** is incorrect because the importance of the sounds is the urgency they convey in the poem. **(D)** is a Misused Detail because, while there is an element of contrast between the noisy train and the calmer countryside, the central focus of the poem is the work of the flying gang.

42. H

Category: Detail

Getting to the Answer: The flying gang is heading to urgent, difficult work, but the children only see the exciting, speeding engine. **(H)** is correct. **(E)** is incorrect because these lines describe the sounds the engine makes as it starts, and these sounds have nothing to do with the children. **(F)** is incorrect because it describes the motion of the speeding pilot engine, not the children. **(G)** is incorrect because children clapping their hands at a thrilling sight does not indicate their misunderstanding. It is the following line that makes the misunderstanding clear.

43. D

Category: Inference

Getting to the Answer: The lines are emphasizing the rapid speed of the pilot engine, "the fiery rush," and the distance it's covering, the "grade marks" flying by; **(D)** is correct. The pilot engine could only be moving so quickly if there were no other trains in the vicinity. **(A)** is incorrect because the "rush" being described in those lines is the winter storm blowing through, not the flying gang. **(B)** is incorrect because these lines illustrate the elders' recognition of the hard work ahead, not of the speed at which the train is traveling. **(C)** is incorrect because it is a description of the lovely countryside, not the speed of the train.

44. F

Category: Function

Getting to the Answer: The rhyme and meter make the poem sound like a train, contributing to the theme of the urgency and importance of the work of the flying gang, so **(F)** is correct. **(E)** and **(G)** are Out of Scope; the poem is not describing different stages of the journey in different stanzas, and the stanzas are not describing different aspects of the work of the flying gang. **(H)** is a Misused Detail because, although the poem opens with a first-person narrator, the narrator does not emphasize the dangers faced by the flying gang.

Passage Analysis: This passage describes the history of how the Panama Canal was built. Paragraph 1 describes how de Lesseps tried to build a canal to connect the Pacific and Atlantic Oceans in 1880, but was unable to complete it. Paragraph 2 provides more details about why he quit: landslides and thousands of deaths from diseases. Paragraph 3 explains how the United States decided to complete the canal around a decade later. Paragraph 4 describes the steps the United States took to support Panama in its efforts to separate from Colombia, in order to acquire the rights to the Canal Zone. Paragraph 5 explains how the United States completed the canal, and paragraph 6 describes the return of the Canal to Panama.

45. D

Category: Global

Getting to the Answer: The passage focuses on the history of the Panama Canal in the period before its construction, lists the obstacles that builders faced, and describes its completion. This outline is summarized in (D), the correct answer. (A) is Extreme, and not supported by the text. There is no mention of the Panama Canal as the most important historical event of the period. (B) is also Extreme; the text never describes the Canal as a "failure of the Panamanian revolution." (C) is only mentioned in the last part of paragraph 5 and is, therefore, too narrow.

46. F

Category: Infographic

Getting to the Answer: The map compares the distance of two trade routes between New York City and San Francisco, with the one through the Panama Canal significantly shorter than the one around South America. The main idea of the passage is the history of building the Panama Canal, with paragraph 1 indicating that the reason behind building the canal was to shorten the voyage between the coasts of the Americas. Predict that the infographic shows how much shorter the voyage is through the Panama Canal rather than around South America; the best match is (F). Because the map does not address Nicaragua at all, (E) is Out of Scope. Though (G) is true, the topic of the passage is not developed by "revealing" this fact. (H) is a Distortion because the Panama Canal was built despite the obstacles; it is not a plan for the future as indicated in this choice.

47. D

Category: Detail

Getting to the Answer: Paragraph 1 claims that de Lesseps faced environmental and logistical problems in building the canal, so the correct answer is (D). No political problems are discussed in connection with de Lesseps, which eliminates (A), and no mention is made of financial problems inhibiting the construction of de Lesseps's canal, which eliminates (B). The Colombian government's resistance was a factor the United States, not de Lesseps, had to overcome; (C) is also incorrect.

48. E

Category: Detail

Getting to the Answer: The question asks about American involvement; in paragraph 3, the United States is deciding between the sites in Nicaragua and Panama. The second sentence says the United States was considering Nicaragua, but experts believed Panama was the better choice. The fourth sentence states that the Nicaraguan site was less expensive. The correct answer will reflect one of these ideas, and (E) is correct. (F) is Opposite; experts recommended Panama, not Nicaragua. (G) is Out of Scope; the passage never reveals that a Nicaraguan canal was nearly completed. (H) is incorrect because paragraph 1 identifies Panama as the location of the shortest span of distance between the two oceans.

49. A

Category: Infographic

Getting to the Answer: Paragraph 1 describes why and how de Lesseps tried to build a canal across the Isthmus of Panama and failed. The infographic compares voyage times from the U.S. Gulf coast to other countries using the Panama canal versus other routes; the Panama Canal takes less or equal time on average in most cases, which supports the idea in the paragraph that the reason behind building a canal would be to cut travel time. (A) is correct. (B) is Opposite of the data in the graph and is incorrect. (C) is a Misused Detail; though it is true according to the data in the graph, it does not support the idea that the Panama Canal cuts down on travel time. Because there is no support in either the passage or the graphic that the leaders of the United States were inspired by de Lesseps, (D) is Out of Scope.

50. H

Category: Inference

Getting to the Answer: Because this question does not provide any clues to the location of the correct answer in the passage, match each choice to the information in the passage and immediately eliminate any choice that is not supported. The United States did spend "nearly half a billion dollars" to build the canal, but the passage does not indicate how this cost compared to the expected cost, so eliminate (E). Diseases are described in the last paragraph as being one of the obstacles that the United States overcame in the project, so **(F)** is also incorrect. **(G)** is incorrect because no mention is made of how de Lesseps felt about the United States' control over the canal. **(H)** is the only choice remaining, so it must be correct. Paragraph 6 supports the inference, because the author describes the start of U.S. involvement as a "devious inception," and Panamanians later rioted and pressured the United States to return the Canal Zone.

51. D

Category: Global

Getting to the Answer: Paragraph 5 describes the steps taken by the United States to successfully complete the Panama Canal. The sentence the question is asking about recognizes that many of the problems faced by de Lesseps also had to be overcome by the United States, but that the canal was completed. **(D)** is correct. **(A)** is incorrect because the text never compares the efforts of de Lesseps and the United States. **(B)** is incorrect because the passage has a neutral tone; the author does not criticize. Similarly, **(C)** is incorrect because the author never compares the cost of the canal with its benefits.

Passage Analysis: The excerpt begins shortly after a visit to Holmes by the distraught daughter of Dr. Grimesby Roylott. Paragraph 1 introduces Dr. Roylott, a large and threatening man who bursts into the room. Paragraphs 2 through 9 follow the prickly introductory conversation between Holmes and Roylott. The confrontation continues in paragraphs 10–15 with a furious Roylott calling Holmes every name he can think of, which merely amuses Holmes. Paragraph 16 describes how Roylott threatens Holmes with violence by bending a poker. In paragraph 17, Roylott warns Holmes to stay away. Paragraph 18 describes Holmes's amused reaction to Roylott and reveals Holmes's equal ability to bend an iron poker. Paragraph 19 features Holmes's opinion of the encounter with Roylott. Paragraph 20 describes Holmes's return from his visit to Doctors' Commons. Paragraph 21 explains the details of the wife's will and Holmes's plans to go to Waterloo.

52. F

Category: Global

Getting to the Answer: The exchange in paragraph 9 illustrates how Holmes maintains his calm in the face of being verbally threatened by Dr. Roylott; **(F)** is correct. Although Holmes is using wit to dismiss Dr. Roylott, that approach is not returned. Dr. Roylott shouts at Holmes. So, **(E)** is incorrect. That Holmes is discussing the weather and its effects on gardening is unimportant. Content aside, he is trying to dismiss Dr. Roylott's angry threats by treating this as an ordinary, everyday conversation; **(G)** is incorrect. Dr. Roylott's anger is not discussed in paragraph 9. The reaction of Holmes to that anger is touched upon, making **(H)** incorrect.

53. A

Category: Inference

Getting to the Answer: In response to learning that his stepdaughter has met with a famous detective, Dr. Roylott attempts to intimidate Holmes and then briefly tries to learn what his stepdaughter said to him; **(A)** is correct. While Dr. Roylott does burst into the room, he merely threatens Holmes and Dr. Watson. He does not physically attack them; **(B)** is incorrect. While Dr. Roylott attempts to learn what his stepdaughter has said to Holmes, Roylott does not deny anything; **(C)** is incorrect. Although he threatens Holmes if the detective does not stop his investigation, Dr. Roylott does not threaten his stepdaughter's life; **(D)** is incorrect.

54. F

Category: Function

Getting to the Answer: In paragraph 10, words like "scoundrel" and "meddler" underline that Dr. Roylott knows that Holmes could unearth the wrongs he has committed toward his stepdaughter. Thus, **(F)** is correct. While Dr. Roylott is violent, he is not totally unhinged. He does not physically attack Holmes or Dr. Watson, he merely threatens to do so; **(E)** is incorrect. Although Dr. Roylott is not taking care to come across as an innocent party, that is not how words like "scoundrel" and "meddler" contribute to the meaning of the excerpt. Instead, they reveal to the reader that Dr. Roylott has knowledge of Holmes's professional background; **(G)** is incorrect. **(H)** is Extreme; it is not clear that Dr. Roylott knows exactly who Holmes is.

55. C

Category: Function

Getting to the Answer: The various insults show that Dr. Roylott is trying and failing to make Holmes afraid of him. Despite Dr. Roylott's repeated hounding, Holmes projects a calm face. Thus, **(C)** is correct. There is no evidence that Dr. Roylott insults every man that he meets. Indeed, his argument with Holmes is rooted in the fact that his stepdaughter has been speaking with Holmes; **(A)** is incorrect. Holmes keeps his calm regardless of what Dr. Roylott says or does; **(B)** and **(D)** are incorrect.

56. H

Category: Global

Getting to the Answer: In terms of the excerpt's structure, paragraph 17 serves to indicate that the conversation between Holmes and Dr. Roylott has ended; **(H)** is correct. The passage is told entirely from the perspective of Dr. Watson; **(E)** is incorrect. There is nothing to suggest that Dr. Roylott and his stepdaughter are working together; **(F)** is incorrect. Although paragraph 17 has Dr. Roylott twist the fireplace poker, this section itself does not provide the practical explanation for why Holmes is not afraid of Dr. Roylott; **(G)** is incorrect. That comes in the next paragraph, when Holmes picks up the solid metal poker and straightens it out.

57. D

Category: Detail

Getting to the Answer: Holmes revealing that "my grip was not much more feeble than his own" (paragraph 18) shows that he and Dr. Roylott would bring equal levels of physical strength to any fight. Thus, **(D)** is correct. While Holmes keeps a calm face when dealing with Dr. Roylott, the reader does not know if Holmes is merely bluffing until he unbends the poker. Since **(A)** and **(B)** occur before Holmes unbends the poker, they are incorrect. Likewise, "He seems a very amiable person" could be another instance of Holmes keeping his calm. It is only after that point that he picks up the twisted poker and unbends it. So, **(C)** is incorrect.

Part 2—Mathematics

58. 10

Subject: Statistics and Probability

Getting to the Answer: Create an organized list of the possible pairs. Use the first letters of the friends' names: C, D, E, F, and G. Keep in mind that the order doesn't matter—Connie and Dale are the same pair as Dale and Connie.

CD, CE, CF, CG

DE, DF, DG

EF, EG

FG

There are a total of 10 possible pairs of friends that Alicia can choose.

59. 5

Subject: Algebra

Getting to the Answer: As with any proportion, cross multiply and isolate the variable:

$$\frac{3m}{5} = \frac{12}{4}$$
$$12m = 60$$
$$m = 5$$

60. 6.49

Subject: Arithmetic

Getting to the Answer: Set up an expression to find the total cost of Sidney's salad: cost of first 8 ounces plus $0.25 times remaining ounces. Next, fill in the missing amounts. The first 8 ounces cost $2.49 and there are 16 ounces in 1 pound, so the total cost is $2.49 + $0.25(16) = $2.49 + $4 = $6.49.

61. 46

Subject: Algebra

Getting to the Answer: Start by substituting 28 for x. This gives the equation $56 + 3y = 194$. From there, solve the equation for y by subtracting 56 from both sides and dividing by 3:

$$56 + 3y = 194$$
$$3y = 138$$
$$y = 46$$

62. 9

Subject: Geometry

Getting to the Answer: Scale drawing questions almost always involve proportions. Here, let x be the missing side of the actual window. Set up a proportion:

$$\frac{x \text{ ft}}{12 \text{ in.}} = \frac{6 \text{ ft}}{8 \text{ in.}}$$
$$8x = 6 \times 12$$
$$8x = 72$$
$$x = 72 \div 8 = 9$$

63. C

Subject: Statistics and Probability

Getting to the Answer: Because 5.5 is half of 11, all the fractions with numerators that are less than 5.5 will have a value that is less than $\frac{1}{2}$. In the list of six numbers provided, there are four of these $\left(\frac{2}{11}, \frac{3}{11}, \frac{4}{11}, \text{and } \frac{5}{11}\right)$. So, the probability that the number Deena chooses is less than $\frac{1}{2}$ is $\frac{4}{6}$, which simplifies to $\frac{2}{3}$.

64. H

Subject: Arithmetic

Getting to the Answer: The circle graph shows that, of the 600 graduates, 12% chose to enter the workforce, and 22% chose to go to vocational school. $12\% + 22\% = 34\%$. 34% of 600 is $\frac{34}{100} \times 600 = 204$, so 204 graduates chose to enter the workforce or go to vocational school.

65. D

Subject: Algebra

Getting to the Answer: You want the value of x. Begin by distributing the 2 over the terms inside the parentheses on the left side of the equation. This gives you $2x + 2y = 8 + 2y$. Subtracting $2y$ from both sides results in $2x = 8$. Dividing both sides by 2 gives you $x = 4$.

66. E

Subject: Geometry

Getting to the Answer: Since point A is at 1 on the number line and point C is at 7, the distance between them is $7 - 1$, or 6 units. Half the distance from A to C is half of 6, or 3, and 3 units from either point A or point C is 4. Therefore, the midpoint of AC is at 4. Point B is at 3, so it is 1 unit from the midpoint of AC.

67. B

Subject: Arithmetic

Getting to the Answer: The machine caps 5 bottles every 2 seconds, and you want to know how many bottles it can cap in 1 minute, or 60 seconds. Dividing 60 seconds by 2 seconds gives you 30, which means that there are 30 of these 5-bottle cycles every minute. If the machine caps 5 bottles in 2 seconds, how many bottles does it cap in 30×2 seconds? Multiply by the same factor of 30 to get $30 \times 5 = 150$ bottles.

68. H

Subject: Algebra

Getting to the Answer: For questions involving percents, you can use the formula Percent $\times$ Whole = Part. The bar graph shows the sales for each month of the second quarter, consisting of April, May, and June. The title on the vertical axis is "Sales (in millions of dollars)," so that's what the heights of the bars represent: $40 million in sales for April, $10 million for May, and $30 million for June. The total sales for the 2nd quarter were $40 + 10 + 30 = 80$ million dollars. Thus, the total, or $80 million, is the whole and the $40 million in April is the part. The formula Percent $\times$ Whole = Part results in Percent $\times 80 = 40$, or Percent $= \frac{40}{80} = \frac{1}{2} = 50\%$.

69. A

Subject: Algebra

Getting to the Answer: The easiest way to do this problem is to use Backsolving. Since each pair of numbers in the answer choices represents possible values of a and b, just add up each a and b to see if $a + b < 5$, and subtract each b from each a to see if $a - b > 6$. If you do this, you'll find that in all four options, $a + b < 5$, but in only 1 option, **(A)**, is $a - b > 6$. In **(A)**, $a + b = 4 + (-3) = 1$ and $a - b = 4 - (-3) = 7$. Therefore, this is the correct answer.

If you think about the properties of negative and positive numbers (drawing a number line can help), you'll probably realize that the only way $a - b$ could be larger than $a + b$ is if b is a negative number, but that would only eliminate **(D)**. In some problems, your knowledge of math only helps you a little bit. In those cases, use the answer choices to solve the problem.

70. E

Subject: Geometry

Getting to the Answer: In the figure, $\angle ABC$ is labeled $(2x - 4)°$, and in the question stem, you're told that $\angle ABC$ measures 60°. So, $2x - 4 = 60$, which leads to $2x = 64$ and $x = 32$. That means that $\angle BAC$, which is labeled $(3x)°$, must measure 3×32, or 96°. Since the measures of the angles of a triangle must add up to 180°, $60° + 96° + y° = 180°$, and $y = 24$.

71. B

Subject: Algebra

Getting to the Answer: Think about the units for each variable. There are 10 floors, R rooms per floor, and C chairs per room. If you multiply 10 floors $\times$ R rooms/floor, the unit "floors" will cancel out, leaving you with $10R$ rooms, and if you multiply $10R$ rooms $\times$ C chairs/room, the unit "rooms" will cancel out, leaving $10RC$ chairs in the building. This matches **(B)**.

Alternatively, you could pick numbers for C and R. Suppose R is 2. Then there would be 2 rooms on each floor, and since there are 10 floors in the building, there would be 2×10 or 20 rooms altogether. If $C = 3$, then there are 3 chairs in each room. Since there are 20 rooms and 3 chairs per room, there are $20 \times 3 = 60$ chairs altogether. Which answer choices equal 60 when R is 2 and C is 3? Only $10RC$, which is again **(B)**.

72. G

Subject: Statistics and Probability

Getting to the Answer: The mean of a set of values is the sum of the values divided by the number of values. In this question, you already know the mean (16) of the original 10 values, so you can find the sum of those values by multiplying.

mean = sum ÷ number of values

sum = mean × number of values

sum = $16 \times 10 = 160$

If 7 and 13 are removed from the set of numbers, the new sum is $160 - 20 = 140$. Find the mean of the remaining 8 numbers by dividing:

$140 \div 8 = 17.5$

73. D

Subject: Algebra

Getting to the Answer: You're given 4% of a number and you have to find 20% of that same number. 4% of r is just a certain fraction, $\frac{4}{100}$ to be exact, times r, and 20% of r is just $\frac{20}{100} \times r$. That means that 20% of r is 5 times as great as 4% of r, since $\frac{4}{100} \times 5$ is $\frac{20}{100}$. Since 4% of r is 6.2, then 20% of r must be 5×6.2, or 31, **(D)**. You could also have figured out the value of r and then found 20% of that value, but this takes a bit longer.

74. F

Subject: Arithmetic

Getting to the Answer: The ratio of teachers to students is 1 to 10, so there might be only 1 teacher and 10 students, or there might be 50 teachers and 500 students, or just about any number of teachers and students that are in the ratio 1 to 10. That means that the teachers and the students can be divided into groups of 11: one teacher and 10 students in each group. So, the total number of teachers and students in the school must be a multiple of 11. If you look at the answer choices, you'll notice that 121 is the only multiple of 11, so **(F)** must be correct.

75. D

Subject: Geometry

Getting to the Answer: Because the distance between each pair of adjacent points is the same, each of the 7 segments $\overline{AB}$, $\overline{BC}$, $\overline{CD}$, $\overline{DE}$, $\overline{EF}$, $\overline{FG}$, and $\overline{GH}$ has the same length. These 7 segments make up segment $\overline{AH}$. Since the length of $\overline{AH}$ is 56, the length of each of the 7 small segments is $56 \div 7$, or 8. The distance between points B and E is the sum of the lengths of the 3 equal segments $\overline{BC}$, $\overline{CD}$, and $\overline{DE}$, so the distance between points B and E is 3×8, or 24.

76. G

Subject: Geometry

Getting to the Answer: A decagon has 10 sides. Here, two of the side lengths are given, so 8 sides remain. Let s be the length of one of the 8 remaining sides. Set up an equation and solve for s:

$$36 + 44 + 8s = 160$$
$$80 + 8s = 160$$
$$8s = 80$$
$$s = 80 \div 8 = 10$$

77. B

Subject: Algebra

Getting to the Answer: When a question involves two consecutive integers, let the smaller integer be x and the larger be $x + 1$. Here, start by using the given sum (-9) to find the two integers, then worry about all the other details.

$$x + (x + 1) = -9$$
$$2x + 1 = -9$$
$$2x = -10$$
$$x = -5$$

Remember, the variable x represents the smaller integer, so the two integers are -5 and -4. Now, work out the rest of the information.

If the smaller integer (-5) is doubled, then that integer becomes $2(-5) = -10$. If 3 is added to the larger integer (-4), then that integer becomes $-4 + 3 = -1$. The sum of the two new integers is $-10 + (-1) = -11$.

78. G

Subject: Arithmetic

Getting to the Answer: The first step to solving this problem is getting both ratios into a form that has the same value for a. If $a{:}b = 4{:}5$ and $a{:}c = 2{:}7$, you can make both values of a equal 4 by multiplying the entire $a{:}c$ ratio by 2. The new form of the ratio becomes 4:14. Now, you can compare b and c. Be careful, however, because the question asks for $c{:}b$, not the other way around. If $a{:}c = 4{:}14$, then $c{:}a = 14{:}4$. Since $a{:}b = 4{:}5$, the ratio $c{:}b$ is therefore 14:5.

79. C

Subject: Algebra

Getting to the Answer: Substitute 15 for each k in the expression and use the order of operations to simplify.

$$[4(15) + 30] - [2(15) + 15]$$
$$= [60 + 30] - [30 - 15]$$
$$= 90 - 45$$
$$= 45$$

80. G

Subject: Statistics and Probability

Getting to the Answer: The median of a set of values is the middle number when the values are arranged from least to greatest. There are 15 prices in the table, so the middle value will be the 8th one. If you think logically, you don't need to list all the values. The first 7 prices in the table are either $60 or $68. That means the 8th value will be the next price, which is $75.

81. B

Subject: Algebra

Getting to the Answer: Scale drawing questions usually involve setting up a proportion. Let d represent the distance, in miles, between the library and the water tower. Set up a proportion and cross multiply to solve for d:

$$\frac{d \text{ miles}}{7 \text{ inches}} = \frac{5 \text{ miles}}{3 \text{ inches}}$$
$$3d = 35$$
$$d = \frac{35}{3} = 11\frac{2}{3} \approx 12$$

82. G

Subject: Arithmetic

Getting to the Answer: 8:00 p.m. is 6 hours after 2:00 p.m. Find the number of degrees the temperature dropped in 6 hours: $6 \times 7° = 42°$. Subtract that from the starting point (40°) to get $40° - 42° = -2°$.

83. C

Subject: Algebra

Getting to the Answer: Use inverse properties to solve for x. The inverse of subtracting 5 is adding 5, so start by adding 5 to both sides of the equation.

$$3x - 5 = y$$
$$3x = y + 5$$

The inverse of multiplying by 3 is dividing by 3, so divide both sides of the equation by 3.

$$3x = y + 5$$
$$\frac{3x}{3} = \frac{y+5}{3}$$
$$x = \frac{y+5}{3}$$

84. H

Subject: Statistics and Probability

Getting to the Answer: Use the formula for finding the mean:

$$\text{Average Score} = \frac{\text{Sum of Scores}}{\text{Number of Quizzes}}$$

If Jung wishes to get an average score of 80 on 3 quizzes, then $80 = \frac{\text{Sum of Scores}}{3}$ and Sum of Scores $= 80 \times 3 = 240$.

So, he needs to score a total of 240 points on all 3 quizzes. Since he had an average score of 70 on the first 2 quizzes, $70 = \frac{\text{Sum of Scores on 2 Quizzes}}{2}$. Thus, Sum of Scores on 2 Quizzes $= 70 \times 2 = 140$. If he scored a total of 140 points on the first 2 quizzes, and he needs to score a total of 240 points on all 3 quizzes, then he must score $240 - 140 = 100$ points on the third quiz.

85. C

Subject: Arithmetic

Getting to the Answer: To convert a decimal to a percent, move the decimal 2 places to the right (multiply by 100) and add the percent sign. Here, 0.0201 is equal to 2.01%, and the answer choice closest to that value is 2%.

86. F

Subject: Algebra

Getting to the Answer: Substitute the values into the expression and simplify.

$$\frac{4(300) - 150}{100}$$
$$= \frac{1,200 - 150}{100}$$
$$= \frac{1,050}{100}$$
$$= 10.5$$

87. C

Subject: Algebra

Getting to the Answer: Substitute 2 for x in both denominators; substitute 3 for y, 4 for z, and then simplify the result.

$$\left(\frac{4y}{2x}\right)\left(\frac{9z}{3x}\right) = \left[\frac{(4)(3)}{(2)(2)}\right]\left[\frac{(9)(4)}{(3)(2)}\right]$$
$$= \left[\frac{12}{4}\right]\left[\frac{36}{6}\right]$$
$$= [3][6]$$
$$= 18$$

88. G

Subject: Arithmetic

Getting to the Answer: List the factors of 120: 1 and 120, 2 and 60, 3 and 40, 4 and 30, 5 and 24, 6 and 20, 8 and 15, and 10 and 12. There are 4 factors greater than 20 and less than 120. Note that you don't include 20 and 120 because they are equal to the two given numbers, not greater or less.

89. D

Subject: Geometry

Getting to the Answer: The formula for finding the volume of a cube is $V = s^3$, where V is the volume of the cube and s is the side length of the cube. If the volume of the cube is 27, its sides must be of length 3, since $3^3 = 27$. There are 6 faces of equal area on a cube, so the surface area equals 6 times the area of a single face. If each face has a length of 3, then each of the 6 faces of the cube has an area of 3 times 3, or 9. The total surface area would be 6 times the area of one face: $6 \times 9 = 54$.

90. G

Subject: Arithmetic

Getting to the Answer: For this question, you have to know not only how to read graphs, but also how to find a percent decrease. The bar above 2016 reaches to 5 on the graph, and the graph is in units of 100,000, so the population in 2016 was 500,000. The population in 2018 was 400,000. To find the percent decrease in population, divide the amount of decrease by the original amount and then multiply by 100%.

$$\left(\frac{500,000 - 400,000}{500,000} \right) \times 100\% = \frac{100,000}{500,000} \times 100\%$$
$$= \frac{1}{5} \times 100\% = 20\%$$

If the percent decrease in population from 2018 to 2020 is the same as the percent decrease from 2016 to 2018, then from 2018 to 2020, the population should also decrease by 20%. 20% of the 2018 population is 20% of 400,000, or 80,000, so the 2020 population should be $400,000 - 80,000 = 320,000$.

91. D

Subject: Algebra

Getting to the Answer: If x is an even number, then the previous two even numbers are $(x - 2)$ and $(x - 4)$.

Add the three expressions by combining like terms.

$$x + (x - 2) + (x - 4) = x + x + x - 2 - 4$$
$$= 3x - 6$$

You could also pick numbers to solve a problem like this. Choose an even number, like 10, for x. The previous two even numbers less than 10 are 8 and 6. The sum of the three even numbers is $10 + 8 + 6 = 24$. The only expression that equals 24 when x is 10 is $3(10) - 6$, which is **(D)**.

92. G

Subject: Arithmetic

Getting to the Answer: Find the difference in the times by subtracting the decimal numbers. Then, convert the result to a fraction.

$$33.24 - 33.09 = 0.15$$

Now, read the decimal: 0.15 is 15 hundredths, so write 15 over 100 and simplify:

$$\frac{15}{100} = \frac{3}{20}$$

93. B

Subject: Algebra

Getting to the Answer: Solve the inequality for x. To do this, subtract 100 from both sides of the inequality and then divide both sides by 4.

$$4x + 100 \geq 20$$
$$4x \geq -80$$
$$x \geq -20$$

Don't answer too quickly—the answer isn't 19 or 20. List the negative **odd** numbers that are greater than or equal to -20. The set includes $-19, -17, -15, -13, -11, -9, -7, -5, -3,$ and -1. There are 10 of them.

94. E

Subject: Geometry

Getting to the Answer: The angle marked 102 degrees is vertical to the interior angle of the triangle at the top. Vertical angles have equal measures, so the interior angle at the top of the triangle has a measure of 102 degrees. The sum of the interior angles of a triangle is 180 degrees, so $b + 2b + 102 = 180$. Solve this equation for b.

$$b + 2b + 102 = 180$$
$$3b + 102 = 180$$
$$3b = 78$$
$$b = 26$$

95. A

Subject: Arithmetic

Getting to the Answer: When working with multiples of numbers over a large range, it's not efficient to list all the multiples, so look for a pattern instead. Start by listing the first several multiples of 10:

10, 20, **30**, 40, 50, **60**, 70, 80, **90**, . . .

Every third multiple (i.e., 30, 60, 90, . . .) is also a multiple of 15. This means that $\frac{1}{3}$ of the multiples of 10 are also multiples of 15. More importantly, $1 - \frac{1}{3} = \frac{2}{3}$ of the multiples of 10 are **not** multiples of 15.

Now, calculate the total number of multiples of 10 that are in the given set of numbers. The last multiple of 10 would be 300, so there are a total of $300 \div 10 = 30$ multiples of 10. Because $\frac{2}{3}$ of those are not multiples of 15, the answer is $\frac{2}{3} \times 30 = 20$.

96. F

Subject: Statistics and Probability

Getting to the Answer: The total number of cards in the box is $7 + 6 + 5 + 8 + 4 = 30$. Set up a proportion to determine which card has exactly a 1 in 5 chance of being picked at random.

$$\frac{x}{30} = \frac{1}{5} \rightarrow 5x = 30 \rightarrow x = 6$$

There are six E cards, so the E has a 1 in 5 chance of being randomly selected.

97. C

Subject: Arithmetic

Getting to the Answer: The greatest allowable thickness is the desired thickness plus the amount of the allowable error. Start by finding 2% of 0.4. Write the percent as a decimal.

$$0.4 \times 0.02 = 0.008$$

Now, add the amount of the allowable error to the desired thickness: $0.4 + 0.008 = 0.408$ centimeters.

98. E

Subject: Geometry

Getting to the Answer: $\angle$PNM is supplementary to $\angle$PNQ, so $m\angle$PNM $+ 105° = 180°$, and $m\angle$PNM $= 75°$. Since $\overline{PM} = \overline{PN}$, triangle MPN is isosceles and $m\angle$PMN $= m\angle$PNM $= 75°$. The interior angles of a triangle sum to 180°, so $75 + 75 + x = 180$, and $x = 30$.

99. D

Subject: Arithmetic

Getting to the Answer: The total number of people who participated in the race was $2 + 7 + 18 + 473 = 500$. The total number who finished the race in 12 minutes or less was $2 + 7 + 18 = 27$.

$$\frac{27}{500} = \frac{54}{1,000} = 0.054 = 5.4\%$$

100. E

Subject: Probability and Statistics

Getting to the Answer: Since Erin does not replace the coins, you must pay careful attention to the numbers of coins each time she chooses a coin. The total number of quarters in the box to start is $6 + 4 + 2 + 3 = 15$. The number of quarters that are **not** from New York is $4 + 2 + 3 = 9$.

The probability that the first quarter is not from New York is $\frac{9}{15}$, or $\frac{3}{5}$. Now, out of the 14 remaining quarters, there are 8 quarters left that are not from New York. The probability that the second quarter is not from New York is $\frac{8}{14}$, or $\frac{4}{7}$. Multiply these two probabilities to find the probability that both coins are not from New York:

$$\frac{3}{5} \times \frac{4}{7} = \frac{12}{35}$$

101. C

Subject: Arithmetic

Getting to the Answer: If you remember your exponent rules, this question is not as complex as it looks. Remember—any non-zero number raised to the 0 power is 1, and any number squared is just that number multiplied by itself.

$$(-1)^0 + 0^2 + (-1)^2 + \left(\frac{1}{2}\right)^2$$

$$= 1 + (0 \times 0) + (-1 \times -1) + \left(\frac{1}{2} \times \frac{1}{2}\right)$$

$$= 1 + 0 + 1 + \frac{1}{4}$$

$$= 2\frac{1}{4} = 2.25$$

102. H

Subject: Algebra

Getting to the Answer: Mixture problems can be very tricky. The important thing to look for in a mixture problem is which quantities stay the same and which quantities change. Here, the water is evaporating but the sand is not. Therefore, the quantity of sand will be unchanged. Start with 4 ounces of sand and 16 ounces of water, and end with 4 ounces of sand and an unknown quantity of water, which you can call w ounces. The final quantities of sand and water are to be in the ratio of 2 to 3. That means that the ratio of 4 to w is equal to the ratio of 2 to 3, or $\frac{4}{w} = \frac{2}{3}$, which is an algebraic equation that can be solved by cross multiplying:

$$4 \times 3 = 2 \times w$$
$$12 = 2w$$
$$6 = w$$

If there are 6 ounces of water left after starting with 16 ounces, then $16 - 6 = 10$ ounces must have evaporated.

103. B

Subject: Algebra

Getting to the Answer: Use algebra to find the solution to this problem. You'll need to solve and substitute several times, so take it one step at time. First, find the numerical values for b and c. Since $2b = 7$, divide both sides of the equation by 2 and you get $b = \frac{7}{2}$. Do the same thing with $3c = 7$, giving you $c = \frac{7}{3}$. Now, substitute these values into the first equation:

$$x\left(\frac{7}{2} - \frac{7}{3}\right) = y + x$$

Now, solve for $\frac{y}{x}$. Start by subtracting x from both sides of the equation. Then, you'll need to find a common denominator for all the x-terms:

$$x\left(\frac{7}{2} - \frac{7}{3}\right) - x = y$$
$$x\left(\frac{7}{2} - \frac{7}{3} - 1\right) = y$$
$$x\left(\frac{21}{6} - \frac{14}{6} - \frac{6}{6}\right) = y$$
$$x\left(\frac{1}{6}\right) = y$$
$$\frac{1}{6} = \frac{y}{x}$$

104. F

Subject: Geometry

Getting to the Answer: If a rectangle has a perimeter of 12, then $2(w + \ell) = 12$, where w is the width of the rectangle and ℓ is its length. If $2(w + \ell) = 12$, then $w + \ell = 6$. If the width is 2 less than the length, then $w = \ell - 2$. You can plug $\ell - 2$ for w into the equation $w + \ell = 6$, so $w + \ell = 6$ becomes $(\ell - 2) + \ell = 6$, and so $2\ell - 2 = 6$, $2\ell = 8$, and $\ell = 4$ inches. If the length is 4 inches, then the width, which is 2 inches less, must be 2 inches. The area of a rectangle with length 4 inches and width 2 inches is $4 \times 2 = 8$ square inches.

105. C

Subject: Arithmetic

Getting to the Answer: Convert the units by setting up ratios of known measures. Start with the given speed, 5 feet per second, and the given conversion, 1 foot = 0.3 meters. Then fill in the ratios needed to convert seconds to hours.

$$\frac{5 \text{ ft}}{1 \text{ sec}} \times \frac{0.3 \text{ meters}}{1 \text{ ft}} \times \frac{60 \text{ sec}}{1 \text{ min}} \times \frac{60 \text{ min}}{1 \text{ hr}}$$

$$= \frac{5 \cancel{\text{ ft}}}{1 \text{ sec}} \times \frac{0.3 \text{ meters}}{1 \cancel{\text{ ft}}} \times \frac{60 \cancel{\text{ sec}}}{1 \cancel{\text{ min}}} \times \frac{60 \cancel{\text{ min}}}{1 \text{ hr}}$$

$$= \frac{5,400 \text{ meters}}{1 \text{ hr}}$$

106. H

Subject: Arithmetic

Getting to the Answer: The multiples of 3 are the integers 3, 6, 9, 12. . . It is useful to think of the multiples of 3 this way: $1 \times 3, 2 \times 3, 3 \times 3, 4 \times 3. . .$

A is the sum of the first 50 multiples of 3. The first 50 multiples of 3 are $1 \times 3, 2 \times 3, 3 \times 3, 4 \times 3, . . . , 48 \times 3$, 49×3, and 50×3. If you factor out $1 + 2 + 3 + . . . + 50$, you can see that $A = (1 + 2 + 3 + . . . + 50) \times 3$.

Because B is the sum of the first 50 multiples of 6, $B = 1 \times 6 + 2 \times 6 + 3 \times 6 + . . . + 50 \times 6 = (1 + 2 + 3 + . . . + 50) \times 6$.

If you call the sum of *all* the first 50 positive integers Y, then $A = 3Y$ and $B = 6Y$. Now, think logically: B is twice A because $6Y = 2 \times 3Y$, which means that B is 200% of A.

107. B

Subject: Arithmetic

Getting to the Answer: Whenever you have a percent problem that doesn't give you a definite amount and asks you a question like "What fraction of the total . . . ?" you should pick a number for the total. Since you're dealing with percents here and will be converting the percents to fractions, a good number for the total is 100. So, say that 100 people were polled. 80% of the 100 people were registered voters, so 80 people were registered voters. 75% of the registered voters voted in the last election, so 75% × 80, or 60 people, voted in the last election. If 60 of the 80 registered voters actually voted in the last election, then 80 − 60 = 20 of the registered voters did **not** vote in the last election. The fraction of

the people surveyed who were registered but did not vote is $\frac{20}{100}$, or $\frac{1}{5}$.

108. F

Subject: Algebra

Getting to the Answer: First, find the values of m and p since they are given in terms of ℓ and you know that $\ell = 24$.

$m = 2\ell + 2 = 2(24) + 2 = 48 + 2 = 50$

$p = \ell - 14 = 24 - 14 = 10$

Next, notice that you can simplify the original expression by canceling the l in the numerator and denominator of the first term. After doing this, substitute the values of l, m, and p. Then simplify.

$$\left(\frac{lm}{lp}\right) + l = \left(\frac{m}{p}\right) + l$$

$$= \left(\frac{50}{10}\right) + 24$$

$$= 5 + 24 = 29$$

109. C

Subject: Geometry

Getting to the Answer: The area of a circle with radius r is πr^2. The area of the large circle is 900π. So, $\pi r^2 = 900\pi$. Then $r^2 = 900$, and $r = 30$. The radius of the large circle is 30. So, the diameter of the large circle is 2×30, or 60. The diameters of the three identical small circles make up the diameter of the large circle, so the diameter of each small circle is one-third of 60, or 20. The circumference of a circle is π times the diameter, so the circumference of the small circle with center C is π times 20, or 20π.

110. H

Subject: Algebra

Getting to the Answer: First, substitute the given expressions for *x* and *y*. Be sure to enclose the expression for *y* in parentheses since it is a quantity. Then, rewrite all three fractions over the same denominator, 12, and follow the order of operations to simplify.

$$x - y = \frac{1}{4} - \left(\frac{1}{2} - \frac{1}{3}\right)$$
$$= \left(\frac{3}{3}\right)\frac{1}{4} - \left[\left(\frac{6}{6}\right)\frac{1}{2} - \left(\frac{4}{4}\right)\frac{1}{3}\right]$$
$$= \frac{3}{12} - \left(\frac{6}{12} - \frac{4}{12}\right)$$
$$= \frac{3}{12} - \left(\frac{2}{12}\right)$$
$$= \frac{1}{12}$$

111. D

Subject: Algebra

Getting to the Answer: Because there are two numbers under the bar in both terms, you can add them just as you do regular decimal numbers. Then, convert the result to a fraction.

$$2.\overline{56} + 1.\overline{32} = 3.\overline{88} = 3.\overline{8}$$

To write this repeating decimal as a fraction, set *x* equal to the repeating decimal, multiply both sides of your equation by 10, then subtract the original equation from the multiplied equation. This will eliminate the repeating part.

$$x = 3.8888\ldots$$
$$10x = 38.8888\ldots$$
$$10x - x = 38.8888\ldots - 3.8888\ldots$$
$$9x = 35$$
$$x = \frac{35}{9}$$

112. E

Subject: Geometry

Getting to the Answer: When finding the area of a shaded region, think about whether you can subtract something from a larger region whose area is easier to calculate.

First, find the area of the rectangle in the graph: $4 \times 6 = 24$.

Then, find the area of each of the two right triangles that are not shaded by multiplying $\frac{1}{2}$ times the base times the height.

Upper triangle: $\frac{1}{2} \times 2 \times 6 = 6$

Lower triangle: $\frac{1}{2} \times 4 \times 4 = 8$

To find the area of the shaded region, subtract the total area of the two right triangles from the area of the rectangle.

$$24 - (6 + 8) = 24 - 14 = 10$$

113. D

Subject: Statistics and Probability

Getting to the Answer: Let $\frac{1}{x}$ be the probability that Diego selects a blue marble the first time. Because he replaces the marble each time, the probability of selecting a blue marble all 4 times is $\frac{1}{x} \times \frac{1}{x} \times \frac{1}{x} \times \frac{1}{x}$, which is given in the question as $\frac{1}{81}$. Because $81 = 3 \times 3 \times 3 \times 3$, the value of *x* is 3, and the probability that Diego selects a blue marble the first time is $\frac{1}{3}$.

114. H

Subject: Arithmetic

Getting to the Answer: Start by finding the total number of parts represented by the mixture. The ratio is 1:12:4:3, so the total number of parts is 20. Since there are 12 parts sand, the fraction of sand is:

$$\frac{12}{20} = \frac{3}{5}$$

Thus, the amount of sand in 200 cubic feet of asphalt (for 1 driveway) is:

$$\frac{3}{5} \times 200 = 120 \text{ cubic feet}$$

To cover 6 identical driveways, that would be $120 \times 6 = 720$ cubic feet.

PRACTICE TEST 3

SHSAT Practice Test 3

ANSWER SHEET

Part 1—English Language Arts

1. (A)(B)(C)(D)	11. (A)(B)(C)(D)	21. (A)(B)(C)(D)	31. (A)(B)(C)(D)	41. (A)(B)(C)(D)	51. (A)(B)(C)(D)
2. (E)(F)(G)(H)	12. (E)(F)(G)(H)	22. (E)(F)(G)(H)	32. (E)(F)(G)(H)	42. (E)(F)(G)(H)	52. (E)(F)(G)(H)
3. (A)(B)(C)(D)	13. (A)(B)(C)(D)	23. (A)(B)(C)(D)	33. (A)(B)(C)(D)	43. (A)(B)(C)(D)	53. (A)(B)(C)(D)
4. (E)(F)(G)(H)	14. (E)(F)(G)(H)	24. (E)(F)(G)(H)	34. (E)(F)(G)(H)	44. (E)(F)(G)(H)	54. (E)(F)(G)(H)
5. (A)(B)(C)(D)	15. (A)(B)(C)(D)	25. (A)(B)(C)(D)	35. (A)(B)(C)(D)	45. (A)(B)(C)(D)	55. (A)(B)(C)(D)
6. (E)(F)(G)(H)	16. (E)(F)(G)(H)	26. (E)(F)(G)(H)	36. (E)(F)(G)(H)	46. (E)(F)(G)(H)	56. (E)(F)(G)(H)
7. (A)(B)(C)(D)	17. (A)(B)(C)(D)	27. (A)(B)(C)(D)	37. (A)(B)(C)(D)	47. (A)(B)(C)(D)	57. (A)(B)(C)(D)
8. (E)(F)(G)(H)	18. (E)(F)(G)(H)	28. (E)(F)(G)(H)	38. (E)(F)(G)(H)	48. (E)(F)(G)(H)	
9. (A)(B)(C)(D)	19. (A)(B)(C)(D)	29. (A)(B)(C)(D)	39. (A)(B)(C)(D)	49. (A)(B)(C)(D)	
10. (E)(F)(G)(H)	20. (E)(F)(G)(H)	30. (E)(F)(G)(H)	40. (E)(F)(G)(H)	50. (E)(F)(G)(H)	

Part 2—Mathematics

58. 59. 60. 61. 62.

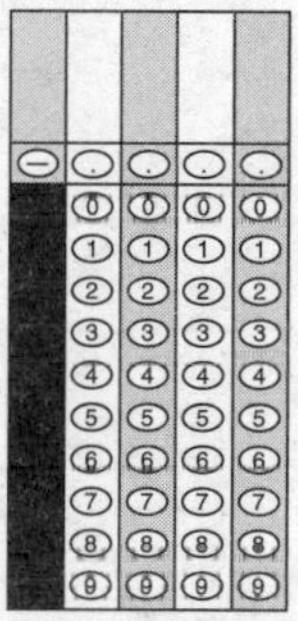

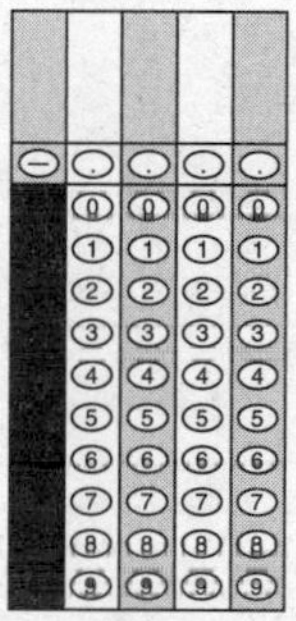

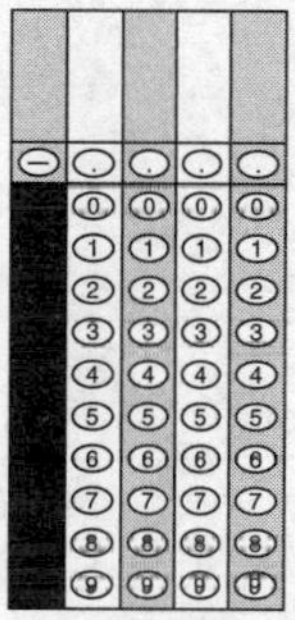

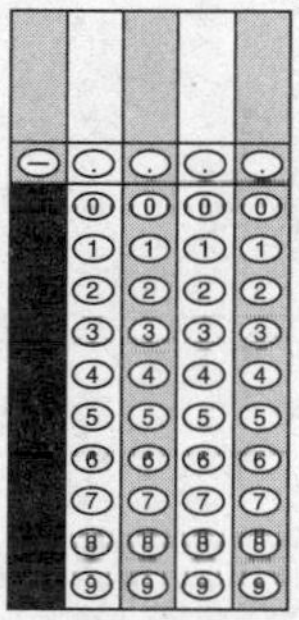

(grid-in response boxes with digits 0–9)

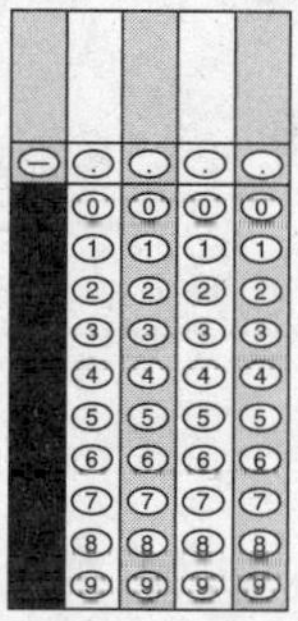

63. (A)(B)(C)(D)	72. (E)(F)(G)(H)	81. (A)(B)(C)(D)	90. (E)(F)(G)(H)	99. (A)(B)(C)(D)	108. (E)(F)(G)(H)
64. (E)(F)(G)(H)	73. (A)(B)(C)(D)	82. (E)(F)(G)(H)	91. (A)(B)(C)(D)	100. (E)(F)(G)(H)	109. (A)(B)(C)(D)
65. (A)(B)(C)(D)	74. (E)(F)(G)(H)	83. (A)(B)(C)(D)	92. (E)(F)(G)(H)	101. (A)(B)(C)(D)	110. (E)(F)(G)(H)
66. (E)(F)(G)(H)	75. (A)(B)(C)(D)	84. (E)(F)(G)(H)	93. (A)(B)(C)(D)	102. (E)(F)(G)(H)	111. (A)(B)(C)(D)
67. (A)(B)(C)(D)	76. (E)(F)(G)(H)	85. (A)(B)(C)(D)	94. (E)(F)(G)(H)	103. (A)(B)(C)(D)	112. (E)(F)(G)(H)
68. (E)(F)(G)(H)	77. (A)(B)(C)(D)	86. (E)(F)(G)(H)	95. (A)(B)(C)(D)	104. (E)(F)(G)(H)	113. (A)(B)(C)(D)
69. (A)(B)(C)(D)	78. (E)(F)(G)(H)	87. (A)(B)(C)(D)	96. (E)(F)(G)(H)	105. (A)(B)(C)(D)	114. (E)(F)(G)(H)
70. (E)(F)(G)(H)	79. (A)(B)(C)(D)	88. (E)(F)(G)(H)	97. (A)(B)(C)(D)	106. (E)(F)(G)(H)	
71. (A)(B)(C)(D)	80. (E)(F)(G)(H)	89. (A)(B)(C)(D)	98. (E)(F)(G)(H)	107. (A)(B)(C)(D)	

Practice Test 3

Directions: Mark your answers on the separate sheet provided. You will receive credit only for answers marked on the answer grid. **DO NOT MAKE ANY STRAY MARKS ON THE ANSWER GRID.** You can write in the test booklet, or use the paper provided for scratchwork.

Each question has only one correct answer. Select the **best** answer for each question. Your score is determined by the number of questions you answered correctly. **It is to your advantage to answer every question, even though you may not be certain which choice is correct.**

You have 180 minutes to complete the entire test. How you split the time between the English Language Arts and Mathematics sections is up to you. **If you begin with the English Language Arts section, you may go on to the Mathematics section as soon as you are ready. If you begin with the Mathematics section, you may go on to the English Language Arts section as soon as you are ready.** It is recommended that you do not spend more than 90 minutes on either section. If you complete the test before the allotted time (180 minutes) is over, you may go back to review questions in either section.

Work as rapidly as you can without making mistakes. Don't spend too much time on a difficult question. Return to it later if you have time. If time remains, you should check your answers.

Part 1—English Language Arts

57 QUESTIONS—SUGGESTED TIMING: 90 MINUTES

REVISING/EDITING

QUESTIONS 1–14 (Part A and Part B)

REVISING/EDITING Part A

DIRECTIONS: Answer the following questions, recognizing and correcting errors so that the sentences or paragraphs are grammatically correct. Reread relevant parts of the text before choosing the best answer for each question, but be mindful of time. You may write in your test booklet to take notes.

---

1. Read this paragraph.

> (1) John Updike wrote many novels, including the Pulitzer Prize-winning *Rabbit Is Rich*. (2) This famous American author studied at Harvard and Oxford before beginning his career in literature and eventually earning more than one Pulitzer Prize. (3) His novels exploring contemporary human relationships in the United States. (4) In addition to creating novels, Updike wrote poems and collections of short stories.

Which sentence contains an error in its construction and should be revised?

A. sentence 1
B. sentence 2
C. sentence 3
D. sentence 4

2. Read this sentence.

> During the intense exchange between the basketball coaches and the referees about a pivotal decision that could change the outcome of the playoff game, the sports journalist calmly and clearly explained to all of the people who were viewing channel KXTV on their televisions what was happening

Which revision uses the most precise language for the words *explained to all of the people who were viewing channel KXTV on their televisions what was happening*?

E. told the people about the events
F. reported on the disagreement for KXTV
G. explained the dialogue for the people at home watching KXTV
H. discussed the issue on live television

GO ON TO THE NEXT PAGE

3. Read this sentence.

> Point Pleasant needed increased revenue, from tourism, and consequently the town built a new park, a large hotel, and a fine restaurant in the main square.

How should the sentence be revised?

A. Insert a comma after **Point Pleasant**, AND delete the comma after **hotel**.

B. Delete the comma after **revenue**, AND insert a comma after **consequently**.

C. Insert a comma after **town**, AND delete the comma after **park**.

D. Insert a comma after **restaurant**, AND insert a comma after **main**.

4. Read this paragraph.

> (1) The reason for the continued interest in Olympic athletes is that their struggle to win draws on experiences with which people can identify. (2) Highlighting legendary feats and memorable occasions, many competitors have participated in Olympic games over the years. (3) Dedicated athletes from all countries have made history and have inspired their fans to pursue their goals. (4) The Olympic games have become a social event and a shared experience among various cultures.

Which sentence contains an error in its construction and should be revised?

E. sentence 1

F. sentence 2

G. sentence 3

H. sentence 4

5. Which revision corrects the error in sentence structure in the paragraph?

> While the learning behavior of many mammals is dictated by instinct, it is also influenced by experience. Complex behaviors can be learned through individual trial-and-error or practice, as long as that practice is motivated by natural instincts. For example, predatory cats aren't born knowing how to hunt, but their instincts prompt them to stalk, pounce on, and bite things they perceive as prey, and they gradually become more skilled and effective hunters. Wolves aren't born knowing how to get along with other wolves, the experience of living in the pack results in their eventual ability to find their place in the hierarchy.

A. instinct, and it

B. instincts, for example, predatory

C. hunters; wolves

D. wolves, but the

6. Which edit should be made to correct this sentence?

> The <u>swift</u> nimble Florence Griffith Joyner set a world record in 1988 when she beat the old record for the 100-meter sprint by 0.27 <u>seconds</u> and improved her <u>previous</u> <u>best</u> by more than half a second.

- **E.** Insert a comma after *swift*.
- **F.** Insert a comma after *seconds*.
- **G.** Insert a comma after *previous*.
- **H.** Insert a comma after *best*.

7. Which pair of revisions need to be made in this paragraph?

> (1) Known for his <u>curiosity</u>, Swiss engineer Georges de Mestral wondered if the burrs that clung to his pants and his dog's fur when they went walking in the woods could be turned into something useful. (2) After nearly eight years of research, de Mestral successfully <u>reproduced</u> the effect with two strips of fabric, one with thousands of tiny hooks and another with thousands of tiny loops. (3) He named the invention <u>Velcro</u> a combination of the words "velvet" and "crochet," and formally patented it in 1955. (4) Early news reports, such as one that appeared in *TIME* magazine in 1958, <u>describe</u> the product as a zipperless zipper.

- **A.** Sentence 1: Delete the comma after *curiosity*.
  Sentence 4: Change *describe* to **described**.
- **B.** Sentence 1: Delete the comma after *curiosity*.
  Sentence 2: Change *reproduced* to **reproduces**.
- **C.** Sentence 3: Insert a comma after *Velcro*.
  Sentence 2: Change *reproduced* to **reproduces**.
- **D.** Sentence 3: Insert a comma after *Velcro*.
  Sentence 4: Change *describe* to **described**.

GO ON TO THE NEXT PAGE ➤

Practice Tests

REVISING/EDITING Part B

DIRECTIONS: Read the passage and answer the questions following it, improving the writing quality and correcting grammatical errors. Reread relevant parts of the text before choosing the best answer for each question, but be mindful of time. You may write in your test booklet to take notes.

Sweat Lodges

(1) Medicines derived from nature have been around for centuries and often complement natural therapies. (2) The most widely used natural therapy is the sweat lodge, a practice established by some groups of indigenous peoples of the Americas; similar practices have evolved in other cultures as well. (3) The Finnish sauna and the Turkish steam room share many characteristics of the sweat lodge. (4) The basic purpose of these therapies is to raise the body's core temperature to between 102 and 106 degrees Fahrenheit. (5) The heat can also ease muscle tension and soreness, the resulting perspiration flushes the system of toxins.

(6) A traditional sweat lodge is often built of willow. (7) Its bark is considered to be medicinal. (8) It also contains the same analgesic as aspirin. (9) Some lodges are covered with animal skins, while others are made with canvas or blankets. (10) Large rocks are heated and brought inside the lodge. (11) Water is then poured over the rocks, filling the lodge with steam.

(12) Traditional sweat lodge ceremonies, which often included songs, prayers, and chants, were believed to purify not only the body but also the mind. (13) "Healing comes on a spiritual level," wrote Dr. Lewis Mehl-Madrona in his book *Coyote Medicine*. (14) "Ceremony and ritual provide the means of making ourselves available."

(15) Mehl-Madrona's focus on ceremony and ritual has influenced many groups. (16) He also improves his mental stamina through the game of chess. (17) These aspects of the sweat lodge have even been adopted by the Jewish group Aquarian Minyan. (18) Incorporating the ceremonial aspect of the traditional *shvitz*, participants gather in a willow structure covered with blankets, one of which bears the Star of David. (19) Regarding this ceremony of mixed Native American and Jewish tradition, Miriam Stampfer, a biologist at U.C. Berkeley, has said, "You purify yourself on the physical level, by cleaning the toxins out of your system, and on a spiritual level, by following ritual paths, which bring in the spirits of the ancestors and the divine presence."

8. Which introductory sentence, if inserted before sentence 1, would best support the argument presented in the passage?

   E. As people become more interested in healthy living, many new trends have emerged.

   F. The twenty-first century has seen a marked increase in the popularity of natural medicines and therapies.

   G. Natural remedies and approaches are an integral part of living the healthiest way possible.

   H. Some people may be skeptical about natural approaches to treating ailments, but many people find them helpful.

9. Which transition should be added to the beginning of sentence 3?

   A. For instance,

   B. Conversely,

   C. On the other hand,

   D. Even though

10. Which sentence would best follow and support sentence 4?

    E. Many indigenous remedies are now being prescribed by medical professionals.

    F. Turkey and Russia also have similar forms of heat therapy.

    G. This is approximately three to seven degrees above normal.

    H. At this temperature, bacterial and viral infections within the body cannot easily survive.

11. Which transition word should be added after the comma in sentence 5?

    A. however

    B. furthermore

    C. but

    D. and

12. What is the best way to combine sentences 6 through 8 to clarify the relationship between ideas?

    E. A traditional sweat lodge is often built of willow, its bark is considered to be medicinal, and it contains the same analgesic as aspirin.

    F. A traditional sweat lodge is often built of willow, having its bark considered to be medicinal and containing the same analgesic as aspirin.

    G. A traditional sweat lodge is often built of willow bark, which is considered to be medicinal and contains the same analgesic as aspirin.

    H. A traditional sweat lodge, often built of willow, with bark considered to be medicinal and containing the same analgesic as aspirin.

GO ON TO THE NEXT PAGE ➡

13. Which concluding sentence would best follow sentence 19 and support the argument presented in the passage?

   A. Research shows that sweat lodges have influenced not only Jewish traditions but also Christian communities.

   B. Mehl-Madrona and Stampfer have recently collaborated on a book about the latest health trends.

   C. Sweat lodges have been a means of purifying the body and the mind for centuries, and recent studies suggest that their influence is expanding and will continue to grow.

   D. Indigenous Americans traditionally used primarily limestones to heat their lodges, and this is very efficient, maintaining high temperatures with very few rocks.

14. Which sentence presents information that shifts away from the main topic of paragraph 4 (sentences 15–19) and should be removed?

   E. sentence 15

   F. sentence 16

   G. sentence 17

   H. sentence 18

Practice Tests

READING COMPREHENSION

QUESTIONS 15–57

DIRECTIONS: Read the six passages and answer the corresponding questions. Reread relevant parts of the text before choosing the best answer for each question, but be mindful of time. Base your answers only on the content within each passage. You may write in your test booklet to take notes.

Murals for Cityscape

1   The modern city has become an increasingly colorless environment. The spread of industry has transformed the urban landscape, covering everything in a thin layer of gray soot. But the monotony of city life is not just due to airborne pollution. Since the Industrial Revolution, city architects have mostly favored the use of somber, neutral colors in their buildings. This may be out of a simple desire to imitate the austere look of the monotone marble and stone materials used in ancient Greece and Rome. If so, that choice is misguided because surprisingly, historians and archaeologists note that these ancient cities were actually very colorful places. For whatever reasons, eschewing the vibrancy of the past and the full array of possibilities, most modern architects have long tended to avoid designing colorful buildings in prominent public places.

2   But simply because city buildings are monotone doesn't mean that cities themselves must be colorless places. Fortunately, the last 30 years have seen an upsurge in the number of urban art projects using decorative color. One especially exciting way to introduce color back into the cityscape is through the use of murals as public art. The mural has a long history of brightening public places. The first important muralists of the twentieth century were three Mexican artists—Diego Rivera, José Clemente Orozco, and David Alfaro Siqueiros. In the 1920s, these artists became famous by creating gigantic paintings that retraced major episodes in the history of Mexico. These paintings covered large portions of the public landscape and brought excitement to cities. The artists received commissions to produce large-scale works later in the United States, inspiring a vast program of publicly financed commissions in the 1930s, which were designed to provide work for unemployed American artists during the Great Depression.

3   While the mural movement during the Great Depression was vigorous, it was also short-lived. Murals enjoyed a resurgence of popularity in the United States during the 1960s, when artists used the medium to make statements about political changes. In 1967, a team of artists led by William Walker created a "collage" of portraits, photographs, and poetic verse on a derelict building in Chicago. Entitled "The Wall of Respect," the work paid tribute to public figures who had fought for civil rights for African Americans. This group effort sparked other similar projects in such American cities as Los Angeles, San Francisco, Baltimore, and New York.

4   The power of murals to inspire and invigorate dull urban centers has been discovered yet again by urban planners, landscape architects, and artists. Much of the street art currently being produced reminds us of important historical events or highlights changes happening in our culture. Murals portraying important political, religious, and artistic events are being employed in otherwise traditional cityscapes. The impact of murals goes far beyond these educational and historical aims, by creating a unique sense of place and establishing a bold spirit of vitality in the urban centers where murals grace the scenery.

GO ON TO THE NEXT PAGE ➡

5 Murals are one piece of a solution to bring color back into cities. Color can help to rehabilitate, revitalize, or even save neighborhoods that might otherwise be doomed to demolition. The aim is to provide
the city-dweller with the opportunity to participate in the rebirth of a more human environment.

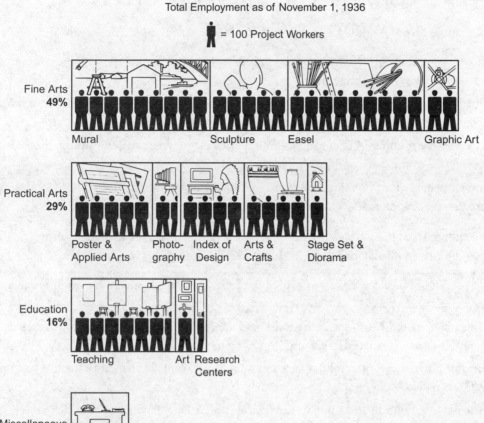

EMPLOYMENT & ACTIVITIES
FEDERAL ART PROJECT

Total Employment as of November 1, 1936

= 100 Project Workers

Fine Arts
49%

Mural   Sculpture   Easel   Graphic Art

Practical Arts
29%

Poster &   Photo-   Index of   Arts &   Stage Set &
Applied Arts   graphy   Design   Crafts   Diorama

Education
16%

Teaching   Art Research
                      Centers

Miscellaneous
6%

Technical &
Coordinating

*Through the Federal Art Project, the United States government's Works Progress Administration commissioned artists, musicians,
educators, and other cultural works as part of a plan to help unemployed American artists during the Great Depression of the 1930s.*

GO ON TO THE NEXT PAGE

15. How does the information about Rivera, Orozco, and Siqueiros in paragraph 2 contribute to the development of the passage?

   A. It illustrates how their success was largely due to a team effort.

   B. It conveys how other artists benefited from their initiative.

   C. It shows how their frescoes were the largest works ever produced.

   D. It highlights how they imitated the colors of ancient Greece and Rome.

16. The infographic provides additional support to the ideas of paragraph 2 mainly by

   E. illustrating that 2,500 artists were encouraged by three influential Mexican muralists in the 1930s to create frescos in American cities.

   F. showing the extent of the Mexican government program inspired by the frescoes of muralists Diego Rivera, José Clemente Orozco, and David Alfaro Siqueiros.

   G. revealing the number of United States mural artists who were assisted through the Federal Art Project due to the work of the Mexican muralists.

   H. providing evidence that many artists were available to decorate modern cities with murals, sculpture, frescoes, and other art forms.

17. Which sentence from the passage best supports the idea that "the use of somber, neutral colors in their buildings" by city architects may be the result of a mistake?

   A. "The spread of industry has transformed the urban landscape, covering everything in a thin layer of gray soot." (paragraph 1)

   B. "This may be out of a simple desire to imitate the austere look of the monotone marble and stone materials used in ancient Greece and Rome." (paragraph 1)

   C. "But simply because city buildings are monotone doesn't mean that cities themselves must be colorless places." (paragraph 2)

   D. "The power of murals to inspire and invigorate dull urban centers has been discovered yet again by urban planners, landscape architects, and artists." (paragraph 4)

18. How does paragraph 2 fit into the overall structure of the excerpt?

   E. It illustrates how the revival of murals can reverse the colorless nature of modern cities.

   F. It discusses how murals reflect changes in culture in both Mexico and the United States.

   G. It contrasts the drab nature of modern cities with the colorful cityscapes of the ancient world.

   H. It demonstrates how colorful murals can save neighborhoods from urban decay.

19. Which sentence from the passage best supports the idea that "color can help to rehabilitate, revitalize, or even save neighborhoods" (paragraph 5)?

   A. "The mural has a long history of brightening public places." (paragraph 2)

   B. "Much of the street art currently being produced reminds us of important historical events or highlights changes happening in our culture." (paragraph 4)

   C. "The impact of murals goes far beyond these educational and historical aims, by creating a unique sense of place and establishing a bold spirit of vitality in the urban centers where murals grace the scenery." (paragraph 4)

   D. "The aim is to provide the city-dweller with the opportunity to participate in the rebirth of a more human environment." (paragraph 5)

20. With which statement would the author of the passage most likely agree?

   E. Colorful urban art can help save condemned buildings.

   F. Urban art projects should avoid political issues.

   G. Murals have caused many important historical events.

   H. The city will always be a colorless environment.

Miles Davis: Legend of Jazz

1   The death of trumpeter Miles Davis in 1991 brought an end to one of the most celebrated careers in the history of jazz. Davis's career spanned six decades and reached heights of enduring influence and popularity that few musicians have ever enjoyed. His legacy in the world of jazz is secure.

2   Davis was born in 1926 in southern Illinois, in a suburb of St. Louis, to a mother who was a music teacher and violinist. His father was a successful dentist and, to many people's surprise—given preconceived notions about jazz musicians—Davis actually enjoyed a very comfortable upbringing. He picked up the trumpet in his early teens and not only showed considerable interest in music but also demonstrated a great deal of musical talent. He arrived in New York City in 1944, and developed his skills at what is now the Juilliard School of Music. He may have enhanced his musical skills by day, but he truly found his musical style at night while haunting the city's jazz clubs. There, Davis received a different kind of education. Bebop, the hot, frantic new style of jazz, was played by such musical revolutionaries as Charlie Parker, Dizzy Gillespie, and Thelonious Monk; Davis was sometimes invited up on the bandstand to play with them. Though obviously talented, Davis had to struggle to keep up with these musicians; there, he found tremendous inspiration, and he worked tirelessly to perfect his technique. Ultimately, he dropped out of Juilliard to focus on his career.

3   Even at this early stage in his craft, Davis's sound and style on the trumpet set him apart. Rather than filling the air with a headlong rush of notes, as other bebop musicians did, Davis played sparingly in a unique, intimate tone. He seemed more interested in the silences between the notes than in the notes themselves. By 1948, Davis was performing and recording music with a small group of jazz musicians. Releasing a dozen singles, the group developed a style that blended the improvisational ideals of bebop with a thickly orchestral sound and paved the way for the West Coast style of jazz.

4   Davis's "less-is-more" approach became the basis of "cool" jazz, a new style of jazz that Davis led and which dominated the genre in the 1950s. The Miles Davis Quintet set the standard for all other jazz groups of the era. Featuring many legendary performers in his work, Davis produced a series of profoundly influential recordings culminating in the classic *Kind of Blue*. That album is notable for its modal style of jazz that features sparse elements and nonstandard scales, as well as complex, frequently changing chords.

5   For many critics, the late 1950s represents the high point of Davis's career. And yet, even though he had developed a very popular and successful brand of music, he soon moved on to play other styles. Indeed, he continued to expand his musical horizons over the next 40 years, always playing with young, emerging musicians in a restless search for new sounds. Although he never topped the critical acclaim of *Kind of Blue*, Davis continued to reach new audiences by dabbling in new genres such as dance music and blues. Davis continued to play and record music up until the last days of his life. His final album, *Doo-Bop*, was released posthumously in 1992.

6   Although, like any enduring artist, Davis's career was faced with uneven critical approval, personal highs and lows, and a changing sound, Davis will always be remembered for his great influence on jazz music, particularly for the way he experimented with style and tone.

GO ON TO THE NEXT PAGE

21. Which statement best describes the central idea of the passage?

    A. Miles Davis sparked the musical revolution of the 1940s.

    B. Miles Davis learned to play jazz in school and in nightclubs.

    C. Miles Davis played a pivotal role in the origins of bebop jazz.

    D. Miles Davis enjoyed a long and artistically notable career.

22. Read this sentence from paragraph 2.

    > His father was a successful dentist and, to many people's surprise—given preconceived notions about jazz musicians—Davis actually enjoyed a very comfortable upbringing.

    The sentence contributes to the development of ideas in the passage by

    E. hinting that Davis's career would be one marked by distinctions from those of other jazz musicians of his era.

    F. highlighting that Davis was a poor fit for the field of jazz music because of his classical training at Juilliard.

    G. justifying why Davis was able to afford to pay to visit so many New York City jazz clubs to meet famous musicians.

    H. revealing that Davis was raised by his father in a middle-class single-parent household.

23. Which sentence from the passage best supports the idea that "For many critics, the late 1950s represents the high point of Davis's career" (paragraph 5)?

    A. "Releasing a dozen singles, the group developed a style that blended the improvisational ideals of bebop with a thickly orchestral sound and paved the way for the West Coast style of jazz." (paragraph 3)

    B. "Featuring many legendary performers in his work, Davis produced a series of profoundly influential recordings culminating in the classic *Kind of Blue*." (paragraph 4)

    C. "And yet, even though he had developed a very popular and successful brand of music, he soon moved on to play other styles." (paragraph 5)

    D. "Although he never topped the critical acclaim of *Kind of Blue*, Davis continued to reach new audiences by dabbling in new genres such as dance music and blues." (paragraph 5)

24. The passage describes Davis's early musical education by stating that he

    E. preferred playing classical music to playing jazz.

    F. learned from playing with club musicians.

    G. rarely needed to practice to keep up with his classmates.

    H. was dissatisfied with his studies at the Juilliard School.

25. Read this sentence from paragraph 3.

> **He seemed more interested in the silences between the notes than in the notes themselves.**

The sentence contributes to the development of ideas in the excerpt by

A. illustrating how Davis first developed "cool" jazz in the 1970s.

B. highlighting how "cool" jazz was unpopular on the East Coast.

C. showing that Davis continued to play "cool" jazz in the 1960s.

D. showing how "cool" jazz was less frantic than bebop jazz.

26. The phrase "expand his musical horizons" in paragraph 5 suggests that

E. Miles Davis went on to explore other art forms.

F. Miles Davis traveled to perform his music all over the world.

G. Miles Davis constantly experimented with new styles of music.

H. Miles Davis rarely let the opinions of his critics influence him.

27. How does the word "haunting" in paragraph 2 contribute to the development of ideas in the paragraph?

A. It highlights how dangerous it was to attend the jazz clubs.

B. It conveys the idea that Davis had to frequent the jazz clubs often in order to learn.

C. It indicates that Davis loomed over junior artists at the jazz clubs.

D. It shows why Davis was unable to gain admission to jazz clubs.

28. The "less-is-more" approach of Miles Davis is best illustrated through the

E. short and concise musical selections he chose to play.

F. limited number of musicians in his band.

G. way he limited playing in jazz clubs to once or twice a week.

H. pauses between notes throughout his performances.

GO ON TO THE NEXT PAGE

The Influence of Immigrant Family Groups

1   Immigrants to the United States during the nineteenth century faced many changes when they reached the New World. Coming from all over Europe and practicing vastly different cultural traditions, they found themselves in a large collective surrounded by others of vastly different backgrounds. Interestingly, most of the immigrant groups at this time were able to remain within the confines of their own small communities even under tremendous external forces. It is notable that while groups of immigrants sometimes bound together through the links of friendship, village, or region, mostly it was blood ties—kinship groups—that formed the basis for these smaller, stable immigrant populations. This coping mechanism of staying with one's own people surely assisted with the transition to the New World, but it assisted with another transition as well: from a rural lifestyle to urban economics. However, the dynamics of these smaller immigrant kinship communities have not always been well understood.

2   Until recently, many historians believed that the immigrant family group broke down upon the transition from a rural to an urban economy. But this argument rested upon assumptions that have proven to be untrue: that families became less important in urban-industrial society and that families operated in isolation from the larger economy of industrial capitalism that surrounded them upon their arrival in the United States. In fact, the family structure continued to thrive during the transition to an urban economy. Further, modern historical scholarship has made it quite clear that the family dynamic fit well with and even supported the underpinnings of American capitalism. In short, the family played an essential role in shaping the urban economy.

3   The immigrant family survived the transition from subsistence agriculture in the home world to an industrial capitalist economy in the new one through its central and enduring attachment to the value of cooperation. What it means to be a "family" is at the root of this. Family members are continually instructed in the necessity of sharing, while notions of reciprocity are constantly reinforced. Thus, in the new world, families, consisting of parents, children, boarders, or others who shared particular households, were ready to share resources and workload. All household members were assigned a series of duties and obligations. By working together, pooling limited resources, and muting individual inclinations, families attempted to assemble the resources sufficient for economic survival and, occasionally, for an improvement in their standard of living.

4   The features of this collaborative interest that helped families thrive served the family's economic interests in this new industrial urban landscape. But immigrant kinship associations didn't just help themselves, they supported the larger machinery of the industrial city. For instance, such groups were able to help organize the movement of workers into different places, facilitate communication, and even to anticipate and meet the demands of the workplace. At times, the relationship between the industrial economy and immigrant families could almost be described as symbiotic, as kinship groups proved very responsive to demands of the workplace, the city, and the individual.

29. Which statement best describes the central idea of the passage?

    A. Immigrant families dissolved over time after moving to the United States.

    B. Immigrant families have been misunderstood in modern history books.

    C. Immigrant families thrived in the urban landscapes of the United States.

    D. Immigrant families enjoyed a high standard of living in the United States.

30. Which sentence best supports the idea that kinship groups served as a "coping mechanism" (paragraph 1)?

    E. "Coming from all over Europe and practicing vastly different cultural traditions, they found themselves in a large collective surrounded by others of vastly different backgrounds." (paragraph 1)

    F. "In short, the family played an essential role in shaping the urban economy." (paragraph 2)

    G. "Family members are continually instructed in the necessity of sharing, while notions of reciprocity are constantly reinforced." (paragraph 3)

    H. "For instance, such groups were able to help organize the movement of workers into different places, facilitate communication, and even to anticipate and meet the demands of the workplace." (paragraph 4)

31. How does paragraph 2 fit into the overall structure of the excerpt?

    A. It contrasts the living standards of Old World countries with those enjoyed by many immigrant families in the New World.

    B. It elaborates on why the assumed breakdown of immigrant families in the United States has been proven to be inaccurate.

    C. It highlights the insubstantial evidence presented in modern history books about immigrant families.

    D. It elaborates on the economic dimension of the family and how it benefits immigrants.

32. How do the details in paragraphs 3–4 help convey a central idea of the excerpt?

    E. They establish how historians have misunderstood immigrant families.

    F. They reveal that immigrant families always prosper in the United States.

    G. They provide concrete examples of how kinship groups operate.

    H. They offer precise definitions of immigrant and native family groups.

33. With which statement would the author of this excerpt most likely agree?

    A. Immigrant families tend to value communal needs over individual needs.

    B. Immigrant families prefer to live in rural communities over urban areas.

    C. Immigrant families work best in isolation from the larger community around them.

    D. Immigrant families have not had much influence on the U.S. economy.

GO ON TO THE NEXT PAGE →

34. The phrase "the larger machinery" in paragraph 4 serves to support the idea that urban life

    E. lacked the sense of belonging common to that of agriculturally-focused rural communities.

    F. depended on a large workforce to maintain its factories and other physical infrastructure.

    G. improved thanks to immigrant families helping to unionize factories and anticipate workers' needs.

    H. benefited in many ways from the influence of immigrant kinship associations.

35. The phrase "muting individual inclinations" in paragraph 3 conveys the idea that immigrant families had to

    A. weather economic declines in the United States.

    B. endure economic hardships after their arrival.

    C. sacrifice their personal wishes to prosper.

    D. resolve their individual disputes to work together.

36. Which sentence from the excerpt best supports the idea that immigrant families succeeded in adapting to the demands of industrial urban work?

    E. "Interestingly, most of the immigrant groups at this time were able to remain within the confines of their own small communities even under tremendous external forces." (paragraph 1)

    F. "It is notable that while groups of immigrants sometimes bound together through the links of friendship, village, or region, mostly it was blood ties—kinship groups—that formed the basis for these smaller, stable immigrant populations." (paragraph 1)

    G. "Thus, in the new world, families, consisting of parents, children, boarders, or others who shared particular households, were ready to share resources and workload." (paragraph 3)

    H. "But immigrant kinship associations didn't just help themselves, they supported the larger machinery of the industrial city." (paragraph 4)

New Hampshire's Old Man

1   On May 3, 2003, the state of New Hampshire lost its most beloved old man. The Old Man of the Mountain, a rock outcropping that had jutted from the side of Cannon Mountain—in New Hampshire's White Mountains region—collapsed. This remarkable and prominent feature had graced the cliff face for thousands of years, long attracting the attention of residents, naturalists, and hikers, but its vulnerability was well understood long before the fateful collapse. In fact, since 1915, steel cables and turnbuckles had been used to shore up the ledges that formed the profile. The forces of erosion couldn't be kept at bay forever and, after the unusually harsh spring of 2003 proved to be too much, portions of the rock profile crumbled and fell to the valley below.

2   Composed of a series of five Conway red granite ledges stacked one on top of the other, the Old Man of the Mountain was about 40 feet high and 25 feet across. Before the rockfall, the granite ledges had jutted out from the rock face of the cliff in striking formation, suggesting the features of a face in profile. Although the natural cliff remains, the distinctive profile is now gone, probably forever. Plans to restore the face have been suggested, but have been deemed impractical and the government of New Hampshire has chosen instead to honor the Old Man of the Mountain with a museum. Though the famous rock face is no more, its history is far from forgotten.

3   The discovery of the Old Man of the Mountain in 1805 has been credited to surveyors Luke Brooks and Francis Whitcomb. However, Native Americans stated long before that time that they had seen a stone face in the White Mountains. As more and more people settled in New Hampshire, the fame of the rocky profile grew. Statesman Daniel Webster, a famed U.S. congressman originally from New Hampshire, is credited with having said, "Men hang out their signs indicative of their respective trades: shoemakers hang out a gigantic shoe, jewelers a monster watch, and the dentist hangs out a gold tooth, but in the mountains of New Hampshire, God Almighty has hung out a sign to show that there, He makes men." In 1945, the Old Man of the Mountain became the state symbol of New Hampshire and has appeared on highway road signs and license plates, as well as the state quarter.

4   Although the remarkable history of the Old Man of the Mountain is as old as the United States, its geologic history is much older. According to geologists, the stone face was the result of processes that began millions of years ago. The White Mountains were created from magma intrusions that, more than 100 million years ago, created the foundational granite that comprises the feature. However, it probably wasn't until the Ice Age, when glaciers descended from the arctic and sculpted the White Mountains, that the surface materials were scrubbed away leaving behind the prominent granite ledges. When the Ice Age ended approximately 10,000 years ago, the glaciers receded and the ice melted. Part of the Old Man's profile was formed by the melting and falling of large chunks of ice from Cannon Mountain during this thawing period. The profile was completed through the eroding process of water collecting and freezing in crevices of the rock face.

5   Erosion moves steadily forward, relentlessly, regardless of human interests. Ironically, the same erosion that formed the Old Man of the Mountain ultimately removed it, and the erosion will continue to shape and reshape the cliffs of New Hampshire for eternity. In time, another "Old Man" could form. In fact, other distinctive rock formations appear all over the world, including Der große Kurfürst (said to look like a nobleman) in Germany, the Heathen Maiden in Slovenia, or the Sleeping Giant in Connecticut. However, few formations possess such a clear, distinctive image, and none hold the special place in the hearts of the citizens of New Hampshire as does that of the Old Man of the Mountain.

GO ON TO THE NEXT PAGE ➡

37. Which statement best describes the central idea of the passage?

   A. The Old Man of the Mountain illustrates how the forces of nature can create lifelike sculptures from rock.

   B. The Old Man of the Mountain can and will be reconstructed by the New Hampshire government.

   C. The Old Man of the Mountain was discovered during the exploration and settlement of the White Mountains.

   D. The Old Man of the Mountain had a long and notable history prior to its collapse in 2003.

38. Read this sentence from paragraph 1.

   > **The forces of erosion couldn't be kept at bay forever and, after the unusually harsh spring of 2003 proved to be too much, portions of the rock profile crumbled and fell to the valley below.**

   Which statement describes the effect of the phrase "proved to be too much" in the passage?

   E. It foreshadows the disastrous effects of ice falling from Cannon Mountain.

   F. It indicates the immediate cause of the collapse of the Old Man of the Mountain.

   G. It establishes why the cables and turnbuckles holding the Old Man of the Mountain in place broke.

   H. It explains why water was collecting and freezing in crevices of the mountain.

39. The author indicates that people in New Hampshire have known about the Old Man of the Mountain for a long time mainly by

   A. demonstrating how Brooks and Whitcomb discovered the Old Man of the Mountain.

   B. presenting the controversy surrounding the proposed efforts at reconstructing this famous landmark.

   C. discussing the construction of the memorial museum for the Old Man of the Mountain.

   D. highlighting how Native Americans knew of a face in the White Mountains.

40. How does the author's use of Daniel Webster's quote in paragraph 3 contribute to the development of ideas in the passage?

   E. It demonstrates the fame and the significance of the Old Man of the Mountain.

   F. It illustrates why Daniel Webster gained a reputation as a superb orator.

   G. It explains why the Old Man of the Mountain was chosen as New Hampshire's state symbol.

   H. It conveys how the loss of the Old Man of the Mountain affects the people of New Hampshire.

41. How does paragraph 4 fit into the overall structure of the passage?

   A. It explains in geological terms how the Old Man of the Mountain collapsed.

   B. It explains how the Old Man of the Mountain rock formation existed long before the state of New Hampshire.

   C. It illustrates how well-formed the profile of the Old Man of the Mountain was prior to its collapse.

   D. It emphasizes how old New Hampshire is compared to other states.

42. Which sentence best demonstrates the cultural importance of the Old Man of the Mountain in the present day?

   E. "Before the rockfall, the granite ledges had jutted out from the rock face of the cliff in striking formation, suggesting the features of a face in profile." (paragraph 2)

   F. "Plans to restore the face have been suggested, but have been deemed impractical and the government of New Hampshire has chosen instead to honor the Old Man of the Mountain with a museum." (paragraph 2)

   G. "Men hang out their signs indicative of their respective trades: shoemakers hang out a gigantic shoe, jewelers a monster watch, and the dentist hangs out a gold tooth, but in the mountains of New Hampshire, God Almighty has hung out a sign to show that there, He makes men." (paragraph 3)

   H. "In fact, other distinctive rock formations appear all over the world, including Der große Kurfürst (said to look like a nobleman) in Germany, the Heathen Maiden in Slovenia, or the Sleeping Giant in Connecticut." (paragraph 5)

43. Which sentence from the excerpt best explains the Old Man of the Mountain's name?

   A. "The Old Man of the Mountain, a rock outcropping that had jutted from the side of Cannon Mountain—in New Hampshire's White Mountains region—collapsed." (paragraph 1)

   B. "Composed of a series of five Conway red granite ledges stacked one on top of the other, the Old Man of the Mountain was about 40 feet high and 25 feet across." (paragraph 2)

   C. "However, Native Americans stated long before that time that they had seen a stone face in the White Mountains." (paragraph 3)

   D. "Ironically, the same erosion that formed the Old Man of the Mountain ultimately removed it, and the erosion will continue to shape and reshape the cliffs of New Hampshire for eternity." (paragraph 4)

GO ON TO THE NEXT PAGE

44. Read this sentence from paragraph 1.

> This remarkable and prominent feature had graced the cliff face for thousands of years, long attracting the attention of residents, naturalists, and hikers, but its vulnerability was well understood long before the fateful collapse.

The sentence contributes to the overall theme of the passage by

E. conveying the sheer age of the Old Man of the Mountain without using specific numbers.

F. highlighting that the structural weakness of this rock formation had been appreciated for many years.

G. revealing that the loss of the Old Man of the Mountain came as a shock to tourists and residents of New Hampshire.

H. shifting the focus from the cultural history of this rock formation to its geological history.

In this excerpt, astronomers in the year 1900 have observed a strange, bright star which, according to the calculations of a master mathematician, seems to be headed for a collision, or close fly-by with Earth, causing a catastrophe. With scholarly detachment, the mathematician, who is also a teacher, explains his findings to his students.

Excerpt from *Tales of Space and Time*
by H. G. Wells

1   The master mathematician sat in his private room and pushed the papers from him. His calculations were already finished. In a small white phial there still remained a little of the drug that had kept him awake and active for four long nights. Each day, serene, explicit, patient as ever, he had given his lecture to his students, and then had come back at once to this momentous calculation. His face was grave, a little drawn and hectic from his drugged activity. For some time he seemed lost in thought. Then he went to the window, and the blind went up with a click. Halfway up the sky, over the clustering roofs, chimneys and steeples of the city, hung the star.

2   He looked at the little phial. "There will be no need of sleep again," he said. The next day at noon—punctual to the minute, he entered his lecture theatre, put his hat on the end of the table as his habit was, and carefully selected a large piece of chalk. It was a joke among his students that he could not lecture without that piece of chalk to fumble in his fingers, and once he had been stricken to impotence by their hiding his supply. He came and looked under his grey eyebrows at the rising tiers of young fresh faces, and spoke with his accustomed studied commonness of phrasing. "Circumstances have arisen—circumstances beyond my control," he said and paused, "which will debar me from completing the course I had designed. It would seem, gentlemen, if I may put the thing clearly and briefly, that—Man has lived in vain."

3   The students glanced at one another. Had they heard aright? Mad? Raised eyebrows and grinning lips there were, but one or two faces remained intent upon his calm grey-fringed face. "It will be interesting," he was saying, "to devote this morning to an exposition, so far as I can make it clear to you, of the calculations that have led me to this conclusion. Let us assume—"

4   He turned towards the blackboard, meditating a diagram in the way that was usual to him. "What was that about 'lived in vain?'" whispered one student to another. "Listen," said the other, nodding towards the lecturer.

5   And presently they began to understand.

6   That night the star rose later. And everywhere the world was awake that night, and throughout Christendom a sombre murmur hung in the keen air over the countryside like the belling of bees in the heather, and this murmurous tumult grew to a clangour in the cities. It was the tolling of the bells in a million belfry towers and steeples, summoning the people to sleep no more, to sin no more, but to gather in their churches and pray. And overhead, growing larger and brighter as the earth rolled on its way and the night passed, rose the dazzling star.

GO ON TO THE NEXT PAGE ➤

7 And the streets and houses were alight in all the cities, the shipyards glared, and whatever roads led to high country were lit and crowded all night long. And in all the seas about the civilized lands, ships with throbbing engines, and ships with bellying sails, crowded with men and living creatures, were standing out to ocean and the north. For already the warning of the master mathematician had been telegraphed all over the world, and translated into a hundred tongues. The new planet and Neptune, locked in a fiery embrace, were whirling headlong, ever faster and faster towards the sun. Already every second this blazing mass flew a hundred miles, and every second its terrific velocity increased. As it flew now, indeed, it must pass a hundred million of miles wide of the earth and scarcely affect it. But near its destined path, as yet only slightly perturbed, spun the mighty planet Jupiter and his moons sweeping splendid round the sun. Every moment now the attraction between the fiery star and the greatest of the planets grew stronger. And the result of that attraction? Inevitably Jupiter would be deflected from its orbit into an elliptical path, and the burning star, swung by his attraction wide of its sunward rush, would "describe a curved path" and perhaps collide with, and certainly pass very close to, our earth. "Earthquakes, volcanic outbreaks, cyclones, sea waves, floods, and a steady rise in temperature to I know not what limit"—so prophesied the master mathematician.

45. Read these sentences from paragraph 2.

> **[He] carefully selected a large piece of chalk. It was a joke among his students that he could not lecture without that piece of chalk to fumble in his fingers, and once he had been stricken to impotence by their hiding his supply.**

The sentences contribute to the development of ideas in the passage by

A. laying the foundation for a contrast between the typical school day routine and the professor's extraordinary news.

B. describing the fussy nature of the professor in order to show that his students did not respect him.

C. alluding to the professor's distress over the implications of his calculations by showing him fidgeting with the chalk.

D. showing that the professor needed to handle the chalk in order to teach as it was coated with the drug that he kept using.

46. How does paragraph 3 fit into the overall structure of the excerpt?

E. It establishes that the students are immediately riveted by the professor's announcement.

F. It showcases the obvious distress, panic, and fear that the students feel toward the professor's announcement.

G. It highlights the confusion the students feel while trying to catch on to what the professor is telling them.

H. It showcases how completely uninterested the students are in the professor's lecture.

47. The phrase "circumstances beyond [his] control" in paragraph 2 conveys the idea that

    A. the frail old professor has fallen ill and is unable to finish teaching the term.

    B. the professor's miscalculation may have actually contributed to the collision that is about to take place.

    C. the professor is not really to blame for the calamity despite his obvious guilt.

    D. the professor is a man who favors exacting precision in his life yet is unable to prevent the calamity that is unfolding.

48. Which sentence best supports the idea that the professor is "serene, explicit, patient as ever" despite the looming calamity?

    E. "He looked at the little phial. 'There will be no need of sleep again,' he said." (paragraph 1)

    F. "It was a joke among his students that he could not lecture without that piece of chalk to fumble in his fingers, and once he had been stricken to impotence by their hiding his supply." (paragraph 2)

    G. "He came and looked under his grey eyebrows at the rising tiers of young fresh faces, and spoke with his accustomed studied commonness of phrasing." (paragraph 2)

    H. "And overhead, growing larger and brighter as the earth rolled on its way and the night passed, rose the dazzling star." (paragraph 6)

49. How does the author's description of wakefulness in paragraph 6 contribute to the development of ideas in the passage?

    A. It highlights how the cosmic rays were preventing people from sleeping.

    B. It conveys how people under stress take substances to prevent them from sleeping.

    C. It foreshadows how the human race was in denial about the events to come.

    D. It establishes that the people everywhere were aware of what was about to happen.

50. Read this sentence from paragraph 6.

> **It was the tolling of the bells in a million belfry towers and steeples, summoning the people to sleep no more, to sin no more, but to gather in their churches and pray.**

The sentence contributes to the development of ideas in the passage by

    E. suggesting there is a religious revival taking place.

    F. confirming that there is to be an important meeting for all to attend.

    G. explaining how the noise of the bells, bees, and clamoring voice prohibit sleep.

    H. conveying that people are likely to soon face death.

GO ON TO THE NEXT PAGE ➤

"Dawn"

by John Gould Fletcher

Above the east horizon,
The great red flower of the dawn
Opens slowly, petal by petal;
The trees emerge from darkness
5 With ghostly silver leaves,
Dew powdered.
Now consciousness emerges
Reluctantly out of tides of sleep;
Finding with cold surprise
10 No strange new thing to match its dreams,
But merely the familiar shapes
Of bedpost, window-pane, and wall.

Within the city,
The streets which were the last to fall to sleep,
15 Hold yet stale fragments of the night.
Sleep oozes out of stagnant ash-barrels,
Sleep drowses over litter in the streets.
Sleep nods upon the milkcans by back doors.
And, in shut rooms,
20 Behind the lowered window-blinds,
Drawn white faces unwittingly flout the day.

But, at the edges of the city,
Sleep is already washed away;
Light filters through the moist green leaves,
25 It runs into the cups of flowers,
It leaps in sparks through drops of dew,
It whirls against the window-panes
With waking birds;
Blinds are rolled up and chimneys smoke,
30 Feet clatter past in silent paths,
And down white vanishing ways of steel,
A dozen railway trains converge
Upon night's stronghold.

51. The details in the first stanza (lines 1–12) contribute to the development of the poem's theme by

    A. describing the surreal imagery from the waking person's dream.

    B. comparing the flower's slowly unfurling petals to a person gradually waking.

    C. establishing the drowsy feeling of sleep that lingers at the start of the day.

    D. illustrating the waking person's dawning realization that he is in a strange bed.

52. Read lines 4–6 from the poem.

> **The trees emerge from darkness**
> **With ghostly silver leaves,**
> **Dew powdered.**

How do these lines contribute to the development of ideas in the poem?

    E. They help connect the flowering dawn imagery to vegetation language throughout the poem.

    F. They show how the night leaves evidence of its passing.

    G. They highlight how the dreamer in the first stanza imagines the trees to have silver leaves.

    H. They are examples of the damage that comes to light with the dawn.

53. Which line from the poem best supports the idea that people in the city react differently to the dawn than those who live in the outskirts?

    A. "Hold yet stale fragments of the night" (line 15)

    B. "Sleep oozes out of stagnant ash-barrels" (line 16)

    C. "Sleep drowses over litter in the streets" (line 17)

    D. "Drawn white faces unwittingly flout the day" (line 21)

54. What impact does the phrase "stale fragments of the night" in line 15 have in the poem?

    E. It establishes that the city's nightlife leaves behind a lot of waste that must soon be collected.

    F. It contrasts the clean, orderly rhythms of city living with life in the countryside.

    G. It highlights how people who live in the city are no different than those living outside of it.

    H. It emphasizes the contrast between those who live in the city and those who live with nature's rhythms.

55. How does the line "It runs into the cups of flowers" contribute to the development of ideas in the stanza?

    A. The line conveys an image of the sun slowly rising on the horizon.

    B. The line highlights that the morning dew is collecting in the flowers.

    C. The line establishes that the open flowers are receiving light from the sun.

    D. The line conveys how beautiful the flowers are in the daytime.

GO ON TO THE NEXT PAGE ▶

56. The line "Blinds are rolled up and chimneys smoke" helps develop the theme of the poem by suggesting that

    E. people outside of the city rise with the morning sun.

    F. people outside of the city resist getting up early in the day.

    G. people outside of the city are disoriented when they first wake.

    H. people outside of the city are woken by the chirping and music of birds.

57. Which line(s) from the poem best support(s) the idea that day is overcoming the night?

    A. "With ghostly silver leaves, / Dew powdered." (lines 5–6)

    B. "No strange new thing to match its dreams," (line 10)

    C. "Drawn white faces unwittingly flout the day." (line 21)

    D. "A dozen railway trains converge / Upon night's stronghold." (lines 32–33)

Part 2—Mathematics

57 QUESTIONS—SUGGESTED TIMING: 90 MINUTES

IMPORTANT NOTES

1. Definitions and formulas are **not** provided.

2. Diagrams are **not** necessarily drawn to scale, with the exception of graphs.

3. Diagrams are drawn in single planes unless the question specifically states they are not.

4. Graphs are drawn to scale.

5. Simplify all fractions to lowest terms.

GRID-IN QUESTIONS

QUESTIONS 58–62

DIRECTIONS: Answer each question. Write your answer in the boxes at the top of the grid on the answer sheet. Start on the left side of each grid, printing only one number or symbol in each box. **DO NOT LEAVE A BOX BLANK IN THE MIDDLE OF AN ANSWER.** Under each box, fill in the circle that matches the number or symbol you wrote above. **DO NOT FILL IN A CIRCLE UNDER AN UNUSED BOX.**

---

58. If $\dfrac{2x+1}{4} = \dfrac{12}{20}$, what is the value of x?

59. A rectangular concrete patio is 20 feet long, 12 feet wide, and 4 inches thick. What is the volume, in cubic feet, of the concrete?

60. If n is a positive odd integer, what value of n satisfies the inequality $-3n + 5 \geq -1$?

61. A salad bar offers vegetable platters in 4 sizes (small, medium, large, and super-sized) and 6 different vegetables to choose from. Different platters can be created by changing the size and/or the choice of vegetables. If Selena wants to order a platter with exactly 2 different vegetables, how many different platters could she create?

62. Samantha grows carrots, peppers, and onions in her garden. She has twice as many carrots as peppers, and she has three times as many onions as carrots. If Samantha grew 36 onions, how many total vegetables did Samantha grow?

GO ON TO THE NEXT PAGE ➤

Practice Tests

MULTIPLE-CHOICE QUESTIONS

QUESTIONS 63–114

DIRECTIONS: Answer each question, selecting the best answer available. On the answer sheet, mark the letter of each of your answers. You can do your figuring in the test booklet or on paper provided by the proctor.

63. If $x = \frac{1}{3}\left(\frac{1}{2} - \frac{1}{8}\right)$, what is the value of x?

   A. $-\frac{1}{8}$

   B. $\frac{1}{24}$

   C. $\frac{1}{12}$

   D. $\frac{1}{8}$

64. A shoe store stocks children's shoes and adult shoes in a ratio of 5:7. How many pairs of adult shoes are stocked if 140 pairs of children's shoes are stocked?

   E. 100

   F. 164

   G. 196

   H. 208

65. Keisha has completed 72 math problems in her SHSAT practice workbook. This is 24% of the total number of math problems in the workbook. How many math problems are in the workbook?

   A. 196

   B. 280

   C. 288

   D. 300

66. A college class is made up of f freshmen and s sophomores. If 5 freshmen drop this class, the number of sophomores in the class would be 3 times the number of freshmen. Which of the following equations represents s in terms of f?

   E. $s = \dfrac{f - 5}{3}$

   F. $s = \dfrac{f + 5}{3}$

   G. $s = 3(f - 5)$

   H. $s = 3(f + 5)$

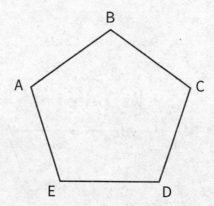

67. In pentagon ABCDE shown above, each side is 1 centimeter. If a particle starts at point A and travels clockwise 723 centimeters along ABCDE, at which point will the particle stop?

   A. A

   B. B

   C. C

   D. D

PIZZA TOPPINGS ORDERED ON LARGE PIZZAS

Number of Toppings Ordered	Percent of Customers
1	25%
2	55%
3	15%
4 or more	5%

68. A pizza place manager recorded the number of pizza toppings that customers ordered when they bought a large pizza. The table above shows the percent distribution for the 120 large pizzas that were sold at the pizza place yesterday. For these 120 large pizzas, how many customers ordered at least 3 toppings?

    E. 18
    F. 20
    G. 24
    H. 96

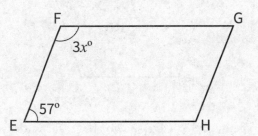

69. In the parallelogram above, what is the value of x ?

    A. 11
    B. 33
    C. 41
    D. 123

70. Which of the following values of s would yield the smallest value for $4 + \frac{1}{s}$?

    E. $\frac{1}{4}$
    F. $\frac{1}{2}$
    G. 1
    H. 4

$$\frac{49}{9} = \frac{7}{x}$$

71. What value of x makes the equation above true?

    A. $\frac{7}{9}$
    B. $1\frac{2}{7}$
    C. 5
    D. $5\frac{1}{9}$

72. If $4x + 2 = 26$, then $4x + 8 =$

    E. 32
    F. 34
    G. 36
    H. 38

73. If a certain train fare costs $5.00 for the first 10 miles of service, $0.25 per mile for the next 40 miles, and $0.10 per mile for each additional mile, what would the train fare be to travel a total distance of 100 miles?

    A. $15.00
    B. $17.50
    C. $20.00
    D. $25.00

GO ON TO THE NEXT PAGE ➡

Practice Tests

74. Mrs. Whitby has a pencil box containing 7 blue pencils, 10 green pencils, and 8 orange pencils. If she removes one pencil at random, what is the probability that it will **not** be green?

    E. $\frac{2}{3}$

    F. $\frac{3}{5}$

    G. $\frac{1}{2}$

    H. $\frac{2}{5}$

75. In a scale drawing of a cruise ship, 0.2 inches represents 200 feet. How many inches represent 10 feet?

    A. 0.001

    B. 0.002

    C. 0.01

    D. 0.02

76. Tariq has $10 and wants to buy 21 oranges at $0.30 each and 12 apples at $0.50 each. If there is no sales tax, how much more money does he need?

    E. $2.00

    F. $2.30

    G. $2.60

    H. $12.00

77. If Thomas went shopping with $15, bought two items that cost the same amount, and ended up with a debt of $5, how much did each of the two items cost?

    A. $5

    B. $10

    C. $15

    D. $20

78. If $2x + 2x + 14 = 2x + 2x + 2x + 6$, then what is the value of x?

    E. 3

    F. 4

    G. 5

    H. 7

79. Darias bought 5 school binders that cost $8.00 per binder. If a back-to-school discount of 40% was applied to his purchase, and then a 6% sales tax was added, what was the total cost of the binders?

    A. $17.12

    B. $25.44

    C. $26.40

    D. $30.40

80. A town's little league program has 108 baseballs, 54 bats, and 72 cases of sunflower seeds left over from last year. The items will be distributed to each team in the league. If each team receives an equal number of each item and there are no items remaining, what is the greatest possible number of teams in the little league program?

    E. 6

    F. 9

    G. 12

    H. 18

Practice Tests

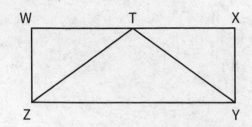

LAST YEAR'S T-SHIRT SALES

Color	Number Sold
White	1,650
Red	600
Blue	750
Total	**3,000**

81. In rectangle WXYZ in the figure above, the length of WZ is 6 units and triangle TYZ has an area of 48 square units. Point T is the midpoint of WX. What is the length of WT?

    A. 6
    B. 8
    C. 12
    D. 16

82. Two boxes can hold the same amount of sand. Box 1 is $\frac{1}{4}$ filled, and Box 2 is $\frac{2}{3}$ filled. If the sand in Box 2 is poured into Box 1, what fraction of Box 1 is still **not** filled?

    E. $\frac{1}{12}$
    F. $\frac{3}{7}$
    G. $\frac{4}{7}$
    H. $\frac{11}{12}$

83. In a room of 33 students, 12 are taking geography, 14 are taking history, and 5 are taking both geography and history. How many of these students are not taking either geography or history?

    A. 7
    B. 10
    C. 12
    D. 14

84. The table above shows the number of each color of T-shirt sold at a particular store last year. If 240 T-shirts were sold in June, and the store only sells white, red, or blue T-shirts, what is the best estimate (based on last year's sales) of the number of blue T-shirts sold in June?

    E. 60
    F. 80
    G. 92
    H. 108

85. How can $\frac{1}{3y} - \frac{1}{6y}$ be rewritten as a single fraction? (Assume $y \neq 0$.)

    A. $-\frac{1}{3y}$
    B. $-\frac{1}{6y}$
    C. $\frac{1}{3y}$
    D. $\frac{1}{6y}$

86. A recipe calls for $\frac{1}{6}$ teaspoon of oregano and $1\frac{1}{4}$ teaspoons of pepper. What is the ratio of oregano to pepper in this recipe?

    E. 1:12
    F. 2:15
    G. 1:3
    H. 2:3

GO ON TO THE NEXT PAGE

87. There are a total of 256 people at a party. If half of the people present leave every 5 minutes, how many people will still remain after 20 minutes?

    A. 80

    B. 64

    C. 32

    D. 16

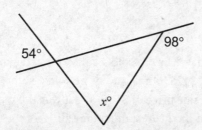

88. In the figure above, what is the value of *x* ?

    E. 24

    F. 28

    G. 36

    H. 44

89. If $x - \dfrac{7}{10} = y$, and $y = 2$, what is the value of x ?

    A. $-\dfrac{3}{10}$

    B. $\dfrac{9}{10}$

    C. $\dfrac{13}{10}$

    D. $\dfrac{27}{10}$

90. One box contains 3 balls, one of which is red. A second box contains 4 balls, one of which is red. If Pilar draws one ball at random from each box, what is the probability that both balls are red?

    E. $\dfrac{1}{14}$

    F. $\dfrac{1}{12}$

    G. $\dfrac{1}{7}$

    H. $\dfrac{2}{7}$

91. If *a* is a positive number, and the product of *b* and *c* is positive, which of the following **must** be true?

    A. $\dfrac{a}{c}$ is negative

    B. $\dfrac{a}{c}$ is positive

    C. $\dfrac{b}{c}$ is negative

    D. $\dfrac{b}{c}$ is positive

92. The spare change on a dresser is composed of pennies, nickels, and dimes. If the ratio of pennies to nickels is 2:3 and the ratio of pennies to dimes is 3:4, what is the ratio of nickels to dimes?

    E. 9:8

    F. 5:7

    G. 4:5

    H. 3:4

PARK PASS CHOICES

Pass Type	Number Purchased
1-Day, 1-Park	84
1-Day, 2-Parks	56
1-Day, 3-Parks	45
2-Day, 2-Parks	49
3-Day, 3-Parks	66

93. The table above shows the number of times that different types of park passes were purchased at a theme park. Based on this information, what is the probability of a customer purchasing a 3-Day, 3-Parks pass?

   A. 22%

   B. 37%

   C. 50%

   D. 66%

94. If an integer is randomly chosen from the first 50 positive integers, what is the probability that the integer selected has at least one digit that is a 3 ?

   E. $\dfrac{7}{25}$

   F. $\dfrac{3}{10}$

   G. $\dfrac{8}{25}$

   H. $\dfrac{2}{5}$

95. If $-1 < y < 0$, which of the following has the greatest value?

   A. y^2

   B. $1 - y$

   C. $1 + y$

   D. $2y$

96. An automobile dealership has only cars, trucks, SUVs, and vans on its lot, of which 179 are vans. The total vehicle-to-van ratio for the entire lot is 15:1. What is the total number of cars, trucks, and SUVs on the lot?

   E. 2,415

   F. 2,506

   G. 2,685

   H. 2,864

97. On Friday, Marvin sold 4 suits that had a mean sale price of $125. On Saturday, he sold 6 suits that had a mean sale price of $140. What was the mean sale price, to the nearest dollar, for all 10 of the suits he sold on Friday and Saturday?

   A. $130

   B. $132

   C. $133

   D. $134

98. Angle K and angle L are supplementary. If the measure of angle L is one-fourth the measure of angle K, how many degrees greater is angle K than angle L?

   E. 36°

   F. 54°

   G. 108°

   H. 144°

99. Andre buys two cedar trees to plant in his back yard. One tree is 4 feet, 9 inches tall and the other is 5 feet, 6.5 inches tall. What is the difference in height, in **inches**, between the two trees?

   A. 8.5

   B. 9.5

   C. 10.5

   D. 11.5

GO ON TO THE NEXT PAGE ➤

100. If $\frac{1}{y} = \frac{x}{3}$, and $y = \frac{1}{5}$, what is the value of x?

    E. $\frac{1}{15}$

    F. $\frac{3}{5}$

    G. $\frac{5}{3}$

    H. 15

101. The average (arithmetic mean) of 16 numbers is 3. The average of these 16 numbers and a seventeenth number is 4. What is the seventeenth number?

    A. 12

    B. 17

    C. 18

    D. 20

102. Given that $20 - (y - x) = 30 - (x - y)$, and $x = 4$, what is the value of y?

    E. -9

    F. -1

    G. 1

    H. Cannot be determined from the information given.

103. To get ready for a craft show, Eric and Agnes are painting magnets. Eric can paint 4 magnets in 10 minutes, working at a constant rate. Agnes can paint 6 magnets in 15 minutes, working at her own constant rate. What is the total number of magnets the two of them can paint in one hour?

    A. 10

    B. 30

    C. 42

    D. 48

104. Martin draws a rectangle that is 4.5 inches by 6 inches to represent his deck. If he used a scale of 1:80, what is the perimeter of his actual deck in **feet**?

    E. 70 feet

    F. 120 feet

    G. 140 feet

    H. 360 feet

$$\{2, 3, 4, 5, 6\}$$

105. Agnes made a list of all possible products of two **different** numbers from the set above. What is the ratio of odd products to even products?

    A. 1:9

    B. 1:4

    C. 1:2

    D. 2:3

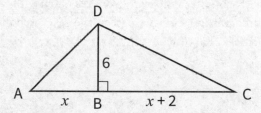

106. In the figure above, triangle ACD has an area of 24 square units, and the lengths of AB and BC are x and $x + 2$, respectively. If the length of BD is 6 units, what is the value of x?

    E. 1

    F. 2

    G. 3

    H. 4

Practice Tests

107. For how many positive integers x is $\frac{130}{x}$ an integer?

    A. 8

    B. 7

    C. 6

    D. 5

108. If $x = 3y(2 - |-4|) + y(3 - |-2|)$, what is the value of y in terms of x?

    E. $-\dfrac{x}{5}$

    F. $-5x$

    G. $-x$

    H. $\dfrac{x}{23}$

109. Two farmers each have a watermelon patch of equal size. Farmer A's patch is divided into 20 equal rows, and Farmer B's patch is divided into 16 equal rows. If Farmer A harvests 14 rows of his watermelon patch, what is the greatest number of whole rows that Farmer B can harvest from his patch without harvesting a greater percentage of a patch than Farmer A harvested?

    A. 9

    B. 10

    C. 11

    D. 12

110. Which statement must be true if x is a whole number such that $1 < x < 3$?

    E. $\dfrac{1}{x-1} < \dfrac{1}{x+1}$

    F. $\dfrac{1}{x-1} > \dfrac{1}{x+1} - 1$

    G. $\dfrac{1}{x-1} + \dfrac{1}{x+1} < 1$

    H. $\dfrac{1}{x-1} + \dfrac{1}{x+1} < -\dfrac{1}{x}$

111. If $x = 4(3 - y)(2^2 - 1)$, what is the value of y in terms of x?

    A. $\dfrac{x-6}{4}$

    B. $\dfrac{x}{4} - 3$

    C. $4 - \dfrac{x}{3}$

    D. $3 - \dfrac{x}{12}$

112. The amount of water in a bucket evaporates in such a way that the amount left at the end of each day is 10% less than the amount at the beginning of that same day. Approximately what percent of the original amount of water is left after three days?

    E. 30%

    F. 67%

    G. 70%

    H. 73%

GO ON TO THE NEXT PAGE

113. A bag contains 8 black chips, 19 green chips, and 23 blue chips. How many more black chips need to be added to the bag so that the probability of randomly drawing a black chip is $\frac{1}{4}$?

   A. 2
   B. 4
   C. 6
   D. 7

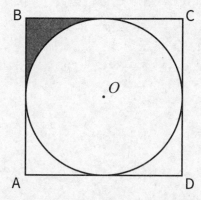

114. In the figure above, circle O is inscribed in square ABCD. If the circumference of circle O is 4π, what is the area of the shaded region?

   E. $\pi - 2$
   F. $4 - \pi$
   G. $4 + \pi$
   H. $16 - 4\pi$

SHSAT Practice Test 1

Answer Key

PART 1—ENGLISH LANGUAGE ARTS

1. C	16. G	31. B	46. G
2. F	17. B	32. G	47. D
3. B	18. E	33. A	48. G
4. F	19. C	34. H	49. D
5. D	20. E	35. C	50. H
6. E	21. D	36. H	51. C
7. D	22. E	37. D	52. F
8. F	23. D	38. F	53. D
9. A	24. F	39. D	54. H
10. H	25. D	40. E	55. C
11. D	26. G	41. B	56. E
12. G	27. B	42. F	57. D
13. C	28. H	43. C	
14. F	29. C	44. F	
15. B	30. G	45. A	

PART 2—MATHEMATICS

58. .7, 0.7, .70, 0.70	73. C	88. H	103. D
59. 80	74. F	89. D	104. G
60. 1	75. C	90. F	105. A
61. 60	76. F	91. D	106. G
62. 54	77. B	92. E	107. A
63. D	78. F	93. A	108. E
64. G	79. B	94. E	109. C
65. D	80. H	95. B	110. F
66. G	81. B	96. F	111. D
67. D	82. E	97. D	112. H
68. G	83. C	98. G	113. C
69. C	84. E	99. B	114. F
70. H	85. D	100. H	
71. B	86. F	101. D	
72. E	87. D	102. F	

Answers and Explanations

Part 1—English Language Arts

1. C

Category: Sentence Structure

Getting to the Answer: As written, the paragraph includes an incomplete sentence. Sentence 3, **(C)**, is a fragment, as it uses the verb "exploring" instead of a correct verb such as "explore" or an appropriate verb phrase like "are known for exploring." **(A)**, **(B)**, and **(D)** are correct as written.

2. F

Category: Knowledge of Language

Getting to the Answer: The correct answer will use clear and precise wording to articulate the phrase in the question. **(F)** correctly identifies that the KXTV journalist is reporting the details of the game. The idea that viewers of KXTV are receiving the explanations of the journalist is implied in the idea of reporting. **(E)** is incorrect because it is vague and contains much less information than the original sentence. **(G)** captures all of the necessary information but uses wordy language that is less clear. **(H)** does not include the fact that the journalist is reporting for KXTV and does not use the most precise wording.

3. B

Category: Punctuation

Getting to the Answer: Both missing and unnecessary punctuation are grammatically incorrect. **(B)** fixes both errors, as it rightly deletes the unnecessary comma after "revenue" and adds a necessary comma after the transition "consequently." **(A)** and **(C)** are incorrect because they each delete one needed comma and add one unnecessary comma. **(D)** incorrectly adds two unnecessary commas.

4. F

Category: Sentence Structure

Getting to the Answer: Modifiers should be near the words they modify. In sentence 2, "Highlighting legendary feats and memorable occasions" incorrectly modifies the subject immediately following, "many competitors." Instead, the modifying phrase should modify "Olympic games." Sentence 2 contains the error,

so **(F)** is correct. **(E)**, **(G)**, and **(H)** all have correctly placed modifiers.

5. D

Category: Sentence Structure

Getting to the Answer: Read each underlined portion, systematically looking for an error. The last sentence is a run-on because "Wolves aren't born knowing how to get along with other wolves" and "the experience of living in the pack results in their eventual ability to find their place in the hierarchy" are each independent clauses that must be properly joined. **(D)** correctly fixes the run-on by adding the coordinating conjunction "but" after the comma. **(A)** and **(C)** are incorrect because even though they do not introduce new errors, they do not fix the error in the last sentence. In addition to not fixing the existing error, **(B)** creates a grammatically incorrect run-on sentence by replacing the period after "natural instincts" with a comma.

6. E

Category: Usage

Getting to the Answer: The answer choices indicate that the sentence is missing a comma; look for specific situations in which commas are needed, such as punctuating nonessential phrases or coordinate adjectives. Coordinate adjectives describe characteristics of the same noun and must be connected with either a comma or the word "and." **(E)** is correct because it places a comma between the coordinate adjectives "swift" and "nimble." In addition to not providing a missing comma, **(F)**, **(G)**, and **(H)** are incorrect because they add unnecessary commas that create grammar errors. **(F)** places a comma before "and," which is incorrect because the combination of a comma and a FANBOYS conjunction is used to separate two independent clauses; "improved her previous best by more than half a second" is not an independent clause because it is missing a subject and cannot stand alone as a separate sentence. **(G)** is incorrect because "previous" is an adjective and "best" is a noun; a comma is not used between adjectives and the nouns they describe. **(H)** places an unnecessary comma between the prepositional phrase "by more than half a second" and the rest of the sentence.

7. D

Category: Punctuation & Usage

Getting to the Answer: Based on the corrections featured in each answer choice, the paragraph contains a comma issue and a verb tense issue. The comma after "curiosity" is necessary to separate the modifying phrase "Known for his curiosity" from the rest of sentence 1, so **(A)** and **(B)** are incorrect. Eliminate **(C)** because it changes the correct past tense "reproduced" in sentence 2 to the incorrect present tense "reproduces." In sentence 3, a comma is needed to separate the nonessential phrase "a combination of the words 'velvet' and 'crochet'" from the rest of the sentence, and sentence 4 references events in the past, so the past tense "described" is needed. **(D)** is correct.

8. F

Category: Topic Development

Getting to the Answer: The correct answer will clearly introduce the topic of the passage. **(F)** correctly focuses on how older traditions of natural therapies have been adopted by different groups of people in the modern world. **(E)** incorrectly characterizes natural therapies as new trends. **(G)** is too extreme, and **(H)** introduces an idea of skepticism that is not discussed elsewhere in the passage.

9. A

Category: Organization

Getting to the Answer: Identify the relationship between sentences 2 and 3. Sentence 2 discusses how the sweat lodge is widely used and that many other cultures have a similar practice. Sentence 3 then follows up with specific examples. The transition "For instance," in **(A)**, correctly connects sentence 2 to 3. **(B)**, **(C)**, and **(D)** are all contrast transitions and, therefore, cannot be correct.

10. H

Category: Topic Development

Getting to the Answer: Determine how the topic develops from sentence 4 to 5. Sentence 4 states that the basic purpose of these therapies is to raise the body's core temperature, and sentence 5 describes additional benefits of heat. The sentence stating that bacteria and viruses cannot easily survive at this temperature supports the idea in sentence 4 and logically connects to the following sentence. Thus, **(H)** is correct. **(E)**, **(F)**, and **(G)** are off-topic and do not logically follow sentence 4.

11. D

Category: Organization

Getting to the Answer: Identify the relationship between the portions before and after the comma in sentence 5. Both the portions before and after the comma describe the benefits of heat. Thus, a sequential transition is needed; **(D)** correctly uses the continuation word "and." **(A)** and **(C)** are contrast transitions that do not convey the intended meaning. **(B)** conveys emphasis but this does not fit the meaning of the sentence, and inserting "furthermore" by itself into the existing sentence would be grammatically incorrect.

12. G

Category: Organization

Getting to the Answer: Since all three sentences describe the structure of a traditional sweat lodge, look for a revision that connects the sentences logically and concisely. The sentences can be concisely combined by making sentence 7 a dependent clause and joining it to sentence 8 with "and," so **(G)** is correct. **(E)** improperly joins the sentences and creates a run-on. **(F)** creates a misplaced modifier, and **(H)** is a fragment that is missing a verb.

13. C

Category: Topic Development

Getting to the Answer: The correct answer will serve as a good concluding sentence for the paragraph, summarizing and supporting the main idea of the passage. **(C)** correctly focuses on the influence of sweat lodges and supports it by mentioning the trends in current research regarding its influence. **(A)** is too narrowly focused on religious traditions and is a poor concluding sentence. **(B)** is not relevant, and **(D)** does not represent the entire passage.

14. F

Category: Topic Development

Getting to the Answer: To determine which sentence is out of place, read in context and identify the topic of the paragraph. This paragraph is about the influence of the sweat lodge ceremony. Thus, sentence 16, **(F)**, is irrelevant and should be deleted. All other sentences work well with the overall idea.

Passage Analysis: This passage is about the use of murals to bring color back to cities to make them more human-friendly environments. Paragraph 1 explains that in contrast to ancient, colorful cities, modern cities tend to be drab. Paragraph 2 traces the history and revival of murals in Mexico and introduces important people. Paragraph 3 addresses the development of mural painting in the United States. Paragraph 4 describes the impact of murals on culture, and the final paragraph provides the author's view of murals as a way to improve city life. Paragraph 5 concludes the passage and restates the way that murals can revitalize cityscapes through color.

15. B
Category: Function

Getting to the Answer: In paragraph 2, the three painters are introduced as "the first important muralists" whose "work inspired a vast program of publicly financed commissions in the 1930s." Others benefited from their initial work, which matches **(B)**. **(A)** and **(C)** are Out of Scope; the muralists did not work as a team, and though their murals were large, the passage does not state that they were the largest paintings ever produced. The muralists were not the people who imitated the colors of ancient Greece or Rome (those were the modern architects), so **(D)** is incorrect as well.

16. G
Category: Infographic

Getting to the Answer: The infographic illustrates how many artists were employed by the "vast program of publicly financed commissions in the 1930s" described in paragraph 2 of the passage. **(G)** is the correct answer. **(E)** is incorrect because the chart indicates 900 artists created murals; 2,500 artists were involved in *all* types of the Fine Arts. **(F)** is a Distortion; the Federal Art Project was a program by the United States, not Mexico. **(H)** is another Distortion; the graphic shows the artists who were employed, not those who were available.

17. B
Category: Detail

Getting to the Answer: The reason for the drab colors of modern cities is in paragraph 1, where the passage states that "architects have mostly favored the use of somber, neutral colors" in an attempt to imitate their ideas of architecture from Roman and Greek

civilizations. The next sentence identifies that desire as "misguided" because ancient cities actually used a lot of color. **(B)** is the correct answer. For the incorrect choices, **(A)** is a fact from the passage that indicates why cities may appear drab, but it is not the choice of the architects. **(C)** describes the overall appearance of the cities, not a decision of the architects. **(D)** describes the power of murals to transform already drab cities, not the architects' decisions to use muted colors.

18. E
Category: Global

Getting to the Answer: Use your notes to predict how paragraph 2 fits into the author's purpose: to describe how murals can enhance city life. After recognizing the issue of drab, colorless cities in paragraph 1, paragraph 2 identifies one solution—murals—and briefly recounts their history. **(E)** is the correct answer. **(F)** and **(G)** are Out of Scope. Although the descriptions of some of the murals include cultural topics, "changes in culture" are not discussed. Similarly, the drab modern cities are not contrasted with colorful ancient cities; the difference is only mentioned. **(H)** Is Extreme; color may be helpful to "save" neighborhoods from demolition, but this is not linked to urban decay.

19. C
Category: Detail

Getting to the Answer: The correct choice will describe a reason or a process by which "color can help to rehabilitate, revitalize, or even save neighborhoods." "Creating a unique sense of place and . . . spirit of vitality" in **(C)**, the correct choice, explains how murals, previously described as an "especially exciting way to introduce color back into the cityscape" in paragraph 2, can improve a neighborhood. **(A)** is incorrect because "brightening public places" is too vague, and there is no connection to improving a neighborhood. **(B)** is also too vague; recollection of historical events or cultural changes may or may not improve a neighborhood. **(D)** describes another goal of providing color in the urban neighborhoods, not support for the idea that color may revitalize these neighborhoods.

20. E
Category: Inference

Getting to the Answer: When a question does not provide a clue to locate the answer in the passage, work through the choices by elimination. The correct answer will be supported by the passage. In paragraph 4, the text states, "Color can help to rehabilitate, revitalize, or even save neighborhoods that might otherwise be doomed to demolition." This matches **(E)**, the correct answer. The author celebrates political murals, such as "The Wall of Respect" in paragraph 3, so eliminate **(F)**. Paragraphs 2 and 4 state that murals can reflect historical events, but not that they can cause them; eliminate **(G)**. The author would not agree with **(H)** because the focus of the passage is how cities are not doomed to be colorless but can, in fact, be improved.

Passage Analysis: This passage describes the career and enduring influence of Miles Davis, a famous jazz musician. Paragraph 1 introduces his importance, and paragraph 2 chronicles his early life and training. Paragraph 3 describes his musical style and early work. Paragraph 4 discusses what many critics consider the high point of Davis's career: his work in the 1950s. Paragraph 5 describes how Davis continued to innovate in later years, and paragraph 6 summarizes and restates Davis's importance to jazz.

21. D
Category: Global

Getting to the Answer: A Global question requires an answer that covers all parts of the passage—in this case, the career of Miles Davis—and the only one to do that is **(D)**, the correct answer. **(A)** is incorrect because Davis's major innovations took place in the 1950s, not the 1940s. **(B)** is a minor detail from paragraph 2, not the focus of the entire passage. **(C)** is a Distortion; Davis played a pivotal role in the origins of West Coast jazz, not bebop.

22. E
Category: Function

Getting to the Answer: Always keep the purpose of the passage—the career and enduring influence of Miles Davis—in mind, and answer the question, "How did the author use this sentence to make that point?" The

sentence in the question indicates that many people thought Davis's upbringing was unusual for a jazz musician, and the author goes on to list other anomalies: he gets his best musical education in nightclubs, not school; he plays "sparingly," not with a lot of notes like other jazz musicians; he develops a new style of jazz; and he continues to innovate throughout his life. **(E)** is correct; Davis's distinctive upbringing is the first of these differences mentioned. **(F)** and **(H)** contradict information in the passage. Paragraph 2 stated Davis had both an interest in music and a talent for it; he was not a "poor fit." Paragraph 2 also mentions Davis's mother, so he was not raised by his father alone. **(G)** is Out of Scope; there is no discussion of how Davis paid to visit nightclubs, or even if he had to pay at all.

23. D
Category: Detail

Getting to the Answer: The clue in the question indicates that you're looking for support for the critics' opinion that the 1950s was "the high point of Davis's career," so start by scanning the choices for one that refers to the critics' view. **(D)**, the correct answer, states that the most "critical acclaim" Davis received was for *Kind of Blue*, released in the 1950s. **(A)**, **(B)**, and **(C)** do not refer to the critics' opinions, and these choices are all incorrect.

24. F
Category: Detail

Getting to the Answer: Davis's early musical education is described in paragraph 2, so return there and research the correct answer. Davis began studying the trumpet, moved to New York and studied at Juilliard, and then started playing with nightclub musicians. **(F)** is correct. The text never compares Davis's preference for jazz over classical music, so **(E)** is Out of Scope. Though he worked hard to keep up with master jazz musicians Charlie Parker, Thelonious Monk, and Dizzy Gillespie, they were not his classmates, so eliminate **(G)**. Finally, **(H)** is Out of Scope because the passage never states Davis was dissatisfied with his studies at the Juilliard School, only that he did study there.

25. D
Category: Function

Getting to the Answer: All of the choices refer to "cool" jazz, so return to the passage and look up what that means. In paragraph 4, it is described as based on

"Davis's "less-is-more" approach." Paragraph 3 notes that Davis's style is played "sparingly" and doesn't fill "the air with a headlong rush of notes as other bebop musicians did." In other words, bebop was "busy" music, frantic and complex, whereas "cool" jazz appreciated the "silences between the notes" and the "less-is-more" approach. Match this with the correct answer, **(D)**. If you are unsure of the correct answer or unable to make a prediction, you can also eliminate other choices to get to the correct answer. Cool jazz became dominant in the 1950s, so it was developed earlier than the 1970s; eliminate **(A)**. It was popular, so eliminate **(B)**. The sentence in the question describes the hallmark of cool jazz, not the period of time when Davis played it, so eliminate **(C)** as well.

26. G

Category: Inference

Getting to the Answer: To expand one's horizons is to seek out new experiences or activities, which, in Davis's case, relates to his "restless search for new sounds" mentioned in paragraph 5. This matches **(G)**, the correct answer. **(E)** may be tempting, but be careful of the words "new art forms." Davis didn't move into painting, dance, or any other art form; he stayed with music, though he sought new ways to express himself musically. Where he played, **(F)**, has nothing to do with expanding his musical horizons, and there is no mention in the passage of his reaction to critics' opinions, eliminating **(H)**.

27. B

Category: Function

Getting to the Answer: Consider how paragraph 2 contributes to the central theme of the passage: how and why Miles Davis is an important and influential jazz musician. Paragraph 2 discusses how that happened—his early life, musical training, and move to playing with professional musicians in jazz clubs. The paragraph states that he "worked tirelessly to perfect his technique," and the word "haunting" emphasizes his regular attendance at night. **(B)** is the correct answer. All of the other choices are Out of Scope. Paragraph 2 does not discuss any danger, Davis's relationship with "junior" artists, or any difficulty in entering the clubs.

28. H

Category: Detail

Getting to the Answer: Davis's "less-is-more" approach is described as more interested "in the silences between

the notes than in the notes themselves." He included pauses in his music rather than fill every moment with bebop-style notes. This matches **(H)**, the correct answer. The remaining choices are Out of Scope; the passage never mentions that his selections were short and concise, that he limited the number of musicians in his band, or that he played only a few times a week.

Passage Analysis: This passage describes how immigrant families survived in the United States. Paragraph 1 details how immigrant groups remained together in the New World and the particular importance of kinship ties. Paragraph 2 corrects the older thinking that immigrant families broke down when moving from a rural to a city environment and presents new scholarship. Paragraph 3 attributes the successful survival of immigrant families to the core value of cooperation. Paragraph 4 details how these immigrant kinship associations not only aided the immigrants themselves, but also served the needs of the industrial economy.

29. C

Category: Global

Getting to the Answer: The answer to a Global question must be broad enough to reflect all the information in the passage. In this case, the major focus is on how relationships, and kinship ties in particular, helped immigrant families adjust to and survive in their new country, the United States. **(C)** is correct. **(A)** is a Misused Detail; paragraph 2 identifies the belief "the immigrant family group broke down" as "untrue." There is no mention of history books or their treatment of immigrant families, so **(B)** is Out of Scope. The passage mentions that occasionally families were able to improve their standards of living, but this is a detail, not the central idea, making **(D)** incorrect.

30. G

Category: Detail

Getting to the Answer: If you don't know what a "coping mechanism" is, stay calm; the passage will tell you. The first part of paragraph 1 describes the difficulties faced by immigrant families, and the "coping mechanism" was "staying with one's own people," which "assisted with the transition." So immigrants stayed together, and this helped them adjust to their new situation. Now, check the choices for one that describes a way or a reason immigrants might stay together. **(G)** is the only match and is the correct answer. **(E)** is incorrect because it describes why immigrant families needed to stay together, but not how they did it. **(F)** and **(H)** are incorrect because they describe benefits to the wider economy, not to the immigrant family.

31. B
Category: Global

Getting to the Answer: Keep the main idea in mind—the dynamics of immigrant families enabled them to adjust to their new lives in the United States and had benefits to the industrial economy as well. Then determine how paragraph 2 contributes to the passage as a whole. Paragraph 2 opens by identifying the assumption "that American immigrant families broke down in the transition from a rural to an urban economy," identifies this assumption as "untrue," and provides the author's support for the argument that "the family played an essential role in shaping the urban economy." This matches **(B)**, the correct answer. **(A)** is incorrect because the passage never compares the living standards in the Old and New Worlds. **(C)** is a Distortion; the original assumption was "insubstantial" but is not identified in the passage as presented in "modern history books." **(D)** is another Distortion. The *community*, not economic, dimension of the family is discussed as benefiting immigrants, and this discussion takes place in paragraph 3, not paragraph 2.

32. G
Category: Function

Getting to the Answer: Refresh your memory of the main idea: the dynamics of immigrant families enabled them to adjust to their new lives in the United States and had benefits to the industrial economy as well. Then determine how paragraphs 3 and 4 contribute to that idea. After introducing the author's view that "the family played an essential role in shaping the urban economy" at the end of paragraph 2, the author supports that opinion by detailing how the family supported its members in paragraph 3, and how the family supported the wider economy in paragraph 4. This matches **(G)**, the correct answer. **(E)** is incorrect because the historians' mistaken assumption is discussed in paragraph 2, not paragraphs 3 or 4. **(F)** is Extreme; the passage states "occasionally" families improved their standard of living, not "always." **(H)** is Out of Scope; the passage only defines

an immigrant family group as a "household" and never defines native family groups.

33. A
Category: Inference

Getting to the Answer: Even for Inference questions that may not be directly stated in the passage, the correct answer will always be supported by information from the passage. Paragraph 3 states that immigrant families endured through cooperation "by working together, pooling limited resources, and muting individual inclinations." This supports **(A)**, the correct answer. The passage mentions the move from rural to industrial economies, but there is no suggestion that immigrant families preferred one location over the other; eliminate **(B)**. The entirety of paragraph 3 refutes the assumption that families worked best in isolation from industrial society; eliminate **(C)**. Paragraph 4 discusses how the dynamics of immigrant family groups benefited the industrial economy, making **(D)** incorrect.

34. H
Category: Function

Getting to the Answer: Refer back to paragraph 4 to see how the author uses the phrase "the larger machinery." Family groups helped workers move, assisted with communications, and helped meet employer's needs; this matches **(H)**, the correct answer. There were different ways immigrant groups benefited the urban economy. **(E)** and **(F)** are not discussed in the passage, and so are Out of Scope. **(G)** is a Distortion; although immigrant family groups did benefit the urban economy, "unionizing factories" is not discussed as one of these benefits.

35. C
Category: Inference

Getting to the Answer: The sentence in which "muting individual inclinations" appears details how the immigrant families survived in the New World. If you don't know what "muting individual inclinations" means, consider the focus of that paragraph: immigrant families managed the transition to their new country by cooperating and working together. The best match is **(C)**. **(A)** and **(B)** are Out of Scope; the passage never mentions economic declines or hardships. **(D)** is a subtle distortion of information in the text. Although in everyday life cooperation may involve resolving individual disputes, the text doesn't mention quarrels, so this choice is also incorrect.

36. H
Category: Detail

Getting to the Answer: The entire passage is focused on explaining how immigrant families succeeded after moving to the United States, so keep the exact question in mind and work through the choices by elimination. The correct choice will provide evidence that immigrant families succeeded in their transition in the United States. **(E)** explains that immigrant families were able to stay together but does not mention their success. Eliminate this choice. **(F)** describes blood relationship as the basis for the formation of immigrant groups but again does not mention the success of immigrant groups; eliminate this choice too. Similarly, **(G)** describes the members of the immigrant groups but not their success, so it cannot be correct. **(H)** is the only choice left and must be correct. **(H)** states that immigrant groups were able to contribute to the wider economy, so the immigrant groups themselves must have been successful. In addition, the previous sentence mentions that immigrant families were able to "thrive" or succeed.

Passage Analysis: This passage is about the history and collapse of the Old Man of the Mountain. Paragraph 1 describes the Old Man of the Mountain and its collapse. Paragraph 2 describes the stone profile. Paragraph 3 gives its history. Paragraph 4 describes the geological formation of the Old Man, and paragraph 5 discusses other notable rock formations around the world.

37. D
Category: Global

Getting to the Answer: Global questions test your understanding of the passage as a whole. When answering a Global question, form a prediction that unifies the ideas discussed throughout the passage. The passage discusses the Old Man of the Mountain, its formation, features, history, and collapse. **(D)** incorporates all this information and is correct. **(A)** is a Misused Detail; although the passage does mention the forces that carved the Old Man of the Mountain, this choice does not reflect its discovery or collapse. **(B)** is Opposite; the passage states that New Hampshire has found plans to rebuild the Old Man of Mountain impractical. **(C)** is

another Misused Detail. This choice does not include the formation or collapse of the Old Man of the Mountain and is incorrect.

38. F
Category: Function

Getting to the Answer: The collapse of the Old Man of the Mountain is discussed in the paragraph 1, which states, "the unusually harsh spring is believed to have proved too much." **(F)** matches and is the correct answer. **(E)** and **(G)** are Distortions; ice falling from the mountain face is cited as a cause for the Old Man's formation in paragraph 4, not its collapse, and the passage mentions that cables and turnbuckles held the face in place since 1915, but the text does not state that they broke. **(H)** is also a Distortion; this is mentioned as a reason for the rocky profile's formation, not its collapse.

39. D
Category: Detail

Getting to the Answer: When a question asks for a detail from the passage, paraphrase the question in your mind, then use your Roadmap or paragraph notes to locate the information in the passage. Here, you're asked how the author indicated that people have known about the Old Man of the Mountain for a long time. Return to paragraph 3, where the discovery of the formation is mentioned. Although the formation was first documented in 1805, the author follows that information with the contrast keyword "however" to indicate that the Native Americans knew of the formation much earlier. **(D)** is correct. **(A)** is a Misused Detail from the passage; although Brooks's and Whitcomb's discovery of the Old Man of the Mountain did take place a long time ago, the author emphasizes that the Native Americans knew of it much longer. **(B)** is Extreme, and doesn't relate to the question. The efforts to preserve the formation are discussed, but there was no "controversy" described. In addition, the preservation efforts were recent, and do not indicate that people have known of the formation for a long time. Similarly, the construction of the museum does not indicate that people have known of the formation for a long time; **(C)** is a Misused Detail.

40. E

Category: Function

Getting to the Answer: Paragraph 3 discusses the history and fame of the Old Man of the Mountain. The quote supports the paragraph topic by showing that the Old Man of the Mountain was appreciated as a proud symbol of New Hampshire even in the 19th century, so **(E)** is correct. **(F)** and **(G)** are Out of Scope; Webster's reputation as an orator is not mentioned in the passage. Furthermore, the passage never discusses why the Old Man was chosen as the state symbol. **(H)** is a Distortion; the passage states that Daniel Webster lived during the 19th century, while the collapse of the Old Man of the Mountain did not occur until 2003.

41. B

Category: Global

Getting to the Answer: When a question asks how a paragraph fits into a passage, recall the central idea of the entire passage. Here, the purpose of the passage is to discuss the formation, history, importance and loss of the Old Man of the Mountain. Paragraph 4 discusses the geological processes which created the formation. The topic sentence of the paragraph emphasizes that, even though people have known about the Old Man of the Mountain for a long time, its history is much older. **(B)** is correct. **(A)** is a subtle Distortion; the paragraph discusses the formation of the Old Man of the Mountain, not its collapse. **(C)** is a Misused Detail. Since it was so distinctive, the profile of the Old Man of the Mountain was well-formed, but that is not mentioned in paragraph 4. **(D)** is Out of Scope. There is no comparison in the text between New Hampshire and any other state.

42. F

Category: Detail

Getting to the Answer: The clue words "present day" in the question focus your attention on what is happening now, after the collapse of the Old Man of the Mountain. **(F)**, describing the construction of the museum, is the correct answer. **(E)**, describing the formation before its collapse, and **(G)**, the words of Daniel Webster from the 19th century, are not happening in the "present day." Eliminate these two choices. **(H)**, describing other rock formations around the world, does not indicate the importance of the Old Man of the Mountain and is also incorrect.

43. C

Category: Detail

Getting to the Answer: The appearance of the Old Man of the Mountain is described in paragraph 2: "the granite ledges had jutted out from the rock face of the cliff . . . suggesting the features of a face in profile," but this sentence is not among the choices. Find the choice that indicates the formation looked like an old man's face. **(C)** is correct. The other choices do not describe the formation's appearance, and are therefore incorrect.

44. F

Category: Global

Getting to the Answer: Paragraph 1 introduces the collapse of the rock formation and its significant impact on the people of New Hampshire. The sentence in the question contrasts the many thousands of years the formation stood with the fact that its weaknesses were well-known—since 1915, equipment had been used to try to stabilize the rocks. So, the author is indicating that the collapse of the Old Man of the Mountain was not surprising. **(F)** is correct. **(E)** is a Misused Detail; the first part of the sentence gives the impression of great age, but the most important idea in the sentence is that of the formation's weakness. **(G)** is Opposite; the author's intention is to announce the weakness of the formation. **(H)** is incorrect because the transition to the geological history of the formation does not happen until paragraph 4. The sentence in the question does not relate that information.

Passage Analysis: This early science fiction passage tells of a professor's discovery of an impending collision of a star with Earth, destroying all mankind. Paragraph 1 introduces the professor who, through mathematical calculations, discovered the coming disaster. In paragraph 2, the professor begins his lecture to his students, but states that for a reason yet to be explained, he will not be able to finish the course, but that "Man has lived in vain." The students' reactions are detailed in the paragraphs 3 and 4, as the professor begins to explain, and it all becomes clear to students in paragraph 5. Paragraph 6 describes how the tolling of the bells that night brings people out to gather and pray, while the menacing star rises, bright in the sky. Paragraph 7 contains more ominous descriptions of how the star will threaten Earth and everyone living there.

45. A

Category: Global

Getting to the Answer: At the beginning of paragraph 2, the professor walks into his classroom, poised to drop a bombshell on his students. Wells repeatedly describes this math teacher as someone who is precise, calm, and punctual. This man who alone knows that the world is about to end—and who is about to share that news with the world—still habitually walks into his classroom, behaving in many ways just as he always has. Wells uses the chalk example as a way of contrasting the mundane daily classroom experience with the profoundly disturbing news he is about to share; **(A)** is correct. There is no suggestion in the passage that the mathematician's students did not respect him or that he was "fussy." **(B)** is incorrect. **(C)** is tempting because it would be understandable if this distressing news made someone fidget; however, Wells uses the chalk fidgeting as an example of how the professor ordinarily behaves, not as something provoked by the news. **(D)** is incorrect because it is not suggested in the passage.

46. G

Category: Global

Getting to the Answer: Paragraph 3 describes the student's reaction as "Raised eyebrows and grinning lips there were," and even raised the question ("Mad?") which indicates that most students were confused. **(G)** is correct. **(E)** and **(F)** might describe the "one or two faces remained intent upon his calm grey-fringed face," but one or two are surely not "most students." All listen to the teacher, so no one seems disinterested; eliminate **(H)**.

47. D

Category: Function

Getting to the Answer: What have the mathematician's calculations proven to him? Why is his face "grave?" Why does he watch the star from his window? All are indications that a great cosmic calamity is about to occur, a circumstance clearly beyond his control. Match this with **(D)**. There is no suggestion that he is frail; eliminate **(A)**. **(B)** and **(C)** are Out of Scope; miscalculation and guilt are not mentioned in the passage.

48. G

Category: Detail

Getting to the Answer: The mathematician's personal characteristics are discussed in numerous places in the passage. Paragraph 1 notes that he has a calm, intentional manner as a teacher. These ideas match the "accustomed studied commonness of phrasing" in the correct answer, **(G)**. **(E)** is incorrect as it has nothing to do with the professor's manner or style of teaching. **(F)** does not support the serene patience at issue here. **(H)** is incorrect in that it does not demonstrate the mathematician's calm, patient personal traits.

49. D

Category: Function

Getting to the Answer: Note the ominous tone of paragraph 6; this sense of doom, along with the theme of cosmic destruction, implies that "the world was awake" because of fear and dread of what was to come. **(D)** is correct. There is no support in the story for **(A)** or **(B)**, and **(C)** is the opposite of what paragraph 6 conveys.

50. H

Category: Function

Getting to the Answer: The tone of paragraph 6 is ominous because people think that the world is about to end. The sentence states that they should "gather in their churches and pray," which shows how people are being urged to prepare for death, as **(H)** states. There is no support in the story for **(E)** or **(F)**, and **(G)** is a Distortion; the noise is mentioned to foretell doom, not to explain why people may not be able to sleep.

Poem Analysis: The poem describes the landscape during the dawning of a new day, as well as the activities of various people, depending on their location. In the first stanza, dawn's effect on nature is described, but by line 7 the focus shifts to a single person. Someone "reluctantly" wakes from dreams of strange things and is surprised to find their bedroom is just as ordinary and familiar as ever. In the second stanza, the dawn's effect on a city center is described. Trash left over from the city's nightlife is still in the streets, and those who were up late ignore the dawn by sleeping in late with their window blinds blocking the light. In the third stanza, the focus shifts to the outskirts of the city. Life there is already up and about: People start kitchen fires to cook breakfast, others are leaving their homes, and trains that had been traveling through the night converge on the city itself.

51. C
Category: Global

Getting to the Answer: The details in the first stanza (lines 1–12) contribute to the development of the poem's theme by establishing the drowsy feeling of sleep that lingers at the start of the day. The person waking is described as being surprised that the world is ordinary, compared to the implicitly strange landscape of the speaker's dreams. Thus, **(C)** is correct. The imagery of the speaker's dreams is not directly described; its nature can only be inferred from the contrast the mundane bedroom is said to make with it. So, **(A)** is incorrect. The dawning sun, not the waking person, is compared to a flower's unfurling petals; **(B)** is incorrect. The person does not wake to find himself in a strange bed. On the contrary, a point is made that the bed is familiar; **(D)** is incorrect.

52. F
Category: Function

Getting to the Answer: Lines 4–6 in the poem describe dew-laden trees in the early morning light. This shows how nighttime leaves evidence of its passing, just as the person waking is marked by the lingering impression of the dream he was having. This development of nighttime leaving evidence is carried into the second stanza, where the author continues to discuss this idea with phrases such as "stagnant ash-barrels," "litter in the streets," and "milkcans by back doors." Thus, **(F)** is correct. While there is a reference to flowers in the third stanza, there are not references to vegetation imagery throughout the poem; **(E)** is incorrect. The dreamer is not imagining the trees to have silver leaves. That is merely a description of the dew in the leaves shining in the morning light; **(G)** is incorrect. The dew is not a form of damage. Dew is merely droplets of water; **(H)** is incorrect.

53. D
Category: Detail

Getting to the Answer: Line 21 best supports the idea that people in the city react differently to the dawn than those who live in the city's outskirts. Their paleness

may be a reference to them not being tanned by working in the sunlight, which was more common in the late nineteenth and early twentieth century of the author's lifetime. This is built upon in lines 22–23, where people at the city's outskirts are described as having their sleep already washed away. That is, they need to get up early and work under the sun. Thus, **(D)** is correct. The line in **(A)** merely describes the setting differing from the outskirts of the city, not the people themselves. **(B)** and **(C)** are incorrect because they describe the evidence of city people sleeping in, not how those city people are reacting to the dawn itself.

54. H
Category: Function

Getting to the Answer: Line 15, which describes "stale fragments of the night" in the heart of the city, points out the contrast between those who live in the city and those who live with nature's rhythms. It serves as evidence to confirm that some city people were up late, before transitioning to show those same people sleeping through the dawn with their blinds pulled shut. Thus, **(H)** is correct and **(G)** is incorrect. Although **(E)** describes the details that line 15 describes, there is no reference to junk needing to be collected—it only suggests that this waste exists. **(F)** is incorrect because "the stale fragments" are not evidence of cleanliness.

55. C
Category: Function

Getting to the Answer: Line 25 contributes to the ideas of the third stanza by establishing that the flowers have woken up for the day, as their petals must have unfurled to allow the sunlight to reach into their cups. This parallels how the people have also woken and started their day. Thus, **(C)** is correct. **(A)** is incorrect because it confuses the flower imagery in the third stanza with that in the first. The third stanza features literal flowers, not a metaphor for the rising sun as the first stanza does. **(B)** is incorrect because sunlight, not dew, is collecting in the flowers. **(D)** is incorrect because the beauty of the flowers is not described; only the flowers' existence is described.

56. E
Category: Global

Getting to the Answer: Line 29 helps develop the theme of the poem by suggesting that people outside of the city wake with the sun and go about their morning routines. The blinds do not roll up themselves, nor do the fireplaces kindle themselves. People have to do those things. Thus, **(E)** is correct and **(F)** is incorrect. While the waking people may be disoriented, given the information in the first stanza, nothing in line 29 gives insight into the state of mind of the people going about their morning routines; **(G)** is incorrect. While the chirping birds are mentioned in the third stanza, they are a mere detail. The majority of the stanza—and the poem—is devoted to emphasizing the importance of sunlight in waking up for the day. Thus, **(H)** is incorrect.

57. D

Category: Detail

Getting to the Answer: Lines 32–33 best support the idea that day is overcoming the night by describing how dozens of early morning trains are converging on the sleepy downtown. In other words, day is not letting the downtown area wake on its own schedule. Thus, **(D)** is correct. **(A)** is incorrect because, while it provides a description of a tree in the morning, it does not describe how the day is overcoming the night. **(B)** is incorrect because it merely contrasts the strangeness of dreams with the ordinary qualities of waking life. **(C)** is incorrect because it describes people who "flout" the day; in other words, people who ignore the sun and fail to rise with the dawn.

Part 2—Mathematics

58. .7, 0.7, .70, 0.70
Subject: Algebra

Getting to the Answer: As with any proportion, start by cross multiplying, then perform the necessary algebra to isolate x. Be sure to distribute the 20 to both terms when you cross multiply.

$$\frac{2x + 1}{4} = \frac{12}{20}$$
$$20(2x + 1) = 12(4)$$
$$40x + 20 = 48$$
$$40x = 28$$
$$x = \frac{28}{40} = \frac{7}{10}$$

Because this is a grid-in question, you can enter .7 a few different ways and still be correct: .7, 0.7, .70, or 0.70. Remember that you must convert any fractions to decimals for grid-in questions.

59. 80
Subject: Geometry

Getting to the Answer: First convert 4 inches to $\frac{1}{3}$ foot. Then, multiply the length times the width times the depth to calculate the volume, in cubic feet:

$$20 \times 12 \times \frac{1}{3} = 20 \times 4 = 80$$

60. 1
Subject: Algebra

Getting to the Answer: Inequalities can be solved just like equations, with one important difference: if you multiply or divide by a negative number, then the direction of the inequality changes.

$$-3n + 5 \geq -1$$
$$-3n \geq -6$$
$$n \leq 2$$

Since you know that n is a positive odd integer less than or equal to 2, n must be 1.

61. 60

Subject: Statistics and Probability

Getting to the Answer: First, figure out how many different vegetable pairs are possible. Use 1, 2, 3, 4, 5, and 6 to represent the vegetables and create a list of possible pairs:

1 and 2; 1 and 3; 1 and 4; 1 and 5; 1 and 6
2 and 3; 2 and 4; 2 and 5; 2 and 6
3 and 4; 3 and 5; 3 and 6
4 and 5; 4 and 6
5 and 6

So, there are 15 different vegetable combinations for one platter. Since there are 4 platter sizes, multiply the total number of combinations by 4 to get the total number of different platters Selena could create: $4 \times 15 = 60$.

62. 54

Subject: Arithmetic

Getting to the Answer: The question states that Samantha grew 36 onions. You are also told that the number of onions, 36, is three times the number of carrots she grew. Thus, she grew $36 \div 3 = 12$ carrots. The number of carrots is twice the number of peppers she grew, so she grew $12 \div 2 = 6$ peppers. Combined, she grew $36 + 12 + 6 = 54$ total vegetables, so grid in 54.

63. D

Subject: Arithmetic

Getting to the Answer: To subtract the fractions inside the parentheses, write $\frac{1}{2}$ as $\frac{4}{8}$ so the denominators are the same. Then subtract the numerators and keep the denominator as 8. Next, multiply the result by $\frac{1}{3}$. To multiply fractions, multiply the numerators and then multiply the denominators. Simplify the final answer if possible.

$$x = \frac{1}{3}\left(\frac{1}{2} - \frac{1}{8}\right)$$
$$= \frac{1}{3}\left(\frac{4}{8} - \frac{1}{8}\right)$$
$$= \frac{1}{3}\left(\frac{3}{8}\right)$$
$$= \frac{3}{24} = \frac{1}{8}$$

64. G

Subject: Algebra

Getting to the Answer: Let x be the number of pairs of adult shoes stocked when 140 pairs of children's shoes are stocked. Set up a proportion and solve for x:

$$\frac{140}{x} = \frac{5}{7}$$
$$5x = 7(140)$$
$$5x = 980$$
$$x = 196$$

When 140 pairs of children's shoes are stocked, 196 pairs of adult shoes are stocked.

65. D

Subject: Algebra

Getting to the Answer: Let x be the total number of math problems in the workbook. Then, 24% of x is 72. Write 24% as the ratio 24 to 100 to set up a proportion and solve for x. To keep the numbers small, don't multiply until you absolutely have to.

$$\frac{24}{100} = \frac{72}{x}$$
$$24x = 72(100)$$
$$x = \frac{72(100)}{24}$$
$$x = 3(100) = 300 \text{ math problems}$$

66. G

Subject: Algebra

Getting to the Answer: To answer this question algebraically, just translate one step at a time. There are f freshmen in the class, but if 5 freshmen drop the class, there would be $f - 5$ freshmen left. The number of sophomores would be 3 times the number of freshmen left: 3 times $f - 5$, or $3(f - 5)$. So, $s = 3(f - 5)$.

You could also try Picking Numbers. If $f = 10$, then there are 10 freshmen in the class. If 5 freshmen drop the class, then there would be $10 - 5$, or 5, freshmen left in the class. The number of sophomores would then be 3 times the number of freshmen left, or $3 \times 5 = 15$. So, there are 15 sophomores in the class and $s = 15$. Which of the answer choices work with $f = 10$ and $s = 15$? All you have to do is plug those numbers into the choices. Only **(G)** works, so **(G)** is therefore the correct answer.

67. D

Subject: Arithmetic

Getting to the Answer: If the particle travels from A to B to C to D to E and then back to A, it has traveled 5 centimeters, since each side of the pentagon measures 1 centimeter. If it goes all the way around the pentagon again, it has traveled another 5 centimeters, for a total of 10 centimeters. In fact, every time the particle makes a complete revolution around the pentagon (from point A back to point A again), it travels an additional 5 centimeters. So, if the number of centimeters the particle has traveled is a multiple of 5, the particle must be at point A. The number 723 is 3 more than a multiple of 5. If the particle had gone 720 centimeters it would be at point A; since it has gone 3 more centimeters, it must be at point D.

68. G

Subject: Arithmetic

Getting to the Answer: First, add the percentage of large pizzas ordered with 3 toppings and 4 or more toppings: 15% + 5% = 20%.

So, 20% of the 120 large pizzas were ordered with at least 3 toppings, so use that to calculate the number of large pizzas: $120 \times 0.2 = 24$.

69. C

Subject: Geometry

Getting to the Answer: In a parallelogram, adjacent angles are supplementary, so $3x + 57 = 180$. Subtracting 57 from both sides of the equation yields $3x = 123$, and dividing both sides by 3 yields $x = 41$.

A less efficient, but perfectly valid, solution would be to use the fact that in a parallelogram, opposite angles are congruent, and that the sum of the interior angles of a parallelogram is equal to 360°. You could solve the equation $2(57) + 2(3x) = 360$ and you would arrive at the same value for x, 41.

70. H

Subject: Arithmetic

Getting to the Answer: When would $4 + \frac{1}{s}$ have the smallest possible value? Certainly if s, and therefore its reciprocal, were negative, $4 + \frac{1}{s}$ would be smaller than 4, since adding a negative number is like subtracting a positive number. However, none of the answer choices are negative, so $4 + \frac{1}{s}$ will be greater than 4. However,

the sum will be as small as possible when $\frac{1}{s}$ is as small as possible. Now, think about how fractions work: when the numerator is 1, the bigger the denominator is, the smaller the fraction is. Thus, you want the biggest possible value for s. The largest of the answer choices is 4; **(H)** is the correct answer.

71. B

Subject: Algebra

Getting to the Answer: Cross multiply to solve for x. Then, divide both sides of the equation by the coefficient of x. Finally, simplify the fraction.

$$49x = 63$$
$$x = \frac{63}{49}$$
$$= \frac{49}{49} + \frac{14}{49}$$
$$= 1\frac{2}{7}$$

72. E

Subject: Algebra

Getting to the Answer: The important thing to remember here is that when solving an algebraic equation, you have to do the same thing to both sides of the equation. You're given an equation with $4x + 2$ on the left side of the equal sign, and the question asks about $4x + 8$. To make $4x + 2$ look like $4x + 8$, just add 6. Now, since you've added 6 to the left side of the equation, you have to add 6 to the right side of the equation also. Adding 6 to the right side of the equation gives you $26 + 6$, or 32.

A more mathematical way of expressing what you just did is to write it out like this:

$$\begin{array}{r} 4x + 2 = 26 \\ +6 = +6 \\ \hline 4x + 8 = 32 \end{array}$$

73. C

Subject: Arithmetic

Getting to the Answer: First, figure out how many miles will be traveled at each price. There are 100 miles total, and the first 10 cost a flat rate of $5.00. That leaves 90 miles, 40 of which cost $0.25 per mile. The last 50 miles cost $0.10 per mile. Now, find out how much each segment costs and add them together:

$$\$5 + 40(\$0.25) + 50(\$0.10) =$$
$$\$5 + \$10 + \$5 = \$20$$

74. F

Subject: Statistics and Probability

Getting to the Answer: There are currently 25 pencils in the box $(7 + 10 + 8)$. Of those pencils, $7 + 8 = 15$ are **not** green. So the probability of choosing a pencil that is **not** green is $\frac{15}{25} = \frac{3}{5}$.

75. C

Subject: Algebra

Getting to the Answer: Let x be the number of inches representing 10 feet. Set up a proportion using the given scale and solve for x:

$$\frac{x}{10} = \frac{0.2}{200}$$
$$200x = 2$$
$$x = \frac{2}{200} = 0.01$$

76. F

Subject: Arithmetic

Getting to the Answer: First, find out how much money Tariq's purchase will cost. 21 oranges at 30 cents each will cost $21 \times \$0.30 = \$6.30$. 12 apples at 50 cents each will cost $12 \times \$0.50 = \$6.00$. The total purchase would cost $\$6.30 + \$6.00$, or $\$12.30$. Since Tariq only has $10, he needs $\$12.30 - \$10.00$, or $\$2.30$ more.

77. B

Subject: Arithmetic

Getting to the Answer: If Thomas wound up in debt, it means that he spent more money than he actually had (perhaps he borrowed some from a friend). A debt of $5 means he spent $5 more than the $15 he originally had, so he spent $20. If he bought two items that cost the same amount, each one must have cost $20 \div 2 = \$10$.

78. F

Subject: Algebra

Getting to the Answer: Start by combining like terms on each side of the equation. The result is $4x + 14 = 6x + 6$. Next, subtract $4x$ from both sides and subtract 6 from both sides. Then divide both sides by 2.

$$4x + 14 = 6x + 6$$
$$8 = 2x$$
$$4 = x$$

79. B

Subject: Arithmetic

Getting to the Answer: Calculate the cost of the binders before the discount and before the tax: $5 \times \$8 = \$40$. Now, apply the discount. If the amount of the discount was 40%, then Darias only paid $100\% - 40\% = 60\%$ of the price: $0.60 \times \$40 = \$24$. Finally, multiply the cost by 1.06 to add in the sales tax: $1.06 \times \$24 = \$25.44$.

80. H

Subject: Arithmetic

Getting to the Answer: The greatest possible number of teams in the little league program is the greatest common factor of 108, 54, and 72. Write the prime factorization of each number:

$$108 = 12 \times 9 = 2 \times 2 \times 3 \times 3 \times 3 = 2^2 \times 3^3$$
$$54 = 6 \times 9 = 2 \times 3 \times 3 \times 3 = 2 \times 3^3$$
$$72 = 8 \times 9 = 2 \times 2 \times 2 \times 3 \times 3 = 2^3 \times 3^2$$

Then, find the factors that all three numbers have in common and multiply: $2 \times 3^2 = 2 \times 9 = 18$.

81. B

Subject: Geometry

Getting to the Answer: The area of a triangle is given by the formula Area $= \frac{1}{2} \times$ Base $\times$ Height. Triangle TYZ has an area of 48 square units, and you know that its height is equal to the length of WZ, which is 6 units. Substitute into the area formula and solve for the base.

$$A = \frac{1}{2}bh$$
$$48 = \frac{1}{2}b(6)$$
$$48 = 3b$$
$$16 = b$$

You now know the length of YZ is 16 units. Opposite sides of a rectangle are equal, so WX also has a length of

16 units. Since T is the midpoint of WX, the lengths of WT and TX are each half of 16, or 8 units.

82. E

Subject: Arithmetic

Getting to the Answer: Add the fractions to determine how much of Box 1 is filled. Write both fractions over a common denominator of 12.

$$\frac{1}{4} + \frac{2}{3} = \left(\frac{3}{3}\right)\frac{1}{4} + \left(\frac{4}{4}\right)\frac{2}{3}$$
$$= \frac{3}{12} + \frac{8}{12} = \frac{11}{12}$$

Since $\frac{11}{12}$ of Box 1 is filled, $1 - \frac{11}{12} = \frac{12}{12} - \frac{11}{12} = \frac{1}{12}$ is not filled.

83. C

Subject: Statistics and Probability

Getting to the Answer: To find the number of students who are not taking either geography, history, or both, first find the number of students taking either geography or history and then subtract this number from the total number of students in the room. In order to find the number of students taking either geography or history, add the number of students taking geography and the number of students taking history and then subtract the number of students taking both geography and history.

So, the number of students taking either geography or history is $12 + 14 - 5$, which is 21. Since 21 students are taking either geography or history, the number of students that are not taking either geography or history is $33 - 21 = 12$.

84. E

Subject: Algebra

Getting to the Answer: Let b represent the number of blue T-shirts sold in June last year. Use the information in the table to set up a proportion. To keep the numbers small, simplify any ratios that you can before cross multiplying.

$$\frac{\text{Blue in June}}{\text{All in June}} = \frac{\text{Blue last year}}{\text{All last year}}$$
$$\frac{b}{240} = \frac{750}{3,000}$$
$$\frac{b}{240} = \frac{1}{4}$$
$$4b = 240$$
$$b = 60$$

85. D

Subject: Algebra

Getting to the Answer: Rewrite the first fraction as a number over $6y$ so that the two terms have the same denominator. Then add the numerators and simplify if possible.

$$\frac{1}{3y} - \frac{1}{6y} = \frac{2}{2}\left(\frac{1}{3y}\right) - \frac{1}{6y}$$
$$= \frac{2}{6y} - \frac{1}{6y}$$
$$= \frac{2-1}{6y}$$
$$= \frac{1}{6y}$$

86. F

Subject: Arithmetic

Getting to the Answer: The amounts involve fractions, so write the ratio of oregano to pepper so that the fractions have the same denominator. Then, compare the numerators.

$$\frac{1}{6} : 1\frac{1}{4}$$
$$\frac{1}{6} : \frac{5}{4}$$
$$\frac{2}{12} : \frac{15}{12}$$

There are 2 parts (twelfths) oregano and 15 parts (twelfths) pepper, so the ratio of oregano to pepper is 2:15.

87. D

Subject: Arithmetic

Getting to the Answer: Since something happens every 5 minutes at this party, look at each five-minute interval. At first, there are 256 people. After 5 minutes, half of them leave. That means that 128 people leave and 128 people are left. 5 minutes after that, or 10 minutes after the starting point, half the remaining people leave. That means that half of 128, or 64, people leave and 64 are left. At 15 minutes, half the remaining 64, or 32, people leave and 32 people are left. Finally, 20 minutes after the start, half of 32, or 16, people leave, and so, ultimately, only 16 people are left at the party.

88. H

Subject: Geometry

Getting to the Answer: Here, the angle marked $x°$ is in a triangle with 2 other unknown angles. However, one of those unknown angles of the triangle, the one to the right of the $x°$ angle, lies on a straight line with an angle measuring 98°. Therefore, that angle must measure $180° - 98° = 82°$. The third angle in the triangle is opposite a 54° angle that is formed by the intersection of two lines, so the third angle of the triangle must also measure 54°. The 3 angles of a triangle add up to 180°, so $54° + 82° + x° = 180°$, and $x = 44$.

89. D

Subject: Algebra

Getting to the Answer: Substitute 2 for y. Then add $\frac{7}{10}$ to both sides. To add the two numbers, write 2 as a fraction with a denominator of 10.

$$x - \frac{7}{10} = y$$
$$x - \frac{7}{10} = 2$$
$$x = 2 + \frac{7}{10}$$
$$= \frac{20}{10} + \frac{7}{10} = \frac{27}{10}$$

90. F

Subject: Statistics and Probability

Getting to the Answer: To find the probability that two events will occur together, simply multiply together the probabilities of the two events. Use the probability formula: Probability $= \frac{\text{Number of Desired Outcomes}}{\text{Number of Possible Outcomes}}$. In the first box, the chance of drawing a red ball is one in three. The probability of drawing a red ball in the second box is one in four. So, the probability of drawing a red ball from each box is $\frac{1}{3} \times \frac{1}{4} = \frac{1}{12}$.

91. D

Subject: Arithmetic

Getting to the Answer: If the product of b and c is positive, then either both numbers are positive or both numbers are negative, but you do not know which is true. The question asks which statement **must** be true, so consider each answer choice carefully before you eliminate it.

(A): You know a is positive, but you do not know whether c is positive or negative, so $\frac{a}{c}$ might or might not be negative.

(B): You know a is positive, but you do not know whether c is positive or negative, so $\frac{a}{c}$ might or might not be positive.

(C): You know b and c have the same sign (either both are positive or both are negative), so $\frac{b}{c}$ cannot be negative.

(D): You know b and c have the same sign (either both are positive or both are negative), so $\frac{b}{c}$ **must** be positive. **(D)** is correct.

92. E

Subject: Arithmetic

Getting to the Answer: Don't fall into the "obvious answer" trap of just taking the number of nickels and the number of dimes from the two ratios to come up with 3:4. To find the ratio of nickels to dimes, you need to get the two ratios in proportion to one another by getting the same number of pennies in each. Multiplying the first ratio (pennies to nickels) by 3 gives you 6:9; multiplying the second ratio (pennies to dimes) by 2 gives you 6:8. Since the number corresponding to pennies is now the same in each ratio (6), the ratio of nickels to dimes can now be found. The ratio of nickels to dimes is 9:8.

93. A

Subject: Statistics and Probability

Getting to the Answer: The total number of park passes purchased is $84 + 56 + 45 + 49 + 66 = 300$. The probability that a 3-Day, 3-Parks pass was purchased is $\frac{66}{300} = \frac{22}{100} = 22\%$.

94. E

Subject: Statistics and Probability

Getting to the Answer: If an integer is chosen randomly from the first 50 integers, the probability of choosing any particular number is 1 divided by 50, and the probability of choosing an integer with at least one digit of 3 is the number of integers with at least one digit of 3, divided by 50. The integers 3, 13, 23, 30, 31, 32, 33, 34, 35, 36, 37, 38, 39, and 43 are the only integers with a 3 in them, for a total of 14 different integers, so the probability is $\frac{14}{50} = \frac{7}{25}$.

95. B

Subject: Algebra

Getting to the Answer: You are given that y is between -1 and 0, so pick an appropriate number for y and plug it into each answer choice. Try $y = -\frac{1}{2}$. Then **(A)** is $y^2 = \left(-\frac{1}{2}\right)^2 = \frac{1}{4}$, **(B)** is $1 - y = 1 - \left(-\frac{1}{2}\right) = 1\frac{1}{2}$, **(C)** is $1 + y = 1 + \left(-\frac{1}{2}\right) = \frac{1}{2}$, and **(D)** is $2y = 2\left(-\frac{1}{2}\right) = -1$. **(B)** is the greatest, and therefore the correct answer. If you are not convinced, you can always try another value, such as $y = -\frac{2}{3}$, or any other fraction that lies between -1 and 0.

96. F

Subject: Algebra

Getting to the Answer: Let x be the number of cars, trucks, and SUVs on the lot. Then the total number of vehicles on the lot is $179 + x$. Set up a proportion and solve for x:

$$\frac{\text{All vehicles}}{\text{Jeeps}} = \frac{\text{All vehicles}}{\text{Jeeps}}$$

$$\frac{15}{1} = \frac{179 + x}{179}$$

$$179 + x = 179(15)$$

$$179 + x = 2,685$$

$$x = 2,506$$

97. D

Subject: Statistics and Probability

Getting to the Answer: The sum of the prices of Marvin's Friday sales is $4(\$125) = \$500$. The sum of the prices of Marvin's Saturday sales is $6(\$140) = \$840$. Add those two sums and divide by 10 to find the mean:

$$\frac{\$500 + \$840}{10} = \frac{\$1,340}{10} = \$134$$

98. G

Subject: Geometry

Getting to the Answer: The sum of the measures of supplementary angles is $180°$, so the measure of angle K plus the measure of angle L is $180°$. Since the measure of angle L is one-fourth the measure of angle K, you can write $L = \frac{1}{4}K$, or $K = 4L$, where K is the measure of angle K and L is the measure of angle L. Set up an equation and solve for L.

$$K + L = 180°$$
$$4L + L = 180°$$
$$5L = 180°$$
$$L = 36°$$

The question asks how many degrees greater angle K is than angle L, so find the measure of angle K (which is 4 times the measure of angle L) and subtract. The measure of angle K is $4(36°) = 144°$, which means the difference is $144° - 36° = 108°$.

99. B

Subject: Arithmetic

Getting to the Answer: First, convert both heights to just inches. To do this, multiply the number of feet by 12 and then add the inches.

First tree: $(4 \times 12) + 9 = 57$ inches

Second tree: $(5 \times 12) + 6.5 = 66.5$ inches

Then, subtract the heights: $66.5 - 57 = 9.5$ inches.

100. H

Subject: Algebra

Getting to the Answer: Substitute $\frac{1}{5}$ for y.

$\frac{1}{y} = \frac{x}{3} \rightarrow \frac{1}{\left(\frac{1}{5}\right)} = \frac{x}{3}$	
$\frac{1}{\left(\frac{1}{5}\right)} = 1 \times \frac{5}{1} = 5$	Simplify the fraction within a fraction. Then, substitute the result for the left-hand side of the equation.
$5 = \frac{x}{3} \rightarrow 15 = x$	Multiply both sides of the equation by 3 to solve for x.

101. D

Subject: Statistics and Probability

Getting to the Answer: Use the average formula in the rearranged form: Sum of the Terms = Average $\times$ Number of Terms. The sum of the 16 terms is 3×16, or 48. When the seventeenth number joins the group, the average of all 17 numbers is 4, so the sum of all 17 numbers is 4×17, or 68. The sum of all 17 numbers is equal to the sum of the first sixteen numbers plus the seventeenth number. Let x equal the unknown number, and solve: $68 = 48 + x$, which means $x = 20$.

Practice Tests

102. F

Subject: Algebra

Getting to the Answer: Substitute 4 for x:

$20 - (y - x) = 30 - (x - y)$ $20 - (y - 4) = 30 - (4 - y)$	
$20 - y + 4 = 30 - 4 + y$	Distribute the negative signs.
$24 - y = 26 + y$ $-2 = 2y$	Combine like terms. Then, add y and subtract 26 from both sides to isolate the variable.
$y = -1$	Divide both sides by -2.

103. D

Subject: Arithmetic

Getting to the Answer: Convert each rate to magnets per hour. Then add the results. There are 60 minutes in 1 hour. Eric can paint 4 magnets in 10 minutes, and there are 6 periods of 10 minutes in 60 minutes. Thus, in 60 minutes, Eric can paint $4 \times 6 = 24$ magnets. Agnes can paint 6 magnets in 15 minutes, and there are 4 periods of 15 minutes in 60 minutes. Thus, in 60 minutes, Agnes can paint $6 \times 4 = 24$ magnets. Together, they can paint $24 + 24 = 48$ magnets in 1 hour.

104. G

Subject: Geometry

Getting to the Answer: Find the perimeter of the rectangle in the scale drawing (in inches), use the scale factor to find the actual perimeter (in inches), then divide by 12 to find the actual perimeter in feet.

$P = 2(4.5) + 2(6) = 9 + 12 = 21$ inches

$21 \times 80 = 1{,}680$ inches

$1{,}680 \div 12 = 140$ feet

105. A

Subject: Arithmetic

Getting to the Answer: First, list the possible products. Since multiplication is commutative, you don't need to list repeat products (for example, 2×3 and 3×2). Don't

forget—the problem states that the two numbers are different.

$2 \times 3 = 6$; $2 \times 4 = 8$; $2 \times 5 = 10$; $2 \times 6 = 12$

$3 \times 4 = 12$; $\mathbf{3 \times 5 = 15}$; $3 \times 6 = 18$

$4 \times 5 = 20$; $4 \times 6 = 24$

$5 \times 6 = 30$

Of the 10 products, only 1 is odd, so the ratio of odd products to even products is 1:9.

106. G

Subject: Geometry

Getting to the Answer: The formula for the area of a triangle is Area $= \frac{1}{2} \times$ Base $\times$ Height. In this problem, you are told that the area of the triangle is 24 square units and that the height, BD, is 6 units. You can also tell from the diagram that the base has length $x + (x + 2)$. Now, substitute these values into the area formula:

$$24 = \frac{1}{2}(x + x + 2)(6)$$
$$48 = (x + x + 2)(6)$$
$$8 = (x + x + 2)$$
$$6 = 2x$$
$$x = 3$$

107. A

Subject: Arithmetic

Getting to the Answer: $\frac{130}{x}$ will be an integer whenever x evenly divides into 130. So, you need to find all of the numbers that will divide evenly into 130—that is, all of the factors of 130. The easiest way to do that is to write down all of the factor pairs of 130:

$130 = 1 \times 130$, 2×65, 5×26, and 10×13. That makes 8 numbers that divide evenly into 130.

108. E

Subject: Algebra

Getting to the Answer: Finding the value of one variable *in terms of* another variable just means to solve for the first variable, y. You won't get a numerical answer, but rather an answer that still has the other variable in it, x. Start by simplifying the right-hand side of the equation. Remember—when you take the absolute value of a number, the number becomes a positive number.

$$x = 3y(2 - |-4|) + y(3 - |-2|)$$
$$x = 3y(2 - 4) + y(3 - 2)$$
$$x = 3y(-2) + y(1)$$
$$x = -6y + y$$
$$x = -5y$$
$$-\frac{x}{5} = y$$

109. C
Subject: Algebra

Getting to the Answer: The fraction of the watermelon patch that Farmer A harvests is $\frac{14}{20} = \frac{7}{10}$. Let x represent the number of rows of watermelon that Farmer B harvests. Then the fraction of the patch that Farmer B harvests is $\frac{x}{16}$. Write an inequality and solve for x:

$$\frac{x}{16} \le \frac{7}{10}$$
$$x \le \frac{7 \times 16}{10}$$
$$x \le \frac{112}{10}$$
$$x \le 11\frac{1}{5}$$

So, the greatest number of whole rows of watermelon Farmer B can harvest from his patch is 11.

110. F
Subject: Algebra

Getting to the Answer: Rather than finding a common denominator and combining the fractions, choose a number that meets the given requirement. The only number that is a whole number such that $1 < x < 3$ (between 1 and 3) is $x = 2$. Substitute that value for x in each inequality to determine which statement is true.

(E) $\frac{1}{2-1} < \frac{1}{2+1} \Rightarrow 1 < \frac{1}{3}$ This is false.

(F) $\frac{1}{2-1} > \frac{1}{2+1} - 1 \Rightarrow 1 > \frac{1}{3} - 1 \Rightarrow 1 > -\frac{2}{3}$
This is true.

(G) $\frac{1}{2-1} + \frac{1}{2+1} < 1 \Rightarrow 1 + \frac{1}{3} < 1 \Rightarrow 1\frac{1}{3} < 1$
This is false.

(H) $\frac{1}{2-1} + \frac{1}{2+1} < -\frac{1}{2} \Rightarrow 1 + \frac{1}{3} < -\frac{1}{2} \Rightarrow 1\frac{1}{3} < -\frac{1}{2}$
This is false.

(F) is the only true statement and is the correct answer.

111. D
Subject: Algebra

Getting to the Answer: Finding the value of one variable *in terms of* another variable just means to solve for the first variable, y. You won't get a numerical answer, but rather an answer that still has the other variable in it, x. Start by simplifying the right-hand side of the equation. Then, solve for y. You may have to manipulate the result to make it match one of the answer choices.

$$x = 4(3 - y)(2^2 - 1)$$
$$x = (12 - 4y)(4 - 1)$$
$$x = (12 - 4y)(3)$$
$$x = 36 - 12y$$
$$x - 36 = -12y$$
$$\frac{x - 36}{-12} = y$$
$$\frac{x}{-12} - \frac{36}{-12} = y$$
$$\frac{-x}{12} + 3 = y$$
$$3 - \frac{x}{12} = y$$

112. H
Subject: Algebra

Getting to the Answer: Let x be the original amount of water in the bucket. It loses 10% after each day, which means 90% of the water remains at the end of each day. So, at the end of the first day, there is $0.90x$ remaining. At the end of the second day, 90% of the amount left at the end of the first day remains, which is:

$0.90(0.90x) = 0.81x$ or 81% of the original amount.

At the end of the third day, 90% of the amount left at the end of the second day remains, which is:

$0.90(0.81x) = 0.729x$ or about 73% of the original amount.

113. C

Subject: Statistics and Probability

Getting to the Answer: Let b represent the number of additional black chips needed. Set the probability of drawing a black chip (after the additional chips have been added) equal to $\frac{1}{4}$ and solve the equation for b:

$$\frac{\text{black} + \text{additional}}{\text{all} + \text{additional}} = \frac{1}{4}$$

$$\frac{8 + b}{19 + 23 + 8 + b} = \frac{1}{4}$$

$$\frac{8 + b}{50 + b} = \frac{1}{4}$$

$$4(8 + b) = 1(50 + b)$$

$$32 + 4b = 50 + b$$

$$3b = 18$$

$$b = 6$$

114. F

Subject: Geometry

Getting to the Answer: The shaded region is one of four equal pieces left when the circle is subtracted from the square. So, to find the area of the shaded region, you must subtract the area of the circle from the area of the square and then take one-fourth of this difference.

You're told that the circumference of the circle is 4π. You also know that the circumference C of a circle is related to its radius r by the formula $C = 2\pi r$. So here, $4\pi = 2\pi r$ and $r = 2$. The area of the circle is πr^2, which equals $\pi(2)^2$ or 4π. To find the area of the square, you must know the length of its side. If you draw in the diameter of the circle whose endpoints are the point where the circle touches side BC of the square and the point where the circle touches side AD of the square, you'll see that the side of the square is equal in length to the diameter of the circle. The radius of the circle is 2, so its diameter, which is twice the radius, is 2×2 or 4. Since the side of the square is 4, its area is 4^2 which is 16. The area of the square is 16 and the area of the circle is 4π, so the area between the circle and the square is $16 - 4\pi$. This means the area of the shaded region is $\frac{16 - 4\pi}{4} = \frac{4(4 - \pi)}{4} = 4 - \pi$.